IMMANUEL KANT

Correspondence

The purpose of the Cambridge Edition is to offer translations of the best modern German editions of Kant's works in a uniform format suitable for Kant scholars. When complete, the edition will include all of Kant's published writing and a generous selection of his unpublished writings such as *Opus postumum, handschriftliche Nachlass*, lectures, and correspondence.

This is the most complete English edition of Kant's correspondence that has ever been compiled. The letters are concerned with philosophical and scientific topics, but many also treat personal, historical, and cultural matters. On one level the letters chart Kant's philosophical development. On another level they expose quirks and foibles, and reveal a good deal about Kant's friendships and philosophical battles with some of the prominent thinkers of the time: Herder, Hamann, Mendelssohn, and Fichte.

What emerges from these pages is a vivid picture of the intellectual, religious, and political currents of late eighteenth-century Prussia, in which there is much to be learned about topics such as censorship, and the changing status of Jews and women in Europe.

Among the special features of this volume are: a substantial introduction, detailed explanatory notes, a glossary, and biographical sketches of correspondents and a considerable number of people referred to in the letters.

This major endeavor will be of importance not only to Kant scholars but also to historians of the Enlightenment and of eighteenth-century Prussia.

THE CAMBRIDGE EDITION OF THE WORKS
OF IMMANUEL KANT

General editors: Paul Guyer and Allen W. Wood

Theoretical Philosophy, 1755–1770
Critique of Pure Reason
Theoretical Philosophy after 1781
Practical Philosophy
Critique of Judgment
Religion and Rational Theology
Anthropology, History, and Education
Natural Science
Lectures on Logic
Lectures on Metaphysics
Lectures on Ethics
Opus postumum
Notes and Fragments
Correspondence

IMMANUEL KANT

Correspondence

TRANSLATED AND EDITED BY

ARNULF ZWEIG

PUBLISHED BY THE PRESS SYNDCATE OF THE UNIVERSITY OF CAMBRIDGE
The Pitt Building, Trumpington Street, Cambridge, United Kingdom

CAMBRIDGE UNIVERSITY PRESS
The Edinburgh Building, Cambridge CB2 2RU, UK   http://www.cup.cam.ac.uk
40 West 20th Street, New York, NY 10011-4211, USA   http://www.cup.org
10 Stamford Road, Oakleigh, Melbourne 3166, Australia

First published 1999

Printed in the United States of America

Typeface Janson Text 10/12 pt.   *System* DeskTop Pro/ux® [BV]

*A catalog record for this book is available from
the British Library.*

Library of Congress Cataloging-in-Publication Data
Kant, Immanuel, 1724–1804.
[Correspondence. English. Selections]
Correspondence / Immanuel Kant ; translated and edited by Arnulf
Zweig.
p.   cm. – (The Cambridge edition of the works of Immanuel
Kant)
ISBN 0-521-35401-3 (hb)
1. Kant, Immanuel, 1724–1804 – Correspondence.   I. Zweig, Arnulf.
II. Title.   III. Series: Kant, Immanuel, 1724–1804.   Works.
English.   1992.
B2797.A4   1999
193 – dc21
[B]   98-30476

ISBN 0 521 35401 3 hardback

Contents

vii

Contents

Contents

Letters 1781–1789

Contents

Contents

Contents

General Editors' Preface

Within a few years of the publication of his *Critique of Pure Reason* in 1781, Immanuel Kant (1724–1804) was recognized by his contemporaries as one of the seminal philosophers of modern times – indeed as one of the great philosophers of all time. This renown soon spread beyond German-speaking lands, and translations of Kant's work into English were published even before 1800. Since then, interpretations of Kant's views have come and gone and loyalty to his positions has waxed and waned, but his importance has not diminished. Generations of scholars have devoted their efforts to producing reliable translations of Kant into English as well as into other languages.

There are four main reasons for the present edition of Kant's writings:

1. *Completeness.* Although most of the works published in Kant's lifetime have been translated before, the most important ones more than once, only fragments of Kant's many important unpublished works have ever been translated. These include the *Opus postumum*, Kant's unfinished *magnum opus* on the transition from philosophy to physics; transcriptions of his classroom lectures; his correspondence; and his marginalia and other notes. One aim of this edition is to make a comprehensive sampling of these materials available in English for the first time.

2. *Availability.* Many English translations of Kant's works, especially those that have not individually played a large role in the subsequent development of philosophy, have long been inaccessible or out of print. Many of them, however, are crucial for the understanding of Kant's philosophical development, and the absence of some from English-language bibliographies may be responsible for erroneous or blinkered traditional interpretations of his doctrines by English-speaking philosophers.

3. *Organization.* Another aim of the present edition is to make all Kant's published work, both major and minor, available in comprehen-

sive volumes organized both chronologically and topically, so as to facilitate the serious study of his philosophy by English-speaking readers.

4. *Consistency of translation.* Although many of Kant's major works have been translated by the most distinguished scholars of their day, some of these translations are now dated, and there is considerable terminological disparity among them. Our aim has been to enlist some of the most accomplished Kant scholars and translators to produce new translations, freeing readers from both the philosophical and literary preconceptions of previous generations and allowing them to approach texts, as far as possible, with the same directness as present-day readers of the German or Latin originals.

In pursuit of these goals, our editors and translators attempt to follow several fundamental principles:

1. As far as seems advisable, the edition employs a single general glossary, especially for Kant's technical terms. Although we have not attempted to restrict the prerogative of editors and translators in choice of terminology, we have maximized consistency by putting a single editor or editorial team in charge of each of the main groupings of Kant's writings, such as his work in practical philosophy, philosophy of religion, or natural science, so that there will be a high degree of terminological consistency, at least in dealing with the same subject matter.

2. Our translators try to avoid sacrificing literalness to readability. We hope to produce translations that approximate the originals in the sense that they leave as much of the interpretive work as possible to the reader.

3. The paragraph, and even more the sentence, is often Kant's unit of argument, and one can easily transform what Kant intends as a continuous argument into a mere series of assertions by breaking up a sentence so as to make it more readable. Therefore, we try to preserve Kant's own divisions of sentences and paragraphs wherever possible.

4. Earlier editions often attempted to improve Kant's texts on the basis of controversial conceptions about their proper interpretation. In our translations, emendation or improvement of the original edition is kept to the minimum necessary to correct obvious typographical errors.

5. Our editors and translators try to minimize interpretation in other ways as well, for example, by rigorously segregating Kant's own footnotes, the editors' purely linguistic notes, and their more explanatory or informational notes; notes in this last category are treated as endnotes rather than footnotes.

We have not attempted to standardize completely the format of individual volumes. Each, however, includes information about the context in which Kant wrote the translated works, a German-English glossary, an English-German glossary, an index, and other aids to comprehension. The general introduction to each volume includes an explanation of specific principles of translation and, where necessary, principles of selection of works included in that volume. The pagination of the standard German edition of Kant's works, *Kant's Gesammelte Schriften*, edited by the Royal Prussian (later German) Academy of Sciences (Berlin: Georg Reimer, later Walter de Gruyter & Co., 1900–), is indicated throughout by means of marginal numbers.

Our aim is to produce a comprehensive edition of Kant's writings, embodying and displaying the high standards attained by Kant scholarship in the English-speaking world during the second half of the twentieth century, and serving as both an instrument and a stimulus for the further development of Kant studies by English-speaking readers in the century to come. Because of our emphasis on literalness of translation and on information rather than interpretation in editorial practices, we hope our edition will continue to be usable despite the inevitable evolution and occasional revolutions in Kant scholarship.

PAUL GUYER
ALLEN W. WOOD

Acknowledgments

When the general editors of the Cambridge Edition of the Works of Immanuel Kant first approached me, suggesting that I revise my earlier collection of Kant's letters, then out of print, for this new edition, I estimated that a revision would be ready in a year. It has taken almost a decade. This resultant volume contains more than twice the number of letters included in Kant's *Philosophical Correspondence: 1755–95* (University of Chicago Press, 1967, 1970) and substantially augments the discussion of the people in Kant's life and letters. Numerous contributions to Kant scholarship have appeared in the last thirty years – a virtual Kant renaissance – and these have extended our understanding of the people in Kant's life and times and the significance of some of the letters. I hope that this shows both in the new translations and in the explanatory notes and biographical sketches. My thanks to all who have helped and instructed me and especially to Henry Allison, Eckart Förster, Ralf Meerbote, and Stephen Palmquist for their meticulous reading of the earlier translations, their discovery of errors and omissions, and their suggestions for revision.

My indebtedness to the late Rudolf Malter, to my colleagues in the North American Kant Society, and especially to Frederick Beiser, Daniel Breazeale, Paul Guyer, Manfred Kuehn, Allen Wood, and Günter Zöller, is great. Alexander Rüger provided invaluable assistance in translating several letters to and from J. S. Beck, letters requiring an understanding not only of philosophy and German but of physics and mathematics as well. Malcolm Wilson and other members of the Classics Department of the University of Oregon helped with the translation of Latin and Greek phrases and allusions. Thomas Hill, Jr., Leah R. Jacobs, Robert N. Johnson, Onora O'Neill, and Thomas Pogge helped to sustain my work, through both their writings and conversations. Support and encouragement from colleagues in the Department of Mathematics at the University of Oregon, especially Peter Gilkey, are appreciated, as are a summer research grant from the Graduate School of the University of Oregon and one from the National Endowment for the Humanities.

My copyeditor, Nicholas Mirra, was enormously helpful in reading the entire manuscript and offering felicitous suggestions for revising the book.

Above all, my warmest gratitude must again be expressed to one who can no longer hear it, my mentor and friend for fifty years, the late Lewis White Beck, who first led me to undertake translating Kant's letters and whose personal influence on my life and work has been immeasurable.

ARNULF ZWEIG

Introduction

ARNULF ZWEIG

Kant's century cultivated letter-writing as an art form. In an age long before telephones, letters were often a necessity even for casual communication with friends and neighbors. But many supposedly private letters were clearly intended for the reading public, and many writers – scientists, philosophers, biographers, novelists – used the medium of letters to present their work. Lessing and Lichtenberg published "letters" on art, Euler and Lambert on physics, Reinhold and Schiller on philosophy and literature. Goethe, F. H. Jacobi, and Rousseau composed *Briefromanen*, novels in the form of letters, and one of Kant's first biographers, R. B. Jachmann, employed the format of "letters to a friend" to depict Kant's life and personality. Important literary feuds and exchanges such as the so-called pantheism controversy between Moses Mendelssohn and Friedrich Heinrich Jacobi were carried on, at least in part, in the style of personal correspondence.[1]

One might therefore expect Kant too to have written his letters with an eye to posterity, composing them with polished elegance and precision. But that was not the case. Kant's private letters were indeed private.[2] Most of them were written hastily, often after much procrastination, and usually in response to some specific question, obligation, or business – a recommendation for a student, a letter of introduction for some traveler, instructions to a publisher,[3] sometimes simply a polite acknowledgment of someone else's letter a year earlier or an expression of thanks for a shipment of his favorite carrots and sausages. Direct, humorless, unadorned by any flights of literary imagination, the letters seldom manifest any sense of pleasure on the part of their author, who clearly regarded letter-writing as a chore and a distraction from more serious work. Though some letters do have significant philosophical content, on several occasions he explicitly refused to allow them to be published, even those addressed to a correspondent of stature such as Moses Mendelssohn or the scientist-philosopher J. H. Lambert.[4]

A good many of the extant letters, it must be admitted, are devoid of philosophical, historical, or biographical interest. Yet a considerable

1

number are either philosophically rewarding or fascinating and treasurable for non-philosophical reasons. Some show the origin of Kant's problems and the evolution of his thinking, the *Entstehungsgeschichte* or working out of the Critical Philosophy. Some reveal aspects of Kant's personality and character, and that of his contemporaries. Others, important for an understanding of Kant's place in the history of philosophy, show Kant's response – and sometimes his lack of response – to questions raised by his disciples and critics. Their questions and astute criticisms – and misunderstandings – often parallel those voiced in our own times.

Since Kant corresponded with some of the leading thinkers of his day and with people close to centers of political power and ferment, his correspondence sometimes provides a perspective not only on philosophical and scientific debates – debates over the possibility of a priori knowledge, the nature of space, time, and matter, the possibility of vindicating religious beliefs – but also on important cultural and political conflicts of the late eighteenth century: the struggle over religious censorship, academic freedom, freedom of conscience, and, more generally, the competition between defenders of "reason" and the Enlightenment on the one hand and their various antagonists – political reactionaries, romantic visionaries, religious zealots, and *Sturm und Drang* champions of faith and feeling – on the other. Occasionally the letters offer eyewitness accounts of political turmoil. A former student writes to Kant of the chaos he sees in his travels through France, a year after the fall of the Bastille;[5] another reports on the marital and spiritualist escapades of Friedrich Wilhelm II in Berlin.[6] We observe also the embattled enlighteners' frustration and loss of power in the last decade of the eighteenth century, under pressure from religious zealots, political reactionaries, and young romantics committed to "the disease of feeling,"[7] or to what Kant derides as *Schwärmerei*.[8]

I. THE LETTERS

History of the Letters' Publication[9]

Ignoring his wishes, Kant's friends and disciples began to gather up and publish his letters almost from the moment of his death, and the task of assembling and editing them continued for over a century. Kant's friend L. E. Borowski included a few letters in his 1804 biography,[10] as did F. T. Rink, Kant's erstwhile dinner companion and editor of some of his lectures.[11] A colleague of Kant's in Dorpat, G. B. Jäsche, who edited and published Kant's lectures on logic in 1800, attempted to recover Kant's letters from various correspondents, asking that they be sent to Kant's publisher Nicolovius in Königsberg. But these letters did not appear in print until Karl Morgenstern obtained Jäsche's collection and published some of it in the *Dörptischen Beiträgen*. Others in the nineteenth century brought out partial collections, e.g., F. Sintenis in the *Altpreußische Monatsschrift*. in 1878. A study of Kant's remarkable correspondence with Maria von Herbert – remarkable for its human interest and for Kant's moralizing – appeared there in 1879. Kant's correspondence with one of his ablest students, J. S. Beck, letters which, along with Kant's letters to Marcus Herz, contain the deepest philosophical discussions to be found in the correspondence, was published by Reicke, Dilthey, and Diederichs in 1885.[12]

In 1900, the Prussian Academy (*Königlich Preußischen Akademie der Wissenschaften*, abbreviated "Ak." in this volume) published the first two volumes of what we refer to as the Akademie edition of Kant's *Briefwechsel*. A third volume appeared in 1902. Since Reicke, the editor, died in 1905, the preparation of a fourth volume, containing explanatory notes, alternative drafts, and a truly impressive amount of background material, the volume which was to become Volume 13 of the complete Akademie edition, was taken over by Paul Menzer and Rose Burger. These scholars worked for the succeeding two decades until, in 1922, they were able to bring out all four volumes, Ak. 10–13, including additional letters that had come to light after the 1910 printing.[13]

While acknowledging that the publication of Kant's letters, especially those disclosing intimate personal matters (such as Kant's digestive problems and constipation or his unflattering opinions about supposedly close friends) would not have met with Kant's approval, the editors of the Akademie edition, aiming at scholarly exhaustiveness, included every available letter, draft, or scrap of correspondence they could find. The resulting Volumes 10–13 of the Akademie edition contain over 2200 pages, 903 letters or fragments of letters, 288 from Kant, 621 to Kant, and over 600 pages of explanatory notes. It is this 1922 edition that is the principal source for the present translation,[14] as it was for the translator/editor's 1967 anthology, Kant's *Philosophical Correspondence: 1759–99*.

The Selection of Letters

The present collection more than doubles the number of letters in the editor/translator's earlier volume.[15] The collection aims to include all letters from Kant that have substantial philosophical content along with most of the letters addressed to Kant that are philosophically noteworthy. In addition to the correspondence with Herz and Beck already mentioned, the most important letters of strictly philosophical interest from Kant are those addressed to Johann Caspar Lavater,

Johann Schultz, Karl Leonhard Reinhold, Christian Gottfried Schütz, and Johann Heinrich Tieftrunk. Letters to Kant, from these and some other correspondents, show how Kant's doctrines and arguments were understood or misunderstood. Some letters have been included because they reveal strikingly and sometimes amusingly the joys and sorrows of academic life in Kant's day – not so different from our own – its fads, academic rivalries, competition for students and promotions, etc. We see Kant's students, worshipful disciples, and hostile critics as they reveal themselves or are gossiped about by their peers. Some letters, from strangers, show how Kant was perceived – often reverentially, but sometimes belligerently – by readers who were not necessarily scholars or philosophers. Jung-Stilling, for example, renowned as a cataract surgeon and writer of devotional poetry, thanks Kant for restoring his religious faith and saving him from the despair engendered by determinism, while another physician, Samuel Collenbusch, challenges Kant to explain how his moral philosophy differs from that of the Devil!

A few of the people who make an appearance in these letters are familiar names in the history of philosophy: Fichte, Herder, and Moses Mendelssohn, for example. Others, such as J. S. Beck, Hamann, and Lambert, were also significant thinkers in their own right. Some important literary contemporaries of Kant – Goethe, for example – are not represented at all, while others such as Wieland and Schiller did correspond with Kant but only in businesslike tones. Many correspondents – Maria von Herbert, Marcus Herz, Salomon Maimon, Carl Leonhard Reinhold, Johann Schultz, to mention only a few, might well be forgotten but for their connection to Kant. Quite apart from their philosophical importance or unimportance, however, they are interesting thinkers and interesting people – some of them blessed or cursed with lives and thoughts full of drama and spiritual turbulence, something that cannot be said of Kant's own. Letters from or about prominent intellectual and literary figures – Jung-Stilling, Lavater, Sophie Mereau, Swedenborg, Jacobi, Lichtenberg, Kästner, various members of the Berlin Academy – enable us to see Kant in the context of the cultural life of his era.

Otto Schöndörffer remarked in his Preface to the *Philosophische Bibliothek* collection of Kant's letters, "Every selection has something subjective about it."[16] Schöndörffer was explaining his own choice of letters from the Akademie edition, but his observation holds for the present collection as well. Not all of the letters selected here can be justified as "objectively" significant. The editor's "subjectivity" shows itself in the inclusion of some letters and persons – e.g., a business letter asking that the Jew Isaac Euchel be permitted to teach Hebrew at the university, a letter from Kant's sister-in-law thanking him for his gift of an instructional book on housewifery, a letter from the poet

Sophie Mereau, soliciting Kant's contribution to a new literary journal – that may be intrinsically unimportant and were very likely deemed unimportant by Kant himself. Yet these seemingly trivial letters, and some offhand remarks by Kant in other letters, are of interest to a late twentieth-century reader for reasons that Kant and his contemporaries could not have foreseen: they tell us something about the equivocal position of women and Jews in the "enlightened" Prussia of Kant's time, the mixture of tolerance, paternalism, and contempt for them displayed by Kant, his friends, and his opponents.[17] A casual anti-Semitic comment by Kant, on the one hand, his affection for Marcus Herz and recommendation of Euchel, on the other, point unwittingly to Kant's own inconsistent attitudes toward the Jews he encountered: respect for emancipated, "enlightened" Jews (as long as they remained appropriately deferential) but disdain and repugnance for the assertive Jew whose academic or commercial ambitions, allegiance to orthodox religious practices, or lack of civility makes him "the vampire of society."[18] Letters, biographical sketches, and editorial notes concerning Jewish intellectuals such as Mendelssohn, Herz, Maimon and Euchel, as well as non-Jews who supported or mocked them – the philo-Semitic Eberhard on the one hand, the anti-Semitic Lavater on the other – are historically and in a broad sense philosophically interesting, quite apart from their metaphysical and epistemological discussions, especially to a post-Holocaust reader.

Some letters, trivial or routine in themselves, reveal something about the status of women in Kant's thinking and in Kant's world. Sophie Mereau and Maria von Herbert are not important names in the history of philosophy, but their letters – and Kant's reaction to them – are moving and revealing. We observe or can infer Kant's ambivalence about the advancement of women, especially intellectual, imaginative women, an ambivalence surprising in a philosopher renowned for championing universal "respect for persons." We see also, especially in his letter to Maria Herbert, what Kant really respects and values in human beings and in human life. The insights into Kant's *Weltanschauung* that we obtain from these letters are not perhaps different from those we could distill from his ethical writings, but here they are presented in concrete, personal terms, as one human being speaking to another.

II. KANT'S LIFE AND CAREER

Kant's Family

Kant was born on April 22, 1724, in Königsberg, East Prussia, a city now under Russian rule and renamed Kaliningrad. His family, stemming originally from Scotland, was poor but not destitute: Kant's father was a harnessmaker. His contribution to Kant's early education was an insistence on work, honesty, and especially the avoidance of lies. Kant's mother played perhaps a more active role in his upbringing, inspiring a respect for his parents' religion – a version of Pietism that rejected the intellectualism, formal ceremonies, and devotional observances of orthodox Lutheranism[19] and instead encouraged prayer, moral earnestness, and the seeking of a personal, heartfelt relation to God through a conversion experience or "rebirth" that would transform one's life. Though Kant's attitude toward Pietism became at least ambivalent if not altogether hostile, some of the uncompromising severity of his later moral philosophy, the demand that human beings strive for "holiness," must certainly be attributed to Frau Kant's instruction and example. Kant's family was not an emotionally close one, at least on his part. As we might expect, the sense of obligation took the place of warmth. According to his friend and biographer Borowski, Kant often expressed gratitude and respect for his parents. "Never, not a single time, did I hear from my parents an improper word, or see them behave unworthily," he told Borowski. In a letter to Kant's brother, late in their lives (December 17, 1796, Ak. [731]), Kant speaks of fulfilling the "duty of gratitude" to their parents for the good upbringing he and his siblings had received.

Kant's four siblings were all younger than he; an older sister, Regina Dorothea, born 1719, is listed in the family album but nothing further is known of her. The three remaining sisters supported themselves as servants until they married. The oldest, Maria Elisabeth, born January 2, 1727, married a shoemaker named Christian Kröhnert. He divorced her in 1768, whereupon Kant supported her with an annual stipend until her death in the summer of 1796. She was for many years an invalid. On her death, Kant doubled this stipend, to provide for her children and grandchildren. Another sister, Anna Luise, born February 1730, died in January 1774. Her husband, Johann Christoph Schultz, was a toolmaker. Kant's youngest sister, Katharina Barbara, born September 1731, was married to a wigmaker named Teyer or Theuer. She died in 1807, having been well maintained by Kant in an old people's home, St. Georgs-hospital, for fifteen years. One biographer reports that she was a capable woman who helped take care of Kant in his last days. All the sisters appear to have been illiterate (they signed their names with an X). Kant had little to do with them and did not often speak of them, though they lived in the same town.[20] Their "lack of culture" made conversation unsatisfactory to him, though, according to his biographers, he was not ashamed of them. (He may have been angered, Karl Vorländer conjectures, at their demanding more support from him, in the early years of his professorship, than he could supply.)

Nor was Kant ever close to his brother, Johann Heinrich Kant (1735–1800). An early letter from him[21] chides Kant for not answering his letters. He tells Kant that he is going to write his own answer and send it to Kant for Kant's signature!

Johann Heinrich, from whom we have several letters, attended the university and became a private tutor in Kurland, then rector of a school in Mitau, 1775, and, in 1781, a country pastor in Altrahden. His letters give us a nice picture of what that sort of life was like. He and his wife, Maria, *née* Havemann, had five children. Although Kant seems never to have met his sister-in-law or her children, he left them a generous legacy. (He had earlier given 100 thaler to each of Krönert's children on the occasion of their marriages.)

Kant's Education and Early Career

Very little of Kant's early life and thinking can be inferred from the correspondence, but we have the reports of his friends and first biographers to provide a sketch.[22] In 1732, when Kant was eight years old, he was enrolled in the Collegium Fridericianum, where, his mother hoped, young boys were taught to be not only clever but pious. He remained until 1740 when he entered the university. The Latin instruction that he received at the Fridericianum must have been excellent: Kant enjoyed reciting various Roman poets and essayists from memory throughout his life. The rigorous religiosity of his teachers at the Fridericianum, on the other hand, left him with an aversion to organized religion that also remained a permanent part of his character. He vowed he would never set foot inside a church again, once he had graduated, and he seems to have kept this promise.

The director of the Fridericianum at that time, Franz Albert Schultz, a follower of Christian Wolff, was also the Kant family's pastor. He became Kant's patron, enabling him to attend the university. Notwithstanding Kant's dislike of church services, Kant initially enrolled as a theology student, and he at least toyed with the idea of becoming a pastor. According to Borowski (in the biographical sketch that Kant himself read and generally approved) it was "weakness of his chest" that discouraged him from such a career. (How serendipitous for the history of philosophy that sermons required more lung power than did lectures on epistemology!) Kant's most important teacher at the university was another Wolffian, Martin Knutzen, who taught him philosophy and mathematics and introduced him to the works of Newton. Kant also heard physics lectures from an ecclesiastical administrator named Teske.[23]

For several years prior to his final examinations and certification as a university lecturer, Kant's impoverished circumstances forced him to take positions as private tutor in various households in and near Königsberg. In 1755, he received his promotion to "Magister," the *Privatdozent* status that licensed him to lecture but, apart from students' fees, carried no salary. He supported himself by offering lectures on logic, metaphysics, physics, mathematics, as well as natural law, ethics, natural theology, anthropology (psychology), and physical geography. We can infer how depressing this teaching schedule, and Kant's poverty, must have been to him from a remark in his letter to his friend Lindner, October 28, 1759, Ak. [13]: ". . . I sit daily at the anvil of my lectern and guide the heavy hammer of my repetitious lectures, always beating out the same rhythm. Now and then I am stirred up somewhere by a nobler inclination, a desire to extend myself somewhat beyond this narrow sphere; but the blustering voice of Need immediately attacks me and, always truthful in its threats, drives me back to hard work without delay . . . I make do finally with the applause I receive and the benefits I derive from that, dreaming my life away."

But for the so-called silent decade of 1770 to 1781, when Kant was at work on the *Critique of Pure Reason*, the list of his publications grew steadily from 1754 onwards (his first published essay was "Thoughts on the True Estimation of Living Forces," 1747). Yet Kant remained a lowly instructor for fifteen years. He applied for various professorships but would not consider positions away from Königsberg. On the death of Martin Knutzen in 1756, Kant sought unsuccessfully to assume his teacher's position, *Extraordinarius* (i.e., associate professor) of philosophy. In 1758 the professor of logic and metaphysics died, but his position went to Friedrich Johann Buck, a more senior *Privatdozent* than Kant. Kant might have had the professorship of poetry, vacated by a death in 1764 – officials in Berlin inquired whether he was interested – but Kant felt that this was not his proper subject. While waiting for the philosophy professorship he coveted, Kant took a job as assistant librarian of the royal library in order to supplement his modest income. Finally, in 1770, Buck vacated his chair in philosophy to become Professor of Mathematics, and Kant, at age 46, received the appointment, Professor of Logic and metaphysics.[24] A year earlier, in 1759, Kant had received his first offer of a philosophy professorship, but it came from Erlangen, not Königsberg.[25] The notes to Kant's reply to Suckow[26] (who had submitted the offer), provide the details of Erlangen's offer and of Kant's efforts to obtain the Königsberg appointment. Kant gives various reasons for his rejecting Erlangen: his anticipating a position at home, his ties to his hometown and his circle of friends and acquaintances, his concern about his weak health and his need for physical and psychological repose, best found in his old home. One additional reason is offered: his aversion to change.

We hear him speak again of his reluctance to move in a letter to

Marcus Herz, April 1778, Ak. [134], some years after his promotion to professor. Kant writes, "All change frightens me . . ." The phrase occurs in the course of an insightful, even poetic account of his own character and temperament: "You know that I am not much moved by the thought of profit and applause on some grand stage. A peaceful situation that just satisfies my need for a variable diet of work, reflection and social intercourse, a situation in which my spirit, hypersensitive but in other respects carefree, and my body, more troublesome but never actually sick, can both be kept busy without being strained – that is all I have wanted and that is what I have managed to obtain. All change frightens me, even one that might offer the greatest prospect of improvement in my circumstances. And I think I must obey this instinct of my nature if I am to spin out to greater length the thin and delicate thread of life which the Fates have spun for me."[27]

Kant's academic life during his remaining 34 years was, in contrast to his philosophical career, routine. Relieved of financial hardship, he gave up his post as librarian in 1772. In 1780 he was elected to membership in the academic senate. At various times, whenever it was his turn, he served as dean or *Dekan* of the philosophical faculty. In 1786 and again in 1788 he became rector of the university, a position full of tedious distractions from the thinking and writing that constituted his real vocation. Academic honors came to him, but so too did reproaches and denunciations. In 1787 the Royal Academy of Sciences in Berlin, which had recognized him as early as 1763 by awarding him second prize, after Moses Mendelssohn, for his *Inquiry concerning the Distinctness of the Principles of Natural Theology and of Morals*, made Kant a corresponding member of the Academy. Ten years later, the Russian Royal Academy of Sciences, in St. Petersburg, did the same, as did the Accademia Italiana di Scienze, Lettere ed Arti in Siena in 1798. But in Marburg a *Kabinettsordre* was issued, August, 29, 1786, forbidding lectures on Kant's philosophy in the university there[28] and from Berlin, in October 1794, a command from Friedrich Wilhelm II condemning Kant's teaching and publishing on religion.[29] The order accuses Kant of "misusing his philosophy to distort and disparage many of the cardinal and foundational teachings of the Holy Scriptures and of Christianity," and names Kant's book, *Religion within the Limits of Reason Alone*, as especially pernicious. On October 14, 1795, the King, or rather his ministers Wöllner and Hillmer, issued an order to the academic senate in Königsberg forbidding all professors to lecture on Kant's book.

With the death of Friedrich Wilhelm II in November 1797, Kant felt himself released from his promise to conform to the censorship edict. Promise keeping and obedience to authority were always two of his firmly held principles, but, perhaps disingenuously, he found a way of interpreting his own words, "as your Majesty's most loyal subject," that, whether sincere or not, overcame whatever misgivings he may have had about again publicizing his views. The promise of obedience, Kant claimed, had been a personal one, made to an individual, not to the world. The previously censured work, *Religion within the Limits of Reason Alone*, had appeared in 1793, a second edition, with a new preface and many added notes, in 1794. Now Kant could publish his final thoughts on religion,[30] in *The Conflict of the Faculties*, published in the fall of 1798.

III. LETTERS BEFORE THE *CRITIQUE OF PURE REASON*

Letters up to the Inaugural Dissertation

Kant's letters before 1770 do not discuss his writings very much, though some are at least mentioned. His early publications included a number of scientific essays, the most famous of which is the *Allgemeine Naturgeschichte und Theorie des Himmels*, (Universal natural history and theory of the heavens, 1755) that anticipated Laplace's nebular hypothesis by 41 years.[31] Kant's "Only Possible Argument in Support of a Demonstration of the Existence of God,"[32] the informal "Observations on the feeling of the beautiful and the sublime,"[33] and the anti-Swedenborg *Dreams of a Spirit-Seer*,[34] 1766, aroused the attention of the *Popularphilosophen* in Berlin. Less so his essay on the concept of negative magnitudes, 1763,[35] but his essay on the different methodologies required by metaphysics and mathematics, "Inquiry concerning the distinctness of the principles of natural theology and morality," was recognized by the Berlin Royal Academy as almost as worthy as Mendelssohn's prize-winning essay. While the correspondence before 1770 tells us little about Kant's philosophical development – for that one must read his letters to Marcus Herz from 1772 onward – there are interesting exchanges with J. G. Herder and J. H. Lambert, the former foreshadowing Herder's subsequent alienation from his teacher, the latter disclosing Kant and Lambert's shared interests in the reform of metaphysics and a certain commonality of approach to this project. Herder, who had revered Kant while auditing his lectures, shows that he is already at odds with the sober, unemotionally cool disposition of his mentor, and Kant shows how little he appreciates the younger man's restless, independent mind. In his letter to Herder, Kant also mentions making progress on "the metaphysics of morals," a work Kant hoped to complete within a year. (In fact Kant's *Groundwork to the Metaphysics of Morals* did not appear until 1785, the *Metaphysics of Morals* not until 1797.)

Other letters of this period that deserve attention are Kant's letter concerning Swedenborg, addressed to a Fräulein von Knobloch, and Kant's exchanges with Mendelssohn and Hamann. There is also a tantalizing note from a certain Frau Maria Charlotta Jacobi, June 12, 1762, hinting very faintly at romance; she and her girlfriend send Kant a kiss and she suggests that Kant may "wind her watch" the next time they meet – a remark that has led at least one scholar to conjecture that Kant may not have been totally chaste throughout his eighty years.[36] The letter to Fräulein von Knobloch, in 1763, Ak. [29], contains some amusing anecdotes concerning Swedenborg's alleged feats of clairvoyance and communication with ghosts, together with Kant's not entirely skeptical comments on these stories. The letter is significantly different in tone from Kant's *Dreams of a Spirit-Seer explained by Dreams of Metaphysics* (1766, Ak.2: 354 hl ff.), which mocks the spiritualist claims that Kant, in this letter, seems to take seriously.

Lambert

J. H. Lambert (1728–77) was a mathematician, physicist, and philosopher whose renown, at the time of his correspondence, exceeded that of Kant. A member of the Berlin Academy, Lambert, in his *Cosmological Letters* (1761), supported an astronomical theory somewhat similar to that of Kant's *Allgemeine Naturgeschichte und Theorie des Himmels* (General natural history and theory of the heavens, 1755).[37] Lambert's *New Organon*, his philosophy of science, appeared in 1764. In his first letter to Kant, November 13, 1765, Ak. [33], he takes note of their common interests and the similarity of their ideas in philosophy and in science. Lambert here makes mention of the need for "an analysis of the elements of human knowledge," which should discuss "the universal and necessary possibilities of synthesizing and uniting of simple concepts." He had read Kant's essay "Only Possible Proof of the Existence of God" (1763) and knew that Kant was working on a reconstruction of the methodology for metaphysics analogous to one that he himself advocated. Lambert suggests that they exchange letters on their research, a proposal which must have flattered Kant (who called Lambert "the greatest genius in Germany"), for he replied to Lambert with unusual alacrity. Lambert's letter is amusing also for its uncharitable observations on Greek scholars, antiquarians, art critics, and literati.

Kant's reply self-confidently announces that he has finally found "the proper method for metaphysics and thereby also for the whole of philosophy," but he says that he is not yet prepared to publish his findings for, as he candidly admits, he lacks examples of propositions that can be demonstrated by means of this method. He has therefore put aside the project in order to devote himself to other essays, the subject of two of these being the metaphysical foundations of natural philosophy and the metaphysical foundations of practical philosophy.[38] Lambert awaited these books impatiently, as he states in his next letter, but as it turned out, in vain. We can only guess what Kant had in mind in 1765, though many scholars regard this as the beginning of Kant's investigations leading to the *Critique of Pure Reason*. It becomes clear that the discovery of the problem to which Kant's letter of 1772 to Herz is devoted was one cause case of Kant's repeated postponement of his project, though undoubtedly the heavy burden of his teaching duties (Kant lectured up to 28 hours a week, in addition to private seminars) was also important.

Lambert's reply, February 3, 1766, Ak. [37], describes his own views on methodology at considerable length, utilizing the distinction between "formal" and "material" cognitions, a distinction that became an important part of Kant's analysis of metaphysics in the Inaugural Dissertation (1770) and also in his later critical writings. Formal cognitions, Lambert suggests, are expressed in "simple concepts" a priori; they are concerned only with the organization of non-formal or material knowledge. Complex, synthesized concepts must be derived from simple concepts. The latter type of concepts, such as space and time, requires direct acquaintance, that is, intuition. The extent of Kant's indebtedness to Lambert is expressed in his letter to Bernoulli, November 16, 1781, Ak. [172].

Hamann

Kant's correspondence with J. G. Hamann (1730–88) does not discuss any technical issues of metaphysics or epistemology but reveals very strikingly the clashing *Weltanschauungen* of these philosophers. Hamann, the "wizard (or Magus) of the North" as he was called, was the most improbable friend one could imagine for Kant. Passionate, mystical, intellectually and physically untidy, he was the antithesis of all that Kant and the Enlightenment represented. His flamboyant style of writing is a language all its own, using a veritable stream of consciousness technique full of classical and biblical allusions along with copious, often brilliant neologisms. Though at one time a deist, Hamann had undergone a sudden conversion and become an intensely fundamentalist "born again" Christian.[39] The long letter of July 27, 1759, expresses Hamann's' stonishment, rage, and amusement at the efforts of Kant and J. C. Berens, a longtime friend of Hamann's, to convert him away from his new faith back to what these men regarded as rational deism. It is a brilliant letter, powerful and sarcastic, and, like several of his other letters, probably intended for publication.

Less theatrical but no less entertaining is Hamann's second letter of 1759, Ak. [14 and 15], and the circumstances that prompted it are again interesting for what they reveal about both Hamann and Kant. Apparently the two men had discussed collaborating on a natural science textbook for children.[40] Hamann lampoons the idea that Kant is capable of such a project and argues that a book by a philosopher, written for children, would have to be as ostensibly simple and babbling as a book by God, written for mere human beings. Hamann suggests that the best way to teach physics is to follow the biblical account of creation, presenting physical phenomena with a view to showing their divine origin. This suggestion could hardly have pleased Kant, and it is not surprising that he failed to reply to this or to Hamann's subsequent effusions on the subject.

Kant's only extant letters to Hamann were written in 1774. They contain a discussion of Herder's *Älteste Urkunde des Menschengeschlechts* The most ancient document of the human race, 1774) that appeared anonymously in that year. The main topic debated in these letters is Herder's intention in discussing the occurrence of common symbols in both the biblical account of creation and the literature of pagan antiquity, and Herder's claim that this concurrence reflected God's effort to instruct the human race. As Frederick Beiser has pointed out, the issue of the divine versus human origin of language, a debate underlying this exchange of letters, is one that parallels in a way a contemporary topic of interest in the philosophy of language and of mind, viz., the issue of pre-linguistic knowledge and whether the human mind is simply a part of nature, its activity subject to physical laws. Herder's essay, *Über den Ursprung der Sprache*, won first prize in the Berlin Akademie of Sciences competition, 1769, on the question whether human beings, left to their natural powers, could invent language. Herder is opposed to Hamann's supernaturalism; the use of reason, Herder maintained, is natural to human beings, and since reasoning requires language, the creation of language must be natural as well. In order to understand God's "instruction" (which Hamann defends as the correct explanation of our linguistic abilities) we would already have to possess language.[41] Though they differ with each other, Hamann and Kant are both opposed to Herder's naturalistic theory of language (and mind).[42]

Besides Hamann's colorful discussion of a possible collaboration on a children's science book, his letters also include some academic gossip. Hamann scoffs at the promotion of a man of dubious piety – he calls him a "Roman-apostolic-catholic-heretic-Crypto-Jesuit" – to the professorship of theology. It is amusing also to read Kant's plea at the conclusion of his letter of April 6, 1774, Ak. [86], asking Hamann to communicate his further ideas "if possible, in the language of men. For

I, poor earthling that I am, have not been properly trained to understand the divine language of an Intuitive Reason."

Mendelssohn and the "Popular Philosophers"

Moses Mendelssohn (1729–86) was the most distinguished of the so-called Popular Philosophers of the German Enlightenment. A group of somewhat unsystematic intellectuals, more or less Leibnizian in outlook though often opposed to learned discourse and technical arguments, they preferred to appeal instead to "common sense," the *gesunder Menschenverstand,* or healthy human understanding. The men usually included under this heading were J. G. H. Feder, C. Meiners, C. Garve, J. J. Engel, C. F. Nicolai, and J. E. Biester. Feder and Meiners taught at Göttingen, where they later founded the *Philosophische Bibliothek,* a journal specifically devoted to combating Kant's critical philosophy. The journal survived only four volumes. Garve, evidently a more sensitive man than his collaborator Feder (Garve's letters to Kant are genuinely moving), worked in Breslau. It was Garve's review of the *Critique of Pure Reason* that provoked Kant's wrath and stimulated him to write certain parts of the *Prolegomena to Any Future Metaphysics* (the appendix of that work refers to the review). The review had been edited and somewhat distorted by Feder before its publication in January 1782, in the *Göttinger Gelehrte Anzeigen.* Nicolai, a friend of Mendelssohn's and of Lessing's, was editor of the *Bibliothek der schönen Wissenschaften* (1757–58), then of the *Briefe, die neueste Litteratur betreffend* (1759–65) and, most important, of the *Allgemeine deutsche Bibliothek* (1765–1805), a propaganda organ of the Enlightenment. Opposed to prejudice, superstition, orthodoxy, pietism, mysticism, and Jesuitism, Nicolai was, for all his zeal, platitudinous and shallow. Kant, who was for a time on cool but friendly terms with him, directed one of his last essays, *Über die Buchmacherei* (On turning out books, 1798),[43] against him, and Nicolai also became a target for Fichte, Goethe, and Schiller. Biester, who published the *Berliner* (or *Berlinische) Monatsschrift,* to which Kant contributed, was secretary to the minister of education, von Zedlitz, as well as librarian of the Royal Library in Berlin. As one of Kant's chief ambassadors in the Prussian capital, his correspondence with Kant during the period 1792–94 tells us much about Kant's difficulties with the censorship of liberal religious views. The French Revolution is also touched on in these letters.

Of all these men, it was Mendelssohn for whom Kant had the greatest respect and affection. Unlike most of the popular philosophers, Mendelssohn did not disdain careful arguments and rigorous demonstration. Like Kant, he deplored the fall of philosophy, once the "queen of the sciences," to the shabby status of a facile, diverting parlor game. In 1763, Mendelssohn and Kant competed for the Berlin Academy Prize. As mentioned, Mendelssohn's entry, "Treatise on Evidence in the Metaphysical Sciences," won the prize, but the judges also praised Kant's essay, "Inquiry into the Distinctness of the Fundamental Principles of Natural Theology and Morals" ("Untersuchung über die Deutlichkeit der Grundsätze der natürlichen Theologie und der Moral") and the two works were to have been published together. The assigned topic of the competition was the question: "Whether metaphysical truths generally, and in particular the fundamental principles of natural theology and morals, are capable of proofs as distinct as those of geometry." Mendelssohn maintained that metaphysics can be as certain as geometry, though it is not as easily comprehended. Kant insisted that there are fundamental differences between metaphysics and mathematics, especially with regard to the role of definition or concept formation. Mathematics arrives at its concepts synthetically, from definitions; its concepts are constructed figures, from which we can derive only what we have originally put into them.[44] Validity is here independent of what exists in nature. Philosophy, however, cannot produce its own objects but must take them as given and try to see them as they are. Definitions are thus the end of philosophy rather than the beginning. "Metaphysics is without doubt the most difficult of human insights; but none has ever been written."

Kant's disagreement with Mendelssohn did not inhibit the start of a warm friendship. Mendelssohn must have written a cordial letter early in 1766 to which Kant's letter of February 7, Ak. [38], is a reply. In this letter he expresses his pleasure at the prospect of a correspondence with Mendelssohn, chats about a Jewish student whom Mendelssohn had recommended to Kant, and asks Mendelssohn to forward copies of his *Dreams of a Spirit-Seer* to various people (including Lambert). Kant refers to the book as "einige Träumerey" (some reveries) and adds: "It is, as it were, a casual piece, containing not so much a working out of such questions as a hasty sketch of the way they should be treated."

Evidently the work estranged Mendelssohn by what the latter took to be an insincere tone, "between jest and earnest." In his answer to Mendelssohn (the latter's critical letter is not extant), April 8, 1766, Ak. [39], Kant forcefully defends his own character. In addition to this extended self-evaluation, unique in Kant's writings, he also indicates his view of the worth of current metaphysics, whose "chimerical insights" lead to folly and error. An exposure of dogmatism is needed, says Kant, an organon, on which he is now at work. Kant speaks of having already reached "important insights" that will define the proper procedure for metaphysics.

The discussion of the soul, in Kant's letter, gives us a brief statement of his position in *Dreams of a Spirit-Seer*. He seems to embrace a mind-body (or spirit-matter) dualism here, for he says that he is interested in the relationship of material and spiritual substances though not optimistic about solving the metaphysical problems concerning their interaction. What are the powers of spiritual substances, he asks, and how are we to discover the precise way in which souls are joined to material substances? Our philosophical fabrications are completely unhindered by any data when we discuss theories that purport to answer these questions. Kant suggests that there are matters (birth, life, and death are his examples) that we can never hope to understand by means of reason. The main theme of the *Dreams of a Spirit-Seer*, to which Kant refers in this letter, is the parallel between the dreams and visions of Swedenborg, on the one hand, and the speculations of supposedly scientific metaphysicians, on the other. Kant tries to show how a clever manipulation of concepts can produce ostensible knowledge of the supersensible. He argues that such structures are mere airy possibilities of thought, undeserving of serious attention. The metaphysician's theories are "dreams of reason," whereas those of the spirit-seer are "dreams of sensation." He writes: "I do not know whether there are spirits; yes, what is more, I do not even know what the word 'spirit' means." Philosophy "excites the suspicion that it is found in bad company" when serious efforts are devoted to explaining fantastic stories.

Kant's deflationary attitude toward traditional metaphysics, as shown in this work and in the letter to Mendelssohn, was, in 1766, quite close to Hume's. The philosopher's task should be to survey the nature and limits of our cognitive powers. Speculative metaphysics offers no possibility of scientific certainty, its principles being based on mere wish fulfillment. The tone of the critical philosophy is there, though Kant had not yet developed the major theses, nor even formulated the main questions, of the *Critique of Pure Reason*.

Kant's Position in the Dissertation of 1770

In 1770, having received his long awaited professorship, Kant sent copies of his Inaugural Dissertation, *The Form and Principles of the Sensible and Intelligible Worlds*, to various scholars whose opinions he respected, among them Lambert and Mendelssohn.[45] In the accompanying letter to Lambert, Kant states some of the main theses of the dissertation. Again, Kant is concerned with the need for a transformation of metaphysics, a program that the separation of non-empirical from empirical principles will help to realize. His position at this time, partly influenced by Leibniz's *Nouveaux Essais* (1765), involved the separation of a "sense world" and an "intellectual world," with a corresponding schism in the structure of our cognitive faculties. In order to reconcile the independence of mathematics from experience with the applicability of mathematics to reality, Kant propounds the theory that space and time are forms of intuition, invariant characteristics of immediate experience.[46] This is essentially the position taken in the Transcendental Aesthetic section of the *Critique of Pure Reason*. The Newtonian view, that space and time are "real beings" existing independently of objects, events, and observers, Kant argued, makes unintelligible how geometry (the science of space) can be known a priori to be valid for everything in space and time. Geometry, on Newton's view of space, would have to have the status of a merely empirical science. Ultimately, Kant attempts to mediate between this absolute theory of space and time and the theory of Leibniz. Though independent of what fills them, space and time are not independent of knowing minds. But Kant believed the consequence of his theory – that space and time are supplied by our own faculty of sensibility – to be that the objects that we perceive in space and time are only phenomenal representations of noumenal realities, and such noumenal entities, if they are to be known at all, would have to be reached by some non-empirical means, viz., pure thought. Thus we have two "worlds": the world of our sensibility is "appearance," and that of our understanding is genuine, "intelligible" reality. As against Leibniz, the distinction between sensibility and understanding is made to be one of kind and not of degree – sensibility is passive; the understanding is active or "spontaneous." In addition, along with the Platonic distinction of two worlds, Kant followed Leibniz in assuming that the categories or non-empirical concepts of the intellect (causality, substance, necessity, and so on) have not only a "logical use," that is, in the organization of experience, but also a "real use," in which they provide knowledge of the world of true Being.

It is this "dogmatic" position (in contrast to the skeptical view of metaphysics in *Dreams of a Spirit-Seer*) against which Kant reacted in the decade between 1770 and the appearance of the *Critique of Pure Reason* in 1781. The change in his thinking is recorded primarily in Kant's letters to Marcus Herz, his friend, physician, and former student. Along with Kant's later correspondence with his apostatic disciples, these letters comprise perhaps the most significant philosophical material to be found in Kant's letters.[47]

Although the dissertation in 1770 certified Kant's standing as a major philosopher, the correspondence with Lambert and Mendelssohn in that year discloses the difficulties that even highly competent philosophers had in accepting Kant's theory of space and time.[48] As already noted, Kant held them to be "forms of intuition," neither attributable to the world apart from human modes of perception nor merely illusory. But Kant's word, *Erscheinung* (appearance), turns out to mislead even Lambert into thinking that Kant meant to reduce empirical objects to *Schein*, 'illusion,' – as generations of readers after Lambert have been similarly misled.

Herz and the Letter of 1772

Herz studied in Königsberg from 1755 to 1770 and acted as "respondent" or "public defender" for Kant's Inaugural Dissertation, a choice indicative of Kant's respect for him. After studying medicine in Halle, Herz returned to Berlin to begin his medical practice. By 1776, he was also giving public lectures on the philosophy of Kant; several letters of 1778 deal with Herz's request for lecture notes from Kant. One of the most distinguished members of Herz's audience was von Zedlitz, the minister of spiritual affairs (which included education) to whom Kant later dedicated the *Critique of Pure Reason*. But Kant's confidence in Herz stemmed not only from the latter's philosophical talents; Herz was a physician, and Kant something of a hypochondriac. Most of Kant's letters to Herz make mention of symptoms and ailments, sometimes very extensively described, with discussions of possible treatments and requests for advice. Though Kant was never seriously ill, he constantly complained about his health and the adverse effects of his indisposition (mainly gastric and intestinal) on his work. (In one of his last works, *The Conflict of the Faculties*, Kant blamed his lifelong sickliness on the narrowness of his chest – apparently one of Kant's favorite medical diagnoses.)

The letter of February 21, 1772, shows Kant's thinking at the point at which the Leibnizian aspects of his theory in the Inaugural Dissertation first became suspect to him. Suddenly Kant is troubled by the uncritical assumption he had made, that categories or "intellectual representations," which he had characterized only negatively as "ideas we employ that are not derived from our experience of objects," could nevertheless be supposed to agree with those objects and thus to represent things as they are. How can concepts that do not produce their objects (the way God's thinking might be supposed to produce corresponding objects) and that are not produced in us by the objects to which they refer (the way empirical concepts purport to do) be applicable a priori to an independent reality? In other words, Kant is asking for a justification or "deduction" of the "real use" of pure concepts when those concepts are to apply not simply to mathematical "objects" that we ourselves construct but to things existing independently of our minds. He asks how we can know that a concept "spontaneously" created by the mind actually corresponds to anything. Kant says that he has found a way to classify these basic concepts "following a few fundamental laws of the understanding" and that in three months he will be ready with his solution – an extraordinarily sanguine prediction, as it turned out. For by the time Kant had completed the *Critique of Pure Reason*, the "recollection of David Hume," as he characterizes it in the Introduction to the *Prolegomena*, had "interrupted [his] dogmatic slumbers . . . ," and the problem stated as it is in this letter to Herz was found to be incapable of solution. The categories could not be shown to agree with the nature of things, if "things" or "facts" – the way the world is – is taken to mean noumenal entities in a non-empirical world.

Though Kant had not yet arrived at the most distinctive argument of his critical position, the Transcendental Deduction, he had evidently reached a form of the table of categories and, more important, a formulation of what was to become one central problem of the *Critique*: how are synthetic a priori judgments possible? Here in the letter to Herz he mentions the *Critique* for the first time by name. It was this momentous work that took up most of Kant's attention in the "silent decade" of the seventies.

Kant published very little between 1770 and 1781, and the number of letters he wrote is also small. His correspondence with Hamann in 1774 has already been mentioned. A few letters to Herz tell of his progress or lack of progress on the *Critique*, along with some very detailed discussion of his physical debilities, and these letters are not only biographically important but help us to see how intimate the friendship of these two men must have been. The correspondence with Lavater, Basedow, and Wolke, however, presents us with an entirely different side of Kant's intellectual interests.

Lavater

J. C. Lavater (1741–1801) was a Swiss poet, theologian, and renowned physiognomist, a man who influenced Goethe and who was also close to Hamann. Lavater was an ardent reader of Kant, whom he called his favorite author, "mein Lieblingsschriftsteller." His letters to Kant indicate that the literary and learned world was awaiting Kant's new writings with great eagerness. "Are you dead to the world?" Lavater asks. "Why is it that so many scribble who cannot write, while you who write so well are silent?" Lavater tells Kant that he and his countrymen are anxious to see the *Critique*. In one letter he asks Kant to evaluate his own book, on faith and prayer, somehow imagining that Kant would approve of it. One can imagine how Lavater's enthusiasm for Kant must have been tempered by the latter's reply (April 28, 1775, Ak. [99] and [100]) for Kant's views were already those of *Religion within the Limits of Reason Alone*.[49] The Lavater letters are in fact a clear and eloquent summary of Kant's position. A certain cooling off on Lavater's part is confirmed by his failure to reply to Kant for almost a year, although the two men afterward remained on good terms and

Lavater later once wrote to Kant of his joy at having found someone to talk with "to satiety and still not to satiety" about Kant's ideas. Though the correspondence between them ended, Kant mentions Lavater a number of times in various works, critically though not disrespectfully. But he had no patience for Lavater's attempt to analyze character by means of the study of facial lines, calling it "indistinct concepts without any order," and in his lectures on anthropology in 1785 Kant maintained that physiognomists are correct in their analyses of character only when they already know the people they are supposedly analyzing. Elsewhere Kant refers to Lavater as a *Schwärmer* – a fanatic or enthusiast inspired by a delusion.

Letters on Education: Basedow and Wolke

Kant's interest in education was always intense, to such an extent that he was even willing to interrupt his work on the *Critique* in order to write and speak in support of the educational reforms of an experimental school, the Philanthropin. This institution was founded in Dessau in 1774 by J. B. Basedow, a man whose views on education Kant regarded highly. Kant used Basedow's *Methodenbuch* as the textbook for his lectures on practical pedagogy in the winter semester of 1776–77. The Philanthropin was based more or less on the liberal principles of Rousseau's *Émile*. The "natural" method of education at the Philanthropin insisted on treating children as children. Powdered hair, swords, gilded coats, and makeup were forbidden. The children had short haircuts and wore sailor jackets. They learned languages in a sort of "immersion" program. The curriculum included Latin, German, French, mathematics, geography, physics, music, dancing, drawing, and physical education. Religion was taught in such a way that sectarian distinctions in theology were completely avoided.

From the very beginning, the school was in serious financial difficulties, for which Basedow's enthusiasm failed to compensate. Kant's correspondence with Basedow and the men who replaced him, C. H. Wolke and J. H. Campe, reflects Kant's efforts to keep the Philanthropin in business.[50] The most important of these letters, for a view of Kant's ideas on education and especially on religious instruction, is the letter to Wolke of 1776, Ak. [109]. Kant believed that a child "must be raised in freedom, but in such a way that he will allow others to be free as well" (*Reflexionen zur Anthropologie*, No. 1473). In the letter to Wolke, he makes explicit his opposition to traditional methods of education and especially to customary religious education. Kant urges that a child not even be introduced to prayer until his understanding has matured to such a degree that he can understand (what Kant regards as) the true purpose of devotional acts, viz., to apprehend his duties as if the latter were divine commands.

IV. LETTERS FROM 1781 ONWARD

Reactions to the Critique of Pure Reason: Mendelssohn and Garve

Readers of Kant who find him difficult to understand may be reassured by the response of Kant's own contemporaries to the publication of the *Critique of Pure Reason*. Mendelssohn, on whom Kant had counted heavily to help disseminate the new philosophy, called it "dieses Nervensaftverzehrendes Werk" – "this nerve-juice-consuming book"! Garve, too, proved disappointingly unsympathetic. To Mendelssohn and to Garve Kant wrote in 1783, carefully setting forth some of the main theses of the *Critique* and defending himself against various criticisms, especially that of "unpopularity" in style of writing. Kant challenges Garve to compose a deduction of the categories that will make pleasant reading, or to try to construct a "whole new science" without the difficult arguments and distinctions in the *Critique* (to Garve, August 7, 1783, Ak. [205]; to Mendelssohn, August 16, Ak. [206]).

These letters taken together provide not only a nice introduction to some of Kant's major theses but also show Kant's view (in 1783) on two matters which his critics have frequently debated and about which it must be admitted Kant himself was never entirely clear: the distinction between "appearances" and "things in themselves," on the one hand, and the distinction between sensible and supersensible "objects." Talking about the first distinction, Kant says to Garve that it is a difference between two concepts or ways of talking about all given objects. Viewed in this light, the distinction does not commit Kant to the "two worlds" theory of the dissertation. One and the same thing can be regarded from the perspective of "appearances" or considered apart from its appearing, i.e., as it may be in itself. In the letter to Mendelssohn, however, Kant speaks of the existence of two radically different kinds of entities. The *Critique*, he says, does not aim to deny the existence of objects (*Gegenstände*) that are not objects of possible experience; in fact, the existence of such entities is required by it! It would seem, then, that the claim that there exist supersensible objects (*übersinnliche Gegenstände*) must be distinguished from the "appearance" versus "thing in itself" distinction, for, as Kant had indicated only a week earlier, in distinguishing appearances from things as they are in themselves, the phrase "thing in itself" refers not to some object other than the object we encounter in experience but to that same object considered apart from its relation to a knowing subject. In the decades following, the problem of the status of the Kantian thing in itself became one of the main targets for Kant's critics. Discussion centered around the question whether Kant's theory of perception entails the claim that unknowable things in themselves are the cause of our sense impressions. Kant's student, J. S. Beck, attempted to save him from inconsistency by interpreting his theory to mean that "thing in itself" is just another way of talking about the object that appears and that it is this same object, not some mysterious supersensible entity, that affects our senses. Kant's answers to Beck's letters do not positively endorse this interpretation – by then Kant was old and, as he told his followers, no longer equipped for overly subtle discussions – but the letter to Garve may be taken as one piece of evidence in support of Beck's interpretation.

Disciples and Critics

The sudden profusion of letters after 1783 attests to the impact of the *Critique of Pure Reason* on the intellectual life of Germany and Europe. Though Kant's reputation in the learned world was already high, his fame now became extended well beyond the sphere of the universities. Kant's philosophy was the topic of discussion in literary salons and court gatherings. Young ladies wrote to him for moral guidance, and religious zealots and political absolutists, deploring the popularity of his liberal ideas, wrote to him to try to convert him. Kant was hailed as the benefactor of mankind, liberator of the human spirit and defender of freedom. Journals were founded to spread the critical philosophy, and several of Kant's students wrote popularizations of his work to make him understandable to the general reading public. The progress of Kant's philosophy did not go unchallenged, however. An upsurge of fanaticism, religious fundamentalism, and political interference in the form of censorship and loyalty oaths was about to begin. As early as 1783 Kant heard from his former student, F. V. .L. Plessing, that the enemies of the Enlightenment were gathering strength, a lament which Plessing repeated in his letter of March 15, 1784, Ak. [226]. Rumor had it that "a Protestant king is supposed secretly to be a J-s-t!" wrote Plessing. The Jesuits, "those hellish spirits," had poisoned the hearts of princes. As far as the government was concerned, Plessing's dire warnings were a few years premature. Kant's most vocal enemies, at this time, were not political figures but the old guard philosophy professors, rationalist defenders of Leibniz and Wolff or empiricist followers of Locke.

Although Kant was attacked and misunderstood by some of the popular philosophers, both empiricists (who assailed Kant for subscribing to synthetic a priori judgments), and rationalists (who assailed him for limiting knowledge to the domain of experience), the fervent support of younger men must have compensated him for these hostile opinions. In Königsburg itself, the mathematician Johann Schultz was a loyal ally. Kantianism was taught and disseminated by dedicated new disciples at the University of Jena, especially C. G. Schütz, K. C. E. Schmid, and K. L. Reinhold. The *Allgemeine Literatur-Zeitung*, to which Kant contributed, did much to promote the critical philosophy. Schütz, whose correspondence with Kant is of interest in tracing the progress of Kant's writings after the *Critique of Pure Reason*, was the author of the first sensible review of the *Critique*, and it was he who persuaded Kant to write a review of Herder's *Ideen* (1785) for the *A.L.Z.*[51] (Schütz was moved to tears by Kant's refusal of the generous honorarium offered by the journal.) Schmid's support of Kantianism came in the form of an elucidatory dictionary of Kantian terminology, *Wörterbuch zum leichteren Gebrauche der Kantischen Schriften* (1788), and Reinhold's *Letters concerning the Kantian Philosophy* (1786/87 in the *Deutsche Merkür*, 1790 as a book) was most important in popularizing Kant.[52] By 1787, when Reinhold was professor of philosophy at the University of Jena, people spoke of the "Kant-Reinhold" philosophy – a phrase that lost its cogency, however, when Reinhold became a follower of Fichte.[53] Reinhold's letters to Kant, in 1787 and 1788, are rhapsodic in praising the critical philosophy and its creator. They also contain some interesting academic gossip, including some anecdotes about Kant's enemy at Jena, J. A. H. Ulrich, who made a practice of inviting Reinhold's students to dinner in order to seduce them away from the study of Kant! Kant's letter to Reinhold, in 1788, expresses his opinion of various contemporaries and states his approval of Reinhold's work. Of greater philosophical interest, however, are Kant's letters in the following year, in which he gives a lengthy account of his objections to the Wolffian philosopher J. A. Eberhard.[54]

Eberhard, professor of philosophy at Halle, was founder of the *Philosophisches Magazin*, another periodical opposed to Kant's philosophy. He denied the originality of Kant's analytic – synthetic distinction, rejected the "Copernican revolution" with its consequent limitation of the understanding to objects of sensible intuition, and argued that reason, being capable of intellectual intuitions, can furnish its own "material" without the aid of the senses. Kant, in his letters to Reinhold, is especially critical of Eberhard's attempt to use the principles f contradiction and sufficient reason as devices for achieving substantive knowledge of objects. Some of the material in these letters was later incorporated into Kant's polemical essay against Eberhard, *Über eine Entdeckung nach der alle neue Kritik der reinen Vernunft durch eine ältere entbehrlich gemacht werden soll* (On a discovery according to which all new critique of pure reason is supposed to be obviated by an earlier one, 1790), in which Kant attacks the metasensible use of reason, refutes Eberhard's objections to his notion of synthetic judgments, and offers an interpretation of Leibniz, arguing that Leibniz's theory requires completion by Kant's own philosophy. The main points in this essay against the philosophical *ancien régime* may be found in the letters to Reinhold of 1789.

Other Opposition: Marburg and Berlin

Eberhard's controversy with Kant was by no means the only occasion on which the partisans of competing philosophies did battle with Kant and his followers. In Marburg, as mentioned earlier, the conflict came to a head sooner than elsewhere. At the probable instigation of the Wolffians, Kant's theories were investigated for alleged impiety and religious skepticism, and in 1786 lecturers were actually forbidden to discuss his philosophy.[55] It may be that Kant's critic, Feder, still stung by the untoward aftereffects of his hostile review of the *Critique*, was one of the main forces behind the ban.

Meanwhile in Berlin, the death of Frederick the Great (1786) and the accession of Friedrich Wilhelm II created a climate that proved to be hostile not only to Kant but to all the Enlightenment, including some of Kant's bitter opponents. Whereas the Wolffians regarded Kant as insufficiently appreciative of the powers of "reason" in metaphysics, the inspired irrationalists who now came to power could see him only as the embodiment of rationalism, an intractable critic of every form of mysticism zealotry, and as the enemy of orthodox, historical Christianity. The actual suppression of heresy did not get seriously started until 1788. As late as December 1787, Kant learned from J. C. Berens that the new king was still allowing the same freedom of the press enjoyed under his predecessor.[56] But one year later, the troubles had begun.[57] Johann Christoph Wöllner (1732–1800) replaced von Zedlitz as *Staatsminister* on July 3, 1788. On July 9, the edict was issued, threatening to punish every deviation from the teachings of "symbolische Bücher" with civil penalties and the loss of office. It was suspected in some quarters that since Kant had claimed that reason was incapable of providing theoretical knowledge of the supersensible, he must be secretly sympathetic to the religious reactionaries. His friends therefore implored him to make his position emphatically clear so as to stop the fanatics. A book merchant named Meyer wrote from Berlin[58] asking Kant to compose an essay on freedom of the press to fight the growing suppression. Kiesewetter and Biester kept Kant informed of developments in the capital, where, for a time, the liberal theologians and clerics paid little attention to the government's repressive edicts on religion.[59] In the decade that followed, the antics of Freidrich Wilhelm II and his pious councilors were to become more than the joking matter they at first appeared to be. The king's mystical visions and sexual escapades are reported with evident relish in a number of Kiesewetter's gossipy letters of 1790 and after.

The heretic-hunting mood reached its climax, for Kant's career, in 1793–94, when Kant's publications on religion were brought under the censorship of the royal Commission on Spiritual Affairs. In 1792, Fichte had sought Kant's advice on how to get his own *Critique of All Revelation* approved by the censor of theology in the University of Halle, for it was not only the government that sought to suppress freedom of thought but some of the theological faculties in the universities themselves. Kant explained to Stäudlin[60] what he had tried to do in his *Religion within the Limits of Reason Alone* and how he had presented the book to the theological faculty in Königsberg to avoid conflict with the authorities. In the fall of 1794, however, the order condemning Kant's book, and any further expression of his unorthodox views, was issued by the king's minister, Wöllner. Kant was obedient, though his response to the king[61] is in no way obsequious. Kant's religion of "rational faith" is given a powerful statement here.

Granting the forcefulness of Kant's letter, one must admit nevertheless that Kant was constitutionally timid.[62] Now in his old age, Kant was unwilling to spend his remaining energy on political (or for that matter philosophical) disputes. His letters of 1789 and after speak repeatedly of his advancing age and increasing frailty. Again and again he excuses himself for failing to act vigorously against his various opponents. Biester respectfully but disappointedly accepted Kant's decision to comply with the royal decree commanding Kant's silence.[63] As we have noted, it was only after the death of Friedrich Wilhelm II in 1797 that Kant felt himself freed from his promise (on the rather casuistic grounds that the pronoun in "Your Majesty's servant" referred specifically to Friedrich Wilhelm II, so that Kant's duty to remain silent was only to that monarch).

Though Kant took a lively interest in the public controversies and political turbulence of the decade following 1789, he devoted himself as much as possible to the completion of his philosophical system. Only on rare occasions did he allow himself to be distracted from this work. One such occasion was the famous Mendelssohn-Jacobi feud in the 1780s. Two others, of more personal than literary or philosophical interest, were the Plessing affair and the tragic case of Maria von Herbert. Each of these three topics requires some explanation.

Mendelssohn, Lessing, and Jacobi.

The literary quarrel between Mendelssohn and Jacobi that came to be known as the *Pantheismusstreit*, or pantheism controversy,[64] dominated the discussions of German intellectuals for several years, until finally Kant himself was drawn into the dispute. Kant's essay "Was heißt: Sich im Denken orientieren?" (What does it mean to orient oneself in thinking? 1786) contains his answer to the disputants, both of whom had attempted to gain his support. The story of this controversy is somewhat complicated. F. H. Jacobi (1743–1819), a *Sturm und Drang* novelist and "philosopher of faith,"[65] had maintained that Spinoza's philosophy contained the only logically acceptable system of metaphysics. Since this system was monistic, however, it entailed the denial of any genuine theism. To accept Spinozism was therefore to become an atheist. Hume, according to Jacobi, had performed an important service by exposing the pretensions of natural theology, for he had made it clear that belief in God is an affair of the heart, not of reason, and that philosophy (that is, Spinozism) must be given up in the name of faith. (Jacobi also argued for the possibility of immediate intuitions of a supersensible reality, and he is famous for a criticism of Kant's doctrine concerning things in themselves – "Without it, I could not get into the system, and with it I could not remain.") Like Kant, however, Jacobi held that the domain of human cognition is restricted to objects of possible experience. Reason is incapable of penetrating beyond the sensible.[66] But so much the worse for reason!

Now Lessing's position was not altogether opposed to Jacobi's. Lessing had published some works of the deist H. S. Reimarus (1694–1768) (under the title *Wolffenbüttel Fragments*) but unlike the deists, Lessing did not believe religious truths capable of proof. A pioneer of the "higher criticism," Lessing believed that faith rests on inner experience and that religious ideas are to be judged by their effect on conduct. Lessing died in 1781 just after he had admitted to Jacobi that Spinoza's theory seemed to him correct. This is what Jacobi wrote to Mendelssohn in 1783, and from this disclosure arose their furious controversy, a controversy on which some were even to put the blame for Mendelssohn's death in 1786.[67] Since pantheism seemed to Jacobi indistinguishable from atheism, he was shocked at Lessing's confession. Mendelssohn, however, took Jacobi's attack on Lessing to be also an attack on himself, and even though Mendelssohn was by no means a pantheist he felt called upon to defend Spinoza and Lessing. In his book Morning Lessons (*Morgenstunden*, 1785, sometimes referred to as Morning Hours), Mendelssohn challenged Jacobi, who replied by publishing his answer to Mendelssohn and their letters to each other.

Herder and Goethe were drawn into the argument, both of them rejecting Jacobi's equation of Spinozism with atheism.

What Lessing had said to Jacobi was that orthodox ideas about God were of no utility to him. God is One and All, and if Lessing had to name anyone as philosophically sound, it would have to be Spinoza. Like Spinoza, Lessing believed human actions to be determined. God is the ultimate cause of the world order, and everything that exists is a part of him. "Why should not the ideas that God has of real things be these real things themselves?" asked Lessing.[68] One consequence of the *Pantheismusstreit* was the revival of interest in the study of Spinoza. Another, as has been mentioned, was Kant's essay on orientation. The main letters mentioning the feud are those from Mendelssohn (October 16, 1785, Ak. [248]), Biester (June 11, 1786, Ak. [275]), and Herz (February 27, 1786, Ak. [260]) as well as Kant's letter to Herz (April 7, 1786, Ak. [267]). In the last of these, Kant adjudges Jacobi guilty of a frivolous and affected "inspired fanaticism" (*Genieschwärmerei*) and goes on to speak of "the excellent Moses," but Kant's defense of reason, in his orientation essay and elsewhere, shows him to be critical of both sides of the dispute.

L'affaire Plessing

When the Akademie edition scholars were assembling manuscripts and copies of Kant's correspondence, it was with considerable reluctance that an indelicate letter of Plessing's (April 3, 1784, Ak. [228]) was included in the published collection. Plessing's friendship with Kant is a significant counterexample for any theory that pictures Kant the "stern moralist" as utterly inflexible, prudish, or inhuman. F. V. L. Plessing (1749–1806) was a fascinating and unstable person who figured not only in Kant's life but also in Goethe's (whose *Harzreise im Winter* depicts Plessing). In his youth, Plessing studied at one university after another, unable to settle on any one subject or in any one place. His life was beset with neurotic and financial difficulties involving his family. In 1782 he came to know Kant and Hamann in Königsberg and decided that it might still be possible to make something of himself, whereupon he studied for the doctorate with Kant. Plessing did in fact become a philosopher,[69] and some of his correspondence with Kant is concerned with his philosophy of history. He was a brooding, troubled man who found himself able to accept Kant's negative doctrines, though he remained basically dissatisfied with Kant's faith grounded on morality.

As Plessing's letters to Kant make clear, Plessing had become involved in (and had lost) a paternity suit, and Kant had helped him by acting as intermediary in transmitting Plessing's maintenance payments. Kant's willingness to become involved in such an unprofessional and undignified assignment reveals a less rigoristic attitude on his part than one might have expected. A careful reading of the letter will disclose that Kant's tolerance of Plessing's human failings did not, however, extend to a condoning of the "unnatural" and calculated practice of birth control. Plessing's arguments against Kant on this matter show a lively wit. It is unfortunate that Kant's answer to Plessing is not available to us. (Kant's highly puritanical attitude toward sex is made very explicit, however, in another letter, where even marital sexual relations are viewed as unsavory and the sexual libertine likened to a cannibal!)[70]

Maria von Herbert

Whatever difficulties Kant's philosophy may have encountered in Prussia and other northern German states, the spread of Kantian ideas in Austria and southern Germany aroused even more opposition. (This may be seen in the letters of M. Reuß, Ak. [699], and C. Stang, Ak. [715], two Benedictine followers of Kant.) In the town of Klagenfurt in southern Austria, however, there lived a Baron Franz Paul von Herbert, one of the few people in conservative Austria who was interested in the philosophy of Kant. The extent of his dedication is shown by the fact that in 1789, "driven by a philosophical itch" (as K. Vorländer puts it)[71] he left his business, wife, and child to journey to Weimar to meet Wieland, then, in 1790, to Jena, to study Kant's philosophy with Reinhold. In 1791, he returned to Klagenfurt, bringing with him some of the revolutionary spirit of the critical philosophy. Herbert's house then became a center for the passionate discussion of Kant's philosophy. It was, in the words of one of Fichte's students, "a new Athens," dedicated to, among other things, the reform of religion, a task that required replacing piety with morality.

Maria, the young sister of Franz Paul, who participated in these discussions, was born in 1769. In family circles she was called "Mizza" and her face was said to be very beautiful. If her physical appearance is somewhat a matter of conjecture to us, the intensity of her emotions and the sensitivity of her intellect (notwithstanding her charmingly bad spelling) are not. In 1791 she wrote her first letter to Kant, a supplication full of anguish, which impressed him so deeply that he showed it to his friend Borowski and prepared a careful preliminary draft of his answer to her plea. Erhard, a friend of her brother's and of Kant's, explained in a letter that she had thrown herself into the arms of a certain man "in order to realize an ideal love." Evidently the man turned out to be a cad for, as Erhard says, he "misused her." Maria fell in love a second time, and for a while she deceived her new lover about her previous relationship. When she finally disclosed her earlier love affair to him, his feeling for her cooled. In her letter, she begs Kant for guidance. Kant's answer is interesting for what it reveals about his own sensitivity to the nuances of emotional and moral problems and about his views on love. He presents his statement in the manner of a sermon, and there is a gently didactic tone throughout. Kant seems willing to make some concessions to the natural weaknesses of human beings. He says in effect that, although we have a duty to abstain from lying and from insincerity, we are to be forgiven for failing to pour out every secret of our hearts to someone we love. An ideal love would consist in mutual esteem and a totally uninhibited sharing, but the inability to be utterly open with another person is a sort of reticence that lies in human nature and does not constitute a weakness of character. These consoling remarks are followed, however, by some more characteristically Kantian moralizing: Maria is not to take pride or any moral credit for confessing her earlier deception, if what motivated her disclosure was only a desire to achieve peace of mind rather than true repentance for having lied. Nor should she brood over the new lover's change of heart; for if his affection does not return, it was probably only sensual in the first place. Besides, the value of one's life does not depend on whether or not one achieves happiness.

The second and third letters Maria sent to her "spiritual physician" are less agitated than the first, but it is not so much resignation as a deeper despair and a sense of overwhelming apathy that breathes through them. The inner emptiness she expresses, the sense of being "almost superfluous" to herself, of being incapable of significant action (even morality has become uninterestingly easy for her, since she feels no temptation to transgress its laws), suggest a beautiful personality destroying itself by the very clarity of its self-awareness. Maria tells Kant, in her third letter (sometime early in 1794, Ak. [614]) that she had in fact been on the point of suicide but that though death would please her she will not take her own life out of consideration for morality and the feelings of her friends. Kant did not answer either of these letters but sent them to Elisabeth Motherby, the daughter of one of his English friends in Königsberg, as a warning to the young woman (whose "good training had, however, made such a warning unnecessary," Kant says) of what happens to women when they think too much and fail to control their fantasies! For all his philosophical acumen, philanthropy and liberalism, Kant was no enthusiast for women's rights; nor was he sensitive to the frustrations suffered by intelligent women in a society that viewed them as merely useful or decorative ornaments.[72] In 1803, nine years after her last letter, Maria did in fact commit suicide.

From Kant to Fichte

Kant's philosophical letters in the 1790s touch on a great number of topics, but some of the most interesting letters are those that show the gradual defection of his once ardent admirers, letters that show the development of Kant's own thinking in response to their questions and criticisms. It is a pity that there are no very serious philosophical exchanges with Fichte in the correspondence, but we do see the beginnings of their relationship and, in a sense, with Kant's open declaration against Fichte's *Wissenschaftslehre*, the end. Kant's letter of February 2, 1792, Ak.[504], contains his advice to Fichte on how to deal with the censorship authorities in Halle and offers a statement of Kant's religious beliefs. A number of other letters in 1792 concern Kant's efforts to help Fichte publish his *Critique of All Revelation* (*Versuch einer Kritik aller Offenbarung*) and, with the subsequent confusion as to its authorship, Fichte's explanation and apologies for the confusion. The book was attributed to Kant himself, partly because it came from his publisher, Hartung. Hartung had inadvertently left out the Preface, in which Fichte spoke of the work as "my first venture before the public," a phrase that would have made clear that the anonymous author was not Kant.

The correspondence with Salomon Maimon, Jakob Sigismund Beck, and Johann Heinrich Tieftrunk provides a wealth of discussion of just those issues – principally the problems concerning the *Ding an sich*, the source of the "matter" of sensibility, and the primacy of *Zusammensetzung* (composition or synthesis) – that make the transition from Kant to Fichte comprehensible.

In 1789 Salomon Maimon (1753–1800) sent Kant the manuscript of his (Essay on the transcendental philosophy, 1790). *Versuch über die Transzendentalphilosophie*. Their mutual friend Herz described Maimon to Kant as "formerly one of the rawest Polish Jews" who by virtue of his brilliance and perseverance had miraculously managed to educate himself in all the sciences.[73] Herz had read the book, and it was on his advice that Maimon asked for Kant's opinion of it. Kant answered Maimon's criticisms in a letter to Herz, May 26, 1789, Ak.[362], and called Maimon's work a book full of "the most subtle investigations" written by an astute critic who, Kant thought, had understood him better than any other. Maimon wrote again in July 1789, expressing his gratitude for Kant's rejoinder, though he was not satisfied with Kant's reply. He wrote several times in 1790, again in 1791 (Ak.[486], 1792 (Ak.[548], and 1793 (Ak.[606]), but Kant did not answer him.[74]

Maimon's criticism of Kant in 1789 already point the way to Fichte and the idealist movement that was soon to take hold. He denied Kant's basic distinction between passive sensibility and the active, spontaneous understanding. He maintained that the human mind is part of an infinite world soul that produces not only the form but also the content of experience. The understanding is intuitive, not merely discursive. Maimon accepted the negative, antidogmatic part of Kant's theory as correct but rejected the positive theory of things in themselves (a theory which he interpreted as claiming the existence of a thinkable entity without any determinate characteristics) as inconceivable. We cannot form a clear concept of either an object-in-itself or of a subject-in-itself. The "thing in itself" loses its character of thinghood, in Maimon's philosophy, and becomes merely an irrational limit of rational cognition, the idea of an endless task whose completion is constantly retreating as knowledge advances. The "self-contradictory" (according to Maimon) assumption of the existence of things independent of all consciousness arose in the attempt to explain the origin of the "content" of appearances; but there is in fact no content or material of experience independent of form. The distinction between the matter and form of knowledge is only a contrast between a complete and an incomplete consciousness of what is present to us, the incomplete consciousness being what we refer to as the given, that irrational residue that we distinguish from the a priori forms of consciousness. The contrast is only one of degree; form and matter are the terminal members of an infinite series of gradations of consciousness. The given is therefore only an idea of the limit of this series.

While on some issues Maimon took Hume's position against Kant's (for example, he maintained that the concept of causality is the product of habit, not a pure concept of the understanding), his indebtedness to Leibniz is also evident. For some reason Maimon called himself a skeptic, but his rejection of Kant's account of things in themselves and the given, along with his conception of the human understanding as part of the divine understanding, clearly foreshadows Fichte and the development of post-Kantian idealism. In fact, Fichte wrote to Reinhold, in 1795, "My esteem for Maimon's talent is boundless. I firmly believe and am ready to prove that through Maimon's work the whole Kantian philosophy, as it is understood by everyone including yourself, is completely overturned. . . . All this he has accomplished without anyone's noticing it and while people even condescend to him. I think that future generations will mock our century bitterly."

Kant's correspondence with Jakob Beck (1761–1840) contains not only some of the most penetrating criticisms of Kant's theory but also an indication of how Kant was himself being influenced by the men he denounced as "my hypercritical friends." By 1799, the 75-year-old Kant (who complained to Garve, September 21, 1798, Ak.[820], that his condition was reduced to that of a vegetable) was so saddened by the independent line taken by his former students that he angrily criticized the position of Fichte (whose books he had not actually read) and Beck (whose position he had virtually adopted as his own) in an open letter or declaration on Fichte's *Wissenschaftslehre* (August 7, 1799, the last letter in this volume of correspondence). There he charged that the *Critique of Pure Reason* had not been intended as a propaedeutic to any future system of metaphysics, that it was in fact the complete statement of pure philosophy, and that no "standpoint" (the allusion is to Beck's *Only Possible Standpoint from which the Critical Philosophy Must Be Judged*) or any interpreter or commentator is required in order to comprehend it.

All of these remarks are either false or misleading. The occasion of the declaration was a challenge put to Kant by a reviewer in the *Erlanger Litteraturzeitung*, January 11, 1799, who asked Kant whether his theories were really meant to be taken literally ("buchstäblich," according to the letter) or as interpreted by Fichte or Beck. Kant's personal attack on Fichte as a "treacherous friend" may have been encouraged by his overly zealous disciple Johann Schultz, on whom Kant relied for an account of Fichte's position and whom Kant had earlier (see the letter to J. A. Schlettwein, May 29, 1797, Ak.[752]) endorsed as his most reliable expositor. Certainly, neither Fichte nor Beck had done anything to deserve it. Fichte's official reply, in the form of an open letter to Schelling, was temperate. Privately, however, he declared Kant's theory to be "total nonsense" unless given a Fichtean interpretation; he even called Kant "no more than three-quarters of a mind" who had "mightily prostituted himself."[75] That the *Critique* was supposed to be a propaedeutic to a reconstruction of metaphysics was not only asserted by Kant himself in numerous passages in the *Critique* but clearly implied by him in his references to the system of metaphysics he intended to compose when "the critical part of [his] task" was finished. This is what he had written to L. H. Jakob, Ak. [303], and to Reinhold, Ak.[322], in 1787 and 1788 in connection with his completion of the third *Critique*.[76] A sketch of Kant's planned system of metaphysics was even included in a letter to Beck in an important letter of 1792, Ak. [500], and the outline Kant gives there agrees with the reorganized form of the *Critique* that Beck recommended in his own letters. It would seem then that the doctrinal gulf between Kant and his erstwhile disciples was not at all as wide as Kant suggests in the declaration against Fichte.

Like Maimon, Beck denied the positive role that Kant's theory of perception seemed to have given to things in themselves. Beck argued that when Kent spoke of objects affecting our sensibility it could only be phenomenal objects that he had meant, not an unknowable thing in itself acting on an unknowable subject in itself. The self that is affected and the object that acts on it must both be viewed as products of a more basic activity of the understanding, an activity that we presuppose when we regard our experiences as produced in us *either* by an independent object *or* by our own power of thinking. This most basic activity Beck equated with the function of producing the transcendental unity of apperception in Kant's deduction of the categories, and it is this "standpoint" one needs to attain in order to understand Kant's theory. It is a unique act of a priori composition, an act whereby the subject constitutes itself as a conscious thinker.

Kant's agreement with Beck is shown most clearly in his willingness to make the activity of composition (*Zusammensetzung*, a word Kant sometimes uses interchangeably with "synthesis" or the Latin *combinatio*) the basic condition of all cognition. Beck used the phrase "original attribution" ("ursprüngliche Beylegung"), which Kant at first (and with justification) found unintelligible; Beck's colleague J. H. Tieftrunk spoke of an act of *Setzen* (positing), Ak. [787]; and in Fichte's *Wissenschaftslehre* the ego "posits" the non-ego in an original *Tathandlung* (a neologism of Fichte's, the "deed-act"). Although each of these philosophers found his own views to be either subtly or dramatically different from those of the others (Beck, for example, tried to convince Kant that he was radically opposed to Fichte), they agreed that Kant's theory of affection must be reconsidered or reformulated. But Kant himself had certainly already modified his position when he wrote to Beck, as early as January, 1792, Ak. [500]: "You put the matter quite precisely when you say, 'The union of representations is itself the object...' [which] must thus ... *be produced*, and by an inner activity ... that precedes a priori the manner in which the manifold is given." Beck thought that Kant's method of exposition in the *Critique* was only a concession to the uninitiated "pre-Critical" reader who had not yet arrived at the "standpoint" of seeing "objects" as the product of that original activity of the understanding. He and Tieftrunk, both of them perhaps reiterating the criticisms of G. E. Schulze, argued that it was inconsistent of Kant to make an unknowable thing in itself that which affects us – inconsistent because "affecting" is a casual relation and the concept of cause is supposed to be meaningful only intraphenomenally, and because Kant seems to know a great deal about unknowables here, for example, that they are real (another category illegitimately used) and efficacious. Beck's suggested reconstruction of Kant's theory, which would begin with the "standpoint," that is, the original activity of mind that first produces the "I think" expressed in the categories, was, as has already been pointed out, not at all uncongenial to Kant, and the extent of Beck's influence on Kant may be seen in Kant's *Opus postumum*.[77]

Kant complained repeatedly about a loss of vigor due to his advancing years, and there is evidence in the letters of his growing inability to think himself into the arguments and theories of his disciples and critics. His writings, however, show no loss of energy or clarity of vision. He had given up seminars and private instruction in 1793, but continued to give public lectures until 1797, the year in which his *Metaphysics der Sitten* (*Metaphysics of Morals*), containing the jurisprudential *Rechtslehre* ("Doctrine of Right" or "Metaphysical Foundations of Justice") and the *Tugendlehre* ("Doctrine of Virtue") finally appeared. The year 1797 also saw the publication of a short essay, "On a supposed right to lie out of altruism," a favored target of critics of Kantian rigorism in ethics – the essay argues that truthfulness is an unconditional, sacred duty, whatever the consequences. Kant's final project, the transition from the metaphysical foundations of natural science to physics, which was to fill a "gap" in the system of his Critical Philosophy, remained unfinished at the time of his death, February 24, 1804.[78]

The apostasy of Kant's ablest disciples may give the impression that Kant's final years were spent in friendless isolation. This was not the case. The love and esteem of his friends and many former students continued throughout their lives and his, and the respect of distinguished writers such as Schiller must have been very pleasing to Kant's old age.[79] From Berlin, Kiesewetter kept him supplied with his favorite carrots,[80] along with the latest court gossip. In a note, July 8, 1800, Ak.[867], Kant thanked Kiesewetter for his two-volume refutation of Herder's *Metakritik* and reassured him that the carrots he sent the previous fall were not damaged by the winter frost. John Richardson, who published English translations of Kant and Beck, kept Kant informed on the progress of his philosophy in England.[81] J. H. I. Lehmann sent sausages from Göttingen (along with gossip and Feder's belated apologies to Kant), as did F. Nicolovius,[82] and Herz wrote movingly to his old friend and mentor.[83] Until 1801, his seventy-seventh year, Kant devoted what energy he had to completing his system, the "gap"-filling transition project already mentioned. But in April of 1802 he wrote,[84] "My strength diminishes daily, my muscles vanish, and even though I have never had any actual illness and have none now, it is two years since I have been out of the house. Nevertheless I view all changes that are in store for me with calm." In April 1803, he celebrated his last (seventy-ninth) birthday with his dinner companions. In October of that year he became ill (after eating his favorite English cheese) but recovered sufficiently to entertain his usual dinner guests later that month. From December until the following February, however, he grew much weaker and his death came on the twelfth of February, "a cessation of life and not a violent act of nature," said his friend and biographer, Wasianski.[85]

Introduction

NOTES

1　E.g., Jacobi's *Über die Lehre des Spinoza in Briefen an den Herrn Moses Mendelssohn* (On the doctrine of Spinoza in letters to Herr Moses Mendelssohn, 1785). Jacobi also wrote a novel which, like Goethe's *Sorrows of Young Werther*, is a *Briefroman*, i.e., a novel composed of letters.

2　The only important exception to Kant's opposition to publication of his letters is his response to Friedrich Wilhelm II's *Kabinettsordre* of Oct. 1, 1794. Both the order condemning Kant's *Religion within the Limits of Reason Alone* and Kant's letter of response were published in the Preface to Kant's *Der Streit der Fakultäten (The Conflict of the Faculties*, 1798), Ak. 7: 1–116. One of three drafts of Kant's letter (for once he did not write hastily!) is included in the present collection. See Ak.[640] and [641]. A little letter by Kant concerning the magician-charlatan Cagliostro was published anonymously in 1790 and reprinted, with Kant's permission, in Borowski's biography of Kant.

　　One might also consider as correspondence various "public declarations" Kant published, e.g., the announcement, July 31, 1792, that Fichte and not Kant was the author of *Attempt at a Critique of All Revelation*, the book that brought initial fame to Fichte. There is also an open letter of Dec. 6, 1796, explaining that Kant's friend Hippel was the author of an anonymously published essay on marriage and of Hippel's novel, which, because it contained material from Kant's lectures, had been attributed to Kant.

3　These include Johann Friedrich Hartknoch the elder (1740–1789) who was also Hamann's publisher, and Hartknoch's son (1768–1819). The Hartknoch firm published the *Critique of Pure Reason*. Other publishers with whom Kant corresponded were Friedrich Nicolovius (1768–1836), and François Théodore de Lagarde (1756–?), publisher of the *Critique of Judgment*. Understandably, there are no letters from or to the publisher Johann Jakob Kanter, for Kant lived in Kanter's house for ten years. All of these people are mentioned in Kant's letters.

4　See, e.g., his letters to J. Bernoulli, Nov. 16, 1781, Ak.[172], and to Marcus Herz, Apr. 7, 1786, Ak.[267]. To G. C. Reccard, a professor of theology in Königsberg, he wrote on June 7, 1781, Ak.[167], concerning the posthumous collection of Lambert's correspondence, subsequently published in 1781. Kant apologized that his work on the *Critique of Pure Reason* had kept him from writing anything useful to Lambert and requested that his letters not be included in the publication. Kant's wishes were however ignored, as was the case also with his correspondence with Salomon Maimon, published in 1792.

5　Johann Benjamin Jachmann, Oct. 14, 1790, Ak.[452].

6　J. G. C. C. Kiesewetter, various letters from 1789 onward.

7　The phrase is Thomas Hardy's, though it might have been Kant's.

8　The word *Schwärmerei* illustrates the difficulty of consistently translating a German word with the same English expression. It is a term of abuse that occurs with considerable frequency in Kant and his correspondents. In some contexts Schwärmerei is the German equivalent of the English "enthusiasm" as that word was used in the seventeenth and eighteenth century, but not as it is used today. "Enthusiasm" meant the supposed experience of being directly inspired or informed by a god, but *Schwärmerei* is broader in meaning. Sometimes it carries the sense of religious fanaticism or mysticism, but in other contexts a penchant for daydreams, delusions, visions or romantic fantasies. In his *Anthropologie* Kant defined *Schwärmerei* as a form of mental illness, the mistaking of one's self-generated psychological state for a cognition coming from some external source. But Kant also uses the word informally, as when he refers to an emotional young lady, Maria von Herbert, as "die kleine Schwärmerin."

9   This abbreviated account of the publication and dissemination of the correspondence relies on notes by Rose Burger and Paul Burger and Paul Menzer, editors of the Akademie edition, and on Rudolf Malter and Joachim Kopper's notes to Otto Schöndörffer's edition of the correspondence. Werner Stark's *Nachforschungen zu Briefen und Handschriften Immanuel Kants* (Berlin: Akademie Verlag, 1993) contains corrections and comments on the Akademie edition and covers the history of publication meticulously. Stark indicates, when possible, where the original manuscripts are located and how the letters were assembled for publication.

10   Borowski's *Darstellung des Lebens und Charakters Immanuel Kants* is one of three biographical sketches in *Immanuel Kant. Sein Leben in Darstellungen von Zeitgenossen* (Immanuel Kant's life in descriptions by contemporaries, 1804). The book has been reprinted by the Wissenschaftliche Buchgesellschaft, Darmstadt, 1978.)

Even before Borowski's publication, some of Kant's correspondents published letters or notes he had written to them, perhaps as a testimonial to show that the recipient was acquainted with and appreciated by the great man. Salomon Maimon, e.g., included a trivial note from Kant, Ak.[361], in his 1793 autobiography, a polite response to Maimon's letter, Ak.[352]. Kant's letter does not mention or attempt to answer any of Maimon's critical questions but contains the flattering remark that Maimon has shown himself to possess no ordinary talent for deep philosophical investigations.

11   Sometimes spelled "Rinck." The letters appeared in Rink's *Ansichten aus Immanuel Kants Leben* (Views from Kant's life, 1805).

12   Rudolf Reicke, *Aus Kants Briefwechsel. Vortrag, gehalten am Kants Geburtstag den 22. April, 1885 in der Kant-Gesellschaft zu Königsberg. Mit einen Anhang enthaltend Briefe von Jacob Sigismund Beck an Kant und von Kant an Beck* (Königsberg, 1885.) Wilhelm Dilthey, *Die Rostocker Kanthandschriften*, in *Archiv für Geschichte der Philosophie*, II (1889), pp. 592–650. Victor Diederichs, *Johann Heinrich Kant*, in *Baltische Monatsschrift* 35, vol. 40 (1893), pp. 535–62. Subsequently the Berlin Akademie called for more letters, augmenting Reicke's collection. Needless to say, these sources are not readily available in the United States. Fortunately the researchers for the Akademie edition and later scholars such as Otto Schöndörffer, Rudolf Malter, and Joachim Kopper have provided excellent German editions that obviate seeking out the earlier publications.

13   The additional letters had been published in *Kant-Studien* and elsewhere. A few letters came to light after 1922 and were printed in Ak. 23, 1955. Various collections based on either the first or second Akademie edition have come out, including Ernst Cassirer's vol. IX and X in his edition of Kant's *Werke* (Berlin, 1921), and Otto Schöndörffer's 1970 edition. The third, revised edi-

tion of Schöndörffer, edited by Rudolf Malter and Joachim Kopper (Hamburg: Meiner Verlag, 1986), includes several additional letters. A letter from Kant to Kiesewetter, Ak.[405a], was published in *Journal of the History of Philosophy*, 3 (1965), pp. 243–6, by P. Remnant and C. E. Schweitzer. The letter "a" after an Akademie number indicates that the Akademie editors knew of the existence of a letter but did not have it. A few more recently discovered letters have no Akademie number at all.

14 The letter numbers in square brackets refer to the 1922 edition as do the marginal page numbers in the text. For the benefit of scholars who may have access only to the earlier Akademie edition, each translation also has the numbering of the 1910 edition, if there is one, given in parentheses in the letter's title. Where letters are unsigned it is because they appear that way in the Akademie edition, presumably because the published text is taken from a copy or draft.

15 Kant's *Philosophical Correspondence: 1759–99*, translated and edited by Arnulf Zweig (Chicago: University of Chicago Press, 1967 and 1970). The translations contained in that volume have been revised and, with the generous assistance of various Kant scholars and friends in the intervening years, corrected. Some of those scholars are mentioned in the editorial notes in this work, as well as in the Acknowledgments. Material that is unchanged in this edition is reprinted with the permission of the University of Chicago Press.

16 Schöndörffer's 1924 collection, augmented in 1972 and more recently in 1986 by Malter and Kopper, is the most readable German edition of Kant's letters, especially for readers who have difficulty with *Fraktur*, the older Gothic script used in the Akademie edition. It contains most of the letters Kant himself wrote but omits or abbreviates many letters addressed to him. Schöndörffer's footnotes convey much of the information in the Akademie edition notes, though in conveniently abbreviated form. Notes to the present edition are derived in many cases from these sources.

17 A considerable amount of information in the biographical sketches and editorial notes in this volume, e.g., material about the lives and careers of Maria Herbert, Maimon, and Mendelssohn, also reflects these contemporary interests.

18 A traveler's diary reports Kant's referring to the "barbaric" practice of circumcision and the commercial nature of Jews, "Jetzt sind sie die Vampyre der Gesellschaft," as making full acceptance into German society presently an impossibility for Jews. See Johann Friedrich Abegg, *Reisetagebuch von 1798* (Frankfurt am Main: Insel Verlag, c. 1976).

19 One can see something of the influence of this upbringing not only in Kant's published writings on religion but, e.g., in his powerful – one might almost say passionate – letters to the Swiss theologian Lavater, Ak.[99] and [100].

20 Borowski, Wasianski, and R. B. Jachmann, in *Immanuel Kant. Sein Leben in Darstellungen von Zeitgenossen*, mentioned in n. 10 above, provide firsthand reports on Kant's relation to his parents and sisters, augmenting the meager disclosures in the correspondence between Kant and his brother.

21 Mar. 1, 1763, Ak.[26].

22 See nn. 10 and 20, above. The biographies in addition to Borowski's *Darstellung* were Jachmann's *Immanuel Kant geschildert in Briefen an einen Freund*, and

Wasianski's *Immanuel Kant in seinen letzten Lebensjahren*. Borowski's is the only source for our knowledge of Kant's instructor years.

23 The combination of divinity and science in one career was not unusual: Kant's favorite expositor, with whom he corresponded on the philosophy of mathematics, was also a pastor, court chaplain, and professor of mathematics, Johann Schultz.

24 Kant's financial situation changed decisively with his appointment as professor in 1770; with the 200 Thaler raise he received a few years later he became the highest paid professor in Königsberg. Of course it is difficult to estimate the contemporary equivalent of his salary or to determine how his total income compared with what he was offered for the positions he declined; some of the latter are stated in different currencies and coinages or included cords of wood for heating or cooking as part of the salary. See the notes to Kant's letters to Suckow, Ak.[47], and to Herz, Ak.[134], for some conjectures, the details of Kant's callings, his strategies and petitions to obtain the Königsberg professorship, and what his academic career might have been.

25 The letter from S. G. Suckow, a professor of mathematics in Erlangen, who had been asked to submit the offer of a newly created chair in philosophy to Kant, expresses enthusiasm for Kant's work but, surprisingly, cites Kant's *Beobachtung über das Gefühl des Schönen und Erhabenen*, (Observations on the Feeling of the Beautiful and the Sublime, 1764) rather than any of his scientific or more deeply philosophical essays.

26 Dec. 15, 1769, Ak.[47].

27 The occasion for these remarks to Herz was a generous offer from his patron in Berlin, Minister von Zedlitz, attempting to persuade Kant to accept a professorship in Halle. A professor of theology at Jena, formerly from Königsberg, also tried to lure him, offering 200 Thaler, another 150 for private instruction, plus royalties from publishers eager for his writings – and only two hours of lecturing per week would be required. As Vorländer remarks, what a prospect, if Kant had agreed – he would have had Goethe and Schiller as neighbors! But Kant was "chained eternally" to his hometown. (Karl Vorländer, *Kants Leben*, 2nd ed, Leipzig, 1921, p. 85.)

28 See J. Bering's letter to Kant, Ak.[279].

29 For the royal rebuke see Ak.[640] and for Kant's reply, Ak.[642].

30 Apart from his highly interesting and ambiguous reflections in the *Opus postumum*, where, e.g., he sometimes seems to entertain the thought that God is a human invention.

31 See Lambert's letter, Ak.[33], n. 8, and Kant's letter to Biester, Ak.[168].

32 *Der einzig mögliche Beweisgrund zu einer Demonstration des Daseins Gottes* (1763).

33 *Beobachtungen über das Gefühl des Schönen und Erhabenen* (1764).

34 *Träume eines Geistersehers* (1766).

35 *Versuch, den Begriff der negativen Größen in die Weltweisheit einzuführen* (1763).

36 The scholar is Rolf George. See Ak.[25], n. 2.

37 Some people erroneously believed, after Lambert's death, that Kant's own theory originated with Lambert. In his letter to J. E. Biester, June 8, 1781, Ak.[168], Kant explained that he wrote his *Natural History of the Heavens* before Lambert published a similar cosmological hypothesis and that Lambert had remarked on this similarity in his letter of 1765, Ak.[33]. Kant's letter to J. F.

Gensichen, Apr. 19, 1791, Ak.[466], also discusses the matter. Kant there explains that his own theory of the Milky Way was formulated six years earlier than Lambert's *Cosmological Letters*. This was in fact accurate.

38 Kant in fact published nothing under these titles until, twenty years later (1786), his *Metaphysical Foundations of Natural Science* appeared.

39 For an account of Hamann's conversion and its background, see the biographical sketches. Kierkegaard must have recognized Hamann as a prefiguration of himself. He quotes Hamann on the title page of *Fear and Trembling*.

40 Kant's interest in education and his views on that topic are also shown in his letters to C. H. Wolke, Mar. 28, 1776, and to the famous educational reformer, J. B. Basedow, June 19, 1776, Ak.[109 and 110]. Basedow was founder of the Philanthropin, a progressive school in Dessau, and Wolke its director. On Basedow, see the biographical sketches.

41 Frederick Beiser, in *The Fate of Reason* (Cambridge, Mass.: Harvard University Press, 1987), p. 135, calls Herder's view a "proto-Darwinisn" account; Beiser discusses the relation of Herder's position to those of Rousseau and Condillac, the former "reducing man to an animal," the latter "raising the animal to man."

42 Kant's mind-body dualism is not explicit here but it is clear from his remarks in *Dreams of a Spirit-Seer* that even in the decade before 1770 he thought the relation of mind and body mysterious. His rejection of Swedenborg's claims is not that "spirits" do not exist but that we cannot understand how "the soul" moves "the body" and we should therefore avoid extravagant pseudo-explanations.

43 A translation, by Allen Wood, of this little known essay may be found in the Cambridge edition of Kant's *Practical Philosophy*, 1996.

44 It is interesting to see how Kant remained true to this early thesis throughout his critical writings. Indeed, the claim is generalized in the *Critique of Pure Reason: all* a priori knowledge depends directly or indirectly on "what we have originally put into" our judgments. See, in the *Critique*, A xx, B ix, B xii, B xiii, B 130.

45 Mendelssohn's response in the letter of Dec. 25, 1770, Ak.[63], offers a number of significant criticisms of the dissertation, for example, of Kant's interpretation of Shaftesbury as a follower of Epicurus. Mendelssohn's criticisms of Kant's theory of time, and similar objections by Lambert, are answered in Kant's most famous letter to Herz, Feb. 21, 1772, Ak.[70], and again in the *Critique of Pure Reason*, A 36–B 53 ff. Kant thought that his view had been misinterpreted as a version of the subjective idealism of Berkeley.

46 Kant was led to this view particularly by the problem of space. His essay *Concerning the Ultimate Foundation of the Distinction of Directions in Space* (1768, Ak. 2: 375–83) defended the thesis that conceptually incongruent but symmetric figures (for example, mirror images) cannot be distinguished without assuming, contrary to Leibniz but in agreement with Newton, an absolute space independent of all matter existing in it.

47 On Herz, see the biographical sketches. Virtually all of the standard commentaries on Kant make some mention of Kant's letter to Herz of 1772, but the rest of their correspondence is also either philosophically or biographically interesting. Some scholars (for example, Norman Kemp Smith) see Kant's

1772 letter as supporting the "patchwork theory" of the deduction of the categories, whereas others (for example, H. J. Paton) opposed this interpretation. There are allusions to this letter in most recent commentaries on the *Critique* and its origins. A debate on the letter's significance, between Wolfgang Carl and the late Lewis White Beck, may be found in Eckart Förster, ed., *Kant's Transcendental Deductions* (Stanford: Stanford University Press, 1989).

48 See Ak.[61] and Ak.[63]. Kant answers Lambert's objection in the famous 1772 letter to Herz, Ak.[70]. See especially 10: 134 f.

49 *Religion innerhalb der Grenzen der bloßen Vernunft* (1793), sometimes translated *Religion within the Boundaries of Mere Reason*. The word "blos" in German is ambiguous; it can mean "mere" in a disparaging sense or "nothing but" in the sense of "pure." It is one of those words that makes difficulties for a translator, and indeed for any reader, as when Kant repeatedly refers to objects of experience as "bloß Erscheinung – " often translated "mere appearance" – which has the negative or reductive tone that paves the way to Schopenhauerian misreadings of Kant's claims. In the title of *Religion . . .* it is not the case, I believe, that "reason" is being disparaged. I therefore prefer "alone" to "mere," contrary to the decision of George di Giovanni in the Cambridge Edition of Kant, *Religion and Rational Theology* (1996).

50 To this end, Kant published several appeals for subscriptions in the *Königsberger gelehrte und politische Zeitung*.

51 In Feb. 1785, Schütz wrote to Kant saying that Herder ought to take pride in Kant's discussion of his book – the review was generally recognized as Kant's even though it appeared unsigned. But Herder's reaction to it was not what Schütz predicted, as can be seen from a letter Herder wrote to Hamann in which he expresses his vexation and accuses Kant of being bitter toward him for having decided not to follow the path of his former teacher's "verbal juggling." Herder objects especially to being treated like a schoolboy now that he is forty years old and a thinker in his own right.

52 On Reinhold's life and checkered career as a Kantian, see the biographical sketches.

53 Reinhold's admirable and uncommon candor is shown by his public pronouncement, while still at the height of his fame, that Fichte had refuted him. He died, virtually forgotten, in 1823.

54 On Eberhard's life – and virtues – see the biographical sketches.

55 See notes to Kant's letter to J. Bering, Apr. 7, 1786, Ak.[266].

56 Berens to Kant, Dec. 5, 1787, Ak.[310].

57 Berens to Kant, Oct. 25, 1788, Ak.[338].

58 Sept. 5, 1788, Ak.[333].

59 See Kiesewetter's long letter of Dec. 15, 1789, Ak.[394].

60 See Kant's letter of May 4, 1793, Ak.[574].

61 See the draft of Kant's letter to Friedrich Wilhelm II, written sometime after Oct. 12, 1794, Ak.[642].

62 We may recall how Kant, 20 years earlier, had shown something of this character when, in 1778, considering an opportunity for a better professorship, he confessed to Herz that "all change frightens me" (Ak.[134]).

63 Dec. 17, 1794, Ak.[646]. Biester writes: "I have had occasion to read your

defense in answer to the department of spiritual affairs' claims against your Religion within the Boundaries of Reason. It is noble, manly, virtuous, thorough. Only everyone regrets that you have voluntarily given your promise to say no more about either positive or natural [philosophy of] religion. You have thereby prepared the way for a great victory for the enemies of enlightenment and a damaging blow to the good cause. It seems to me also that you need not have done this. You could have continued to write in your customary philosophical and respectable way about these subjects, though of course you would have had to defend yourself on this or that point. Or you could have remained silent during your lifetime without giving people the satisfaction of being released from the fear of your speaking."

64 This name, as Beiser has pointed out, is something of a misnomer. For the issue debated was not pantheism and its putative viciousness but whether the great Enlightenment writer Lessing had subscribed to this "vice" and, more important, whether "reason" (as worshipped by the enlighteners) inevitably led to fatalism and the repudiation of orthodox religious beliefs. Ch. 2 of Beiser's *The Fate of Reason* offers an excellent account of the controversy and its significance for German intellectual history.

65 On Jacobi, see his letters to Kant and the biographical sketches.

66 Unlike Kant, Jacobi maintained that we perceive things as they are in themselves. He also rejected Kant's formalism in ethics and defended the possibility of immediate moral intuitions.

67 See the biographical sketches of Mendelssohn and Jacobi, as well as Herz's letter, Feb. 27, 1786, Ak.[260], and notes thereto.

68 "On the Reality of Things outside God," an essay for Mendelssohn.

69 In 1788 he accepted a professorship at Duisberg, one of the smallest universities in Germany, far removed from the frontiers of intellectual debate, which was just as he wished.

70 See Kant to C. G. Schutz, July 10, 1797, Ak.[761].

71 K. Vorländer, *Immanuel Kant, der Mann und das Werk* (Leipzig: Felix Meiner, 1924), vol. 2, p. 116.

72 Kant's views on women were even less progressive than this discussion might suggest. His early *Observations on the Feeling of the Beautiful and the Sublime* (1764) betray sentiments close to misogyny. I have discussed "Kant's Antifeminism" in "Kant and the Family," an essay first published in *Kindred Matters*, ed. by Diana Tietjens Meyers, K. Kipnis, and C. F. Murphy, Jr. (Ithaca and London: Cornell University Press, 1993) and reprinted as "Kant's Children," in *The Philosopher's Child*, ed. by Susan M. Turner and Gareth B. Matthews (Rochester: University of Rochester Press, 1998). Kant's behavior in response to Maria Herbert's letters and to a letter from Sophie Mereau, Ak.[689], are two pieces of relevant evidence.

73 See Herz's letter, Apr. 7, 1789, Ak.[351]. On Maimon's remarkable life, see the biographical sketches.

74 In 1794, Kant spoke disparagingly of Maimon, in a letter to Reinhold on Mar. 28, Ak.[620]. It is one of the relatively few occasions on which Kant indulged in anti-Semitic remarks. (Another occurs in his comment on a portrait of Kant made by a Jewish artist, where Kant reports the opinion, probably that of his friend Hippel, that Jewish painters always make people look like Jews, stretch-

ing their noses. This comment too is in a letter to Reinhold, Apr. 23, 1789, Ak.[356]).

75 Vorländer, op. cit., II, 265.

76 Kant's statement to Jakob that on completion of the critical part of his plan he could proceed to the dogmatic is puzzling if one thinks of Kant's customary use of the word "dogmatic" to stigmatize the philosophical method he rejected, viz., one that proceeds without a prior investigation of reason's competence to answer the questions it is asking. But Kant was probably thinking of "dogmatic" in the sense in which he distinguished "dogmata" from "mathemata" in the *Critique of Pure Reason*, A 736=B 764, and not in the derogatory sense. A "dogma" is one sort of non-analytic apodeictic proposition, viz., a synthetic proposition that can be "directly derived from concepts." Mathemata are the other sort of synthetic a priori proposition, not found in philosophy, which can be "directly obtained through the construction of concepts." There are no dogmata "in the whole domain of pure reason, in its merely speculative employment," Kant argued (loc. cit.).

77 There are a number of letters exchanged with Beck that concern other topics. Included here are several dealing with physics and the nature of matter and how variation in density affects gravitational attraction.

78 See the *Opus postumum* volume in the Cambridge Kant edition, edited by Eckart Förster.

79 Kant's correspondence with Schiller unfortunately deals not with substantive matters but with Schiller's request that Kant contribute an article to the journal *Die Horen*. Kant declined. The letters are respectful on both sides. It is not clear whether Kant was aware of Schiller's poetry and dramas.

80 Curious gourmets may be interested in Kiesewetter's advice on how to cook these Teltow carrots, Nov. 25, 1798, Ak.[827]. They must be washed in warm water, dropped at once into boiling water, and then cooked for no more than fifteen minutes. They must be stored in a dry place. One of the last exchanges between Kant and Kiesewetter reports on the survival of carrots through a hard winter. Kant was not indifferent to food, even in his last years.

81 The translation was published in two volumes in London, 1798–99. See Richardson's letter of June 22, 1798, Ak.[808], and the notes to it.

82 Friedrich Nicolovius (1768–1836) was a publisher in Königsberg.

83 Dec. 25, 1797, Ak.[791].

84 To the fiancé of his brother's daughter, Pastor K. C. Schoen, Apr. 28, 1802, Ak.[892].

85 Wasianski, op. cit., p. 303. Wasianski's detailed account of Kant's death is a little like Plato's account of the last moments of Socrates. Kant's sister stood at the foot of the bed. His friend Borowski was called into the room. Kant's breathing became weaker and less audible. The clock struck 11.

Letters before 1770

[1a–47]

1749

1 [1a¹]

To Leonhard Euler.

August 23, 1794

Noble Sir,
Learned and renowned Herr Professor,
Esteemed Sir,

The universal indebtedness to you of all the world for your great accomplishments[2] may excuse my boldness in asking for your illuminating evaluation of these modest *Thoughts on the [True] Estimation of Living Forces*.[3] The same audacity that prompted me to seek out the true quantity of natural force and to pursue the reward of truth, notwithstanding the laudable efforts of the followers of Herr von Leibnitz and of des Cartes [*sic*], prompts me to submit this work to the judgment of a man whose discernment qualifies him better than anyone to carry forward the efforts I have begun in these wretched essays and to reach a final and full resolution of the division among such great scholars. The world sees in you, esteemed sir, the individual who better than others is in a position to rescue the human understanding from its protracted error and perplexity concerning the most intricate points of Mechanics, and it is just this that moves me to solicit most respectfully your precise and gracious appraisal of these poor thoughts. I shall be honored to send you, sir, a short appendix to this book which will soon be ready as well, an appendix in which I develop the necessary explanations and certain ideas that belong to the theory but which I could not include in the work itself without rendering the system too disjointed. If you do me the honor of either publishing or sending me privately your treasured judgment of this modest work, I shall then

begin to have a certain respect for it. I am, with all due veneration for
your merits,

your noble, honored, learned, renowned sir's
most obedient servant,

I. Kant

Judtschen[4] behind Insterburg in Prussia

23rd August, 1749

---

1   This letter, published in Rudolf Malter's appendix to the third, augmented
edition of Schöndörffer's selection of Kant's letters (Kant's *Briefwechsel*), ed. by
Malter and Joachim Kopper, Hamburg: Felix Meiner Verlag, 1986) is not to
be found in the Akademie edition of Kant's *Werke*.

    The letter was first published in a Russian translation by T. N. Klado and
N. M. Raskin, in *Istoriko-astronomiceskie issledovanija*, vol. II, p. 371. (Moscow,
1856). A German version appeared in Leonhard Euler, *Briefe an eine deutsche
Prinzessin*, 2nd ed., pp. 195 f. (Leipzig, 1968).

2   Euler (1707–83), the renowned mathematician and physicist, was born in Basel,
lived in Petersburg after 1727 and, from 1741 on, was a member of the Berlin
Academy of Sciences. At the time of this letter, he had already produced over
100 publications. Kant's "Versuch den Begriff der negativen Grössen in die
Weltweisheit einzuführen" (1763) refers to Euler's "Reflexions sur l'espace et
le temps" (1748). Euler is also mentioned to in Kant's essay "Von den ersten
Grunde des Unterschiedes der Gegenden im Raume" (1768), in the Inaugural
Dissertation (1770), in the *Metaphysische Anfangsgründe der Naturwissenschaft*
(1786), the *Critique of Judgment* (1790), and in the reply to Soemmerring,
"Über das Organ der Seele" (1796).

3   *Gedanken von der wahren Schätzung der lebendigen Kräfte* (1747), Kant's first
publication. Kant here omits the word "true" (*wahren*), thereby giving a somewhat misleading impression of his work.

4   Judtschen was a village inhabited at that time by French settlers. The local
pastor, Daniel Andersch (1701–71), employed Kant as a private tutor for his
three sons from about 1747 to 1750. Kant was twice listed as a witness in the
baptismal records of the village, with the identifying phrase "studiosus Philosophiae." Cf. Ak. 10: 2, n. 2.

1759

2 [11]

From Johann Georg Hamann.[1]

July 27, 1759.

Honored Herr Magister,   <10:7 placeholder>10:7</10:7 placeholder>

I do not hold it against you that you are my *rival* or that you have   10:8
enjoyed your new friend[2] for weeks during all of which I only saw him
for a few scattered hours, like a phantom or even more like a clever
scout. I shall however bear this grudge against your friend, that he
ventured to import you even into my seclusion; and that he not only
tempted me to let you see my sensitivity, wrath, and jealousy but even
exposed you to the danger of getting quite close to a man whom the
disease of his passions has given an intensity of thinking and of feeling
that a healthy person does not possess. This is what I wanted to say to
your sweetheart right into his face when I was thanking you for the honor
of your first visit.

If you are Socrates and your friend wants to be Alcibiades, then for
your instruction you need the voice of a daimon.[3] And that role is one
I was born for; nor can I be suspected of pride in saying this – an actor
lays aside his royal mask, no longer walks and speaks on stilts, as soon
as he leaves the stage – allow me therefore to be called "daimon" and
to speak to you as a daimon out of the clouds, for as long as I have to
write this letter. But if I am to speak as a daimon, I beg that you give
me at least the patience and attentiveness with which an illustrious,
handsome, clever, and informed public recently heard the farewell
address of a mortal concerning the fragments of an urn on which one
could with effort make out the letters BIBLIOTHEK.[4] The "project" was
to teach beautiful bodies how to think. Only a Socrates can do that,
and no count; no legislature will create a daimon out of a Watson,

whatever the power of their governing offices and the authority of its election.

I write in epic style since you do not yet understand lyric language. An epic author is a historian of unusual creatures and their still more unusual lives. A lyric author is the historian of the human heart. Self-knowledge is hardest and highest; the easiest and most disgusting natural history, philosophy, and poetry. It is pleasant and profitable to translate a page of Pope – into the fibers of the brain and of the heart – but vanity and a curse to leaf through a part of the *Encyclopédie*.[5] I

10:9 finished the work you proposed to me only last night. The article concerning beauty is a piece of chattering and a summarizing of Hutchinson [*sic*].[6] The one about art is less harsh and thus sweeter than the Englishman's discourse concerning nothing but a *word*. So only one article remained that really deserved translation. It had to do with forced labor.[7] Every perceptive reader of my heroic letter will appreciate from experience the effort required to be in charge of such people but will also have the sympathy for all forced laborers that the writer of my article has for them and will look for the amelioration of the abuses that make it impossible for them to be good forced laborers. Since I, however, have no desire to become one or to hold any office of that sort on this earth, where I have to be dependent on the mood of those under me, this article will find enough other translators who have a calling for that job. A man of the world who knows the art of making visits will always put enterprises in charge of a good superintendent.

To return to our dear cousin [Berens]. You cannot love this old man out of inclination; the motive must be vanity or self-interest. You should have known him in my day, for I loved him. In those days he thought the way you do, most honorable Herr Magister, about natural law; he knew nothing but generous tendencies in himself and in me.

You have it, this final contempt is a leftover bit of affection for him. Let yourself be warned and let me parrot Sappho:

Ah, send me back my wanderer,
Ye Nisaean matrons and Nisaean maids,
Nor let the lies of his bland tongue deceive you![8]

I think your association with him is still innocent and that you are merely passing the long summer and August evenings. Could you not see me as a girl, confused and shamed, a girl who has sacrificed her honor to her friend, who entertains his company with her *weaknesses* and *nakedness*, of which I have made no secret to him, privately.

France, the life of the court, and his present association with a pack

10:10 of Calvinists, these are responsible for all the trouble. He loves the human race as a Frenchman loves a woman, for his mere personal enjoyment and at the expense of her virtue and honor. In friendship as in love, he casts aside all secrets. But that means that he denies the god of friendship; and when Ovid, his heart's poet, writes to a corrupt friend, he is still tender enough to prefer to her love-making the intimacy of *a third party*.

> Those kisses are common to you with me,
> And common to me with you – why does
> Any third attempt to share those goods?[9]

That he thinks differently than he talks, writes differently than he talks, I shall be able to show you more clearly when we have occasion to talk and walk. Yesterday everything was supposed to be open, and in his last love letter he wrote me: "I beg you not to make us a laughingstock by misusing in any way what I, as an honest friend, am writing to you – our domestic affairs are none of your business now – we live quietly here, cheerful, human, and Christian." I have lived up to this condition so scrupulously that I have plagued my conscience over innocent words that escaped my lips and that no one could have understood. Now everything is supposed to be public. But I shall keep to what he has written.

We are not going to reach an understanding. I am not going to put up with having to justify myself. Because I cannot justify myself without damning my judges, and these are the dearest friends I have on earth.

If I had to justify myself, I would have to argue:

1) that my friend has a false conception of himself,
2) an equally false conception of all his *fellow men*,
3) has had and still has a false conception of me,
4) has unfairly and one-sidedly judged the issue between us as a whole and in its context,
5) has not the slightest conception or sensitivity about what he and I have heretofore done and are still doing.

Because I know all the principles and motivations of his actions, I can forgive what I know and don't know that he has done and still does, since he, according to his own confession, cannot make head or tail of anything I say or do. This must seem like bragging to you and   10:11
happens quite naturally in the course of events. I am still too modest, but I can certainly boast with my bleary red eyes against one with cataracts.

It would be a simple matter, compared with all my work and effort, to get myself acquitted. But to be condemned to the poison cup while innocent! Acquittal is what all Xantippes and Sophists think of – but not Socrates; for to him it was more a matter of the innocence of his conscience than of its reward, staying alive.

So that sort of Apology is out of the question for me. The God I serve, whom scoffers take to be clouds, fog, mist and hallucinations, will not be appeased by means of rams' blood and calves' blood;[10] otherwise I could prove very quickly that your friend's reason and wit, as my own, is a lascivious calf and his noble intentions a ram with horns.

What your friend doesn't believe is as little my affair as what I believe is his affair. On this subject we are thus divided, and the talk remains simply a matter of trade. A whole world full of handsome and profound minds, were they nothing but morning stars and Lucifers, could be neither judge nor expert witness here, and such a world is not the public of a lyric poet, who smiles at the applause of his eulogy and remains silent at its faults.

Peter the Great was called upon by the gods to have his own people imitate the handsome spirit of other nations in certain petty details. But do we get younger by shaving off our beards? The truth is not found in mere sensuous judgments.

A subject of a despotic government, says Montesquieu, does not need to know what is good and evil.[11] Let him be fearful, as though his prince were a god who could cast down his body and soul into hell. Were he to have insights, he would be an unhappy subject for his state; if he has any virtue, he is a fool to let himself be noticed.

A patrician in a Greek *republic* could not have connections with the Persian court, if he were to avoid being rebuked as a traitor to his fatherland.

10:12 Are the laws of the vanquished proper for the conqueror? Was the subject repressed by those laws? Do you grant your fellow citizens a similar fate?

Abraham is our father[12] – do we work according to Peter's plan? as the ruler of a little free state in Italy learned to babble of "commerce" and "the Public" – do your father's works, understand what you are saying, use your knowledge judiciously, and put your "alas!" in the right place. We can do more harm with truths than with errors, if we use the former absurdly and, by luck or by habit, know how to rectify the latter. That is why many an orthodox soul can ride to the devil, in spite of the truth, and many a heretic gets to heaven, despite excommunication by the ruling church or the public.

How far a man can be effective in the order of the world is an assignment for you, an assignment, however, to which one dare not turn until one understands how our soul may be effective in the system of its little world. Whether "pre-established harmony" is not at least a *happier sign* of this miracle than *"influxus physicus"* manages to express, you may decide for yourself. Meanwhile I am pleased that I can infer from this, that the Calvinistic church is as little in a position to make an adherent of your friend as is the Lutheran.

These impressions are nothing but apples that I toss as Galatea did to tease her lover. I am as little concerned with truth as is your friend; like Socrates, I believe everything that others believe – but I aim to disturb other people's faith. That is what the wise man had to do, because he was surrounded with Sophists and priests whose *sound reason* and good works existed only in the imagination. There are people who imagine themselves healthy and honorable, just as there are *malades imaginaires*.

If you want to judge me from Herr B's reviews and my writings, that is as unphilosophical a judgment as if one were to survey Luther from head to toe by reading one brochure to the Duke of Wolfenbüttel [*sic*].[13]

He who trusts another man's reason more than his own ceases to be a man and stands in the front ranks of a herd of mimicking cattle.[14] Even the greatest human genius should seem to us unworthy of imitation. Nature, said Batteux;[15] one mustn't be a Spinozist in matters of fine arts or in those of government. 10:13

Spinoza led an *innocent mode of life*, too timid in reflection; had he gone farther, he would have expressed the truth better than he did. He was incautious in whiling away his time and occupied himself too much with spider webs; this taste revealed itself in his thinking, which can only entangle small vermin.

Of what use are the archives of all kings and of all centuries, if a few lines out of this great fragment, a few motes in a sunbeam out of this chaos, can give us knowledge and power. How happy is the man who can visit daily the archives of him who can guide the hearts of all kings like brooks,[16] who does not desire in vain to inspect his marvelous economy, the laws of his kingdom, and so on. A pragmatic author says about this: "The statutes of the Lord are more precious than gold, even than the finest gold, sweeter than honey and the dripping honeycomb."[17] "I put the Law you have given before all the gold and silver in the world." "I have more understanding than all my teachers, for I meditate on your decrees. I understand more than the ancients, for I respect your precepts. Through your law you have made me wiser than my *enemies*, for it is ever with me."[18]

What do you think of this system? I want to make my neighbors happy. A rich merchant is happy. So that you might become rich – you need insight and moral virtues.

In my mimicking style, a sterner logic prevails and a connection more coherent than in the concepts of lively minds. Your ideas are like the playing colors of shot silk, says Pope.

At this instant I am a Leviathan, the monarch or prime minister of Ocean, on whose breath depends the ebb and flow of the tides. The next instant I see myself as a whale, created by God, as the mightiest poet says, *to sport in the sea.*[19]

I must almost laugh at the choice of a *philosopher* to try to change my mind. I look upon the finest logical demonstration the way a sensible girl regards a love letter and upon a Baumgartian explanation[20] as a witty courtesan.

10:14

I have been imposed upon with dreadful lies, most honored tutor. I wonder whether your reading so many travel books has made you credulous or incredulous. One forgives the original authors, since they do it unaware and, like a comic hero, "speak prose without knowing it."[21] Lies are the mother tongue of our reason and wit.

One mustn't believe what one sees – let alone what one hears. When two people are in different situations, they must never fight about their sense impressions. A stargazer can tell a person on the fourth story a great deal. The latter must not be so stupid as to claim the other man's eyes are sick. Come on down: then you'll be convinced that you didn't see anything. A man in a deep ditch without water can see stars at bright noon. The man on the surface does not deny the stars – but all he can see is the lord of the day. Because the moon is closer to the earth than the sun is, you tell your moon fairy tales about the glory of God. It is God's glory to conceal a thing; it is the glory of kings to search out a matter.[22]

As one knows the tree by its fruits, so I know that I am a prophet from the fate that I share with all witnesses: slander, persecution, contempt.

All at once, my dear tutor!, I want to deprive you of the hope of bargaining with me about certain matters that I can judge better than you. I have more *data,* I base myself on *facts,* and I know my authors not out of journals but by carefully and repeatedly wallowing in them; I have not read extracts but the Acts themselves, wherein the "interests" of the king as well as that of the country are discussed.

Every animal has its characteristic gait in its thinking and writing. One proceeds by leaps and bounds like a grasshopper; the other, in a cohesive connection, like a slow worm in its track, for the sake of security, which his construction may need. The one straight, the other crooked. According to Hogarth's system, the snake line is the basis of all beautiful painting, as I read in the vignette on the title page. [23]

10:15

The Attic philosopher, Hume, needs faith if he is to eat an egg and drink a glass of water.[24] He says: Moses, the law of reason, to which the philosopher appeals, condemns him. Reason is not given to you to make you wise but to make you aware of your folly and ignorance, just as the Mosaic law was given to the Jews, not to make them righteous, but rather to make their sins more sinful to them.[25] If he needs faith for food and drink, why does he deny faith when he judges of matters that are higher than sensuous eating and drinking?

To explain something by means of *custom* – custom is a composite thing consisting of monads. Custom is called "second nature," and its phenomena are just as perplexing as nature itself, which it imitates.

If Hume were only sincere, consistent with himself – All his errors aside, he is like a Saul among the Prophets.[26] I only want to quote one passage that will prove that one can preach the truth in *jest*, and without consciousness or desire, even if one is the greatest doubter and, like the serpent,[27] wants to doubt even what God said. Here it is: "The Christian religion not only was at first attended with miracles, but even at this day cannot be believed by any reasonable person without one. Mere reason is insufficient to convince us of its veracity. And whoever is moved by *Faith* to assent to it, is conscious of a continued miracle in his own person, which subverts all the principles of his understanding, and gives him a determination to believe what is most contrary to *custom* and *experience*."[28]

Beg your friend that it becomes him least to laugh at the eyeglasses of my aesthetic imagination, for I must arm the naked eyes of my reason with those same spectacles.

A tender lover never worries about his expenses, when an affair breaks up. So if perhaps, according to the new natural law of old people, the question were one of money, tell him that I have nothing and must myself live on my father's generosity; that nevertheless every- thing belongs to him that God may want to give me – which, however, I do not follow, because I might then lose the blessing of the fourth commandment. If I should die, I want to bequeath my corpse to him, which he can then, like the Egyptians, treat as a forfeit, as is supposedly written in the pleasant *Happelio* of Greece, Herodotus.[29]

10:16

The lyre for lyric poetry is the *tireli* of the lark. If only I could sing like a nightingale sings. So there will at least have to be art critics among the birds, who always sing, and boast of their incessant dili- gence.

You know, most honored tutor, that daimons have wings and that they sound just like the applause of the multitude.

If one is permitted to mock God with grace and strength, why shouldn't one be able to amuse oneself with idols?

Mother Lyse sings: Make mockery of idols false.[30] A philosopher however looks at poets, lovers, and visionaries the way a man looks at a monkey, with amusement and pity.

As soon as men can understand one another, they can work. He who confused the languages – who punished the exemplars of pride out of love and also for the sake of political ends, for the good of the populace as a friend of humanity – joined them together again on the day that they slandered men with tongues of fire, as if intoxicated by sweet wine.[31] Truth did not want highway robbers to get too close to her; she wore dress upon dress, so that they had misgivings about ever finding her body. How terrified they were when they had their wish and saw Truth, the terrible ghost, before them.

I shall come and pick up this letter in person at the earliest possible date.

---

1 Hamann (1730–88), the so-called "Magus of the North." See biographical sketches.

2 Behrens = Johann Christoph Berens (1729–92), a merchant in Riga, friend of Kant's and Hamann's.

3 "Genii." Hamann's reference must allude to Socrates' guiding spirit, the "daimon" that informed him of evils to be avoided.

4 The allusion is to the academic farewell address of Matthias Friedrich Watson, professor of poetry in Königsberg, 1756–9. Hamann thought the speech incredible. Evidently it consisted largely of autobiographical anecdotes, together with extracts from a book entitled *Critical Outline of a Selected Library [Bibliothek] for Friends of Philosophy and Belles-Lettres.*

5 Diderot's famous *Encyclopédie ou Dictionnaire Raisonée des Sciences, des Arts et des Métiers* (1751).

6 The article "Beau" is by Diderot. In its historical introduction, there is a discussion of Francis Hutcheson's aesthetics.

7 N. A. Boulanger's article, "Corvée."

8 Ovid, *Heroides*, Epis. XV, v. 53–6 (trans. by Grant Showerman; Cambridge, Mass.: Loeb Classical Library, 1914).

9 Ovid, *Amores* 2, 5, 31 f. (trans. by Grant Showerman; Cambridge, Mass.: Loeb Classical Library, 1914).

10 Hebrews, 9:12

11 See Montesquieu, *De l'Esprit des Lois*, Bk. III, ch. 9, and Bk. IV, ch. 3.

12 John 8:39.

13 Luther's polemic "Wider Hans Worst," Wittenberg, 1541.

14 "servum pecus." Horace, *Epistles* I, 19,19: "O imitatores, servum pecus."

15 Charles Batteux, *Les Beaux Arts Reduits à un Même Principe* (Paris, 1747), p. 9: "The spirit which is father to the arts must imitate nature."

16 Proverbs 21:1.

17 Psalms 19:10–11.

18 Psalms 119:72, 99–100, 98.

19 Psalms 104:26.

20 Alexander Gottlieb Baumgarten (1714–62), professor of philosophy in Frankfurt an der Oder, originated the conception of aesthetics as the study or doctrine of beauty. Kant used Baumgarten's *Metaphysics* (published in 1739) as the textbook for his lectures.

21 Monsieur Jourdain, in Molière's *Le Bourgeois Gentilhomme*, Act II, scene 6.

22 Proverbs 25:2.

23 William Hogarth's *The Analysis of Beauty* (London, 1753). The title page has a snake line with the subscript "Variety."

24 See Hume's *Treatise of Human Nature*, Bk. I, Pt. III, vi and vii.

25 Romans 7:7–8.

26 I Samuel 10:11;19:24.

27 Genesis 3:1–5.

28 Hume, *Enquiry concerning Human Understanding*, Sec. X, concluding paragraph; *"custom"* and *"experience"* italicized by Hamann.

29 The allusion is to Herodotus' account of the treasure of Rhampsinitos. See his *History*, Bk. II, ch. 121.

30 From the eighth stanza of the song "Sei Lob und Ehr' dem Höchsten Gut," by the famous composer Johann Jakob Schütz (1640–90).

31 Gen. II:7–9.

3 [13]
To Johann Gotthelf Lindner[1]

October 28, 1759.

Noble Sir,   10:18
Esteemed Magister,

I take advantage of Herr Behrens'[2] willingness to transmit to you my sincerest thanks for the kind regard you have often expressed for me; I am all the more grateful to you for I suspect that my good fortune in acquiring such a worthy and treasured friend is partly due to the kind impression of me which you must have given him beforehand. I acknowledge the recommendations of the students who were sent here from Riga as a compliment which obligates me to give an account or news of their conduct, and I can do this very easily for Herren Schwartz and Willmsen, since these two gentlemen have shown an unusual amount of eagerness at the start of their studies (which usually does not last very long) and have sustained that eagerness with such regularity that I anticipate the best results from them. I wish I could praise Herr Holst as well and say that, besides being pleasant and winning people's affection on account of his pleasantness, he is also mindful of and similarly devoted to his main purpose for being here. I do not know what little temptations or unnecessary entertainments may have drawn him away, but to my mind it would be helpful in alleviating these obstacles were he to dine in our company, as Herr Schwartz does. For since he would then have to give an account of himself every day, the excuses would soon be used up.

I am very pleased to hear from everyone that you have managed to display your talents in a place where people are capable of appreciating them and that you have succeeded in getting away from the sick wooing of approval and the tasteless arts of ingratiation which pretentious little masters around here, who can only do harm, lay on to those people who are eager to earn this reward and have no desire to hide it. For my part, I sit daily at the anvil of my lectern and guide the heavy 10:19 hammer of repetitious lectures, continuously beating out the same rhythm. Now and then I am stirred up somewhere by a nobler inclination, a desire to extend myself somewhat beyond this narrow sphere; but the blustering voice of Need immediately attacks me and, always truthful in its threats, drives me back to hard work without delay – intentat angues atque intonat ore.[3]

Yet in this town where I find myself and the modest prosperity for which I allow myself to hope, I make do finally with the applause I receive and the benefits I derive from that, dreaming my life away.

Recently a meteor has appeared here on the academic horizon. In a rather disorganized and incomprehensible dissertation attacking optimism, Docent Weymann[4] tried to make his solemn debut in this theater, a theater that includes harlequins just as Herferding's[5] does. I refused to argue against him, since he is known to be a presumptuous man; but in a short piece that I distributed the day after his dissertation – Herr Behrens will give you a copy, along with a few other little essays – I offered a brief defense of optimism, against Crusius, without having Weymann in mind. That galled him immediately. The following Sunday he published a sheet in which he defended himself against my supposed attacks; I shall send it to you soon, since I don't have it right here. It was full of distortions, insolence and the like.

When I thought of how the public would judge me, and the obvious impropriety of getting into a boxing match with a Cyclops, and the very idea of rescuing an essay that would probably already be forgotten by the time its defense came out, I was driven to the conclusion that silence would be the best answer. These are the weighty matters with which we little spirits concern ourselves, puzzled that the world at large is indifferent to them.

Please greet Herr Freytag,[6] Prof. Kypke,[7] and Dr. Funck[8] for me. I hope that all is well with you and I remain

yours truly,
Kant.

Königsberg, Oct. 28, 1759.

---

1 Johann Gotthelf Lindner (1729–76) studied in Königsberg and became a teacher at the Friedrichskollegium in 1748, then lecturer (*magister legens*) in philosophy, 1750, rector of the cathedral school in Riga, 1755, and professor of poetry in Königsberg. He was a friend of Hamann's as well.

The present letter is a reply to Lindner's letter of August 20, 1759, from Riga, Ak. 10:6–7, discussing students Schwartz, Willemsen, and von Holst, whom Lindner had recommended to Kant, and inquiring about their progress.

2 Behrens = Johann Christoph Berens. See Hamann's letter Ak.[11], n. 2.

3 Kant is playing on Virgil's *Aeneid*, VI, ll. 572 and 607. Tisiphone, one of the Furies in hell, "brandishing fierce snakes in her left hand, she calls upon the savage ranks of her sisters."

4 Daniel Weymann (1732–95) submitted his *habilitations* thesis, *De mundo non optimo*, October 6, 1759. The following day Kant's "Versuch einiger Betrachtungen über den Optimismus" appeared, intended as an invitation to Kant's lectures. The essay, which Kant later disparaged – he told Borowski he wished it had been destroyed – is a polemic against Christian August Crusius (1712–75), the most influential opponent of Christian Wolff. Weymann sought to reconcile reason and revelation but disputed "best of all possible worlds" optimism. Kant at this time disagreed with him, though without mentioning him by name.

5 Johann Peter Hilferding, an impresario whose theatrical troupe often played in Königsberg.

6 Theodor Michael Freytag (1725–90), a schoolmate of Kant's.

7 Georg David Kypke (1724–79), professor of Oriental languages.

8 Johann Daniel Funck (1721–64), professor of law (*Rechte*) from 1749.

4 [14 & 15][1] (13 & 14)
From Johann Georg Hamann.

1759.

As Horace writes: "Oh, unfortunate one! With what a vortex of calamity must you struggle, youth, you who are worthy of a better flame!"[2] 10:20

Your patrons would shrug their shoulders with pity if they knew that you were going around pregnant with a physics book for children.[3] This idea would strike many a man as so childish that he would jeer at your ignorance and the misuse of your own powers or he might even fly into a rage. Since I do not think that you give satirical lectures with your textbooks, I doubt that you mean to include people of good social background among the children for whom your nature-instruction is intended.

I therefore assume, dear sir, that you are serious about this project and this presupposition has led me to a web of reflections which I cannot analyze all at once. I hope you will at least take what I am writing with as much seriousness as we recently remarked that the games of children deserve to receive and have received from sensible people. If there is nothing so absurd that some philosopher has not taught it,[4] so nothing must appear so absurd to a philosopher that he should be unwilling to test and examine it before *daring* to reject it. Disgust is a sign of a ruined stomach or a spoiled imagination.

You want to perform a miracle, my dear Magister. A good and useful and beautiful book that does not exist is to come into being through your pen. If it existed or if you knew that it existed, you would not dream of this project. You say, "The title or name of a children's physics book exists, but the book itself is lacking." – You have certain grounds for suspecting that something will work for you which has failed to work for so many others. Otherwise you would not have the heart to embark on a path from which the fate of your predecessors might well frighten you away. You are indeed a master in Israel if you think it a trivial matter to change yourself into a child, despite all your learning! Or do you have more faith in children, while your adult auditors struggle to have the patience and quickness to keep up with your thinking? Since in addition your project requires an excellent knowledge of the *child's world*, which can be obtained neither in the gallant nor in the academic world, it all seems so marvelous to me that out of pure inclination toward marvels I would risk a black eye just to take such a crazy, daring ride.

Supposing that appetite alone gave me the courage to write this, a philosopher like you would know how to take advantage even of that and be able to exercise his morality where it would be pointless to display his theories. But you will be able to read my intentions this time; for the lowliest machines demand a mathematical insight if they are to be used properly.

It is as easy for the learned to preach as it is for them to deceive honest people! And there is neither danger nor accountability in doing it; not in writing for scholars, because most of them are already so wrongheaded that the most mischievous author cannot render their

10:21

thinking any more confused than it already is. But even blind heathens had respect for *children*, and a baptized philosopher will know that it takes more to write for children than having the wit of a Fontanel and a seductive literary style. What petrifies beautiful minds and inspires beautiful marble pillars[5] – that sort of thing would offend the *majestic innocence* of a child.

To secure praise out of the mouths of children and sucklings![6] It is no ordinary business to join in this ambition and taste, not something to start with by *stealing colored plumes* but by voluntarily renouncing all concern about age and wisdom and by denying all vanity. A philosophical book for children would therefore have to appear as simpleminded, foolish and tasteless as a *divine* book written for human beings. Now examine yourself to see whether you have the heart to be the author of a simple-minded, foolish and tasteless science book. If you have, then you are a philosopher for children. "Farewell and dare to be intelligent."[7]

[*Continuation*]   10:22

To make judgments about children from what we know of adults, I attribute more vanity to the former than to us, because they are more ignorant than we are. And that may be why the writers of catechisms, in accord with this instinct, put the most foolish questions into the mouths of the teacher and the wisest answers into the pupils' responses. So we must adapt ourselves to the pride that children have, as Jupiter adapted to the inflated Juno, whom he is said to have approached in no other guise than that of a cuckoo half-dead and dripping with rain, addressing her about the *duty* of her *love*, while he chose very respectable and ingenious disguises for his amorous intrigues.

The most important methodological principle in dealing with children consists thus in condescending to their weaknesses; one must become their servant if one wants to be their master, must follow them if one would rule them, must learn their language and their soul if one wants to move them to imitate one's own. It is impossible to *understand* or in fact to *fulfill* this practical principle if one hasn't as the saying goes been crazy about them and loved them, without really knowing why. If you feel the weakness of such a love of children is concealed in your womb's desire, then that "Dare" will come easily to you, and the "to be intelligent" will come too. So, dear Sir, you can become in six days the creator of an honest, useful and beautiful children's book, which however no T – [8] will see as that, let alone will a courtier or a Phyllis, out of recognition for your work, embrace you for it.

The point of these observations is to move you to use no other plan for your physics book than one that is already present in every child that is neither heathen nor Turk, a plan that as it were awaits the cultivation of your instruction. The best plan you could now adopt would contain human defects, and perhaps greater defects than the rejected cornerstone of the Mosaic history or story.[9] For it contains in itself the origin of all things; so a historical presentation of a science is always to a certain extent superior to a logical one, however artificial it may be. The idea of nature according to the six days of its birth thus presents the best schema for a child that believes in the legends told 10:23 by its nurse, until the child can *calculate*, *designate*, and *prove*, and is then justified in believing in numbers, figures, and logical inferences the way it first believed its wet-nurse.

I am surprised that it occurred to the wise Architect of the world to give us, right along with the great work of creation, an account of His work; for no clever human being would readily take the trouble to inform children and idiots about the mechanism of his actions. Nothing but love for us sucklings of creation could have moved Him to this foolishness.

How would a great mind begin to illuminate either a child who still went to school, or a simple-minded servant girl, with an understanding of his systems and projects? But that it should have been possible for *God* to let us hear two words about the origin of things, that is incomprehensible; and the actual revelation concerning this is as beautiful an argument for His wisdom as the seeming impossibility of it is proof of our imbecility.

A philosopher however reads the three chapters of Genesis with the sort of eyes with which that crowned star-gazer[10] looks at heaven. It is natural therefore that nothing but eccentric concepts and anomalies should appear to him; he prefers to find fault with holy Moses rather than doubt his own educated fads and his systematic spirit.

So if you want to write for children, dear sir, don't be ashamed to ride the wooden horse of Mosaic history and to present your physics in the order that every Christian child has learned about the origin of nature:

1. Of light and fire.
2. Of the sphere of vapors and all airy appearances.
3. Of water, the sea, rivers
4. Of solid ground and of what grows in the earth and on it.
5. Of the sun, moon and stars.
6. Of the animals.
7. Of human beings and society.

I will say more when I speak to you!

As Horace writes – "You turn again, ancestor, to the despised race of grandchildren, sated with the game of war that lasts too long."[11]

1 Hamann published these two letters under the title "Zugabe zweener Liebes-
   briefe an einen Lehrer der Weltweisheit, der eine Physik für Kinder schreiben
   wollte" (Two love letters to a teacher of philosophy who wanted to write a
   physics book for children) as a supplement to his book *Fünf Hirtenbriefe das
   Schuldrama betreffend*, 1763.

2 Horace, *Carmina* I, 27, 18–20:

> " – Ah! miser,
> Quanta laboras in Charybdi
> Digne puer meliore flamma!"

3 Kant initiated the project, aimed at popularizing Newton. In a letter to Hamann, evidently in Dec. 1759 (not extant), Kant invited Hamann to collaborate
   with him.

4 Cicero, *De divinatione*, II, 58, 119. "Heaven knows that nothing so foolish can
   be said that some philosopher or other has not maintained it."

5 Hamann's word-play is difficult to capture in English: "Was schöne Geister
   versteinert und schöne Marmorsäulen begeistert . . ." "What turns lovely spirits to stone and fills lovely stones with spirit" conveys the verbal trick but loses
   the sense.

6 Matthew 21:16.

7 "Vale et sapere aude!" Horace, *Epistles*. I, 2, 40. The motto "Sapere aude" is
   sometimes translated "Have the courage to use your own reason," as in Kant's
   essay, "What Is Enlightenment?"

8 Hamann's "T – " might be short for "Devil" (Teufel).

9 "The stone which the builders rejected is become the chief cornerstone."
   Psalms 118, 22; Matthew 21:42.

10 Alphonso X (1221–84), King of León and Castile, called "the wise" or "astrol-
    ogus."

11 Horace, *Carmina* I, 2, 35–7:

> "Neglectum genus et nepotes
>   Respicis AUTOR
> Heu nimis longo satiate ludo."

5 [17] (16)

From Johann Georg Hamann.

Late December 1759.

Dear Friend,

This title is not an empty word for me but a source of duties and 10:26
delights – the two are related. Please judge my enclosure accordingly.

The alliance we call friendship doesn't always call for a bushel of salt. I trust that a handful is sufficient, the handful with which I have had to season this letter.

Your silence concerning certain matters about which sincerity would be enough to loosen a dumb person's tongue is an insult to me which I find as difficult to explain, or which I must explain as unpleasantly, as you must my vehement passion.

I really want to work on the book we have been discussing. It is too hard for one person alone, and it would be easier for two people than for three. We must also perhaps have a certain amount of talent for it and our styles must fit together. But we need to become so precisely aware of our *weaknesses* and *vulnerabilities* that no jealousy or misunderstanding is possible between us. Love grounds itself on weaknesses and vulnerabilities, and fecundity grounds itself on love. So you must hit back at me with the same blows with which I attack you, and put down my prejudices with the same force with which I attack yours. Otherwise your love of truth and virtue will seem to me as contemptible as artful coquetry.

Unity is what our project requires, unity not just in ideas, where unity cannot be sought or maintained, but unity in the strength and in the spirit to which even ideas are subject – as the images of the right and the left eye are made to coalesce by means of the unity of the optic nerves.

I wished therefore that you had interrogated me about the issues in my two letters. But it does not matter to you whether you understand me or not as long as you can explain me more or less so that you will not be disgraced and so that I do not lose every good opinion of you. That is not behaving philosophically, not sincerely, not with friendship.

10:27

My offer was to represent the position of a child. You ought to ask me therefore, "How far did I get? What and how did I discover?" and adjust your building accordingly. But you assume from the outset that what I have learned is childish stuff. That assumption is in opposition to all the love of humanity of a teacher, who ought to endure even the poorest explanation from a student and who encourages the student, by means of what he already knows, to see that he knows and who leads him thereby to broader and better learning. Sapienti sat.[1] Now do you know why Jesuits are such good school teachers and fine statesmen?

[*Enclosure*]

Should I not *feel pain* if someone is *angered* at me? And at what? At my pride. I tell you, you must feel this pride or at least counterfeit it, yes, be able to exceed it. Or you must take my humility as a model and give up your desire to be a writer. Otherwise prove to me that your vanity is better than the pride that angers you and better than the humility you despise.

There is a certain *pride* in Caesar, from what I know, that made him feel dissatisfied with anything until he had done everything and nothing remained. Where others are too weak to create obstacles he himself puts the Alps in his own path in order to display his patience, his courage, his greatness. He loves honor more than life. A clever spirit would not think like that and behaves entirely otherwise; much less a wise man.

If you are *ashamed* or perhaps *powerless* to be *proud*, then let your pen sleep, at least give up the book on which I am to collaborate. In that case it is beyond your vision and your strength.

Don't worry about your pride. It will be humbled enough in carrying out the project. How would you be able to endure the *troubles* and *danger* on your journey without this emotion?

It takes pride to *pray;* it takes pride to *work. A vain man* can do neither; or his praying and working are fraud and imposture. He is *ashamed* to dig and to beg, or he becomes a begging babbler and a polypragmatic sluggard. Alembert and Diderot wanted to honor their country by producing an *Encyclopédie;* they achieved *nothing.* Why did they fail? And why was their work suppressed? The two questions are connected and have a common solution. The mistakes in their project can teach us more than can its successful pages.

10:28

If we wish to pull with one yoke we need to be of one mind. The question is thus: whether you wish to raise yourself to my pride or whether I ought to lower myself to your vanity? I have already demonstrated to you that we will find obstacles which vanity is too weak to face, let alone overcome.

My pride seems to you unbearable; I judge your vanity much more mildly. An axiom has priority over an hypothesis; the latter however is not to be spurned. Only one must not use it like a cornerstone but like *scaffolding.*

The spirit of our book is supposed to be moral. If we ourselves are not, how can we impart morality to our book and to our readers? We shall obtrude ourselves as blind men leading the blind; I say obtrude, without vocation and need.

Nature is a book, a written message, a fable (in the philosophical sense) or whatever you wish to call her. Supposing we know all the letters in it as well as is possible, and we can spell and sound out every word, we even know the language in which it's written – is all that enough, in order to understand the book, to judge it, to make sense of it, to epitomize it? So we need more than physics in order to interpret nature. Physics is nothing but the alphabet. Nature is an equation with unknown quantities, a Hebrew word that is written with nothing but consonants, for which the understanding must supply the vowels.

We write for a nation, as did the Encyclopaedists, but for a people that wants an artist and poet.

> Mediocribus esse poetis
> Non homines, non di, non concessere columnae.[2]

This is not some brain wave of Horace's but a law of nature and of good taste. But all ideas appear in your mind the way images in your eyes: upside down. You take fancies for truths, and the latter for the former. With this upside down way of thinking it will be impossible for us to make progress together.

You are proud of telling people the truth; not I, though I must seem like that to you. With Weymann[3] you can behave as you like; as a friend I demand a different treatment. Your silence in response to him is more insidious and contemptuous than his stupid critique of your essay. You treat me on a similar footing, but I won't let you get away with that unpunished.

You think it not worth the while to rebut his objections. You think there is more honor in coming up with a new, irrefutable demonstration. You have not responded to my objections and perhaps you are thinking of a new plan. My plan does not belong to me – it is rather the property of every child and it has Moses for its author, whose reputation I would rather defend, if necessary, than my own.

If you wish to be a teacher of children, you must have a fatherly heart toward them, and then you will know, without blushing, how to seat yourself on the old hack, the wooden horse of Mosaic history. What seems to you to be a wooden horse is perhaps a winged one. I see that philosophers unfortunately are not better than children and that, like children, one has to lead them into a fairyland to make them wiser or to get them to keep paying attention.

I say it to you with vexation: you did not understand my first letter. And it must be true that my writing is more difficult than I realize and that you want to admit. It isn't only my letter but also the Platonic Dialogue on Human Nature[4] that you also fail to understand. You suck on gnats and swallow camels.[5]

Isn't it written there and thoroughly demonstrated that no ignorance can harm us, only that ignorance which we mistake for wisdom? I will add to that that no ignorance can damn us, except when we mistake truths for errors and discard and abhor them. Has it not been said to thee? Yes it has been said but I did not want to believe, or it seemed to me tasteless, or I preferred my lies.

Look upon my candor as the insolence of a Homeromastyx[6] or as outrageous cynicism. You are lord and can name things as you wish –

10:29

10:30

Not your language, not mine, not your reason, not mine; here it is one timepiece versus another. But the sun alone is correct; and if it should *err*, it is still its noonday shadow alone that divides time beyond all dispute.

If you want to be a learned conqueror like Bacchus, it is well that you take along a Silen[7] to accompany you. I don't like wine for its own sake but because it loosens my tongue enough to tell you the truth as I sit drunkenly on my donkey.

Because I cherish you and love you, I am your Zoilus,[8] and Diogenes looked for a man who had inclinations similar to his own, however unlike were the roles that everyone later played.

One who puts forth an ideal world, like Rousseau, but denies an individual, indivisible and omnipresent Providence, contradicts himself. If coincidence is possible in the smallest things, then the world cannot be good nor can it endure. If the smallest things flow from eternal laws, and the way an age exists of itself out of an unlimited number of days, it is really Providence in the *smallest* parts that makes the whole good.

The creator and ruler of the world is that sort of being. He likes himself in his plan and is unconcerned about our opinions. If the masses with clapping hands and shuffling feet say polite things to him about the goodness of the world and shout their approval, he is embarrassed like Phocion[9] and asks the little circle of friends standing around his throne with eyes and feet covered up whether he spoke something foolish when he said, "Let there be light!" because he sees his work admired by the common herd.

We ought not to be enthusiastic about the applause of this century which we see but about the coming one which is invisible to us. We do not want only to shame our predecessors but to be a model for the world to come.

As our book is supposed to be written for all classes of youth, we want to become such authors that our great grandchildren will not reject us as childish writers.

A vain being exerts itself therefore because it wants to please; a proud god does not think of that. If it is good, let it look anyway at all; the less it pleases the better it is. Creation is thus not a work of vanity but of humility, of lowering. Six words will taste so sour to a great genius that he needs six days and rests on the seventh.

10:31

> Ex noto fictum carmen sequar; ut sibi quivis
> Speret idem; sudet multum, frustraque laboret
> Ausus idem.[10]

Ex noto fictum carmen sequar; if Thou wouldst write a Heidelbergian catechism, don't talk about Lord Christ with a philosopher, for he doesn't know the man. And if you want to prove to your auditors that the world is good, don't start from the whole, for no one can see it, nor from God, for that is a being that only a blind person with staring eyes can behold and whose way of thinking and moral character only a vain human being would think he could understand. An honest Sophist says, "The more I think about it, the less wisdom I get."[11]

I want to close my argument with a dilemma, and thereby encourage you to be sincere and candid with me. Why are you so aloof and shy with me? And why can I speak so impudently to you? Either I have greater friendship for you than you for me or I have more insight into our work than you have. You are afraid to expose yourself and to bare the impurity of your intentions or the deficiency of your powers. Think of the brook that shows its sludge to everyone who looks into it. I believe, therefore I speak. You cannot convince me, for I am not one of your auditors, I am an accuser, one who contradicts. You don't *want* to believe. If you can only *explain* my notions you don't even see that your explanation is as idiotic and remarkable as my notions. I will gladly be patient with you as long as I can hope to win you over, and to be *weak* because you are *weak*. You must ask me, not yourself, if you wish to understand me.

---

1   "For one who understands, it suffices." Plautus, *Persa*, IV, 7, 19.
2   "To be mediocre is not permitted to poets, neither by men, nor by gods, nor by booksellers." Horace, *Ars Poetica*, v. 372 f.
3   Daniel Weymann, a colleague, philosophy instructor invited by Kant to attend his lectures.
4   The reference is to Hamann's translation of Plato, published in 1755.
5   Matthew 23: 24: "Ye blind guides, which strain at a gnat, and swallow a camel."
6   See note 8.
7   In Greek mythology, Silenus was a jolly old philosopher, father of the Satyrs and guardian of Dionysus/Bacchus, a water-dispensing god of fertility.
8   A Greek rhetorician, notorious for trivial fault-finding in Homer, and therefore called "Homeromastyx," Scourge of Homer.
9   Cf. Plutarch's *Lives*. Phocion was a Greek general and statesman of the fourth century, B.C. According to Plutarch he once spoke to the people and, on receiving friendly applause from his audience, he asked his friends, "Did I, without knowing it, say something bad?"
10 "My aim shall be poetry, so moulded from the familiar that anybody may hope for the same success, may sweat much and yet toil in vain when attempting the same." Horace, *Ars Poetica*, v. 240–42. Transl. by H. Rushton Fairclough, Loeb Classical Library (Cambridge and London, 1926).
11 Simonides is said to have asserted, when asked why he asked for more and more time to answer the question of God's existence, "Because the subject seems more obscure to me the more I consider it." Cicero, *De natura deorum*, I, 22, 60.

1762

6 [25] (24)
From Maria Charlotta Jacobi, née Schwinck.[1]
June 12, 1762.

Dear Friend, 10:39

Aren't you surprised that I dare to write to you, a great philosopher? I thought I would find you in my garden yesterday, but since my girlfriend and I crept through all the alleys and failed to find our friend under this circle of heaven I spent my time finishing a rapier ribbon, it is dedicated to you. I make claim on your company tomorrow afternoon. I hear you say, "Yes, yes, I'll come." Well good, we shall await you and then my watch will get wound.[2] Forgive me this reminder. My girlfriend and I send you a kiss by means of sympathy[3] – surely the air must be the same in Kneiphoff, [4] so our kiss won't lose its sympathy-power. May you live happily and well

Jacobin.

from the garden, June 12, 1762.

---

1 Frau Jacobi was the young wife – married at age 13 – of Kant's friend, a banker and privy commercial councillor named Johann Conrad Jacobi. She divorced him in 1768 and married Johann Julius Gösche, director of the mint, until that time also a good friend of Kant's. According to a biography of Kant by his student Reinhold Bernhard Jachmann, Kant "held it to be forbidden and unethical to be on friendly terms with both men at the same time, thinking this an insult to the first man and suggesting to the second that Kant approved of his blameworthy behavior." Cf. Ak. 13: 19.

2 Rolf George, reviewing Arsenij Gulyga, *Immanuel Kant* (Moscow, 1977), interprets this remark in the light of Laurence Sterne's *Tristram Shandy* and con-

cludes that Kant's friendship with Frau Jacobi was more than Platonic. Cf. George, "The Lives of Kant," a Critical Notices article in *Philosophy and Phenomenological Research*, XLVII, No. 3 (March 1987). Tristram's father would wind the house-clock every Sunday night, in time to attend to his marital duties. The "tomorrow" referred to by Frau Jacobi is a Sunday since the present letter was sent on a Saturday, as Rolf George mentions. George points out too that Wolfgang Ritzel, *Immanuel Kant, Zur Person* (Bonn, 1975), p. 42, and *Immanuel Kant*, pp. 112, ff., had noticed the allusion to Shandy before Gulyga.

On the other hand, Karl Vorländer, *Immanuel Kant, Der Mann und das Werk*, vol. 1, p. 133, suggests that the watch-winding refers to a joking remark about women and watches that Kant made in his lectures on *Anthropologie:* "Scholarly women use their books the way they use their watches, namely to show people that they have one, even if generally the watch doesn't move or doesn't agree with the time of day" (Ak. 7: 307). But, as George points out, the *Anthropologie* was not published until 1797.

3 In this context, perhaps the "secret power" whereby one body affects another.
4 The district in which Kant lived at that time.

1763

7 [27] (26)
To Johann Heinrich Samuel Formey[1]
June 28, 1763

I have had the pleasure of discovering by way of the Berlin newspaper that my essay,[2] with the motto *"Verum animo satis haec,* etc." from Lucretius,[3] an essay that was delivered to you, dear sir, by the merchant Abraham Gottlieb Ficker and a receipt for which, signed by you, sir, and dated Berlin, 31 October, 1762, was transmitted to me, was pronounced worthy of Second Place after the winning Prize Essay by the Royal Academy of Sciences assembly.

10:41

I am all the more moved by this favorable judgment in view of how little care in preparing its appearance and ornamentation went into the work, since a somewhat too lengthy delay left me with hardly enough time to present some of the most important arguments on this subject on which I have been reflecting for several years and the goal of which reflections, I flatter myself, I am near to reaching.

I take the liberty of inquiring, dear sir, whether my work will be published by the Academy along with the winning Prize Essay and whether in that case the inclusion of a supplement containing considerable elaboration and a more precise explication might be acceptable to your excellent society. Leaving aside any motive of vanity, publication seems to me to be the best means of encouraging scholars to inspect a method from which alone, I am convinced, a happy outcome for abstract philosophy can be awaited, if that inspection be supported to some extent by the authority of a highly esteemed learned society.

10:42

In case the Academy should approve of this suggestion, I beg you most respectfully to determine the date by which these additions should be submitted. With confidence, sir, in your honoring me with a reply without taking offense at the liberty I take, I am with the greatest respect

your most obedient servant
Immanuel Kant
Magister legens in the University of Königsberg
Königsberg, the 28th of June, 1763.

---

1 Formey (1711–97) was permanent secretary of the Royal Academy of Sciences in Berlin (Berliner Akademie der Wissenschaften). His one extant letter to Kant, dated Dec. 9, 1786, written in French, informs Kant of his election to the Academy. In a letter to Mendelssohn, Kant refers to Formey as Professor Formey.

2 Kant's "Inquiry into the Distinctness of the Principles of Natural Theology and of Morals" ("Untersuchung über die Deutlichkeit der Grundsätze der natürlichen Theologie und der Moral"), 1764, was submitted to the Berlin Academy's essay competition. An essay by Moses Mendelssohn, "Treatise on Evidence in the Metaphysical Sciences ("Abhandlung über die Evidenz inden metaphysischen Wissenschaften") won first prize, but as the present letter indicates, Kant's essay was judged to be almost as good. It was subsequently published, though without the changes and additions Kant here asked to have appended. A fuller discussion of the Academy's decision may be found in Kant's *Werke*, Ak. 2:. 492–5.

3 *De rerum natura* i. 403–4. The passage Kant quotes reads, in the translation by W. H. D. Rouse, Loeb Classical Library, "But for a keen-scented mind, these little tracks are enough to enable you to recognize the others for yourself."

8 [29] (28)
To Charlotte von Knobloch.[1]

August 10, 1763.[2]

10:43 I would not have denied myself for so long the honor and pleasure of obeying the command of a lady who is an ornament to her sex and giving her the requested report, were it not for the fact that a much more complete investigation of this matter seemed to me to be necessary. The tale I am about to write is of a totally different sort from those that have the charm normally required of stories that are allowed to penetrate the chambers of lovely women. If this report should cause a moment of solemn seriousness to interrupt the customary air of gaiety with which all innocent creatures are entitled to look upon the whole of creation, I would have to accept responsibility for this. But I am sure that even if my pictures activate a shudder, the sort of horror evoked by a repetition of one's childhood experiences, the intelligent lady who reads these words will not fail to find a pleasant use for them. Allow me to justify my procedure in this matter, gracious lady, since it may look as though an ordinary sort of madness had predisposed me to seek out such tales and led me to want to believe in them without careful testing.

I doubt that anyone has ever perceived in me a trace of mystical bent, an inclination to believe in marvels or a weakness for giving in easily to credulity. So much is certain: that regardless of the many tales of apparitions and actions in the realm of spirits that I have heard, I have always submitted these stories to the test of sound reason and have been inclined to regard such tales with skepticism. Not that I see such things as impossible (for how little do we know about the nature of a spirit?) but, taken all in all, we simply do not find sufficient evidence to validate them. Further, considering how incomprehensible this sort of appearance is, and how useless, and how many difficulties there are in supposing these stories to be true – whereas there are no difficulties at all in supposing that we have been deceived and there are plenty of instances in which fraud has in fact been discovered – I am therefore not inclined to be afraid of graveyards or of the dark. That was my position for a long time, until I became acquainted with the stories about Herr Swedenborg.[3]

10:44

This report came to me from a Danish officer, a friend and formerly my pupil. He himself, along with other guests, was able to read a certain letter about Herr Swedenborg while a guest in the house of Dietrichstein[4] in Copenhagen, the Austrian envoy to Copenhagen. His host had received the letter just then from Baron von Lützow,[5] the Mecklenburg Ambassador to Stockholm. Von Lützow reported a remarkable incident that he, along with the Dutch Ambassador[6] at the Court of the Queen of Sweden,[7] had witnessed, an incident about Herr von Swedenborg with which you, gracious lady, are probably familiar. The credibility of such a report stunned me. For one could scarcely believe that an ambassador would transmit to another ambassador a story *meant for publication*, a story that reports something untrue about the Queen of a country in which he is stationed, and that describes an incident at which he and other distinguished persons were supposedly present. In order to avoid replacing a blind prejudice against visions and apparitions with another prejudice, I thought it sensible to make further inquiries concerning this story. I wrote to the aforementioned officer in Copenhagen and asked him to make all sorts of investigations for me. He responded that he had once again spoken to Count von

Dietrichstein and that the facts of the matter were such that even Professor Schlegel[8] thought it beyond doubt. He advised me, since he himself had been placed under the command of General St. Germain[9] and was about to leave town, that I should write directly to von Swedenborg myself to get more details about the case. I did write to this strange man, and my letter was delivered to him personally in Stockholm by an English merchant. I received word that Herr von Swedenborg accepted the letter politely and promised to reply to it. However, no reply has arrived. Meanwhile, I made the acquaintance of a fine gentleman, an Englishman, who was staying here in Königsberg last summer. On the strength of our friendship I asked him to make further inquiries, on his forthcoming trip to Stockholm, into the amazing gifts of Herr von Swedenborg. According to his first letter, the most respectable people in Stockholm say that the story took place just as I have described it to you. He did not get to speak with Herr von Swedenborg at that time but hoped to do so, though he found it difficult to convince himself that all those stories about Swedenborg's secret communication with the invisible spirit world, told by the most sensible people in town, were true.

His second letter sounded quite different. He had managed not only to speak to Herr von Swedenborg but had visited him at his home, and he expressed the greatest astonishment about the whole, strange affair. Swedenborg, he said, is an intelligent, gracious and open-hearted man; he is a scholar, and my friend has promised to send me some of his writings before long. He told my friend without any reservation that God had given him a wonderful power enabling him to communicate with the souls of the dead whenever he pleased. He cited some quite notorious examples as proof. On being reminded of my letter he answered that he had received it with pleasure and would have answered it were it not for his intention to submit this whole remarkable affair to the eyes of the public. He intended to go to London in May of this year and there publish his book.[10] An answer to my letter, point by point, is supposed to be included in it as well.

To give you a few more examples, gracious lady, that many still living people witnessed, examples that could be examined then and there by the man who reported them, let me cite the two following incidents.

Some time after her husband's death, Madame Harteville [*sic*], the widow of the Dutch ambassador to Stockholm,[11] was approached by a goldsmith named Croon, who wanted payment for a certain silver service which he had produced for her late husband. The widow was quite convinced that her departed husband was much too meticulous and orderly in his affairs to leave this debt unpaid, but she could not find a receipt. In her distress and because the sum was considerable,

10:45

10:46

she asked Herr von Swedenborg for assistance. After some apologies she asked that if he really possessed those extraordinary gifts communicating with the souls of the departed, as everyone said he did, would he be kind enough to get in touch with her deceased husband and find out the truth about the bill for the silver service. Swedenborg was not at all reluctant to comply with her request. Three days later the lady had some guests at her house for coffee. Herr von Swedenborg came in and, in his chilly manner, informed her that he had had a talk with her deceased husband. The bill had been paid seven months before his death and the receipt was to be found in a cabinet located in an upstairs room. The lady replied that this cabinet had been thoroughly emptied out and that no receipt had been found among all the papers in it. Swedenborg said that her husband had told him that if one pulled out a drawer on the left side, a board would appear that one would have to push aside, which would then expose a concealed drawer, in which his secret Dutch correspondence was secured, as well as the receipt. On hearing this the lady, together with all her company, proceeded to the upstairs room. The cabinet was opened and, following the instructions precisely, the concealed drawer appeared, of which she had known nothing; the papers were in it, just as described, to the great amazement of everyone who was present.

However, the following incident seems to me to have the greatest weight of any of these stories and really removes any conceivable doubt. It happened in the year 1756, when Herr von Swedenborg was returning from England toward the end of September, on a Saturday at 4 in the afternoon. He had just landed in Gothenburg [=Göteborg]. Herr William Castel[12] invited him to his house with a party of fifteen other people. About 6 in the evening Herr von Swedenborg left the group, returning to the company a little later looking pale and disturbed. He said that a dangerous fire had just broken out in Stockholm on the Südermalm (Stockholm is about 50 miles from Gothenburg) and that it was spreading fast. He was worried and left the room several times during the evening. He said that the house of a friend, whom he named, was already in ashes and that his own house was in danger. At 8 o'clock, after having left the room again, he announced joyfully that Thank God! the fire had been put out, and that it actually reached to within three doors of his house.

10:47

This story excited the whole city, especially those who had been present, and people told the Governor[13] about it that same evening. Sunday morning Swedenborg was summoned to the Governor. The latter questioned him about the case. Swedenborg described the fire precisely, how it began, how it had ended and how long it had lasted. That same day the news spread through the whole city, occasioning even more excitement than before, since the Governor had taken note of it and many people were worried about their friends or their goods. Monday evening a messenger arrived in Gothenburg, sent by the merchants' guild of Stockholm at the time of the fire. The letters he brought depicted the fire exactly as described by Swedenborg. Tuesday morning a royal courier arrived and informed the Governor fully about the fire, the damage it had caused, and the houses it had affected. There was not the slightest deviation from Swedenborg's report, which he had given at the same time as the fire, for the fire was put out at 8 o'clock.[14]

What objections can one raise against the authenticity of such a story? The friend who wrote me this investigated the whole matter personally, not only in Stockholm but as recently as two months ago in Gothenburg. He is very well acquainted with the most distinguished families in Gothenburg where everyone concerned told him the same story about this incident and most of the eyewitnesses of 1756, which is not so long ago, are still alive today. He also gave me a report of how, according to Herr von Swedenborg, the latter's communication with other spirits takes place, and his ideas about the state of departed souls. This is a very strange portrait; but I lack the time to give you a detailed description of it. How I wish I could have questioned this singular man personally, for my friend is not so well trained in asking the questions that would shed the most light on a subject such as this. I eagerly await the book Swedenborg intends to publish in London. All arrangements have been made so that I will receive it at soon as it leaves the press.

This is all I can report for now to satisfy your noble curiosity. I don't know, gracious lady, whether you wish to have my own judgments about this slippery business. People who possess far greater talents than mine will be unable to draw any reliable conclusions from it. Whatever my verdict may be, I shall obey your command and keep you informed by letter, since your need to remain in the country so long makes it impossible for me to give you my explanations in person. I fear I have misused your kind permission to write to you by taking up too much of your time with my hasty and clumsy scribbling. I remain with deepest devotion,

I. Kant.

10:48

---

1 Charlotte Amalie von Knobloch (1740–1894), was the daughter of General Karl Gottfried von Knobloch in whose house Borowski, Kant's student, friend, and later biographer served as *Hofmeister*. The translation of this letter is indebted to a translation made by John Manolesco, included in Manolesco's

Dreams of a Spirit-Seer by Immanuel Kant and other Related Writings (New York: 1969).

2 There has been a good deal of debate over the date of this letter. The letter was first published by Borowski, who presented it under the heading, "How did Kant think of Swedenborg in the year 1758?" The editors of the Akademie edition of Kant's letter point out, however, that Kant's letter could not have been written in 1758, since it alludes to Madame Marteville as a widow; her husband did not die until Apr. 25, 1760. There is further evidence of a later date: Baron von Lützow, mentioned in the letter, was in Stockholm from the end of May 1761 until mid June 1762. His conversation with the Queen of Sweden must have taken place during this period. Kant, in *Dreams of a Spirit-Seer* (Ak.2: 354, f.), speaks of the test of Swedenborg's powers as taking place near the end of 1761. Kant's specific mention of the year 1761 shows decisively that Borowski's date was mistaken. For a fuller discussion of this and other pieces of evidence regarding the letter's date see Ak. 13:21.

3 Emanuel Swedenborg (1688–1772). Swedenborg (spelled Schwedenberg by Kant in *Dreams of a Spirit-Seer*) is famed not only for his theology and clairvoyant powers – he predicted the precise moment of his own death – but also for a variety of scientific activities, e.g., the discovery of the function of endocrine glands. He published the first work on algebra in Swedish, helped to found the science of crystallography, devoted himself for 30 years to metallurgy, and is said to have made suggestions toward the invention of the submarine and the airplane. The New Jerusalem Church, following his religious and spiritualist teachings, was founded by some of his disciples around 1784 and still has branches today.

There is now a fairly extensive literature, mainly in German, on the relation between Swedenborg and Kant. The third edition of Rudolf Malter's reworking of Otto Schöndörffer's selections from Kant's correspondence (*Kant's Briefwechsel*, Hamburg: Felix Meiner, 1986) lists some of the important studies. See op. cit., p. 956, f., n. 2. An English-language discussion may be found in Georgio Tonelli, "Kant's Ethics as a Part of Metaphysics: A Possible Newtonian Suggestion? With Some Comments on Kant's *Dreams of a Seer*," in *Philosophy and the Civilizing Arts. Essays Presented to Herbert W. Schneider*, edited by Craig Walton and John P. Anton (Athens, Ohio, 1975), pp. 236–63. There is also an interesting discussion in C. D. Broad's "Kant and Psychical Research," a chapter in his *Religion, Philosophy and Psychical Research* (New York: Harcourt, Brace & Company, Inc., 1953).

The scholarly puzzle posed by the present letter and its dating is philosophically interesting as well. We see that Kant told Fräulein Knobloch that he had been a skeptic about Swedenborg's supernatural powers until he learned of the incidents reported in this letter and became convinced of their credibility. In the *Dreams of a Spirit-Seer* Kant tries to convince the reader that Swedenborg's visions must be the concoctions of a diseased brain. Since the letter to Fräulein Knobloch shows Kant taking very seriously the reports of Swedenborg's occult powers, what led Kant to change his mind and adopt the mocking stance of *Dreams of a Spirit-Seer*? Kant's Apr. 8, 1766, letter to Mendelssohn states that he "can't help suspecting that there was some truth in the stories mentioned" but speaks of the explanations that people have given as "absurd" and "incomprehensible." Kant says further that he is convinced of the impossibility of our coming to understand "spirits" or their capacity to act either on other spirits or on bodies.

John Manolesco offered an interesting conjecture concerning Kant's change of attitude toward Swedenborg: wounded pride occasioned by Swedenborg's failure to reply to the young Magister's letter.

Regarding Swedenborg, see also the translation and a discussion of Kant's *Dreams of a Spirit-Seer* in vol. I of *The Cambridge Edition of the Works of Immanuel Kant, Theoretical Philosophy, 1755–1770*, translated and edited by David Walford and Ralf Meerbote (Cambridge University Press, 1992).

4 Karl Johann Baptist Walter, Count von Dietrichstein-Proskau-Leslie (1728–1808), served as envoy and minister in Copenhagen during the Seven Years' War, until 1763.

5 Johann Joachim, Freiherr von Lützow (1728–92), served as envoy in Stockholm from the end of May 1761, until mid June 1762.

6 Frans Doublet van Groenevelt, envoy in Stockholm from June 27, 1760, until May 22, 1762.

7 Luise Ulrike (1720–82) sister of Frederick the Great.

8 Johann Heinrich Schlegel (1726–80), historian, brother of Johann Elias Schlegel, professor of philosophy in Copenhagen from 1760.

9 Claude Louis, Comte de St. Germain (1709–78), commanded the Danish army in 1762.

10 Swedenborg went to Amsterdam in 1762 and published various writings there on "angelic wisdom" and the Christian religion: *Sapientia angelica de divino amore et de divina sapientia* (Amsterdam, 1763); *Sapientia angelica de divino providentia* (Amsterdam, 1764); *Vera christiana religio* (Amsterdam, 1771).

11 Ludwig von Marteville (not Harteville) came to Sweden in 1752, died in Stockholm, April 25, 1760. The story of the missing receipt for a silver tea-service and Swedenborg's remarkable assistance is told in the second part of Kant's *Dreams*, Ak. 2:355.

12 Swedenborg's vision was generally reported to have occurred in the home of Niclas Sahlgren. Records in the municipal library of Göteborg indicate that no William Castel resided in the city at that time. The Akademie edition of Kant's *Werke* conjectures that Castel might have been an English traveling companion of Swedenborg's. Cf. Ak.13:23.

13 Baron Johann Fredrik von Kaulbars (1689–1762).

14 The story of the fire and Swedenborg's vision is also referred to in *Dreams*, Ak. 2:356, where Kant however speaks of himself not as reporting stories that have "great weight" but of "spreading fairy-tales."

1765

9 [33] (31)
From Johann Heinrich Lambert.[1]
November 13, 1765.

Dear Sir: 10:51

I believe that the similarity of our ways of thinking will excuse this letter, its frankness, and the omission of customary circumlocutions. I need no such artificial mannerisms, since Professor and Pastor Reccard's[2] trip to Königsberg gives me such a fine opportunity to express to you the pleasure I feel at our agreement on so many new thoughts and investigations. You may already have learned from the Reverend Dr. Reccard, dear sir, that he lives for the sake of astronomy, and finds his pleasure in the depths of the firmament. I need not recommend him further.

A year ago Professor Sulzer[3] showed me your *Only Possible Proof for the Existence of God*.[4] I found in it my own thoughts and even the phrases I would choose to express them, and I decided at once that if you were to see my *Organon*[5] you too would find yourself mirrored in most of its pages. Since then, I had worked out my *Architektonic*[6] and the book was already prepared for publication a year ago. And now I learn, dear sir, that you are going to publish a *Proper Method for Metaphysics* this coming Easter. What could be more natural than my desire to see whether what I have done is in accord with the method you propose? I have no doubts as to the correctness of the method. The only difference will be that I do not count under "architectonic" all the things heretofore treated in metaphysics and that, on the other hand, I maintain that a complete system of metaphysics must include 10:52 more than has previously been thought. I take "architectonic" to include all that is *simple* and *primary* in *every* part of human cognition, not only the *principia* which are grounds derived from the *form*, but also the *axiomata* which must be derived from the *matter* of knowledge and actually only appear in simple concepts, thinkable in themselves and without self-contradiction, also the *postulata* which state the universal and necessary possibilities of composition and connection of simple concepts. We do not get to any material knowledge from form alone, and we shall remain in the realm of the *ideal*, stuck in mere nomenclature, if we do not look out for that which is primary and thinkable in itself in the matter or objective material of cognition.

If the *Architectonic* were a novel, I think it would already have found numerous publishers, so true is it that booksellers and readers corrupt each other, both of them wanting to avoid any thorough thinking. Hereabouts one philosophizes exclusively about so-called belles-lettres. Poets, painters and musicians find the vocabulary of their own arts too lowly, and each one therefore borrows the artistic terms of the other. The poet speaks of nothing but coloration, the mixing of hues, brush strokes, composition and design, style, shade, and so on. The musician speaks of coloration, expression, wording, the fiery and witty "ideas" expressed by the notes, the "pedantry" of the fugue, and so on. He has, just like the painter, a "style" in which he can sound sublime, moderate, middle-class, heroic, crawling, and so on. It is such metaphors, which no one understands or explains, that give these arts their refined and elevated character; and just for that reason one acquires a learned and "sublime" appearance when one uses them. Since no one has yet troubled to sift out what is intelligible in such expressions and restate it in its proper terms, one can use them all the more boldly. Explication cannot be carried out to the point where colors become comprehensible to the blind or sounds to the deaf. Yet this is evidently the intention of such metaphors.

But I come back to the *Architektonic*. I see from various indications that Herr Kanter[7] is a man who will also publish philosophy and larger works, and for this reason I wanted to give him a number of things to print, though at the moment I have no other manuscript. Whether it would be advantageous or all the same to him, because of the costs, to have it printed in Leipzig would depend on the equivalence or difference in price and on the freight charges. If it could be done in Leipzig, there are various other reasons why that would be best. In my ignorance I take the liberty of forwarding the enclosed sheet, in case Herr Kanter might be inclined to publish the work and could get it out by Easter. The honorarium would be around two hundred Reichsthalers and is the more moderate because the work will necessarily create a stir.

I can tell you with confidence, dear sir, that your ideas about the origin of the world, which you mention in the preface to *The Only*

10:53

Possible Argument . . . [8] were not known to me before. What I said on page 149 of the *Cosmological Letters*[9] dates from 1749. Right after supper I went to my room, contrary to my habit then, and from my window I looked at the starry sky, especially the Milky Way. I wrote down on a quarto sheet the idea that occurred to me then, that the Milky Way could be viewed as an ecliptic of the fixed stars, and it was this note I had before me when I wrote the *Letters* in 1760. In 1761 I heard in Nürnberg that an Englishman had had similar thoughts a few years before,[10] which he had had printed in letters to other Englishmen, but I was told that these ideas were quite undeveloped and the translation that someone in Nürnberg had begun had not been completed. I answered that the *Cosmological Letters* would not arouse interest until perhaps some future astronomer discovers something in the sky that cannot be explained in any other way. And then, if the system will have been verified *a posteriori*, the lovers of Greek *literature* will come and labor without rest until they can prove that the whole system was already known to Philolaus or Anaximander or some Greek wise man or other and that it has only been rediscovered and polished up in more recent times. For these people can find everything among the ancients, as soon as you tell them what to look for. I am more surprised, however, that Newton did not stumble on the idea, since he did think about the gravitational attraction of the fixed stars.

10:54

I have a number of wishes, dear sir. One of them I shall not express, since I don't know whether and how far the present constitution of things will let it be so. However, I can say that the wish is not mine alone. The other thing is that it would be very pleasant, if time and your affairs allow it, to exchange letters with you. Cosmology, metaphysics, physics, mathematics, belles-lettres, and their principles, and so on, in short, every quest of new ideas, and every occasion that I might be of service to you. We have heretofore hit upon almost the same investigations without knowing it. Would we not make better progress by advising one another in advance? How easily one reaches agreement in the consequences when one is agreed in the starting points, and how emphatic one can then be! Wolf has brought approximately half of the method of mathematics into philosophy. The other half remains to be worked on, so we know what to strive for.

I am honored to be, with sincere respect, dear sir, your most devoted servant.

J. H. Lambert
Professor and member of the Royal Academy of Sciences
Berlin, the 15th of November, 1765
In the Bethgenschen house at the corner of Cronenstraße and Schinkenbrücke.

1 Johann Heinrich Lambert (1728–77), renowned mathematician and philosopher. A draft of this letter, differing from it considerably, may be found in Ak. 13:28–30. It contains further remarks on Lambert's conception of how a reform of metaphysics should proceed. His detailed suggestions are reiterated in his letter to Kant, Feb. 3, 1766, Ak.[37], below.

2 Gotthilf Christian Reccard (1735–98) came to Königsberg from Wernigerode in 1765 as professor of theology and pastor of the Sackheimer Church. In 1775 he became director of the Collegium Fridericianum.

3 Johann Georg Sulzer (1720–79), aesthetician, a follower of Christian Wolff and member of the Berlin Academy of Sciences, was one of the men to whom Kant sent his 1770 Inaugural Dissertation for review. See his letter to Kant of Dec. 8, 1770, Ak. [62], containing remarks on Kant's theory of space and time. His publications included *Allgemeine Theorie der schönen Künste* (Leipzig, 1771–4) and a two-volume collection of articles, *Vermischte philosophische Schriften* (1773).

4 *Der einzig mögliche Beweisgrund zu einer Demonstration des Daseins Gottes*, 1763, Ak. 2:63–163.

5 *Neues Organon oder Gedanken über die Erforschung und Bezeichnung des Wahren und dessen Unterscheidung vom Irrthum und Schein* (New Organon, or thoughts on the discovery and designation of truth and its differentiation from error and appearance; Leipzig, 1764).

6 *Anlage zur Architektonic oder Theorie des Einfachen und des Ersten in der philosophischen und mathematischen Erkenntniss* (Outline of architectonic, or theory of the simple and primary elements of philosophical and mathematical knowledge) (Riga, 1771).

7 Johann Jakob Kanter (1738–86), bookseller and publisher in Königsberg. He published a weekly newspaper, *Königsberger Gelehrte und Politische Zeitungen*, and had contact with the leading intellectuals in Königsberg. At one time Kant lived in Kanter's house.

8 See Ak. 2: 68 hl f., the preface to Kant's *The Only Possible Argument in Support of a Demonstration of the Existence of God*, in which a footnote refers to his earlier *Universal Natural History and Theory of the Heavens (Allgemeine Naturgeschichtel und Theorie des Himmels*; Königsberg and Leipzig, 1755) and to Lambert's agreement, in the latter's *Cosmologische Briefe* (1761) with Kant's ideas on the formation of the world, the Milky Way, and the fixed stars. Kant's *Universal Natural History* was published in 1755, but the publisher went bankrupt just as the book came out. As a result, Kant's theories, specifically the nebular hypothesis, were not well known to Lambert and other physicists. Laplace, 41 years later, does not mention Kant's book.

9 *Cosmological Letters on the Establishment of the Universe (Kosmologische Briefe über die Einrichtung des Weltbaues*; Augsburg, 1761).

10 *An Original Theory and New Hypothesis of the Universe*, by Thomas Wright of Durham (1750). Kant credits this work with stimulating his own composition of the *Universal Natural History*. Kant knew of Wright's ideas from a 1751 review of the book in a Hamburg newspaper.

10 [34] (32)
To Johann Heinrich Lambert.
December 31, 1765.

Dear Sir:

Nothing could have been more welcome and pleasant for me than to receive the letter with which you have honored me; for, in all sincerity, I hold you to be the greatest genius in Germany, a man capable of important and enduring contributions to the investigations on which I too am working. I beg you also not to think me negligent for my delay in answering. Herr Kanter, whom I informed of your proposal, asked me to postpone my letter until he might indicate his final decision to you in a letter of his own. He recognizes very well the significance of an association with such a distinguished writer as you, and he is willing enough to undertake the publication. But he would like to postpone it, since he does not have enough time before the Easter book fair and he is overwhelmed with other commitments. He has gone into partnership with his former employee, Herr Hartknoch, who managed his affairs in Riga till now, and he has assured me that he will send you his explanation of the matter just mentioned right away.

10:55

It is no small pleasure for me that you have noticed the fortunate agreement of our methods, an agreement that I have often observed in your writings. It has served to increase my confidence, since it is a logical confirmation that shows that our methods satisfy the touchstone of universal human reason. I value greatly your invitation to share our plans with each other, and since I feel highly honored by this proposal I shall not fail to make use of it. For unless I deceive myself I think I have finally reached some conclusions I can trust. But the talent one sees in you, dear sir, combining an exceptional acuteness for details with a breadth of vision of the whole, is universally admitted, so that your willingness to join your powers with my paltry endeavors allows me to hope for important instruction, for myself and perhaps for the world as well.

For a number of years I have carried on my philosophical reflections on every earthly subject, and after many capsizings, on which occasions I always looked for the source of my error or tried to get some insight into the nature of my blunder, I have finally reached the point where I feel secure about the method that has to be followed if one wants to escape the cognitive fantasy that has us constantly expecting to reach a conclusion, yet just as constantly makes us retrace our steps, a fantasy

10:56 from which the devastating disunity among supposed philosophers also arises; for we lack a common standard with which to procure agreement from them. Now, whatever the nature of the investigation before me, I always look to see what it is I have to know in order to solve a particular problem, and what degree of knowledge is possible for a given question, so that the judgment I make is often more limited but also more definite and secure than is customary in philosophy. All of my endeavors are directed mainly at the proper method of metaphysics and thereby also the proper method for philosophy as a whole. Apropos, I must tell you, dear sir, that Herr Kanter, in true bookseller's fashion, did not hesitate to announce the title, somewhat distorted,[1] in the Leipzig catalog when he heard from me that I might have a work with that title ready for the next Easter book fair. I have, however, departed so widely from my original plan that I now want to postpone this book a little while, for I regard it as the culmination of my whole project. My problem is this: I noticed in my work that, though I had plenty of examples of erroneous judgments to illustrate my theses concerning mistaken procedures, I lacked examples to show in concreto what the proper procedure should be. Therefore, in order to avoid the accusation that I am merely hatching new philosophical schemes, I must first publish a few little essays, the contents of which I have already worked out. The first of these will be the "Metaphysical Foundations of Natural Philosophy" and the "Metaphysical Foundations of Practical Philosophy."[2] With the publication of these essays, the main work will not have to be burdened excessively with detailed and yet inadequate examples.

The moment for ending my letter has arrived. I shall in the future have the honor of presenting you, dear sir, with parts of my project, and I shall request your very respected judgment.

You complain with reason, dear sir, of the eternal trifling of punsters and the wearying chatter of today's reputed writers, with whom the only evidence of taste is that they talk about taste. I think, though, that
10:57 this is the *euthanasia* of erroneous philosophy, that it is perishing amid these foolish pranks, and it would be far worse to have it carried to the grave ceremoniously, with serious but dishonest hairsplitting. Before true philosophy can come to life, the old one must destroy itself; and just as putrefaction signifies the total dissolution that always precedes the start of a new creation, so the current crisis in learning magnifies my hopes that the great, long-awaited revolution in the sciences is not too far off. For there is no shortage of good minds.

Professor Reccard,[3] who pleased me with his kind visit and also with your honored letter, is well liked here and universally respected as he deserves to be, though certainly there are few people able to appreciate his full worth. He sends his regards, and I am, with the greatest respect, dear sir,

your most devoted servant,
I. Kant

P.S. As I had finished this letter, Herr Kanter sent over the letter he owes you, which I am enclosing.

---

1 As Lambert's letter, Ak.[33], indicates, the announced title was *Eigentliche Methode der Metaphysic*, i.e., "The Proper Method of Metaphysics."

2 "Metaphysische Anfangsgründe der natürlichen Weltweisheit, und die metaph: Anfangsgr: der praktischen Weltweisheit." Kant's *Metaphysische Anfangsgründe der Naturwissenschaft* did not in fact appear until 20 years later, in 1786. No "metaphysical foundations of practical philosophy" was ever published by Kant. See L. W. Beck, *Commentary on Kant's Critique of Practical Reason* (Chicago: University of Chicago Press, 1960), ch. 1, for a full account of Kant's plans, and changes of plans, for a book on the foundations of ethics.

3 Gotthilf Christian Reccard (1735–98), professor of theology in Königsberg.

1766

11 [37] (35)
From Johann Heinrich Lambert.
February 3, 1766.

10:62   Dear Sir,

I am in every way obliged to you for your most treasured letter of December 31 and should like especially to render my sincerest thanks for your efforts in connection with Herr Kanter. If it suits him I should be very pleased to see him here at Easter and to make the necessary appointments with him. I shall also have various matters to discuss with him in connection with the calendar revision that I have undertaken for the Academy. Might I beg you, sir, to inform Herr Kanter of all this when you have time. I have nothing else to say in answer to his letter. But do think up ways in which, perhaps because of my location [in Berlin], I can be of service to you, so that I shall not remain your debtor.

There is no denying it: whenever a science needs methodical reconstruction and cleansing, it is always metaphysics. The universal, which is supposed to reign in that science, leads us to suppose ourselves omniscient, and thus we venture beyond the limits of possible human

10:63   knowledge. I think this shows that if we want to avoid omissions, premature inferences, and circular reasoning, we had better work piecemeal, demanding to know at every step only what is capable of being known. I think it has been an unrecognized but perennial error in philosophy to force the facts and, instead of leaving anything unexplained, to load up with conjectures, thus actually delaying the discovery of the truth.

The method that your writings exhibit, sir, is undeniably the only method that one can use with security and progress. I see it approximately as follows (and this is also how I set it forth in the last part of my *Dianoiologie*.[1] First, I write down in short sentences whatever occurs to me, and in just the order that it occurs to me, be it clear or conjectural or doubtful or even in part contradictory. Second, I continue until it looks as though something can be made out. Third, I consider whether the contradictory propositions can be made consistent by limiting or more closely determining them . . . [2]

But I wanted to make some more general remarks. The first concerns the question whether or to what extent knowing the *form* of our knowledge leads to knowing its *matter*. This question is important for several reasons. First, our knowledge of the form, as in logic, is as incontestable and right as is geometry. Second, only that part of metaphysics that deals with form has remained undisputed, whereas strife and hypotheses have arisen when material knowledge[a] is at issue. Third, the basis of material knowledge[b] has not, in fact, been adequately shown. Wolf assumed nominal definitions and, without noticing it, shoved aside or concealed all difficulties in them. Fourth, even if formal knowledge[c] does not absolutely determine any material knowledge, it nevertheless determines the ordering of the latter, and to that extent we ought to be able to infer from formal knowledge what would and what would not serve as a possible starting point. Fifth, a knowledge of form can also help us to determine what belongs together and what must be separated, and so on.

In thinking over these relationships of form and matter I arrived at the following propositions, which I only want to list here.

10:64

10:65

1. Form gives us *principles*, whereas matter gives us *axioms* and *postulates*.
2. Formal knowledge must begin with simple concepts, which, just because these are in themselves simple, cannot as such contain any inner contradiction, and which are in themselves conceivable[d] and free of contradiction.
3. Axioms and postulates actually contain only simple concepts. For complex concepts[e] are not conceivable a priori in themselves. The possibility of combining[f] must first of all be derived from the principles[g] and postulates.
4. Either no complex concept is conceivable or the possibility of combining must already be conceivable in the simple concepts.
5. The simple concepts are singular concepts. For genera and species contain the *fundamenta divisionum et subdivisionum* within them and, just for that reason, are more highly complex the more

---

[a] *Materie unsers Wissens*
[b] *Materie*
[c] *die Form*
[d] *für sich gedenkbar*
[e] *zusammengesetze Begriffe*
[f] *Zusammensetzen*
[g] *Grundsätzen*

abstract and universal they are. The concept of "thing," *ens*, is of all concepts the most complex.

6. According to the Leibnizian analysis, which proceeds by way of abstraction and analogies, one arrives at more highly complex concepts the more one abstracts, and for the most part, at *nominal* relational concepts that concern the form more than the matter.

7. On the other hand, since form consists of nothing but relational concepts, it can provide nothing but simple relational concepts.

8. Accordingly, the really objectively simple concepts must be found by a direct inspection[b] of them, that is, we must, in good anatomical fashion, assemble all the concepts and let each one pass through inspection, in order to see whether, when we ignore all the relations of a given concept to other concepts, there are several concepts included in it or whether it is indeed simple.[i]

9. Simple concepts are like space and time, that is to say, totally different from one another, easily recognizable, easy to name, and practically impossible to confuse, if we abstract from their degrees and concentrate only on their kind.[j] And thus I believe that not a single one of those concepts remains unnamed in our language.

10:66

With these propositions in mind I have no hesitation in saying that Locke was on the right track when he sought the simple elements in our knowledge. But we need to eliminate the distortions caused by linguistic usage. For example, there is an undeniably individual, simple something in the concept of *extension* – something that is not found in any other concept. There is something simple in the concepts of *duration, existence, movement, unity, solidity*, and so on, something belonging uniquely to each of these concepts, that can readily be distinguished in thought from the many relational concepts that may accompany them. Axioms and postulates that lay the groundwork for scientific knowledge are also indicated by these simples and are all of the same type as Euclid's.

The other remarks I wanted to make concern the comparison of philosophical and mathematical knowledge. I realized that where mathematicians have succeeded in opening up a new field that philosophers previously thought they had constructed in its entirety, the mathematicians not only had to reverse everything the philosophers had done but also had to reconstruct everything on simple foundations, so much so that philosophy was entirely useless and contemptible to them. The single condition that only homogeneous elements can be added implies

[b] *Anschauen* [i] *einförmig*
[j] *Quale*

that all philosophical propositions whose predicates do not apply uniformly to their subjects are rejected by the mathematician. And there are entirely too many such propositions in philosophy. A watch is called "gold" when even the casing is hardly made of gold. Euclid does not derive his elements from either the definition of space or that of geometry but begins instead with lines, angles, and so on, the simple elements in the dimensions of space. In mechanics, we make little use of the definition of *motion*; rather, we immediately consider what *accompanies* motion, viz., a body, the direction, velocity, time, force and space, and then we *compare* these things with one another in order to discover *principles*. I have been led to the conclusion that as long as a philosopher does not carry his analysis of measurable objects to the 10:67 point where the mathematician can find unities, measures, and dimensions he must surely still be hanging on to some confusion, or at least the predicates of his propositions do not apply uniformly to the subjects.

I await impatiently the publication of both your "Foundations of Natural Philosophy" and the "Foundations of Practical Philosophy" and I agree entirely that a genuine method commends itself most effectively when displayed in actual examples, since one can then illustrate it with individual cases, whereas it might well be too abstract when expressed logically. But once the examples are there, logical remarks about them become highly serviceable. Examples perform the same job that figures do in geometry, for the latter, too, are actually examples or special cases.

I close now and want to assure you that our continued correspondence would be exceptionally pleasing to me. I remain most eagerly at your service, sir,

Sir most devoted servant,

J. H. Lambert

Berlin

At the corner of Cronenstraße and Schinkenbrücke in the Bethgenschen house.

---

1 Lambert, *Neues Organon* I, 386–450. Lambert's account of his method is lengthy. He warns against hasty generalization and the overlooking of ambiguities and urges that philosophical investigations begin with "simple" rather than "complex" things.

2 Lambert's summary of his 13-step "Allgemeine der Methode" would, as he admits, be clearer if examples were offered. As it stands, the method is no more than an exhortation to look out for ambiguities, inconsistencies, and "Dissonanzen" in composing one's metaphysical theory.

12 [38] (36)
To Moses Mendelssohn.[1]
February 7, 1766.

Dear Sir:

There is no need for fashionable circumlocutions between two persons whose ways of thinking are, because of the similarity of their intellectual concerns and the mutuality of their principles, in such agreement. I was so happy to receive your gracious letter[2] and I accept with pleasure your proposal that we continue our correspondence.

10:68 Herr Mendel Koshmann brought me the Jewish student Leo and your recommendation of him. I was glad to assist him and allow him to attend my lectures. But a few days ago he came to me stating that he wished to take advantage of the opportunity afforded by an available Polish supply wagon and take a little trip to visit his relatives, and that he planned to be back sometime around Easter. It seems that he has made himself somewhat unpopular with the local Jewish community by neglecting some of the required observances. I take it that you will give him the instruction he needs to have for the future, in anticipation of which I have already given him some prudential reminders.

I have sent you *via* the postal service some daydreams[3] and I humbly request that, after retaining a copy for yourself, you be kind enough to have the remaining copies conveyed to Court Chaplain Sack, High Consistory Councillor Spalding,[4] Provost Süsmilch, Prof. Lambert, Prof. Sultzer and Prof. Formey. It is as it were a casual piece, containing not so much a working out of these questions as a hasty sketch of the way they ought to be considered. Your judgment in these and other matters will be highly treasured.

It would please and profit me to hear news of the intellectual life and the bright people in your area. I wish that I for my part could offer you something entertaining and I am

with sincere respect, sir,
your most devoted servant,
I. Kant

---

1 Moses Mendelssohn (1729–1786), the renowned German Jewish philosopher, often identified with the so-called Popular philosophers of the period. He was important politically and socially for his advocacy of the separation of church

and state and his defense of freedom of conscience. His philosophical connection with Kant came via the so-called pantheism controversy and Mendelssohn's attempt to provide rationalistic proofs for the existence of God and the immortality of the soul. The latter argument is examined and attacked by Kant in the Paralogisms section of the first *Critique*.

On Mendelssohn, see *inter alia* Alexander Altmann, *Moses Mendelssohn, A Biographical Study* (Philadelphia: Jewish Publication Society of America, 1973); Lewis White Beck, *Early German Philosophy* (Cambridge, Mass.: Harvard University Press, 1969), especially chs. XIII and XIV; and Frederick Beiser, *The Fate of Reason* (Cambridge, Mass., and London: Harvard University Press, 1987), chap. 3.

2 The letter, obviously dating from sometime before Feb. 7, is not extant.

3 Kant refers to his gift as "einige Träumerei" playing on the actual title of his book, *Träume eines Geistersehers, erläutert durch Träume der der Metaphysik (Dreams of a Spirit-seer explained by Dreams of Metaphysics*; Königsberg, 1766).

4 Friedrich Samuel Gottfried Sack (1738–1812) and Johann Joachim Spalding (1714–1804) were two prominent liberal Protestant theologians. Spalding, pastor of the Nikolaikirche in Berlin, gave up his ecclesiastical position in 1788, following the religious censorship edict issued by Wöllner, the Minister of Spiritual Affairs under the anti-Enlightenment monarch Friedrich Wilhelm II.

13 [39] (37)
To Moses Mendelssohn.
April 8, 1766.

Dear Sir,   10:69

For your kind efforts in forwarding the writings I sent you, I again send my sincerest thanks and my readiness to reciprocate in any way that I might be of service.[1]

The unfavorable impression you express[2] concerning the tone of my little book proves to me that you have formed a good opinion of the sincerity of my character, and your very reluctance to see that character ambiguously expressed is both precious and pleasing to me. In fact, you shall never have cause to change this opinion. For though there may be flaws that even the most steadfast determination cannot eradicate completely, I shall certainly never become a fickle or fraudulent person, after having devoted the largest part of my life to studying how to despise those things that tend to corrupt one's character. Losing the self-respect that stems from a sense of honesty would therefore be the greatest evil that could, but most certainly shall not, befall me. Although I am absolutely convinced of many things that I shall never have the courage to say, I shall never say anything I do not believe.

I wonder whether, in reading this rather untidily completed book, you noticed certain indications of my reluctance to write it. For since I had made some inquiries after learning of Swedenborg's visions first from people who knew him personally, then from some letters, and finally from his published works, I knew that I would never be at peace from the incessant questions of people who thought I knew something about this subject until I had disposed of all these anecdotes.

10:70 It was in fact difficult for me to devise the right style with which to clothe my thoughts, so as not to expose myself to derision. It seemed to me wisest to forestall other people's mockery by first of all mocking myself; and this procedure was actually quite honest, since my mind is really in a state of conflict on this matter. As regards the spirit reports, I cannot help but be charmed by stories of this kind, and I cannot rid myself of the suspicion that there is some truth to their validity, regardless of the absurdities in these stories and the fancies and unintelligible notions that infect their rational foundations and undermine their value.

As to my expressed opinion of the value of metaphysics in general, perhaps here and again my words were not sufficiently careful and qualified. But I cannot conceal my repugnance, and even a certain hatred, toward the inflated arrogance of whole volumes full of what are passed off nowadays as insights; for I am fully convinced that the path that has been selected is completely wrong, that the methods now in vogue must infinitely increase the amount of folly and error in the world, and that even the total extermination of all these chimerical insights would be less harmful than the dream science itself, with its confounded contagion.

I am far from regarding metaphysics itself, objectively considered, to be trivial or dispensable; in fact I have been convinced for some time now that I understand its nature and its proper place among the disciplines of human knowledge and that the true and lasting welfare of the human race depends on metaphysics – an appraisal that would seem fantastic and audacious to anyone but you. It befits brilliant men such as you to create a new epoch in this science, to begin completely afresh, to draw up the plans for this heretofore haphazardly constructed discipline with a master's hand. As for the stock of knowledge currently available, which is now publicly up for sale, I think it best to pull off its dogmatic dress and treat its pretended insights skeptically. My feeling is not the result of frivolous inconstancy but of an extensive investigation. Admittedly, my suggested treatment will serve a merely

10:71 negative purpose, the avoidance of stupidity (*stultitia caruisse*),[3] but it will prepare the way for a positive one. Although the innocence of a healthy but uninstructed understanding requires only an *organon* in order to arrive at insight, a *katharticon* [cathartic] is needed to get rid of the pseudo-insight of a spoiled head. If I may be permitted to mention something of my own efforts, I think I have reached some important insights in this discipline since I last published anything on questions of this sort, insights that will establish the proper procedure for metaphysics. My notions are not merely general ones but provide a specific criterion. To the extent that my other distractions permit, I am gradually preparing to submit these ideas to public scrutiny, but principally to yours; for I flatter myself that if you could be persuaded to collaborate with me (and I include in this your noticing my errors) the development of science might be significantly advanced.

It suffices for my not inconsiderable pleasure that my superficial little essay will have the good fortune to entice "Basic Reflections"[4] from you on this point, and I regard it as useful enough if it occasions deeper investigations in others. I am sure that the main point of all these considerations will not escape you, though I could have made it clearer if I had not had the book printed one page at a time, for I could not always foresee what would lead to a better understanding of later pages; moreover, certain explanations had to be left out, because they would have occurred in the wrong place. In my opinion, everything depends on our seeking out data for the problem, *how is the soul present in the world, both in material and in non-material things.* In other words, we need to investigate the nature of that power of external agency in a substance of this kind, and the nature of that *receptivity* or capacity of being affected, of which the union of a soul with a human body is only a special case. Since we have no experience through which we can get to know such a subject in its various relationships (and experience is the only thing that can disclose the subject's external power or capacity), and since the harmony of the soul with the body discloses only the reciprocal relationship of the *inner* condition (thinking or willing) of the soul to the *outer* condition of the material body (not a relation of one *external* activity to another *external* activity) and consequently is not at all capable of solving the problem, the upshot of all this is that one is led to ask whether it is really possible to settle questions about these powers of spiritual substances by means of a priori rational judgments. This investigation resolves itself into another, namely, whether one can by means of rational inferences discover a *primitive* power, that is, the primary, fundamental relationship of cause to effect. And since I am certain that this is impossible, it follows that, if these powers are not given in experience, they can only be the product of poetic invention. But this invention (an heuristic fiction or hypothesis) can never even be proved to be possible, and it is a mere delusion to argue from

10:72

the fact of its conceivability (which has its plausibility only because no impossibility can be derived from the concept either). Such delusions are Swedenborg's daydreams, though I myself tried to defend them against someone who would argue that they are impossible; and my analogy between a real moral influx by spiritual beings and the force of universal gravitation is not intended seriously; it is only an example of how far one can go in philosophical fabrications, completely unhindered, when there are no *data*, and it illustrates how important it is, in such exercises, first to decide what is required for a solution of the problem and whether the necessary data for a solution are really available. If, for the time being, we put aside arguments based on fitingness or on divine purposes and ask whether it is ever possible to attain such knowledge of the nature of the soul from our experience – a knowledge sufficient to inform us of the manner in which the soul is present in the universe, how it is linked both to matter and to beings of its own sort – we shall then see whether *birth* (in the metaphysical sense), *life*, and *death* are matters we can ever hope to understand by means of reason. Here we must decide whether there really are not boundaries imposed upon us by the limitations of our reason, or rather, the limitations of experience that contains the *data* for our reason. But I shall stop now and commend myself to your friendship. I beg also that you convey to Professor Sultzer my particular respect and the desire to hear from him. I am, most respectfully,

10:73

Your most devoted servant,
I. Kant

Königsberg

---

1   This letter is a reply to Mendelssohn's letter, not extant, of some time between Feb. 7 and Apr. 8. On the former date, Kant replied to another letter of Mendelssohn's (also not extant). See letter Ak.[38] above, in which Kant expresses his pleasure at the prospect of a correspondence with Mendelssohn and asks him to forward some copies of Kant's *Traüme eines Geistersehers* to various people. He asked for Mendelssohn's opinion. As is evident from Kant's reply to Mendelssohn in the present letter, it was not the opinion for which Kant had hoped. Mendelssohn was offended by what he took to be the tone of Kant's essay, "between jest and earnest."

2   In his discussion in the *Allgemeine deutsche Bibliothek* IV, 2, 1767, p. 281, Mendelssohn wrote: "The jocular profundity with which this little book is written leaves the reader for a time in doubt whether Herr Kant intended to make metaphysics ridiculous or spirit-seeing credible."

3   Horace, *Epistle* I, 1, 41hl f. "Virtus est vitium fugere et sapientia prima stultitia

caruisse" (It is the beginning of virtue and wisdom to flee from vice and free oneself from folly).

4   A reference to Mendelssohn's *Phaidon* (1767). In the second dialogue, Mendelssohn argues that a material thing cannot think.

1768

14 [40] (38)
To Johann Gottfried Herder.[1]
May 9, 1768.

10:73 Reverend, esteemed Sir,

I seize this opportunity to express to you the respect and friendship which my customary negligence in letter writing might otherwise have made you doubt. It is with a certain vanity that I observed the discriminating approbation which your recent essays[2] have received from the public, even though they are entirely your own achievement and owe nothing to my instruction.[3] If criticism did not have the unfortunate tendency to make a man of genius timorous, and if nicety of judgment did not make self-approval so difficult, I would venture the hope, based on the fragments I have from you,[4] that I might live to see you become in time a master of that sort of philosophical poetry in which Pope excels. Observing the precocious development of your talents I anticipate with pleasure the time when your fertile mind, no longer so buffeted by the warm winds of youthful feeling, will achieve that gentle

10:74 but sensitive tranquility which is the contemplative life of a philosopher, just the opposite of the life that mystics dream about. I look forward to that epoch of your genius with confidence – confidence being a frame of mind that is most beneficial both to its possessor and to the world; it is a frame of mind that Montange [*sic*] possessed hardly at all and Hume, as far as I know, exemplifies to the highest degree.[5]

As for my own work, since I am committed to nothing and with total indifference to my own and others' opinions, often turn my whole system upside down and observe it from a variety of perspectives in order finally perhaps to discover one which I can hope to point me in the direction of the truth, I have, since we parted, exchanged many of my views for other insights. My principal aim is to know the actual nature and limits of human capacities and inclinations, and I think I have finally more or less succeeded as far as ethics is concerned. I am now working on a Metaphysics of Ethics in which I fancy I shall be able to present the evident and fruitful principles of conduct and the method that must be employed if the so prevalent but for the most part sterile efforts in this area of knowledge are ever to produce useful results. I hope to be finished with this work this year, unless my fragile health prevents it.

Please give my best regards to Herr Behrens[6] and assure him that one can be very loyal in friendship even if one never writes about it. Herr Germann[7] who is forwarding this letter to you is a well brought up and diligent man who will know how to profit from your kindness and who will make a capable student in the Riga school.[8] I am respect-fully

your most devoted friend and servant,
I. Kant

Königsberg
the 9th of May
1767[9]

---

1   Johann Gottfried Herder (1744–1803), the distinguished writer and philoso-pher. He was Kant's student in 1762–4 but became one of the leading *Sturm und Drang* opponents of "Kantian rationalism" and of academic philosophy generally. It is probable that Herder's eventual antagonism to Kant was fos-tered by Hamann, whom Herder came to regard with great respect.

    Kant's dislike of Herder's philosophical development may be seen in his reaction to Herder's *Älteste Urkunde des Menschengeschlechts* (1774), which Kant discusses in an exchange of letters with Hamann (see Ak.[86], [87] and [88], below) and in Kant's published review of Herder's *Ideen (Ideas for a Philosophy of the History of Mankind)*. Herder's *Gott. Einige Gespräche* (1787) also elicits a critical comment from Kant. See his letter to Jacobi, Ak. [389] below, where he calls Herder "this great sleight of hand artist" ("dieser grosser Künstler von Blendwerken"). Herder's 1799 *Eine Metakritik zur Kritik der reinen Vernunft* (Part 1 of his *Verstand und Erfahrung*) was criticized by Kant's disciple Kiesew-etter as "Herderish babbling, unworthy of refutation." Cf. Ak.[848].

2   Herder's *Über die neuere deutsche Litteratur* (Fragments concerning recent German literature; Riga, 1767).

3   Herder studied medicine and then theology in Königsberg, 1762–4; Kant allowed him to attend his lectures *gratis* and to read some of his unpublished manuscripts.

4   Kant must refer here to Herder's poem written while he was Kant's student. Herder had tried to put some of Kant's ideas into verse. This so pleased Kant that he recited them to his class.

5 Kant's sentence, with the phrase, "eine Gemütsverfassung . . . worin Montange den untersten und Hume . . . den obersten Platz einnehme," is syntactically ambiguous and somewhat perplexing to translate, since "untersten Platz" sounds disparaging. Taking "frame of mind" (*Gemütsverfassung*) to refer to "confidence" (*Zuversicht*) rather than to the "tranquility" (*Ruhe*) praised in the previous sentence is more in keeping with Kant's ostensible aim, viz., to *commend* both Montaigne and Hume to Herder. So Herder interprets him, in his responding letter. Vorländer and Cassirer remark that Kant was especially taken with Montaigne in this period. Cf. K. Vorländer, *Immanuel Kant, Der Mann und das Werk*, I, 173. Nor did Kant's respect for Montaigne lessen as he reached old age. In a 1793 letter to his publisher Lagarde, Ak. [593], Kant asks that a copy of a German translation of Montaigne be sent to him in place of copies of the *Critique of Judgment* that Lagarde owed him. It is therefore highly unlikely that Kant meant "den untersten Platz" to be pejorative.

6 Johann Christoph Berens, a merchant in Riga and a good friend of Kant's. See notes to Hamann's letter to Kant, July 27, 1759.

7 Alberecht Germann, a student, matriculated in Königsberg, Apr. 1763.

8 Herder held a teaching position at the cathedral school in Riga.

9 Kant wrote "1767" but the correct date must be 1768 since Germann, mentioned in the letter, did not go to Riga until then.

15 [41] (39)
From Johann Gottfried Herder.
November 1768.

10:75 Noble Herr Magister,
Treasured teacher and friend,

I hope and trust that you have too kind an understanding of my way of thinking to interpret my previous silence as slackness or something even worse. It is only my incredibly burdensome work, a huge number of distractions, and particularly that "uneasiness of soul"[1] which Locke regards as the mother of so many enterprises but which for me has been the mother of a paralyzed inactivity, from which I am just now beginning to emerge.

I cannot tell you how much joy your letter gave me. My teacher's remembrance of me, the friendly tone of your letter, its contents – all these added up to a gift, quite unlike any of the letters I often get from Germany, even from the worthiest people, or even from as far away as Switzerland. Your letter was all the more precious to me since I know your disinclination to letter-writing (a trait I seem to have inherited from you somewhat). But how silly of me to try to enumerate the grounds of my pleasure!

It is so kind of you to describe my authorship in terms that I myself would not think of using. I regard it as little more that a youthful first step, one that certainly has done me no harm or on the whole any dishonor, but which for several reasons I wish I could take back. Not that what I wrote was irresponsible; what troubles me rather is mainly that my name has become so associated with this work and is bandied about by so many people that your good landlord and my good friend Herr Kanter,[2] has, through a series of events, unintentionally played me a dirty trick, since he was the first cause of this notoriety. My firm resolve, and I say this calmly and deliberately, was to publish everything anonymously until I could surprise the world with a book that would be worthy of my name. For this and no other reason did I hide myself behind the floral façade of an ornate style of writing, a style that is not really my own, and publish fragments that are insufferable if not taken as mere preludes.   10:76

As far as it is up to me, I shall continue to be silent and anonymous. But how can I help it that the impetuous kindness of my friends has spoiled my plan? You, my friend, must be one of those who know that materials of the sort contained in my previous little volumes are not supposed to be the final resting place of my Muse. Yet why shouldn't I apply my little bit of philosophy to the fashionable topics of this third quarter of a century, if that application (or so I flatter myself) could promote a healthy philosophy in so many ways? I don't know to what extent philology and criticism and the study of antiquity would have to be cut back if philosophers themselves were to philologize and criticize and study the ancients. But what a pity it is that in Germany this word is starting to become almost a term of abuse and that the sort of sciences that are becoming popular are those in which the most unphilosophical heads can chatter away.

But there I go again, writing almost like an art critic and a fragmentist, so let me stop abruptly.

My cherished friend, the path which you recommend for my future, to follow Montaigne, Hume and Pope, is (except for a slight detour) at least the one that my Muse *desires*, even if the *hope* of joining that company is too flattering. I have spent many sweet and lonely hours reading Montaigne, reading with that quiet reflexion which one needs if one is to follow his shifting moods and see each of his stories, one after the other, and each detached and flowing thought which he reveals, as either a product of nature or as an artful experiment of the human soul. What an achievement it would be for someone to discuss Baumgarten's rich psychology[3] with the wisdom of a Montaigne! I was less patient with Hume, since Rousseau still enthralled me, but now

10:77 that I have gradually come to see that, whatever else might be the case, human beings are social animals, I have learned to appreciate Hume as well, he who can be called in the true sense a philosopher of human society. And I took up British history at school mainly because I wanted to work through the historical writings of this greatest modern history writer. It makes me angry that his new History of England has fallen into the hands of such a semi-competent translator who is very inaccurate even if he leaves us half-informed, here and there.[4]

But why do you mention only two people and forget a third name, my dear philosopher, one whose human wisdom and social temper are just as great? The friend of our old Leibniz who owes so much to him and whom he loved to read – the philosophical scoffer whose laughter contains more truth than do other people's coughs and spittle – in short, Lord *Shaftesburi* [*sic*].[5] It is a sickness that his moral philosophy and his investigations of virtue and recently his essays on enthusiasm and temper have been taken up by such mediocre minds, people who almost make him seem disgusting, among whom I reckon particularly that most recent translator with his mishmash of long and absurd refutations. But apart from the fact that his criterion of truth – to be worthy of ridicule – seems itself to be ridiculous, this author is such a favorite of mine that I would love to hear your opinion of him as well.

Do let that obscure, rough poem of mine die in the night. It is less likely that one will find any Pope in it than that our Lindner[6] will become another penetrating Aristotle and Schlegel[7] the model of urbanity.

You send me news of your forthcoming Moral [Philosophy]. How I wish it were finished. May your account of the Good contribute to the culture of our century as much as your account of the Sublime and the Beautiful have done. On the latter topic I am currently reading with pleasure a work by a very philosophical Britisher, which you can get in French as well. I just happen to have the book in front of me, *Recherches philosophiques sur l'origine des Idées, que nous avons du Beau et du Sublime.*[8] He presses his analysis in many places, whereas you on many pages are inclined to generalize and draw contrasts among our observations; it is a pleasure to see two such original thinkers each pursue his own path and in different ways meet each other again.

10:78 There are so many things I would tell you if I thought you would have the patience to answer me. Misgivings about several of your philosophical hypotheses and proofs, especially when you touch on the science of the human, are more than speculations. This human philosophy is my favorite occupation as well, for I assumed my spiritual office for no other reason than that I knew (and I confirm it every day with new experience) that under the conditions of our civic constitution I could use this position most effectively to bring culture and human understanding to the noble segment of mankind that we call the People [*Volk*]. It would be unjust of me were I to complain that I had not reached this goal. For at least I am given the gentle hope that my existence is not without some purpose when I see the love that I enjoy from many good and noble people, the joyful and willing intrusion into my life of the most educable part of the public, the young people and the ladies – all these things are not just flattering to me but reassure me that my life on earth has a purpose.

But since love begins with ourselves, I cannot conceal my wish that I might get the opportunity as soon as possible to leave this place and to see the world. The aim of my life is to know more people and learn more about things than Diogenes could from his jar. If I should get an invitation from Germany, I would hardly feel bound to my present position. I don't know why I shouldn't accept a call, and I upbraid myself for having turned down the invitation from Petersburg, a position which it seems it has been very poorly filled.[9] Right now I feel myself a constrained force and I try at least to remain a living force, though I don't exactly see how constraint is supposed to nourish my inner drive. But who does know that? And where am I to go? Do love me, my dearest, esteemed Kant, and accept as heartfelt my signing myself as

your

Herder.

P.S. I know I should hesitate to ask for your letters, since I know your feelings of discomfort about writing; but if you knew how I long to make use of your letters in the absence of live contact, you might overcome your feeling of discomfort.

1　John Locke, *An Essay concerning Human Understanding*, Book II, ch. 21, sec. 40: "The greatest present uneasiness is the spur to action, that is constantly felt, and for the most part determines the will in its choice of the next action."

2　On Kanter, see Lambert's letter above, Ak. [33], n. 7.

3　Kant used Baumgarten's *Psychologia empirica* (Halle, 1739) in his *Anthropologie* lectures.

4　*Hume's History of England*, translated by Johann Jakob Dusch (Breslau and Leipzig, 1762).

5　Anthony Ashley Cooper, third Earl of Shaftesbury (1671–1713). His *Characteristics of Men, Manners, Opinions and Times* appeared in 1711. German translations of some of these essays were published by J. J. Spalding in 1747. The essay on enthusiasm (Treatise I) was translated by von Wichmann (Leipzig, 1768). Herder praised Shaftesbury as the "beloved Plato of Europe" and called him "this virtuoso of humanity." Cf. Herder's *Briefe zu Beförderung der Hu-*

manität, Letter 33 (1794). Leibniz refers to Shaftesbury in *Philosophical Papers and Letters*, ed. Leroy Loemker (Chicago, 1956), II, 1030.

6 Johann Gotthelf Lindner (1729–76), rector of the cathedral school at Riga, 1755, and professor of poetry in Königsberg from 1765.

7 Gottlieb Schlegel (1739–1810), superintendent of Herder's school in Riga, 1765, and professor of theology in Greifswald. Herder's opinion of him, stated in a letter to Hamann, May 4, 1765: "S. is invariably stupid in what he thinks, what he wants, and what he says, and before Riga he was nothing, as a businessman, as a talker, as a preacher."

8 Edmund Burke's well-known essay, *A Philosophical Inquiry into the Origin of our Ideas of the Sublime and the Beautiful* (1757) appeared in a French translation by Abbé Des François in 1765.

9 Herder refused the position of inspector of Protestant schools in St. Petersburg in Apr. 1767.

1769

16 [47] (44)
To Simon Gabriel Suckow.[1]
December 15, 1769.

Dear Herr Privy Councillor, 10:82
Esteemed and learned Herr Professor,

The unexpectedly prompt result of your kind efforts on my behalf
have filled me with both consternation and gratitude. In thinking about
your kind proposal, which would involve a change at your university
which His Highness,[2] at first thought might take place sometime in the
future, I found myself moved not to reject too hastily the opportunity   10:83
to gain a small but secure amount of prosperity;[3] but I am also put into
a state of perplexity by this immediate and kind offer of an opportunity
which I coveted just a little while ago. My resolution, I beg you to
forgive me, has in the meantime vacillated.

Renewed and much stronger assurances, the growing likelihood of
a possibly imminent vacancy here,[4] attachment to my native city and a
rather extended circle of acquaintances and friends, above all however
my weak physical constitution – these suddenly present themselves as
such strong counter-arguments, that my peace of mind seems possible
to me only where I have heretofore always found it, even if only in
burdensome circumstances. And since it appears that a definite answer
is required right away, I make it now with most earnest apologies for
the trouble that I may have occasioned: I hereby decline the honor and
the appointment intended for me. I am exceedingly worried that I have
brought your displeasure and that of the distinguished nobleman upon
myself by occasioning a vain expectation. But you, dear sir, know the
weaknesses of the human character too well not to understand that
some minds suffer from an aversion to change that is as uncontrollable
as fortune is, an aversion even to changes that seem trifling to others.

I shall think of you forever, dear sir, with the greatest respect and, if you do not judge me to be fickle, I beg permission to hope for your continued goodwill and I remain

your most obedient servant

Immanuel Kant

Königsberg, the 15th of December, 1769

---

1   Simon Gabriel Suckow (1721–86) was professor of mathematics and physics in Erlangen.

2   Margrave Carl Alexander (1763–1806).

3   Kant was to have received 500 Rhenish guilder and five cords of wood annually, as well as 100 talers for moving expenses.

4   A professor of theology in Königsberg, Christoph Langhansen, had been ill for some time. He died Mar. 15, 1770. On Mar. 16 Kant wrote to Carl Joseph Maximilian, Freiherr von Fürst and Kupferberg (1717–90), the *Oberkurator* of Prussian universities, asking that Langhansen's professorship be given to Carl Andreas Christiani, who was then professor of moral philosophy. Kant suggested that, since Christiani, Langhansen's son-in-law, was very knowledgeable in mathematics, the deceased man's chair should go to Christiani, thereby opening up a philosophy professorship for Kant himself. If that should fail, Kant suggested Buck, the professor of logic and metaphysics, be given Langhansen's chair; Buck had been an associate (*extraordinarious*) professor of mathematics for some years and, according to Kant, had become professor of philosophy only because of the occupying Russian government.

In that letter, Kant complains that he is about to be 47 years old and still lacks a secure position. He mentions turning down an offer from Erlangen in hopes of remaining in his native city. (Cf. Ak.[51], 10:90–9.)

In a petitioning letter to Frederick the Great, Mar. 19, Kant repeated his suggestion, mentioning also the rejected Erlangen position and its salary. Kant does not mention the "feeler" he had received, Jan. 12, 1770, from Jena, a position whose salary would have been more than 200 Reichstaler, with no more than two hours per week of public lecturing required. Three hours of private lecturing per day would have yielded an addtional 150 Reichstaler per year. The Jena inquiry came from Ernst Jacob Danovius (1741–82), professor of theology in Jena. (Ak.[49], 10: 87–8.)

It is interesting to compare these salaries with a 1778 offer from Halle where, according to von Zedlitz, Kant would receive "only" 600 Reichstaler. (Zedlitz's letter, Feb. 28, 1778, Ak.[129], 10:224–5.) On Mar. 28, 1778, Zedlitz raised the offer to 800 Taler, adding that Halle had a better climate than Königsberg, that Kant would have 1000–1200 students (and their considerable lecture fees) and would be in the intellectual center of Germany.

As we know, Zedlitz could not persuade Kant to move. Kant's professorship in Königsberg, awarded Mar. 31, 1770, stipulated 166 Reichstaler plus "60 g. Pr." (probably Prussian goldpieces) from the university plus all the emoluments that Professor Buck had enjoyed. The total salary came to approximately 400 thalers, in addition to the lecture fees. The king increased this sum by an additional 220 talers in 1789. Stuckenberg's 1882 biography of Kant estimates that this was equivalent to about £90. It is difficult to say what the equivalent salary in Great Britain or America in the last decade of the twentieth century would be, but Kant's income must have been considerable, a great contrast to his difficult life before 1770.

Letters 1770–1780

[57–146]

1770

17 [57] (54)
To Johann Heinrich Lambert.
September 2, 1770.

Noble Sir,   10:96
Honored Herr Professor,

I am taking advantage of the opportunity I have of sending you my [Inaugural] Dissertation by way of the respondent of that work, a capable Jewish student of mine.[1] At the same time, I should like to destroy an unpleasant misunderstanding caused by my protracted delay in answering your valued letter. The reason was none other than the striking importance of what I gleaned from that letter, and this occasioned the long postponement of a suitable answer. Since I had spent much time investigating the science on which you focused your attention there, for I was attempting to discover the nature and if possible the manifest and immutable laws of that science, it could not have pleased me more that a man of such discriminating acuteness and universality of insight, with whose method of thinking I had often been in agreement, should offer his services for a joint project of tests and   10:97 investigations, to map the secure construction of this science. I could not persuade myself to send you anything less than a clear summary of how I view this science and a definite idea of the proper method for it. The carrying out of this intention entangled me in investigations that were new to me and, what with my exhausting academic work, necessitated one postponement after another. For perhaps a year now, I believe I have arrived at a position that, I flatter myself, I shall never have to change, even though extensions will be needed, a position from which all sorts of metaphysical questions can be examined according to wholly certain and easy criteria, and the extent to which these questions can or cannot be resolved will be decidable with certainty.

I could summarize this whole science, as far as its nature, the sources of its judgments, and the method with which one can progress in it are concerned; and this summary could be made in a rather small space, namely, in a few letters, to be submitted to your sound and instructive judgment. It is that judgment for which I beg here, anticipating the most excellent results from your criticism. But since in a project of such importance a little expenditure of time is no loss at all, if one can thereby produce something complete and lasting, I must beg you again to believe my good intentions to be unaltered but again to grant me more time to carry them out. In order to recover from a lengthy indisposition that has bothered me all summer, and at the same time to keep busy during odd hours, I have resolved this winter to put in order and complete my investigations of pure moral philosophy, in which no empirical principles are to be found, as it were the Metaphysics of Morals. It will in many respects pave the way for the most important views involved in the reconstruction of metaphysics and seems to be just as necessary in view of the current state of the practical sciences, whose principles are so poorly defined. After I have completed this work I shall make use of the permission you gave me, to present

10:98   you with my essays in metaphysics, as far as I have come with them. I assure you that I shall take no proposition as valid which does not seem to you completely warranted. For unless this agreement can be won, the objective will not have been reached, viz., to ground this science on indubitable, wholly incontestable rules. For the present it would please and instruct me to have your judgment of some of the main points in my dissertation, since I intend to add a few pages to it before the publisher presents it at the coming book fair. I want both to correct the errors caused by hasty completion and to make my meaning more determinate. The first and fourth sections can be scanned without careful consideration; but in the second, third, and fifth, though my indisposition prevented me from working them out to my satisfaction, there seems to me to be material deserving more careful and extensive exposition. The most universal laws of sensibility play a deceptively large role in metaphysics, where, after all, it is merely concepts and principles of pure reason that are at issue. A quite special, though purely negative science, general phenomenology (*phaenomologia* [sic] *generalis*), seems to me to be presupposed by metaphysics. In it the principles of sensibility, their validity and their limitations, would be determined, so that these principles could not be confusedly applied to objects of pure reason, as has heretofore almost always happened. For space and time, and the axioms for considering all things under these conditions, are, with respect to empirical knowledge and all objects of sense, very real; they are actually the conditions of all appearances and of all empirical judgments. But extremely mistaken conclusions emerge if we apply the basic concepts of sensibility to something that is not at all an object of sense, that is, something thought through a universal or a pure concept of the understanding as a thing or substance in general, and so on. It seems to me, too (and perhaps I shall be fortunate enough to win your agreement here by means of my very inadequate essay), that such a propaedeutic discipline, which would preserve metaphysics proper from any admixture of the sensible, could be made usefully explicit and evident without great strain.

I beg your future friendship and favorable interest in my still modest scientific efforts. I hope I may be permitted to commend to you Herr Marcus Herz, who is delivering this letter and who would like your help with his studies. He is a young man of excellent character, industrious and capable, who adheres to and profits from every piece of good advice. I am, most respectfully,   10:99

Your most devoted servant,
I. Kant

---

1   Marcus Herz.

18 [58] (55)

From Marcus Herz.

September 11, 1770.

Eternally unforgettable teacher,
Esteemed Herr Professor,

Forgive me, dearest Herr Professor, for only now paying my respects to you, though I have been here since last Thursday. The unusual wakefulness, the five days' journey and the uninterrupted agitation that one experiences on the stage coach had so weakened my body, spoiled as it is by comfort, that I was unfit for any other important business, and how much more unfit for communication with you! The mere thought of you fills my soul with reverential amazement, and it is only with great effort that I am thus able to collect my distracted consciousness and resume my thinking. It is you alone that I must thank for my change of fortune, and to you alone am I indebted for what I am; without you I would still be like so many of my kinsmen,

10:100 pursuing a life chained to the wagon of prejudices, a life no better than that of any animal. I would have a soul without powers, an understanding without efficacy, in short, without you I would be that which I was four years ago, in other words I would be nothing. Certainly the role that I now play is a very small one, if I consider the substance of what I know or compare it to what many others know; yet it is an infinitely elevated role compared to the one I played only a few years ago. Let the ignorant always seek to console themselves by claiming that with all our science we have not progressed beyond them; and let hypochondriacal savants complain that our knowledge only increases our misery. I scorn the former and pity the latter; I shall never cease to regard the day that I dedicated myself to the sciences as the happiest and the day that you became my teacher as the first day of my life.

My first visit here was to Herr Mendelssohn. We conversed for four whole hours over certain things in your Dissertation. We have very different philosophies; he follows Baumgarten to the letter and he gave me to understand very clearly and distinctly that he could not agree with me on a number of points because they did not agree with Baumgarten's opinions. On the whole he likes the Dissertation and he only regrets that you were not somewhat more expansive. He admires the penetration shown in the proposition that, if the predicate of a proposition is sensuous it is only subjectively valid of the subject, while on the other hand if the predicate is intellectual etc.[1] Similarly the development of the infinite,[2] the solution to Kästner's problem.[3] He is about to publish something in which, as he says, it will look as though he has simply copied your whole first section; in short he thinks the whole Dissertation an excellent work, though there are certain points with which he does not totally agree. One of them is that in explaining the nature of space one must use the words "at the same time" [*simul*], and in explaining time the word "after" [*post*]; he also thinks that "at the same time" ought not to be put into the principle of contradiction.[4] I shall have further opportunities to discuss these things with him and I shall never fail to keep my dear teacher informed of them. This man's favorite entertainment is conversation about metaphysical issues, and I

10:101 have spent half of my time here with him. He will write to you himself, but only with brevity, for he thinks that subtle disagreements cannot be resolved in correspondence. I am occupied just now with a little essay for him in which I want to show him the error of an a priori proof of the existence of God. He is very taken with this proof; small wonder, since Baumgarten accepts it.

In the near future Herr Mendelssohn's *Freundschaftliche Briefe* will appear[5] and his *Phädon*,[6] in which the third dialogue is quite revised, also his *Philosophische Schriften* with an Appendix in which he will be concerned with the issue on which you, Herr Professor, once worked, namely the contradiction among realities[7] and finally his translation of 15 Psalms into German verse. I shall send you all this as soon as it is available.

Incidentally Herr Mendelssohn has been very hospitable to me and I wish that I really were what he takes me to be.

I have not yet visited the other scholars or the Minister, for I have not received the letters yet. You were kind enough to promise to send them by mail, so I await them impatiently.

It troubles me that you, dearest teacher, are not feeling well. Is it really impossible for you to reduce the burden of your lectures? If you spent half the afternoon reading or if you just lectured less strenuously? For it is only this and not your sitting that seems to me to be the cause of your weakness. After all there are teachers in Königsberg who sit from morning till evening and move their mouths without ever having to complain about their physical condition. If you think it desirable that I consult physicians here then be so good as to describe to me in detail the whole condition of your body. How fortunate I would deem myself if I could make the smallest contribution to your well-being!

I have bothered you with a very long letter this time. Forgive me for misusing your permission. It is for me a pleasurable hour spent with you, and where is the mortal who can be moderate in such experiences?

Do continue to honor me by your goodwill, and be assured that I shall never cease to be proud to be allowed to venerate you.

10:102

Your most humble pupil and
most obedient servant
Marc. Hertz

Berlin,
the 11th of Sept. 1770
My compliments to Herr Kanter.

---

1 Cf. Kant's Inaugural Dissertation, Section II, especially § 3 and § 4.

2 Cf. Kant's Inaugural Dissertation, Section II, Ak. 2:399, ll. 21 ff.

3 Cf. Kant, op. cit., Ak. 2: 400, ll. 3 ff. and Mendelssohn, *Philosophische Schriften*, Parts 1 and 2 (Berlin, 1771).

4 Cf. Mendelssohn's letter to Kant, Dec. 25, 1770, Ak. [63].

5 Mendelssohn's letters "On the Sentiments" ("Über die Empfindungen") were published separately in 1755, and subsequently in several editions of his *Philosophischen Schriften*, 1761, 1771, etc.

6 Herz must be referring to the third edition of *Phädon*, which appeared in 1769.

7 "von dem Wiederstreit der Realitäten untereinander." Manfred Kuehn has suggested that the "contradiction among realities" referred to here is that of the different cognitive faculties with each other, an early version of the antinomies, except that it is here a contradiction between the reality of sense and reason, or between what different faculties tell us. The editors of both the Akademie edition and of the Schöndörffer/Malter edition of Kant's letters however assert Herz's reference to be to Kant's distinction between logical opposition and real opposition, as set forth in his 1763 essay, "An Attempt to Introduce the Concept of Negative Magnitudes into Philosophy" ("Versuch, den Begriff der negativen Grössen in die Weltweisheit einzuführen"), Ak. 2: 168–204. Section I begins with Kant's distinction between logical vs. real opposition. Cf. Kant, *Theoretical Philosophy, 1755–1770*, trans. and ed. by D. Walford and R. Meerbote (Cambridge and New York: Cambridge University Press, 1992), pp. 207–41. A translation of the Inaugural Dissertation may be found in the same volume.

19 [59] (56)
To Marcus Herz.
September 27, 1770.

My dearest Herr Hertz,

Each of us painfully awaited the other's letter. My letter, with its enclosures, was supposed to leave for Berlin on the 4th of September, and Stalbaum, the lad who works for Kanter,[1] took it (along with the postage) to be mailed. My suspicions were aroused, since your answer did not arrive for so long, but what confused me was that there really was a postal record of a letter to M. Hertz dated the 4th. Finally I no longer doubted that some fraud had occurred and Herr Kanter, on my advice, had the lad's suitcase opened, wherein among a number of other embezzled letters my own was discovered.

The lad himself hurried away and is at the moment still unavailable for questioning.

And now I beg you to be kind enough to see that the enclosed letters reach the Minister, Professor Sultzer[2] and Professor Lambert. Please explain to the first of these the reason for the old postmark and apologize to him. Apart from this I shall always be much obliged to you for your friendly letters and news. Your most recent letter, which spoke the language of the heart, made a deep impression on my own. Herr Friedländer[3] has transmitted to me a new piece by Koelbele.[4] If anything new can be sent to me through that sort of channel, please let me share it. I am, most sincerely,

your

dear friend and servant

I. Kant

Königsberg,
the 27th of September, 1770

---

1 On Kanter, see Lambert's letter, Ak. [33], n. 7. The employee referred to, Christian Ludwig Stahlbaum, later became a book dealer in Berlin.

2 On Sulzer, see Ak. [33], n. 3.

3 David Friedländer (1750–1834), was born in Königsberg to one of the most highly educated families in town. In 1771 he moved to Berlin where he befriended Mendelssohn and Herz, became a banker and *Stadtrat* (city councillor). Schiller referred to him in a letter of September 19, 1795, as "a wealthy and respected Berlin Jew."

4 Johann Balthasar Koelbele (1722–78), a jurist and an unbridled anti-Semite, injected himself into the feud between Lavater and Mendelssohn. He attacked Mendelssohn in several pamphlets so scurrilously that Lavater, himself an outspoken critic of Mendelssohn and of Judaism, decided that continued public combat with Mendelssohn would be disadvantageous to his cause, since it would possibly alienate more liberal Christians. For a full discussion see Alexander Altmann, *Moses Mendelssohn*, ch. 3, especially pp. 234–9.

20 [61] (57)

From Johann Heinrich Lambert.

October 13, 1770.

Noble Sir, 10:103

Your letter and also your treatise, *Concerning the Sensible World and the Intelligible World*[1] gave me great pleasure, especially because I regarded the latter as a demonstration of how metaphysics and ethics[2] could be improved. I hope very much that your new position may occasion more of such essays, unless you have decided to publish them privately.

You remind me, noble sir, of my suggestion of five years ago, of a *possible future collaboration.* I wrote to Herr Holland[3] about it at that

113

10:104 time, and would have written to some other scholars, too, had not the book fair shown me that belles-lettres are displacing everything else. I think that the fad is passing, however, and that people are ready to take up the serious disciplines once more. I have already heard from some people at the universities who never read anything but poems, novels, and literary things that, when they had to get down to business, they found themselves in an entirely new country and had to start their studies all over again. These people are in a position to know what needs to be done at the universities.

In the meantime I planned, on the one hand, to write little treatises myself, to keep in reserve, and on the other hand to invite the collaboration of some scholars with similar views, and thus to create a private society where all those things that tend to ruin public learned societies would be avoided. The actual members would have been a small number of selected philosophers, who would, however, have had to be at home in physics and mathematics as well, since in my view an *authentic metaphysician* is like a man who lacks one of his senses, as the blind lack sight. The members of this society would have exchanged their writings or at least an adequate concept of them, so as to help each other in those cases where several eyes can see better than just one. If each member remained convinced of his own view, however, each would still have been able to get his opinion published, with suitable modesty and the awareness that anyone can be mistaken. Most of the papers would have been philosophical treatises or papers on the theory of language and on belles-lettres, though physics and mathematics could have been included as well, especially if they bordered on philosophy.

The first volume especially would have had to be excellent, and because of the contributions that were to be expected, the right of returning such papers as the majority opposed would always have been reserved. On difficult subjects, the members would have expressed their views in the form of questions or in such a way that objections and counter-arguments could always be voiced.

You could still inform me now, noble sir, to what extent you regard such a society as a genuine possibility and one that might last. What I 10:105 imagine is something like the *Acta eruditorum*[4] as they originally were, exchanges of letters among some of the greatest scholars . . .

But I turn now to your excellent dissertation, since you particularly wanted to have my thoughts about it. If I have correctly understood the matter, certain propositions are basic, and these are, briefly, as follows:

The first main thesis is that *human knowledge*, by virtue of being *knowledge* and by virtue of *having its own form*, is divided in accordance with the old *phaenomenon* and *noumenon* distinction and, accordingly, arises out of two entirely different and, so to speak, *heterogeneous* sources, so that what stems from the one source can never be derived from the other. Knowledge that comes from the senses thus is and remains sensible, just as knowledge that comes from the understanding remains peculiar to the understanding.

My thoughts on this proposition have to do mainly with the question of *generality*, namely, to what extent these two ways of knowing are so completely *separated* that they *never* come together. If this is to be shown a priori, it must be deduced from the nature of the senses and of the understanding. But since we first have to become acquainted with these a posteriori, it will depend on the classification and enumeration of [their] *objects*.

This seems also to be the path you take in the third section. In this sense it seems to me quite correct to say that truths that integrally involve *space* and *location* are of an entirely different sort from truths that must be regarded as eternal and immutable. I merely mentioned this in my *Alethiology*, No. 81.87,[5] for it is not so easy to give the reason why truths integrally involve time and location in this way and in no other, though the question is extremely important.　　　　　10:106

But there I was talking only of *existing* things. The truths of geometry and chronometry, however, involve time and location essentially, not merely accidentally; and in so far as the *concepts* of space and time are eternal, the truths of geometry and chronometry belong to the class of eternal, immutable truths also.

Now you ask whether these truths are sensible? I can very well grant that they are. The difficulty seems to lie in the concepts of time and location and could be expressed without reference to this question. The first four statements in your No. 14 seem to me quite correct[6] and it is especially good that you insist on the true concept of *continuity*, which metaphysics seems to have completely forgotten,[7] since people wanted to bring it in as the idea of a set of connected simple entities [*complexus entium simplicium*] and therefore had to alter the concept. The difficulty actually lies in the fifth statement. It is certainly true that you do not offer the statement, time is the subjective condition [*Tempus est subiectiva conditio*] and so on, as a definition.[8] It is nevertheless supposed to indicate something peculiar and essential to time. Time is undeniably a necessary condition [*conditio sine qua non*] and belongs therefore to the representation of every sensible object and of every object integrally involving time and location. Time is also particularly necessary in order that any human being have such representations. It is also a pure intuition [*Intuitus purus*], not a substance, not a mere relation. It differs from *duration* in the way *location* differs from *space*. It is a particular determination of duration. Moreover, it is not an *accident* that perishes along with substances, and so on. These propositions may all be correct. They lead to no definition, and the best definition will always be that time is time, since we do not want to involve ourselves in logical circularity by defining it in terms of its relations to things that are in time. *Time* is a more determinate concept than *duration*, and for that reason, too, it leads to more negative propositions. For example, whatever is in time has some duration. But the reverse does not hold, in so far as one demands a beginning and an end for "being in time." Eternity is not in time, since its duration is absolute. Any substance that has absolute duration is likewise not in time. Everything that exists has duration, but not everything is in time, and so on. With a concept as clear as that of *time*, we do not lack propositions. The trouble seems to lie only in the fact that one must simply think time and duration and not define them. All changes are bound to time and are inconceivable without time. *If changes are real, then time is real*, whatever it may be. *If time is unreal, then no change can be real.* I think, though, that even an idealist must grant at least that changes really exist and occur in his representations, for example, their beginning and ending. Thus time cannot be regarded as something *unreal*. It is not a substance, and so on, but a finite determination of duration, and like duration, it is somehow real in whatever this reality may consist. If this cannot be identified, without danger of confusion, by means of the words we use for other things, it will either require the introduction of a new primitive term or it will have to remain nameless. The reality of time[9] and of space seems to have something so simple and peculiar about it that it can only be thought and not defined. Duration appears to be inseparable from existence. Whatever exists has a duration that is either absolute or of a certain span, and conversely, whatever has duration must necessarily, while it lasts, exist. Existing things that do not have absolute duration are temporally ordered, in so far as they begin, continue, change, cease, and so on. *Since I cannot deny reality to changes*, until somebody teaches me otherwise, I also cannot say that time (and this is true of space as well) is only a helpful device for human representations. And as for the colloquial phrases in use that involve the notion of time, it is always well to notice the ambiguities that the word "time" has in them. For example,

A long time is an interval of time or of two moments [*intervallum temporis vel duorum momentorum*] and means "a definite duration."

At this or that time, and so on, is either a definite moment, as in astronomy, the time of setting, of rising [*tempus immersionis, emersionis*], and so on, or a smaller or larger interval preceding or following a moment, an indefinite duration or point in time, and so on.

You will gather easily enough how I conceive location and space. Ignoring the ambiguities of the words, I propose the analogy,

Time: Duration = Location: Space

The analogy is quite precise, except that space has three dimensions, duration only one, and besides this each of these concepts has something peculiar to it. Space, like duration, has absolute but also finite determinations. Space, like duration, has a reality peculiar to it, which we cannot explain or define by means of words that are used for other things, at least not without danger of being misleading. It is something simple and must be thought. The whole intelligible world is non-spatial; it does, however, have a spatial counterpart [*Simulachrum*], which is easily distinguishable from physical space. Perhaps this bears a still closer resemblance to it than merely a metaphoric one.

The theological difficulties that, especially since the time of Leibniz and Clarke,[10] have made the theory of space a thorny problem have so far not confused me. I owe all my success to my preference for leaving undetermined various topics that are impervious to clarification. Besides, I did not want to peer at the succeeding parts of metaphysics when working on ontology. I won't complain if people want to regard time and space as mere pictures and appearances. For, in addition to the fact that constant appearance is for us truth, though the foundations are never discovered or only at some future time; it is also useful in ontology to take up concepts borrowed from appearance[11], since *the theory must finally be applied to phenomena again.* For that is also how the astronomer begins, with the phenomenon; deriving his theory of the construction of the world from phenomena, he applies it again to phenomena and their predictions in his *ephemerides* [star calendars]. In metaphysics, where the problem of appearance is so essential, the method of the astronomer will surely be the safest. The metaphysician can take everything to be appearance, separate the empty appearance from the real appearance, and draw true conclusions from the latter. If he is successful, he shall have few contradictions arising from the principles and win much favor. Only it seems necessary to have time and patience for this.

10:109

I shall be brief here in regard to the fifth section. I would regard it as very important if you could find a way of showing more deeply the ground and origin of truths integrally involving space and time. As far as this section is concerned with method, however, I would say here what I said about time. For if *changes*, and therefore also *time* and *duration*, are something real, it seems to follow that *the proposed division in section five must have other, and in part more narrow, intentions*; and according to these, the classification might also have to be different. This occurred to me in No. 25–26. In regard to No. 27, the "whatever exists, exists in some place and at some time" [*Quicquid est, est alicubi et aliquando*] is partly in error and partly ambiguous, if it is supposed to mean located at a time and in a place [*in tempore et in loco*]. Whatever has *absolute* duration is not in time [*in tempore*] and the intelligible

117

world is only "located in" the aforementioned counterpart [*Simulachri*] of space or in the "place" of intelligible space.

What you say in No. 28, and in the note on pages 2–3 concerning the mathematical infinite, that it has been ruined by the definitions in metaphysics and that something else has been substituted for it, has my full approval. In regard to the "simultaneous being and not being" mentioned in No. 28. I think that a counterpart of time exists in the intelligible world as well, and the phrase "at the same time" is therefore used in a different sense when it occurs in the proofs of absolute truths that are not tied to time and place. I should think that the counterpart of space and time in the intelligible world could also be considered in the theory you have in mind. It is a facsimile of real space and real time and can readily be distinguished from them. Our symbolic knowledge is a thing halfway between sensing and actual pure thinking. If we proceed correctly in the delineation of the simple and the manner of our composition, we thereby get reliable rules for producing designations of compounds that are so complex that we cannot review them again but can nevertheless be sure that the designation represents the truth. No one has yet formed himself a clear representation of all the members of an infinite series, and no one is going to do so in the future. But we are able to do arithmetic with such series, to give their sum, and so on, by virtue of the laws of *symbolic* cognition. We thus extend ourselves far beyond the borders of our "real" thinking. The sign $\sqrt{-1}$ represents an unthinkable non-thing. And yet it can be used very well in finding theorems. What are usually regarded as specimens of the pure understanding can be viewed most of the time as specimens of symbolic cognition. This is what I said in No. 122 of my *Phaenomenology* with reference to the question in No. 19.[12] And I have nothing against your making the claim quite general, in No. 10.

But I shall stop here and let you make whatever use you wish of what I have said. Please examine carefully the sentences I have underlined and, if you have time, let me know what you think of them. Never mind the postage. Till now I have not been able to deny all reality to time and space, or to consider them mere images and appearance. I think that every change would then have to be mere appearance too. And this would contradict one of my main principles (No. 54, *Phaenomenology*). If changes have reality, then I must grant it to time as well. Changes follow one another, begin, continue, cease, and so on, and all these expressions are temporal. If you can instruct me otherwise, I shall not expect to lose much. Time and space will be *real* appearances, and their foundation an existent something that truly conforms to the appearance just as precisely and constantly as the laws of geometry are precise and constant. The language of appearance will

10:110

thus serve our purposes just as well as the unknown "true" language. I must say, though, that an appearance that absolutely never deceives us could well be something more than mere appearance. . . . [13]

I have the honor of being, very respectfully,

Your most devoted servant,
J. H. Lambert.

Berlin

---

1   Lambert refers to Kant's dissertation in German, "Von der sinnlichen und Gedankenwelt," rather than by its Latin title.

2   Cf. §9 of Kant's dissertation: "Moral philosophy, therefore, in so far as it furnishes the first principles of judgment, is only cognized by the pure understanding and itself belongs to pure philosophy. Epicurus, who reduced its criteria to the sense of pleasure or pain, is very rightly blamed, together with certain moderns, who have followed him . . . such as Shaftesbury . . ." Ak. 2: 396 (trans. D. Walford, in Kant, *Theoretical Philosophy, 1755–1770*, ed. Meerbote and Walford (Cambridge Univ. Press, 1992), p. 388.

3   Georg Jonathan Holland (1742–84), mathematician and philosopher.

4   The *Acts eruditiorum Lipsiensium* was the oldest learned journal in Germany. Written in Latin, it was published in Leipzig, from 1682 to 1782.

5   In Lambert's *Neues Organon* (1764).

6   The propositions are as follows: (1) *"The idea of time does not arise from but is presupposed by, the senses."* (2) *"The idea of time is singular, and not general."* (3) *"The idea of time, therefore, is an intuition . . . not a sensuous but a pure intuition."* (4) *"Time is a continuous magnitude . . . ."* (Kant's *Werke*, Ak. 2:398 ff.)

7   In discussing the fourth proposition (see the preceding note), Kant argues: "A *continuous* magnitude is one that does not consist of simple parts . . . The metaphysical [Leibnizian] law of *continuity* is this: *All changes are continuous* or flow, that is, opposite states succeed one another only through an intermediate series of different states." Lambert is criticizing Wolffian metaphysics, which maintained that "if in a composite the parts are arranged next to each other in turn in such an order that it is absolutely impossible that others be placed between them in some other order, then the composite is called a continuum. By the agency of God, continuity precludes the possible existence of a distinct part intermediate between two adjoining parts." (See Christian Wolff, *Philosophia prima Sive Ontologia*[1736], No. 554, and *Cosmologia Generalis* [1731], Nos. 176 ff.

8   "Time is the subjective condition necessary, because of the nature of the human mind, for co-ordinating any sensible objects among themselves by means of a certain law." (Kant's *Werke*, Ak. 2:400.)

9   "Das Reale der Zeit . . ." Lambert might mean "Real things in time and space . . ."

10 Samuel Clarke (1675–1729). The Leibniz-Clarke correspondence of 1715 and 1716 was published in London, 1717, and in German translation, Frankfurt, 1720. For one discussion of the controversy, see Robert Paul Wolff, *Kant's Theory of Mental Activity* (Cambridge, Mass.: Harvard University Press, (1963), pp. 4–8. There is a short, lucid account as well in L. W. Beck, *Early German Philosophy*, pp. 200 and 449 f.

11 *Schein.* See n. 13 below.

12 "Phänomenologie oder Lehre von dem Schein" is a part of Lambert's *Neues Organon.* The claim made by Kant, to which Lambert refers, is that man is "incapable of any intuition of intellectual concepts," so that our cognition must be "symbolical." Since "all the material of our cognition is given only by the senses, but the noumenon, as such, is not conceivable by representations drawn from sensations, the intellectual concept is destitute of all data of human intuition" (*Werke*, Ak. 2: 396). In Lambert's book, the question is raised "to what extent it is possible for us to have a distinct representation of truths without any sensuous images?" He argues that words and signs must be used as substitutes for images and that by means of them it is possible to transcend the limits of our power of imagination. Algebra is said to be a perfect example of this.

13 It is tempting to translate Lambert's "Schein" as "illusion" rather than "appearance," as one would in everyday German. That is clearly the sense of the word in this context. However, since Lambert calls his "Phänomenologie" "die Lehre von dem Schein" and in that context does *not* mean "illusion" it seems preferable to stick with "appearance," though that word normally translates "Erscheinung." Kant responds to Lambert's argument in the *Critique of Pure Reason* in §7 of the "Transcendental Aesthetic". Kant often stresses that by "appearance" he does *not* mean "illusion."

21 [62] (58)
From Johann Georg Sulzer.[1]
December 8, 1770.

10:111   Noble and most esteemed Sir.

You have made me very indebted to you by sending me your Inaugural Disputation and have given the public an important gift. Of that much I am certain, from what I have been able to understand of your work, though a confluence of many chores, including my daily labor on a book I am about to publish on the fine arts,[2] has kept me from grasping completely all of the new and important ideas which abound in your book. I think that you would give new vitality to philosophy

with these ideas if you would take the trouble to develop each particu- 10:112
lar concept fully and show its application somewhat explicitly.

These concepts appear to me to be not only well founded but highly significant. In only one small detail have I found myself unable to share your way of thinking about things. I have always thought Leibniz's concepts of space and time to be correct, for I held time to be something different from duration, and space something different from extension. Duration and extension are absolutely simple concepts, incapable of analysis, but, as I see it, concepts having genuine reality. Time and space, on the other hand, are constructed concepts which presuppose the concept of order. My understanding of the natural influence of substances, or its necessity, has for quite some time coincided roughly with yours. And I have reasonably clear ideas about the distinction between the sensible and the intelligible, as I intend to show explicitly when I get the time to do so. But in this matter, sir, you will undoubtedly obviate my work, and that will please me very much. For at present I really have little time and, since I am occupied with entirely different subjects, little mental disposition to work on abstract matters of that sort.

I really wished to hear from you whether we may hope to see your work on the Metaphysics of Morals soon. This work is of the highest importance, given the present unsteady state of moral philosophy. I have tried to do something of this sort myself in attempting to resolve the question, "What actually is the physical or psychological difference between a soul that we call virtuous and one which is vicious?" I have sought to discover the true dispositions to virtue and vice in the first manifestations of representations and sensations, and I now regard my undertaking of this investigation as less futile, since it has led me to concepts that are simple and easy to grasp, and which one can effortlessly apply to the teaching and raising of children. But this work too is impossible for me to complete at present.

I wish you success, sir, with all my heart in the illustrious career that 10:113
you yourself have initiated, good fortune, also health and leisure, so that you may carry it through with distinction.

J. G. Sulzer.

Berlin, the 8th of December, 1770.[3]

---

1 Johann Georg Sulzer (1720–1829), aesthetician, a disciple of Wolff, was born in Switzerland and resided in Berlin where he was a member of the Academy of Sciences.

2 Sulzer's *Allgemeine Theorie der schönen Kunste* (Leipzig, 1771–1774) was long regarded as a standard work in aesthetics.

3 The editors of the Akademie edition of Kant's letters, 13:51, conjecture that this letter is the one to which Kant alludes in a note in the *Grundlegung zur Metaphysik der Sitten*, Ak. 4:411, where Kant mentions a letter from "the late excellent Sulzer." But the question Kant there attributes to Sulzer is not raised in the present letter.

22 [63] (59)
From Moses Mendelssohn.
December 25, 1770.

Noble Sir,
Distinguished Herr Professor,

Herr Marcus Herz, who is indebted to you for your instruction and even more for the wisdom you imparted to him in your personal association, continues gloriously on the path that he began under your tutelage. I endeavor to encourage his progress a little through my friendship. I am sincerely fond of him and have the pleasure of almost daily conversations with him. Nature has truly been generous to him. He has a clear understanding, a gentle heart, a controlled imagination, and a certain subtlety of mind that seems to be natural to his nation. But how lucky for him that these natural gifts were so early led on the path of truth and goodness. How many people, without this good fortune, left to themselves in the immeasurable region of truth and error, have had to consume their valuable time and best energies in a hundred vain attempts, so that they lacked both time and power to follow the right road when at last, after much groping about, they found it. Would that I might have had a Kant for a friend before my twentieth year!

Your dissertation has now reached my eager hands, and I have read it with much pleasure. Unfortunately my nervous infirmities make it impossible for me of late to give as much effort of thought to a speculative work of this stature as it deserves. One can see that this little book is the fruit of long meditation and that it must be viewed as part of a whole system, the author's own creation, of which he has only shown us a sample. The ostensible obscurity of certain passages is a clue to the practiced reader that this work must be part of a larger whole with which he has not yet been presented. For the good of metaphysics, a science that, alas, has fallen on sad days, it would be a shame for you to keep your thoughts in stock for long without offering them to us. Man's life is short. How quickly the end overtakes us, while

10:114

we still cherish the thought of improving on what we have. And why do you so carefully avoid repeating what you have said before? Old ideas are seen in another light, suggesting new and surprising views, when they appear in the context of your new creations. Since you possess a great talent for writing in such a way as to reach many readers, one hopes that you will not always restrict yourself to the few adepts who are up on the latest things and who are able to guess what lies undisclosed behind the published hints.

Since I do not quite count myself as one of these adepts, I dare not tell you all the thoughts that your dissertation aroused in me. Allow me only to set forth a few, which actually do not concern your major theses but only some peripheral matters.

Pages 2–3.[1] You will find some thoughts concerning the infinite in extended magnitude, similar though not as penetratingly expressed, in the second edition of my *Philosophische Schriften*,[2] now in press. I shall be honored to send you a copy. Herr Herz can testify that everything was ready for the printer before I received your book, and I told him of my pleasure at finding that a man of your stature should agree with me on these points.

Page 11.[3] You regard Lord Shaftesbury as at least a distant follower of Epicurus. But I have always thought that one must distinguish carefully between Shaftesbury's "moral instinct" and the sensual plea-sure of Epicurus. The former, for Shaftesbury, is just an innate faculty for distinguishing good from evil by means of mere feeling.[4] For Epi-curus, on the other hand, the feeling of pleasure is not only a criterion of goodness [*criterium boni*] but is itself supposed to be the highest good [*summum bonum*].

Page 15.[5] *quid significet vocula post.* etc. [What does the little word *after* mean . . .][6] This difficulty seems to demonstrate the poverty of language rather than the incorrectness of the concept. The little word "after" [*post*] originally signifies a temporal succession; but it is possible to use it to indicate any order in general where A is possible only when or in case B does not exist, where A and B are actual things. In short, the order in which two absolutely (or even hypothetically) contradic-tory things can yet be present. You will object that my unavoidable words "when or in case" presuppose once more the idea of time. Very well, then, let us shun those little words, too, if you like. I begin with the following explication:

If A and B are both real and are the immediate (or even the remote) consequences (*rationata*) of a single ground, C, I call them hypotheti-cally compatible things (*compossibilia secundum quid*); if they are une-qually remote consequences or *rationata* I call them hypothetically incompatible. I continue:

Hypothetically compatible things (things that also in this world are

10:115

compossibilia) are simultaneous [*simultanea*]; hypothetically incompatible real things [*Actualia*], however, are successive, to wit, the nearer consequence or *rationatum* precedes, and the more remote one follows.

Here, I hope, there occurs no word presupposing the idea of time. In any case, it will rest more in the language than in the thoughts.

For several reasons I cannot convince myself that time is something merely subjective. Succession is after all at least a necessary condition of the representations that finite minds have. But finite minds are not only subjects; they are also objects of representations, both those of God and those of their fellows. Consequently it is necessary to regard succession as something objective.

Furthermore, since we have to grant the reality of succession in a representing creature and in its alterations, why not also in the sensible object, the model and prototype of representations in the world?

10:116 On page 17[7] the way you find a vicious circle in this way of conceiving time is not clear to me. Time is (according to Leibniz) a phenomenon and has, as do all appearances, an objective and a subjective aspect. The subjective is the *continuity* thereby represented; the objective is the succession of alterations that are *rationata* or consequences equidistant from a common ground.

On page 23[8] I don't think the condition "at the same time," *eodem tempore*, is so necessary in the Law of Contradiction. In so far as something is the same subject, it is not possible to predicate A and non-A of it at different times. The concept of impossibility demands no more than that the *same subject* cannot have *two predicates, A and non-A*. Alternatively, one could say: it is impossible that non-A be a predicate of the subject A.

I would not have been so bold as to criticize your book with such abandon had not Herr Herz made known to me your true philosophical spirit and assured me that you would never take offense at such frankness. This attitude is so rare, among imitators, that it frequently serves as a distinguishing mark of men who think for themselves. He who has himself experienced the difficulty of finding the truth, and of convincing himself that he has found it, is always more inclined to be tolerant of those who think differently from himself. I have the honor of being, noble sir and revered Herr Professor, most respectfully,

Your most devoted servant,
Moses Mendelssohn

---

1 Ak. 2:388.
2 *Philosophische Schriften, verbesserte Auflage* (Berlin, 1771), Part I, 3rd *Gespräch*, pp. 247 ff. Cf. Herz to Kant, Ak.[58].
3 Ak. 2:396.

4 I.e., the feeling of pleasure or displeasure that good and evil arouse.
5 Ak. 2:399.
6 "For I understand what the word 'after' means only by means of the prior concept of time." Kant argues that time therefore cannot be defined by reference to the series of actual things existing one after the other.
7 Ak. 2:401.
8 Ak. 2:406.

1771

23 [67] (62)

To Marcus Herz.

June 7, 1771.

10:121   Dearest friend,

What do you think of my negligence in corresponding? What does your mentor, Herr Mendelssohn and what does Professor Lambert think of it? These brave people must certainly imagine me to be a very rude person for reciprocating so badly the trouble they have taken in their letters. I could hardly blame them if they decided never again to allow themselves to be coaxed into troubling to answer a letter from me. But if only the inner difficulty one personally feels could be as perspicuous to other eyes, I hope that they would sooner take anything 10:122   in the world to be the cause of my silence, rather than indifference or lack of respect. I beg you therefore to forestall or disabuse these worthy men of any such suspicion; for even now I feel the same hindrance that kept me from answering them for so long. My delay however really has two causes, not counting the bad habit of thinking that tomorrow is always a more convenient day to post a letter than today. The sort of letters with which these two scholars have honored me always lead me to a long series of investigations. You know very well that I am inclined not only to try to refute intelligent criticisms but that I always weave them together with my judgments and give them the right to overthrow all my previously cherished opinions. I hope that in that way I can achieve an unpartisan perspective, by seeing my judgments from the standpoint of others, so that a third opinion may emerge, superior to my previous ones. Besides that, the mere fact that men of such insight can remain unconvinced is always a proof to me that my theories must at least lack clarity, self-evidence, or even something more essential. Long experience has taught me that one cannot compel

126

or precipitate insight by force in matters of the sort we are considering; rather, it takes quite a long time to gain insight, since one looks at one and the same concept intermittently and regards its possibility in all its relations and contexts, and furthermore, because one must above all awaken the skeptical spirit within, to examine one's conclusions against the strongest possible doubt and see whether they can stand the test. From this point of view I have, I think, made good use of the time that I have allowed myself, risking the danger of offending these scholars with my seeming impoliteness while actually motivated by respect for their judgment. You understand how important it is, for all of philosophy – yes even for the most important ends of humanity in general – to distinguish with certainty and clarity that which depends on the subjective principles of human mental powers (not only sensibility but also the understanding) and that which pertains directly to the facts.[a] If one is not driven by a mania for systematizing, the investigations which one makes concerning one and the same fundamental principle in its widest possible applications even confirm each other. I am therefore now busy on a work which I call "The Bounds of Sensibility and of Reason." It will work out in some detail the foundational principles and laws that determine the sensible world[b] together with an outline of what is essential to the Doctrine of Taste, of Metaphysics, and of Moral Philosophy. I have this winter surveyed all the relevant materials for it and have considered, weighed, and harmonized everything, but I have only recently come up with the way to organize the whole work.

10:123

The *second cause* of my delay in writing will seem to you as a physician even more valid, namely, that since my health has noticeably suffered, I find it compellingly necessary to assist my nature to a gradual recovery by avoiding all exertions for a while and to exploit only my moments of good mood, dedicating the rest of my time to comforts and little diversions. Even my acquaintances agree that this regimen, and the daily use of quinine since October of last year, have already visibly improved my condition. I am sure that you will not condemn a negligence that conforms to the principles of the medical arts.

I am delighted to learn that you intend to publish a work on the nature of the speculative sciences. I anticipate your book with pleasure and since it will be finished before mine, I will be able to take advantage of all sorts of suggestions which I shall surely find in it. The pleasure which I shall take at the applause that your first published treatise will presumably receive, though it may have more than a little vanity behind it, is still a pleasure that has a strong taste of unselfish

[a] *Gegenstände*   [b] *Sinnenwelt*

and friendly interest. Herr Kanter sent out my Dissertation rather late and in small numbers, and without even listing it in the Leipzig Book Fair Catalogue; I did not want to make any changes in it, since I had formulated my plan for a fuller treatment later on. Since the Dissertation, about which more will be said in my next book, contains a number of separate ideas which I shall not have a chance to present again, it depresses me a little to think that this work must so quickly suffer the fate of all human endeavors, namely oblivion; for with all its errors it seems unworthy of reprinting.

10:124

If you could bring yourself to write, even though you receive only rare replies from me, your most wide ranging letter will help my quinine nicely to produce a spring tonic. Please convey my apologies and highest devotion to the Herren *Mendelssohn* and *Lambert*. I anticipate that when my stomach comes to do its duty, my fingers will do so as well. I conjoin to all your undertakings the good wishes of your
sincere, devoted friend,
Immanuel Kant

24 [68] (63)

From Marcus Herz.

July 9, 1771.

Berlin, the 9th of July, 1771

Most esteemed Herr Professor,

Aside from the usual pleasure of seeing that my dear teacher's memories of me have not yet been extinguished, your last letter had another effect on me of much greater importance than you might have imagined. My friend Herr Friedländer[1] said to me on his arrival that you are no longer such a great devotee of speculative philosophy as you used to be. What's that I am saying – "not a devotee"? He said that you had told him explicitly on a certain occasion that you took metaphysics to be pointless head scratching, a subject understood only by a handful of scholars in their study chambers but far too removed from the tumult of the world to bring about any of the changes that their theorizing demands. Since most of the rest of the world has no comprehension of metaphysics at all, it cannot have the slightest effect on its well-being. You supposedly said to him that moral philosophy for the common man is thus the *only* appropriate subject for a scholar, for here one may penetrate the heart, here one may study human feelings and try to regulate them by bringing them under the rules of common experience. How I trembled at this news! What? I thought, was it all just deception when my teacher on so many occasions extolled the value of metaphysics? Or did he then really feel what he claimed to feel, though time has given him a more penetrating insight into the essential nature of science, an insight that has all at once converted his warmest dispositions into cold aversion? So the fate of all our enjoyments is the same, be they physical enjoyments or mental, call them what you will – they all intoxicate us for a few moments, agitate our blood, allow us for a little while to be Children of Heaven, but soon afterwards we experience the most painful torments of all: Disgust, which imposes penance after penance on us for our transitory moments of delight. Why then all that shouting about the pleasures of the mind, all that noise about the happiness that springs from the works of the understanding, happiness which is closest to that of the gods themselves? Away with that rubbish, if theorizing can accomplish nothing more than can the fulfillment of any other desire – or indeed far less, since the disgust that follows, disgust over wasted time and effort, necessarily awakens in us an unending regret! I was really prepared to accept this fate and renounce all the sciences, even to smother my "child," already half-born;[2] but your letter called me back in the nick of time from my rashness: You are still the same devotee of metaphysics as ever, it must have been only a bad mood that made you say otherwise. You are once again engaged in producing a great work for the public, and you still maintain that the happiness of the human race depends on the truths that you are going to demonstrate concerning the bounds of knowledge![3] O what a secure pledge has been put into my hands by this confession from the greatest friend of humanity: that he can never cease to treasure the subject which constitutes the only remedy to bring about human happiness!

 You will receive my book[4] by regular mail and I suspect you will find little in it that should cause you to make any changes in the work you have at hand. I need hardly tell you, dearest Herr Professor, how little I deserve credit for my book. I have merely had your own book[5] before my eyes, followed the thread of your thoughts and only here and there have I made a few digressions, things that were not part of my original plan but that occurred to me while I was working. I hope you will therefore be kind enough to share in whatever applause I may expect to receive. It is all due to you, and the only praise I deserve is for being a conscientious auditor. But let me be disgraced, eternally

10:125

10:126

disgraced, if I have misunderstood you, if I have substituted inauthentic wares for the genuine article, let the whole world's censure be upon me!

I could use this opportunity to discuss various matters in my book, but I shall wait until you have read it and written me your opinion. In developing the concepts of space and time I digressed to discuss the nature of the principles of the beautiful; my investigation of relations led me to a proof of the reality of the soul, a proof that perhaps deserves attention;[6] in the second part of the book I merely followed you and only made a small gesture in the direction of further progress.

My style of writing will seem clumsy and forced to you; I lack charm and precision but I am not sure whether my lack of clarity in a number of places is due entirely to my incapacities or also to the nature of the subject-matter. I await your judgment, dearest Herr Professor, both concerning the individual points and the work as a whole, and I especially want to know whether you approve of my whole project of publication.

I have various comments to make about the Englishman Smith[7] who, Herr Friedländer tells me, is your favorite. I too was unusually taken with this man, though at the same time I greatly prefer the first part of Home's *Criticism*.[8] I assume you will have read Herr Mendelssohn's *Rhapsody*.[9] He has greatly expanded the new edition and has discovered a new way of looking at the topic of mixed sensations. A great deal of it is still difficult for me, but I cannot now discuss it with him. For the last six months he has suffered from an attack of a nervous disorder which makes it impossible for him to read, write or think about philosophical matters. Thank God that, through a strict diet (both mental and physical) he has recovered more or less and will be able to resume his work this coming winter. In the meantime I shall turn to my dear teacher and submit to you whatever occurs to me as I read those books I mentioned.

10:127

I am so pleased to have your picture over my study table. What delight it gives me by reminding me of those instructive hours! I am eternally grateful to you and to my friend Herr Friedländer for it.

I have only started to read Lambert's *Architektonik*[10] so I cannot yet make any judgments about it. Besides, I have only a few spare hours to devote to non-medical studies.

I have chattered long enough. Be well, unforgettable Herr Professor, and write to me soon and at length about my book. For, I swear to God! your judgment alone will determine its worth for me. In the meantime think of

your
most obedient servant and pupil
Marcus Herz

---

1 On Friedländer see Kant's letter to Herz, Ak. [59], n. 4.

2 Herz's book, *Betrachtungen aus der spekulativen Weltweisheit* (Königsberg, 1771). The work has recently been reprinted (Hamburg: Felix Meiner Verlag, 1990).

3 *"den Wahrheiten . . . die über den Grenzen der Erkenntnis festgesetzt werden."* There is a possible ambiguity in Herz's word "über" ("concerning" – or "going beyond"? – the bounds of knowledge). I believe Kant himself could only have meant "concerning" here, though what Herz or Friedländer took him to mean is less certain, i.e., perhaps that the happiness of the human race depends on establishing truths about matters that lie beyond the limits of human knowledge. It would not be surprising if Herz, in 1771, had little inkling of Kant's philosophical reasons for feeling ambivalent about metaphysics.

4 See n. 2 above.

5 The Inaugural Dissertation (1770).

6 Herz argues in the Appendix to his book that there can be no relations without a subject who perceives them: ". . . kein Verhältnis findet statt, wenn nicht ein Subjekt vorhanden ist, das es wahrnimmt." Op. cit., p. 80. He takes the perceiving subject to be simple and non-spatial, hence, he maintains, a soul.

7 Adam Smith (1723–90), *Theory of Moral Sentiments* (1759). A German translation by Christian G. Rautenberg was published in Braunschweig in 1770.

8 Henry Home, Lord Kames, the Scottish philosopher (1696–1782), *Elements of Criticism* (Edinburgh, 1762). A German translation by J. N. Meinhard was published in Leipzig, 1763–66.

9 Moses Mendelssohn, *Rhapsody, or Appendices to the Letters concerning Sensations* (*Rhapsodie oder Zusätze zu den Briefen über die Empfindungen*), expanded edition, 1771.

10 Johann Heinrich Lambert, *Anlage zur Architektonic* (Riga, 1771). The work was written in 1764. See L. W. Beck, *Early German Philosophy* (Cambridge, Mass.: Harvard University Press, 1969), pp. 402–12.

1772

To Marcus Herz.

February 21, 1772.

Noble Sir,

10:129   Esteemed friend,

You do me no injustice if you become resentful at my total failure to reply to your letters; but lest you draw any disagreeable conclusions from it, let me appeal to your understanding of my turn of mind. Instead of excuses, I shall give you a brief account of the sorts of things that have occupied my thoughts and that cause me to put off letter-writing in my leisure hours. After your departure from Königsberg I examined once more, in the intervals between my professional duties and my sorely needed relaxation, the project that we had debated, in order to adapt it to the whole of philosophy and the rest of knowledge and in order to understand its extent and limits. I had already previously made considerable progress in the effort to distinguish the sensible from the intellectual in the field of morals and the principles that spring therefrom. I had also long ago outlined, to my tolerable satisfaction, the principles of feeling, taste, and power of judgment, with their effects – the pleasant, the beautiful, and the good – and was then making plans for a work that might perhaps have the title, *The Limits of Sensibility and Reason*. I planned to have it consist of two parts, a theoretical and a practical. The first part would have two sections, (1) general phenomenology and (2) metaphysics, but this only with regard to its nature and method. The second part likewise would have two sections, (1) the universal principles of feeling, taste, and sensuous desire and (2) the first principles of morality. As I thought through the

10:130   theoretical part, considering its whole scope and the reciprocal relations of all its parts, I noticed that I still lacked something essential, something that in my long metaphysical studies I, as well as others, had failed to consider and which in fact constitutes the key to the whole secret of metaphysics, hitherto still hidden from itself. I asked myself this question: What is the ground of the relation of that in us which we call "representation" to the object? If a representation comprises only the manner in which the subject is affected by the object, then it is easy to see how it[2] is in conformity with this object, namely, as an effect accords with its cause, and it is easy to see how this modification[a] of our mind can *represent* something, that is, have an object. Thus the passive or sensuous representations have an understandable relationship to objects, and the principles that are derived from the nature of our soul have an understandable validity for all things insofar as those things are supposed to be objects of the senses. Similarly, if that in us which we call "representation" were active with regard to the object, that is, if the object itself were created by the representation (as when divine cognitions are conceived as the archetypes of things), the conformity of these representations to their objects could also be understood. Thus the possibility of both an *intellectus archetypus* (an intellect whose intuition is itself the ground of things) and an *intellectus ectypus*, an intellect which would derive the data for its logical procedure from the sensuous intuition of things, is at least comprehensible. However, our understanding, through its representations, is neither the cause of the object (save in the case of moral ends), nor is the object the cause of our intellectual representations in the real sense (*in sensu reali*). Therefore the pure concepts of the understanding must not be abstracted from sense perceptions, nor must they express the reception of representations through the senses; but though they must have their origin in the nature of the soul, they are neither caused by the object nor do they bring the object itself into being. In my dissertation I was content to explain the nature of intellectual representations in a merely negative way, namely, to state that they were not modifications of the soul brought about by the object. However, I silently passed over the further question of how a representation that refers to an object without being in any way affected by it can be possible. I had said: The sensuous representations present things as they appear, the intellectual representations present them as they are. But by what means are these things given to us, if not by the way in which they affect us? And if such intellectual representations depend on our inner activity, whence comes the agreement that they are supposed to have with objects – objects that are nevertheless not possibly produced thereby? And the axioms of pure reason concerning these objects – how do they agree with these objects, since the agreement

10:131

---

[a] *Bestimmung*

has not been reached with the aid of experience? In mathematics this is possible, because the objects before us are quantities and can be represented as quantities only because it is possible for us to produce their mathematical representations (by taking numerical units a given number of times). Hence the concepts of the quantities can be spontaneous and their principles can be determined a priori. But in the case of relationships involving qualities – as to how my understanding may, completely a priori, form for itself concepts of things[b] with which concepts the facts[c] should necessarily agree, and as to how my understanding may formulate real principles concerning the possibility of such concepts, with which principles experience must be in exact agreement and which nevertheless are independent of experience – this question, of how the faculty of the understanding achieves this conformity with the things themselves[d] is still left in a state of obscurity.[3]

Plato assumed a previous intuition of divinity as the primary source of the pure concepts of the understanding and of first principles. Mallebranche[4] [sic] believed in a still-continuing perennial intuition of this primary being. Various moralists have accepted precisely this view with respect to basic moral laws. Crusius[5] believed in certain implanted rules for the purpose of forming judgments and ready-made concepts that God implanted in the human soul[6] just as they had to be in order to harmonize with things. Of these systems, one might call the former the Hyperphysical Influx Theory [influxum hyperphysicum] and the latter the Pre-established Intellectual Harmony Theory [harmoniam praestabilitam intellectualem]. However, the deus ex machina is the greatest absurdity one could hit upon in the determination of the origin and validity of our cognitions. It has – besides its vicious circularity in drawing conclusions concerning our cognitions – also this additional disadvantage: it encourages all sorts of wild notions and every pious and speculative brainstorm.

10:132   As I was searching in such ways for the sources of intellectual knowledge, without which one cannot determine the nature and limits of metaphysics, I divided this science into its naturally distinct parts, and I sought to reduce transcendental philosophy (that is to say, all the concepts belonging to completely pure reason) to a certain number of categories, but not like Aristotle, who, in his ten predicaments, placed them side by side as he found them in a purely chance juxtaposition. On the contrary, I arranged them according to the way they classify themselves by their own nature, following a few fundamental laws of the understanding. Without going into details here about the whole

[b] Dingen
[c] Sachen. In previous translations this word was rendered "things."
[d] den Dingen selbst

series of investigations that has continued right down to this last goal, I can say that, so far as my essential purpose is concerned, I have succeeded and that now I am in a position to bring out a critique of pure reason[7] that will deal with the nature of theoretical as well as practical knowledge – insofar as the latter is purely intellectual. Of this, I will first work out the first part, which will deal with the sources of metaphysics, its method and limits. After that I will work out the pure principles of morality. With respect to the first part, I should be in a position to publish it within three months.

In an intellectual project of such a delicate nature, nothing is more of a hindrance than to be occupied with thoughts that lie outside the field of inquiry. Even though the mind is not always exerting itself, it must still, in its quiet and also in its happy moments, remain uninterruptedly open to any chance suggestion that may present itself. Encouragements and diversions must serve to maintain the mind's powers of flexibility and mobility, whereby it is kept ever in readiness to view the subject matter from other sides and to widen its horizon from a microscopic observation to a general outlook in order that it may see matters from every conceivable position and so that views from one perspective may verify those from another. No other reason than this, my worthy friend, explains my delay in answering your pleasant letters – for you certainly don't want me to write you empty words.

With respect to your discerning and deeply thoughtful little book, several parts have exceeded my expectations.[8] However, for reasons already mentioned, I cannot let myself go into discussing details. But, 10:133 my friend, the effect that undertakings of this kind have on the educated public, undertakings relating to the status of the sciences, is such that when, because of the indisposition that threatens to interrupt its execution, I begin to feel anxious about my project (which I regard as my most important work, the greater part of which I have ready before me) – then I am frequently comforted by the thought that my work would be just as useless to the public if it is published as it would be if it remains forever unknown. For it takes a writer of greater distinction and eloquence than mine to move his readers to exert themselves to reflect on his writing.

I have found your essay reviewed in the *Breslauische Zeitung* and, just recently, in the *Göttingischen Zeitung*.[9] If the public judges the spirit and principal intent of an essay in such a fashion, then all effort is in vain. If the reviewer has taken pains to grasp the essential points of the effort, his criticism is more welcome to the author than all the excessive praise arising from a superficial evaluation. The Göttingen reviewer dwells on several applications of the system that in themselves are trivial and with respect to which I myself have since changed my views – with the result, however, that my major purpose has only gained thereby. A single letter from *Mendelssohn* or *Lambert* means more to an author in terms of making him reexamine his theories than do ten such opinions from superficial pens. Honest Pastor Schultz,[10] the best philosophical brain I know in this neighborhood, has grasped the points of the system very well; I wish that he might get busy on your little essay, too. According to him, there are two mistaken interpretations of the system lying before him. The first one is that space, instead of being the pure form of sensuous appearance, might very well be a true intellectual intuition and thus might be objective. The obvious answer is this: there is a reason why space is claimed not to be objective and thus also not intellectual, namely, if we analyze fully the representation of space, we find in it neither a representation of things (as capable of existing only in space) nor a real connection (which cannot occur without things); that is to say, we have no effects, no relationships to regard as grounds, consequently no real representation of a fact or anything real that inheres in things, and therefore we must conclude that space is nothing objective. The second misunderstanding leads him to an objection that has made me reflect considerably, because it seems to be the most serious objection that can be raised against the system, an objection that seems to occur naturally to everybody, and one that Herr Lambert has raised.[11] It runs like this: Changes are something real (according to the testimony of inner sense). Now, they are possible only if time is presupposed; therefore time is something real that is involved in the determinations of things in themselves. Then I asked myself: Why does one not accept the following parallel argument? Bodies are real (according to the testimony of outer sense). Now, bodies are possible only under the condition of space; therefore space is something objective and real that inheres in the things themselves. The reason lies in the fact that it is obvious, in regard to outer things, that one cannot infer the reality of the object from the reality of the representation, but in the case of inner sense the thinking or the existence of the thought and the existence of my own self are one and the same. The key to this difficulty lies herein. There is no doubt that I should not think my own state under the form of time and that therefore the form of inner sensibility does not give me the appearance of alterations. Now I do not deny that alterations have reality any more than I deny that bodies have reality, though all I mean by that is that something real corresponds to the appearance. I cannot even say that the inner appearance changes, for how would I observe this change if it did not appear to my inner sense? If someone should say that it follows from this that everything in the world is objective and in itself unchangeable, then I would reply: Things are neither changeable nor unchangeable, just as *Baumgarten* states in his *Metaphysics*, § 18: "What is absolutely impossible is neither hypothetically possible nor impossi-

10:134

ble, for it cannot be considered under any condition"; similarly here, the things of the world are objectively or in themselves neither in one and the same state at different times nor in different states, for thus understood they are not represented as in time at all. But enough about this. It appears that one doesn't obtain a hearing by stating only nega-   10:135 tive propositions. One must rebuild on the plot where one has torn down, or at least, if one has disposed of the speculative brainstorm, one must make the understanding's pure insight dogmatically intelligible and delineate its limits. With this I am now occupied, and that is the reason why, often contrary to my own resolve to answer friendly letters, I withhold from such tasks what free time my very frail constitution allows me for contemplation and abandon myself to the drift of my thoughts. So long as you find me so negligent in replying, you should also give up the idea of repaying me and suffer me to go without your letters. Even so, I would count on your constant affection and friendship for me just as you may always remain assured of mine. If you will be satisfied with short answers then you shall have them in the future. Between us the assurance of the honest concern that we have for each other must take the place of formalities. I await your next delightful letter as a sign that you have really forgiven me. And please fill it up with such news as you must have aplenty, living as you do at the very seat of learning, and please excuse my taking the liberty of asking for this. Greet Herr *Mendelssohn* and Herr *Lambert*, likewise Herr *Sultzer*, and convey my apologies to these gentlemen with similar reasons. Do remain forever my friend, just as I am yours,

I. Kant

Königsberg
February 21, 1772

---

1   This is the letter referred to by many Kant scholars as "the" Herz letter – the document which in a sense reports the birth of the *Critique of Pure Reason*.

2   The sense here is obscured by Kant's pronouns. He writes "er" but this must be a mistake. "Es" is possible, in which case the referent is "the subject" and the "easily comprehensible correspondence" is between the subject and the object causing its state. But "sie" referring to "the representation" and "ihrer" would make even more sense, i.e., "it is easy to see how the representation can conform to its cause."

3   An exchange of papers between Lewis White Beck and Wolfgang Carl in *Kant's Transcendental Deductions*, ed. by Eckart Förster (Stanford, 1989), pp. 24, f., points out that it is not clear whether the "things" or "facts" referred to in this sentence are noumenal objects or objects of experience.

4   Nicolas Malebranche (1638–1715), the well-known French philosopher.

5 Christian August Crusius (1715–75), philosopher and theologian, studied in Leipzig and became professor of theology there in 1750. He was an important opponent of Christian Wolff.

6 On Kant's later view of this "preformation" theory, cf. *Critique of Pure Reason*, § 27 in the second edition.

7 We may assume that "eine Critick der reinen Vernunft" is not here a title but a description, since Kant has already announced another intended name for the work.

8 Herz's *Betrachtungen aus der spekulativen Weltweisheit* (Königsberg, 1771), reprinted in *Philosophische Bibliothek Bd. 424* (Hamburg: Felix Meiner Verlag, 1990). Kant's opinion of the book, as expressed in a note to the publisher Friedrich Nicolai, was not very favorable. Kant compares Herz's exposition of the dissertation's new ideas with the portrait of Kant published in Nicolai's *Allgemeine deutsche Bibliothek* and complains that neither one captured its subject properly. See Ak. [77] below. Kant there states that Herz has had "wenig glück" in expressing Kant's meaning.

9 The reviewer in the Göttingen journal was Feder, the same man whose review (with Garve) of the *Critique* aroused Kant's anger and occasioned the writing of the *Prolegomena*.

10 Johann Schultz (1739–1805), whom Kant later (see Kant's Open Declaration concerning Schlettwein, Ak. [752]) declared to be his ablest expositor. Schultz was pastor in Löwenhagen near Königsberg at the time of the present letter. In 1776 he was appointed court chaplain in Königsberg and in 1786 professor of mathematics. His publications included a review of the Inaugural Dissertation in the Königsberg *Gelehrten und Politischen Zeitungen* (1771), *Erläuterungen über des Herrn Prof. Kant Kritik der reinen Vernunft* (1784), and *Prüfung der Kantischen Kritik der reinen Vernunft* (2 volumes, 1789/92). Several of Schultz's writings have recently been translated into English, e.g., *Exposition of Kant's Critique of Pure Reason*, trans. James C. Morrison (Ottawa: University of Ottawa Press, 1995), a volume that includes Schultz's reviews of Kant's Inaugural Dissertation, Garve's review of the *Critique*, and the Gotha Review of the *Critique* by S. H. Ewald.

11 See Lambert's letter of Oct. 13, 1770, Ak. [61].

1773

26 [79] (71)
To Marcus Herz.

Toward the end of 1773.

Noble Sir,
Esteemed friend,

10:143

It pleases me to receive news of the good progress of your endeavors, but even more to see the signs of kind remembrance and of friendship in the communications imparted to me. Training in the practice of medicine, under the guidance of a capable teacher, is exactly what I wish. The cemetery must in the future not be filled before the young doctor has learned how to attack the disease properly. Do make many careful observations. Here as elsewhere, theories are often directed more to the relief of the idea than to the mastery of the phenomenon. Macbride's *Systematic Medical Science*[1] (I believe you are already acquainted with it) appealed to me very much in this regard. In general, I now feel much better than before. The reason is that I now understand better what makes me ill. Because of my sensitive nerves, all medicines are without exception poison for me. The only thing I very occasionally use is a half teaspoonful of fever bark with water, when I am plagued by acid before noon. I find this much better than 10:144 any absorbentia. But I have given up the daily use of this remedy, with the intention of strengthening myself. It gave me an irregular pulse, especially toward evening, which rather frightened me, until I guessed the cause and, adjusting it, relieved the indisposition. Study the great variety of constitutions. My own would be destroyed by any physician who is not a philosopher.

You search industriously but in vain in the book fair catalog for a certain name beginning with the letter K. After the great effort I have made on the not inconsiderable work that I have almost completed, nothing would have been easier than to let my name be paraded therein. But since I have come this far in my projected reworking of a science that has been so long cultivated in vain by half the philosophical world, since I see myself in possession of a principle that will completely solve what has hitherto been a riddle and that will bring the misleading qualities of the self-alienating understanding under certain and easily applied rules, I therefore remain obstinate in my resolve not to let myself be seduced by any author's itch into seeking fame in easier, more popular fields, until I shall have freed my thorny and hard ground for general cultivation.

I doubt that many have tried to formulate and carry out to completion an entirely new conceptual science. You can hardly imagine how much time and effort this project requires, considering the method, the divisions, the search for exactly appropriate terms. Nevertheless, it inspires me with a hope that, without fear of being suspected of the greatest vanity, I reveal to no one but you: the hope that by means of this work philosophy will be given durable form, a different and – for religion and morality – more favorable turn, but at the same time that philosophy will be given an appearance that will make her attractive to shy mathematicians, so that they may regard her pursuit as both possible and respectable. I still sometimes hope that I shall have the work ready for delivery by Easter. Even when I take into account the frequent indispositions that can always cause interruptions, I can still promise, almost certainly, to have it ready a little after Easter.

10:145

I am eager to see your investigation of moral philosophy appear. I wish, however, that you did not want to apply the concept of reality to moral philosophy, a concept that is so important in the highest abstractions of speculative reason and so empty when applied to the practical. For this concept is transcendental, whereas the highest practical elements are pleasure and displeasure, which are empirical, and their object may thus be anything at all. Now, a mere pure concept of the understanding cannot state the laws or prescriptions for the objects of pleasure and displeasure, since the pure concept is entirely undetermined in regard to objects of sense experience. The highest ground of morality must not simply be inferred from the pleasant; it must itself be pleasing in the highest degree. For it is no mere speculative idea; it must have the power to move. Therefore, though the highest ground of morality is intellectual, it must nevertheless have a direct relation to the primary springs of the will. I shall be glad when I have finished my transcendental philosophy, which is actually a critique of pure reason, as then I can turn to metaphysics: it has only two parts, the metaphysics of nature and the metaphysics of morals. I shall bring out the latter of these first and I really look forward to it.

I have read your review of Platner's *Anthropologie*.[2] I would not have guessed the reviewer myself but now I am delighted to see the evident progress of his skill. This winter I am giving, for the second time, a lecture course on *Anthropologie*,[3] a subject that I now intend to make into a proper academic discipline. But my plan is quite unique. I intend to use it to disclose the sources of all the [practical] sciences, the science of morality, of skill, of human intercourse, of the way to educate and govern human beings, and thus of everything that pertains to the practical. I shall seek to discuss phenomena and their laws rather than the foundations of the possibility of human thinking in general. Hence the subtle and, to my view, eternally futile inquiries as to the manner in which bodily organs are connected with thought I omit entirely. I include so many observations of ordinary life that my auditors have 10:146 constant occasion to compare their ordinary experience with my remarks and thus, from beginning to end, find the lectures entertaining and never dry. In my spare time, I am trying to prepare a preliminary study for the students out of this very pleasant empirical study, an analysis of the nature of skill (prudence) and even wisdom that, along with physical geography and distinct from all other learning, can be called knowledge of the world.

I saw my portrait on the front of the [issue of the *Allgemeine deutsche*] Bibliothek. It is an honor that disturbs me a little, for, as you know, I earnestly avoid all appearance of surreptitiously seeking eulogies or ostentatiously creating a stir. The portrait is well struck though not striking. But it pleases me to see that this sort of gesture stems from the amiable partisanship of my former students.

The review of your work that appears in the same issue[4] proves what I feared: that it takes quite a long time to put new thoughts into such a light that a reader may get the author's specific meaning and the weight of his arguments, until the reader may reach the point where such thoughts are fully and easily familiar.

I am, with most sincere affection and regard,

Your devoted servant and friend,
I. Kant

---

1   David Macbride (1726–78), a physician in Dublin. A German translation of his *A Methodical Introduction to the Theory and Practice of Physic* (London, 1772) was published in 1773.

2   Herz reviewed Ernst Platner's *Anthropologie für Ärzte und Weltweise* (Leipzig, 1772) in the *Allgemeine deutsche Bibliothek*, XX (1773), No. 1, pp. 25–51.

3   What Kant means by *Anthropologie* is clearly quite different from what the English word "anthropology" suggests. It seems wise therefore to retain the German word.

4   Lambert's review of Herz's commentary on Kant's dissertation, Herz's *Betrachtungen aus der spekulativen Weltweisheit*.

1774

27 [86] (78)
To Johann Georg Hamann.
April 6, 1774.

10:154

The author of The Oldest Document[1] has taken the famous Hermes figure ⊗ supposedly abbreviated with dots to form the representation of a six-sided regular figure

```
                    *

          *                   *

                    *

          *                   *

                    *
```

the seventh point of which is the center. He compares this at last to the seven days of the creation story and, since Hermes seems not to have been a person but rather the first ground-plan of all human science, he therefore imagines that the whole of creation, along with the thought of its author, can be represented by such a figure.

```
                     1
                   Light

            2                    3
          Heaven                Earth

                     4
                   Lights
              (Sun, Moon, Stars)

          5                        6
  Heaven's Air and Water    Earthly Creatures

                     7
                   Sabbath
```

Now he has viewed this chapter not as a history of how the world came about but as a plan for the first *instruction* of the human race, hence as a kind of *methodo tabellari*[2] which God has used to form the concepts of the human race by means of a division of all natural objects such that the recollection of any class of these objects is attached to a particular day; and the seventh day which would complete the section could serve to comprehend the whole. Here God has bound up the figure, that all-encompassingly meaningful stroke of the pen presented above – a figure which is no Egyptian invention but comes directly from God – with language. Written as well as spoken language were united in this initial, divine instruction from which all human knowl- edge is descended. The Oldest Document is, in the author's opinion, not the first chapter of the Books of Moses, for the latter is only the most adequate representation of the divine method of teaching; rather, it encompasses a kind of handing down to posterity that all the nations of the earth have received, their first instruction, which various nations have disclosed, each according to its racial line. Consequently even if Moses has revealed the sense [of this instruction] to us better than others have, we can thank the Egyptians alone for the preservation of the *figure* which as a supplement to all written language has come directly from the hand of God. The utility of the week's divisions is thus especially connected to the introduction of the Sabbath, actually only insofar as it is supposed to serve to disclose all the elements of knowledge and to remind us of them, as well as to be a measure of time and thus the simplest preparation for numerical concepts. The figure serves to inaugurate the art of measurement, etc.

10:155

This figure, the mystical number 7, the days of the week, etc., constituting the universal monument to the first instruction which God himself gave to human beings, is thus expressed in different symbolism by different nations, each according to its taste. Moses clothed the monument in the allegory of the creation story. The Greeks did it with the vowels

$$\begin{matrix} & & \alpha & & \\ \varepsilon & & & & \eta \\ & & \iota & & \\ o & & & & \upsilon \\ & & \omega & & \end{matrix}$$

the lyre with its seven tones. The theogony of the Phoenicians and Egyptians, even the shape of the pyramids and obelisks, was only a somewhat altered image of that holy monogram ⊗ of God's stroke of the pen and of the primer of humanity.

As science, e.g., astronomy, developed, people arranged the sup- posed seven planets (among other things) in accordance with the ancient model. All the authors who previously maintained that that great symbol was borrowed from these seven planets, from the seven tones of the octave, etc., were dreadfully mistaken.

The capacity to count to 7 and beyond, as well as the capacity for all other knowledge and science, was rather a derivation from that symbol, etc.

If, dear friend, you discover a way of improving on my conception of the author's main intention, please write me your opinion, but if possible in the language of human beings. For I, poor earthling, am not at all equipped to understand the divine language of *intuitive reason*. What can be spelled out for me with ordinary concepts in accordance with logical order I can pretty well comprehend. And I ask nothing more than to understand the author's main point, for to recognize the worth of the whole theory in all its dignity as true is not something to which I aspire.

Kant.

---

1   Herder's *Älteste Urkunde des Menschengeschlechts* (1774).
2   In Kant's *Logic*, § 118, "tabular" (*tabellarisch*) is explained as "a method of representing in the form of a table an already finished doctrinal edifice [*Lehrgebäude*] in its totality." The tabular method is contrasted with the syllogistic: "that method whereby a science is presented in a chain of syllogisms."

28 [87] (79)
From Johann Georg Hamann.
April 7, 1774.

10:156   P. P.[1]

Just after I received my book[2] I took it to my friend Dr. Lindner[3] and I am not in a position to understand and evaluate by a precise comparison the skeleton you sent to me. For now, without having the book, using merely the impressions in my memory of it, I analyze my concept of our author's main intention into the following points:

I. The Mosaic creation story is not written by Moses himself but by the ancestors of the human race. This *antiquity* alone makes it worthy of respect; but it reveals at the same time the true infancy of our *race*.

II. These origins are no poems nor an Easter allegory, least of all Egyptian hieroglyphics. Rather, they are an historical document in *the most real sense* – a genuine heirloom – yes, more reliable than *the most common physical experiment*.

III. This Mosaic archeology is the sole and best key to all previous riddles and fables of the oldest eastern and Homeric wisdom which were from time immemorial unreservedly admired and scorned without ever having been understood by the most impudent and fawning critics. The light reflected from this cradle of the human race illuminates the holy night in the fragments   10:157 of all *traditions*. Here lies the only sufficient ground of the inexplicable partition wall and fortress that separates savage from civilized peoples.

IV. In order to recover for every sympathetic reader of the Mosaic writings their original, artless, extravagantly fruitful meaning, nothing more is needed than to blast all the fortifications of the most recent Scholastics and Averroists whose history and whose relation to their father Aristotle can serve as the clearest proof and example of such recovery.

This is what my friend Herder has done, not with the dead critique of an earth-son like Longinus[4] who is stirred on the spot by the lightning bolt of a single, Mosaic bon mot, but rather with a *conqueror's passion* in whose **magnanimity** I have taken just as much delight as our criminal prosecutor Hippel[5] has in the gamy taste of a roasted hare.

This letter is at the same time the outline of a publishing contract for some pages which I mean to submit to your censorship, since you are the Expert Judge of the Beautiful and the Sublime, as I have provisionally written to my friend Herder. Your Imprimatur will move our friend, the printer in Marienwerder,[6] both to publishing and to seeing the political wisdom of not judging writers in accordance with his estimate of their market value, an estimate which Heaven understands best.

For the present, the merit of our compatriot as an author seems to me so decided that I can with good conscience advise that as a creative mind he rest from his labor, and his rest will be honor. I shall still appear in print soon enough when the precocious spirits of our critical philosophical-political century will have shot off their powder and lead a bit, since in any case it is possible to make a fairly precise estimate of their supplies.

But it sticks in my kidneys that the theological faculty of the Albertina could confer a doctorate on a Roman-apostolic-catholic heretic

10:158 and crypto-Jesuit[7] – and that this man, without even knowing the Christian catechism, is allowed the pretense of insights into the arcane doctrines of paganism, in the German defense of his Freemasonry[8] and in a dissertation[9] whose total theological-historical-antiquarian knowledge consists of words taken from the pagans and besides that, nothing.

I don't know whether my uterus will have room enough for twins, and this question can be answered only by

Socrates Insane [ΣΟΚΡΑΤΗΣ ΜΑΙΝΟΜΕΝΟΣ]

or

Being a Midwife [ΜΑΙΟΜΕΝΟϹ] [*sic*]

Am alten Graben, the 7th of April, 1774.
I have not received Lavater's letter and the other incidentals.

Hamann.

---

1 Possibly "Pontius Pilate," an ironic salutation consistent with Hamann's way of addressing Kant.

2 Herder's *Aelteste Urkunde*. See Kant's preceding letter to Hamann, Ak.[86].

3 On Lindner, see Kant's letter to him, Oct. 28, 1759, Ak. [13].

4 Longinus, in *On the Sublime*, marveled at the magnificence of the words in Genesis, "And God said, Let there be light! And there was light."

5 Kant's good friend, the author and administrator Theodor Gottlieb von Hippel. On Hippel, see the biographical sketches.

6 The book dealer Johann Jakob Kanter of Königsberg in 1772 received permission to open a court publishing house in Marienwerder. He expressed his displeasure with Hamann's and Herder's writings on account of their failing to earn him money. On Hippel, see Hamilton H. H. Beck, *The Elusive "I" in the Novel* (New York: Peter Lang, 1987).

7 Johann August Starck (1741–1816) secretly converted to Catholicism in Paris, 1766, but later returned to Protestantism. He took his degree in Königsberg in 1774.

8 In 1769 Starck published "Apologie des Ordens der Freimauer."

9 Starck's dissertation was entitled *De tralatitiis e gentilismo in religionem christianam: (On that which has been transferred into the Christian religion from the pagans)*. Hamann plays on this title in his insulting reference to Starck.

29 [88] (80)
To Johann Georg Hamann.
April 8, 1774.

The author's[1] theme is: to demonstrate that God himself taught the first human beings spoken and written language and, by means of these, instructed them in the beginnings of all knowledge or science. The author means to show this not by an appeal to rational grounds, at least that is not the characteristic virtue of his book, nor does he appeal to the testimony of the Bible, for there is no mention of it; rather, his proof is an ancient memorial that occurs in almost all civilizations and whose explication he maintains is contained quite specifically and explicitly in the first chapter of Genesis, and thereby the secret of many centuries is unlocked. The Mosaic narrative would receive from this a trustworthy and wholly decisive proof, a proof that derives from a genuine and invaluable document that is founded not on the respect of a single nation but on the agreement of the most holy symbols maintained by every ancient people from the beginning of human learning and which are thereby collectively deciphered. Thus the archive of nations contains the proof of the correctness and at the same time of the meaning of this document, namely the *universal* meaning that it has. For, after this meaning has disclosed itself, the people's symbol conversely gets the explanation of its own *special* meaning from this document, and the endless speculations about this are suddenly eliminated. For the controversy is immediately transformed into harmony when it is shown that these were only so many different appearances of one and the same archetype.

Now the issue is not at all whether the author is right or not, nor is it whether this supposedly discovered master key will unlock all the chambers of the historical-antiquarian critical labyrinth. The question is only: 1) what is the meaning of this document, 2) what is the proof, taken out of the most ancient archival reports of all peoples, that this document is in the intended sense the most trustworthy and the purest?

10:159

And on this our author's opinion is as follows:

Concerning the first question, the first chapter of the Bible is not the story of creation but rather, in accordance with this image (which additionally may also be the most natural way of picturing the formation of the world) a division of the instruction given by God to the first human beings, in seven lessons as it were, whereby God first led people to think and from which the use of language must be learned, so that the first stroke of writing was bound up with this and the seven

147

days (above all through their being concluded with a Sabbath) were themselves a glorious aid to memory as well as to chronological astronomy, etc.

Concerning the second question, the actual proof is derived from the fact that Hermes meant to the Egyptians nothing but the beginning of all human learning, and that the simple symbol of this, which is a representation of the number seven, must, together with all the other allegories which represent this mystical number as the totality of all knowledge of the universe, be a memento not only of the origin of all human knowledge but even of the method of the first instruction – a sign that the latter would become totally certain when one came upon the true objects of human learning in the Mosaic story, methodically placed there, conveyed in the same figure, and sealed up with the selfsame solemnity. From this he concludes that since this important Mosaic piece is the only one that can make all those ancient symbols intelligible, it is the only genuine and the most sacred document that can inform us most reliably about the origin of the human race.

From the main features of the writer's intentions that I have gathered, your second comment, dearest friend, does not as far as I recall agree with the author's opinion. For certainly he takes the creation story to be only a Mosaic allegory concerning the division of creation in the divine instruction, as human knowledge in regard to this allows itself to be developed and extended.

10:160

I only ask that in rereading the book you take the trouble to point out to me whether the meaning and the grounds of demonstration that I found in it are really there, and whether my perception may still need important addition or improvement.

Getting to read some pages from your pen is sufficient incentive for me to use all the influence I may have with our self-critical publisher to promote them. But he is so confidant about his conception of what he calls the tone of the book, the taste of the public, and the secret intention of the author that, even if it were not in itself a rather lowly service, so as not to lose the little bit of credit I have with him I would in no way want to accept the office of a House Censor. I must therefore reluctantly decline the honor demanded of the humble writer by the powerful status appertaining to a censor. You must also be aware that what goes beyond the moderate would be just his thing if only he did not smell political danger, for the stock market quotation is probably not what counts in this matter.

I find nothing surprising in the new academic presence.[2] If a religion once reaches the point where critical knowledge of old languages, philological and antiquarian erudition, constitute the foundation on which that religion must be constructed through every age and among all nations, then he who is most at home in Greek, Hebrew, Syrian,

Arabian, etc., and in the archives of antiquity, will drag the orthodox (they may look as sour as they please) like children wherever he wants; they mustn't grumble; for they cannot compare themselves to him in what according to their own confessions carries the power of proof, and they look shyly at a Michaelis[3] as he recasts their ancient treasure into an entirely different coinage. If theological faculties should in time become less insistent on maintaining this sort of literature among their pupils, which seems to be the case at least here, if philologists indepen-   10:161 dent in their faith should only master this volcanic weapon, then re-spect for those demagogues will be totally finished and they will have to take instruction from the literary people on what they have to teach. In contemplating this I have great fear about the long duration of triumph without victory for the reviver of The Document [*Urkunde*]. For there is a tightly closed phalanx of masters of oriental scholarship opposing him, who will not so easily allow such a prey to be led astray from their own territory by one who is not ordained. I am

your loyal servant
Kant.

the 8th of April, 1774.

---

1   Herder's *Älteste Urkunde des Meschengeschlechts* (1774) is the subject of this and the preceding letter from Hamann.

2   The conferring of a doctorate on Johann August Starck, alluded to in Ha-mann's previous letter.

3   Johann David Michaelis (1717–91), a famous Orientalist and theologian in Göttingen who was one of the founders of the movement of historical-critical analysis of the Old Testament.

30 [90] (82)

From Johann Caspar Lavater.[1]

April 8, 1774.

Dearest Herr Professor,   10:165

Many thanks, from me and from Sulzer's relatives, for the trouble, care, and loyalty you have shown.[2] Just this minute his sister left here, saying, on behalf of her mother (for his father died a few weeks ago –

would you be willing to tell him this?) that they are totally satisfied with your advice; they wanted to send him two gold pieces, but on the condition that you yourself advised, viz., that before they could think about his release you first wanted to see evidence of improvement in his behavior, especially his industriousness. Do write me a brief note at your convenience, telling me how the fellow looks a few months from now.

I am eagerly awaiting your *Critique of Pure Reason*, as are many people in my country. Without meaning to sound like a flatterer – for many years you have been my favorite author, the one with whom I identify most, especially in metaphysics but also with your style and method of thinking in general.

And now, since you are after all writing a critique of pure reason, I want to ask you: will you maintain the following things in it?

That our critique could hardly be more remote from pure reason than it is. I mean our principles – or rather our maxims (for the two are always confused with each other) in *all* non-mathematical sciences – are as remote from pure reason as our particular judgments which so often contrast absurdly with our most respected maxims.

That until we fix our *observations* more on *human beings*, all our wisdom is folly.

That the reason we always fall so horribly into error is that we seek to find outside of us what is only within us.

That we cannot and may not have any knowledge whatsoever of the inner nature of things but only of their *relations* to our needs.

That any and every occupation, writing, meditation, reading is childishness and foolishness unless it be a means of sedation and a means of satisfying human needs.

10:166   That manifestly out of a thousand books and ten thousand bookish judgments there is hardly one that is not a would-be sedative of the author's needs – though this is by no means noticed by particular readers.

That – Oh, what a fool I am – you will say all of this twenty times more powerfully, more clearly, with embellishing examples, so much more humanly, more popularly, with more appropriate humility, more *epoch-makingly* – so that I shall have nothing more to desire.

I will gladly temper my longing to see your book here in this humble locality, if you think that it will become riper and more decisive thereby. A thousand authors fail to bring their works to the epoch-making critical point. You are the man to do it. Your writings are so full of insight, erudition, taste – and that *humanity* which innumerable writers lack, and which today's critics do not even consider taking into account – that I anticipate more from you in this regard than from any other writer.

I hope that you will come to like Pfenninger, my close friend, a great deal. His *Lectures*[3] have for me that rare stamp of *luminous humanity* – When light is focused on a single spot, it ignites. This secret of the writers', preachers', orators' art – how few possess it!

I am indiscreet, I sense it powerfully – but I believe just as powerfully in your *strength*, your ability to endure indiscretions, and in your kindness, your willingness to tolerate them. It is an indiscretion to ask you to tell me, in just a single page, and with all possible severity and most adamantine candor, when you have read the first volume of my *Miscellaneous Writings*,[4] whether or not you think that my actual view of scriptural faith and prayer agrees essentially with the teaching of Scripture. For me the latter is not cold dogma. It is the most intimate matter of the heart. But rather than answer me, the readers, non-readers, and reviewers (but one should count the latter as readers least of all) will turn in their tracks and shout "That's a *pet opinion!*" And they will suppose that this is an *answer*.

There is so much I still want to say. I have already taken too much of your time with my chatter. Fare you well. I am truly your sincere and devoted

Lavater

Zürich, the 8th of April, 1774

---

1 Lavater (1741–1801), Swiss poet, mystic, theologian and physiognamist.

2 Johann Rudolf Sulzer was a musketeer in Königsberg, originally from Winterthur, Switzerland. In a previous letter Lavater had asked Kant to inquire about Sulzer's condition and see whether his release from the army could be purchased.

3 Johann Conrad Pfenninger, *Fünf Vorlesungen von der Liebe der Wahrheit* (Five lectures on the love of truth. On the influence of the heart on the understanding. On the infallible and correct method of studying the holy scriptures; Zürich, 1774).

4 *Vermischte Schriften* (Winterhur, 1774).

31 [99] (90)
To Johann Casper Lavater.
April 28, 1775.

My worthy friend,

. . .

10:175   You ask for my opinion of your discussion of faith and prayer. Do you realize whom you are asking? A man who believes that, in the final moment, only the purest candor concerning our most hidden inner convictions can stand the test and who, like Job, takes it to be a crime
10:176 to flatter God and make inner confessions, perhaps forced out by fear, that fail to agree with what we freely believe. I distinguish the *teachings* of Christ from the *report* we have of those teachings. In order that the former may be seen in their purity, I seek above all to separate out the moral teachings from all the dogmas of the New Testament. These moral teachings are certainly the fundamental doctrine of the Gospels, and the remainder can only serve as an auxiliary to them. Dogmas tell us only what God has done to help us see our frailty in seeking justification before Him, whereas the moral law tells us what we must do to make ourselves worthy of justification. Suppose we were totally ignorant of what God does and suppose we were convinced only of this: that, because of the holiness of His law and the insuperable evil of our hearts, God must have hidden some supplement to our deficiencies somewhere in the depth of His decrees, something we could humbly rely on, if only we should do what is in our power, so as not to be unworthy of His law. If that were so, we should have all the guidance we need, whatever the manner of communication between the divine goodness and ourselves might be. Our trust in God is unconditional, that is, it is not accompanied by any inquisitive desire to know how His purpose will be achieved or, still less, by any presumptuous confidence that the soul's salvation will follow from our acceptance of certain Gospel disclosures. That is the meaning of the
10:177 moral faith that I find in the Gospels, when I seek out the pure, fundamental teachings that underlie the mixture of facts and revelations there. Perhaps, in view of the opposition of Judaism, miracles and revelations were needed, in those days, to promulgate and disseminate a pure religion, one that would do away with all the world's dogmas. And perhaps it was necessary to have many arguments χατ' ανθροπον,[1] which would have great force in those times. But once the doctrine of the purity of conscience in faith and of the good transformation of our lives has been sufficiently propagated as the only true

religion for man's salvation (the faith that God, in a manner we need not at all understand, will provide what our frail natures lack, without our seeking His aid by means of the so-called worship that religious fanaticism always demands) – when this true religious structure has been built up so that it can maintain itself in the world – then the scaffolding must be taken down. I respect the reports of the evangelists and apostles, and I put my humble trust in that means of reconciliation with God of which they have given us historical tidings – or in any other means that God, in His secret counsels, may have concealed. For I do not become in the least bit a better man if I know this, since it concerns only what God does; and I dare not be so presumptuous as to declare before God that this is the real means, the only means whereby I can attain my salvation and, so to speak, swear my soul and my salvation on it. For what those men give us are only their reports. I am not close enough to their times to be able to make such dangerous and audacious decisions. Moreover, even if I could be sure, it would not make me in any way more worthy of the good, were I to confess it, swear it, and fill up my soul with it, though that may be of help to some people. On the contrary, nothing is needed for my union with this divine force except my using my natural God-given powers in such a way as not to be unworthy of His aid or, if you prefer, unfit for it.

When I spoke of New Testament dogmas I meant to include everything of which one could become convinced only through historical reports, and I also had in mind those confessions or ceremonies that are enjoined as a supposed condition of salvation. By "moral faith" I mean the unconditional trust in divine aid, in achieving all the good that, even with our most sincere efforts, lies beyond our power. Anyone can be convinced of the correctness and necessity of moral faith, once it is made clear to him. The auxiliary historical devices are not necessary for this, even if some individuals would in fact not have reached this insight without the historical revelation. Now, considered as history, our New Testament writings can never be so esteemed as to make us dare to have unlimited trust in every word of them, and especially if this were to weaken our attentiveness to the one necessary thing, namely, the moral faith of the Gospels, whose excellence consists in just this: that all our striving for purity of conscience and the conscientious conversion of our lives toward the good are here drawn together. Yet all this is done in such a way that the holy law lies perpetually before our eyes and reproaches us continually for even the slightest deviation from the divine will, just as though we were condemned by a just and unrelenting judge. And no confession of faith, no appeal to holy names nor any observance of religious ceremonies can help – though the consoling hope is offered us that, if we do as much good as is in our power, trusting in the unknown and mysterious

10:178

153

help of God, we shall (without meritorious "works" of any sort) partake of this divine supplement. Now, it is very clear that the apostles took this biblical doctrine of divine aid as the fundamental thesis of the Gospels, and whatever might be the actual *basis* of our salvation from God's point of view, the apostles took the essential requirement for salvation to be not the honoring of the holy teacher's religious doctrine of conduct but rather the veneration of this teacher himself and a sort of wooing of favor by means of ingratiation and encomium – the very things against which that teacher had so explicitly and repeatedly preached. Their procedure was in fact more suitable for those times (for which they were writing, without concern for later ages) than for our own. For in those days the old miracles had to be opposed by new miracles, and Jewish dogmas by Christian dogmas.

10:179

Here I must quickly break off, postponing the rest till my next letter (which I enclose). My most devoted compliments to your worthy friend Herr Pfenniger.[2]

> Your sincere friend,
> I. Kant

---

1   Kat' anthropon. An argument that is not universally valid but is convincing to a
    limited audience.
2   See Ak. [90], n. 3.

32 [100] (91)
To Johann Casper Lavater.

After April 28, 1775,

[Draft]

I would rather add something incomplete to my interrupted letter than nothing at all. My presupposition is that no book, whatever its authority might be – yes, even one based on the testimony of my own senses – can substitute for the religion of conscience. The latter tells me that the holy law within me has already made it my duty to answer for everything I do and that I must not dare to cram my soul with devotional testimonies, confessions, and so on, which do not spring from the unfeigned and unmistaking precepts of that law. For although statutes may bring about the performance of rituals, they cannot beget inner convictions. Because of this presupposition, I seek in the Gospels not the ground of my faith but its fortification, and I find in the moral spirit of the Gospels a clear distinction between what I am obligated to do and the manner in which this message is to be introduced into the world and disseminated, a distinction, in short, between my duty and that which God has done for me. The means of disclosure of my obligations may be what it will – nothing new is thereby provided for me, though my good convictions are given new strength and confidence. So much for the clarification of that part of my letter in which I spoke of the separation of two related but unequivalent parts of the holy scriptures and of their application to me.

As for your request that I give my opinion of the ideas on faith and prayer expressed in your "Miscellaneous Writings,"[1] the essential and most excellent part of the teachings of Christ is this: that righteousness is the sum of all religion and that we ought to seek it with all our might, having faith (that is, an unconditional trust) that God will then supplement our efforts and supply the good that is not in our power. This doctrine of faith forbids all our presumptuous curiosity about the manner in which God will do this, forbids the arrogance of supposing that one can know what means would be most in conformity with His wisdom; it forbids, too, all wooing of favor by the performing of rituals that someone has introduced. It allows no part of that endless religious madness to which people in all ages are inclined, save only the general and undefined trust that we shall partake of the good in some unknown way, if only we do not make ourselves unworthy of our share of it by our conduct.

10:180

---

1   Lavater, *Vermischte Schriften* (1774).

1776

33 [109] (98)
To Christian Heinrich Wolke.[1]
March 28, 1776.

10:191 Noble Sir,
Esteemed Herr Professor,

With sincerest pleasure I take this opportunity, while carrying out an assignment I have been given, to let you know of my great sympathy for your excellent school, the Philanthropin.

Herr Robert Motherby,[2] a local English merchant and my dear friend, would like to entrust his only son, George Motherby,[3] to the care of your school. Herr Motherby's principles agree completely with those upon which your institution is founded, even in those respects in which it is farthest removed from ordinary assumptions about education. The fact that something is unusual will never deter him from freely agreeing to your proposals and arrangements in all that is noble and good. His son will be six years old on the seventh of August this year. But though he has not reached the age you require, I believe that his natural abilities and motivations are already such as to satisfy the 10:192 intent of your requirement. That is why his father wants no delay in bringing the boy under good guidance, so that his need for activity may not lead him to any bad habits that would make his subsequent training more difficult. His education thus far has been purely negative, which I regard as the best that can be done for a child in those years. He has been allowed to develop his nature and his healthy reason in a manner appropriate to his years, without compulsion, and has been restrained only from those things that might set his mind in a wrong direction. He has been brought up without inhibitions, but not so as to be troublesome. He has never experienced force and has always been kept receptive to gentle suggestions. Though his manners are not the finest, he has been taught not to be naughty, but without his being

156

reprimanded into bashfulness and timidity. This was all the more necessary in order that a real ingenuousness might establish itself in him and especially so that he would not come to feel a need to lie. Some of his childish transgressions have therefore been excused so as not to give him the temptation to break the rule of truthfulness. Besides this, the only thing he has been taught is to write in Latin script when the letters are recited for him. He can do this (but only with a lead pencil). He is thus a blank slate on which nothing has yet been scribbled, a slate that should now be turned over to a master hand, so that the unerasable characteristics of sound reason, of knowledge and righteousness, may be inscribed upon it.

In matters of religion, the spirit of the Philanthropin agrees perfectly with that of the boy's father. He wishes that even the natural awareness of God (as the boy's growth in age and understanding may gradually make him arrive at it) should not be aimed at devotional exercises directly but only after he has realized that these are valuable merely as a means of animating an effective conscience and a fear of God, so that one does one's duties as though they were divinely commanded. For it is folly to regard religion as nothing more than a wooing of favor and an attempt to ingratiate oneself with the highest being, since this results in reducing the differences among various religions to differences of opinion as to what sort of flattery is most appealing to God. This illusion, whether based on dogmas or independent of them, is one that undermines all moral dispositions, for it takes 10:193 something other than a conversion to righteousness to be the means of surreptitiously currying favor with God, as though one need not be too fastidious about righteousness since one has another exit ready in case of emergency.

It is for this reason that our pupil has been kept ignorant of religious ceremonies. It may take a certain amount of skill, therefore, to give him a clear idea of their meaning when, at your discretion, he first attends such ceremonies. But he is being placed in the charge of a man who is accustomed to finding wisdom whence it truly springs, a man whose judgment can always be trusted. It would also please the boy's father very much if in the future the Philanthropin were also to teach English according to your easy and reliable method, for the boy will be going to England when his education is completed.

The child has already had measles and the pox, and no particular care need be taken about illnesses.

The father will be happy to pay the 250 thaler annual boarding fee, according to whatever arrangements you wish.

He asks your advice about what clothes, beds, and necessary equipment are customary in your school. He hopes that it may be possible to send the boy this summer, so that the amusements you have organized for your pupils will make him like his new surroundings. If you have no one who could escort him, there is a reliable foreign merchant who can bring him along toward the end of July.

All of these are firm decisions, not just tentative plans. I therefore 10:194 hope to hear from you soon, even if only a brief reply, for I realize how busy you are with your important work. I am most sympathetic to the noble labors to which you have dedicated yourself.

Your sincere admirer, friend, and servant,

Immanuel Kant
Professor of Philosophy

P.S. The enclosed paper should serve as a bit of evidence to demonstrate the renown your school is coming to have in these parts.[4]

---

1 Christian Heinrich Wolke (1741–1825) was director of the Philanthropin school in Dessau. As this letter and Kant's lectures on pedagogy demonstrate, Kant took a lively interest in education and in Wolke's school. See also the following letter to Basedow, Ak. [110].

2 Robert Motherby (1736–1801), Kant's close friend and frequent dinner companion.

3 George Motherby (1770–99) was one of Robert Motherby's nine children – five sons and four daughters. George died shortly before his planned marriage to Betsy Avenson whom Kant, even in his 70s, found so appealing that, according to R. B. Jachmann, Kant's student and later biographer, "he invariably seated her beside him at dinner on the side of his good eye." (Jachmann, quoted in the Schöndörffer/Malter 3rd edition of Kant's *Briefwechsel*, p. 828, and in Ak. 13:78.)

4 Kant refers to the first of his two essays concerning the Philanthropin, "Zwei Aufsätze, das Philanthropin betreffend". It was printed, without attribution to Kant, in the *Königsbergischen Gelehrten und Politischen Zeitungen* on the date of this letter.

34 [110] (99)
To Johann Bernhard Basedow.[1]

June 19, 1776.

Dear Sir,
Esteemed Herr Professor,

Herr Motherby,[2] who thinks that every day his son is not at the Philanthropin is a total waste, has decided not to wait any longer for a more propitious opportunity but to deliver his son himself into the trusted hands of the boy's second father who will educate and care for him. He will be leaving here in four or five days. Since this journey is going to take place at the earliest possible moment, I wanted to take the liberty of informing you ahead of time, for I saw from previous correspondence with the Philanthropin that this promising pupil would not be unwelcome in your institution. I hope only that all is well with you, who have become so important to the world, and with the institution you have founded, deserving the gratitude of all posterity; that hope is at the same time the hope for the child's best interests. I remain most respectfully

10:195

your devoted servant,
I. Kant.

---

1 Basedow (1723–90), educator and founder of the Philanthropin school in Dessau, devoted to Rousseau's educational theories. Kant used Basedow's *Methodenbuch* as a textbook when lecturing on *Pädagogik* in the winter semester of 1776/77. See also the preceding letter, Ak. [109], to Wolke, director of the Philanthropin.

2 On Motherby see notes to the preceding letter, to Wolke, Ak. [109].

35 [112] (101)
To Marcus Herz.
November 24, 1776.

Dear Herr Doctor,   10:198
Worthiest friend,

It pleases me to learn from Herr Friedländer that your medical practice is making good progress. Quite apart from the benefits it bestows, medicine is a field in which new insights provide continual nourishment to the understanding, since moderate activity keeps the understanding busy without exhausting it in the way that our greatest analysts, people like Baumgarten, Mendelssohn, Garve,[1] whom I follow from a distance, have been exhausted. They spin their brain nerves into the most delicate threads and thereby make themselves excessively sensitive to every impression or tension. I hope that with you this sort of mental activity will be only a refreshing play of thoughts and never become a burdensome occupation.

I observed with pleasure the purity of expression, the charm of your prose style, and the subtlety of observations in your book on the differences of taste.[2] I cannot now give you any detailed comments on it for the book was lent to me, I don't remember by whom. I still recall one passage in it which compels me to object to your partisan friendship toward me: I am uncomfortable that you praise me as comparable to Lessing. For in fact I have not yet accomplished anything to deserve such comparison, and I feel as though a mocking observer were beside me, attributing such pretensions to me and finding in them a justification for malicious rebuke.

As a matter of fact I have not given up hopes of accomplishing something in the area in which I am working. People of all sorts have been criticizing me for the inactivity into which I seem to have fallen for a long time, though actually I have never been busier with systematic and sustained work since the years when you last saw me. I might well hope for some transitory applause by completing the matters I am working on; they pile up as I work on them, as usually happens when one is on to a few fruitful principles. But all these matters are held back by one major object that, like a dam, blocks them, an object with which I hope to make a lasting contribution and which I really think I have in my grasp. Now it needs only finishing up rather than thinking through. After I acquit myself of this task, which I am just now starting to do (after overcoming the final obstacles last summer) I see an open field before me whose cultivation will be pure recreation. I must say it takes persistence to carry out a plan like this unswervingly, for difficulties have often tempted me to work on other, more pleasant topics. I have managed to recover from such faithlessness from time to time partly by overcoming some difficulty that comes along, partly by thinking about the importance of this business. You know that it must be possible to survey the field of pure reason, that is, of judgments that are independent of all empirical principles, since this lies a priori in ourselves and need not await any exposure from our experience. What we need in order to indicate the divisions, limits, and the whole content of that field, according to secure principles, and to lay the road marks so that in the future one can know for sure whether one stands on the floor of true reason or on that of sophistry – for this we need a critique, a discipline, a canon, and an architectonic of *pure reason*, a formal science, therefore, that can require nothing of those sciences already at hand and that needs for its foundations an entirely unique technical vocabulary. I do not expect to be finished with this work before Easter and shall use part of next summer for it, to the extent that my incessantly interrupted health will allow me to work. But please do not let this intention arouse any expectations; they are often troublesome and hard to satisfy.

And now dear friend, I beg of you not to be offended by my negligence in writing but I hope that you will honor me with news, especially literary, from your region. My most devoted regards to Herr Mendelssohn, and also to Herr Engel, Herr Lambert, and Herr Bode, who greeted me via Dr. Reccard.

10:200

Your most devoted servant and friend,
I. Kant

---

1 On Garve, see his letter to Kant, July 13, 1783, Ak.[201], n. 1.
2 Herz's *Versuch über den Geschmack und die Ursachen seiner Verschiedenheit* was published anonymously in Leipzig and Mitau, 1776.

1777

36 [120] (108)
To Marcus Herz.

August 20, 1777.

Dear Herr Doctor,
Dearest friend,

Today Herr Mendelssohn, your worthy friend and mine (for so I flatter myself), is departing. To have a man like him in Königsberg on a permanent basis, as an intimate acquaintance, a man of such gentle temperament, good spirits, and enlightenment – how that would give my soul the nourishment it has lacked so completely here, a nourishment I miss more and more as I grow older! For as far as bodily nourishment goes, you know I hardly worry about that and I am quite content with my share of earthly goods. I fear I did not manage to take full advantage of my one opportunity to enjoy this rare man, partly because I worried about interfering with his business here. The day before yesterday he honored me by attending two of my lectures, taking potluck, so to speak, since the table was not set for such a distinguished guest.[1] The lecture must have seemed somewhat incoherent to him, since I had to spend most of the hour reviewing what I had said before vacation. The clarity and order of the original lecture were largely absent. Please help me to keep up my friendship with this fine man.

You have made me two presents, dear friend, that show me that both in talent and in feeling you are that rare student who makes all the effort that goes into my often thankless job seem amply rewarded.

Your book *For Doctors* was thoroughly appealing to me and gave me genuine pleasure, though I cannot take the slightest credit for the honor it will bring you.[2] An observant, practical mind shines through the book, along with that subtle handling of general ideas that I have

10:212

162

noticed in you before. You are sure to achieve distinction in the medical profession if you continue to practice the art not simply as a means of livelihood but as a way of satisfying the curiosity of the experimental philosopher and the conscientiousness of the humanitarian within you.

Of the various indispositions that constantly plague me and often make me interrupt my intellectual endeavors (heartburn seems to be the general cause, though I seem to all my acquaintances just as healthy as I was twenty years ago), there is one complaint you may be able to help me with: I am not exactly constipated, but I have such a difficult and usually insufficient evacuation every morning that the remaining feces that accumulate become the cause, as far as I can tell, not only of that gas I mentioned but also of my clouded brain. To counteract this, I have sought relief in the past three weeks (when nature did not help me out with an unusual evacuation) through gentle purgatives. They did sometimes help, by accelerating an unusual movement. Most of the time, though, they produced a merely fluid evacuation, without dislodging the bulk of the impure stuff, and caused not only a feeling of weakness (which diuretic purgatives always do) but also an ensuing constipation. My doctor and good friend did not know what prescription would be exactly right for my condition.[3] I notice in Monro's book   10:213 on dropsy a classification of purgatives that corresponds exactly to my idea.[4] He distinguishes *hydragogic* (diuretic) and *eccoprotic* (laxative) and notices correctly that the former cause weakness. He says that the strongest of diuretics is jalap resin [*resinam Jalappae*] and that senna leaves and rhubarb are milder, though both of them are classified as hydragogic purgatives. On the other hand, he regards *crystals of cream of tartar* and *tamarinds* as eccoprotic, which is what I need. Herr Mendelssohn says that he himself has found the latter useful and that it consists of the pulp of the tamarinds. I would be most grateful to you if you would write me a prescription for this, which I could use from time to time. The dosage must be small for me, for I have usually reacted more than I wanted to from a smaller dosage than the doctor prescribed. Please arrange it so that I can take more or less, as necessary.

I think your second gift robs you of an enjoyable and expensive collection, just to prove your friendship for me, a friendship that is all the more delightful because it springs from the pure sources of an excellent understanding. I have already entertained some of my friends with this book, a stimulant to good taste and the knowledge of antiquity. I wish that this pleasure of which you have deprived yourself could be replaced in some way.

Since we parted company my philosophical investigations, gradually extended to all sorts of topics, have taken systematic form, leading me slowly to an idea of the whole system. Not until I have that will it be possible to judge the value and interrelationships of the parts. There is a stone that lies in the path of my completion of all these projects, the work I call my *Critique of Pure Reason*, and all my efforts are now devoted to removing that obstacle and I hope to be completely through with it this winter. The thing that detains me is the problem of pre-10:214 senting these ideas with total clarity, for I know that something can seem clear enough to an author himself and yet be misunderstood even by knowledgeable readers, if it departs entirely from their accustomed way of thinking.

Every news of your growing success, honors, and domestic good fortune is received with the greatest interest by

Your always devoted friend and servant,

I. Kant

---

1 Mendelssohn's visit to Kant's classroom is described by August Lewald in *Ein Menschenleben*, I (1844), p. 99. Malter quotes it at some length, in the Schöndörffer 3rd edition of Kant's *Briefwechsel*, pp. 829, f. Evidently the unruly students did not know that this "warped little Jew with a goatee" was the renowned philosopher until Kant himself took notice, uttered a few words, then warmly shook hands and embraced Mendelssohn. At that point the word spread like wildfire through the class: "Moses Mendelssohn! It's the Jewish philosopher from Berlin!" and the students made a path to honor the two philosophers who left the auditorium hand in hand.

2 Herz's *Briefe an Ärzte* (Mitau, Berlin, 1777).

3 Johann Gerhard Trummer (1729–93), physician in Königsberg and Kant's school friend, the only friend, according to Wasianski, who could address Kant as "Du."

4 Donald Monro (1729–92), *An Essay on the Dropsy and Its Different Species* (London, 1756). A German translation by K. C. Krause was published in Leipzig, 1777.

1778

37 [133] (870)
To Johann Gottlieb Immanuel Breitkopf.[1]
April 1, 1778

Königsberg, April 1, 1778

Noble esteemed Sir,   10:229

I am very pleased to make your acquaintance through your letter. I certainly think that the subject of human races could be treated both with greater thoroughness and illumination and with more detail; I am wholly content to entrust this project to your publishing company. 10:230 Firstly, however, I am for now still busy with pressing work of an entirely different sort and it would be difficult for me to turn my attention to the subject before the later part of the summer. Secondly, I think it would have to be a separate book; it could not easily become part of a natural history to be composed by other people, for in that case my views would have to be expanded and the play of races among animal and plant species considered explicitly, which would require too much attention from me and necessitate new and extensive reading rather outside my field, since natural history is not my specialty but only a hobby and my principal aim with respect to it is to use it to extend and correct our knowledge of mankind.

It would please me at any time to become personally and intellectually acquainted with Dr. Oehme.[2] I could indeed contribute something to a general section of natural history, some general ideas rather than their detailed application. But my decision in this regard depends on a more precise account of what this project aims to do.

I have the honor of remaining with full respect
your most devoted servant
I. Kant

1 Johann Gottfried Immanuel Breitkopf (1719–94), publisher and book merchant in Leipzig, is more famous in the history of music than in philosophy. In 1750 he invented a system of movable music type. Breitkopf makes an appearance in Goethe's *Dichtung und Wahrheit* (Part 2, Book 8).

Breitkopf founded the journal *Allgemeine musikalische Zeitung*. The publishing firm of Breitkopf and Härtel produced complete editions of the works of Mozart, Haydn, and other renowned composers. The firm survived into the twentieth century with numerous important composers in its catalog.

2 Oehme was Breitkopf's son-in-law.

38 [134] (121)
To Marcus Herz.

Early April 1778.

Choice and priceless friend,

Letters of the sort that I receive from you transport me into a state of feeling that sweetens my life as I should like it to be sweetened, a feeling that gives me a kind of foretaste of another life. That is how I feel when, if my hopes are not deceived, I see in your honest and grateful soul the reassuring evidence that the central aim of my academic life, which is always before my eyes, has not been pursued in vain: the aim, that is, of spreading good dispositions based on solid 10:231 principles, securing these dispositions in receptive souls, and thereby directing people to cultivate their talents in the only useful direction.

In this regard, my pleasure is however mixed with a certain feeling of melancholy when I see opening up before me a scene in which I might promote that aim in a much larger arena and yet see myself shut off from that prospect by the limited vitality that is my portion. You know that I am not much moved by the thought of profit and applause on some grand stage. A peaceful situation that just satisfies my need for a variable diet of work, reflection and social intercourse, a situation in which my spirit, hypersensitive but in other respects carefree, and my body, more troublesome but never actually sick, can both be kept busy without being strained – that is all I have wanted and that is what I have managed to obtain. All change frightens me, even one that might offer the greatest prospect of improvement in my circumstances. And I think I must obey this instinct of my nature if I am to spin out to greater length the thin and delicate thread of life which the Fates have spun for me. My greatest thanks therefore to my friends and supporters who have such a generous opinion of me and devote themselves to my welfare. But at the same time I beg sincerely that they direct this kind disposition to protecting and maintaining me in my present situation – in which, till now, I have been fortunate enough to be free of disturbances.

I am glad to have your prescriptions for medicine, dearest friend, in case of emergency, but since they include laxatives which generally affect my constitution severely and which are inevitably followed by intensified constipation, and since, as long as my morning evacuation is regular, I am really in good if somewhat fragile health – at least in my own manner, given that I have never enjoyed much better health than this – I have therefore decided to leave matters to nature's care and turn to artificial remedies only when nature fails me.

The news that some sheets from the book I am working on have already been printed is premature. Since I don't want to strain myself by forcing the book out (for I would like to continue my labors on this earth for a while longer) I let various other projects interrupt my work on it. My progress continues nevertheless and I expect to have it finished by this summer. I hope that you recognize from the nature 10:232 and aim of the project that there are good reasons why a book like this, though not extraordinarily large in number of pages, has taken me so long. *Tetens*,[1] in his diffuse work on human nature, made some penetrating points; but it certainly looks as if for the most part he let his work be published just as he wrote it down, without corrections. When he wrote his long essay on freedom in the second volume, he must have kept hoping that he would find his way out of this labyrinth by means of certain ideas that he had hastily sketched for himself, or so it seems to me. After exhausting himself and his reader, he left the matter just as he had found it, advising his reader to consult his own feelings.

If my health does not deteriorate I think I shall be able to present my promised little book to the public this summer.

While writing this letter I have received another gracious letter from His Excellency, Minister von Zedlitz, repeating his offer of a chair in Halle.[2] I must decline it for the reasons I have already mentioned to you.

Since I have to respond immediately to Breitkopf[3] in Leipzig who asked me to work out my essay on the races of mankind more extensively, I must delay sending the present letter until the next post.

Please greet Mr. Mendelssohn for me and tell him that I hope his health improves and that I wish him the enjoyment that his naturally cheerful heart and ever fertile spirit deserve. Do retain your affection and friendship for me,

your always devoted and faithful servant,
I Kant.

P.S. Please mail the enclosed letter for me with whatever postage is necessary, etc.

---

1 Johann Nicolaus Tetens (1736–1807), philosopher and psychologist, was a professor in Kiel and lived for a time in Copenhagen. It is said that he was the first philosopher/psychologist to recognize the faculty of feeling as equally important as the faculties of understanding and will. Under "feeling" he included pleasure and pain, but also two sorts of impressions: sensuous impressions and impressions that the mind produces on itself. It has been urged by T. D. Weldon, R. P. Wolff and others that a good deal of Kant's theory, e.g., the representational character of inner sense and the "self-affection" theory in the first *Critique*, is indebted to Tetens. Henry Allison, in *Kant's Transcendental Idealism*, p. 260, takes a different view. Tetens' *Philosophische Versuche über die menschliche Natur and ihre Entwicklung, two* volumes, was published in Leipzig, 1777. The justice of Kant's criticism of Tetens is shown, e.g., on pp. 129–48 of volume 2 of that work. Hamann wrote to Herder, May 17, 1779, "Kant is hard at work on his Moral of Pure Reason and Tetens lies open constantly before him."

2 Karl Abraham von Zedlitz (1731–93), minister of education in the Department of Spiritual Affairs, from 1771, the man to whom Kant dedicated the first *Critique*.

The position Zedlitz offered would have given Kant 800 Reichsthaler per year. In an earlier letter from Zedlitz, the offer was 600. Zedlitz's second invitation, Ak. [132], also praises the Halle faculty, which included according to Zedlitz the best theological faculty in Europe. Halle, he says, is the intellectual center of Europe and has a better climate than "up there on the Ost See." Ironically, it was Kant's opponent, Johann August Eberhard, who got the professorship that Kant turned down.

3 See Kant's letter to Breitkopf, Ak. [133].

39 [140] (127)
To Marcus Herz.

August 28, 1778.

Most worthy friend,

10:240   I should be very pleased to gratify your wish, especially when the purpose is connected with my own interest.[1] However, it is impossible

10:241   for me to do so as quickly as you ask. Whatever depends on the diligence and aptitude of my students is invariably difficult, because it is a matter of luck whether one has attentive and capable students during a certain period of time and also because those whom one has recently had disperse themselves and are not easily to be found again. It is seldom possible to persuade one of them to give away his own transcript. But I shall try to attend to it as soon as possible. I may yet find something here or there on the logic course. But metaphysics is a course that I have worked up in the last few years in such a way that I fear it must be difficult even for a discerning head to get *precisely* the right idea from somebody's lecture notes. Even though the idea seemed to me intelligible in the lecture, still, since it was taken down by a beginner and deviates greatly both from my formal statements and from ordinary concepts, it will call for someone with a head as good as your own to present it systematically and understandably.

When I have finished my handbook on that part of philosophy on which I am still working indefatigably, which I think will be soon, then every transcription of that sort will also become fully comprehensible, through the clarity of the overall plan. In the meantime I shall make an effort to find a serviceable set of lecture notes for your purposes. Herr Kraus[2] has been in Elking for several weeks but will return shortly, and I shall speak to him about it. Why don't you start with the logic? While that is progressing, the materials for the remaining work will be gathered. Although this is supposed to be a task for the winter, it may be possible to gather the supplies before the summer is over, thus allowing you time for preparation. Herr Joel[3] says that he left me in good health, and that is so, for I have accustomed myself for many years to regard a very restricted degree of well-being as good health, a degree of which the majority of people would complain, and, to whatever extent I can, I take recreation, rest, and conserve my strength. Without this hindrance my little projects, in the pursuit of which I am otherwise content, would have been brought to completion long ago.   10:242
I am, in immutable friendship and dedication,

> Your most devoted
> I. Kant

P.S. Did you also receive my letter of about a half a year ago, with its enclosure for Breitkopf in Leipzig?

---

1 Herz had requested a set of lecture notes that he might use in Berlin for his own lectures on Kant's logic and metaphysics.
2 Christian Jakob Kraus (1749–1814), Kant's student and later one of his most trusted friends. He became Professor of Practical Philosophy and Political

Sciences (*Staatswissenschaften*) in Königsberg. Before that, from 1777 to 1778, he served as *Hofmeister* in the palace of Count Keyserling in Königsberg (Kant had secured him the position as tutor to the count's 18-year-old son), where Kant was often entertained.

3 Aron Isaak Joel (1749–?) was an auditor of Kant's whom he recommended to Mendelssohn. Joel became a physician at the Jewish hospital in Berlin.

40 [141] (128)
To Marcus Herz.
October 20, 1778.

Dearest and worthiest friend,

To be of service to my upright and indefatigable capable friend, in a matter that will reflect back some approbation on myself as well, is always pleasant and important to me. However, there are many difficulties in carrying out the commission you gave me. Those of my students who are most capable of grasping everything are just the ones who bother least to take explicit and verbatim notes; rather, they write down only the main points, which they can think over afterwards. Those who are most thorough in note-taking are seldom capable of distinguishing the important from the unimportant. They pile a mass of misunderstood stuff under what they may possibly have grasped correctly. Besides, I have almost no private acquaintance with my auditors, and it is difficult for me even to find out which ones might have accomplished something useful. My discussion of empirical psychology is now briefer, since I lecture on anthropology. But since I make improvements or extensions of my lectures from year to year, especially in the systematic and, if I may say, architectonic form and ordering of what belongs within the scope of a science, my students cannot very easily help themselves by copying from each other.

However, I do not abandon the hope of gratifying your wish, especially if Herr Kraus[1] helps me. He will arrive in Berlin toward the end of November. He is one of my favorite and most capable students. Please have patience until then. Especially I beg you to do me the favor of announcing to His Excellency, Herr von Zedlitz,[2] through his secretary, Herr Biester,[3] that the aforementioned Herr Kraus will deliver the requested transcript.

My letter to Breitkopf may actually have arrived there, but perhaps

10:243

he had nothing to reply to the rather negative answer I had to give him; otherwise no reason.

I close hurriedly and am still

Your true friend and servant,

I. Kant

---

1 On Kraus see Kant's preceding letter to Herz, Ak. [140], n. 2.
2 On Zedlitz see Kant's letter to Herz, Ak. [134], n. 2.
3 Johann Erich Biester (1749–1816) taught at the Pädagogium and as privatdozent at the University of Bützow in Meklenburg-Schwerin, became secretary to von Zedlitz in 1777, and, in 1777, first librarian of the Royal Library in Berlin and member of the Berlin Academy of Sciences. He published the *Berliner Monatsschrift*. Like Zedlitz, he was introduced to Kant's philosophy by Herz's lectures.

41 [143] (130)
From Marcus Herz.
November 24, 1778.

Honored Herr Professor,
Revered teacher,

Here I am again, dunning. Isn't it true, dearest sir, I'm an obstreperous person? Forgive me, by assuming that I know the man to whom   10:244
I dare to be obstreperous; it can be no one else than he who dwells constantly in the center of my thoughts and my heart!

I am enjoying a degree of happiness this winter to which I never aspired even in my dreams. Today, for the twentieth time, I am lecturing on your philosophical teachings to approbation that exceeds all my expectations. The number of people in my audience grows daily; it is already over thirty, all of them people of high status or profession. Professors of medicine, preachers, lawyers, government administrators, and so on, of whom our worthy minister [Zedlitz] is the leading one; he is always the first to arrive and the last to leave, and until now he has not missed a single session, as neither have any of the others. It seems to me that this course is in many ways a remarkable thing, and not a day passes that I do not reflect on the impossibility of ever repaying you, through any act of mine, the tenth part of the happiness I enjoy in a single hour, which I owe to you and to you alone!

I have now completed half of the logic and hope to be finished with the other half by January. I have several very complete notebooks of your lectures on logic, and to these I owe my audience's applause; here and there your fruitful ideas led me to other views that appeal to my listeners. But the foundations of it all are yours.

It will all depend on you whether I can carry off the metaphysics course. I don't even have complete copies of your lectures, and certainly the whole business will be virtually impossible for me without them. To build up the course from scratch, all alone, is not within my powers, nor have I the time, since most of my time is taken up with my practical work.

10:245   I beg you again, therefore, to send me, with the earliest mail, at least some incomplete notebooks, if the complete ones are not to be had. Diversity, I think, will compensate for incompleteness, since each set of notes will have noticed something different. I beg you especially for an ontology and a cosmology.

I take the liberty of recommending to you a young nobleman, Herr von Nolte, of Kurland, who is passing through here. He is a very clever and well-educated young man, who has been in the service of France for a year and now is going into that of Russia. He will bring you something that should go with your anthology.

From certain letters that Herr Kraus wrote to his friends, I see how troubled the good man is about his stay here. Please be good enough to assure him that everything will be done to make his stay as pleasant as possible. He is always welcome to dine at Friedländer's, and free lodging has also been arranged.

I am and shall always be, with the greatest respect,

    Your honored sir's most devoted servant,

      M. Herz

1779

42 [145] (132)
To Marcus Herz.
January 1779

Dear Sir, 10:247
Worthiest friend,

I received your kind gift, the plaster cast of Herr Mendelssohn's medallion,[1] via Herr von Nolte, a pleasant young gentleman, and I thank you for it.

Dr. Heintz[2] assures me, through letters from Secretary Biester,[3] that your lectures have been received with unusual and universal applause. Now Herr Kraus[4] tells me exactly the same thing and informs me of the thoroughgoing respect you have earned from the Berlin public. I need not assure you of the exceptional pleasure that this evokes in me; it is obvious. What is unexpected in this is not your astuteness and insight, which I already have cause to believe in completely, but the popularity you have achieved that, in a project of this sort, would have made me fearful. For some time I have been reflecting in idle moments on the principles needed to achieve popularity in the sciences generally (obviously I mean sciences that are capable of popularity, for mathematics is not), especially in philosophy, and I think that from this perspective I can not only describe a different selection but also a wholly different organization than the methodical, scholastic one that always remains fundamental requires. However, your success shows that you have the knack for this even in your first attempts.

How I wish I had a better manuscript[5] to give you than the one Herr Kraus will deliver to you. If I could have foreseen this last winter I would have made some arrangements with my auditors. Now you will get very little out of these paltry notes, which your genius can nevertheless turn to advantage. When you have no further use for them,

Herr Toussaint who is now staying in Berlin will ask for them to return them shortly before Easter.

10:248 If, as I do not doubt, your influence can help Herr Kraus, I beg you to use it and count it as evidence of the friendship with which you honor me and of which you have never allowed me to have the slightest doubt. He is a modest, highly promising and grateful young man. He will bring no dishonor to your recommendation, should you wish to give it on his behalf to the minister,[6] nor will he be insensitive to it. Nothing stands in his way but hypochondriacal worries with which young, thinking minds like his often plague themselves without cause. Your medical arts undoubtedly contain a remedy for that as well, but even more important is your friendship, if you will condescend to give it to him. I receive every direct and indirect news of your growing good fortune with additional pleasure and I am in eternal friendship

your
sincerely devoted servant,
I. Kant

---

1   The plaster cast pictured on one side the head and shoulders of Mendelssohn with his name inscribed, on the reverse side a skull on which a butterfly was perched, with the inscription "Phaedon," the title of Mendelssohn's book on the immortality of the soul. The medallion was the work of the royal medallion maker, Abramson or Abrahamson (1754–1811).

2   Karl Reinhold Heintz (1745–1807), professor of law in Königsberg from 1779.

3   On Biester, see Kant to Herz, Ak. [141], n. 3.

4   On Kraus see Kant to Herz, Ak. [143], n. 1.

5   Herz had requested some of Kant's lecture notes. See the previous letters, e.g., Ak. [140].

6   Presumably Zedlitz.

43 [146] (133)

To Marcus Herz.

February 4, 1779.

In response to your expressed wish, dear friend, I have mailed the very poorly drafted manuscript and, with the next post, I hope to send you still another perhaps more extended one, to help you as best as I can.

A certain misology that you, as I, detected and regretted in Herr Kraus derives, as does much misanthropy, from this: that in the first instance one loves philosophy, in the second, people, but one finds both ungrateful, partly because one expected too much of them, partly because one is too impatient in awaiting the reward for one's efforts from the two. I know this sullen mood also; but a kind glance from either of them soon reconciles us with them again and serves to make our attachment to them even stronger.

I thank you sincerely for extending your friendship to Herr Kraus so obligingly. Please return my compliments to Secretary Biester. I would have taken the liberty of writing him to ask that he be gracious 10:249 to Herr Kraus if I had not felt some hesitation about causing him trouble right at the start of our acquaintanceship. I remain with steadfast respect and friendship

your most devoted servant,
I. Kant.

Königsberg, February 4, 1779.

Letters 1781–1789

[164–394]

1781

44 [164] (151)
To Marcus Herz.

May 1, 1781.

In the current Easter book fair there will appear a book of mine, 10:266
entitled *Critique of Pure Reason*. It is being published by *Hartknoch's*
firm, printed in *Halle* by Grunert, and distributed under the direction
of Herr *Spener*,[1] the Berlin book dealer. This book contains the result
of all the varied investigations, which start from the concepts we debated together under the heading "the sensible world and the intelligible world" [*mundi sensibilis und intelligibilis*]. I am anxious to hand
over the summation of my efforts to the same insightful man who
deigned to cultivate my ideas, so discerning a man that he penetrated
those ideas more deeply than anyone else.

With this in mind I beg you to deliver the enclosed letter[2] in person
to Herr Carl Spener and to arrange the following matters with him;
after you talk with him, please send me news with the earliest possible
mail, if my demands are not too extravagant.

1. Find out how far along the printing is and on which day of the
fair the book will appear in Leipzig.

2. Since I intended that four copies go to Berlin – a dedicatory copy
to His Excellency, Minister von Zedlitz, one for you, one for Herr 10:267
Mendelssohn, and one for Dr. Sell,[3] which last should please be delivered to the music master, Herr Reichard[4] (who recently sent me a copy
of Sell's *Philosophische Gespräche*), I beg that you ask Herr Spener to
write to Halle immediately and see to it that these four copies be sent
to Berlin, at my expense, as soon as the printing is done and that they
be delivered to you. Please lay out the postage money for me, have the
dedicatory copy elegantly bound, and present it in my name to His
Excellency, Herr von Zedlitz. It is of course taken for granted that this
copy will reach Berlin so early that no other could possibly have

reached the Minister before it. Please lay out the expenses for me or sign for them in my name. For the copies themselves, there is nothing to pay, for I arranged with Herr Hartknoch to have ten or twelve of them at my disposal.

As soon as I hear from you about all this I shall take the time to write to you and Herr Mendelssohn somewhat more fully about this work. Until then, with greatest respect and friendship,

Your devoted servant,
I. Kant

---

1   Johann Carl Philipp Spener (1749–1847), book merchant in Berlin; the firm's name was Haude-Spener. In a brief letter to Spener, May 11, 1781, Ak. [165], Kant expresses approval of the printing of the *Critique of Pure Reason*, noting only that places in the text which he had underlined, to be printed in "Schwabacher" type, were printed in a font that made them almost indistinguishable from the rest of the text. Kant was annoyed but thought it not a matter of great consequence.

2   The letter, Ak. [163], is a brief note instructing Spener to send four copies of the *Critique* to Grunert, the printer in Halle, one of them, the dedicatory copy, on excellent paper. Kant also asked Spener to send him, via Herz, the remaining proof sheets as soon as they were ready.

3   Christian Gottlieb Selle (1748–1800), member of the Berlin Academy and physician at the Berlin Charité. Selle, an empiricist in the Lockean tradition, became an opponent of Kant's philosophy, though they remained on friendly terms. See Kiesewetter's letter to Kant, Ap. 20, 1790, Ak. [420], and Kant's letter to Selle, Feb. 24, 1792, Ak. [507].

4   Johann Friedrich Reichardt (1752–1814), composer and *Kapellmeister* in Berlin, came from Königsberg where, as a boy of 15, he had entered the university and attended Kant's lectures.

45 [166] (153)

To Marcus Herz.

After May 11, 1781.

10:268 Noble Sir,
Dearest friend,

Sincere thanks for your efforts in distributing the four copies of my
10:269 book. I am even more thankful that you are determined to study this

work thoroughly, despite the fact that you are busy with your own writings (for I hear that you are working on a medical encyclopedia.)[1] I can count on such effort only from a very few readers now, though I am most humbly convinced that in time this will become more general; for one cannot expect a way of thinking to be suddenly led off the beaten track into one that has heretofore been totally unused. That requires time, to stay that style of thinking little by little in its previous path and, finally, to turn it into the opposite direction by means of gradual impressions. But from a man who as a student delighted me by grasping my ideas and thoughts more quickly and exactly than any of the others – from this man I can hope that shortly he will grasp those concepts of my system that alone make possible a decisive evaluation of its worth. He, however, who becomes entirely clear about the condition in which metaphysics lies (not only at present, but always), that man will find it worthwhile, after only a cursory reading, at least to let everything lie fallow until the question here at issue is answered. And in this, my work, may it stand or fall, cannot help but bring about a complete change of thinking in this part of human knowledge, a part of knowledge that concerns us so earnestly. For my part I have nowhere sought to create mirages or to advance specious arguments in order to patch up my system; I have rather let years pass by, in order that I might get to a finished insight that would satisfy me completely and at which I have in fact arrived; so that I now find nothing I want to change in the main theory (something I could never say of any of my previous writings), though here and there little additions and clarifications would be desirable. This sort of investigation will always remain difficult, for it includes the *metaphysics of metaphysics*. Yet I have a plan in mind according to which even *popularity* might be gained for this study, a plan that could not be carried out initially, however, for the foundations needed cleaning up, particularly because the whole system of this sort of knowledge had to be exhibited in all its articulation. Otherwise I would have started with what I have entitled the "Antinomy of Pure Reason,"[2] which could have been done in colorful essays and would have given the reader a desire to get at the sources of this controversy. But the school's rights must first be served; afterwards one can also see about appealing to the world.

10:270

I am very uncomfortable at Herr Mendelssohn's putting my book aside; but I hope that it will not be forever.[3] He is the most important of all the people who could explain this theory to the world; it was on him, on Herr Tetens, and on you, dearest man, that I counted most. Please give him, in addition to my highest regards, a diathetic observation that I made on myself, which, because of the similarity in our studies and our resultant weak health, might serve to restore this excellent man to the learned world, this man who for so long has withdrawn from it, finding that attention to it was incompatible with his health. [The observation is this:] during the past four years my health has noticeably improved. I discovered that studying in the afternoon and especially evenings – even engaging in light books – was bad for my health. Therefore, even though I am at home every evening, I entertain myself exclusively with light reading, taking numerous intermissions, reading about subjects that happen to present themselves, never anything important. In the morning, on the other hand, after a restful night, I am busy with reflection and writing until I get tired. The distractions of what is left of the day compensate for all the attacks on my energy. I would be interested to hear what my advice does for this excellent man who certainly doesn't need my advice, for his genius . . . 4

---

1 Herz's *Grundriß aller medizinischen Wissenschaften*, (Berlin, 1782).
2 In a late letter to Garve, Ak. [820], Kant states that it was the discovery of the antinomies that first drove him to work on the *Critique of Pure Reason*.
3 Mendelssohn wrote, in a letter to Elise Reimarus, Jan. 5, 1784: "Very nice to hear that your brother does not think much of the 'Critique of Pure Reason.' For my part, I must admit that I didn't understand it. The summary that Herr Garve put in the *Bibliothek* is clear to me, but other people say that Garve didn't understand him properly. It is therefore pleasant to know that I am not missing much if I go thence without understanding this work."
4 The letter breaks off here. What we have is possibly only a draft.

46 [168] (155)
To Johann Erich Biester[1]
June 8, 1781.

Königsberg, the 8th of June, 1781

10:271 Dear Herr Doctor,
Most honored friend,

That you regard the little bit of assistance I gave to good-natured Etner[2] as a favor to yourself, sir, is proof of your kind disposition and obliges me to undertake any services which you may wish to ask of me

in the future. Exactly the same disposition, so pleasing to me, must   10:272
presumably have motivated your announcement[3] in the *deutsche Bib-*
liothek, which was reported to me but which I have not yet received,
concerning my competition with the late Lambert on matters of physical astronomy.[4] I am however somewhat troubled by the effect that
Herr *Goldbeck*'s remark may have on certain reviewers, because the
news was imparted to him by his friend here who received it in a
conversation with me and presumably did not grasp precisely what I
said; Herr Goldbeck, through the same friend, then inquired of me
again concerning this matter and I expressed myself to this person
approximately in the same terms *that I have used in the appended note to*
this letter. The aforesaid Herr Goldbeck may make use of this, either
in a new edition of his *Literary News* or in the next issue thereof. If
you, sir, would be kind enough to print this appended correction in
the next issue of the *deutsche Bibliothek*, with an introduction which I
leave to your discretion, all misunderstanding would thereby be prevented in a timely manner.[5]

What now concerns me most is to find out speedily whether the
dedication copy of my *Critique of Pure Reason* has been delivered to His
Excellency Herr von Zedlitz via Dr. Hertz. I have received no letter
from him since the 8th of May and I worry over the possibility that,
because of my publisher's agent, this copy may have been delivered to
Herr Hertz either very late or not at all. Though this book has occupied my thinking for a number of years, I have put it down on paper
in its present form in only a short time. That is also why certain
stylistic infelicities and signs of haste as well as certain obscurities still
remain, not to mention the typographical errors which I could not
avoid, since because of the propinquity of the book fair it was impossible to mark them. In spite of that I boldly allow myself to believe
that this book will lead every treatment of this subject in a new direction and that the doctrines propounded in it can hope for an endurance
which until now one has been accustomed to deny to all metaphysical
endeavors. I could not delay the publication of the book any longer to   10:273
sharpen the presentation and render it more easily intelligible. For
since, as concerns the subject matter itself, I have no more to say, and
since clarifications will be more readily given when the judgment of
the public has called attention to the places that seem to need them
(and for these places I shall not fail to supply clarification in the future),
and since I hope also that this subject will still occupy various writers
and therefore me as well, and considering besides this my advancing
age (I am in my 58th year) and the troublesome illnesses that charge
me to do today what may be impossible tomorrow, the completion of
the book had to be pursued without delay. Nor do I find that there is
anything in what I have written that I would want to take back, though

now and again clarifications could be brought to bear, a task to which I shall turn at the first opportunity.

Among the errors – I don't know whether they are due to the printing or to my transcriber – the one that disturbed me most is one that occurs right in the dedication! The sixth line should read: "Through the more intimate *relation*." But perhaps the majority of readers will overlook this error and, I flatter myself, it will be forgiven by His Excellency.

Might I then ask that you kindly inform me by return mail (omit the postage) how things stand with the commission that Herr Hertz was supposed to carry out and, in case (as I can well imagine) the expected has not been accomplished, please convey my sincerest apologies to His Excellency. I am most respectfully

your most devoted and loyal servant
I. Kant

The announcement in Herr *Goldbeck's Literary News from Prussia*, pp. 248–49, shows the trace of a kind but somewhat too favorable disposition of the writer toward his erstwhile teacher. My *Natural History of the Heavens* could never be taken for a product of *Lambert's* mind, he whose deep insights in astronomy are so distinctly different that no confusion could arise over this. In any case the confusion 10:274 concerns the genesis of my weak silhouette prior to that of his masterful and entirely original abstract of the cosmological system, whose outlines indeed could easily coincide with those of the former without there being any other commonality except the analogy with the planetary system to cause such a misunderstanding, something of which the excellent man took notice in a letter with which he honored me in the year 1765 when this agreement of our conjectures accidentally came to his attention. Moreover, since Herr *Bode*, in his very useful Introduction,[6] did not intend to note historical differences in the propounded propositions, he took my opinion concerning the analogy of the *nebulae* (which appear as *elliptical formations*) with the Milky Way system, together with Herr Lambert's thesis and subsumed them both under those ideas that were common to our hypothesis, even though Herr Lambert had not taken notice of this analogy but had rather divided our Milky Way itself, in those places where it discloses intervals, into several levels of Milky Ways. But the elliptical shape of these constitutes an essential ground of the conjecture I ventured about the Milky Way's being a mere limb of a still larger system of similar world-orders. But the correction of conjectures which must always remain conjectures is only of limited consequence.

1 On Biester see Ak. [141], n. 3.
2 Biester had recommended a young student named Ettner to Kant.
3 In his *Literarischen Nachrichten von Preussen*) Literary news from Prussia), (Leipzig and Dessau, 1781) Part I, pp. 248, f., Johann Friedrich Goldbeck (1748–1812) asserted that "Kant's *Natural History and Theory of the Heavens*, published anonymously in 1755, became known only later when certain propositions in it were afterwards advanced by other scholars, namely Herr Lambert in his *Cosmological Letters*, which came out in 1761; these propositions were attributed to Lambert and therefore their original author did not get credit for his discovery." Goldbeck claimed that the Nebular Hypothesis was attributed to Lambert by the astronomer Johann Elert Bode, though Lambert never stated it. "One might almost come to think that this Kantian Natural History accidentally came to be regarded as a product of Lambert's mind."
4 Biester discussed Goldbeck's book in the Supplement to Vols. 37–52 of the *Allgemeine deutsche Bibliothek*, (1783). The announcement read: "What the author says on pp. 248 f. about Kant's and Lambert's cosmological propositions coinciding and about Bode's ascribing to the latter a hypothesis of the former is not quite correct; we know how Kant himself thinks about this, he who is too modest to usurp anything of Lambert's fame."
5 Biester in fact did not publish the notice.
6 *Anleitung zur Kenntnis des gesternten Himmels* (*Introduction to knowledge of the starry heavens*), 3rd ed., 1777, p. 658 n.

47 [172] (158)
To Johann Bernoulli.[1]
November 16, 1781

Esteemed Sir,

I received your letter of November 1st on the 10th. I feel it is incumbent on me to satisfy your request in regard to Lambert's correspondence, not only because of my duty to the distinguished man's literary estate but for the sake of my own interests as well, since the latter are bound up with your proposed publication.[2] It is, however, not entirely within my power to satisfy your expectations. I can tell you the exact date of his first letter: November 13, 1765. But I cannot seem to find his last letter,[3] written in 1770, though I am certain I kept it. However, since I received a letter from the late Herr Sulzer on December 8, 1770, in answer to one that I wrote to him on the same

10:277

occasion on which I wrote to Herr Lambert, namely, when I sent him my dissertation, I suspect that Herr Lambert's reply may have arrived at about the same time. The excellent man had made an objection to the ideas concerning space and time that I had expressed, an objection that I answered in the *Critique of Pure Reason*, pages 36–38.[4]

You are fully justified in expecting that I would keep a copy of my replies to letters from such an important correspondent, but unfortunately I never wrote him anything worth copying – just because I attached so much importance to the proposal that this incomparable man made to me, that we collaborate on the reform of metaphysics. I saw at that time that this putative science lacked a reliable touchstone with which to distinguish truth from illusion, since different but equally persuasive metaphysical propositions lead inescapably to contradictory conclusions, with the result that one proposition inevitably casts doubt on the other. I had some ideas for a possible reform of this science then, but I wanted my ideas to mature first before submitting them to my deeply insightful friend's scrutiny and further development. For that reason the projected collaboration was postponed again and again, since the enlightenment I sought seemed always to be near, yet always distanced itself on further investigation. In the year 1770 I was already able clearly to distinguish *sensibility* in our cognition from the *intellectual*, by means of precise limiting conditions. The main steps in this analysis were expressed in my Dissertation (mixed with many theses that I should not accept today), which I sent to the great man, hoping to have the remainder of my theory ready before long. But then the problem of the *source of the intellectual* elements in our cognition created new and unforeseen difficulties, and my postponement became all the more necessary as it stretched on, until all the hopes I had set in anticipation of his brilliant counsel were shattered by the untimely death of that extraordinary genius. I regret this loss all the more since, now that I think I have found what I was looking for, Lambert would be just the man whose bright and perceptive mind – all the more free of prejudice because of its very *inexperience* in metaphysical speculations and therefore all the more skillful – could have shown me the possible mistakes in my *Critique of Pure Reason* after examining its propositions in their total context; and with his disposition for achieving something enduring for human reason, the union of his efforts with mine might have brought about a truly finished piece of work. Even now I do not discount the possibility of such an achievement, but since the project has been deprived of his fine mind, it will be more difficult and more protracted.

These are my reasons for begging pardon of you and the public for not having used better the opportunity that pleased me so and the reasons why my answers to the departed man's kind letters are lacking.

10:278

To Johann Bernoulli. November 16, 1781

I thank you, sir, for the use which you wish to make of the recollections I transmitted to Herr Goldbeck. It will avert a misunderstanding that might be unfortunate for me, though not for Herr Lambert. I cannot allow you to assume any of the costs of shipping the first volume of Lambert's correspondence to me. I played no part in its completion, so that it would be presumptuous of me to accept your kind offer . . .

Your obedient servant,
I. Kant

---

1 Johann Bernoulli, mathematician and astronomer (1744–1807), one member of an extraordinary family of scientists and mathematicians. This is Johann III, oldest son of Johann II (1710–90), mathematician and jurist, brother of another brilliant Bernoulli, Daniel (1700–82). Johann III was educated by his father and his uncle; at age 13 he gave lectures, at 14 he was awarded an instructorship, and at 19 he completed a law degree, at which point Frederick the Great called him to Berlin to the Academy of Sciences. There Bernoulli did research in astronomy and translated Euler's *Algebra* into French.

2 Bernoulli was preparing an edition of Lambert's correspondence, which appeared between 1782 and 1785.

3 Oct. 13, 1770, Ak.[61].

4 See Lambert's letter mentioned above and *Critique of Pure Reason*, A 36–9 = B 53–5.

1782

48 [180] (165)
From Johann Heinrich Kant with Postcript from his wife.

Sept. 10, 1782

10:287 Dearest brother,

My wife was delighted by the book you sent, *The Housewife in All Her Tasks*,[1] for she had gotten it into her head that you were offended by her bold request and that you would henceforth disregard her. She intends to use this book to teach herself how to become a truly competent farmer. That is a new subject for me as well, since Providence has seen fit to transfer me from schoolroom to plough. I am now a preacher in a loamy diocese that covers a lot of territory. A considerable number of Protestants who live in the adjoining part of Lithuania belong to my congregation and this requires that I make frequent excursions for sick visits. This part of my office is very tiring but I am strong and healthy enough not to pay attention to my fatigue. In other respects my new situation is much more pleasant than my previous teaching position whose depressingly massive work and minimal pay made it hard to make ends meet and support my family. I endured that burden for six years; thank God for letting me rest from it. Now I enjoy contentment and my prospects will be even better when I get out from under the debts I have had to incur as a budding farmer – for cattle, horses, wagon, and a thousand other necessities. My pastorate is six miles from Mitau and ten from Riga and I travel to the latter city where I try to sell my produce.[2] The region in which I live is so charming that a painter touring Courland who wanted to capture the sights would not omit ours. My fields are fertile and there is a nice garden next to my house which people in Courland have noticed. The only flaw in my dwelling place is that there are almost no visitors. My diocese is in the princely domain in which no nobility resides. But I am so busy with my work and my reading that I hardly feel this solitude. I live harmoniously and contentedly with my honest, home-loving, kind wife. This domestic happiness is made even more appetiz-ing by two clever and lively daughters, Charlotte and Mina, and then, in place of my Eduard whom I lost several years ago, a fresh Friedrich Wilhelm who will soon be one year old. That is a quick sketch of my current situation. I beg you, dear brother, to send me news of you, the state of your health and happiness, your literary accomplishments, and news also of our dear relatives, Uncle and Aunt Richter, and of our sisters. I am not yet so much an emigrant that the welfare of my father-city, my siblings, and my relatives have become a matter of indifference to me. Your Critique of Purified Reason [*Critique der gereinigten Ver-nunft*] [*sic*] is talked about by all intellectuals hereabout. I am sure you have not yet retired from authorship. Couldn't your brother then ask for a little privilege, namely, that you let me be instructed by your writings before you give those gifts to the public to read? Be well and happy, my brother, and give me the joy of a letter, for which I yearn, and do love your brother

10:288

Joh. Heinrich Kant.

Altrahdensches Pastorat, the 10th of September, 1782.

Dearest Herr Brother,

I include my own sincerest thanks for the excellent book that you gave me, from which I shall try to make myself into a professor of housekeeping.

Do love your sister-in-law who is devoted to you even without the hope of ever being able to embrace you in person. My little daughters commend themselves to their uncle and, were it possible, would gladly fly to you to kiss your hand. Do be well disposed also to my little son. He is a good boy who will not dishonor your name. Think of us and especially of your

warmly devoted sister
Maria Kant.

---

1   *Die Hausmutterin in allen ihren Geschäften*, 3 volumes, Leipzig, 1778–81, author anonymous; a book of selections from these volumes appeared in 1782.

2   The translation is conjectural, for "nach der letzteren Stadt verführe ich meine Kreszentien" is puzzling: *Kreszentien* can mean growing, blossoming things, *die Wachsende, Aufblühende*, hence this possible reading.

1783

49 [190] (174)
From Moses Mendelssohn.
April 10, 1783.

10:307 Esteemed Sir,

10:308 He who has the pleasure of delivering this letter to you is the son of one of the *finest* men serving Frederick the Great.[1] His worthy father, who knows you, thought that to this significant recommendation my own recommendation would make an additional contribution. Since this opinion of how you estimate my worth is so flattering to me, I would like in any case to be able to preserve it among good people, and you, dearest Herr Professor, you love me really too well to impute this to my vanity. In any case, every young person who strives after wisdom is recommended like a son to you and this one has authenticated witnesses testifying that he is worthy of your guidance.

I don't know what persons from Königsberg assured me several months ago that you were going to visit us this summer, traveling beyond here to Pyrmont or Spa. Can your friends hope for this? Such a journey would on the whole be good for you, even without bath and springs, and I should think that you were obligated to sacrifice to Aesculapius your convenience and the whole army of scruples which a clever hypochondria can bring up to oppose the journey. You would find many open arms in Berlin, but also many an open heart, among them one that belongs to a man who voices his admiration for you even if he cannot follow you. For many years I have been as though dead to metaphysics. My weak nerves forbid me every exertion and I amuse myself with less stressful work of which I shall soon have the pleasure of sending you some samples. Your *Critique of Pure Reason* is also a criterion of health for me. Whenever I flatter myself that my strength has increased I dare to take up this nerve-juice consuming book,[2] and I am not entirely without hope that I shall still be able to think my way through it in this life. I am

your

Berlin, the 10th of April, 1783.   Moses Mendelssohn

---

1   Friedrich von Gentz (1764–1832) attended Kant's lectures in 1784–6. His father was general director of the mint in Berlin.

2   In the Preface to his *Morgenstunden oder Vorlesungen über das Dasyn Gottes* (Morning lessons or lectures on the existence of God) (Part I, Berlin, 1785) Mendelssohn mentions his "so-called weakness of nerves" and continues: "I am therefore only imperfectly acquainted with the metaphysical writings of great men such as Lambert, Tetens, Plattner and even of the all-destroying Kant [*des alles zermalmenden Kants*], whose works I know only from the incomplete reports of my friends or from scholarly announcements which are seldom very informative."

50 [201] (184)

From Christian Garve.[1]

July 13, 1783.

Esteemed Sir,   10:328

You demand that the reviewer of your book in the Göttingen journal[2] identify himself.[3] I cannot in any way recognize that review, in the form that it was published, as my own. I would be distressed if it were wholly the product of my pen. Nor do I believe that any other contrib-   10:329 utor to this journal, working alone, would have turned out anything this incoherent. But I do bear some responsibility for it. And since I am concerned that a man whom I have long respected should at least regard me as an honest person, even if he also takes me to be a shallow metaphysician, I therefore step out of my incognito, as you demanded in one place in your *Prolegomena*.[4] In order to put you in a position to judge correctly, however, I must tell you the whole story.

I am not a regular contributor to the Göttingen journal. Two years ago, after many years of indolence, sickness and obscurity in my homeland, I made a journey to Leipzig, through the state of Hannover, and on to Göttingen. Since I had received such cordial and friendly treatment from Heyne,[5] the editor of this journal, and from several contributors to it, some sort of feeling of gratitude mixed with a certain

191

amount of vanity prompted me to volunteer to contribute a review. Since your *Critique of Pure Reason* had just come out and I anticipated great pleasure from a major work having Kant as its author (for his previous short writings had already given me so much pleasure) and since I thought it would be useful to me to have an incentive to read this book with more than usual care, I agreed therefore to review your book before I had even seen it. This commitment was rash, and it is actually the only foolishness of which I am conscious in the matter, one which I still regret.

Everything that followed is a consequence either of my actual incapacity or bad luck. I recognized as soon as I started to read the book that I had made the wrong decision and that this work was too difficult for me, especially then, distracted as I was by my travels, busy with other work, and as always weak and sickly. I confess to you that I know of no other book in the world that was so strenuous for me to read, and if I had not felt myself to be bound by my promise I would have postponed the reading until better times, when my head and my body might be stronger. Nonetheless I did not undertake my labors frivo-lously. I applied all my strength and all the attention of which I am capable to the book; I read it through completely. I think I grasped the meaning of most of the individual parts correctly, but I am not so certain that I correctly understood the whole.

10:330

The first thing I did was to make myself a complete abstract, over 12 pages long, interspersed with the ideas that occurred to me during my reading. I regret that this abstract is lost; it may have been better (as my first ideas often are) than what I made of it later on. From these 12 pages (which could never become a journal review article) and with great effort (for on the one hand I wanted to be concise and on the other hand comprehensible enough to do the book justice) I worked out a review. But that too was very prolix; for it is actually impossible to give a short account that is not absurd of a book whose language must first be explained to the reader. I sent this review in, even though I realized that it would be longer than the longest reviews in the Göttingen journal. I did so because in fact I didn't know how to abbreviate it myself without mangling it. I flattered myself that either the people in Göttingen would suspend the usual policy, because of the size and importance of the book, or, if the review were just too long for them, they would know better than I how to shorten it. I mailed the review from Leipzig when I returned from my journey. For a long time after I had returned to my homeland, Silesia, nothing appeared. Finally I received the issue that supposedly contained what was called my review. Your own resentment and displeasure could not have exceeded mine at the sight of it. Certain phrases of my manuscript were in fact retained; but they constituted less than a tenth of my words and less than a third of the published review.[6] I saw that my work, which had not been without difficulty, was as good as in vain and not merely in vain but pernicious. For it would have been better if the Göttingen scholar[7] had written something of his own after a cursory reading of your book; at least it would have been more coherent. To justify myself to my close friends who knew that I had worked for Göttingen, and in *this* way at least to mitigate the unfortunate impression that this review must make on everyone, I sent my manuscript (after a while I received it back from Göttingen) to Counselor Spalding in Berlin. After that, Nicolai asked me to let him publish it in his *Allgemeine deutsche Bibliothek*.[8] I agreed, on condition that one of my Berlin friends compare it to the Göttingen review to determine whether it was worth the trouble. For I am now wholly unwilling to touch the thing.

That is all I know about it.

Along with this letter I am also writing to Herr Spalding,[9] asking him to have a copy made of my manuscript, since it has not yet been printed, and have it sent to you with my letter. Then you may compare. If you are as dissatisfied with my review as with the Göttingen one, it will prove that I lack the penetration to judge so difficult and profound a book and that it was not written for a reader like me. All the same, even if you are dissatisfied with my manuscript I believe you will see yourself as owing me some respect and indulgence; with even greater confidence I hoped that you would be my friend if we came to know each other personally.

I do not want to absolve myself totally of the charge you make against the Göttingen reviewer, that he became resentful of the difficulties he had to overcome. I confess that now and then I did. For I believed that it must be possible to render more easily comprehensible (to readers not wholly unaccustomed to reflection) the truths that are supposed to bring about important reforms in philosophy. I marveled at the great strength needed to think through such a long series of extremely abstract ideas without fatigue, resentment, or distraction from the trail of the argument. I did also find instruction and nourishment for my spirit in many parts of your book, for example, even where you show that there exist certain contradictory propositions which are nevertheless capable of proof. But my opinion, perhaps mistaken, is still this: that your whole system, if it is really to become useful, must be expressed in a popular manner, and if it contains truth then it can be expressed. And I believe that the new language which reigns throughout the book, no matter how much sagacity is shown in the coherence with which its terms are connected, nevertheless often creates a deceptive appearance, making the projected reform of science itself or the divergence from the ideas of others seem greater than it really is.

10:331

10:332

You demand that your reviewer come up with a proof of just one of those contradictory propositions such that its negation is not capable of an equally good proof. This challenge must concern my Göttingen colleague, not me. I am convinced that there are limits to our knowledge, and that these limits reveal themselves just when contradictions of that sort can be developed with equal cogency out of our sensations. I think it is highly useful to learn these limits and I see it as one of the most generally useful accomplishments of your work to have analyzed these limits more distinctly and completely than has ever been done. But I do not see how your *Critique of Pure Reason* has contributed to overcoming these difficulties. At least the part of the book in which you bring these contradictions to light is incomparably clearer and more illuminating (you yourself will not deny this) than are those parts where the principles for resolving these contradictions are supposed to be established.

Since I am presently traveling and without books and have neither your book nor my review at hand, please take what I say here as fleeting thoughts not to be judged too strictly. If I have here or in my review misrepresented your meaning and purpose, it is because I have misunderstood them or because my memory is unreliable. The malicious intention to distort the thing is not mine, and I am incapable of it.

Finally I must ask you not to make any public use of this information. Notwithstanding the fact that from the first moment that I perceived the mangling of my work I felt insulted, I have nevertheless fully forgiven the man who thought it necessary to do this mangling. I forgave him partly because I am myself responsible, having authorized it, and partly because I have other reasons to feel affection and respect

10:333   for him. Still, he would have to view it as a sort of vindictiveness if I protested to you that I was not the author of the review. Many people in Berlin and Leipzig know that I wanted to do the Göttingen review, and few know that only the smallest part of it is mine, even though the dissatisfaction that you (justifiably, but somewhat harshly) express against the Göttingen reviewer throws an unfavorable light on me, in the eyes of these people, so I would rather carry this burden as a punishment for my rashness (for that is what the promise to do a job whose range and difficulty I did not fathom was) than receive a sort of public vindication that would compromise my Göttingen friend.

    I am with true respect and devotion

        Esteemed sir

            Your most obedient friend and servant,

                Garve

Leipzig

13 July, 1783

1 Christian Garve (1742–98), famous representative of so-called popular philosophy, was born in Breslau and became professor of philosophy in Leipzig in 1770. Two years later, for reasons of health, he returned to Breslau and lived there, without any official academic position, until his death. There is an excellent discussion of Garve's position and of the controversy over the Garve-Feder review of Kant's *Critique* in Frederick Beiser, *The Fate of Reason* (Cambridge, Mass., and London: Harvard University Press, 1987). See especially Beiser's chapter, "The Attack of the Lockeans."

2 *Göttlugische gelehrte Anzeigen*, Suppl. to Part 3, Jan. 19, 1782, pp. 40 h.l., ff.

3 Kant's challenge is in the Appendix to the *Prolegomena*, Ak. 4: 378–9.

4 Ibid.

5 Christian Gottlob Heyne (1729–1812), philologist, professor of rhetoric in Göttingen from 1763.

6 According to E. Arnold (cf. "Kritischen Exkursen im Gebiete der Kantforschung," *Gesammelte Schriften* IV, pp. 1–118, Berlin, 1908) as cited by Malter in Kant's *Briefwechsel* (1986 edition), p. 836, Garve is not telling the truth here; Garve's review is only three times as long as the published review, not ten times, and two-thirds of the review are his, only one-third of it Feder's.

7 I.e., Feder.

8 Garve's review did appear, but Kant (according to Hamann's letter to Herder, Dec. 8, 1783) was displeased with it and complained that he was treated like an imbecile.

9 On Spalding (1714–1804), a pastor in Berlin and friend of Garve's, see Kant's letter to Mendelssohn, Ak. [39], n. 4, above. Spalding's letter to Kant, July 20, 1783, Ak. [202], explains the delay in Kant's receiving a copy of Garve's review.

51 [205] (187)
To Christian Garve.
August 7, 1783.

Esteemed Sir,   10:336

I have long noticed in you an enlightened philosophical spirit, and I have appreciated your refined taste, the product of wide reading and worldly experience, so that I, along with Sultzer, have regretted the illness that has hampered you from rewarding the world with the total fecundity of your excellent talents. Now I experience the still greater pleasure of finding in your letter clear evidence of your fastidious and conscientious honesty and of your humane manner of thinking, which   10:337
bestows genuine value upon those intellectual gifts. This last is some-

thing I think I cannot say of your friend in Göttingen, who, entirely without cause, has filled his review (which I can call "his" since it mutilates your essay) with the breath of pure animosity.[1] There were, after all, some things in my book that should have deserved mention, even if he did not immediately approve of the explanation of the difficulties I discovered; he should have mentioned them if only for the reason that I first showed those difficulties in their proper light and in their proper context, because I reduced the problem, so to speak, to its simplest terms, even if I did not solve it. Instead, he tramples everything with a certain impetuosity, yes, I can even say with visible rage. I mention only one small example: he deliberately omits the word "Herr," which customarily prefaces the word "author" in this journal to sweeten a criticism a little bit. I can guess very well who this man is, from his style, especially when he tells us his own ideas. As a contributor to a famous journal, he has, if not the honor, at least the reputation of an author in his power for a little while. But he is at the same time himself an author and thereby jeopardizes his own reputation in no small way. But I shall speak no more of this, since you are pleased to call him your friend. Actually he ought to be my friend as well, though in a broader sense, if common interest in the same science and dedicated if misdirected effort to secure its foundations can constitute literary friendship. It seems to me though that here as elsewhere it has failed; this man must have feared to forfeit something of his own pretensions at such innovations as mine, a fear that is entirely groundless. For the issue here does not concern the limitedness of authors but the limitedness of human reason. . . .

[Kant breaks off here, apologizing for the poor paper on which he is writing.]

You can believe me, esteemed sir, and you can also make inquiries any time with my publisher, Hartknoch, at the Leipzig book fair, that I never believed any of his assurances that you were responsible for the review; and so I am highly pleased to obtain confirmation of my view, through your good letter. I am not so pampered and egotistic that criticism and reprimand – even assuming them to be directed against what I think are the most excellent merits of my work – would provoke me, if the deliberate intent to injure and to distort what is worthy of approval (which may still be found here and there) did not stare one in the face. And I await with pleasure your unmutilated review in the *Allgemeine deutsche Bibliothek*. You have presented your action to me in a most favorable light, with an uprightness and integrity of principles that characterize the true scholar and always fill me with respect, whatever your judgment may turn out to be. Furthermore, I must admit that I have not counted on an immediately favorable reception of my work. That could not be, since the expression of my ideas – ideas that

10:338

I had been working out painstakingly for 12 years in succession – was not worked out sufficiently to be generally understandable. To achieve that I would have needed a few more years instead of the four or five months I took to complete the book, out of fear that such an extensive project would finally become a burden, were I to linger any more, and that my advancing years (I am already 60) would perhaps make it impossible for me to finish the whole system that I still have in my mind. And I am now actually satisfied with my decision, as the work stands, to such an extent that I should not wish it unwritten for any price, though neither would I want to take on again for any price the long labors that it took to produce it. People will get over the initial numbness caused unavoidably by a mass of unfamiliar concepts and an even more unfamiliar language (which new language is nonetheless indispensable). In time, a number of points will become clear (perhaps my *Prolegomena* will help this). These points will shed light on other passages, to which of course a clarifying essay from me may be requisite from time to time. And thus, finally, the whole work will be surveyed and understood, if one will only get started with the job, beginning with the main question on which everything depends (a question that I have stated clearly enough), gradually examining every part with con- 10:339 certed effort. In a word, the machine is there, complete, and all that needs to be done is to smooth its parts, or to oil them so as to eliminate friction, without which, I grant, the thing will stand still. Another peculiarity of this sort of science is that one must have an idea of the whole in order to rectify all the parts, so that one has to leave the thing for a time in a certain condition of rawness, in order to achieve this eventual rectification. Had I attempted both tasks simultaneously, either my capability or my life would have proved insufficient.

You choose to mention, as a just criticism, the lack of popular appeal in my work, a criticism that can in fact be made of every philosophical writing, if it is not to conceal what is probably nonsense under a haze of apparent cleverness.* But such popularity cannot be attempted in studies of such high abstraction. If I could only succeed in getting people to go along with me for a stretch, in concepts that accord with those of the schools together with barbarisms of expression, I should

---

* In order to clear myself of the charge that my innovations of language and my impenetrable obscurity cause my readers unnecessary difficulty in grasping my ideas, let me make the following proposal. It is of the highest importance to give a deduction of the pure concepts of the understanding, the categories, that is, to show the possibility of wholly a priori concepts of things in general; for, without this deduction, pure a priori knowledge can have no certainty. Well then, I should like someone to try to do this in an easier, more popular fashion; he will then experience the great difficulties that are to be found in this field of speculation. But he will never deduce the categories from any other source than that which I have indicated, of that I am certain.

like to undertake a popular yet thorough exposition myself (though others will be better at this), for which I already have a plan. For the time being, let us be called dunces [*doctores umbratici*], if only we can make progress with the insight, with whose development the sophisticated public will of course not sympathize, at least until the work

10:340 emerges from its dark workshop and, seen with all its polish, need not be ashamed of being judged. Be so kind as to have another fleeting glance at the whole and to notice that it is not at all metaphysics that the *Critique* is doing but a whole new science, never before attempted, namely, the critique of *an a priori judging* reason. Other men have touched on this faculty, for instance, Locke and Leibnitz, but always with an admixture of other faculties of cognition. To no one has it even occurred that this faculty is the object of a formal and necessary, yes, an extremely broad, science, requiring such a manifold of divisions (without deviating from the limitation that it consider solely that uniquely pure faculty of knowing) and at the same time (something marvelous) deducing out of its own nature all the objects within its scope, enumerating them, and proving their completeness by means of their coherence in a single, complete cognitive faculty. Absolutely no other science attempts this, that is, to develop a priori out of the mere concept of a cognitive faculty (when that concept is precisely defined) all the objects, everything that can be known of them, yes, even what one is involuntarily but deceptively constrained to believe about them. Logic, which would be the science most similar to this one, is in this regard much inferior. For although it concerns the use of the understanding in general, it cannot in any way tell us to what objects it applies nor what the scope of our rational knowledge is; rather, it has to wait upon experience or something else (for example, mathematics) for the objects on which it is to be employed.

And so, my dearest sir, I beg you, if you should wish to apply yourself any further in this matter, to use your position and influence to encourage my enemies (not my personal enemies, since I am at peace with all the world), the enemies of my book, but not the *anonymous* ones, encourage them not to grab everything or anything at all at once, out of context, but to consider the work in its proper order: first, to examine or grant my theory concerning the distinction between analytic and synthetic knowledge; then, to proceed to the consideration

10:341 of the general problem, how synthetic a priori knowledge is possible, as I have clearly stated it in the *Prolegomena*; then, to examine successively my attempts to solve this problem, and so on. For I believe I can demonstrate formally that not a single truly metaphysical proposition, torn out of the whole system, can be proved except by showing its relation to the sources of all our pure rational knowledge and, therefore, that it would have to be derived from the concept of the possible system of such cognitions. But regardless of how kind and eager you may be in carrying out my request, I am reconciled to the prevailing taste of our age, which imagines difficult speculative matters to be easy (but does not make them easy), and I believe your kind efforts in this regard will be fruitless. *Garve, Mendelssohn,* and *Tetens* are the only men I know through whose cooperation this subject could have been brought to a successful conclusion before too long, even though centuries before this one have not seen it done. But these men are leery of cultivating a wasteland that, with all the care that has been lavished on it, has always remained unrewarding. Meanwhile people's efforts continue in a constant circle, returning always to the point where they started; but it is possible that materials that now lie in the dust may yet be worked up into a splendid construction.

You are kind enough to praise my presentation of the dialectical contradictions of pure reason, though you are not satisfied with the solution of these antinomies.** If my critic from Göttingen had pre- 10:342 sented only a single judgment of this sort, I should at least have assumed him to be of goodwill and would have put the blame on the (not unexpected) failure of most of my sentences to express my meaning, that is, mainly on myself, instead of allowing a certain bitterness into my reply. Or perhaps I would have made no answer at all – in any case, only a few complaints at his absolutely condemning everything without having grasped the basic points. But such an insolent tone of contempt and arrogance ran through the review that I was necessarily moved to draw this great genius into the open, if I could, in order to decide, by comparison of his work to my own, however humble the latter may be, whether there really is such a great superiority on his side or whether, perhaps, a certain literary cunning may not lie behind it, an attempt to make people praise whatever agrees with him and condemn whatever opposes. Thus he achieves somewhat of a dominion

---

** The key is already provided, though its initial use is unfamiliar and therefore difficult. It consists in this: that all objects that are given to us can be interpreted in two ways [*nach zweierlei Begriffen nehmen kann*] on the *one hand*, as appearances, *on the other hand*, as things in themselves. If one takes appearances to be things in themselves and demands of those [*als von solchen*] [appearances] the *absolutely unconditioned* in the series of conditions, one gets into nothing but contradictions. These contradictions, however, fall away when one shows that there cannot be anything wholly unconditioned among appearances; such a thing could exist among things in themselves. On the other hand, if one takes a *thing in itself* (which can contain the condition of something in the world) *to be an appearance*, one creates contradictions where none are necessary, for example, in the matter of freedom, and this contradiction falls away as soon as attention is paid to the variable meaning that objects can have.

over all the authors on a given subject (who, if they want to be well thought of, will be compelled to scatter incense and extol the writings of their presumed critic as their guide), and without extravagant effort, he manages to make a name for himself. Judge from this whether I have argued my "dissatisfaction" with the Göttingen critic, as you are pleased to call it, *"somewhat harshly."*

After your kind explanation of this matter, according to which the actual reviewer must remain incognito, my expectation concerning a challenge comes to nothing, for he would have to submit himself to it voluntarily, that is, reveal himself; but even in that case, I would be bound *not to make the slightest public use* of the information you have given me as to the true course of the affair. Besides, a bitter intellectual quarrel is so repugnant, and the frame of mind one has to assume in order to carry it on is so unnatural to me, that I would rather assume the most extensive labors in explaining and justifying what I have already written against the sharpest opponents (but against those who base their attacks only on reasons) than to activate and nourish a feeling in myself for which my soul would otherwise never have room. If the reviewer in Göttingen should feel it necessary to answer the statement I made in the journal – if he should do this without compromising his person – then I would feel called upon (though without prejudice to my obligation to you) to take appropriate measures to remove this burdensome inequity between an invisible assailant and one who defends himself before the eyes of all the world. A middle course is still open, namely, to reveal himself if not publicly then at least to me in writing (for the reasons I indicated in the *Prolegomena*) and to announce and settle publicly but peacefully the point of the controversy as he picks it out. But here one would like to exclaim: O cares of men! [*O curas hominum!*] Weak men, you pretend that you are only concerned with truth and the spread of knowledge, whereas in fact it is only your vanity that occupies you!

And so, esteemed sir, let this occasion not be the only one for pursuing our acquaintance, which I so much desire. The sort of character you reveal in your letter (not to mention your excellent talents) is not so abundant in our literary world that a man who values purity of heart, gentleness, and compassion as greater than all science can help but feel a lively desire for closer ties with one who combines in himself these virtues. Any advice, any suggestion, from such an insightful, fine man, will always be treasured by me; and if there is ever any way in which I can reciprocate this favor, the pleasure will be doubled. I am, with true respect and devotion, esteemed sir,

Your most obedient servant,
I. Kant

1 J. G. H. Feder (see Garve's letter to Kant, Ak.[201] above). The Garve-Feder review appeared in the *Zugaben zu den Göttinger gelehrten Anzeigen*, Jan. 19, 1782. As is well known, Kant wrote his *Prolegomena to Any Future Metaphysics* partly in answer to the review (see the appendix to that work). Feder attempted to justify his actions in a letter to Garve of May 7, 1782, on the grounds that abbreviation was necessary and that "certain changes will be of help to some of the readers." Garve's review, as originally written, appeared in the *Allgemeine deutsche Bibliothek*, suppl. to vols. XXXVII – LII, pt. II, pp. 838–62. But according to Hamann's letter to Herder, Dec. 8, 1783, "Kant is not satisfied with it and complains of being treated like an imbecile. He won't answer it; but he will answer the Göttingen reviewer, if the latter dares to review the *Prolegomena* as well." To Johann Schultz, Kant wrote on Aug. 22, 1783, Ak.[209], "I have only been able to skim it, because of various distracting tasks; but leaving aside the many scarcely avoidable errors in getting my meaning, it seems to be something quite different and much more thought out than what was in the Göttingen *Anzeige* (which was supposed to be Garve's)." A recent English translation of the review, along with Garve's original version, may be found in James C. Morrison's edition and translation of Schultz's *Exposition of Kant's Critique of Pure Reason* (Ottawa, Canada: University of Ottawa Press, 1995).

52 [206] (188)
To Moses Mendelssohn.
August 16, 1783

Esteemed Sir,

Certainly there could be no more effective recommendation for the hopeful young son of Herr Gentz[1] than one from a man whose talents and character I treasure and love so greatly. I am delighted to see that you anticipate my feelings and count on them without my having to assure you of them. And I can now assure the worthy father of this young man whom I have come to know very well that he will come home from our university with heart and mind cultivated in just the way he had hoped. I delayed responding to your kind letter until I could give you this guarantee.

Rumors about my trip to the baths, which you were kind enough to mention in such a way that my mind was filled with pleasant images of much more attractive surroundings than I can ever hope to have here, have also been bandied about locally without my ever having given the least incentive to such conjecture. There is a certain medical principle that I discovered long ago in some English writer whom I can't recall and which I have long adopted as the foundation of my diathetic: *Every human being has his own particular way of preserving his health, which he must not alter if he values his safety.* Although I have had to battle against constant indispositions in following this principle, I have never actually been sick. Furthermore, I find that one lives longest if one eschews struggling to lengthen one's life but strives carefully not to shorten it by disturbing the benign nature within us.

That you feel yourself dead to metaphysics does not offend me, since virtually the entire learned world seems to be dead to her, and of course, there is the matter of your nervous indisposition (of which, by the way, there is not the slightest sign in your book, *Jerusalem*).[2] I do regret that your penetrating mind, alienated from metaphysics, cannot be drawn to the *Critique*, which is concerned with investigating the 10:345 foundations of that structure. However, though I regret this, and regret that the *Critique* repels you, I am not offended by this. For although the book is the product of nearly twelve years of reflection, I completed it hastily, in perhaps four or five months, with the greatest attentiveness to its content but less care about its style and ease of comprehension. Even now I think my decision was correct, for otherwise, if I had delayed further in order to make the book more popular, it would probably have remained unfinished. As it is, the weaknesses can be remedied little by little, once the work is there in rough form. For I am now too old to devote uninterrupted effort both to completing a work and also to the rounding, smoothing, and lubricating of each of its parts. I certainly would have been able to clarify every difficult point; but I was constantly worried that a more detailed presentation would detract both from the clarity and continuity of the work. Therefore I abstained, intending to take care of this in a later discussion, after my statements, as I hoped, would gradually have become understood. For an author who has projected himself into a system and become comfortable with its concepts cannot always guess what might be obscure or indefinite or inadequately demonstrated to the reader. Few men are so fortunate as to be able to think for themselves and at the same time be able to put themselves into someone else's position and adjust their style exactly to his requirements. There is only one Mendelssohn.

But I wish I could persuade you, dear sir (granted that you do not want to bother yourself further with the book you have laid aside), to use your position and influence in whatever way you think best to encourage an examination of my theses, considering them in the following order: One would first inquire whether the distinction between analytic and synthetic judgments is correct; whether the difficulties concerning the possibility of synthetic judgments, when these are supposed to be made a priori, are as I describe them; and whether the completing of a deduction of synthetic a priori cognitions, without which all metaphysics is impossible, is as necessary as I maintain it to be. Second, one would investigate whether it is true, as I asserted, that we are incapable of making synthetic a priori judgments concerning anything but the formal condition of a possible (outer or inner) experience in general, that is, in regard to both its sensuous intuition and the concepts of the understanding, both of which are presupposed by experience and are what first of all make it possible. Third, one would inquire whether the conclusion I draw is also correct: that the a priori knowledge of which we are capable extends no farther than to objects of a possible experience, with the proviso that this field of possible experience does not encompass all things in themselves; consequently, that there are other objects in addition to objects of possible experience – indeed, they are necessarily presupposed, though it is impossible for us to know the slightest thing about them. If we were to get this far in our investigations, the solution[3] to the difficulties in which reason entangles itself when it strives to transcend entirely the bounds of possible experience would make itself clear, as would the even more important solution to the question why it is that reason is driven to transcend its proper sphere of activity. In short, the Dialectic of Pure Reason would create few difficulties any more. From there on, the critical philosophy would gain acceptability and become a promenade through a labyrinth, but with a reliable guidebook to help us find our way out as often as we get lost. I would gladly help these investigations in whatever way I can, for I am certain that something substantial would emerge, if only the trial is made by competent minds. But I am not optimistic about this. Mendelssohn, Garve, and Tetens have apparently declined to occupy themselves with this sort of business, and where else can anyone of sufficient talent and good will be found? I must therefore content myself with the thought that a work like this is, as Swift says, a plant that only blossoms when its stem is put into the soil. Meanwhile, I still hope to work out, eventually, a textbook for metaphysics, according to the critical principles I mentioned; it will have all the brevity of a handbook and be useful for academic lectures. I hope to finish it sometime or other, perhaps in the distant future. This winter I shall have the first part of my [book on] moral [philosophy] substantially completed.[4] This work is more adapted to popular tastes, though it seems to me far less of a stimulus to broadening people's minds than my other work is, since the latter tries to define the limits and the total content of the whole of human reason. But moral philosophy, especially when it tries to complete itself by stepping

10:346

10:347

over into religion without adequate preparation and definition of the critical sort, entangles itself unavoidably either in objections and misgivings or in folly and fanaticism.

Herr Friedländer[5] will tell you how much I admired the penetration, subtlety, and wisdom of your *Jerusalem*. I regard this book as the proclamation of a great reform that is slowly impending, a reform that is in store not only for your own people but for other nations as well. You have managed to unite with your religion a degree of freedom of conscience that one would hardly have thought possible and of which no other religion can boast. You have at the same time thoroughly and clearly shown it necessary that every religion have unrestricted freedom of conscience, so that finally even the Church will have to consider how to rid itself of everything that burdens and oppresses conscience, and mankind will finally be united with regard to the essential point of religion. For all religious propositions that burden our conscience are based on history, that is, on making salvation contingent on belief in the truth of those historical propositions. But I am abusing your patience and your eyes, and shall add nothing further except to say that news of your welfare and contentment cannot be more welcome than to your

most devoted servant,
I. Kant

---

1 See n. 1 of Mendelssohn's letter to Kant, Ak.[190], above.

2 Mendelssohn, *Jerusalem oder über religiöse Macht und Judentum* (Berlin, 1783).

3 Ernst Cassirer inserts "of the Antinomies" after "solution" (*Auflösung*).

4 Possibly the *Grundlegung*, which appeared in Apr. 1785.

5 David Friedländer (1750–1834), friend of Herz and Mendelssohn, a merchant in Königsberg who later became a banker and city councillor in Berlin.

53 [208] (190)
From Johann Schultz.
August 21, 1783.

10:348   Since the last two weeks of vacation finally gave me the long awaited spare time to think my way through your *Critique*, dear sir, I wanted without further delay to make the public not only aware of your book but also informed in a comprehensible fashion about its purpose and content. With works of highly abstract content it is only too easy to misunderstand the author. It would therefore be no slight gain for the sciences if every reviewer, before he allowed his review to be published, would ask the author who is the best expositor of his own words whether his true meaning has been correctly captured. In that way neither would the author be imposed upon nor would the public be deceived. Now there are sometimes a number of circumstances that make this impossible. But since in the present instance it is possible, I did not want to let my review become known until I was first assured by you, dear sir, that I have adequately expressed your thoughts. As soon as I know this I shall send along my own humble judgment of this so treasurable book and, since my concern is only with truth, I shall submit it to you first for your scrutiny. I beg you most respectfully to indicate on a separate slip of paper the places where I may not have grasped your meaning, and I beg you to add just briefly your true   10:349 opinion, so that I can improve my manuscript accordingly. Because of lack of time I have had to leave out what little needs to be added concerning the moral theology which crowns your book; but I shall write it as soon as I can. With greatest respect I remain.

Your most devoted servant

J. Schultz.

Königsberg, the 21st of August, 1783

P.S. May I ask you to be kind enough to clarify the following: In the four classes of categories, might not every third category be derived from the first two, in the following way:

totality is a plurality in which no unity is lacking or denied;

limitation is a reality containing negations;

community is that relation of substances in which each is at once cause and effect with respect to the others;

necessity is the impossibility of non-existence.

I do not have the time just now to add more questions.[1]

---

1 For Kant's response to Schultz's question, see his letters Ak.[210] and Ak.[221] below. Kant also speaks to the question in § 39 of the *Prolegomena* and in the second edition of the *Critique*, B 109–13.

54 [209] (191)
To Johann Schultz.
August 22, 1783.

I have the honor, dear sir, of transmitting for your evaluation the Garve review[1] forwarded to me yesterday by Herr *Oberconsistorialrat* Spalding.[2] I have only been able to skim it quickly, there being various other distracting tasks lying in the way; however, despite his frequently mistaking my meaning, which is hardly avoidable, I found the review quite different and far more thought through than what is contained in the *Göttinger Anzeige* (which was supposed to be by him).

Since you, as is your custom, esteemed sir, have honored this matter with your thorough analysis and, as Herr Jenisch[3] informs me, have already prepared a draft of the result of your judgment, I view this cooperation of yours as so important that I wish you would postpone the completion of your work a bit in order, if possible, to provide the metaphysically inclined public with a hint of how to begin their investigation of it and in what order to proceed; I wish you would call their attention at first only to the essential points in order that they see how the limits of all our insight in this field may be securely determined. For only in this way, with the collaboration of such men as you (who are certainly rare) can we hope for success in science, however much or little may remain of my efforts.

I shall take the liberty of making a few little proposals for your consideration, dear sir, suggesting how such investigations might be abbreviated, namely, by first introducing certain general problems which can be described without going into the way I have tried to solve them. If your work could be published as an independent piece, so as not to be buried among the mass of reviews of other sorts, this would serve our purpose much more effectively. But all this is left to your mature discretion and to your judgment as to the importance or unimportance of this business, as well as whether it is compatible with the time you can devote to it. I remain, most respectfully

your obedient servant

I. Kant

10:350

---

1 The reference is to Garve's original review, published in the *Allgemeine deutsche Bibliothek*, Appendix to Vols. 37–52, 2nd Div., 1783, pp. 838–62. On this, see the biographical sketch of Garve. A translation of this review as well as of the

Göttingen Garve-Feder review and one by S. H. Ewald, published in the *Gothaische gelehrte Zeitungen*, Aug. 1782, may be found in the appendices to James C. Morrison's translation of Schultz's *Exposition of Kant's Critique of Pure Reason* (University of Ottawa Press, 1995).

2 Johann Joachim Spalding (1714–1804), preacher at the Nikolai Kirche in Berlin. The title *Oberconsistorialrat*, abbreviated by Kant as "O.C.R.," signifies an ecclesiastical administrative position.

3 Daniel Jenisch (1762–1804), friend of Schultz and Hamann, later also a preacher at the Nikolai Kirche in Berlin. Depression led him to suicide by drowning in the Spree River. Schiller regarded him as a fool who poked his nose into everything. There are quite a few allusions to him, mainly unflattering, in various Kant letters – Kiesewetter, for example, writing to Kant, Nov. 15, 1799, Ak. [848], refers to Jenisch's "Diogenes' Laterne" (Leipzig, 1799) and its clever but apocryphal anecdotes about Kant. See the biographical sketch of Jenisch.

55 [210] (192)
To Johann Schultz.
August 26, 1783.

It gives me extraordinary pleasure to see a person of your penetrating intelligence, sir, applying himself to my work, but above all to see how correct is your grasp of the totality of my thoughts, how everywhere you sift out the most important and most useful points and precisely capture my meaning. It offers me great consolation for the pain I feel at being almost universally misunderstood and it relieves me of the fear that I may have too little, or perhaps may lack altogether, the gift of making myself comprehensible in such a difficult subject; I feel relieved of the fear that all my labor may have been in vain. Now, a most discerning man has turned up who furnishes proof that I can indeed be understood and at the same time offers an example to show that my writings are not unworthy of being thought through so as to be understood and only then to be judged as to their merit or lack of merit. I hope that this will have the effect I desire and bring new life and decisive results to the long-neglected project of metaphysics. 10:351

I can see from the postscript to your esteemed letter (as well as from other things you say) how deeply and correctly you have entered into the spirit of the project.[1] You suggest that each third category might well be derived from the preceding two – an entirely correct opinion and one at which you arrived all by yourself, for my own statement of this property of the categories (*Prolegomena* § 39, Remark 1) could easily be overlooked.[2] This and other properties of the table of categories that I mentioned seem to me to contain the material for a possibly significant invention, one that I am however unable to pursue and that will require a mathematical mind like yours, the construction of an *ars characteristica combinatoria*.[3] If such a thing is at all possible, it would have to begin principally with the same elementary concepts. And since the conditions of a priori sensibility are entirely distinct from these concepts (sensation in general, empirically undetermined, would have to be added as their material), the former conditions would take on an entirely different character from the latter. Rules would be possible that would make it perspicuous how objects of sensibility (in so far as they are regarded as objects of experience) can have a category as predicate, but also vice versa: it would be clear that categories in themselves can contain no spatial or temporal determinations unless a condition is added to them that enables them to be related to sensible objects. I have touched on similar points already in my dissertation "On the Sensible World," in the section entitled "De methodo circa sensibilia et intellectualia." Perhaps your penetrating mind, supported by mathematics, will find a clearer prospect here where I have only been able to make out something hovering vaguely before me, obscured by fog, as it were.

10:352   I shall also be pleased to return the excellent essay[4] you sent me, for I have almost nothing to suggest in the way of changes as far as the correct representation of my meaning is concerned. However, I have another idea that might not be displeasing to you to pursue and that moves me to ask to keep the essay a few more days. Your essay could be published as a review in one of the journals such as the *Deutsche Bibliothek* just as it stands, or with whatever additions you may find agreeable; if presented as a review, no one could demand that a reader understand it adequately without consulting the book. But then the attention it would receive from the public is limited and slow in coming.

On the other hand, if the essay were to be fashioned into a self-sufficient work (and I think this is a better idea), then it seems to me that there are a few places in it, for example on the Dialectic, where certain little insertions are needed in order to make it easier for the reader to understand and to prevent misinterpretation, as you have thus far so excellently endeavored to do. I would like to take the liberty of sending you, in a few days, some such insertions to use at your discretion. I would have done this already but for the current atmospheric conditions which I think are having a troublesome influence on my body as well as on my power of concentration, making me disinclined and unfit for all intellectual work. If however you should prefer to pursue another plan, I shall return the essay to you forthwith. I remain with greatest respect,

Your most obedient servant,

I. Kant.

Königsberg, the 26th of August, 1783.

---

1 See the postscript to Schultz's letter of Aug. 21, 1783, Ak. [208].

2 Kant also added this remark to the second edition of the *Critique*, B 110 f.

3 The "Art of Combination" to which Kant alludes was proposed by Leibniz. In his *Dissertation de arte combinatoria* (1666) Leibniz suggested a sort of universal algebra that would exhibit the relations among simple ideas. The basic claim was that all complex ideas are compounded from a certain number of simple or primitive ideas and that, by constructing an ideal language, the properly selected name of a complex idea would show immediately what its constituent simple ideas were, i.e., the analysis of a complex idea could be seen at a glance. Since all the possible combinations of simple ideas would be exhibited by this method, the combinatory art would provide a table of all the possibilities in the world.

4 Kant must mean the manuscript of Schultz's *Erläuterungen über des Herrn Professor Kant Critik der reinen Vernunft*, published the following year (Königsberg, 1784).

56 [211] (193)
From Johann Schultz.

August 28, 1783.

You will be kind enough to forgive me, dear sir, for failing to answer your two most excellent letters right away, but business and other distractions kept me from doing so. Thank you for sending me the Garve review.[1] I was very eager to see it and it was pleasant to have my desire satisfied sooner than I expected. The review is far better than 10:353 that wretched Göttingen review[2] and shows in fact that Herr Garve has thought his way through your *Critique* with considerable care. Nonetheless, it is so inadequate to your great book that, on the whole, it still casts an unfavorable shadow on it. It seems therefore that my modest essay[3] is not made superfluous by Garve's, all the more so since you are kind enough to assure me that I have been so fortunate as to grasp your meaning almost everywhere. I may therefore hope to realize my goal and make the public aware of the true purpose and meaning of your excellent work, in a way that does not cost it too much exertion – something that our philosophers nowadays seem almost to fear. This has made me resolve to follow your suggestion and publish my treatise not as a review but as an independent book. In this way I need not worry so much about the length and can thus make the announcement of the contents somewhat more complete, not confining myself to the doctrine of the schematism, the concepts of reflection, and the necessary proofs for the principles of the pure understanding, the paralogisms, and the antinomies of pure reason. Now I can also discuss the Dialectic somewhat more clearly and fully. With regard to the latter, I look forward to your promised clarification of what still needs to be inserted, which I know in advance will greatly facilitate my work. With equal pleasure I await your promised suggestions as to how the investigation of the whole subject can be presented most convincingly and what general problems might be introduced at the outset before presenting your own way of solving them. For even though I had already drawn up a rough plan to disclose, prior to making any evaluation, the main points on which everything depends if the boundary of our metaphysical insight is to be securely presented, I am sure that my plan will be greatly improved, perhaps even set in a completely different direction, by your broader vision. I really did overlook the place in your 10:354 *Prolegomena*,[4] which shows me once more how not even the smallest particular of your system has eluded your acute mind. Since I see from this that you actually do recognize every third category to be a concept derivable from the preceding two, it seems to me that the idea I had in mind when I raised this question is quite correct: the third category in each group should be eliminated, and the total number reduced by one-third, since I take "category" to mean simply a basic concept that is not derived from any prior concept.

The ingenious idea of using the table of categories to invent an *artis characteristica combinatoria*, which you were kind enough to suggest to me,[5] is most excellent and I agree completely that if such an invention were possible at all it would have to be done in this way. But except for you, I know of no man with sufficient creative genius to carry out such a project.

I return herewith the Garve review with all due thanks. If you should have the kindness to lend it to me again for a short while, I would be very grateful. I commend myself to your kindness and friendship and have the honor of remaining, with greatest respect,

Your most obedient servant,

J. Schultz

Königsberg, the 28th of August, 1783.

1 As indicated in the Garve-Kant letters above, Garve's review of the *Critique*, not the version of it that Feder edited, appeared originally in the *Allgemeine deutsche Bibliothek*, appendix to vols. 37–52, 2nd div., 1783, pp. 838–62.

2 That is, the version of the review of the *Critique* written by Garve but altered by Feder, published originally in the Supplement (*Zugaben*) to the *Göttinger Anzeigen von gelehrten Sachen*, Stück 3, pp. 40–48, Jan. 19, 1782.

3 Schultz's *Erläuterungen über des Herrn Professor Kant Critik der reinen Vernunft* (Königsberg, 1784).

4 See Kant's letter of Aug. 26, 1783, Ak. [210], above.

5 In the letter just cited.

1784

57 [218] (199a)
To Friedrich Victor Leberecht Plessing.[1]
February 3, 1784.

10:363   Dear Sir,

I have the honor of sending you herewith the receipts for the business matters that I have transacted, together with the letters from Herr Hamann and Herr Brahl.[2] I would have responded sooner if these letters had been delivered to me earlier; they arrived only the day before yesterday. I wanted to advise you, concerning the monies to be transferred, of course with great fastidiousness, by Herr John,[3] that all care should be taken in the future to see that these monies are also paid out very punctually and correctly from this end.

Sincerest thanks for your *Osiris*.[4] For reasons already largely anticipated by Herr Meiners,[5] I cannot agree with your judgment concerning the great wisdom and insight of the ancient Egyptians, but I am more inclined to share your ingenious conjecture that Socrates intended nothing less than a political revolution with his attempted transformation of religion. There is much that is new and well thought out in this

10:364   book, but I think that a certain diffuseness and repetitiousness (caused, it seems, by a lack of appropriate prior planning), making the book bloated and more expensive, might work to its disadvantage and to that of your publisher. But I leave this to your judgment of the reading public's taste.

I cannot guess the source from which mysticism[a] and ignorance[b] again threaten to break out; it must be certain lodges[6] but the danger there seems to me not especially great. However, I fail too to understand what danger is supposed to lie in our openly discussing the

---

[a] *Schwärmerei*   [b] *Unwissenheit*

matter and I hope you will be kind enough to share your thoughts with me when you can. I wish you good luck in the very insecure academic career on which you want to embark. If it should happen that you know any young men whose travels you direct, that would unquestionably be a preferable proposal.[7] Sincere but, to be sure, powerless good wishes accompany you in your undertakings from

your devoted servant

I. Kant

---

1   Friedrich Victor Leberecht Plessing (1749–1808), a student of Kant's, has been immortalized by Goethe. Reclusive, neurotic, troubled, he provided the inspiration for Goethe's *Harzreise im Winter* and thus, indirectly, for Johannes Brahms' *Alto Rhapsody*, which utilizes some of Goethe's text, descriptive of the despairing Plessing whom Goethe encountered and sought to restore to human society.

Kant's efforts on Plessing's behalf are shown in his humane assistance with Plessing's child support payments (see letters Ak. [226] and Ak. [228]) and, earlier in Plessing's career, in Kant's petition to the Philosophical Faculty to suspend certain rules in connection with Plessing's degree requirements. Kant described him, in a letter to the university rector, as "well-mannered, industrious and clever" ("wohlgesitteten, fleißigen und geschickten Mann").

Earlier, in 1777, Goethe had described him, after their meeting in the Harz mountains, in rather different terms: "He never took any notice of the outer world but, through manifold reading, he has educated himself; yet all his energy and interest are directed inwardly and, since he has found no creative talent in the depths of his life, he has virtually condemned himself to destruction."

Plessing came to Königsberg in 1779 after studying in various universities. He concentrated on ancient history and philosophy. In 1788, Plessing became professor of philosophy in Duisberg, where Goethe visited him again in 1792.

2   Johann Brahl (1754–1812), originally a needle maker, educated himself to become editor of Hartung's newspaper and, later on, municipal revenue officer in Königsberg. He was an acquaintance and frequent dinner guest of Kant's, a poet, and an ardent champion of truth in public life.

3   Georg Friedrich John, *Kammersekretär* in Königsberg, also an active writer, arranged for Plessing's payment of 6 thalers a year to a woman with whom Plessing had had a liaison. See Plessing to Kant, Ak. [198], Ak. 10:323.

4   *Osiris und Sokrates* (Berlin, 1783). Cf. Ak. 10: 311, f.

5   Christoph Meiners (1747–1812), professor of philosophy in Göttingen, *Geschichte des Ursprungs, Fortgangs und Verfalls der Wissenschaften in Griechen und Rom* (History of the origin, development and decline of the sciences in Greece and Rome), 2 vols. (Lemgo, 1781/82). His judgment was that "none of the nations of Asia or Africa, whose venerable and enlightened character is so highly praised, possessed scientific knowledge; neither philosophy nor any of

the other sciences was brought to Greece from any of the barbaric peoples who lived in these parts of the world" (I, 377, quoted Ak. 13: 130). Meiners stresses the great differences between Greek and Egyptian art, maintaining also that Egyptian monuments show no trace of the "simplicity, order, and beauty" of Greek columns.

6   A note in Ak. 13:131 conjectures that Kant is referring to the Berlin lodge *Zum Roten Löwen* which, under the leadership of Johann Christoph Wöllner, became the main seat of the Rosicrucian Order in Germany. Wöllner, officially an orthodox Lutheran theologian, accepted the secret teachings of the Rosicrucians concerning magic, alchemy, and communion with spirits, as did Bischoffswerder who initiated the crown prince, Friedrich Wilhelm, into the order in 1782. On Wöllner's character and his role in Kant's censorship problems, see n.4 to Kiesewetter's letter to Kant of Apr. 20, 1790, Ak.[420].

7   A "preferable proposal" for what? Possibly Kant means for transmitting the child support payments, or perhaps a preferable way of sending news.

58 [221] (202)
To Johann Schultz.
February 17, 1784.

It gives me special pleasure to learn from Herr Dengel that your thorough and at the same time popular treatment of the *Critique* is ready for publication. I had intended to put at your disposal certain suggestions that might help to prevent misunderstanding and make my book easier to grasp; but external and internal distractions, among them my usual indisposition, have interrupted this plan several times. And now I am glad that none of those things has had any influence on your work, which is so much the more uniform and hence original in the presentation of your ideas, ideas which you formed by yourself in thinking through the entire work.

10:366

Allow me just one observation, dear sir, which I intended to communicate to you in answer to your note of August 22[1] last year but which only now occurred to me again as I read through your manuscript. I beg you to consider this question more closely in order that a possible major divergence in our views of one of the basic parts of the system may be avoided. This observation concerns the thought you expressed at that time, dear sir, *that there might well be only two categories in each class*, since the third category arises out of the union of the first with the second [in each group]. You came to this insight by means of your own acute thinking. However, it does not, in my opinion, have the consequence that you draw from it; and thus your suggested change in the system is not required. (It would rob the system of an otherwise very uniform, systematic character.)

For although the third category does certainly arise out of a uniting of the first and second, it does not arise out of their mere conjunction but rather out of a *connection whose possibility itself constitutes a concept*, and this concept is a particular category. Therefore the third category is sometimes not applicable when the first two are valid. For example, *one year*, *many years* in future time – these are real concepts; but the *totality* of future years, the collective unity of a future eternity, which is   10:367 to be thought as a whole (completed, as it were) cannot be conceived. And even when the third category is applicable, it always contains something more than the first and second alone or taken together, viz., the *derivation* of the second from the first (and this is not always possible); for example, necessity is nothing else than existence *insofar as* it could be inferred from possibility; community is the reciprocal *causality* of *substances* with respect to their determinations. But the fact that determinations of one substance can be produced by another substance is an idea that one cannot absolutely presuppose; rather, the idea is one of the syntheses without which no reciprocal relation of objects in space, and consequently no outer experience, would be possible. In short, I find that just as a syllogism shows in its conclusion something more than the operations of the understanding and judgment required by the premises, viz., *a further particular operation belonging specifically to reason*, so, too, the third category is a particular, to some extent original, concept. (In a syllogism a general rule is stated by the major premise whereas the minor premise ascends from the particular to the universal condition of the rule; the conclusion descends from the universal to the particular, that is, it says that what was asserted to stand under a universal condition in the major premise is also to be asserted of that which stands under the same condition in the minor premise.) For example, the concepts of *quantum, compositum, and totum* belong under the categories of unity, plurality, and totality; but a *quantum*, thought as a *compositum*, would not yet yield the concept of a *totality*, except insofar as the concept of the *quantum* is thought as *determinable* by composition, which is not the case of every *quantum* – for example, infinite space.[2]

I hope, dear sir, that you will find this remark correct and that you will think the issue of whether the system of categories needs to be modified an issue important enough to warrant your attention before your manuscript is printed. For nothing could please our opponents more than to detect dissension over fundamental principles.

But why do I dwell on these things when perhaps you have long ago abandoned this passing thought on the basis of your own reflection   10:368

and are besides completely free, here as elsewhere, to do as you wish. I have no doubts that your book, as also your ingenious theory of parallel lines,[3] will broaden and extend human knowledge and contribute to your deserved fame. With full respect I am
Your most obedient servant,
I. Kant

P.S. Since I now anticipate reading your work in print, I have the honor of returning with my most devoted thanks the pages you sent to me.

---

1 See the footnote to Schultz's letter, Aug. 21, 1783, Ak. [208], above.
2 I.e., the totality of infinite space cannot be thought as determined by the composition of particular regions or *quanta* of space.
3 *Entdekte Theorie der Parallelen nebst einer Untersuchung über den Ursprung ihrer bisherigen Schwierigkeit* (Königsberg, 1784).

59 [226] (207)
From Friedrich Victor Leberecht Plessing.[1]
March 15, 1784.

Since there is mail leaving for West Prussia I shall send along this note to you, to express my eternal esteem for you and to assure you that I think of you always with the deepest feelings of which my soul is capable. I have been very ill this winter and am still suffering from eye trouble that makes me utterly unfit for work. But now I hope to get better. Because my father happens to be sending letters to Graudenz today, I am writing these few words to thank you for your kindness in carrying out my request, as your letter of February 3 informed me.[2] Trusting in the very noble sentiments I know you to have, I am taking the liberty again of sending three thalers to that same woman, with my most humble request that you deliver them to Herr John[3] so as to take care of the quarterly compensation. This money is coming via Graundenz. I think that Herr John can be trusted always to pay the money correctly, but I don't know whether he gets a receipt from that person or not. He has not written me for a year and a day. If I knew some other way to arrange it, I would not bother him with this chore.

From Friedrich Victor Leberecht Plessing. March 15, 1784

As far as I am able and as far as the nature of the case permits, I shall answer your question as to what I meant in saying that fanaticism and superstition are now again threatening us with great restrictions on freedom of thought, indeed, something even worse, and all men of integrity who love humanity are trembling. You have guessed one of the directions from which danger threatens, only you do not picture the magnitude of it. Particularly Jesuits, those enemies of reason and 10:372 human happiness, are now carrying on their work in every possible manner. Their organization is more powerful than ever, and they infiltrate *M–r–n* [*Freimauren*, i.e., Freemasons], Catholics, and Protestants. A certain Protestant king is himself supposed to be secretly a J–s–t. These hellish spirits have poisoned the hearts of princes and lords. They are responsible for the pretended toleration the Catholics are evincing, whereby they hope finally to convert the Protestants to Catholicism. Exorcism and similar fanatical nonsense, also alchemy and the like, are things in which the most distinguished people believe. I myself have heard sophisticated people in Berlin talking this way. Also, a former associate of Schröpfer's [*sic*][4] is staying with an important person in Potsdam or Berlin. The Emperor's edict of toleration[5] is of little consequence, and Belial carries on his game even there.

Just as mankind has always raged against its own welfare, against reason and enlightenment, so, too, it is happening now. The Protestants are trying to combat the Enlightenment (they call it atheism and the work of the devil) by forming societies: one of them has spread its branches through Switzerland, Holland, Germany, and Prussia – even Königsberg. Here, in this locality where sound reason is completely contraband, where the inhabitants are nothing but Abderites,[6] there is also a lodge of this society (Urlsperger[7] of Augsburg is the founder, and in Berlin the members whom one may mention publicly include Silberschlag and Apitsch).[8] The Jesuits are behind these societies too, trying to nip reason in the bud as much as they can and to plant the seed of ignorance. How great our king seems to me! And how grateful to him must human reason be! If only he could live another 20 years.[9] It seems that despotism, fanaticism, and superstition are trying to conquer all of Europe. Catholicism and Jesuitism are reaching even England, Denmark, and Sweden. England will soon be overcome.

Forgive me for expressing all these thoughts so crudely. I cannot write more coherently at present. . . .

Plessing

---

1 On Plessing, see his letter to Kant, Ak.[218], n. 1, and the biographical sketches.

2   Kant acted as intermediary in transmitting money from Plessing to a woman whose child Plessing was accused of fathering. See Plessing's letter of Apr. 3, 1784, Ak. [228], for Plessing's dispute over his paternity and, indirectly, for Kant's views on birth control.

3   George Friedrich John (1742–1800), author and financial officer.

4   Johann Georg Schrepfer (1739–74), a leading apostle of Rosicrucianism, also a café proprietor in Leipzig. He was influential in the highest government circles, for example, with Bischoffswerder, a favorite of Friedrich Wilhelm II 's.

5   Joseph II of Austria (1741–90) issued his toleration edict in 1781.

6   The inhabitants of Abdera were considered proverbially stupid by the ancient Greeks, though Protagoras and Democritus also lived in this Thracian town.

7   Johann August Urlsperger (1728–1806). The society was the Deutsche Christentums Gesellschaft zur Beforderung reiner Lehre und wahrer Gottseligkeit (German Christian society for the advancement of pure doctrine and true piety).

8   Johann Esaias Silberschlag (1721–91), *Oberkonsistorialrat*, director of the Realschul, and preacher in Berlin; Apitsch was a merchant there.

9   Frederick the Great died in 1786.

60 [228] (209)

From Friedrich Victor Leberecht Plessing.

April 3, 1784.

Dear Sir,
Esteemed Sir,

My heartfelt thanks for the trouble and the care that you have until now always taken on my behalf. I shall never cease to acknowledge my indebtedness for it. The thought of you will be with me always.

I want to answer your letter immediately.[1] You are a just man and have an ardent feeling for the duties of humanity, and therefore your displeasure is aroused against a certain unnamed man, because you believe that he has not adequately done his duty toward a certain woman. Any vivid feeling tends, at some moments, to displace all our other feelings: let us now consider the conduct of that unnamed man more closely, so that perhaps those feelings for him that have been silenced in you for some time might be reawakened. For that man also deserves justice, and a man with your heart will not deny it to him.

10:375

First of all, I must assure you, *on my honor and conscience*, that the unnamed one used not the slightest artifice to seduce the person in question. He used neither persuasion nor protestations of love. The woman in question was subdued by the momentary feeling of a merely animal impulse; the unnamed one encountered no resistance. As little as I excuse the unnamed one for sinking into this weakness, he is nevertheless innocent of the offense of leading virtue astray, and he is innocent of this both in the present case and throughout his life. I can swear on the soul of the unnamed one that, had he found even the slightest sign of resistance, which might have betrayed a noble sense of virtue, he would have honored that sentiment. There is still another assurance I can give you in the name of the unnamed one: of the young people of today, he is one who least deserves the charge of leading a dissolute life devoted to the satisfaction of animal instincts in the love of the opposite sex. He could rather be blamed for having been excessive in his nobler metaphysical love, in the most unhappy way, thereby having lost virtually the total health of his body and soul. Only a few times did he give in to animal feelings with that person, and afterward he lived strictly removed from her and felt disgust and inner displeasure with himself.

The unnamed one is supposed to have behaved immorally in that, while engaging in this animal experience, he sought to guard against the unfortunate consequences of his action. Now I regard such illicit satisfactions of love as on the whole impermissible, but if a man has once succumbed to this natural weakness, is it immoral of him to be moved by the fear of tragic consequences and thus not wholly to give himself up to his instincts in those moments? The confines of this letter do not permit any further discussion of this delicate matter, which can be viewed from so many sides. I only want to ask this one thing: Are married people immoral when, after conception, they continue to satisfy the drive of physical love nevertheless, even though the purpose of procreation cannot thereby be achieved any longer? I think this example is pertinent to the case of the unnamed one; for if it is a moral law, when satisfying this natural impulse, to do it only for the sake of procreation, then married people are immoral when they continue to practice the works of love after the goal of procreation can no longer be achieved. If, however, the unnamed one has really erred in this, I believe that one should not seek the source of this error in his heart – in his moral depravity. He must certainly not have believed at the time (in fact his mental state was highly unusual then, and it would be difficult to find examples of other people with whom to compare his mental state) that he had committed himself to a significantly immoral principle. This can be inferred from his whole behavior. However evil a man may be, he will yet try to have the appearance of a just man, assuming he has not yet been totally unmasked as a scoundrel. He will not freely reveal his innermost thoughts, admitting his evil intentions. The unnamed one, on the other hand, did reveal his

10:376

thoughts to a distinguished man.[2] So there are only two possibilities: either the unnamed one must be the most simple-minded man in the world, not understanding that he exposes himself to the bitterest scorn by revealing his bad principles; or he must be the most shameless scoundrel, whose insensitivity and impudence have gone so far that disgrace and honor mean nothing to him. I doubt that the unnamed one has in any way given you cause to suspect that he is either entirely simple-minded or a thoroughgoing scoundrel . . .

10:377   Furthermore, the unnamed one is supposed to have acted immorally in that he lied to the woman in question, since, in view of the resemblance between the child and the unnamed man, who has so many *distinguished* features, the truth of her testimony [that he is the father] is thereby confirmed. If the unnamed one has been unfair to that person, he sincerely begs her forgiveness. But having done that, I can assure you with the greatest certainty that the unnamed one had much evidence to support his suspicion. For in the first place, the unnamed one had an experience that is very common in Königsberg; there are so very many lewd females in Königsberg who misuse the names of people they don't know. I know a respected merchant in Königsberg who, within the space of a year, was accused by seven females of having

10:378   got them pregnant; he swore to me on his honor and conscience that he had not even met all of them, especially the seventh one whom he had never seen in his life. He gave money to six of these lewd women, to avoid a spectacle. But he lost his patience with the seventh and threw her out the door, whereupon she sued him (for there are lots of those whore-lawyers in Königsberg; Herr H.[Hippel] himself intervened in a praiseworthy manner, so that a few of these wicked men were suspended from practicing law). The woman testified as to the place, the hour, everything very precisely, and the man lost the case. He appealed to Berlin and finally won, but it cost him several hundred thalers. The unnamed one thus at least knew of many cases in which females of that sort practice deceit. True enough, this would not in itself justify his stating positively that her testimony was false. But there was another reason, which he explained to Herr H., that persuaded him that what she said was false: if in fact her testimony should actually have some basis, he would have to admit his conviction that the male sex does not supply the cause but only the remote occasion of procreation.

Or can the alleged resemblance of the child constitute an adequate proof against the unnamed one? I don't think that this could be defended either on legal or on physical grounds. If it were [considered proof], then, for example, some mothers could be accused of sexual intercourse with animals – for I once saw in Leipzig a nine-year-old child whose body was almost wholly covered with deer hair and who also had other deer-like characteristics, especially the feet.[3] This phenomenon is also illustrated by the example of the late elector of Saxony.[4] Besides this, there are hundreds of cases where numerous resemblances between strangers have been noticed, without the suspicion being warranted that one of them owed his existence to the other. And then one would have to investigate to see whether this resemblance between the child and the unnamed one really exists; the power of the imagination often makes people see things. . . . [5]

---

1 Sometime in Mar. 1784; that letter is not extant.

2 Theodor Gottlieb von Hippel.

3 Perhaps Anna Marie Herrig, b. 1771. An engraving of her is said to show her skin covered with fur spotted like a deer.

4 Perhaps Friedrich Christian (1722–63), who suffered from congenital lameness.

5 To summarize the remainder of this letter, Plessing agrees to double the child support payments to one Reichsthaler every month, even though he questions his paternity. He promises to pay more when his circumstances permit. He regrets having been weak and causing trouble thereby. His whole life has been a chain of ills; the path of his life has always been over thorns. Evil always triumphs; goodness is defeated. The woman's present sad circumstances are not his fault, for he gave her a great deal of money, which she has mismanaged, etc. Finally, he refers again to the threat of fanaticism and fear of despotism, mentioned in his previous letter.

   Plessing is not given to brevity. There are ten more pages of this letter in the Akademie edition, Ak. 10:374–88.

61 [232] (213)
To Theodor Gottlieb von Hippel.[1]
July 9, 1784

Your grace was kind enough to wish to ease the complaints of   10:391
residents on the Schlossgraben concerning the stentorian singing of prayers by hypocritical inmates of the jail. I do not think they would have any cause for lamentation – as though their spiritual rehabilitation were in jeopardy – if they were required to modulate their singing so that they could hear themselves even with the windows shut and with-

out yelling with all their might. They can still obtain the jailer's testimony (which seems to be what they are really concerned about) to the effect that they are very God-fearing people, for he will hear them all right and in essence they will only be retuned to lower the pitch of the note by which the pious citizens of our good city feel themselves to be sufficiently awakened in their homes.[2] A word to the jailer, if you should wish to summon him and make the foregoing a permanent rule for him, would remove an annoyance from one whose peace you have often been so kind as to promote and who is ever with the greatest respect

your most obedient servant
I. Kant

---

1 On Hippel, see the biographical sketches. As the present letter makes clear, Hippel was at this time police superintendent in Königsberg.
2 Kant's annoyance with the prisoners' loud singing is expressed also in the *Critique of Judgment*, § 53. See also *Anthropologie*, Ak. 7: 158.

62 [233] (214)
From Christian Gottfried Schütz.[1]
July 10, 1784.

10:392   Noble Sir,
Esteemed Herr Professor,

Before I disclose the specific purpose of this letter, please allow me to give you my thanks for the instruction I have long enjoyed from your writings, and especially the daily nourishment that your *Critique of Pure Reason* imparts to my spirit. For this I offer my true and sincere gratitude.

Even before the appearance of your *Prolegomena*, I was very sorry to see this excellent book presented in such a totally false light in the Göttingen review. I was upset even more by the news that this truly remarkable misunderstanding could occur in a philosopher who is held in the highest esteem by the public.

I don't know whether the history of this review is already familiar to you. Professor Garve came to Göttingen for a visit. People wanted to honor him in some sort of literary way, so they offered to let him review the most important philosophical book that has appeared in a long time. Unfortunately, his distractions, his depression, his mental indisposition, and the magnitude of the book led to his misinterpreting it so drastically that, as the saying goes, none of it fit the facts.[2] In addition, the review was much too long for even the lengthiest review accepted for the *Göttinger Zeitung*, so that Herr Feder was called upon to shorten it. Perhaps those cuts made the piece even more confused.

I am not sure whether Herr Garve knows anything of your just challenge in the *Prolegomena*. I have enough confidence in his sense of honor, however, to be sure that he will admit his error and thus give you satisfaction.

What makes the reading of your book somewhat hard, other than the difficulty and sublimity of the philosophical speculation in it, is that the book always drives ahead in a single direction, without paragraphs or cross-references. I divided it up into paragraphs for myself and managed thereby to make it much less obscure to me. I take the liberty however of mentioning a few troubling passages to you. 10:393

On p. 80,[3] it seems to me that the third category, Community, under the heading Relation, does not stand to the corresponding moment of thought, the disjunctive relation, in the same relation that the other categories stand in relation to their corresponding moments of thought. Besides that, it seems to me that Community and Reciprocity are only empirically and not internally distinct from the second category, Causality. For reciprocity always involves a causality in one thing and dependence in the other, or vice versa.

You have introduced a number of very appropriate technical terms in the *Critique of Pure Reason* and given a clearer meaning to many terms that are already in use; yet I wished that you had used another expression for the distinction between those who admit a merely transcendental theology and those who also assume a natural theology, some expression other than "Deists" and "Theists."[4] For besides the fact that these terms sound hardly at all different, they both derive from the same root. Perhaps it would be best to ban entirely from philosophy all words that end in "ists" and "ians."

I am dying of curiosity about and eagerness for your Metaphysics of Nature. After that you must certainly give us a Metaphysics of Morals. However slowly your works may become known (what with the frivolous tastes of our age), they will surely take root and their effects will be felt in times to come if there are still thinkers then. They are not showpieces to win the applause of the moment but possessions for all time.[5] I would not have wasted your precious time with all this chatter, excellent man, if I were not commissioned by a typographical society to ask you if you would contribute at least a few papers to a new

10:394 *Allgemeine Literaturzeitung* that will be published in the coming year. For each printed sheet the publishers will pay 3 Louis d'or; they will of their own accord (though without actually binding themselves to this raise) pay as much as 6 ducats per sheet for really excellent reviews. This will be a respectable society of reviewers since the publishers are inviting only men of real distinction for each subject.

Please be kind enough to let me know as soon as possible whether you will participate and specifically whether you would review Herder's *Ideas for a Philosophy of the History of Mankind.*[6] The directors of the publishing house also want to know whether you would cover physics or whether you prefer to review only in the area of speculative and moral philosophy.

If you have any questions about these matters I shall certainly inform you of anything you may wish to know as soon as I receive your reply.

Let me return to the *Critique* once more. The book is dear to my heart. Various commentators have offered to write popular versions of it. I would not be opposed to this if it were carried out under your supervision. Without that, I fear that your book, like the Bible, will be subjected to countless false exegeses and paraphrases. In general I believe that those who have a calling to *make use* of your book will read it *for themselves* and *think themselves into it*. I have already tried to draw the attention of some capable minds to it in some of my courses and have read certain parts of it to them, such as pp. 753–6, p. 312, etc.,[7] (when I read these I wanted to *worship* you). I am sure that these efforts will bear fruit.

With sincere esteem I am

> your most obedient servant,
> Schütz
> Professor of Eloquence

Jena, July 10, 1784.

---

1 Christian Gottfried Schütz (1747–1832) was professor of rhetoric and poetry in Jena. In 1785 Schütz, with the help of Wieland and Bertuch, founded the *Allgemeine Literaturzeitung* (often referred to as the *A.L.Z.*), a journal devoted to Kantian philosophy. Schütz became one of Kant's strongest champions. Other prominent people who supported the journal were Gottlieb Hufeland, a renowned legal scholar, and Goethe.

2 Schütz uses a Greek expression here, ουδεν προς Διονυσον.

3 Page 80 of the first edition = B 106.

4 Kant calls a Deist one who believes in God as an impersonal First Cause of the world, while a Theist thinks of God as a creator who is a living "Author of the world." Cf. *Critique of Pure Reason*, B 659–61.

5 Schütz quotes these two phrases in Greek; they are from Thucydides, *Peloponnesian War*, I, 22.

6 Kant's review was published anonymously in the *A.L.Z.*, Jan. 5, 1785; Karl Leonhard Reinhold, at that time Herder's friend, replied to it, prompting Kant's rejoinder, published in Mar. 1785. Later that year, Kant published a review of Part Two of Herder's work, which had included a critical discussion of Kant's "Idea for a Universal History." For Kant's reviews, see Ak. 8: 45 ff. and pp. 471 ff. The review incurred Herder's hatred, destroying any friendship that remained between the two men.

7 Pp. 753–6 and 312 = B 780 ff. and B 371 ff. In the first, Kant is discussing the "sacred right" to freedom of thought and open discussion concerning the existence of God, freedom of the will, the hope of a future life. Kant attacks the idea that the youth need to be protected from "dangerous propositions" and kept for a period under tutelage. The second alluded to is the first book of the Transcendental Dialectic where Kant discusses Plato, the unchanging Idea of virtue, and rejects the notion that concepts of virtue are derived from empirical archetypes such as Jesus.

1785

63 [237] (217)
From Christian Gottfried Schütz.
February 18, 1785

Most esteemed Herr Professor,

You can't believe how I have been longing to have the time to answer your priceless letter. The various matters of business connected with starting up the *Allgemeine Literatur Zeitung* have kept me from writing.

You have probably seen a copy of your review of Herder by now. Everyone who has read it with impartial eyes thinks it a masterpiece of precision and – are you surprised? – many readers recognized that you must be the author. I can tell you that this review, since it came out in the trial issue of the journal, has certainly accounted for much of the favorable response to the *A.L.Z.*

They say that Herr Herder is very sensitive to the review.[1] A young convert by the name of Reinhold[2] who is staying in Wieland's house in Weimar and who has already sounded an abominable fanfare in the *Merkur* about Herder's piece intends to publish a refutation of your review in the February issue of that journal.[3] I will send you the sheet as soon as I receive it. The directors of our journal would be delighted if you would undertake an answer to it right away. If it seems to you not worth the effort, I will try to find someone else to reply.

Good Heavens – it boggles my mind that you can write that you "would relinquish the honorarium, in case etc.," that you could believe that a review like yours might not be acceptable! When I was reading what you said I could not keep the tears from coming to my eyes. Such modesty from a man like you! I cannot describe the feeling it gave me. It was joy, fright and indignation all at once, especially the last, when I think of the conceit of many scholars of our age who are not worthy of unfastening the shoe strings of a *Kant*.

10:399

Would you be kind enough, esteemed man, to let me know as soon as possible whether you might still want to review some of the best philosophical books that have come out this half-year, e.g., Platner's *Aphorisms*, or Eberhard's *Miscellaneous Writings* or some other works.[4]

In the March or April issue of the *A.L.Z.* we shall publish Court Chaplain Shultz's account of the revolution in metaphysics that you have brought about.[5] Your book is truly not "a showpiece to win the applause of the moment, but a possession for all time."[6]

Though people all believe that you are the *A.L.Z.* reviewer of Herder's book, I heard today that Herr H. intends to write to you himself. I would love to know whether that is a fact. Oh how true what you say is – there are so few people to whom philosophy really *matters*. If I had written Herder's book I would take more pride in your review than in the diseased, panegyrical twaddle of shallow pates.

I have a burning desire to see your new book.[7] Believe me, your work quietly exerts more influence than you perhaps imagine. I must tell you a pleasant anecdote. Herr Platner is publishing a new edition of his aphorisms; the book is being printed a sheet at a time and on one sheet there was some perplexity expressed about a place in your *Critique* and an announcement on the same sheet that your *Critique* would be carefully examined in the Appendix. Now that the aphorisms are published, that sheet has been cut out of the book, a cartoon printed in its stead and the Appendix has not appeared at all. Presumably Herr P. found his perplexity dissolved when he thought it over.

I must break off now and ask you please to deliver the enclosure to Hartung's bookstore, and please do it as soon as you receive this.

I shall write you again a few post days from now; meanwhile I beg you to let me know in a few words (omit the postage) whether you wish to review the books mentioned above, and tell me also what else you might offer to the *A.L.Z.*

I must thank you also for your excellent essays in the *Berliner Monatschrift* which I found genuinely edifying. I am sure that innumerable readers must be as grateful as I am.

Be well, most esteemed man, and be assured that I am with sincerest   10:400
affection and reverence

your most obedient servant

Schütz

Jena, the 18th of Feb., 1785.

---

1 Herder's letter to Hamann, Feb. 14, 1785, attests to his displeasure at Kant's review, which he accuses of totally misunderstanding the spirit of his book from beginning to end. Herder accuses it of being "so malicious and distorting

and metaphysical and totally alien to the spirit of the book" that he is "astonished, never thinking that Kant, my teacher, whom I have never knowingly insulted, could be capable of writing such a contemptible piece . . . His final preceptorial instructions to me are wholly improper: I am 40 years old and no longer a schoolboy on his metaphysical schoolbench. What causes his boil is that I have not followed the Professor's beaten track of verbal juggling, and that is why he complains so absurdly about my peculiarities and immoderate inspiration . . ."

2   Karl Leonhard Reinhold (1758–1823), Viennese by birth and educated by Jesuits, became professor of philosophy in the Barnabite college in 1774, fled to Germany in 1783, converted to Protestantism, and married Wieland's daughter. He became a devoted disciple of Kant's and, through the publication of "Briefe über die Kantische Philosophie," published first in the *Deutsche Merkur*, 1786/87, he contributed greatly to the spread Kantianism. Reinhold eventually became convinced that Fichte, not Kant, was the philosopher to worship.

3   Reinhold's announcement in the *Anzeiger des Teutschen Merkur* proclaimed that Herder's *Ideen* was the first real philosophy of history. Reinhold effusively praised Herder's book for being unlike the dry, graceless writings of academic philosophers.

   The projected refutation of Kant's review was published anonymously in the *Merkur* under the title "Schreiben des Pfarrers zu * * * an den Herausgeber des Teutschen Merkur" to which Kant replied in an Appendix to the March issue of the *A.L.Z.* in 1785 under the title "Erinnerungen des Rezensenten der Herderschen Ideen . . ." See Kant's *Werke*, Ak. 8:471 ff.

4   Kant did not review these books.

5   The published piece was written by Schütz himself, in *A.L.Z.*, July 1785. Schütz appends a summary and defense of Kant's ideas in the *Critique* and the *Prolegomena* to an announcement of Johann Schultz's *Erläuterungen über des Herrn Prof. Kant Kritik der reinen Vernunft.*

6   Thucydides, *Peloponnesian War*, I, 22. Schütz seems fond of this Greek quotation, which he used also in his previous letter, July 10, 1784, Ak. [233].

7   Kant's *Grundlegung.*

64 [243] (223)
To Christian Gottfried Schütz.[1]
September 13, 1785.

10:406   Your great sympathy for my modest literary efforts, which you demonstrate so illuminatingly in the *A.L.Z.* as well as in your accurate account of my ideas, especially your excellent and instructive Table of the Elements of our Concepts,[2] moves me to offer my great thanks and make me at the same obligated to carry our my plan as you have announced it. You may count on it that I shall not disappoint you or the expectation you have aroused in the public.

I owe you a review that I promised to write. Dearest friend! You will forgive me for having been prevented from writing it by a feeling of obligation to work on something else, something on which I have felt obliged to work partly by its relationship to my whole project and partly because of the train of my thoughts. Before I can compose the metaphysics of nature that I have promised to do, I had to write something that is in fact a mere application of it but that presupposes an *empirical* concept. I refer to the metaphysical foundations of the theory of body*[a]* and, as an appendix to it, the metaphysical foundations of the theory of soul.*[b]* For the metaphysics [of nature], if it is to be wholly homogeneous, must be a completely pure science. But I wanted to have some concrete examples available to which I could refer in order to make my discourse comprehensible; yet I did not want to bloat the system by including these examples in it. So I finished them this summer, under the title "Metaphysical Foundations of Natural Science" [*Metaphysische Anfangsgründe der Naturwissenschaft*], and I think the book will be welcomed even by mathematicians. It would have been published this Michaelmas, if I hadn't injured my right hand and been prevented from writing the ending. The manuscript must now lie till Easter.

Now I am proceeding immediately with the full composition of the Metaphysics of Morals.[3] Pardon me, therefore, dearest friend, if I cannot send anything to the *A.L.Z.* for a long time. I am already rather old and find it more difficult now to adjust quickly to different kinds of work. I have to hold my thoughts together without interruption, lest I lose the thread that unites the whole system. But I shall in any case undertake the review of the second part of Herder's *Ideen.*[4]

10:407

I have not yet seen any reviews of *Die Betrachtungen über das Fundament der Kräfte*, etc. The author, Privy Councillor von Elditten[5] of Wickerau in Prussia, asked me to request that you have it reviewed and, if the review turns out to be more or less favorable, to feel free to name him as the work's author.

I must break off here. I commend myself to your good collaborative friendship and good disposition. Yours, etc.

---

1 Christian Gottfried Schütz (1747–1832), professor of rhetoric and poetry in Jena. Founder, in 1785, with the aid of Wieland and Bertuch, of the *Allgemeine Literaturzeitung*, a journal devoted to the cause of Kant's philosophy.

[a] Körperleher   *[b] Seelenleher*

229

2 In the 1785 *A.L.Z.*, Nos. 162, 164, 178, and 179, Schütz had published a discussion of Johann Schultz's *Erläuterungen* with a lengthy discussion and defense of Kant's theory.

3 In fact it was not until 1797 that Kant published a work with this title.

4 See Kant's *Werke*, Ak. 8:58–66.

5 Ernst Ludwig von Elditten (1728–97), privy *Justizrat* in Mohrungen and then in Angerburg, wrote to Kant, Aug. 5, 1783, Ak. [204]. The full title of his work is *Betrachtungen über das Fundament der Kräfte und die Methoden, welche die Vernunft anwenden kann, darüber zu urtheilen* (Königsberg, 1784). The editor of Ak. 13 refers to it as thoroughly "dilettantisch."

65 [248] (228)
From Moses Mendelssohn.
October 16, 1785.

10:413   Esteemed Sir,

I have taken the liberty of sending you, via the book merchant Voss and Son, a copy of my *Morning Lessons, or Lectures on the Existence of God*.[1]

Though I no longer have the strength to study your profound writings with the necessary concentration, I recognize that our basic principles do not coincide.[2] But I know too that you tolerate disagreement, indeed that you prefer it to blind worship. From what I know of you, the intention of your *Critique* is just to drive blind worship out of philosophy. Apart from that, you permit everyone to have and to express opinions that differ from your own.

I intended to postpone until the second part of my book informing people of the circumstances that prompted my publishing these *Morning Lessons*, for I want to prepare readers for certain contentions – claims that seemed to me somewhat risky when I considered how the reading public would take them. Herr Jacobi[3] hurried to anticipate me and published a work, *On the Doctrine of Spinoza, in Letters to Moses Mendelssohn*,[4] that discloses these circumstances. He publicizes a correspondence there between him, a third person,[5] and myself. According to Jacobi, our Lessing[6] is supposed to have announced himself to be a Spinozist. Jacobi claims to have demonstrated the truth of Spinozism to him; Lessing supposedly found it to agree with his principles and is alleged to have been glad that finally, after a long search, he had found a brother in pantheism who knew how to clarify so beautifully the whole system of "One and All."[7]

He [Jacobi] for his part elects finally to arm himself with the canon of faith and finds salvation and certainty in one of the beatific Lavater's fortifications, from whose "angel pure"[8] mouth he cites a passage at the end of his work that is rich in solace; it conveys no solace to me, however, because I cannot understand it. All in all this work of Herr Jacobi is an unusual mixture, an almost monstrous birth, with the head of *Goethe*,[9] the body of *Spinoza*, and the feet of *Lavater*.

10:414

I find it incredible that people nowadays think anyone has the right to publish a private exchange of letters without the consent of the correspondents.[10] Still more: Lessing is supposed to have confided in him, namely Jacobi, that he had never revealed his true philosophical principles to me, his most trusted philosophical friend for 30 years. If that were true, how could Jacobi bring himself to disclose his deceased friend's secret, disclose it not only to me but to the whole world? He protects himself and leaves his friend naked and defenseless on the open field, to be the object of his enemies' assault and mockery. I cannot countenance such behavior and I wonder what men with a sense of justice think of it. I fear that philosophy has its fanatics who are just as inclined to persecute and proselytize as are the fanatics of positive religion.

Moses Mendelssohn

---

1 *Morgenstunden, oder Vorlesungen über das Dasein Gottes.*

2 Kant's letter to Schütz, Ak. [256], certainly confirms Mendelssohn's opinion that he and Kant are not philosophically at one, for Kant there refers to Mendelssohn's book as "a masterpiece of deception of our reason."

3 Friedrich Heinrich Jacobi (1743–1819), the famous "philosopher of faith." On Jacobi, see the biographical sketches. For a full discussion of Jacobi and the so-called pantheism controversy between Jacobi and Mendelssohn, and its significance for Kant and the Enlightenment, see Frederick Beiser, *The Fate of Reason*, ch. 2. As Beiser points out, the name "Pantheism Controversy" or "*Pantheismusstreit*" is a misnomer, since the controversy was not really over pantheism.

4 *Über die Lehre des Spinoza in Briefen an den Herrn Moses Mendelssohn* (Breslau, 1785). See Kant's letter to Jacobi, Aug. 30, 1789, Ak.[375], where Kant expresses a highly favorable view of Jacobi's work.

5 Margarete Elisabeth [Elise] Reimarus, friend of Lessing as well as of Jacobi and Mendelssohn. It was she to whom Jacobi confided the scandalous news that Lessing was committed to Spinoza. Given the prevailing view in Germany, before 1785, that Spinozism was equivalent to atheism, this was a shocking

revelation, bound to be disturbing to the late Lessing's dear friend, Mendelssohn.

6 Ephraim Lessing (1729–81), the renowned author.

7 This phrase, or the Greek *"hen kai pan,"* used by Lessing in conversation with Jacobi to describe his own Spinozism, became the general slogan of Spinozists in Germany.

8 In the second edition Jacobi replaced the word *engelrein* with the more moderate *aufrichtig* (upright or sincere).

9 Jacobi gave Goethe's poem "Prometheus" to Lessing to read; their conversation about pantheism is connected with this. Kant's opinion of the principles underlying the pantheism controversy is expressed in "What Is Orientation in Thinking?" (1786).

10 One hopes that Mendelssohn's righteous judgment would not condemn the publication of letters 200 years later, when obtaining the correspondents' consent would pose some problems.

66 [251] (231)
From Johann Erich Biester.
November 8, 1785.

I hasten to send you all I know about the stone "Sophronister," dearest man. I have copied the citation in Winkelmann for you. I added the passage from Pausanias to which he alludes and I include it together with my grammatical and lexicographic research. It is little, but all I could find. Please excuse my sending it on individual pages but I wrote this while I was in the library.

10:416

I just received a note from my friend Gedike,[1] whom I consulted. Because I am so busy, I think it best to send it on to you just as it is.[2]

I hope these materials are sufficient for your purpose. I doubt that I can improve on them.

Please accept my sincerest thanks for your excellent essay on the history of mankind that you sent me recently for the *Monatsschrift*.[3] It is an example of the most sublime and noble philosophy, uplifting to the soul. You supply us with a lofty perspective from which we can survey the whole and from which the greatest contradictions resolve themselves into harmony. You offer a valuable gift to the public via our journal, and I am all the more sorry that it cannot be printed immediately in December. Herr Garve, God knows why, is trying once more to defend the Catholics, even the Jesuits and the Pope, in a long letter to me, which I shall answer.[4] This letter and my reply will leave

10:417

no room for any major pieces in the December issue [of the *Berliner Monatsschrift*]. As amusing as it usually is to argue against Catholics and their friends, the game becomes sour when a Garve puts himself on their team . . .

I shall recommend Herr Pörschke[5] to the minister, as you suggest, and I have no doubt that he will gladly approve the proposal, since it came originally from you.

But where can one find an orientalist to take Köhler's place,[6] now that he is determined to leave? My dear friend Professor Kraus once suggested a Herr Hill,[7] with a letter of recommendation from Lavater that he paraded, but the man is far too inexperienced for such an important position. He may one day become quite a useful man when his understanding has ripened.

Do you know any other orientalists? I would really be happy to arrange matters in such a way that the minister appoints someone from there instead of my sending him a foreigner, since foreigners seem not at all to flourish there.

Please don't forget to write something about philosophical fanaticism,[a] as you once mentioned you would in connection with Jakobi's letter to Moses Mendelssohn.[8] Truly a strange letter! It was supposed to deal with philosophy and ends up with words from Lavater's angelpure mouth prescribing *faith*!

Be well and be always assured of my warmest respect.

Biester

The letter you wanted sent to Jena was taken care of right away.

[a] *philosophische Schwärmerei*

---

1   Friedrich Gedike, director of a *Gymnasium* and co-founder of the *Berliner Monatsschrift*.
2   Cf. Kant's *Werke*, Ak. 10: 418–20, for Biester's enclosures. What they say, briefly, is as follows: Hercules, having gone mad, tried to kill Amphitryon (his mortal step-father). Athena/Minerva stopped him by throwing a stone against his chest, which put Hercules to sleep. The myth of Minerva's pacifying Stone of the Wise (*Stein der Weisen*, also called *Sophronister* or the Stone of Minerva) is reported by the Greek traveler and geographer Pausanias (fl. c. 150 A.D.) as a Theban legend. There is a reference to the stone in Euripides' *Hercules furens*, 1.1004.
3   "Mutmaßlicher Anfang der Menschengeschichte" (Conjectural beginning of human history) was published in the *Berliner Monatsschrift*, Jan. 1786. Schiller developed the ideas expressed in this essay in his own essay, "Etwas über die erste Menschengesellschaft" (Concerning the first human society) in *Thalia*, Heft II, 1790.

4 Garve's letter, "Über die Besorgnisse der Protestanten in Ansehung der Verbreitung des Katholizismus" (Concerning the Protestants' anxieties about the spread of Catholicism), appeared in the July 1785 issue of the *Berliner Monatsschrift* along with Biester's reply.

5 Karl Ludwig Pörschke (1751–1812), professor of poetry in Königsberg, was Kant's student, dinner companion, and friend. He did not receive his doctorate until 1787.

6 Johann Bernhard Köhler (1742–1802), professor of Greek and other "eastern" languages. Cf. Kant's petition to the philosophy faculty, Feb. 20, 1787, suggesting a Jewish candidate named Euchel be hired to teach Hebrew.

7 Christian Hill (d. 1809) was a theology student in Königsberg, much admired by Hamann. Lavater had written in Hill's *Stammbuch*, "Whoever does not love Hill is not loved by Lavater."

8 Kant's "What Is Orientation in Thinking?" answers Biester's request.

67 [253] (233)
From Christian Gottfried Schütz.
November 13, 1785.

10:421   Eight days ago, esteemed Herr Professor, I mailed you Part II of Herder's *Ideen*. I await the review of it that you were kind enough to offer to write.

I would be extremely grateful too if you would give me a report on *Ulrich's textbook*[1] which he himself sent you. Would you please indicate what seems to you to need correcting in it. If this is not possible for you, perhaps Court Chaplain Schultz could undertake it.[2]

10:422   I am writing to him now as well; I beg you to forward the enclosed letter to him. I hear that there are two Herren Schulz, both of them court chaplains;[3] this letter of course is meant for the author of the *Erläuterungen*[4] to your *Critique*.

I repeat my request for a review, by early next year, of Dr. Hufeland's *Foundation of Natural Law*.[5] If you don't wish to be bothered with having to make an abstract of the book, just include a page of notes with references to the page numbers and I shall rewrite it in the standard form of a review. That will save you time while still giving the public and the author the benefit of your instruction. Your own handwriting is completely legible so I beg you to send me your first thoughts without bothering to have them transcribed.

Now I must tell you about some contributions to the history of the *Critique of Pure Reason* at our university.

Near the start of this term I was asked to submit a plan for the course of studies that new students should pursue. For philosophy, I presented your outline of the subject, using your name. No one had any objections except Herr Hennings[6] who was terrified that he would lose all his acclaim. He demanded that the traditional divisions of philosophy be observed and your name not be mentioned. He even protested my proposal and took his appeal to the highest academic tribunal. My answer was that those who have the title "professor of philosophy" would have to come to some agreement about this, and I left the matter to Herr Hennings and Herr Ulrich. In the letters they exchanged over this issue, Herr Hennings exposed very clearly how much he had read or understood of your *Critique*. He "did not at all see how *construction of concepts* could distinguish mathematics from *philosophy*, since after all the whole of philosophy involved *making* concepts."

My idea finally won out, only Herr Hennings still inserted something about Monadology, Somatology, etc., that certainly did not fit in, and he insisted that since in the announcement no one else was mentioned by name, yours should not be mentioned either. Herr Ulrich however countered with "The honor devolves not only upon those who are honored but upon those who honor."[7]

10:423

Since the new courses have begun I hear that Herr Hennings often refers to you, saying that there is much good in your *Critique* but that most of it was known already.

A young instructor named Schmid[8] is now lecturing on the *Critique of Pure Reason*, using a little abstract he has published.

I finally read the review of your Metaphysics of Morals in the Göttingen paper[9] and was not very pleased with it.

As I was thinking once more of your excessively kind waiver of the honorarium, it occurred to me that perhaps you were trying to *spare me*. I owe it to you to report therefore that it would in no way be to my advantage even if all contributors were to decline their honoraria. I am not one of the entrepreneurs who govern the institute but am hired by the society of entrepreneurs to be editor. The society has made it a matter of principle not to accept any essays gratis, their reason being that a policy of no honoraria could not work in the long run and would bring no honor to the entrepreneurs; and since one cannot be inconsistent, giving an honorarium to some and not others, one must unfortunately conform to the popular style of most commercial firms and endorse avarice. I really wish therefore that you would not be an exception here and least of all if you want to accept one of the compromises I suggested in my last letter[10] of designating your honorarium to some charity.

Herr Moses Mendelssohn sent me his *Morgenstunden* as well. I don't doubt that it contains some lovely passages but I am convinced in advance from what he himself says about his nervous condition that he has not been able to study the recent developments in philosophy and that no new arguments against the *Critique* will show up in his book. In a few days I shall start to work on it myself.

I await with great eagerness the appearance of your new books and wish that Easter were already here.

10:424

With sincerest esteem and genuine interest in your well-being I remain, most estimable teacher,

yours,
Schütz

Jena, November 13, 1785

---

1 Johann August Heinrich Ulrich, *Institutiones logicae et metaphysicae* (Jena, 1985). Ulrich (1744–1807) was professor of philosophy in Jena. Cf. Ulrich's letter to Kant, Ak.[239]. Kant had sent Ulrich his *Grundlegung*; and Ulrich, at that point a follower of Kant's though later an antagonist, sent his textbook in return, along with a confused question about Kant's relating of causality to the possibility of experience.

2 Schultz did so, in the *A.L.Z.*, Dec. 13, 1785, pp. 297 ff. See Kant's footnote in the *Metaphysische Anfangsgründe der Naturwissenschaft*, Ak. 4:474–6, and the editor's notes, 4: 638 ff.

3 There were indeed two, the Johann Schultz (1739–1805) mentioned here, court chaplain and professor of mathematics in Königsberg, author of the *Erläuterungen*, the man whom Kant later designated as his favorite expositor (the name is sometimes spelled Schultze or Schulz), and Johann Ernst Schulz (1742–1806) who was preacher at the Royal Orphanage in Königsberg and, among other positions, professor of theology. A third Schultz, Johann Heinrich Schultz (1739–1823), pastor in Gielsdorf in der Mark, is also of interest for Kant studies: he was known as *Zopfschulz* – "pig-tail Schulz" – because of his refusal to wear a wig when conducting church services. This last Schulz, a rebel in more ways than one, composed a work entitled "Attempt at an introduction to a doctrine of morals for all human beings regardless of different religions," which was published in Königsberg in a journal called *Rässonierenden Bücherverzeichnis* (1783) and which Kant reviewed in the same year. His unorthodox behavior and liberal theological leanings were tolerated under Friedrich II but not under his successor, Friedrich Wilhelm II, whose reactionary minister of spiritual affairs, Wöllner, saw to *Zopfschulz*'s dismissal. Kant's review, Ak. 8:10–14, is available in the Cambridge edition of Kant's *Practical Philosophy* (1996).

4 Johann Schultz, *Erläuterungen über des Hrn. Prof. Kant Kritik der reinen Vernuft* (1784).

5 Gottlieb Hufeland (1760–1817) was co-editor of the *A.L.Z.* and professor of law, first in Jena, then in Würzburg, Landshut, and Halle; he was also for a

short time mayor of Danzig, his native city. Hufeland is known also for his association with Schiller. The book Schütz mentions, whose correct title was *Versuch über den Grundsatz des Naturrechts* Essay on the principle (or foundation) of natural right; (Leipzig, 1785), was discussed by Kant in the *A.L.Z.*, Apr. 18, 1786. A translation of Kant's review by Allen Wood is included in the Cambridge edition of Kant's *Practical Philosophy* (1996).

Gottlieb Hufeland was a cousin of a famous physician, Christoph Wilhelm Hufeland, inventor of macrobiotics, the science of prolonging life. Kant corresponded with both Hufelands. See, e.g., Ak. [796].

6 Justus Christian Hennings (1731–1815), professor in Jena, the man who bestowed the Imprimatur on Kant's *Religion within the Limits of Reason Alone*. Goethe wrote to Carl August, June 1, 1786, "Hennings is a good man, but weak."

7 "Honor est non tantum honorati, sed etiam honorantis."

8 Carl Christian Erhard Schmid (1761–1812), *Magister* in Jena, later professor of philosophy. In 1786 he published an introduction and lexicon to the *Critique, Kritik der reinen Vernuft im Grundrisse zu Vorlesungen nebst einem Wörterbuch zum leichteren Gebrauch der Kantischen Philosophie*.

9 *Göttinger Anzeigen*, Oct. 29, 1785. The review (of the *Grundlegung*, obviously not the Metaphysics of Morals which was yet to appear) was by Feder and supported "Eudaemonism."

10 In his letter of Nov. 8, 1785, Ak. [252], Schütz suggested that if Kant declined the honorarium he could instead have a year's subscription to the *A.L.Z.* or he could order that the money be given to some charity in Kant's name.

68 [256] (237)
To Christian Gottfried Schütz.
End of November 1785.[1]

Although the worthy M[endelssohn]'s book[2] must be regarded in 10:428 the main as a masterpiece of the self-deception of our reason, insofar as it takes the subjective conditions of our reason's determination of objects in general for conditions of the possibility of these objects themselves, a self-deception whose true character it is no easy task to expose and from which it is not easy to liberate our understanding completely, this excellent book will nevertheless be highly useful – not only for what is said with penetration, originality, and exemplary clarity in its "Preliminary Notions" concerning truth, appearance, and error,[3] things that can be used very well in any philosophy lecture, but also for its second part, which has significant value for the critique of human reason. For since the author, in presenting the subjective conditions of the use of our reason, finally reaches the conclusion that something is *conceivable* only if it is *actually conceived* by some being or other, and that without a *conception* no *object* really exists (p. 303),[4] from which he deduces that an infinite and at the same time active understanding must really exist, since only in relation to it can possibility or reality be meaningful predicates of things; since in fact there is also an essential need in human reason and its natural dispositions to support its freely floating arch with this keystone, this extremely penetrating pursuit of our chain of concepts, extending itself until it embraces the whole of reality, provides us with the most splendid occasion and at the same time challenge to subject our faculty of pure reason to a total critique, in order that we may distinguish the merely subjective conditions of its employment from those from which something valid about objects can be inferred. Pure philosophy must certainly profit from this, even assuming that after a complete investigation illusion intervenes, so that something may appear to be victory over a field of highly remote objects when it is really only (though very usefully) the direction of the subject to objects that are very close by. One can regard

10:429 this final legacy of a dogmatizing metaphysics at the same time as its most perfect accomplishment, both in view of its chain-like coherence and in the exceptional clarity of its presentation, and as a memorial, never to detract from his worth, to the sagacity of a man who knows and controls the full power of the mode of reasoning that he has adopted, a memorial that a Critique of Reason, which casts doubt on the happy progress of such a procedure, can thus use as an enduring example for testing its principles, in order either to confirm or to reject them.

---

1 Schütz reviewed Mendelssohn's *Morgenstunden* in the *A.L.Z.*, No. 7, January 1786, closing his discussion with an introduction to Kant's verdict, the letter here translated, though without specifically naming Kant as its author. That Kant was indeed the author was discovered by Benno Erdmann in 1878. Cf. the latter's *Kants Kriticismus* (Leipzig, 1878,) pp. 144 ff. In his essay "What Is Orientation in Thinking?" (1786) Kant elaborates his criticism of Mendelssohn in a less sarcastic tone.

2 *Morgenstunden.*

3 Mendelssohn's *Morgenstunden* consists of two parts: the *"Vorerkenntniss"* or Part I contains seven introductory lectures, on truth, appearance, and error, notions which have to be presupposed in justifying belief in God. The ten lectures of the second part contain the justification itself, the "doctrine of God."

4   Kant refers to an argument that may be found on p. 303 of Mendelssohn's
    Gesammelte Schriften, Bd. II (Leipzig, 1843–5). Mendelssohn sought to develop
    a new proof of the existence of God, from the incompleteness of self-
    knowledge and the idea of the possible. Cf. Ak. 13: 159, f.

1786

69 [259] (240)
From Christian Gottfried Schütz.
February 1786.

10:430 Esteemed Friend and Teacher,

I learn from you every week, so once again I submit my sincerest thanks for your excellent essay in the January issue of the *Berlinische Monatschrift*.[1]

I beseech you now most respectfully for

1. the review of Dr. Hufeland's book,[2] please send it soon,

2. a declaration stating whether Privy Councillor Jacobi has misunderstood you when, in his book on Spinoza, he introduces your ideas about space and says that they are *"wholly in the spirit* of Spinoza."[3]

It is truly incomprehensible how often you are misunderstood; there exist people who are really in other respects not imbeciles yet who take you to be an atheist.[4]

I am sure that you too sincerely regret the unexpected death of the excellent Mendelssohn. But can that be why you hesitate to publish your work? You can tell how diligently the students here are studying

10:431 your *Critique of Pure Reason* from the fact that, a few weeks ago, two students fought a duel because one of them had said to the other that he didn't understand your book and that it would take another thirty years of study before he would understand it and another thirty before he would be able to say anything about it.

If I should die before long, I think the only thing to which I could not easily reconcile myself would be to have missed seeing the completion of your labors. I await Easter[5] with the most intense longing.

Let me know sometime in a few words whether you found the notice about Mendelssohn's book in the *A.L.Z.* offensive.[6]

With the greatest veneration I am

your most obedient servant

Schütz

---

1 Kant's essay, "Mutmaßlicher Anfang der Menschengeschichte" (Conjectural beginning of human history) appeared in the *Berliner Monatsschrift*, Jan. 1786. Schiller's essay, "Etwas über die erste Menschengesellschaft" (Something concerning the first human society), in *Thalia*, issue #11, 1790, takes off from Kant's ideas here.

2 Gottlieb Hufeland. On Hufeland, see Schütz's letter to Kant, Ak. [253], n. 5, above.

3 F. H. Jacobi, *Über die Lehre Spinoza in Briefe an den Herrn Moses Mendelssohn* (Concerning the teaching of Spinoza, in letters to Mr. Moses Mendelssohn; Breslau, 1785), p. 123 f. In the second edition (1789) the words "die ganz im Geiste des Spinoza sind," i.e., "which are wholly in the spirit of Spinoza," are omitted. Instead, Jacobi adds, "No sensible person needs to be told that the Kantian philosophy is not thereby indebted to Spinozism." On Jacobi, see Mendelssohn's letter to Kant, Ak. [248], n. 3, and the biographical sketches.

4 Until the revival of Spinozism occasioned by the pantheism controversy, it was not unusual to equate Spinoza's pantheism with atheism.

5 Schütz must be referring to the Easter book fair.

6 Schütz himself was the author.

70

To the Philosophical Faculty.

February 20, 1786.

[from Kant's *Amtlicher Schriftverkehr*
(official correspondence) #6])

A Jewish student, Herr Euchel,[1] who is already well known as the author of a Hebrew periodical, has presented himself to me, requesting permission to teach Hebrew to a group of young people. He asks for this in view of the vacancy, which I myself reported to him, created by Professor Köhler's leaving. Since instruction in Hebrew will now and presumably for a considerable time be completely neglected, the Theo-

12:426

12:427

logical Faculty will doubtless be pleased to have this interim appointment to the orientalist position, even by a Jewish scholar, especially since he has voluntarily agreed to abstain from all exegesis in his teaching and to limit himself entirely to imparting thorough linguistic competence. I therefore request the faculty's judgment in this matter. My own opinion, since I know this clever young man as one of my auditors, is that there is no reason to oppose his certification as language teacher and I think he should be given approval so that students can more easily find out about him from the bulletin board, i.e., that he is a linguist. The fact that this is unusual is no objection, since it is also unusual that our university should for an extended period of time be lacking instruction in a necessary subject.

I am with complete respect the faculty's wholly devoted servant,

I. Kant

Königsberg, February 20, 1786.

---

1   Isaac Abraham Euchel (1758–1804), a student, served as a tutor with a Jewish family. He published, from 1784 on, a journal called *Der Sammler* in which he sought to oppose exclusively rabbinical learning and tried to spread German culture among the Jews. Since Köhler, the professor of Oriental languages (actually Greek was his specialty) in Königsberg, left the university early in 1786 and no successor was appointed, Euchel appealed to Kant, at that time *Dekan* (Dean) of the Philosophical Faculty, with the request Kant states here. Despite Kant's personal recommendation, Euchel was turned down, with Kant's concurrence, on the grounds that the statutes of the university required all members of the teaching faculty to swear allegiance to the doctrines of the Augsburg Confession and Euchel was unwilling to convert to Christianity.

No Jew was licensed to teach in Königsberg until 1848.

71 [260] (241)
From Marcus Herz.
February 27, 1786.

10:431   Esteemed teacher,

You will receive, dearest teacher, via Dr. Joel,[1] a copy of my *Essay on Vertigo*[2] which I mentioned in my letter of November 25th.[3] I once expressed the main idea of the work in one of the conversations I was

fortunate enough to have with you – I still recall all of them with delight. The idea lay in my mind awaiting adequate knowledge of physiology before it could have whatever modest influence it may have on practice. You see, dearest sir, that I am not entirely disloyal to you, that I am much more a deserter who still wears your uniform and who, while associating with other powers (not hostile to your cause), is still in your service. Or, to express myself less Prussianly, I enjoy wandering around along the borders of both provinces, philosophy and medicine, and it gives me joy when I can make suggestions and arrangements for their common government. I think it would be a good thing if similar   10:432
border areas between philosophy and its neighboring territories were diligently visited by philosophers as well as by practical scholars and artists of all sorts. The former would avoid thereby the frequently valid charge of useless rumination, the latter the charge of being empirical.

What do you say to the uproar that has started up among our preachers and inspired heads, exorcists, droll poets, enthusiasts and musicians, since and concerning Moses' [Mendelssohn's] death, an uproar for which the Councillor of Pimplendorf[4] gave the signal?[5] If only a man like you would say "Shut up!" to this swarm of rascals, I bet they would scatter like chaff in the wind. Above all, I wish I had guessed the mischievous character of that foolish lyricist of Wansebeck; in his entire life and thought, the only things that rhyme are the endings of his childish verses. With what resolute malice he misinterprets our Moses, toward whom he had "a certain tenderness," just to destroy his fame and esteem. They have been saying here lately that you are going to publish a short essay against Jacobi's book, which seemed all the more probable to me since you did not answer Moses' last letter. If only you would take the opportunity to say something on behalf of your deceased friend against the contemporary and, I suppose, future irrational Jacobites!

We are now busy putting our Moses' papers in order. His correspondence is perhaps the only important thing that might be given to the public, if his friends will give us their letters from him, since he himself copied only a very few. Will you be so good as to let us have   10:433
yours, dearest sir? . . .

To be esteemed by you as you are by me is my warmest desire. Your faithful student and servant,

M. Herz

---

1   Aron Isaac Joel (b. 1749), a student of Kant's, later a physician in Königsberg. Kant had introduced him to Mendelssohn.

2 *Versuch über den Schwindel* (Berlin, 1786). Herz refers to it, in his previous letter, as "a psychological-medical essay."

3 Herz's letter, Ak. [255], responds to Kant's request, Ak. [254], for medical assistance for a friend who was suffering from skin eruptions. Herz's letter informs that the veterinary whom Kant had asked him to consult was a lazy alcoholic and that the man had died suddenly, presumably from an excess of brandy. In the letter Herz also expresses his customary veneration for his former teacher.

4 Correctly, Pempelfort, a village near Düsseldorf – the reference is to F. H. Jacobi.

5 For a general account of the Mendelssohn-Jacobi feud, see the Introduction to this volume of letters and the letters, from Mendelssohn (Ak. [248]) and others, concerning the pantheism controversy. The uproar to which Herz refers is enormously complicated. Shortly before his death in Jan. 1786, Mendelssohn had replied to Jacobi's book, *On the Doctrine of Spinoza in Letters to Herr Moses Mendelssohn* (Breslau, 1785). The reply, *To Lessing's Friends: An Appendix to Herr Jacobi's Correspondence on the Doctrine of Spinoza*, appeared after Mendelssohn's death. The editor, J. J. Engel, one of the *Popularphilosophen*, wrote an introduction to the book, saying that the event that prompted Mendelssohn's writing of this work was also the cause of his death. Mendelssohn's agitation over Jacobi's book had so stirred up his blood, according to Engel, that, what with his nervous system already weakened, only the slightest external stress was needed to kill him. (In fact, Mendelssohn himself had told Herz that his illness was caused by a cold caught while on a walk to his publisher.) A newspaper article written by K. P. Moritz in Jan. 1786 claimed that Mendelssohn died nobly, a martyr to his defense of the suppressed rights of reason against fanaticism and superstition; Lavater had given him the first blow (by demanding that he either "refute" Christianity or become a Christian) and Jacobi had finished the job.

In defense of the beleaguered Jacobi, the composer and *Kapellmeister* J. F. Reichardt, an erstwhile auditor of Kant's, wrote in the *Berliner Zeitung* that Mendelssohn had indicated in a conversation with him in Dec. 1785 that he had not actually taken the controversy with Jacobi seriously though he regarded Jacobi and Hamann as birds of a feather. Engel replied that Reichardt had no right to consider himself one of Mendelssohn's confidants. Herz agreed and wrote as a physician, pointing out the difference between the immediate and dispositional causes of death. Herz and David Friedländer contradicted Reichardt as to Mendelssohn's sensitivity to Jacobi's charges. Moritz wrote another newspaper article, asking that Mendelssohn's ashes be allowed to rest in peace.

But the arguments continued, with a poet named M. Claudius joining in on Jacobi's side; he is "that foolish lyricist of Wansebeck" to whom Herz alludes. An anonymous essay (actually by the eccentric atheist-preacher Johann Heinrich Schulz [1739–1823], known as "Zopfschulz" because he wore a pigtail instead of a wig, as a symbol of his anti-establishment position) mocked Mendelssohn and maintained that Mendelssohn mistakenly thought himself to have refuted atheism once and for all in his *Jerusalem.*, but when he was confronted with a work (also by Schulz) entitled *Philosophische Betrachtung über Theologie und Religion überhaupt, und über die jüdische insonderheit* (Philosophic contemplation on theology and religion in general and on Judaism in particular, 1784) that attacked him for having denounced atheism as undermining morality, he, Mendelssohn, saw his defense of theism threatened. He therefore became concerned that Lessing would be branded an atheist. Therefore he conspired against Jacobi, but without success, and his death was the result of the anger he felt at seeing his plans miscarry!

Hamann, who had accused his "old friend Mendelssohn" of atheism – Hamann's *Golgotha* describes Mendelssohn as "a circumcised fellow-believer in the spirit and essence of pagan, naturalistic, atheistic fanaticism" – gave a number of impressions of Kant's reactions to the dispute. In a letter of Oct. 25, 1786, Hamann wrote that Kant was not at one with the Berliners (that is, Herz, Engel, the pro-Mendelssohn group, et al.).

In his letter to Herz, Apr. 7, 1786, Ak. [267], Kant expresses his opinion of the feud, and in Oct. 1786 Kant published his essay *"What Does It Mean to Orient Oneself in Thinking?" "(Was Heißt: Sich im Denken Orientieren?")* in the *Berliner Monatsschrift*. There Kant, who had no desire to serve as referee in the dispute, shows his opposition both to Jacobi's philosophy of faith and feeling and to Mendelssohn's attempt to establish rational theology on the foundation of "healthy common sense." Kant is closer to Mendelssohn than to Jacobi in that he regards Jacobi's conception of faith as a dangerous endorsement of *Schwärmerei*, but Kant insists that philosophers in both camps must defend freedom of conscience and inquiry against religious orthodoxy and the enemies of reason.

For additional details on the pantheism controversy and its background, see ch. 9, "Guardian of the Enlightenment," in A. Altmann's *Moses Mendelssohn*, Lewis Beck's *Early German Philosophy*, and the account of the *Pantheismusstreit* in F. Beiser's *The Fate of Reason*. as well as the biographical sketches of Mendelssohn, Lavater, et al., in this volume.

72 [264] (245)
From Ludwig Heinrich Jakob.[1]

March 26, 1786.

Halle, the 26th of March, 1786

Illustrious Herr Professor,   10:435

I believe that the intimacy I have enjoyed with your writings for some time now may to some extent justify my approaching you with greater familiarity than customary formality demands. It is to seek the   10:436 benefit of your advice on a matter on which I do not trust my own judgment and on which others either cannot or will not advise me. If the gratitude and warm veneration I feel toward a man who has so greatly illuminated my pessimistic dissatisfaction with previous metaphysical systems should constitute another reason for your excusing my boldness, then I take joy in being able to make this acknowledgment – an acknowledgment I have made so often in the circle of friends and students, with no greater warmth but with greater voice – to this man himself.

The immediate occasion of this letter is Mendelssohn's book[2] and a journal announcement[3] giving the impression that you were going to refute it. Mendelssohn deserves to have his book favorably received, and I believe that everyone, even those who disagree with him, will thank him for his illuminating discussion of previous proofs of the existence of God. But right away I heard some triumphal songs, stemming to be sure more from hearts than from minds, though gaining acceptance all the sooner just for that reason, songs that celebrate a victory that Herr Mendelssohn, according to his own statements, never even had in mind. Yes, one could even make out from certain reviews that his book is thought to have dealt a serious blow to the Kantian critique, which to me proves very clearly that people are still only skimming the *Critique*, not studying it thoroughly. I must confess that in my reading of Mendelssohn's book I found not the slightest thing that would strengthen the old proofs or make them more valid. Everywhere he makes precisely those assumptions that you in your *Critique* so justly attack. Herr Mendelssohn's complaints, in his Preface, about the current way of philosophizing, also seem to me totally groundless, especially if as is customary one takes them as directed against those that demand sense perception for every convincing existence claim. Nor did I find that Herr Mendelssohn said anything important that might justifiably be used against your *Critique*, and therefore I quite believed him when he said that he knew your work only through hearsay.[4] There was just a single passage that seemed to me to give the appearance of being intended as an arrow aimed against your *Critique*, namely p. 115, where he denies the concept of a thing in itself.[5] But I think the passage is easily rebutted, for Herr Mendelssohn concedes the central claim of your *Critique*, that it is impossible to assign predicates to a thing in itself, and merely disagrees with the implication of this thesis. For when Herr Mendelssohn, on p. 116, says, "You wish to know something that is absolutely not an object of knowledge," he says exactly what you say. But when he adds: "We stand at the limits not only of human cognition but of any cognition at all," he clearly asserts something that can in no way be proved. In short, the whole book seemed to me to be a really striking proof that nothing can be determined about existence a priori, and I wished therefore, right from the

10:437

start, that someone would come along who would examine it, not with such beautiful writing but with comparable clarity. Now I cannot conceal that, seeing here and there so many uninsightful comparisons between this book and your *Critique*, with general rejoicing on the one hand and total silence on the other, I myself had the idea of contributing something, with whatever powers I possess, toward a clear analysis. However, since I heard that you yourself were willing to undertake this project, I restrained myself and at the same time took delight in the thought that my wish would be fulfilled by one who could do it in the most uncontentious way. Meanwhile I was still a bit uneasy about this rumor. For it seems to me that all the counter-arguments are already fully contained in the *Critique*, and that therefore what is needed is more to display these arguments to the public rather than to invent them. For even the supposedly new proof rests on the undemonstrated presupposition that things in themselves are dependent on a necessary being and that only the concept of necessary being accords with the most complete understanding. This proof means nothing to the fatalist and establishes nothing more than that *appearances* are not possible without a thinking being, which must be conceded in any case; leaving that aside it seemed to me that some third party for a change should try to explain your ideas in his own way, because, unfortunately, people still look upon the *Critique* as a large beast that they fear but cannot trust. Yes, the prejudice in favor of the old system is so great that philosophers of great talent will privately though not openly pass 10:438 judgment on the *Critique*, and because they fear the destruction of the edifice in which they have till now securely resided, they try to convince others that the building is fireproof, so that people can regard any attack on it as a priori powerless. Young readers in particular are frightened by the description of the opaque curtain supposedly drawn before the sanctuary of your thoughts, and thus the truly beneficial spread of your ideas is hindered more than one would think. At least that is how matters stand in the circle where I live. That is why I think it not superfluous that a third party should try to demonstrate that understanding the propositions of your *Critique* does not require more than the powers of an ordinary intelligence, so that the naturalness and truth of your claims will be made that much more evident. What I must ask you then is whether you yourself will undertake the closer examination of Mendelssohn's book and, in case you do not take the partnership of others as superfluous, whether you would be kind enough to inspect my thoughts and to judge whether they might deserve to be presented to the world. For an incorrect account of your ideas would in fact be more harmful than none at all, since people will judge the value of the *Critique* from it. I hope, for the sake of the good cause, that I can expect your candid opinion, in the event that you do undertake to offer one. Nor will my vanity mislead me into mistrust toward you, however severe your judgment may turn out to be. I shall begin by examining Mendelssohn's axioms, then continue to the proof itself and show above all that his new turn does not strengthen the proof in the slightest. But I fear that this has already taken up too much of your time. So I await first of all your kind permission informing me to what extent I may turn to you again. I am with greatest respect

your

student and admirer
Jakob
Magister in Halle.

---

1 Ludwig Heinrich Jakob (1759–1827) studied at the Lutheran *Gymnasium* in Halle, became an instructor at the university, and eventually professor of philosophy in Halle. He attempted to provide a popular presentation of Kant's philosophy. The *Philosophischen Annalen,* or *Annalen der Philosophie und des philosophischen Geistes,* of which he was the editor, was a principal publication of loyal Kantianism at a time when Kant's doctrines were under attack. The *Annalen* attacked Fichte's work and criticized Schiller's writings on aesthetics, thus earning Jakob mockery in Schiller's *Xenien* where he is caricatured as a thief who stole 20 concepts from Kant.

2 Moses Mendelssohn, *Morgenstunden oder Vorlesungen über das Dasein Gottes* (Morning lessons, or lectures on the existence of God; Berlin, 1785).

3 The *Gothaische gelehrte Zeitungen* of January 25, 1786, contained a notice: "One expects a refutation by Professor Kant of Mendelssohn's proof of the existence of God, the proof which the latter has given in his most recent work, entitled *Morgenstunden.*"

4 In his preface Mendelssohn wrote that he knew the works of great men – Lambert, Tetens, Plattner, and even "the all-destroying Kant" ("der alles Zermalmender" became a famous phrase) only from incomplete reports of friends and from inadequate scholarly notices.

5 Mendelssohn there discusses the conflict between "idealists" and "dualists." The former, he claims, regard all sensuous appearances as accidents of the human mind and refuse to believe that there is an external material prototype (*Urbild*) to which they correspond. The passage Jakob refers to reads: "Are you not rather yourself an adherent of the intellectual [*geistigen*] system with which I am at odds, the system that confounds our language and tries to confuse us? For you grant that all characteristics which you ascribe to this prototype are mere accidents of the soul. But we want to know what this prototype itself is, not what it does. Friend, I answer, if you are serious then, I think, you want to know something that is not an object of knowledge. We stand at the limits not only of human cognition but of all cognition in general; and we want to go on from there without knowing where. If I tell you what

sort of concept you must make of a thing, the question of what that thing is in and for itself has no further meaning."

73 [266] (247)
To Johann Bering.[1]
April 7, 1786.

[*Kant thanks Bering for the gift of his dissertation and for his letters. He praises*   10:440
Bering's thoroughness and regrets that the work was not available at the book
fair, as it deserved to be more widely known.]

. . . Herr Tiedemann's supposed refutation[2] has shown so little understanding of the question at issue, so little insight into the principles relevant to deciding that issue and, if I may say so, so little talent for pure philosophical investigations, and your circumspection in all these matter shows so clearly in your work, that I imagine he will desist from further attempts of this sort. On the other hand I hope and trust with pleasure, from the evidence you, sir, have sent me, that your efforts will eventually come to arouse more enthusiasm for research on these   10:441 matters, and help to bring about new creativity in an ancient science that has fallen on hard times and much misunderstanding of late.

You ask how soon my Metaphysics will appear. I now feel it will be another two years. In the meantime, if I remain healthy, I shall publish something to take its place temporarily, viz., a new, highly revised edition of my *Critique*, which will come out soon, perhaps within half a year; my publisher, hearing of my intention, quickly sold his entire stock of the book and is now spurring me on. In it I shall attend to all the misinterpretations and misunderstandings that have come to my attention since the book began circulating. A number of things will be condensed and many new things that will clarify the theory will be added. I shall not change any of its essentials, since I thought out these ideas long enough before I put them on paper and, since then, have repeatedly examined and tested every proposition belonging to the system and found that each one stood the test, both by itself and in relation to the whole. Since, if I am successful with this project, almost any insightful person would be able to construct a system of metaphysics in conformity with my theory, I am therefore putting off my own composition of such a system for a while longer, in order to gain time for my system of practical philosophy, which is the sister of the former system and requires a similar treatment, though the difficulties are fewer.

May you continue, dearest sir, with your youthful strength and lovely talent, to correct the claims of speculative reason that seek to overstep its bounds and to combat the fanaticism that is always aroused by those claims; continue your work but without damaging the soul enlivening theoretical and practical uses of reason and without providing a cushion to lazy skepticism. Recognizing clearly reason's powers and at the same time the limits of its use makes one secure, stout-hearted and decisive; it is a good and useful thing. By contrast, it leads to undervaluing of reason and thus to laziness or fanaticism to be incessantly deceived by sweet hopes and by constantly renewed and just as constantly failed attempts to achieve something that lies beyond our powers.

10:442

I commend myself to your goodwill and remain your

Kant

---

1 Johann Bering (1748–1825), professor of logic and metaphysics in Marburg from 1785. He had asked Kant, in a letter dated Mar. 5, 1785, Ak. [238], for a transcription of Kant's lectures on metaphysics. In a subsequent letter, Sept. 24, 1785, Ak. [245], Bering sent Kant his dissertation, "Dissertatio philosophica de regressu successivo," a work directed largely against Dietrich Tiedemann's criticisms of Kant.

Bering became a strong disciple of Kant, and it was he who informed Kant, Sept. 21, 1786, Ak.[279], of the "Cabinets Ordre" forbidding anyone to lecture on Kant's philosophy at Marburg during the coming winter semester – an interesting irony, in view of that university's later fame as a center of Kant scholarship. Bering did not know the source of the opposition to Kant – he suspected Professors Christoph Meiners and J. G. H. Feder in Göttingen. See Ak. 13:182–187 for a fuller discussion. The editor suggests that the ban on Kant might have been issued without any specific scholar's responsibility, though the theologian Samuel Endemann's denunciation is conjectured to be the probable source.

The philosophical faculty of Marburg was instructed to report to the government by the end of the year whether Kant's philosophy encouraged (religious) skepticism, and whether it sought "to undermine the certainty of human knowledge." The report sent on Oct. 11, 1786, praised Kant's genius and depth of thinking but stated that his difficult terminology, obscurity, and unusual ideas insured his innocuousness, since he could never have any influence on the public even if his works did contain errors. The report then notes the distinction between doubt and skepticism and points out that the former is essential for scientific progress: Kant has in fact sought to refute the profound and dangerous doubts of the illustrious Hume; but having rejected the traditional proofs of God and the immortality of the soul, he has nevertheless sought to establish these truths on a surer foundation. The report is signed by eight men, including Bering. They did not all agree on the correctness of Kant's views, but all of them favored freedom of inquiry for the university. For the full texts, see Kant's *Werke*, Ak. 13: 182 f. An announcement in the *Allgemeine Literatur-zeitung* in Oct. 1787 removed the injunction against lectures on Kant's philosophy, though the lectures were to be "privatissime," that is, restricted to advanced students.

2   Dietrich Tiedemann (1748–1803), professor in Cassel, one of Kant's critics, published an essay on the nature of metaphysics, attacking the *Critique of Pure Reason* and the *Prolegomena*. "Über die Natur der Metaphysik; zur Prüfung von Herrn Prof. Kants Grundsätzen, in *Hessischen Beiträgen zur Gelehrsamkeit und Kunst*," I Band (Frankfurt, 1785).

   Frederick Beiser (*The Fate of Reason*, pp. 135 f.) calls attention to another work of Tiedemann's, *Versuch einer Erklärung des Ursprungs der Sprache*, attacked by Hamann because of its historical, empiricist, non-supernaturalistic account of the origin of language.

74 [267] (248)
To Marcus Herz.

April 7, 1786.

I found the lovely work[1] with which you have once again made me a present worthy of you, my dearest friend, as far as I have read – for my current distractions (on account of which I beg you also to forgive the brevity of this letter) have not allowed me the time to read it through completely.

The Jacobi [-Mendelssohn] controversy is nothing serious; it is only an affection of *inspired fanaticism*[a] trying to make a name for itself and is hardly worthy of a serious refutation. It is possible that I shall publish something in the *Berliner Monatsschrift* to expose this humbug.[2] Reichard,[3] too, has been infected with the genius-epidemic[b] and associates himself with the chosen ones. It is all the same to him how he does it, as long as he can make a big impression, as an author no less, and as to that too much has been granted him. I regret very much that no usable manuscripts from the excellent Moses [Mendelssohn] are to be found. But I can contribute nothing to the publication of his correspondence, since his letters to me contain nothing really scholarly, and a few general remarks of that nature do not provide material for a scholarly *opus postumum*. I must ask you also please to leave out completely any letters of mine that might turn up among his papers. They were never intended to be read by the public.

---

[a] *Eine affectierte Genieschwärmerei*   [b] *Genieseuche*

My friend Heilsberg[4] is almost fully recovered. I reproached him for neglecting your advice and he promised to make up for it very soon.

10:443 There are great difficulties here in collecting money for the monument in Berlin.[5] But I shall see what can be done.

Do maintain your love and habitual kind feeling for him who remains always, with warmth and respect,

Your loyal, devoted servant and friend,

I. Kant

---

1 Herz's "Versuch über den Schwindel" (Essay on vertigo, 1786). See Herz's letter of Feb. 27, 1786, Ak. [260].

2 As mentioned in Ak.[260], n. 2, Kant's essay, "What Does It Mean to Orient Oneself in Thinking?" (1786) presents his opinion of the controversy and takes issue with both Mendelssohn's and Jacobi's views. A full account of the events leading up to Kant's publication may be found in Allen W. Wood's introduction to his translation of the "Orientation" essay, in the Cambridge Edition of Kant, *Religion and Rational Theology* (1996).

3 The composer Johann Friedrich Reichardt. On Reichardt see Kant's letter to Herz, Ak.[164], n. 4, and the biographical sketches. The "genius-epidemic" was a feature of the early Romantic movement in literature and aesthetics.

4 Christoph Friedrich Heilsberg (1726–1807), a friend and schoolmate of Kant's. He served as both war and school councillor and he is the author of a descriptive account of Kant as a student. Herz had given some medical advice for him in a previous letter.

5 A monument in the shape of a pyramid, in Berlin, dedicated to Leibniz, Lambert, and Sulzer. The fourth side was to feature a portrait of Mendelssohn. Hamann wrote to Jacobi, Apr. 27, 1786, perhaps falsely, that Kant thought the Jewish community should bear all the costs of the monument alone, for the honor given to a Jewish philosopher in putting him among such men.

75 [269] (249)
From Friedrich Gottlob Born.[1]
May 7, 1786.

Noble Sir,
Most esteemed Herr Professor,

I hope most fervently, sir, that you will forgive my boldness in bothering *you* with this letter, since you do not know me. For a long

time I have had the idea of eventually translating *your* excellent writings   10:444
into old classical Latin. My reasons for this are the following: works of
this kind, which are certainly not brought forth by every century, and
from which one may expect the most important revolutions in the
domain of philosophy, are not only worthy of being introduced to
foreigners but cannot indeed be made available to them too soon.
Rarely do foreigners possess enough knowledge of the German language to enable them to read such profound works in the original and
to understand them completely. The usual translators have, on the
whole, only a very limited knowledge of the language, especially when
it comes to rigorous philosophy. Their translations are therefore shallow, incorrect, puzzling and not infrequently patent nonsense. But old
classical Latin is easily comprehensible to everyone. As an indication
of how my translation would read I have enclosed my prospectus. I
would begin with the *Critique of Pure Reason* and then eventually do
the rest of your masterful works. I do not however feel justified in
proceeding until I have your permission. If you do not approve of my
idea, then it is my duty to suppress it. But should it find favor with
you, please let me know as soon as possible. In that case I would also
wish that you might think it useful to offer here and there some brief
additions and clarification, or corrections of the often wholly insignificant criticisms made by Tiedemann[2] and be kind enough to share them
with me so that I can insert them into the proper places in my translation. If your publisher should agree to accept this translation I would
be all the more pleased.[3] I beg you for the gift of your goodwill and
for your kind permission to allow me to prove my devotion to you in
writing, and I remain with immeasurable respect and reverence

your wholly obedient servant
Friedrich Gottlob Born

---

1 Born (1743–1807) was professor of philosophy in Leipzig.
2 Dietrich Tiedemann. On Tiedemann and Kant's view of him see Kant's letter
   to Bering, Apr. 7, 1786, Ak.[266], where Kant writes very insultingly of Tiedemann.
3 The saga of efforts to get a Latin translation of Kant's *Critique* published is
   complicated. Born did not complete his translation for ten years. It was finally
   published in 1796. Hartknoch, son of Kant's publisher in Riga, wrote to Kant
   that he thought Born was working on the translation and had received an
   advance of 150 thalers but Born was impossible to contact. Born wrote to Kant
   (Kant never answered him directly) on May 10, 1790, Ak.[429], addressing
   Kant as "Your Magnificence," expressing an interest in doing another book, a

"pragmatic history of critical philosophy," and asking Kant to send him an autobiography. His translation work, he said, was interrupted by the need to work on a lexicon of church Latin. He explained to Kant that he needed the money and complained that Hartknoch's fee for Born's Kant translation, 3 thalers per page, was insufficient. Born asked whether Kant could get Hartknoch to agree to 5, in which case the first part of his book could be done by Michaelmas. Kant sympathized with Born's poverty, but, writing to Rudoph Gottlob Rath in Halle (see his letter of Oct. 16, 1792, Ak.[536]), he asked Rath to undertake the Latin translation, mentioning Schütz's offer to review it. Born's translations of Kant appeared in four volumes (Leipzig, 1796–8).

76 [273] (253)
To Ludwig Heinrich Jakob.
May 26, 1786.

10:450   Your worthy letter, sir, conveyed to me by a student traveling through here, gave me great pleasure, what with the interest you take in my philosophical efforts. I hope you will not come to regret your commitment to my cause, seeing the outcries and even intrigues currently opposing it. For it is part of human nature for people to defend a madness in which they have been raised, and it is only young, strong men that one can expect to have enough freedom of thought and
10:451   courage to liberate themselves from it. I am just now occupied with a second edition of the *Critique*, at the request of my publisher, and with it I shall clarify certain parts of the work whose misunderstanding has occasioned all the objections so far brought against it. It is irksome to me that an extensive academic business that has fallen on my shoulders this half year has robbed me of virtually all my time. For the present I must ignore all the distorted and even malicious judgments; their strength will subside of itself once the pretext of their mistaken interpretation is removed.

As for my supposed promise to refute Mendelssohn's *Morgenstunden*, the report is false and got into the Gotha paper through a misunderstanding. Nor do I now have the time for it; therefore, if you wish to take the trouble to show the fruitlessness of attempting to extend the bounds of pure reason in this manner, you will have the reward of guiding the reflections of good minds to a position from which they can hope for better success. And it is not at all necessary to have my judgment of your work in advance (besides which, I hardly have time for that now), except for what concerns p. 116 of Mendelssohn's book, about which, as soon as you wish to send me information about your project, I shall be honored to send you a sufficient correction.[1] Please excuse my brevity . . .

Your most devoted servant,
I. Kant

---

1 Kant wrote comments on Jakob's examination of Mendelssohn: *Einige Bemerkungen zu L. H. Jakobs Prüfung der Mendelssohnschen Morgenstunden* (Leipzig, 1786), Ak.8:149, ff. Jokob's essay bore the title *Prüfung der Mendelssohnschen Morgenstunden oder aller spekulativen Beweise für das Daseyn Gottes . . . nebst einer Abhandlung von Herrn Prof. Kant.*

77 [275] (255)
From Johann Erich Biester.

June 11, 1786.

Berlin, the 11th of June, 1786

When I received (via Herr Jenisch[1] whom, on your recommenda-   10:453
tion, I shall certainly try to help with all my might) your latest important letter yesterday, dearest Herr Professor, I was almost glad that a coincidence had prevented me from sending you the most recent issue of the [*Berliner.*] *Monatsschrift* any sooner. I would still have had to write you about a matter on which you yourself touch in the letter and concerning which I can now (having seen what you said about it) speak more explicitly.

The controversy now unfortunately raging so fiercely between (or about) Moses Mendelssohn and Herr Jakobi[2] involves, as far as I can see, two main points. The first is a question of *fact*: whether Lessing really was an atheist, and, connected with that, the question, whether Moses M[endelssohn] first agreed to have this fact publicized and thereafter sought to suppress it? But this is essentially only a side issue and is seen and treated as only a side issue even by Herr Jakobi and his friend[3] (the author of *Kritische Resultate*, etc.). For these gentlemen start with this factual question only in order to dogmatize emphatically about Reason, Philosophy, Deism, Revelation, Faith, etc. Only close friends who know Moses M. very intimately can get involved in this controversy. I confess that from what Herr Jakobi alleged about Lessing in his most recent work,[4] I take it to be highly probable that Lessing was inclined toward atheism. But as for Mendelssohn's conduct in this matter, if one is going to make a full appraisal of that one needs two things, both of which I lack: a precise knowledge of his character and above all an inspection of all the letters exchanged on this subject. Herr Jakobi, if one wanted to challenge him about this, seems still to have certain fragments of letters up his sleeve with which he would then come forth. For in fact one wishes that he had immediately published everything, totally and in chronological order, not (as in his latest work) the answering letters first and the earlier letters last. In short, the whole subject seems to me not worth resolving. For even assuming it were completely proved that Lessing was an atheist and that Moses M. was a weak person, what of it?

10:454

More important is the second point that these philosophical fanatics now so hotly pursue: the burial and mocking of any rational knowledge of God, the glorifying and virtual idolizing of the incomprehensible Spinozistic phantom of the brain, and the intolerant recommendation that one accept a positive religion as the only alternative that is necessary and at the same time befitting to every reasonable person. This point of contention must be important to every thinking friend of mankind, quite apart from any particular hypothesis or particular personality, especially in these times when fanaticism already confounds half of Europe, when gross, foolish, dogmatic atheism is taught and greeted with applause, and when now, with this most remarkable development, both of these confusions of the human understanding are actually united in the minds of these hare-brained people who have come along. I say: quite apart from any particular personality. For, like many things Herr Jakobi says, his allegations about the idolizing of Moses Mendelssohn are false and purely malicious. Scholars hereabouts have recognized the worth of this agreeable and capable philosopher, and the moral excellence of the man. But no one has ever meant to present him to the world as omniscient; what people here say about him is no different from what the best minds of Germany have always said of him. Zöllner[5] has written against his *Jerusalem*, and Engel[6] frequently engaged in oral arguments with him about the main theme of the book. He [Mendelssohn] knew quite well that neither Herz nor Engel was happy with his a priori proof of the existence of God. – It is really very strange to see what different people from other places have recently said about the "Berlin style of thinking," and what Herr Jakobi says with the most intense bitterness and in totally undeserved terms. There may be no place on earth where intellectuals are less cliquish, less partisan, and more open in expressing their disagreements. Nowhere are intellectual disputes handled more casually and with less rancor than here. What is he up to, this fanatic screamer, with his accusation of Crypto-Jesuitism, Papism, and widespread illegal dealing?

But, as I said, as far as I am concerned Moses M. and Berlin can stand or fall! It is only *truth* and *reason* that I would want to defend against these visible threats. And when conceited genius-fanatics[7] pose such threats in such a proud, haughty, dictatorial manner, I would wish that men who till now have held the helm of philosophy and been recognized by the entire intellectual world as reliable and experienced leaders would declare themselves in public, so that readers not be led astray by ignorant and officious coxswains who steer them to disastrous reefs instead of fertile islands. How it would gladden us all to hear right now that you have decided to speak out against this truly dangerous philosophical fanaticism. Only from you, excellent man, could one hope to get a thorough, instructive correction. But now this altogether strange Jakobi, who will do anything it takes to make himself important, portrays himself as solitary and oppressed and persecuted, but then also represents his opinion as that of all sensible people and of the greatest thinkers (Leibnitz, Lessing, Kant, Hemsterhuis, the author of the *Resultate*[8]) and of all worthwhile, pious Christians (Lavater, Hamann, et al.); in that way he is equally well served by martyrdom or by the agreement of the best witnesses. This fierce, impetuous man, it seems to me, has now drawn you into the controversy, esteemed sir, and in a most indiscreet manner, making you seem even more obliged to explain your position, for the sake of the good cause and the reassuring of your contemporaries.[9] Naturally, only the smallest number of readers are familiar with philosophical systems or have them at their command, especially a system as new, profound, and unusually penetrating as yours. If readers now find that *you* are cited as a corroborating witness by a writer who is contemptuous of truth and innocence, they won't know what to think, and finally they may well believe what he says. I can assure you that this is already the case with many highly noteworthy persons who have been deceived by this maneuver. But there is no more hateful accusation for an enlightened philosopher than that his principles *resolutely support dogmatic atheism and therefore fanaticism. Fanaticism through atheism!* That is Jakobi's teaching; and having *you* as a partner he has the impudence to maintain that he is not out to deceive the world.

You exhort me to avoid any hurtful attack on Herr Jakobi. What is really hurtful is only the personal attack and from that sort my friends and I will always strive to refrain. But Herr Jakobi has not restrained himself from anything, even lowering himself to insults and slanders, he has allowed himself (something that is always effective in his clique)

10:455

10:456

to treat *Nikolai*[10] most indecently. Nikolai's extended travel book[11] has to be brought into the controversy too, even the unfortunate and wholly false anecdote about the epigram,[12] which was as little Nikolai's work as yours or mine – the epigram was really an impromptu performance by the local chief of police, Philippi, at a dinner with the governor. Not only that but the book is written in such an arrogantly ignoble, childishly vain, contemptibly egoistic tone – it is hard to think of its equal in the German language. Anyone who writes in that *form* and with that *content* offends not only his contemporaries but reason itself to such a degree that an appropriate response is hardly possible.

However, let reviewers and whoever is an actual participant in this fight determine that. Only you, dearest, most excellent man, I implore you to throw your healing Stone of Minerva[13] on the raving fanatics; reject your initial plan and at least tell the public explicitly and immediately that Herr J. has misunderstood you and that you can never be an ally of the Christian Society for the Advancement of Atheism and Fanaticism. You probably find repugnant the idea of any public declaration against another person; all the more rude is Herr Jakobi's importunity. Whether your opposition to controversy should here balance out the love of truth I leave to your own decision. Allow me only to add two somewhat more personal remarks. It is in fact insulting to you to have a fanatic like Herr J. who writes with the bitterness of gall present himself as your intimate associate. The public naturally takes notice and what should it think if you say nothing in opposition to this suggestion? Might it not come to the insulting suspicion that words of praise from a Jakobi are capable of determining your action or inaction?

10:457

Furthermore: we are likely to experience a change[14] of which we cannot know (as with all future events) whether it will be favorable to freedom of thought or not. But everyone must be pained by the damage to the good cause and to the person if it can be made to appear that the greatest philosopher of our country and philosophy in general can be accused of supporting dogmatic atheism. This loathsome accusation might then make an impression, an impression which would however be totally weakened if you had previously declared your distance from any connection with this fanatic atheism.

You write to me of a defense that you want to make against the attacks of Herren Feder and Tittel.[15] Like everything from your pen, it will be instructive and useful to the public. But I cannot convince myself at all that Herr Jakobi, caught between suspicious signs from two different places on the literary horizon, has understood the feud aroused by Herren Feder and Tittel. He is here most likely only referring to *his* view; as arrogant as he is, he cannot regard *you* and himself, your system and his trickery, as equivalent. I also think that your rebuttal [of Feder and Tittel] cannot possibly be as important as that declaration for which I ask. Every sensible person shrugs his shoulders when he sees that a Feder (and Tittel is really only a weak shadow of a weak Feder) hopes to educate a Kant. A correction for this can do no harm. But the danger posed by Jakobi and the author of *Resultate* is certainly more urgent; and in fact too urgent, I think, for you to treat *this* matter only incidentally in an essay in which you mean to correct F. and T.

I hope and trust that your usual kindness will forgive the candor and diffuseness of this letter. Decide this matter as you wish; only never withdraw your kind friendship from me.

I have nothing to report to you about appointments to positions in your university. Because of the situation in Potsdam all business is in suspension. We hope at least to use this intervening period of time to   10:458 seek out capable people.

Your sincerest admirer and most devoted friend,

Biester

---

1   Daniel Jenisch (1762–1804) was a friend of Schultz and Hamann, later appointed preacher at the Nikolaikirche in Berlin. His letter to Kant of May 14, 1787, Ak.[297], from Braunschweig, contains some interesting gossip on the reception of Kant's writings and their popularity in Holland and Göttingen. In 1804 Jenisch's depression led him to drown himself in the Spree river. Schiller did not think highly of him; to Goethe he wrote, "Jenisch, that idiot who insists on poking his nose into everything" (Schiller's letter, Nov. 21, 1795).

2   Friedrich Heinrich Jacobi.

3   Thomas Wizenmann (1759–87), instructor of philosophy and friend of Jacobi. *Die Resultate der Jacobischen und Mendelssohnschen Philosophie, kritisch untersucht von einem Freywilligen* (The results of Jacobi's and Mendelssohn's philosophy critically examined by an impartial [observer]), published anonymously (Leipzig, 1786). Wizenmann's tract created a great stir and stimulated interest in the pantheism controversy. For a full discussion of Wizenmann and his *Resultate*, see Beiser, *The Fate of Reason*, ch. 4. Wizenmann attacked Mendelssohn, claiming that the latter's appeal to "healthy human understanding" ("bon sens") could mean nothing more than Jacobi's claim that all certainty rests on faith. He then refutes Mendelssohn's attempt to prove the existence of God on rational grounds and appeals in this connection to Kant, whom he calls "The German Philosopher." A Kantian objection to Jacobi's position is not pursued; it is simply presented as the product of "sober examination." In the final part of his book, Christian faith is defended against Jewish faith, with numerous personal attacks.

On Wizenmann see also Kant's "What Is Orientation in Thinking?" where Kant refers to him and "the not insignificant conclusions of the penetrating author of the *Resultate*." Kant's footnote in the *Critique of Practical Reason* (Ak. 5:143) also mentions and praises Wizenmann, "a fine and bright mind whose early death is to be regretted."

4 Jacobi, *Wider Mendelssohns Beschuldigungen bettrefend die Briefe über die Lehre des Spinoza*, (Leipzig, 1786).

5 Johann Friedrich Zöllner (1753–1804), a pastor in Berlin. *Über Moses Mendelssohns Jerusalem* (Berlin, 1784).

6 Johann Jacob Engel, one of the men responsible for the feud between Jacobi and Mendelssohn. See Herz's letter to Kant, Feb. 27, 1786, Ak.[260], n. 1.

7 It is interesting that Biester's phrase, "affectierte Genieschwärmer," is almost exactly Kant's characterization of the Jacobi partisans in his Apr. 7, 1786, letter to Herz.

8 Wizenmann's book. Cf. n. 3, above.

9 Jacobi wrote: "It is not my intention here to lower the Kantian philosophy to my own nor to raise mine to the level of the Kantian. I am content that this Hercules among thinkers must in all fairness stand even more condemned by my opponents (especially as to the impossibility of proving the existence of God) as do I in these matters." Jacobi, *Werke*, vol. IV, 2, p. 259 (quoted in Schöndörffer's edition of Kant's *Briefwechsel*, p. 845).

10 Christoph Friedrich Nicolai (1733–1811), publisher, book dealer, and author in Berlin, identified with the *Popularphilosopher* there, of whose journal, the *Allgemeine deutsche Bibliothek*, Nicolai was founding editor.

Nicolai is known also for his takeoff on Goethe's *Sorrows of Young Werther* – *Freuden* (Joys) *des Jungen Werthers* (1775). He was a friend of Lessing and Mendelssohn, an enemy of Kant, Schiller, and Goethe. See the biographical sketch of Nicolai.

11 *Beschreibung einer Reise durch Deutschland und die Schweiz* (Berlin and Stettin, 1783–96).

12 Jacobi quoted a verse, attributing it to Nicolai and claiming that it had already appeared in a number of newspapers: "Es ist ein Gott, das sagte Moses schon/ Doch den Beweis gab Moses Mendelssohn" (There is a God, Moses already said/But the proof was given by Moses Mendelssohn).

13 Cf. Biester's letter of Nov. 8, 1785, Ak. [251], n. 2.

12 Biester must be alluding to the impending death of Frederick the Great; it occurred on Aug. 17, 1786.

15 Gottlob August Tittel (1739–1816) was a professor in Karlsruhe, an associate of Feder's. Both men attacked Kant's moral philosophy and supported "eudaimonism." Cf. Ak 5:505, f. and Kant's correspondence with Garve, especially Garve to Kant, July 13, 1783, Ak. [201].

1787

78 [300] (280)
To Christian Gottfried Schütz.
June 25, 1787.

I hope that a copy of the second edition of my *Critique* will have 10:489 been conveyed to you, dear friend, by Herr Grunert of Halle; if not, the enclosed letter to him, which I beg you to post, should take care of it.

If you think it necessary to arrange for a review of this second edition, I would be very grateful if it took note of an error in transcription that troubles me. Something like this:

"In the Preface, p. xi, the third line from the bottom contains a copying error, since "equilateral" is written instead of "equiangular" triangle. (Euclid's Elements, Bk. I, Prop. 5.)"

For even though in Diogenes Laertes' version one can easily see that the latter is intended, not every reader has a copy of Diogenes readily available.

My publisher commissioned a Latin translation of the second edi- 10:490 tion of my *Critique*, by Professor Born[1] in Leipzig. You were kind enough to offer to inspect his completed translation if it is sent to you a section at a time, to make sure that the style, which might aim too much at elegance, be more or less Scholastic if not quite Old Latin in its precision and correctness. If your kind offer is still valid, please let me know what my publisher will owe you for your trouble. From me you will have the greatest gratitude. I have sought to inform Prof. Born of this plan in my enclosed letter.

I am so far along with my *Critique of Practical Reason* that I intend to send it to Halle for printing next week. This work will better demonstrate and make comprehensible the possibility of supplementing, by pure practical reason, that which I denied to speculative reason – better than all the controversies with Feder and Abel[2] (of whom the first maintains that there is no a priori cognition at all while the other one maintains that there is some sort of cognition halfway between the empirical and the a priori). For this is really the stumbling block that made these men prefer to take the most impossible, yes, absurd path, in order to extend the speculative faculty to the supersensible, rather than submit to what they felt to be the wholly desolate verdict of the *Critique*.

Someone else will have to undertake a review of the third part of Herder's *Ideen*, and will have to explain that he is another reviewer. For I haven't the time for it, since I must start on the Foundations of the Critique of Taste right away.

With immutable respect and devotion, I am . . .

---

1   See Born's letter to Kant, Ak. [269], especially nn. 1 and 3.
2   Jakob Friedrich Abel (1751–1829), professor of philosophy in Karlsruhe, then Tübingen, was a friend of Schiller's. He published a critique of Kant, *Versuch über die Natur der spekulativen Vernunft zur Prüfung des Kantischen Systems* (Frankfurt and Leipzig, 1787).

79 [303] (283)
To Ludwig Heinrich Jakob.
September 11(?), 1787.

10:493   Esteemed Sir,

I take this opportunity to thank you for sending me your very successful book and for the good news you mentioned in your last
10:494   letter.[1] My congratulations on your new professorship.[2] Toellner's manual is quite good for a logic text.[3] In my humble opinion, it is necessary to present logic in its purity, as I said in the *Critique*, that is, as consisting merely of the totality*a* of the formal rules of thinking, leaving aside all materials that belong to metaphysics (concerning the origin of concepts as far as their content is concerned) or to psychology; in this way, logic will become not only easier to grasp but also more coherent and comprehensive. Feder thinks this fastidiousness

a Inbegriff

pedantic and useless. I have never written a metaphysics; please tell Herr *Hemmerde*[4] that I am opposed to the publication of my minor writings at present. I might revise them when I have the time for it and will then announce it, but don't expect this for another two years. – My *Critique of Practical Reason* is at Grunert's now.[5] It contains many things that will serve to correct the misunderstandings of the [Critique of] theoretical [reason]. I shall now turn at once to the *Critique of Taste*, with which I shall have finished my critical work, so that I can proceed to the dogmatic[b] part. I think it will appear before Easter.[6] – I wish you would try to compose a short system of metaphysics for the time being; I don't have the time to propose a design for it just now. The ontology part of it would begin (without the introduction of any critical ideas) with the concepts of space and time, only insofar as these (as pure intuitions) are the foundation of all experiences. After that, there are four main parts that would follow, containing the concepts of the understanding, divided according to the four classes of categories, each of which constitutes a section. All of them are to be treated merely *analytically*, in accordance with Baumgarten,[7] together with the predicables, their connection with time and space, and how they proceed, just as Baumgarten presents them. For every category, the corresponding synthetic principle (as presented in the second edition of the *Critique*) indicates how experience must conform to the category, and thus the whole of ontology is covered. Now after all this, the critical conception of space and time as form[s] of sensibility and the deduction of the categories are to be presented. For the latter, as well as the former, cannot be understood completely before this, and neither can the only possible way of proving the principles, as has been seen. Then come the transcendental ideas, which pertain either to *cosmology*, psychology, 10:495 or theology, and so on. I must close now, and I am, with friendship,

Your devoted servant,

I. Kant

---

[b] *dogmatisch* in this context could also be rendered "doctrinal."

---

1 Jakob's examination of Mendelssohn's *Morning Lessons* (*Prüfung der Mendelssohnschen Morgenstunden*, 1786). Jakob sent it to Kant "the moment it was printed," according to his letter of July 28, 1787, Ak. [301].

2 Jakob was advanced from Magister to *außerordentlicher* professor "by his Majesty" on Mar. 8, 1787. He reported to Kant that his lecture courses on logic and metaphysics were "rather well attended."

3 Johann Gottlieb Toellner (1724–74), professor of theology in Frankfurt and elsewhere, editor of A. G. Baumgarten's *Acroasis logica* (1765). Jakob had asked Kant for advice on a logic text, saying that Feder's book, which he had previ-

263

ously used, was unsystematic and totally inadequate, as was Ulrich's; Baumgarten's seemed to Jakob the best, in Toellner's edition.

4 Carl Hemmerde, printer in Halle.

5 Friedrich August Grunert, printer in Halle.

6 As usual, Kant was overly optimistic. The *Critique of Judgment*, containing Kant's theory of taste, appeared in 1790.

7 Alexander Gottlieb Baumgarten (1714–62), aesthetician, professor of philosophy in Frankfurt and elsewhere, whose works Kant used as textbooks.

80 [305] (285)
From Carl Leonhard Reinhold.[1]

October 12, 1787.

10:497   Esteemed Sir,

My passionate desire to approach **you** via a written visit has finally triumphed over the shy scruples I have been fighting for over a year. Yet even now I cannot help but worry whether the good intentions that animated the struggle are enough to justify my taking a quarter of an hour of your valuable time.

If I had nothing more in mind than to express my heart's gratitude, affection, esteem and admiration, I would have remained silent like *Klopstock*'s young man

who, as yet unwithered by many springtimes, is eager to tell the silver-haired, venerable old man *how much he loves him*, wanting to let that blazing expression pour forth. Impetuously he starts up at midnight, his soul aglow; the wings of dawn flutter; he hurries to the old man – and says it not![2]

And still I say it not; for how could words on a piece of paper convey it to you.

I am the author of the "Letter of a Priest from * * * concerning the *A.L.Z.* Review of Herder's *Ideen*"[3] which was published in the February 1785 issue of the *Deutsche Merkur*. I have nothing to add to this confession except that that letter was as well intentioned as my "Ehrenrettung der Reformation," which appeared in the *Merkur* in February 1786, and the two months following, concerning the two chapters of the historian Schmidt's book[4] and I am also the author of the "Letter 10:498   concerning the Kantian Philosophy"[5] that appeared in August 1786 and January of this year.

I know that *you* have read the former miserable letter[6] and from it have become acquainted with the unphilosophical philosophy of the obnoxious priest; unfortunately I don't know whether you have read the last "Letters" to which I referred. If I did know, I could just appeal to that and say nothing further about the salutary revolution in my thinking that occurred two years ago, a revolution through which *you* became the greatest and best benefactor to me that ever one human being could be to another.

I was first led to study the *Critique of Pure Reason* by *your* development of the *moral foundation* of our knowledge of religious fundamentals, which I encountered in the abstract of *your book*[7] published in the [*Allgemeine*] *Literaturzeitung*, the only part of the whole abstract that was comprehensible to me. I sensed, I sought and I found in the *Critique* the medicine – people hardly think it possible anymore – to relieve me of the unfortunate disjunction: either superstition or unbelief. I was well acquainted with both of these diseases from my own experience. I don't know whether I suffered from the second, from which the *Critique* cured me, as much as from the first, which I absorbed with my mother's milk – I was placed in a Catholic hot-house of fanaticism[8] in my fourteenth year, which powerfully amplified my superstitions. My joy at the radical recovery from these illnesses and my desire to spread the valued remedy I had discovered, a remedy which my contemporaries for the most part still misunderstood, led me to write the aforementioned "Letters concerning the Kantian Philosophy."

I gained confidence in my work from the good reception these "Letters" received from that part of the reading public to which they were directed, and from their good effect on my excellent father-in-law[9] who now plans to prepare himself for the *Critique of Pure Reason* by reading Schultz's *Erläuterungen*.[10] I asked myself whether it was only a sweet dream of mine that I felt the calling to be a voice in the wilderness preparing the way for the second Immanuel.[11]

I know how greedy it is of me to ask you at least to read the third (in the January issue) and the eighth (in the September issue) of my "Letters," and then, if you think it possible, to give me a simple testimonial, to be published in the place I shall mention, stating *that I have understood the Critique correctly*.[12] Your testimonial will put the seal of authenticity (I hope I am not dreaming) on my professional work, and will gain more conscientious and more numerous readers for my "Letters"[13] and an audience for my lectures, *Beginners' Introduction to the Critique of Reason*, which I shall be starting in two weeks. An improved edition of the "Letters" will appear at the next Easter book fair, published by the firm of Blumauer (my friend) and Gräffer in

10:499

Vienna. I hope that this first little volume will be followed by several others. I chose this publisher in order to have access not only to the usual audience reached by the Leipzig fair but also to the Imperial states where, as Blumauer assures me, the "Letters" seem to have an excellent reception.

Hardly was the word out that I would be giving the lectures that I mentioned concerning the Introduction when Professor Ulrich[14] here (who, as you probably know, attempted in his textbook to combine previously accepted metaphysics with the conclusions that follow from the *Critique of Pure Reason* but who, as you probably don't know, now, *since the day I arrived*, keeps finding contradictions in the *Critique* and has been submitting these to his auditors) announced that he would give a polemical lecture course on the *Critique*, for the benefit of his οντος οντων.[15] But since he had already used up all his available time for the coming half year with his scheduling of six different courses, and since the schedule of lectures was already in print, *he nailed a notice to the door of his lecture hall announcing that in the term after Easter* he would take on the *Critique*. In the meantime he tries to spread among the students the same mockery he advanced in his review on *space and causality* in the *Jena gelehrte Zeitung*, viz., that the *young gentlemen* (I am now in my thirties) who are currently *affected by the Kantian fever* and driven by idolatry for Kantian nit-picking *understand* their idol hardly at all. As a beginner I cannot be wholly indifferent to this compliment from an old and rather renowned teacher.

10:500

I venture to suggest the following way in which you might tell the public that I have, as far as you gather from my "Letters on the Kantian Philosophy," understood you correctly: a *fragment* of your reply to my letter, should you be kind enough, which I shall reprint in the *Teutscher Merkur* that my father-in-law and I have been publishing for the last year and a half. I hope you can also answer the following perplexity that several readers of the *Critique* have already voiced:

In the Note beneath the text of the Preface to the *Metaphysical Foundations of Natural Science*[16] you write very pointedly that the main foundation of your system is secure "even without a complete deduction of the categories" – on the other hand in both the first and second editions of the *Critique of Pure Reason*[17] in Chapter II of the Transcendental Analytic, Section I, "the indispensable necessity" of that deduction is asserted and demonstrated. The author of the "Letters on Kantian Philosophy" would feel himself richly rewarded, as would the publisher of the *Merkur* (who often assures me that he wishes his *Merkur* would carry *your name*) if you would resolve this seeming difficulty.[18]

If you find my forwardness unworthy of forgiveness or my request

unworthy of being granted, your silence will rebuke me. But I shall be
no less proud to call myself in truth

your sincere, devoted admirer
Carl Leonhard Reinhold Mpr[19]
Councillor of Weimar-Saxony and Professor of Philosophy in Jena.

Jena, October 12, 1787.

---

1 On Reinhold, see the letter from C. G. Schütz, Ak. [237], n. 2. While most of
  Reinhold's writings are available only in German, there is a recent English
  edition of his *Fundamental Concepts and Principles of Ethics*, translated by Sabine
  Roer (University of Missouri Press, 1995).

2 Reinhold here quotes Klopstock's ode "Mein Vaterland":

  > dem wenige Lenze verwelkten,
  > und der dem silberhaarigen, thatenumgebenen Greis
  > *wie sehr er Ihn liebe* das Flammenwort hinströmen will.
  >
  > Ungestüm fährt er auf um Mitternacht;
  > glühend ist seine Seele;
  > die Flügel der Morgenröthe wehen; Er eilt
  > zu dem Greis – und saget es nicht!

3 "Brief von dem Pfarrer aus * * *über die Rezension von Herders *Ideen* in der
  A.L.Z." This was Reinhold's reply to Kant's review of Herder's *Ideen*. Reinhold
  was a friend of Herder's at the time of his writing this piece.

4 Michael Ignaz Schmidt (1736–94), director of the state archives in Vienna,
  author of *Geschichte der Teutschen* (1778–85) and *Neuere Geschichte der Teutschen*
  (1785). Reinhold's discussion is of the latter work.

5 "Briefe über die Kantische Philosophie" (1786, ff). Reinhold published this
  anonymously, signing his work only with "R."

6 Kant replied to it; see "Errinerungen des Recensenten der Herderschen Ideen
  über ein im Februar des *Teutschen Merkuk* gegen diese Recension gerichtetes
  Schreiben," Ak. 8: 56–8.

7 Review of Johann Schultz's *Erläuterungen über des Hrn. Prof. Kant Kritik der
  reinen Vernunft* (1784) in the *A.L.Z.* (1785). The "only comprehensible part"
  was the discussion of Kant's critique of rational theology, the final part of the
  review, July 30, 1785, pp. 127–8.

8 In 1772 Reinhold was enrolled in the Jesuit school of St. Anna in Vienna.

9 The famous author Christoph Martin Wieland (1733–1813), whose daughter
  Reinhold had married in 1784.

10 The reference is to Johann Schultz's *Erläuterungen über des Herrn Professor Kant
   Critik der reinen Vernunft* (Exposition of Kant's *Critique of Pure Reason*, 1784
   and 1791), the first published commentary on the*Critique*.

11 Reinhold plays on Isaiah 40:3.

12 Kant compliments Reinhold at the end of "Über den Gebrauch teleologischer
   Principien in der Philosophie" (1788), Ak. 8: 184.

13 They were published in a greatly revised version, in the form of a book in two volumes (Leipzig, 1790/92).

14 Johann August Heinrich Ulrich (1746–1813), professor of philosophy in Jena. Cf. Ak.[239]. Until Reinhold's appearance in Jena, Ulrich was a follower of Kant's, but jealousy and rivalry seem to have converted him into an opponent. Friedrich Gedicke, a schoolmaster in Berlin and, with Biester, one of the founders of the *Berliner Monatsschrift*, wrote, "Though Court Councillor Ulrich has recently found a tremendous rival in Prof. Reinhold, he still has a great following. Before Reinhold came here, he was a devoted admirer of Kantian philosophy, but now he is all the more excitedly opposed to it. His lecture contains much that is enjoyable and instructive. Too bad that he plays the fool and even allows himself smutty jokes." The passage is quoted in Ak. 13: 204.

15 "being of beings"; the Greek phrase Reinhold uses here makes no grammatical sense, but Reinhold's meaning must be that Ulrich sought to puff himself up by attacking Kant.

16 See the long footnote in the preface of the *Metaphysische Anfangsgründe der Naturwissenschaft*, Ak. 4: 474 f., where Kant takes up Ulrich's objection.

17 Ak. 3: 99 ff., i.e., A 84=B 117 ff.

18 Kant responds in the penultimate paragraph of "Über den Gebrauch teleologischer Principien in der Philosophie," Ak. 8: 184.

19 "Mpr" is possibly an abbreviation for "manu propria reinholdi," i.e., "not a transcription."

81 [310] (290)
From Johann Cristoph Berens.[1]
December 5, 1787.

[Berens tells of his travels through West Prussia. Kant and his Critique are taking hold in Halle, Leipzig, and elsewhere. As yet there is no actual intrigue against Kant's philosophy, but teachers are reluctant to abandon their old ways and dislike seeing the foundations of their system undermined.]

. . . Plattner[2] refused to discuss your philosophy; he said only "We teach Kant."[a] His elegant lectures are more on philosophizing than on philosophy as such. The season was drawing to a close; otherwise I would have liked to look up Wieland[3] and Reinholdt [*sic*],[4] both of

---

[a] *wir lesen Kanten*

whom are very enthusiastic about [the Critique of] Pure Reason, or so their countrymen told me. The former [Wieland] maintains that if it is Kant who has defined the limits of the understanding we can all rest contented with that position. The second man [Reinhold], a former Capuchin monk or even Jesuit[5] but a thoroughly intelligent, unprejudiced man (he was in Berlin recently), weeps, or so Dr. Biester[6] told me, when he hears that your holy doctrine is not yet universally recognized. Prof. Eberhard[7] fears the consequences of your new philosophy for morality and thinks you should have followed the old view. Your former admirer, Prof. Ulrich,[8] is becoming your enemy, since Reinhold has taken away his laurels . . . So far we still have freedom of   10:508 thought and freedom of the press. The Secret Letters[9] concerning people in the current regime are circulated openly at court and in town. . . .

> Your
> J. C. Berens

---

1   Johann Cristoph Berens (1729–92), merchant, friend of Kant's and Hamann's.

2   Ernst Plattner (1744–1818), professor of medicine and physiology in Leipzig.

3   Christoph Martin Wieland (1733–1813), the famous German author.

4   Karl Leonhard Reinhold (1758–1823), son-in-law of Wieland, who became one of Kant's most famous disciples and popularizers. See the various letters to and from him in this collection.

5   Reinhold joined the Jesuits as a novice in 1772 but became a Barnabite monk when the Jesuit order was dissolved one year later.

6   On Biester see his letter to Kant, Ak.[168], and the biographical sketches.

7   Johann August Eberhard (1738–1809), professor of philosophy in Halle, a fervent opponent of Kant's critical philosophy who claimed it was anticipated and obviated by Leibniz. On Kant's response to Eberhard's criticisms, see Kant's letters to Reinhold of May 12 and 19, 1789, Ak.[359 and 360], and, for a full discussion of the issues raised in these letters and in Kant's lengthy essay on Eberhard, see Henry Allison, *The Kant-Eberhard Controversy* (Baltimore and London: The Johns Hopkins University Press, 1973).

8   Johann August Heinrich Ulrich (1744–1807), professor of philosophy in Jena. For Kant's response to Ulrich, see *Metaphysische Anfangsgründe der Naturwissenschaft,* Kant's *Werke,* Ak. 4: 474n.

9   *Geheime Briefe über die Preußische Staatsverfassung seit der Thronbesteigung Friedrich Wilhelms des Zweyten* (Secret letters concerning the Prussian constitution since the accession of Friedrich Wilhelm II; Utrecht, 1787). The letters contained critical discussions of the first royal edicts and attacked Bischoffswerder and Wöllner, two of the king's favorites, who became important in the censorship movement against liberal theologians.

82 [312] (291)
To Marcus Herz.
December 24, 1787.

10:512 Dearest friend,

One again you have made me a gift of a lovely essay, I mean the one on the Jewish custom of early burial.[1] I forgot to arrange in time for a copy of my *Critique of Practical Reason*, which has just been published, to be sent to you from Halle. I wanted to reciprocate your previous literary gifts to me, and that would have been a start. I must see whether I can still have this done.

Hasn't Herr David Friedländer[2] forwarded something to you that I sent him, information about a spinning machine that was invented here? I was hoping for your kind assistance. He has not answered me, though it has been several weeks. Do you think he might have been offended that I wrote on the envelope, next to his name, *the renowned Jewish merchant*? The reason I did this was that I was unsure whether his name was David and I feared that the letter might be delivered to some Christian who happened to have the name Friedländer. If you would be kind enough to speak to him about this, please ask him to reply as soon as he can whether the matter I asked about can be arranged or not.

I have got myself involved with philosophical work of a rather demanding and extensive sort for a man of my age. But I am making excellent progress, especially as regards the remaining part that I am now working on. It cheers me up and strengthens me to see this, and I have high hopes of putting metaphysical issues onto such a secure path as to bring my project to completion.

10:513 I commend myself to your continued good will and generous disposition toward me, and I remain, with greatest respect and sincere concern for your welfare,

your most devoted servant,
I. Kant

Königsberg, the 24th of December, 1787.

---

1 Herz's *An die Herausgeber des Hebräischen Sammlers, über die frühe Beerdigung der Juden* (Berlin, 1787).
2 On Friedländer, see Kant's letter to Herz, Ak.[59], n. 1. In Kant's letter to Friedländer, Nov. 6, 1787, Ak.[307], Kant described the problems of a friend

named Böttcher who sought a royal license or patent for a new spinning wheel that worked faster and easier than any previous model. It had been tested successfully, under official police scrutiny, by an arthritic spinner, using various sorts of yarn and thread. Kant asked Friedländer and, through him, Herz, if they could find financial backers for the inventor. Friedländer replied on Jan. 8, 1788, Ak.[317], that no one was interested in purchasing the new spinning wheel.

83 [313] (292)
To Carl Leonhard Reinhold
December 28 and 31, 1787.

I have read the lovely *Letters*,[1] excellent and kind sir, with which you have honored my philosophy. Their combination of thoroughness and charm are matchless and they have not failed to make a great impression in this region. I was therefore all the more eager somehow to express my thanks in writing, most likely in the *Deutscher Merkur*, and at least to indicate briefly that your ideas agree precisely with mine and that I am grateful for your success in simplifying them.[2] However, an essay in that very journal, written by the younger Herr Forster[3] and directed against some other ideas of mine, made it difficult to do this without taking on both projects together.[4] As far as the latter is concerned, namely my argument with Herr F, I was prevented from publishing a clarification of my hypothesis, in part by my official duties and in part by the indispositions that often attend my age, so the matter got postponed till now, and I take the liberty now of sending you an essay, with the request that you find room for it in the *Deutscher Merkur*.

I was very pleased to find out with certainty at last that you are the author of those excellent *Letters*. I had asked the printer, Herr Grunert in Halle, to send you a copy of my *Critique of Practical Reason* as a small token of my respect, but till now I did not know your exact address and Grunert was therefore unable to carry out my request.

10:514

If you would please mail him the enclosed letter he will do it if he still has copies. This little book will sufficiently resolve the many contradictions that the followers of the old-guard philosophy imagine they see in my *Critique*, and at the same time the contradictions in which they themselves are unavoidably caught up if they refuse to abandon their botched job are made perspicuous.

I hope you will pursue your new path with confidence, dear man. Only jealousy, not superiority in talent or insight, can stand in your way, and jealousy can always be conquered.

Without becoming guilty of self-conceit, I can assure you that the longer I continue on my path the less worried I become that any individual or even organized opposition (of the sort that is common nowadays) will ever significantly damage my system. My inner conviction grows, as I discover in working on different topics that not only does my system remain self-consistent but I find also, when sometimes I cannot see the right way to investigate a certain subject, that I need only look back at the general picture of the elements of knowledge, and of the mental powers pertaining to them, in order to discover elucidations I had not expected. I am now at work on the critique of taste, and I have discovered a new sort of a priori principles,[5] different from those heretofore observed. For there are three faculties of the mind: the faculty of cognition, the faculty of feeling pleasure and displeasure, and the faculty of desire. In the Critique *of Pure* (theoretical) *Reason*, I found a priori principles for the first of these, and in the Critique *of Practical Reason*, a priori principles for the third. I tried to find them for the second as well, and though I thought it impossible to find such principles, the analysis of the previously mentioned faculties of the human mind allowed me to discover a systematicity, giving me ample material at which to marvel and if possible to explore, material sufficient to last me for the rest of my life. This systematicity put me on the path to recognizing the three parts of philosophy, each of which has its a priori principles, which can be enumerated and for which one can delimit precisely the knowledge that may be based on them: theoretical philosophy, teleology, and practical philosophy, of which the second is, to be sure, the least rich in a priori grounds of determination. I hope to have a manuscript on this completed though not in print by Easter; it will be entitled "The Critique of Taste."

Please convey to your esteemed father-in-law[6] not only my highest regard but also my sincerest thanks for the manifold pleasures that his inimitable writings have given me.

If you have time, I would appreciate any news of the learned world, from which we are here rather removed. The learned world has its wars, alliances, and secret intrigues just as much as does the political world. I am neither willing nor able to play that game, but it is entertaining and it gives one a useful slant to know something of it.

Your *Letters* produced such friendly feelings in me, even without my knowing you, and gave such excellent proof of your talents and goodness of heart, making both me and the public indebted to you. I hope

10:515

that my letter will arouse similar feelings of friendship in you, and I remain with greatest respect

your wholly devoted and loyal servant,

I. Kant

P.S. This is as far as I got with the present letter when unavoidably I missed the postal departure. I have used the additional time to make some notes and insertions in the text of the enclosed essay that seemed to me needed. You will need a competent editorial assistant who understands the subject to make the connections on pages 6 and 7 correctly, where the marks indicate. Please don't forget to attend to this; also, when the piece is delivered from the printer, please be kind enough to send it to me by regular mail. I don't think that Councillor Wieland will have misgivings about publishing it in his journal because of its somewhat polemical character. I have scrupulously avoided such a tone, which is in any case unnatural to me. I have only tried to dispel   10:516
misunderstandings by providing clarifications.

December 31.   I. K.

Please forward the enclosed letter to Prof. Schütz.

----

1   Reinhold's "Briefe über die Kantische Philosophie," first published in the *Deutscher Merkur*, 1786/87.

2   In his essay, "On the Employment of Teleological Principles in Philosophy" ("Über den Gebrauch teleologischer Principien in der Philosophie"), Kant compliments the author of "Briefe über die Kantische Philosophy," i.e., Reinhold. Cf. Ak. 8:183.

3   Johann George Adam Forster (1754–94) was a world traveler and author, son of a professor in Halle, Johann Reinhold Forster.

4   The essay mentioned discusses Georg Forster's criticism of Kant's earlier essay, "Determination of the Concept of a Human Race" ("Bestimmung des Begriffs einer Menschenrasse, 1785. Kant's essay on teleological principles appeared in the *Teutsche Merkur*, Jan. and Feb. 1788. See also Kant's letter to Reinhold, Mar. 7, 1788, Ak.[322].

5   As often in Kant's writings, the word "a priori" comes after the word "Prinzipien"; "a priori" could, grammatically, be an adverb modifying "discovered" (*gefunden*), though in the context of this paragraph "I have discovered a priori a new sort of principles" seems a most unlikely translation of Kant's meaning.

6   The famous author Christoph Martin Wieland (1733–1813).

1788

[318] (297)
From Carl Leonhard Reinhold.[1]

January 19, 1788.

[*Abbreviated*]

10:523 Finally my wish is fulfilled – my strongest wish ever since my heart and mind were brought into concord by that man who among all men of present and past ages is most significant to me, and who becomes and must become more significant to me with every progressive step my liberated spirit takes, he who is attached to my soul with a love as pure and indelible as is the light of cognition that he has kindled in me – in a word, my wish to be known and loved by *you*. And it is you to whom I shall owe not only the tranquillity and the most blessed employments but also the sweetest joy of my life, which I have been fortunate enough to find in having the respect and good favor of noble human beings.

My distinguished father-in-law[2] takes joy in my joy. I conveyed your kind letter and the manuscript[3] to him right away along with your flattering references to him. He asked me to write to you. He would be proud to think that his writings contributed to *your* entertainment. Your essay, an excellent adornment to his *Merkur*, was most welcome to him. For that reason he regrets that when the manuscript arrived the first sheet of the *Merkur* already had Jenner's work along with a historical essay by Schiller[4] printed on it, so that the current new series had to be initiated with another name than yours. Since Schiller's essay
10:524 took up so much space, part of *your* essay had to be held for next month's issue, with which it will begin. Wieland undertook to make the division; but at my request he sent the last proof pages to me in Jena, and I have looked them over most conscientiously in case the print setter should err. As unhappy as I am about that division, I have

274

to concede that my father-in-law has a point when he maintains that the division will have the effect of increasing rather than decreasing the number of readers.

What can I say about this essay, about the passages in it that concern my modest efforts? What can I say about the *Critique of Practical Reason*, a copy of which I received today but which I had already devoured eight days ago? I have you to thank that I am presently struck dumb, and you to thank for my whole future life. If heaven grants me a son – it has already given me a gracious young lady – *your letter* and that *copy of your book* will be the inalienable treasures I shall bequeath to him, and they shall be sacred to him as reliable documentation of his father's worth.

I am so glad that in my "Letters on the Kantian Philosophy" I did not yet take up the actual explication of the *moral epistemic grounds of the basic truths of religion*. I would have kindled a tiny light where *you* with your *Critique of Practical Reason* have called forth a sun. I must admit that I had not anticipated finding such a degree of proof or such complete satisfaction as you provide.

Now I await with redoubled anticipation the Critique of Taste . . .

. . . Professor Jakob in Halle recently offered to collaborate with me on a new journal wholly dedicated to the Kantian Philosophy.[5] I asked   10:526
my local friends Schütz, Hufeland, and Magister Schmidt for advice, and with their agreement I made the following proposals to Herr Jakob: *First*, that the publication be announced in the name of a *society* of academic teachers and friends of philosophy, the aforementioned people being members with other people to be invited to join. We shall be content to call ourselves *editors*. *Secondly*, to name the journal *Philosophische Zuschauer* (Philosophical observers). But I abuse your valuable time – let me hold off more details until the project is ripe. So that the society not resemble an *alliance*, which would not be right, we should invite opponents and publish their essays as well, provided they are more than shallow twaddle.

An alliance between Göttingen and Würzburg becomes more and more striking to me. I hope to be able to send you news about it soon. There should be plenty to tell about the zeal the confederates are showing in their attacks.

Since I came here, Prof. U[lrich] has radically changed his mind about the *Critique of Reason*. Since the catalogue of lectures was already printed, he just now found out about my intention to lecture on the *Introduction* [to the *Critique*]. In order to beat me out, he put an announcement on the *door of his lecture room* even before the start of winter term that he would be giving his polemical lecture course against the *Critique of Pure Reason* in the summer term, which would meet four times a week and without any lecture fee required. To give you a sample of the tone in which this man speaks of his plan, I include here the end of his last lectures (he lectures daily for *six* hours):

"Kant, I shall be your stinger, Kantians, I shall be your pestilence. What Hercules promises, he will accomplish."

You will find it as difficult as I did to believe this silly nonsense. But the witnesses who heard this are too numerous, and Prof. Schütz wants to publish this story under Literary News in the *A.L.Z.*, without naming the university. You will have noticed how seriously your doctrine concerning freedom is distorted by this charlatan in his so-called *Eleutherologie*.[6] There were times when this man held up one of your letters on the podium – and now he complains often on the same podium that you have never answered his charges.

10:527

Forgive my entertaining you with such pathetic anecdotes. They hardly deserve to be discussed.

It is high time that I close, assuring you that my respect, which is must sincere and devoted, will be eternal.

Yours,

Reinhold mpr.[7]

Jena, the 19th of January, 1788

---

1 On Reinhold, see Schütz's letter of Feb. 18, 1785, Ak. [237], n. 2, and the biographical sketches.

2 Christoph Martin Wieland (1733–1813), the renowned author.

3 Kant's essay, "Über den Gebrauch teleologischer Principien in der Philosophie," appeared in the *Teutsche Merkur*, January and February issues, 1788.

4 The opening of Schiller's "Der Abfall der vereinigten Niederlande von der spanischen Regierung," 1788.

5 *Annalen der Philosophie und des philosophischen Geistes von einer Gesellschaft gelehrter Männer* was founded by Jakob in 1795, connected with the *Philosophischen Anzeiger* that Reinhold mentions. The journal lasted only till 1797. Cf. L. H. Jakob's letter to Kant, June 22, 1795, Ak. [667].

6 *Eleutheriologie, oder über Freiheit und Notwendigkeit* (Jena, 1788). A review of the work, by Kraus, appeared in the *A.L.Z.* in Apr. 1788. Kant contributed to this review. Cf. Ak. 8: 453–60. An English translation may be found in the volume *Practical Philosophy* (1996), ed. Mary J. Gregor, pp. 121–31, in the *Cambridge Edition of the Works of Immanuel Kant*.

7 Possibly an abbreviation for "manu propria reinholdi," i.e., written with his own hand.

85 [322] (301)
To Carl Leonhard Reinhold.
March 7, 1788.

Please accept my warmest thanks, dearest man, for the trouble and 10:531
even persecution you have experienced in taking on a cause for which
I perhaps am originally responsible, whose completion however will
depend on the work of elucidation and dissemination by younger men,
gifted and at the same time disposed to candor, men such as you.
There is something so illuminating and ingratiating in your style of
presentation, at the same time something so thoroughly thought out in
drawing together important applications, that I am delighted in advance at your *Introduction to the Critique*.[1] Herr Ulrich[2] is destroying
his own reputation with his efforts at opposition. He is not going to
increase his following with his recent proclamation of a mechanistic
theory of nature, supported as it is by those old, familiar sophistries. It
is really instructive and reassuring, at least for people who are reluctant
to get involved in controversies, to see how those who reject the
Critique cannot at all agree among themselves how to do it better. One
has only to look on quietly and if need be take notice of the main
moments of misinterpretation when the opportunity presents itself, but
otherwise continue on one's path without deviating from it, confident
that eventually everything will settle nicely into the right track. Profes- 10:532
sor Jacob's proposal to start a journal dedicated to these investigations
seems to me a happy inspiration, assuming that one has sufficiently
come to an understanding beforehand about the first appointments
that are to be made. For without making the advocacy or clearer
explication of the system the explicit goal of the journal, this would be
an as yet unseen inducement to examine thoroughly and *systematically*
the most controversial points of the whole of speculative and practical
philosophy; in time a good many quiet, thoughtful minds would join
in, people who don't want to commit themselves to extensive projects
but who would not refuse to present their ideas in short essays (which
of course would have to be mostly grain and not husk). Right now I
would propose as collaborators Professor Bering in Marburg and certainly our Court Chaplain Schultz. Personalities must be entirely ignored and even men like *Schlosser*[3] and *Jacobi*, even if a bit eccentric,
would have to have places set aside for them. I shall say more of this in
the future.

I am burdened this summer semester with unaccustomed work – the
job of rector of the university (which, along with the position of dean

of the faculty of philosophy, I have had to take on twice in three consecutive years). Nevertheless I hope to be able to publish my Critique of Taste by Michaelmas and thus to complete my critical projects.

I thank you sincerely for your efforts in securing the inclusion in the D[eutsche] Merkur of my somewhat dry essay; it has been printed more fastidiously than it deserves. Please convey my great respect and devotion to your esteemed father-in-law whose mind is still functioning with such youthful liveliness.

I. Kant

---

1 In a previous letter, Mar. 1, 1788, Reinhold had spoken of writing a work with this title. In fact he never published anything by that name. Perhaps he meant his essay, "Über das bisherige Schicksal der kantischen Philosophie," published in the Deutsche Merkur and separately, 1789.

2 Johann August Ulrich (1746–1813), professor of philosophy in Jena, discussed in Reinhold's preceding letter, Ak. [318], above.

3 Johann Georg Schlosser (1739–99), Goethe's brother-in-law; Kant later directed an essay against him: "Von einem neuerdings erhobenen vornehmen Ton in der Philosophie" (1796).

86 [330] (309)
From Christian Gottfried Schütz.

June 23, 1788.

Jena. June 23, 1788.

10:540   I came down with an illness last summer which made me weak and unable to take care of all sorts of accumulated business. I had to take
10:541   off four weeks in May for travels to restore my health. Thus almost for a year and a day I was robbed of the inexpressible pleasure of letting you know how my admiration for your mind and your heart increases with every new book that you produce. I do it now with this brief announcement: I felt myself truly *blessed* when I read your *Critique of Practical Reason*. My joy is further enhanced by the thought that a great many excellent men with whom I dare not even compare myself agree completely with my sentiments.

What prompts my writing to you now is a review of your most

recent book, to be published in the *A.L.Z.* and authored by Herr Rehberg of Hannover.[1] I enclose a copy of it. Before I allow anything of this sort to be printed, I should like *either* your comments on it *or* at least your declaration stating that you would be pleased:

> to submit an *essay* to the *Allgemeine Literatur Zeitung* clearing up the *penetrating* reviewer's principal misunderstandings (for the misinterpretations of dull-witted pates need no refutation from you).

The *A.L.Z.* is the best journal you can find right now to publicize such a clarification, for according to the most reliable estimates it presently has around 40,000 readers. Over 2,000 copies of each issue are actually sold, and a single copy is read not by 10 or 20 people but 30, 40, 50.

You notice that one of the things on which Herr Rehberg focuses is the Category of Freedom with respect to [the category of] *modality.*[2]

There is however *another problem* I find perplexing which I should like to ask you to resolve.

It seems to me that this portion of your Table ought to read:

1. that which *can* be commanded[a] – that which cannot be commanded, e.g., sensuous love;
2. that which *actually* is commanded, – that which is *not* actually commanded;
3. that which is *necessarily* commanded, e.g., (to each his own) – that which is only contingently commanded, e.g., (to give alms);   10:542

or, expressed in technical terms:

Possibility of the Law (*permitted* action)	*Impossibility* of a Law (*forbidden action*[b]).
Reality of a Law (duty)	*Unreality* of a Law (non-duty)
Necessity of a Law (unavoidable duties)	*Contingency*[c] of a Law (meritorious duties).

Under the category of *Possibility of a Law* there are two sorts of actions: actions which are actually specified by a law and actions which are not specified by a law. In other words, *permitted* actions. That I drink wine – something that I am not *bound* by a law to do – and that I maintain my life – something that a law does *bind* me to do – these actions are equally to be classified under *Permitted Actions* although

---

[a] "geboten"; the verb *gebieten* however carries with it the suggestion of something commanded by a ruler or lawful authority, i.e., the issuing of a commandment, not simply a command.

[b] "Nicht zu gebietende Handlung," an action that cannot be legitimately commanded.

[c] *Zufälligkeit*

if the wine were part of a prescribed therapy I *might* be bound to drink it.

Anything that *could not possibly* be binding on me to do is either: a) not at all *determined* by a law, or b) it is already determined by a *necessary* law that I *abstain* from doing it. Consequently two sorts of things belong here: a) physically necessary actions and physically impossible ones, in general those which do not fall within the domain of freedom, and b) an action whose opposite is necessarily binding, or which itself is necessarily forbidden. It can never be *binding* on one to kill oneself.[d]

That negation of *duty* is not only that which is *contrary* to duty but, just as in the *Critique of Pure Reason* "Existence" and "Non-existence" are [the opposing categories of modality], so here the contrast must be

Duty and Non-duty.

Non-duty includes 1) all actions that are impossible, 2) all actions that are not determined by any law or which are neither commanded nor forbidden, 3) all actions that are opposed to duty.

In the Preface to the *Critique of Pure Practical Reason* the example of a permitted action that is introduced there,[3] what an orator is permitted to do, etc. seems to me to belong under a different genus,[4] namely under *Rules of Skill*, which you yourself have wisely distinguished from ethical *Laws*.

10:543

I enclose also the two reviews of Rehberg's essay *Concerning the Relation of Metaphysics to Religion*[5] and beg you to examine the criticisms of Rehberg in both reviews and tell me whether you are satisfied with what is claimed there.

My friend and helper Dr. Hufeland sends you his best regards. I am distressed that your worthy colleague Professor Kraus does not submit his essays to the *A.L.Z.* more often.

I await your answer with great longing, wish you the most enduring good health, and remain eternally with greatest esteem

your obedient servant
Schütz

---

[d] The translation of *geboten* as "binding" rather than "commanded" seems preferable in this paragraph, in order to avoid attributing to Schütz the obviously false claim that no one can be commanded to kill himself.

---

1 *A.L.Z.*, 1788, Bd. III, pp. 353 ff. August Wilhelm Rehberg (1757–1836), author and statesman in Hannover, reviewed Kant's *Critique of Practical Reason*, question how "the world of Ideas could be connected with the real world." He challenged Kant's claim that pure practical reason and the feeling of respect

for the moral law could serve as a motivating principle. To Biester, Ak. [621], Kant wrote an answer to another of Rehberg's questions concerning Kant's ethical theory, viz., whether the principle that human beings must always be treated as ends is valid in the real world. Kant's own letter to Rehberg, Sept. 25, 1790, Ak. [448], concerns other matters entirely, the understanding of irrational numbers.

2 Cf. *Critique of Practical Reason*, Ak.5: 66–7, Kant's "Table of Categories of Freedom with Reference to the Concepts of Good and Evil." Under #4, "Categories of Modality," Kant lists three distinctions: The permitted and the forbidden, duty and that which is contrary to duty, and perfect and imperfect duty. Rehberg wants to replace this with the following: "1. The permitted (what can be consistent with duty) and what is not permitted; 2. What is in accord with duty or virtue (what is really determined by duty) and its opposite: and finally, the holy (which is thoroughly and necessarily in agreement with the moral law, because it is nothing but a pure expression of the latter) and the unholy. The division between perfect and imperfect duty, in the ordinary sense, belongs rather to the subjective and objective determination and thus to the category of Quantity."

3 Cf. Ak. 5: 11, n.: "For instance, an orator is not permitted to forge new words or constructions, but this is permitted, to some extent, to a poet. In neither case, though, is there any thought of duty, for if anyone wishes to forfeit his reputation as a speaker, no one can prevent it." Kant is elucidating what he means by "permitted" and "forbidden" in the table of categories of practical reason.

4 Schütz writes μεταβασις εις αλλο γενος (metabasis eis allo genos).

5 *Über das Verhältnis der Metaphysik zur Religion* (Berlin, 1787). The reviews in the *A.L.Z.* are 1788, II, pp. 617 ff. and pp. 689 ff. For a summary of Rehberg's position, see Ak. 13: 220.

87 [333] (312)
From Meyer[1]
September 5, 1788.

Esteemed Herr Professor,   10:545

Various people who are thoroughly well-informed and very strongly concerned about the preservation of freedom of thought have urged me to engage a respected scholar of great standing to write a clarification of the limits of freedom of the press and the beneficial consequences of that freedom even from a political point of view, and including a discussion of the power of the sovereign in religious matters.

I realize that much has been written about these matters in recent times, but this subject is so important that it always deserves to be considered from a new angle. It would be of enormous utility to have such an analysis now, since there are good reasons for fearing restrictions on the freedom of the press and the freedom to publish. You would make another great contribution to the cause of enlightenment, and to the welfare of humanity that is so closely tied up with it, if you would undertake such a book. And I would certainly earn the gratitude of all sensible people if I were even remotely responsible for your doing this.

10:546   Such a book would make an even greater impression if it came from your hands, in view of your long and distinguished reputation among scholars. Fanatics of every kind would be less able to support their stand by an appeal to your philosophical system, claiming as they do that since our reason has limits we must finally have recourse to blind faith. I am sure that many of them really imagine that you secretly hold this view.

If you should decide to compose such a piece, I beg you to let me publish it. I am going to open my bookstore around Christmas, for which opening I have just received a license from the king. Of course I would like to be able to start out with an important book.

I leave the conditions entirely to you, for I am already convinced of your fairness. At the same time let me be so bold as to commend myself to your good will if you have anything else to publish; fairness in such matters will always be my guiding principle.

Hoping for a speedy and kind reply I have the honor of remaining

your obedient servant

Meyer

Book merchant

(return address at Herr Pauli's book shop[2]

---

1   Evidently a book merchant in Berlin. Nothing else is known of him.
2   Joachim Pauli, bookseller and Privy *Kommerzienrat* in Berlin.

88 [340] (318)
To Johann Schultz,
November 25, 1788.

Reverend and esteemed Sir,   10:554

When I consider writings that aim at the rectification of human
knowledge, especially at the clear, unobscured presentation of our faculties, I am entirely opposed to any factional or rhetorical concealment
of whatever errors in one's own system may be brought to one's
attention. Here as elsewhere, my motto is rather: Honesty is the best
policy. Therefore my motive in wanting to look over before its publi-   10:555
cation the solid book[1] you have started was only to make it easier to
forestall future controversies, many of which might be avoided by
resolving some misunderstanding, an easy thing to do since we live so
close to each other and can exchange our views so readily.

Allow me therefore to state certain doubts I feel about your contention that, contrary to my own thesis, there are no synthetic a priori
cognitions in arithmetic, only analytic ones.

Universal arithmetic (algebra) is an *ampliative* science to such an
extent that one cannot name a single rational science equal to it in this
respect. In fact the remaining parts of pure mathematics [*Mathesis*]
make progress largely because of the development of that universal
doctrine of magnitude. If the latter consisted of merely analytic judgments, one would have to say at least that the definition of "analytic"
as meaning "merely explicative" was incorrect. And then we would face
the difficult and important question, How is it possible to extend our
knowledge *by means of merely analytic judgments*?

I can form a concept of one and the same magnitude by means of
several different kinds of composition and separation, (notice, however,
that both addition and subtraction are syntheses). Objectively, the concept I form is indeed identical (as in every equation). But subjectively,
depending on the type of composition that I think, in order to arrive
at that concept, the concepts are very different. So that at any rate my
judgment goes beyond the concept I have of the synthesis, in that the
judgment substitutes another kind of synthesis (simpler and more appropriate to the construction) in place of the first synthesis, though
it always determines the object in the same way. Thus I can arrive
at a single determination of a magnitude $= 8$ by means of $3 + 5$, or
$12 - 4$, or 2×4, or 2^3, namely 8. But my thought "$3 + 5$" did not include the thought "2×4." Just as little did it include the concept "8,"
which is equal in value to both of these.

It is true that arithmetic has no *axioms*, since its object is actually not any *quantum*, that is, any object of intuition as a quantity, but merely *quantity as such*, that is, it considers the concept of a thing in general by means of quantitative determination.[2] On the other hand, 10:556 arithmetic does have *postulates*, that is, immediately certain practical judgments. For if I regard 3 + 4 as the setting of a *problem*, namely, to find a third number = 7 such that the one number will be seen as that which completes the sum [*complementum ad totum*] of that number with the other, the solution is found by means of the simplest operation, requiring no special prescription, namely by the successive addition generated by the number 4, simply continuing the counting up from the number 3. The judgment "3 + 4 = 7" does seem to be a merely theoretical judgment, and, objectively regarded, that is what it is; but subjectively regarded, the sign "+" signifies the synthesis involved in getting a third number out of two other numbers, and it signifies a task to be done, requiring no rule prescribing its solution and no proof. Consequently the judgment is a *postulate*. Now assuming it were an analytic judgment, I would have to *think* exactly the same thing by "3 + 4" as by "7," and the judgment would only make me more clearly conscious of what I thought. But since 12 − 5 = 7 yields a number = 7 that is actually the same number I thought when I was adding 3 + 4, it would follow, according to the principle "things equal to the same thing are equal to each other," that when I think "3 and 4" I must at the same time be thinking "12 and 5." And this does not jibe with my own consciousness.

All analytic judgment *by means of concepts* have this characteristic: they can represent a predicate only as a constituent concept contained in the subject concept; only the definition demands that both concepts be reciprocal [*conceptus reciproci*]. But in an arithmetical judgment, namely, an equation, both concepts must be absolutely reciprocal concepts and objectively completely identical, for example, the concepts "3 + 4" and "7." The number 7 must thus not have arisen from the task "Conjoin 3 and 4 in one number" by means of an analysis. Rather, it must have arisen by means of a construction, that is, synthetically. This construction presents the concept of the composition of two numbers in an *a priori* intuition, namely a single counting up. – Here we have the construction of the concept of quantity, not that of a quantum. For the idea that the conjoining of 3 and 4, considered as distinct concepts of magnitude, could yield the concept of a *single* quantity was only a thought. The number 7 is thus the presentation of this concept in one act of adding together.

Time, as you correctly notice, has no influence on the properties of 10:557 numbers (considered as pure determinations of magnitude), as it may have on the property of any alteration (considered as alteration of a quantum) that is itself possible only relative to a specific state of inner sense and its form (time); the science of number, notwithstanding succession, which every construction of magnitude requires, is a pure intellectual synthesis that we represent to ourselves in thoughts. But insofar as specific magnitudes (quanta) are to be determined in accordance with this, they must be given to us in such a way that we can apprehend their intuition successively; and thus this apprehension is subject to the condition of time. So that when all is said and done, we cannot subject any object other than an object of a possible *sensible* intuition to quantitative, numerical assessment, and it thus remains a principle without exception that mathematics applies only to *sensibilia*. The magnitude of God's perfection, of duration, and so on, can only be expressed by means of the *totality* of reality; it cannot possibly be represented by means of numbers, even if one wanted to assume a merely intelligible unity as a measure. – I take this opportunity to note that, since the enemies of the *Critique* like to gnaw on every phrase, it would be advisable to change the passage on page 27, line 4, 5, 6, a little, where there is a reference to a *sensuous* understanding and the divine understanding appears to have a sort of *thinking* ascribed to it.

It would be greatly to your credit, esteemed sir, if you were to work out a statement of the grounds that explain why the pure doctrine of magnitude is capable of such an extensive a priori expansion (the explanation given on pages 68 and 69 itself requires such a deduction). No one could do a better job of this than you.

My humble suggestion is thus that you suppress Number II, from page 54 to 71 and (if you don't have time to carry out the desirable investigation I mentioned) just replace it with an indication of the importance of such an investigation. A claim such as you make in that section, a claim that contrasts so sharply with everything that follows, will be only too useful to people who are just looking for an excuse to abandon all deep investigations; it will encourage them to deny the existence of all synthetic *a priori* cognitions and say that the old principle of contradiction is everywhere sufficient.

Please forgive the liberty I have taken and also the haste with which,   10:558 in the interest of promptness, I have expressed my thoughts. I hope above all that you will not let your publisher pressure you. The time that otherwise will have to be devoted to controversies can be cut in half by taking care ahead of time to obviate misunderstandings.[3]

I hope to have the honor of discussing these matters with you in person, and I remain with total respect

Your most obedient servant,

I. Kant.

1 Schulz (or Schultz) *Prüfung der Kantischen Kritik der reinen Vernunft* (Königsberg), pt. I (1789) and pt. II (1792).

2 Cf. *Critique of Pure Reason* A 164 = B 204 f.; A 732 = B 760 ff.

3 Schultz seems to have been won over completely by Kant's argument. In Schultz's *Prüfung der Kantischen Kritik der reinen Vernunft*, 1. Teil (Königsberg, 1789, published by Hartung), 2 Teil (1792, published by Nicolovius), Teil I, p. 211, has virtually a quotation of some of Kant's remarks in this letter, asserting the a priori but amazingly "ampliative" character of the science of "allgemeine Mathesis."

1789

89 [346] (324)
From Heinrich Jung-Stilling.[1]
March 1, 1789.

Esteemed Sir, 11:7

This is the second time in my life that I write to you; you will recall that some years ago I sent you a little tract, "Glimpses into the Secrets of Natural Philosophy,"[2] which I had had printed anonymously. But now I speak to you in an entirely different tone; now what I must do is to thank you with my whole heart.

The total story of my life, which has been published by Decker in Berlin under the title "Stilling," demonstrates how much reason I have to believe in a God, a Redeemer, a teacher of mankind, and in a special 11:8 providence. My biography shows how dreadful philosophical confusion and nonsense, Pro and Contra rationalizing, made it necessary to hold fast to the New Testament if I were to avoid sinking into a bottomless, groundless abyss. Yet my reason struggled perpetually for apodictic certainty, which neither the Bible nor Wolf nor mystics nor Hume nor Loke [*sic*] nor Swedenborg nor Helvetius could give me. Unconditional, fearful, anxious faith was thus my lot, while at the same time Determinism with all its conquering power pressed on my heart, my understanding, my reason, imprisoning me completely and gradually subduing me. No foe was ever more horrible to me than determinism; it is the greatest despot of humanity, strangling every incipient attempt at goodness and every pious trust in God, and yet determinism is so reliable, so certainly true, so evident to every thinking mind, that the world is inescapably lost, religion and morality are destroyed, just as soon as we isolate our sense world and believe the world to be in itself exactly as we imagine it and think it to be. But who in the world even dreams that there is such a thing as a Kantian Transcendental Idealism? If you had not constructed and revealed this secret to the human soul, what would have happened? All the refined determinism that the great thinkers of our time dream up is nothing but soap bubbles which finally dissolve into fatalism; there is no deliverance, no other escape.

In this state of anxiety last autumn I came upon some essays in the German Museum, discussing the moral law, and suddenly I felt a glow of warmth.[3] The opacity that everyone decries in your writings and the chatter of your opponents who talk as if YOU were a danger to religion had frightened me away. But now I started to work, first reading Schulz's *Explication of the Critique of Pure Reason*,[4] and then the *Critique of Practical Reason* as well, and after a number of re-readings I now understand, I grasp everything and I find apodictic truth and certainty everywhere. God bless YOU! You are a great, a very great tool in the hand of God; I do not flatter – your philosophy will bring about a much more blessed and universal revolution than Luther's Reformation. For as soon as one comprehends the *Critique of Reason* one sees that no refutation of it is possible. Consequently your philosophy must be eternal and immutable, and its beneficent effects will lead the religion of Jesus – whose only purpose is holiness – back to its original purity. Every science will become more systematic, purer and more certain, and there will be extraordinary gains especially in the field of legislation.

11:9

I am a certified teacher of political economy in the full sense of the phrase; I have published a whole series of textbooks on this subject and they have generally been well received. Nevertheless I see deficiencies and errors everywhere, for I lack a true and pure Metaphysics of Legislation, which I take to be most important. How I wish that YOU could compose such a work as well! May we hope for that?

It occurred to me recently in reading Montesquieu's *Spirit of the Laws* that four principles of natural law can be based on the four classes of categories. (1) Preserve yourself. (2) Satisfy your needs. (3) Be a member of civil society. (4) Perfect yourself. Now I want to study the *Critique of Practical Reason* again and see whether I find the clue there. May I hope to receive your thoughts about these principles? I certainly don't wish to rob you of your time any more than necessary, but since I am just starting to work out my System of Political Economy I would like to secure it on firm ground and to build on your philosophical foundations.

God, how peaceful, how full of blessed expectation you can be as you approach the evening of your life! May God make you cheerful and full of the sense of a joyful future. Fare you well, great and noble man! I am eternally

your

true, devoted admirer

Dr. Jung

---

1 Johann Heinrich Jung-Stilling (1740–1817) is known to history from his autobiography and from Goethe's *Dichtung und Wahrheit*, Book 16.
At the time of this letter he was professor of government (or political
economy – *Kameralwissenschaft*) in Marburg. Jung-Stilling thought Kant his
savior because Kant had shown the incompetence of natural reason to speak
on spiritual matters. Kant's answering letter (Ak. [347]) reassures Jung-Stilling,
agreeing that the Gospels are a source of truth. But Jung-Stilling saw every
moral postulate as a direct revelation of God; Kant could not sympathize with
that sort of *Schwärmerei*. Jung-Stilling's view of Kant's philosophy later became
less favorable.
Jung-Stilling was also renowned as an ophthalmologist, a specialist in cataract surgery. He was pro-rector of a university, had 5 children to support, 15
dependents in his household. To assist him with his domestic responsibilities
he married for the third time at age 51. His mystical writings, e.g., "Scenes
from the Realm of Spirits," led to opposition. A book entitled *Heimweh*
(Homesickness) was popular, translated into all European languages and, according to the *Allgemeine deutsche Biographie*, was still read in Christian homes
in 1880. Between 1803 and 1817, Jung-Stilling was regarded as a Christian
herald. He won a following for his anti-sectarian religious views.
Recent and contemporary philosophers may have heard of them through
C. D. Broad, who mentions him as "the German occultist" on account of his
book *Theorie der Geisterkunde*. See Broad, *Religion, Philosophy and Psychical Research* (New York: Harcourt, Brace & Co., 1953), p. 154, for an interesting
chapter entitled "Kant and Psychical Research."

2 *Blicke in die Geheimnisse der Naturweisheit denen Herrn von Dalberg, Herdern und
Kant gewidmet* (Berlin and Leipzig, 1787). Hamann wrote to Hartknoch, Feb.
17, 1787, that Kant had given him his copy as a present but that he (Hamann)
could neither endure it nor read it, though he was pleased with the gift.

3 "Versuche über die Grundsätze der Metaphysik der Sitten des Herrn Prof.
Kant," Deutsches Museum (Leipzig, 1787/88).

4 Johann Schultz, *Erläuterungen über des Herrn Professor Kant Kritik der reinen
Vernunft*, 1784.

90 [347] (325)[1]
To Heinrich Jung-Stilling.
After March 1, 1789.

Your interest in every investigation into the vocation of man does   23:494
honor to you, dear sir; it stands in contrast to the attitude of the
majority of speculative minds, whose interests are motivated only by
partisanship or vanity. And it is quite right of you to seek in the

Gospels the final satisfaction of your striving for a secure foundation of wisdom and hope, since that book is an everlasting guide to true wisdom, one that not only agrees with a Reason which has completed her speculations but also sheds new light on the whole field surveyed by that reason, illuminating what still remains opaque to it.

That the *Critique of [Pure] Reason* has been useful to you in this quest must be owing not to me but to your own keen mind, which manages to draw something of value out of even an imperfect work. But I was quite surprised that the system of categories, which must indeed be the a priori foundation for any classification of the principles of scientific knowledge based on concepts, would be the place you would look for help in setting up a system of civil law. I think that here, too, you are not mistaken.

The principles that you suggest as foundational for a system of legislation cannot serve that purpose properly, since they are valid also as precepts for *human beings in the state of nature*, even the third of your principles, "Be a member of civil society." One might raise the question how laws should be given in a civil society that is already presupposed; and in that case, I think one might say, following the order of the categories:

23:495

> (1) as regards *quantity*, the laws must be of such a nature that one [citizen] might have decreed them for all, and all for one;
>
> (2) as regards *quality*, it is not the citizen's *purpose*[a] that the laws must decide, for all citizens may be allowed to pursue their own happiness in conformity with their own inclination and power; but laws concern only the freedom of every person and the forcible limitation on that freedom imposed by the condition that each person's freedom must be compatible with that of every other person;[2]
>
> (3) as regards the category of *relation*, it is not those of the citizen's actions that relate to that person or to God that are to be condemned but only those external actions that restrict the freedom of a person's fellow citizens;
>
> (4) as for *modality*, the laws (qua coercive) must not be given as arbitrary and accidental commandments required for the sake of some purposes that happen to be desired; they must be given only insofar as they are *necessary* for the achievement of universal freedom.

But the general problem of civil union is this: To unite freedom with a coercion that is yet consistent with universal freedom and its preservation. In this manner there arises a state of external justice

---

[a] *Zweck*

(*status iustitiae externae*) whereby that which was only an *Idea* in the state of nature (namely, the notion of law^b as the mere *entitlement*^c to coerce) is *actualized*.

Around the end of this summer I shall begin to work on my "Metaphysics of Morals," and by next Easter I should be finished with it. In it the a priori principles for any civil constitution in general will also be discussed.

In view of the integrity of your thinking and the lively concern for all that is good that I perceive in your letters to me, I am sure that the peace of mind with which, not without justification, you are pleased to credit me, in the evening of my life, will brighten the days of your own life, and may there be many of them still to be lived through.

With respect and friendship, I am

Your most devoted servant,
I. Kant

^b *Recht*   ^c *Befugnis*

---

1 Ak. 11:10 contains a fragment of Kant's reply to Jung-Stilling's letter of Mar. 1, 1789, Ak.[346], Ak. 23:494–5 the fuller version utilized in this translation.

2 Cf. *Critique of Pure Reason*, A 316 = B 373. "A constitution allowing the greatest possible human freedom in accordance with laws by which the freedom of each is made to be consistent with that of all others. . . ."

91 [351] (329)
From Marcus Herz.
April 7, 1789.

Esteemed Sir,   11:14
Unforgettable teacher,

Herr *Salomon Maimon*,[1] whose manuscript, containing penetrating reflections on the Kantian system, is being sent to you by regular mail, has asked me to write an introduction to you, to accompany his letter. I am delighted that he has given me an opportunity to assure my unforgettable teacher once more of my respect. Unfortunately my mind has so degenerated since I studied with you that I cannot show you through the exercise of those mental powers that you nurtured so excellently in me that I am even worthy of expressing my esteem for you! So I must express it in another way, seizing the first, best opportunity of this sort. My total entanglement in the practical sphere that surrounds me increases daily; unfortunately it renders me physically and morally incapable of pursuing those sweet, sublime philosophical speculations with which you now grace the world – speculations that make humanity aware of itself and its worth, and that tempt me most powerfully to participate in them. Your immortal books stand perpetually before me; I open them almost daily and discuss them diligently with my friends. But the demands of my practical life have made me completely incapable of grasping your system as a whole and really assimilating it. I can confess to you that the thought of this incapacity depresses many an hour of my life.

11:15

Herr *Salomon Maimon*, formerly one of the crudest of Polish Jews, has managed to educate himself in the last few years to an extraordinary degree. By means of his genius, shrewdness, and diligence he has achieved a command of virtually all the higher disciplines and especially, just lately, a command of your philosophy or at least of your manner of philosophizing. Indeed he has achieved this to such an extent that I can confidently assert him to be one of the very, very few people on earth who comprehend you so completely. He lives here in pitiful circumstances, supported by some friends, devoted entirely to philosophy. He is also my friend and I love and treasure him uncommonly. It was my urging that caused him to send these essays, which he means to publish, for you to review beforehand. I took it upon myself to ask you to look over his writings and convey your opinion of them and, if you find them worthy of publication, to let the world know of this in a brief statement. I know full well the audacity of this request; but, praise God, I also know the man of whom I make it.

How are you faring, estimable man? How is your health? Are you over-exerting yourself, at your age? God, if only I might have the good fortune to hear your answer to these and countless other questions face to face while life lasts! I remain

my unforgettable teacher's wholly devoted servant,

Marcus Herz.

Berlin, the 7th of April, 1789.

---

1 Salomon ben Joshua, known as Salomon Maimon (1753–1800). Herz and Kant spell Maimon's name "Maymon." A Polish-Lithuanian Jew, Maimon raised himself by his own bootstraps from extraordinarily impoverished circumstances. He was married at the age of 11 and became a father at 14. His languages were Hebrew and the Polish-Latvian dialect spoken in his region;

the only books available to him were Talmudic and Old Testament studies. Driven by a thirst for knowledge – Maimon seems to have had a photographic memory for whatever he read – he made his way to Berlin as a penniless beggar. Rejected as "uncouth" by the Berliners, he managed to reach Posen (or Poznan) and to be hired as a private tutor in a Jewish family. On his second trip to Berlin, he succeeded this time in meeting Moses Mendelssohn and, largely through him, in gaining acceptance.

92 [352] (330)
From Salomon Maimon.[1]
April 7, 1789.

Esteemed Sir,   11:15

Filled with the veneration owed to a man who has reformed philosophy and thereby reformed all other sciences as well, I am emboldened to approach you only by the love of truth.

Condemned at birth to live out the best years of my life in the woods of Lithuania, deprived of every assistance in acquiring knowl- 11:16
edge, I finally had the good fortune to get to Berlin, late though it was. Here the support of certain noble-minded persons has put me in a position to study the sciences. It was natural, I think, that my eagerness to arrive at my main goal – the truth – should make me neglect to some extent those subordinate studies, language, method, and so on. Therefore, for a long time I dared not make any of my thoughts public, to expose them to a world whose taste is currently so sophisticated, even though I had read various systems of philosophy, had thought through them and, now and then, discovered something new. Finally I was lucky enough to see your immortal book, to study it, and to reconstruct the whole of my thinking in order to come into accord with it. I have tried as hard as I can to draw the final implications from this work, to impress them on my memory, and to seek out the track of the main argument, so that I might penetrate the author's mind. With this end in view, I have written down my results and have made a few comments, mainly concerning the following points:

1. The distinction you draw between analytic and synthetic propositions and the reality of the latter.
2. The question, *Quid Juris?* This question, because of its importance, deserves the attention of a Kant. If one spells it out the

way you yourself do, it becomes: How can something a priori be applied with certainty to something a posteriori? The answer or deduction that you give in your book is, as the answer of only a Kant can be, totally satisfying. But if one wishes to amplify the question, one asks: How can an a priori concept be applied to an intuition, even an a priori intuition? This question must await the master's attention, if it is to be answered satisfactorily.

3. I define a new class of ideas that I call *ideas of the understanding*[a] which signify *material totality*, just as your Ideas of Reason signify *formal totality*. I believe I have opened the way to a new means of answering the aforementioned *Quid Juris* question.

4. The question, *Quid facti*? You seem to have touched on this, but it is, I think, important to answer it fully, on account of the Humean skepticism.

These comments summarize the content of the manuscript that I venture to submit to you. My good friends have urged me for a long time to publish this book, but I did not want to comply without having subjected it to your priceless judgment. If a Kant should find the book not utterly unworthy of his attention, he will certainly not scorn him who approaches so reverentially. He will answer, will instruct where errors are committed, or give his approval if the work is found to deserve it, and he will thereby make its author doubly happy.[2]

Your wholly devoted servant and admirer,
Salomon Maimon

Berlin

---

[a] *Verstandesideen*

---

1 Salomon ben Joshua, known as Salomon Maimon (1753–1800). On Maimon, see the preceding letter from Herz, ak. [351], n. 1, and the biographical sketches.

2 For Kant's reply, see his letter to Herz, May 26, 1789, Ak. [362]. Kant's brief note to Maimon, May 24, 1789, Ak. [361], praises his "unusual talent for profound investigations" and refers him to his letter to Herz.

93 [354] (332)
From Johann Benjamin Jachmann.[1]
April 15, 1789.

[Abbreviated]

... Last Tuesday I presented my paper on the distinction between synthetic and analytic judgments to the Speculative Society. What I said was mainly what you said in the Introduction to your *Critique*, and I also tried to acquaint the Society with the overall intent and plan of your book. I especially tried to put the question, "How are synthetic a priori judgments possible?" in its most conspicuous light. My intention was to show the solution to this question and thus at the same time to discuss space and time. I had previously worked out my lecture in German with this end in mind, but I put off making an English translation so long that I was unable to finish it on time. I found it particularly difficult to find the right words for your ideas, and this was all the more difficult for me since I had never read any philosophical books in English. Besides this, I thought my essay too long for the occasion, and since the subject is so speculative, I feared it would fatigue the audience, since they would be unable to follow the arguments. As far as my reading of the essay went, it was highly successful. People marveled at the originality of the plan, the importance of the subject, the unusual precision in the definition of concepts, and so on. But they regretted that, after I had aroused their curiosity, I had not satisfied it, for I did not tell them the solution to this important question. They requested unanimously that I relate it to them as soon as possible. – Hume's views, and especially those of a certain Hardley [*sic*][2] (I don't know whether this book has been translated into German), are strongly admired and defended in this Society and also among most of the philosophers in Scotland. A priori judgments are totally impossible, according to Hardley, whom I have, however, not read myself – I know him only from conversations. All our concepts rest on sensation, reflection, and association, and so on. All necessary judgments, for example, are mere identities, as, for example, in mathematics, the proposition 7 + 5 = 12. So that when I say "7 and 5," I am at the same time saying "12." Twelve is only another way of expressing "7 + 5," just as "Deus" is another word for God. They also talk a great deal about "common sense." The proposition that everything that happens has a cause is not a necessary proposition. It depends merely on the uniformity of experience, and so on. Dr. Reid of Glasgow[3] does not agree. ... Hardley's theory of the passions[4] is especially popular here; I am convinced that

11:21

the theory is without foundations. He maintains that all depressing passions are only abstractions or negations of stimulating passions. For example, fear is only an abstraction derived from hope, as cold is the abstraction of heat, and therefore not truly a real thing. I have had some extraordinarily strong arguments over this, in the Medical Society as well as in the Speculative Society. . . .

Your most obedient friend and servant,
Joh. Benj. Jachmann

Edinburgh

---

1 Johann Benjamin Jachmann (1765–1832), Kant's student and amanuensis. This excerpt is from a letter that runs seven pages in the Akademie edition. Jachmann writes of his personal circumstances, his election to an honorary membership in the Glasgow Chemical Society, his lectures to medical and philosophical societies, etc. He explains his financial problems and asks Kant to send him some books by Reinhold and Jakob.

2 David Hartley (1705–57). The book referred to is his *Observations on Man, His Frame, His Duty, and His Expectations* (London, 1749). Part I, ch. 111, sec. 11, deals with mathematical judgments.

3 Thomas Reid (1710–96).

4 Joseph Priestley, *Hartley's Theory of the Human Mind: On the Principle of the Association of Ideas* (London, 1775), ch. III, sec. III, prop. 41.

94 [359] (337)
To Karl Leonhard Reinhold.

May 12, 1789.

11:33 Sincerest thanks, my most cherished and dearest friend, for the communication of your kind opinion of me,[1] which arrived together with your lovely present on the day after my birthday! The portrait of me by Herr Loewe, a Jewish painter, done without my consent, is supposed to resemble me to a degree, from what my friends say. But a man who knows painting said at first glance: a Jew always paints people to look like Jews. And the proof of this is found in the nose. But enough of this.

I couldn't send you my judgment of Eberhard's new attack earlier,[2] since our shop did not even have all three of the first issues of his

296

magazine, and I could find them only in the public library. Whence the delay in my answer. *That Herr Eberhard, along with a number of people*, has not *understood me* is the least you can say[3] (for that might be partly my fault). But I shall show you in my following remarks that he actually sets out to misunderstand me, and even to make me incomprehensible.

In the first issue of the magazine he tries to appear as a man who is aware of his own importance in the eyes of the philosophical public. He speaks of "sensations" aroused by the *Critique*, of "sanguine hopes" that were "surpassed," of the many people were stupefied and of the many who have not yet recovered (as if he were writing for the theater, or the boudoir, about some rival), and like a man who is fed up with watching the show, he determines to put a stop to it. – I wish that this insolent charlatanry might be shoved under his nose a bit. – The first three issues of the magazine more or less make up a unit, of which the   11:34 third, from page 307 on,[4] attacks the main contention of my Introduction in the *Critique* and closes triumphantly with "We should therefore now. . . ." I cannot fail to make a few remarks about this, so that those readers who take the trouble to check up on it will not overlook the fraud with which this man, who is dishonest in every line he writes – on those matters where he is weak and on those where his opponent is strong – puts everything in an equivocal light. I will only indicate the pages and the opening words of the places I discuss and beg you to look up the rest for yourself. The refutation of the fourth part of the third issue will serve to reveal the whole man, as far as his "insight" as well as his character are concerned. My remarks concern mainly pages 314–19.

On pages 314 f. he writes, "According to this the distinction would be," and so on, to "insofar as we can make anything definite out of this."[5]

His explanation of an a priori synthetic judgment is pure deception, namely, a flat tautology. For in the expression "an a priori judgment" it is already implied that the predicate of the judgment is necessary; and the expression "synthetic" implies that the predicate is not the essence nor an essential part of the concept that serves as subject of the judgment, for otherwise the predicate would be identical with the subject concept and the judgment would thus not be synthetic. Whatever is thought as necessarily connected with a concept, but is not thought through identity, is thought through something necessarily connected with, but *distinct* from, the essence of the concept, that is, connected with the essence through some ground. For it is one and the same thing to say that the predicate is not thought as part of the essence of the concept but yet as necessarily through it, or to say that it is grounded in the essence, that is, it must be thought as an attribute of the subject. Therefore his pretended great discovery is nothing but a shallow tautology in which by surreptitiously substituting other meanings for the technical terms of logic, one creates the illusion of having offered a real *basis of explanation.*

But this sham discovery has yet a second inexcusable flaw: as an alleged definition, it is not convertible. For I can say in any case: In every synthetic judgment the predicates are attributes of the subject, but I cannot say conversely: Every judgment that asserts an attribute of its subject is a synthetic a priori judgment – for there are also *analytic* attributes. Extension is an essential part of the concept of a body, for it is a *primitive* mark of the latter concept, which cannot be derived from any other inner mark. Divisibility, however, is also a necessary predicate of the concept of body, and therefore an *attribute*, but only in the sense that it can be inferred (as subaltern) from the former predicate (extension). Now divisibility can be derived from the concept of something extended (as composite) according to the principle of identity; and the judgment "Every body is divisible" is an a priori judgment that has an attribute of the thing for its predicate (the thing itself for its subject) and thus is not a synthetic judgment. Consequently, the fact that the predicate in a judgment is an attribute does not at all serve to distinguish synthetic a priori judgments from analytic judgments.

All similar errors, which start out as confusions and end up as deliberate deceptions, are based on this point: the logical relation of ground and consequent is mistaken for the real relation. A ground is (in general) that whereby something else (distinct from it) is made *determinate (quo posito **determinate*** ponitur aliud).*[a] A consequent *(rationatum)* is *quod non ponitur nisi posito alio.*[b] The ground must thus always be something distinct from the consequent, and he who can provide no ground but the given consequent itself shows that he does not know (or that the thing does not have) any ground! Now this distinction of ground and consequent is either merely *logical* (having to do with the manner of representation) or *real,* that is, in the object

---

* This expression must never be left out of the definition of "ground." For a *consequent* too, is something that, if I posit it, I must at the same time think something else as posited, that is, a consequent always belongs to something or other that is its ground. But when I think something as consequent, I posit only *some* ground *or other; which* ground is undetermined. (Thus the hypothetical judgment is based on the rule, "a positione consequentis ad positionem antecedentis non valet consequentia" [the movement from the consequent to the antecedent is not valid].) On the other hand, if the ground is posited, the consequent is determined.

[a] that which being posited *determines something else*
[b] that which is not posited unless *something else* is posited

itself. The concept of the extended is logically distinct from the concept of the divisible; for the former contains the latter, but it contains much more besides. In the thing itself,^{c} however, the two are identical, for divisibility really is contained in the concept of extension. But it is   11:36
real distinctness that is required for a synthetic judgment. When logic says that all (assertoric) judgments must have a ground, it does not concern itself with this real distinction at all. Logic abstracts from it, because this distinction relates to the content of cognition. If, however, one asserts that every *thing* has its ground, one always means by this the real ground.

Now when Eberhard names the principle of sufficient reason as the principle for synthetic propositions generally, he must mean by this nothing other than the logical axiom.^{d} This axiom, however, allows also for analytic grounds, and it can indeed be derived from the principle of contradiction; but then it is a clumsy absurdity on his part to justify his so-called *non-identical* judgments on the basis of the principle of sufficient reason, a principle which on his own view is merely a consequence of the principle of contradiction (a principle that is absolutely incapable of grounding any but identical judgments).

In passing I remark (so that in the future people may more easily take notice of Eberhard's wrong track) that the real ground is again twofold: either the *formal* ground (of the *intuition* of the object) – as, for example, the sides of a triangle contain the ground of the angle – or the *material* ground (of the *existence* of the thing). The latter determines that whatever contains it will be called *cause*. It is quite customary that the conjurers of metaphysics make sleights of hand and, before one realizes it, leap from the logical principle of sufficient reason to the transcendental principle of causality, assuming the latter to be already contained in the former. The statement *nihil est sine ratione*, which in effect says "everything exists only as a consequence," is in itself absurd – either that, or these people give it some other meaning. Thus the whole discussion of *essence*, *attributes*, and so on, absolutely does not belong to metaphysics (where Baumgarten, along with several others, has placed it) but merely to logic. For I can easily find the logical essence of a given concept, namely its primitive *constitutiva*, as well as the attributes, as *rationata logica* of this essence, by means of the analysis of my concepts into all that I think under them. But the **real** essence (the nature) of any object, that is, the primary *inner* ground of **all** that **necessarily belongs** to a given thing, this is impossible for man to discover in regard to any object. For example, extension and impen-   11:37
etrability constitute the whole logical essence of the concept of matter, that is, they are all that is necessarily and primitively contained in my,

---

^{c} *in der Sache selbst* ^{d} *Grundsatz*

and every man's, concept of matter. But to know the real essence of matter, the primary, inner, sufficient ground of *all* that *necessarily belongs* to matter, this far exceeds all human capacities. We cannot discover the essence of *water*, of *earth*, or the essence of any other empirical object; but leaving that aside, even the real essence of space and time and the basic reason why the former has three dimensions, the latter only one, are unknowable. And the reason for this is precisely that since the logical essence is to be known analytically and the real essence must be known synthetically and a priori, there must be a ground of the synthesis for the latter, which brings *us* at least to a standstill.

The reason that mathematical judgments yield only synthetic attributes is not that all synthetic a priori judgments have to do exclusively with attributes; it is rather that mathematical judgments cannot but be synthetic and a priori. On page 314, where Eberhard introduces such a judgment as an example, he writes, cautiously: "The question as to whether there are such judgments outside mathematics may for the present be set aside." Why did he not offer at least one of the various examples from metaphysics for purposes of comparison? He must have found it difficult to find one that could withstand such a comparison. On page 319, however, he ventures to consider one, which he claims to be obviously synthetic. But it is obviously analytic, and the example fails. The proposition is: *Everything necessary is eternal; all necessary truths are eternal truths.* The latter judgment says no more than that necessary truths are not restricted by any accidental conditions (and therefore are also not restricted to any position in time); but this is exactly what the concept of necessity is, so that the proposition is analytic. But if what he wanted to assert is that necessary truth *exists* at all times, this is an absurdity to which we cannot be expected to assent. He couldn't possibly have intended the first proposition to refer to the eternal existence of a *thing*, for then the second proposition would be totally unrelated to it. (At first I thought the expression "*eternal* truths" and its *opposite*, "*temporal* truths," were merely affectations employing figurative terminology, rather improper for a transcendental critique. Now, however, it seems as though Eberhard really takes them literally.)

On pages 318–19, we read: "Herr K. seems to understand 'synthetic judgment' to mean judgments that are not absolutely necessary truths and, of absolutely necessary truths, just those whose necessary predicates can only be discovered a posteriori by the human understanding. For, except for mathematical judgments, *only experiential judgments are necessary*."[6] This is such a crude misunderstanding, or rather a deliberate misrepresentation of my view, that one can predict how "genuine" the consequences are going to be.

Of his opponents he says repeatedly that their distinction between synthetic and analytic judgments has already been known for a long

11:38

time. Maybe so! But the importance of the distinction was not been recognized, because all a priori judgments were regarded as analytic, whereas only experiential judgments were reckoned as synthetic, so that the whole point of the distinction was lost.

And finally, Herr Eberhard says on page 316: "One seeks in vain for Kant's *principle for synthetic judgments.*" But that principle is unequivocally presented in the whole *Critique,* from the chapter on the schematism on, though not in a specific formula. It is this: *All synthetic judgments of theoretical cognition are possible only by the relating of a given concept to an intuition* . . . If the synthetic judgment is an experiential judgment, the underlying intuition must be empirical; if the judgment is a priori synthetic, the intuition must be pure. Since it is impossible (for us human beings) to have pure intuitions other than merely of the form of the subject (since no object is given) and of his receptivity to representations, that is, his capacity to be affected by objects, the reality of synthetic a priori propositions is itself sufficient to prove that these propositions concern only sensible objects and cannot transcend appearances. This is shown even without our having to know that space and time are those forms of sensibility and that the a priori concepts to which we relate our intuitions, in order to make synthetic a priori judgments, are categories. However, once we recognize these categories and their origin as mere forms of thinking, we become convinced that they cannot by themselves provide any genuine knowledge, and that, when supplied with intuitions, they do not give us any *theoretical knowledge,* of the supersensible, though they can be used as Ideas for a practical purpose without transcending their proper sphere. This is so just because the limitation of our power of conferring objective reality upon our concepts is not a limitation on the possibility of things. Nor does this limitation restrict the use of the categories, as concepts of things in general, when considering the supersensible, a use which grounds genuinely given practical Ideas of reason. Thus the principle of synthetic a priori judgments has infinitely greater fruitfulness than the principle of sufficient reason, which determines nothing and which, considered in its universality, is merely logical.

11:39

These then, dear friend, are my remarks on the third issue of Eberhard's magazine, which I put wholly at your disposal.[7] The delicacy to which you have committed yourself in your projected work, and which is so in accord with your restrained character, may not only be undeserved by this man but actually disadvantageous, if you are driven too far. I shall have the honor of sending you the conclusion of my remarks on the second issue during the next week, which will serve to reveal his truly malicious character along with his ignorance. Since he is inclined to regard every gentleness a weakness, he can only be stopped by a blunt confrontation with his absurdities and misrepresentations. Please use my remarks as you see fit, for they are only hints to help you recall what your own diligent study of this material must already have disclosed. I give you full permission even to use my name wherever and whenever you please.

For your lovely book,[8] which I have not yet had time to read, my sincerest thanks. I am eager to hear of your theory of the faculty of representation, which should appear at the same book fair as my *Critique of Judgment* (a part of which is the "Critique of Taste") next Michaelmas. My compliments to Herren Schütz, Hufeland, and your distinguished father-in-law.[9]

With the greatest respect and sincere friendship, I am

Your devoted

I. Kant

See enclosure

---

1 Kant refers to Reinhold's letter of Apr. 9, 1789, Ak. [353]. The letter was accompanied by a gift – for Kant's 66th birthday – an etching by Charles Townley of 1789, based on a 1784 portrait of Kant painted by Johann Michael Siegfried Loewe (1756–1831), along with a poem by R. B. Jachmann and Kiesewetter. The poem may be found in Ak. 12: 407–9.

2 Johann August Eberhard (1738–1809), a Wolffian philosopher, professor at Halle, and founder of the *Philosophisches Magazin*, a journal specifically devoted to attacking Kant's philosophy. Eberhard's claim that whatever is true in the *Critique of Pure Reason* had already been said by Leibniz provoked Kant's important polemical essay, *On a Discovery According to which Any New Critique of Pure Reason Has Been Made Superfluous by an Earlier One (Über eine Entdeckung nach der alle neue Kritik der reinen Vernunft durch eine ältere entbehrlich gemacht werden soll, 1790). See Ak. 8:187–251 and 492–7.

Henry Allison's *The Kant-Eberhard Controversy* (Baltimore and London: The Johns Hopkins Press, 1973) contains a translation and thorough discussion of the work and of its connection with Kant's letters to Reinhold, Ak.[359 and 360]. The arguments contained in these letters were incorporated into Kant's "On a Discovery." The present translations incorporate some of Allison's felicitous modifications of the translator's earlier published versions (in *Kant's Philosophical Correspondence: 1759–99*, pp. 136–150).

3 Reinhold had asked Kant to make a public declaration to this effect.

4 "On the Distinction between Analytic and Synthetic Judgments."

5 Eberhard wrote: "According to this the distinction between analytic and synthetic judgments would seem to be this: analytic judgments are those whose predicates state the essence or some of the essential parts of the subject; those whose predicates assert no determination belonging to the essence or to the essential parts of the subject are synthetic. This is what Herr Kant must mean to say, if he presents the contrast so that the first are merely explicative and

the latter are ampliative, insofar as we can make anything definite out of his explanation."

6 The whole passage is given here, in place of Kant's brief reference. The last word, however, should be "synthetic" rather than "necessary" – Kant misread Eberhard here.

7 Reinhold used Kant's replies to Eberhard in the *Jena Allgemeine Literaturzeitung* (1789).

8 Part I of Reinhold's "Über das bisherige Schicksal der Kantischen Philosophie," which appeared in the April issue of the *Neue Deutsche Merkur* (1789).

9 C. M. Wieland.

95 [360] (338)
To Karl Leonard Reinhold.
May 19, 1789.

I am adding to the remarks I sent you on the 12th some additional   11:40
ones concerning the first two issues of the *Philosophisches Magazin*. This is a disgusting job as it involves exposing pure equivocations. It is one which you did not demand of me but which nevertheless still seems necessary in order to show the public right at the start the shallowness and fraud of an author [Eberhard] whose only commitment is to deceit.

Page 12. Eberhard writes: "Plato and Aristotle denied the certainty of any sense knowledge and restricted certainty to the area of non-sensible ideas or ideas of the understanding. The newest philosophy banishes it from this region and limits it only to the world of the senses."[1] Just the opposite is true of Aristotle. The *principle nihil est in intellectu, quod non antea fuerit in sensu* [nothing is in the intellect which was not first in the senses] (a principle that agrees with Locke's) is actually the criterion for distinguishing the Aristotelian school from the Platonic.

P. 23: "The metaphysics of this philosophy (Leibniz-Wolffian) is regarded by Kant as useless, and he refers to a future metaphysical system. There can, however, be no likelihood of its construction since the *Critique* has already precluded any access to the materials which are necessary for it." The materials are completely, without any exception, to be found in the *Critique*.

Pages 25–26. Eberhard writes: ". . . If it is said that sensible concepts are intuitive,[a] this is quite true: they are *immediately* intuitive. But

---

[a] *anschauend*

303

concepts of the understanding are also intuitive, only they are *mediately* intuitive. For they are derived from sensible concepts and can be intuited in the latter; and even if they are constructed out of abstract concepts, they still bring with them the mediately intuitive marks[b] of the abstract concepts out of which they have been constructed. . . ." Here there is a double absurdity. Pure concepts of reason,[c] which Eberhard identifies with pure concepts of the understanding,[d] he interprets as concepts that have been drawn from sensuous concepts (like extension or color, which are initially situated in sense representations). This is exactly the opposite of what I gave as the criterion for pure concepts of the understanding.[2] And then the notion of "mediate intuition" is self-contradictory. I say only that to a pure concept of the understanding a *corresponding* intuition can be given. This intuition, however, contains nothing of that concept. It contains only the manifold to which the concept of the understanding applies the synthetic unity of apperception; it is therefore the concept of an object in general, be the intuition what it may.

11:41   Page 156. [Eberhard speaks of necessary truths that have objects "lying entirely outside the sphere of sense-knowledge, which can neither be warranted nor refuted by experience." Later he says, "their logical truth follows necessarily from their metaphysical truth; the two are indivisibly united. That is, as soon as the power of representation has, in accordance with its necessary laws, thought something as possible and as independently actual, that thing must be possible and independently actual."] Here he talks of necessary laws, and so on, without noticing that in the *Critique* the task is just this: to show which laws are objectively necessary, and how we are authorized to assume them valid for the nature of things, that is, how they can possibly be synthetic and yet a priori. For otherwise we are in danger (like *Crusius*,[3] whose language Eberhard uses here) of taking a merely subjective necessity (based either on habit or on our inability to imagine an object any other way) for an objective necessity.

Pages 157–8. [Eberhard insists on the possibility of progress in metaphysics.] Here one might ask, as the foreign scholar did when they showed him the Sorbonne lecture hall, "They've argued here for three hundred years; *what have they found out?*"

Page 158. "We can always work to extend it (metaphysics), without committing ourselves. . . ." Here we mustn't let him get by. For his declaration concerns an important point, viz., whether or not a critique of pure reason must precede metaphysics. From page 157 to 159 he demonstrates his confusion as to what the *Critique* is trying to do, and

---

[b] *Merkmale*   [c] *reine Vernunftbegriffe*
[d] *Verstandsbegriffen*

he displays his ignorance just when he tries to parade as learned. This passage also reveals by itself the trickery he is up to. He sounds off about metaphysical truth and its demonstration (at the start of the section it was transcendental truth), contrasting this with logical truth and its demonstration. But all judgmental truth,^{e} insofar as it rests on objective grounds, is logical, whether the judgment itself belongs to physics or to metaphysics. We are in the habit of contrasting logical truth with aesthetic truth (that of a poet), for example, to represent heaven as a vault and the sunset dipping into the sea. In the latter case we require only that the judgment have the appearance of truth for all men, that is, that it agree with subjective conditions of judgment. When we speak of the objective determining grounds of a judgment, however, we make no distinction between geometric truth, physical or metaphysical truth, and logical truth.

Now he says (p. 158) "We can always continue to work for its extension, without having to first concern ourselves with the transcendental validity of these truths." Previously (p. 157) he had said that the genuineness of logical truth was being called into question, and now (p. 158) he says that we don't have to concern ourselves with transcendental truth (by which he presumably means the very same thing which he had just said was being questioned). When he says, on page 158, "In this way the mathematicians have completed the design of whole sciences *without even discussing the reality of the objects of these sciences*," and so on, he shows himself to be supremely ignorant, not only in his make-believe mathematics, but in his utter lack of comprehension of what it is that the *Critique* demands with respect to the intuitions without which the objective reality of concepts cannot be secured. We must therefore pause a moment to discuss his own examples.

Herr Eberhard wants to free himself from the demand, so troublesome to all dogmatists yet so unavoidable, that no concept be admitted to the rank of cognitions if its objective reality is not made evident by the possibility of the object's being exhibited in a corresponding intuition. He thus calls upon the mathematicians, who are supposed not to have said a single word about the reality of the objects of their concepts, and who nevertheless have succeeded in designing entire sciences. He could hardly have hit upon a more unfortunate example for his purpose. For the situation is exactly the opposite: the mathematician cannot make the smallest assertion about any object whatsoever without exhibiting it in intuition (or, if we are considering only quantities without qualities, as in algebra, exhibiting the quantitative relationships for which the symbols stand). As usual, he has, instead of investigating the subject himself, merely leafed through some books,

^{e} *Wahrheit eines Urteils*

which he has not understood, and has hunted up a place in Borelli[4] (the editor of Apollonius's *Conica*) that just accidentally seems to suit his purpose: *"Subjectum enim . . . delineandi."* Had he the slightest grasp of what Borelli was talking about, he would find that the definition that Apollonius gives, for example, of a parabola is itself the exhibition of a concept in intuition, viz., the intersection of a cone under certain conditions, and that in establishing the objective reality of the concept, here as always in geometry, the definition is at the same time the construction of the concept. If, however, in accordance with the property of the conic section derived from this definition – viz., that the semi-ordinate is the mean proportional between the parameter and the abscissa – the problem is set as follows: given the parameter, how do you draw the parabola? (that is, how are the ordinates to be applied upon the given diameter?), the solution, as Borelli correctly says, belongs to art, which follows science as a practical corollary. For science has to do with the properties of objects, not with the way in which they can be produced under given conditions. If a circle is defined as a curve all of whose points are equidistant from a center, is not this concept given in intuition? And this even though the practical proposition that follows, viz., to *describe a circle* (as a straight line is rotated uniformly about a point), is not even considered. Mathematics is the most excellent model for all synthetic use of reason, just because the intuitions *with which* mathematics confers objective reality upon its concepts are never lacking. In philosophy, however, and indeed, in theoretical knowledge, this demand for intuitions is one with which we cannot always sufficiently comply. When intuitions are lacking, we must be resigned to forgo the claim that our concepts have the status of cognitions of objects. We must admit that they are only Ideas, merely regulative principles for the use of reason directed toward objects given in intuition, objects that, however, can never be completely known in terms of their conditions.

Page 163. "Now this principle of sufficient reason can only be demonstrated a priori; for a demonstration through induction is impossible . . . If the principle of sufficient reason is to be demonstrated, then we must derive it from a higher principle. Now there is no higher principle than the principle of contradiction. The universal truth of the principle of sufficient reason can therefore only be demonstrated from this higher principle." Here he makes a confession that will not appeal to many of the empiricists who are his allies in attacking the *Critique*, viz., *that the principle of sufficient reason is only possible a priori*. He explains, though, that the principle could only be demonstrated by means of the principle of contradiction, which makes it *ipso facto* a principle of analytic judgments and thus demolishes right at the outset his projected attempt to account for the possibility of synthetic a priori

judgments by means of that principle. The demonstration thus turns
out pathetically. First he treats the principle of sufficient reason as a   11:44
logical principle (which it must be if he wants to derive it from the
principle of contradiction), so that the principle says in effect, "Every
assertoric judgment must have a ground"; but then he proceeds to use
the principle as if it had a metaphysical meaning, that is, in the sense
of "Every event has its cause,"*f* which is an entirely different sense of
"ground"; in the latter proposition, it refers to the real ground or
principle of causality, the relation of which to the consequent cannot
in any way be thought according to the principle of contradiction, as
can the relation of logical ground. The demonstration begins on p. 164
with: "Two propositions which contradict one another at the same
time cannot both be true." If this principle is compared to the example
given earlier on page 163, "An amount of air moves eastward," the
application of the logical principle of sufficient reason would read: The
proposition, "the air moves eastward," must have a ground. For without having a ground, i.e., a representation other than the concept of
air and that of an eastward movement, the subject is wholly undetermined in respect to this predicate. But this proposition is an experiential one, and consequently it is not merely thought problematically but
assertorically, as *grounded*, and grounded in experience, as a cognition
through connected perceptions. But this ground is identical to that
stated in the proposition (I refer to what is present according to perceptions, not to what is merely possible according to concepts); it is
consequently an analytic ground of *judgment*, in accordance with the
principle of contradiction, and thus has nothing in common with the
real ground, which concerns the synthetic relationships between cause
and effect in the objects themselves. So Eberhard starts with the analytic principle of sufficient reason (as a logical principle) and leaps to
the metaphysical principle of causality, which is always synthetic and
which is never mentioned in logic. His argument is thus a crude fallacy
of *ignoratio Elenchi*, it does not prove what he wants it to but only
shows something that was never in fact disputed. But this is not the
reader's only problem: the paralogism on pages 163–4 is too awful for
words.[5] Put in syllogistic form it would read: If there were no sufficient
reason why the wind moves eastward, it could just as well (*instead of*   11:45
that – Eberhard has to mean this, otherwise the conclusion of the
hypothetical proposition is false) move toward the west; now there is
no sufficient reason why, and so on. Therefore the wind could just as
well move *both* eastward and westward at the same time, which is self-
contradictory. This syllogism walks on all fours.

The principle of sufficient reason, so far as what Herr Eberhard has

f Ursache

307

shown, is thus still only a logical principle and analytic. Viewed from this perspective, there are not two but three principles of knowledge: (1) the principle of contradiction, for categorical judgments, (2) the principle of (logical) ground, for hypothetical judgments, and (3) the principle of division (excluded middle between two mutually contradictory propositions), for disjunctive judgments. All judgments must first, as *problematic* (as mere judgments) insofar as they express *possibility*, conform to the principle of contradiction; second, as *assertoric* (*qua* propositions) insofar as they express logical *actuality*, that is, *truth*, they must conform to the principle of sufficient reason; third, as *apodictic* (as certain knowledge), they must conform to the principle of excluded middle. The reason for the last point is that an apodictic truth can only be thought possible by negating its contrary, that is, by dividing the representation of a predicate into two contradictories and excluding one of them.

On page 169 the attempt to demonstrate that the simple, as the intelligible, can nevertheless be made intuitive, turns out to be even more pathetic than all the other arguments. For he speaks of *concrete* time as something composite,[g] whose simple elements are supposed to be representations, and he does not notice that in order to conceive the succession of this concrete time one would already have had to presuppose the *pure* intuition *of time* wherein those representations are supposed to succeed one another. But since there is nothing simple in this pure intuition, which the author calls non-pictorial[b] (or non-sensible), it follows without question that the understanding does not in any way elevate itself above the sphere of sensibility when it is representing time. With his would-be primary elements of the com-

11:46 posite in space, his "simples," (p. 171) he repudiates not only Leibniz' actual opinion[6] but also crudely the whole of mathematics. From my remarks concerning page 163 you can determine the value of pages 244–56 and the claimed *objective* validity of his logical principle of sufficient reason.[7] He wants to infer, from the subjective necessity of the principle of sufficient reason (which he really construes as the principle of causality) and from the representations and connections of representations that make up the principle, that the ground of this principle must lie not merely in the subject but in the objects; however, I am not sure I understand this confused discussion. But why does he need such circumlocutions, when he thinks he can deduce it from the principle of contradiction?

I don't remember whether in my previous letter I mentioned this man's strange and thoroughly provocative misinterpretation or misrepresentation of my account of *Ideas of Reason* (Ideas for which no corre-

---

[g] *Zusammengesetzten*   [b] *unbildlich*

sponding intuition can be given) and of my discussion of the supersensible in general. (It is on his pp. 272 to 274, from "I must here use an example" to "have no reality?") He maintains that the concept of a chiliagon is such an idea and that nevertheless we can have a good deal of mathematical knowledge concerning it. Now this is so absurd a misrepresentation of the concept of "supersensible" that a child would see through it. For the question is just whether there can be an exhibition of the idea in a possible intuition, in accordance with our *kind* of sensibility; the degree thereof – i.e., the power of the imagination to grasp the manifold – may be as great or small as he wishes. Even if something were presented to us as a million-sided figure and we were able to spot the lack of a single side at first glance, this representation would still be a sensible one. Only the possibility of exhibiting the concept of a chiliagon in intuition can ground the possibility of this object itself in mathematics; for then the construction of the object can be completely prescribed in accordance with all its requirements, without our having to worry about the size of the tape measure that would be needed to make this figure, with all its parts, observable to the eye. You can tell what sort of a man Eberhard is from this example of his misrepresentation.

He is also good at giving false citations, for example pp. 19–20 and especially on page 301. But on pages 290 and 298 ff. he surpasses   11:47
himself, for there he becomes a veritable *Falsarius*. He cites A 44 of the *Critique* where I said, "The philosophy of Leibniz and Wolff, in thus treating the difference between the sensible and the intelligible as merely logical, has given a completely wrong direction to all investigations into the nature and origin of our knowledge," and expounds it thus: "Here Herr Kant accuses the philosophy of Leibniz and Wolff of falsifying the concept of sensibility and appearance by making the distinction between the sensible and the intellectual a merely logical one." Just as certain people are inclined to believe lies that they themselves have often repeated, so Eberhard becomes so zealous with regard to the alleged use of this presumptuous expression against Leibniz that he attributes the word *"falsified"*[i] to me, when the word in fact exists only in his brain. He does this three times on one page (p. 298) in discussing my supposedly unrestrained attack on Leibniz.[8] What do you call someone who deliberately falsifies a document in a legal trial?

I content myself with these few remarks and beg you to use them as you see fit but, where possible, in a vigorous fashion. You must not expect restraint from this man who has made braggadocio his maxim in order to trick people into granting him recognition. I would fight him myself, but for the time it would take, which I must rather use to

[i] *verfälscht*

complete my project; for already I feel the infirmities of age and must therefore leave the struggle to my friends, if they deem it worth the effort to defend my cause. Basically I cannot help but be pleased by the general commotion that the *Critique* has inspired and still arouses, even with all the alliances that are formed against it (although the opponents of the *Critique* are split and will remain so); for all this serves to call attention to the book. Besides, the unending misunderstandings and misinterpretations provide a stimulus to the further clarification of the expressions that occasion the misunderstandings. So I really do not fear these attacks, as long as we remain calm under fire. Still, it is a good deed to the community to unmask at the outset a man composed entirely of deceit, who uses nimbly, from long experience, every device that can seduce a casual reader into blind faith in him, for example, the appeal to misinterpreted passages in the writings of distinguished men. Feder is for all his limitations at least honest, a property totally absent from Eberhard's thinking.

11:48

  With warmth and friendship, and with the greatest respect for the integrity of your character, I am, faithfully,

Your entirely devoted friend and servant,
I. Kant

Königsberg

---

1 The full passages from Eberhard are inserted here, in place of Kant's brief references.

2 Though the abbreviation "r. V" in Kant's letter could signify either "pure reason" (*Vernunft*) or "pure understanding" (*Verstand*), the context makes *Verstand* the only plausible interpretation.

3 Christian August Crusius (1712–75), professor of philosophy and theology in Leipzig. According to the editors of the Akademie edition, Kant's reference is probably to Crusius's *Entwurf der nothwendigen Vernunftwahrheiten* (Leipzig, 1753), § 16.

4 Giovanni Alfonso Borelli (1608–79), distinguished Italian physicist, published Books V–VII of *Apollonii Pergaei conicorum*, (1661). The passage to which Kant alludes states: "Subjectum enim definitum assumi potest, ut affectiones variae de eo demonstrentur, licet praemissa non sit ars subjectum ipsum efformandum delineandi." (Roughly. "An object can be assumed to be defined in order that various properties be demonstrated of it, though previously no way of presenting an actual constructive presentation of it was available.)"

5 "Either everything has a ground or not everything has a ground. If the latter, something could be possible and thinkable though its ground is nothing. But if, of two opposing things, it were possible for one of them to be without a sufficient reason, then the other one could also be without a sufficient reason. If, for example, an amount of air could move eastward, so that the wind is

eastward, even though the air was not warmer and thinner in the east, this amount of air could just as well move westward as eastward; the same air would thus simultaneously be able to move in two opposing directions, east and west, and thus both east and not-east, that is, something could simultaneously be and not be, which is contradictory and impossible."

6 "Leibnitz's *wahre Meinung*" could mean his "true opinion."

7 Eberhard attacks the question, "Can we attribute external reality – a possibility or actuality – beyond our cognitive power" to objects that we judge to be external? His proof that external objects are actual is then derived from "healthy reason" (*gesunden Vernunft*) which requires "true objects external to it," corresponding to those representations that are not grounded in the subject himself.

8 Henry Allison has noticed, op. cit., p. 170, n. 14, that Kant did in fact write, in the paragraph preceding A 44, that the concept of sensibility and of appearance would be falsified "if we were to accept the Leibnizian view."

96 [362] (340)
To Marcus Herz.

May 26, 1789.

Every letter that I receive from you, dearest friend, gives me genuine pleasure. Your noble feeling of gratitude for the small contribution I made to the development of your excellent native talents sets you apart from the majority of my students. What can be more consoling, when one is close to leaving this world, than to see that one has not lived in vain, since one has brought up some, even if only a few, to be good human beings.   11:48

But what are you thinking of, dearest friend, in sending me a large package of the most subtle investigations, not only to read through but to think through, I who in my 66th year am still burdened with the extensive work of completing my plan (partly in producing the last part of the Critique, namely, that of *judgment*, which should appear soon, and partly in working out a *system of metaphysics*, of nature as well as of morals, in conformity with those critical demands). Besides, I am continuously kept on the move by many letters, demanding special explanations of certain points, and my health grows progressively worse. I had half decided to send the manuscript back immediately, with the aforementioned, totally adequate apology. But one glance at the work made me realize its excellence and that not only had none of my critics understood me and the main questions as well as Herr Maimon does   11:49

311

but also very few men possess so much acumen for such deep investigations as he; and this moved me to lay his book aside till I might have a few moments of leisure, which I have found only now, and then only enough to get through the first two parts of which I can write only briefly.

Please convey this to Herr Maimon. I assume it is taken for granted that this is not meant for publication.

If I have correctly grasped the sense of his work, the intention is to prove that if the understanding is to have a law-giving relationship to sensible intuition (not only to the empirical but also to the a priori sort), then the understanding must itself be the originator not only of sensible forms but even of the material of intuition, that is, of objects. Otherwise the question, *quid juris?* could not be answered adequately; that question could, however, be answered according to Leibnizian-Wolfian [*sic*] principles, if one grants the view that sensibility is not specifically different from the understanding but differs from it only in degree of consciousness, belonging to the understanding *qua* knowledge of the world. The degree is infinitely small, in the first kind of representation; it is of a given (finite) magnitude in the second. An a priori synthesis can have objective validity only because the divine understanding, of which ours is only a part (or as he expresses it, "though only in a limited way"), is one with our own understanding; that is, it is itself the originator of forms and of the possibility of the things (in themselves) in the world.[1]

11:50

However, I doubt very much that this was Leibniz' or Wolf's opinion, or that this could really be deduced from their explanations of the distinction between sensibility and the understanding; and those who are familiar with the teachings of these men will find it difficult to agree that they assume a Spinozism; for, in fact, Herr Maimon's way of representing *is* Spinozism and could be used most excellently to refute the Leibnizians *ex concessis*.

Herr Maimon's theory consists basically in the contention that an understanding (indeed, the human understanding) not only is a faculty of thinking, as our understanding and perhaps that of all creatures essentially is, but is actually a faculty of intuition, where thinking is only a way of bringing the manifold of intuition (which is obscure because of our limitations) into clear consciousness. I, on the other hand, conceive of the understanding as a *special* faculty and ascribe to it the concept of an object in general (a concept that even the clearest consciousness of our intuition would not at all disclose). In other words I ascribe to the understanding the synthetic unity of apperception, through which alone the manifold of intuition (of whose *every feature* I may nevertheless be *particularly* conscious), in a unified consciousness, is brought to the representation of an object in general (whose concept is then determined by means of that manifold).

Now Herr Maimon asks: How do I explain the possibility of agreement between a priori intuitions and my a priori concepts, if each has its specifically different origin, since this agreement is given as a fact but the legitimacy or the necessity of the agreement of two such heterogeneous manners of representation is incomprehensible. And vice versa, how can I prescribe, for example, the law of causality to nature, that is, to objects themselves, by means of my category (whose possibility in itself is only problematic). Finally, how can I even prove the necessity of these functions of the understanding whose existence is again merely a fact, since that necessity has to be presupposed if we are to subject things, however conceived, to those functions.

To this I answer: All of this takes place in relation to an experiential   11:51
knowledge that is only possible for us under these conditions, a subjective consideration, to be sure, but one that is objectively valid as well, because the objects here are not things in themselves but mere appearances; consequently, the form in which they are given depends on us, – on the one hand, in its subjective aspect, [objects are] dependent on the specific character of our kind of intuition; on the other hand, they are dependent on the uniting of the manifold in a consciousness, that is, on what is required for the thinking and cognizing of objects by our understanding.[2] Only under these conditions, therefore, can we have experiences of those objects; and consequently, if intuitions (of objects of appearance) did not agree with these conditions, those objects would be nothing for us, that is, not objects of *cognition* at all, neither cognition of ourselves nor of other things.

In this way it can be shown that if we are able to make synthetic judgments a priori, these judgments are concerned only with objects of intuition as mere appearances. Even if we were capable of an intellectual intuition (for example, that the infinitely small elements of those objects were noumena), it would be impossible to show the necessity of such judgments according to the nature of our understanding in which such concepts as "necessity" exist. For such an intuition would still be merely a perception; for example, the perception that in a triangle two sides taken together are larger than the third side – not the recognition that this property would have to belong to a triangle of necessity. But we are absolutely unable to explain further how it is that a sensible intuition (such as space and time), the form of our sensibility, or such functions of the understanding as those out of which logic develops are possible; nor can we explain why it is that one form agrees with another in forming a possible cognition.[3] For we should have to have still another manner of intuition than the one we have and another understanding with which to compare our own and with which everyone could perceive things in themselves. But we can only judge an understanding by means of our own understanding, and so it is, too, with all intuition. It is, however, entirely unnecessary to answer this question. For if we can demonstrate that our knowledge of things, even experience itself, is only possible under those conditions,

11:52 it follows that all other concepts of things (which are not thus conditioned) are for us empty and utterly useless for knowledge. But not only that; all sense data for a possible cognition would never, without those conditions, represent objects. They would not even reach that unity of consciousness that is necessary for knowledge of myself (as object of inner sense). I would not even be able to know that I have sense data; consequently for me, as a knowing being, they would be absolutely nothing. They could still (if I imagine myself to be an animal) carry on their play in an orderly fashion, as representations connected according to empirical laws of association, and thus even have an influence on my feeling and desire, without my being aware of them (assuming that I am even conscious of each individual representation, but not of their relation to the unity of representation of their object, by means of the synthetic unity of their apperception). This might be so without my knowing the slightest thing thereby, not even what my own condition is.

It is difficult to guess the thoughts that may have hovered in the mind of a deep thinker and that he himself could not make entirely clear. Nevertheless I am quite convinced that Leibniz, in his pre-established harmony (which he, like Baumgarten after him, made very general), had in mind not the harmony of two different natures, namely, sense and understanding, but that of two faculties belonging to the same nature, in which sensibility and understanding harmonize to form experiential knowledge. If we wanted to make judgments about their origin – an investigation that of course lies wholly beyond the limits of human reason – we could name nothing beyond our divine creator; once they are given, however, we are fully able to explain their power of making a priori judgments (that is, to answer the question, *quid juris?*).

I must content myself with these remarks and cannot, because of my limited time, go into details. I remark only that it is not necessary to assume, with Herr Maimon, *"ideas of the understanding."* Nothing is thought in the concept of a circle other than that *all* straight lines drawn between it and a single point (the center) are equal. This is a

11:53 merely logical function of the universality of judgment, in which the concept of a line constitutes the subject and signifies only as much as *"any line,"* not the *totality* of lines, that could be inscribed on a plane from a given point. Otherwise every line would, with equal justice, be an idea of the understanding; for the idea includes all lines as parts that can be thought between two points (thinkable only in it) and whose number is also infinite. That this line can be infinitely divided is also not an idea, for it signifies only a continuation of the division unlimited by the size of the line. But to see this infinite division in its totality, and consequently as completed, is an idea of reason, the idea of an absolute totality of conditions (of synthesis) demanded of an object of sense, which is impossible since the unconditioned is not at all to be found among appearances.

Furthermore, the possibility of a circle is not merely *problematic*, dependent, as it were, on the practical proposition "to inscribe a circle by the movement of a straight line around a fixed point"; rather, the possibility is *given* in the definition of the circle, since the circle is actually constructed by means of the definition, that is, it is exhibited in intuition, not actually on paper (empirically) but in the imagination (a priori). For I may always draw a circle freehand on the board and put a point in it, and I can demonstrate all properties of the circle just as well on it, presupposing the (so-called) nominal definition, which is in fact a real definition, even if this circle is not at all like one drawn by rotating a straight line attached to a point. I assume that the points of the circumference are equidistant from the center point. The proposition "to inscribe a circle" is a practical corollary of the definition (or so-called postulate), which could not be demanded at all if the possibility – yes, the very sort of possibility of the figure – were not already given in the definition.

As for defining a straight line, it cannot be done by referring to the identity of direction of all the line's parts, for the concept of direction (as a *straight line*, by means of which the movement is distinguished, *without reference to its size*) already presupposes this concept. But these are incidentals. 11:54

Herr Maimon's book contains besides this so many acute observations that he could have published it at any time, with no small advantage to his reputation and without offending me thereby, though he takes a very different path than I do. Still, he agrees with me that a reform must be undertaken, if the principles of metaphysics are to be made firm, and few men are willing to be convinced that this is necessary. But, dearest friend, your request for a recommendation from me, to accompany the publication of this work, would not be feasible, since it is after all largely directed *against me*. That is my judgment, in case the work were published. But if you want my advice about publishing the work as it is, it seems best to me, since Herr Maimon is presumably not indifferent to being fully understood, that he use the time required for the publication to work up a complete theory. There he should indicate clearly not merely the manner in which he thinks of the principles of a priori knowledge but also what his system implies concerning the solution of the tasks of pure reason, which constitute the essential part of the goals of metaphysics. The antinomies of pure reason could provide a good test stone for that, which might convince him that one cannot assume human reason to be of one kind with the divine reason, distinct from it only by limitation, that is, in degree – that human reason, unlike the divine reason, must be regarded as a faculty only of *thinking*, not of *intuiting*; that it is thoroughly dependent on an entirely different faculty (or receptivity) for its intuitions, or better, for the material out of which it fashions knowledge; and that, since intuition gives us mere appearances whereas the fact itself is a mere concept of reason, the antinomies (which arise entirely because of the confusion of the two) can never be resolved except by deducing the possibility of synthetic a priori propositions according to my principles.

I remain as ever your loyal servant and friend,

I. Kant

---

1 Maimon, *Versuch über die Transzendentalphilosophie mit einem Anhang über die symbolische Erkenntnis* (Berlin, 1790), pp. 62, f.

2 As R. Malter and J. Kopper note in their edition of Kant's *Briefwechsel*, p. 857, n. 6, to this letter, that Kant's sentence here is grammatically impossible to construe. The meaning is fairly clear, however: the form of appearances depends on us; it depends on the one hand on the kind of intuition we human beings have (that is the "subjective" aspect of appearances) and, second, on our understanding, which supplies the "objective" part of appearances.

3 Cf. *Critique of Pure Reason*, conclusion of § 21 in the second edition.

97 [373] (350)
From Johann Heinrich Kant.

August 21, 1789.

11:71   My dearest brother,

It seems fitting that, after letting so many years pass by without any letters, we should come closer to each other again. We are both old, and who knows when one of us may pass into eternity; only fair, then, that we should both renew our memories of the years that have gone by, with the proviso that in the future we keep in touch, if only now and then, and let each other know how we live and *quomodo valemus* [however we fare].

Though I gave up the yoke of school teaching eight years ago, I still live the life of a primary school teacher in a farming community in my Altrahden pastorate, feeding myself and my honest family frugally and sufficiently from my farmyard.

"A peasant, a philosopher unschooled and of rough mother-wit." *(Rusticus abnormis sapiens crassaque Minerva.)*[1]

With my good and worthy wife I have a happy, loving marriage and I am pleased that my four well-mannered, good-natured, obedient children give every indication of becoming decent, upright human beings. I don't find it irksome, even with all my tiring official duties, to be their sole teacher. That teaching role with our dear children, here in this lonely place, compensates me and my wife for the lack of social life. There you have a sketch of my monotonous life.

Now then, dearest brother! As laconic as you always are as a scholar and writer "so as not to sin against the public weal" (*ne in publica commoda pecces*),[2] do let me know how your health has been and how it is at present, what scholarly plans of assault you have to enlighten the world of today and of tomorrow. *But also!* do tell me how things are going with my dear, surviving sisters and their families, and how the only son of my departed, esteemed paternal *Uncle Richter* is. I will gladly pay the postage for your letter, even if you only write an octavo page . . .[3]

. . . "Stay! That's enough!" (*Ohe! jam satis est!*)[4] May God sustain you for a long time and may I soon receive from your hand the pleasant news that you are well and contented. With sincerest heart and not superficially I sign myself your genuinely loving brother,

Johann Heinrich Kant.

My dear wife sends you a sisterly embrace and thanks you again for the book, *The Housewife*,[5] which you sent her some years ago. And here come my dear children who all want to send their greetings.

Yes, esteemed uncle, yes, beloved aunts, we all want you to know about us, and to love us, and not to forget us. We shall love you sincerely and respect you, all of us, who sign ourselves

Amalia Charlotta Kant.
Minna Kant.
Friedrich Wilhelm Kant.
Henriette Kant.

11:72

11:73

1 Horace, *Satires* II, 2, 3.
2 Horace, *Epistles* II, 1, 3. "I should sin against the public weal if with long talk I were to delay your busy hours, O Caesar."
3 The letter goes on to mention various acquaintances whom Kant might have met or who could transmit a letter from Königsberg.
4 Horace, *Satires* I, 5, 12.
5 Cf. J. H. Kant's letter of Sept. 10, 1782, Ak.[180], n. 1.

98 [375] (352)
To Friedrich Heinrich Jacobi.
August 30, 1789.

Esteemed Sir:

11:75   The gift from Count von Windisch-Graetz,[1] containing his philosophical essays, has arrived (thanks to you and to Privy Commercial Councillor Fischer,[2] and I have also received the first edition of his *Histoire métaphysique* . . . etc., from the book dealer Sixt.

Please thank the Count for me and assure him of my respect for his philosophical talent, a talent that he combines with the noblest attitudes of a cosmopolite. In the last-mentioned work, I observed with pleasure that the Count discusses, with the clarity and modesty of one who is at home in the great world, the same matters with which I in my scholastic fashion have also been concerned, viz., the clear definition and encouragement of human nature's nobler incentives, incentives that have so often been confused with (and even taken for) physical incentives that they have failed to produce the results that one rightfully expects of them. I long passionately to see him complete this work, for it obviously is systematically related to his other two books (the one on secret societies and the one on voluntary changes of the constitution in monarchies). This system would certainly have great influence, partly as a wonderfully realized prophecy, partly as sage counsel to despots, in the current European crisis. No statesman has heretofore inquired so deeply into the principles of the art of governing men or has even known how to go about such an inquiry. But that is why none of the proposals of such people have succeeded in convincing anyone, much less in producing results.

For the newest edition of your handsome book on Spinoza's theory,

318

my warmest thanks. You have earned distinction, first of all for having clearly presented the difficulties of the teleological road to theology, difficulties that seem to have led Spinoza to his system. To dash with hasty, enterprising steps toward a faraway goal has always been injurious to a thorough insight. He who shows us the cliffs has not necessarily set them up, and even if someone maintains that it is impossible to pass through them *with full sails* (of dogmatism), he has not on that account denied every possibility of getting through. I think that you do not regard the compass of reason as unnecessary or misleading in this venture. The indispensable supplement to reason is something that, though not part of speculative knowledge, lies only in reason itself, something that we can name (viz., freedom, a supersensible power of causality within us) but that we cannot grasp. The question whether reason could only be *awakened* to this conception of theism by being instructed with historical events or whether it would require an incomprehensible supernatural inspiration,[a] this is an incidental question, a question of the origin and introduction of this idea. For one can just as well admit that if the gospels had not previously instructed us in the universal moral laws in their total purity, our reason would not yet have discovered them so completely; still, *once we are in possession of them*, we can convince anyone of their correctness and validity using reason alone.

11:76

You have thoroughly refuted the syncretism of Spinozism and Deism in Herder's *God*.[3] All syncretistic talk is commonly based on insincerity, a property of mind that is especially characteristic of this great artist in delusions (which, like magic lanterns, make marvelous images appear for a moment but which soon vanish forever, though they leave behind in the minds of the uninformed a conviction that something unusual must be behind it all, something, however, of which they cannot catch hold).

I have always thought it my duty to show respect for men of talent, science, and justice, no matter how far our opinions may differ. You will, I hope, appraise my essay on orientation, in the *Berlinische Monatsschrift*, from this perspective. I was requested by various people to cleanse myself of the suspicion of Spinozism, and therefore, contrary to my inclination, I wrote this essay.[4] I hope you will find in it no trace of deviation from the principle I have just affirmed. With inner pain I have read some other attacks upon your views and those of some of your worthy friends, and I have even spoken out against such attacks. I do not understand how it is that otherwise good and reasonable men are often inclined to regard as meritorious an attack that they would

11:77

[a] *Einwirkung*

take to be highly unfair were it directed against themselves. Yet true merit cannot be diminished by such shadows cast on its gleaming brilliance; it will not be mistaken.

Our Hamann[5] has accepted the position of private tutor at Count von Keyserling's in Curland, principally with the intention of systematizing his many-sided knowledge by presenting it to others, and he likes it there. He is a decent, honest soul. He is thinking of devoting himself to school teaching since he recently lost his father and mother and needs to help his orphaned sisters at home.[6]

I wish you many years of good health, good cheer, and good fortune to pursue the work you so love, the noblest task of all, viz., reflection on the serious principles on which the general welfare of mankind depends, and I am, most respectfully,

Your most devoted servant,
I. Kant

---

1 Joseph Nicolaus, Reichsgraf von Windisch-Graetz (1744–1802), for a time *Reichshofrat* in Vienna, a philanthropist and writer on political philosophy. Kant asked his publisher de la Garde to send a complimentary copy of the third *Critique* to Windisch-Graetz and mentions him also in *Perpetual Peace*, calling him wise and penetrating. His position resembled Kant's on several points; for example, he insisted that human activity could not be understood in terms of merely passive sensations, he rejected eudaemonism, and he argued that the idea of immortality must be based on virtue, not vice versa. The writings to which Kant alludes are: *Solution provisoire d'un Problème, ou Histoire métaphysique de l'organization animale* (1789), *Objections aux sociétés sécrètes* and a discourse on the question whether a monarch has the right to change an apparently vicious constitution (both published in London, 1788, though Windisch-Graetz usually wrote in French).

2 Karl Konrad Fischer, *Kommerzienrat* and *Admiralitätsrat* in Königsberg.

3 Kant refers to Herder's *Gott, einige Gespräche* (Gotha, 1787).

4 "What is Orientation in Thinking?" ("Was heißt: Sich im Denken Orientieren?" 1786.

5 Johann Michael Hamann (1769–1813), son of Johann Georg Hamann. The Count Keyserling to whom Kant alludes is Albrecht Johann Otto von Keyserling (1747–1809), elder son of Count Heinrich Christian von Keyserling (1727–87) by his first wife.

6 J. G. Hamann died June 21, 1788, his wife in Apr. 1789, leaving three daughters.

99 [377] (354)
To Johann Wilhelm Andreas Kosmann.[1]

September 1789.

[Draft]

Answer to Kosmann.[2] We can attempt to give a psychological deduc-   10:81
tion of our representations, for we regard them as effects which have
their cause in the mind where they are linked with other things; on the
other hand, we can attempt to give a transcendental deduction, for, if
we have grounds for assuming that they are not empirical in origin, we   10:82
then merely search for the grounds of the possibility of this, i.e., how
nevertheless these representations [whose origin is not empirical] have
objective reality a priori. In regard to space, we need not ask how our
power of representation first came to use the representation of space
in experience; it is sufficient that, since we have now developed that
representation, we can prove the necessity of thinking it, and of thinking it with these and no other determinations; it is enough that we can
prove this from the rules of its employment and the necessity of presenting grounds of that employment that are independent of experience, though [they]³ are in fact of such a nature that they cannot be
developed out of a concept but are instead synthetic.

I can perceive the fall of a body without so much as thinking of
what causes it, but I cannot even perceive that things are outside and
beside one other without presupposing the representation of space as
sensible form (wherein alone spatial distinctness can be thought) and
regarding certain given representations as related to each other accordingly. The concept of space may not and cannot be presupposed, for
concepts are not innate but are only acquired. Outer representations as
such – and the representation of the body of a fetus is an example – are
only produced in that sensations affect the power of representation in
accordance with this form.

---

1 Johann Wilhelm Andreas Kosmann (1761–1804) was a teacher in the Latin
   School at Schweidnitz and later a professor at the Artillery Academy in Berlin.
   He was the publisher of a journal, *Allgemein Magazin für kritische und popüläre
   Philosophie.* He wrote to Kant, Aug. 20, 1789, Ak. [376], telling of his life and
   of his work on a thesis defending the a priori character of space against the
   empirical-psychological objections of Feder. Feeling himself unclear on the
   matter, he asked Kant for help. It has been established, Kosmann thought,

"that the representation of space develops through and with [the development of] feeling [*Gefühl*]" and that feeling already exists in the embryo, even before the soul is capable of thinking. Kant's answer stresses the distinction between a psychological and a transcendental inquiry.

2   This fragment was inscribed on the back of Kant's note dated Nov. 1788 (Ak.[341]) addressed to Carl Daniel Reusch, professor of physics in Königsberg.

3   The word "sie" is needed here grammatically, but its referent is unclear: "rules" or "grounds" both fit, and either would make sense.

100 [389] (366)
From Friedrich Heinrich Jacobi.
November 16, 1789.

Pempelfort, the 16th of November, 1789

11:101   Esteemed Kant,

11:102   Since the day[1] that I was so delightfully surprised to receive a letter from you and, as our Hamann expressed it on a similar occasion, "felt something like dizziness as I experienced a delicious little stupor," I have become someone who picks days or at least who counts the days. The day is coming, it came not, and – it will not come: the day on which I shall be capable of expressing to you the joy I feel and the gratitude that I so much want to convey.

As you are my teacher! As you are a man whom I already admired with a pounding heart when I was young and before whom I would now bow with veneration as before a great conqueror and wise lawgiver in the realm of science, were I to say this of you publicly at a time and in circumstatnces in which no shadow of suspicion could be aroused that I was guilty of self-serving flattery. You yourself, most esteemed Kant, mention your essay "On Orientation," that appeared in the *Berliner Monatsschrift;* and you mention it in such a way as not only to silence any complaint from my lips but to erase completely and forever even the faintest grievance that might yet be stirred up in my heart. None of your admirers can exceed me in the reverence and affection which I feel for you.

I immediately conveyed to Count von Windisch-Graetz[2] the kind compliment you paid him, for I knew how pleased he would be to hear it. I have only recently become acquainted with this excellent man.

Last winter he sent me his *Objections aux sociétés sécrètes* and his *Discours* and expressed great interest in my essay, *Something that Lessing Said,*[3] which had been given to him in Vienna by a mutual friend, Count Carl von Sickingen.[4] The *Discours* was originally written only for the emperor[5] and was given to him in manuscript form. Since the continuing troubles in Brabant[6] showed that the emperor's having the *Discours* was useless, its author wrote to his crowned friend that he now found it desirable to make this essay public. He is at present in his estates in Bohemia. The usual place he stays has for years been Brussels, where he got married for a second time to a certain Princess von Aremberg. Several days after I received your letter he visited me on his way to Bohemia. I had received his first visit in May and at that time he stayed until I left for Pyrmont. Windisch-Graetz is very sensitive to the value of a favorable report from a man like Kant and he asked me to express his heartfelt respect and total devotion to you. The second part of his *Histoire métaphysique de l'âme* was already in print at that time. I have since received copies of it and shall have the one intended for you sent to Königsberg as soon as possible. The writings of this noble thinker can be very useful in improving the state of French philosophy. For since he always starts from this philosophy – it is really the foundation of his own, and he merely concerns himself with repairing those parts of it that are incomplete or incorrect – the adherents of that philosophy can not only understand him but even follow along with him and quite willingly, without their actually realizing that they are taking his lead. Unfortunately the Parisian philosophers have a bit of a grudge against their German half-brother because it seems to them that he subscribes to prejudices here and there and delays the progress of the good cause. Remarkable how human beings always recognize fanaticism only in a particular instance and never in themselves.

11:103

Among the remarks, most esteemed Kant, which you were kind enough to make about the new edition of my book on Spinoza's doctrine, the following especially drew my attention and preoccupied me for a long time: You say: "The question whether reason could only be *awakened* to this conception of theism by being instructed with historical events or whether it would require an incomprehensible supernatural inspiration, this is an incidental question, a question of the origin and introduction of this idea . . . It is enough that *once we are in possession of this idea*, we can convince anyone of its correctness and validity using reason alone."

What kept me thinking about this passage was the question, how does this relate to my theory, or how might it not relate to my theory?

Since I have derived my theism exclusively from the omnipresent fact of human intelligence, from the being of reason and freedom, I could not see the possible relevance of your remark to my theory. I

11:104

know that the first edition of my book contained some obscure passages, but I believe I have since then resolved all ambiguity and have now in the newest edition made my convictions sufficiently clear. What I ascribe to human beings is a self-evident but incomprehensible union of the sensible with the supersensible, the natural with the supernatural, a union which, as soon as it is perceived and recognized as certain, provides a satisfying resolution to the seeming contradiction of reason with itself. Just as the conditioned is ultimately related to the unconditioned, just as every sensation is related to a pure reason, to something that has its life in itself, so every mechanistic principle is ultimately related to a non-mechanistic principle of the expression and interlinking of its forces; every composition to something not composed but indivisible; everything that is a consequence of laws of physical necessity to something that is not a consequence, something primordially active, free; universals to particulars; individuality to personality. And this cognition, I believe, has its source in the direct intuition that rational beings have of themselves, of their connection with the primordial being and a dependent world. The difference between your theory and my conviction becomes striking when one asks whether these cognitions are real or only imaginary, whether truth or ignorance and illusion correspond to them. According to your doctrine, nature in general assumes that which is represented, the form of our faculty of representation (in the broadest sense), which is at the same time inner and inscrutable, and thereby not only all contradiction of reason with itself is resolved but also a thoroughly coherent system of pure philosophy is made possible. I on the other hand am more inclined to seek the form of human reason in the universal form of things; and I believe I have to some extent seen, and in part to have shown, how the various instances which the contradictory assertions of everything hypothetical are supposed to remove, may perhaps be resolved. Our knowing may well be so completely fragmentary that even the *knowing* of our not-knowing is no exception. Meanwhile what I am really doing is testing my credo again seriously by means of Professor Reinhold's theory of the faculty of representation. I cannot be so very mistaken, since my results are almost entirely the same as yours. And so it might well be possible that my error, if I were to become more and more firmly rooted in it, might nevertheless make the transition to truth easier for others.

11:105

Do forgive me, dear, esteemed sir, my prolixity in disclosing what is in my heart. I did not want you to take me for a supernaturalist the way Professor Reinhold describes me.[7] I inferred the seriousness of this danger from another passage in your letter, where you spoke of a possible passage between the cliffs of atheism, saying "I think that you will not find the compass of reason to be unnecessary or misleading in this venture." So some of my anxiety about this will surely be forgiven.

I am eager to see the fourth part of Herder's *Ideen* and the sarcastic remarks about me I shall probably find there. But the man is unjust if he is dissatisfied with me. I could have burned his golden calf into powder, like Aaron, and given it to him to drink. Truly Herder's *Gespräch*[8] is, as *philosophical critique*, beneath criticism and contains hardly a word of truth. Of course it is full of lovely things, especially the dialogue and the form of the whole work.

Be well, noble sir, and let me hear via your worthy friend Kraus that you still think well of me.

With a heart full of respect, thanks, and love

Your most devoted

Friedrich Heinrich Jacobi.

---

1 Aug. 30, 1789, Ak. [375].

2 On Windisch-Graetz see Kant's letter to Jacobi, Aug. 30, 1789, Ak. [375], to which the present letter is a reply.

3 The full title of Jacobi's essay is *Etwas, was Lessing gesagt hat. Ein Kommentar zu den Reisen der Päpste nebst Betrachtungen von einem Dritten* (Something that Lessing said. A commentary on the travels of popes, along with observations of a third party (published anonymously in Berlin, 1782). The subject is a remark of Lessing's concerning the infallibility of popes.

4 Karl Heinrich Joseph von Sickingen (1737–91), a chemist.

5 Joseph II of the Austro-Hungarian Empire.

6 The suspension of the constitution of Brabant in 1789–90 provoked an insurrection.

7 Reinhold characterizes the supernaturalist as one who holds that the grounds on which an answer to the question of God's existence must be based lie outside the province of reason. *Versuch einer neuen Theorie des menschlichen Vorstellungsvermögen* (1789), p. 80 A. On p. 86 Reinhold names Jacobi along with Johann Georg Schlosser, Goethe's brother-in-law, as defenders of supernaturalism.

8 Jacobi's reference is to Herder's *Gott. Einige Gespräche* (1787).

101 [394] (371)
From Johann Gottfried Carl Christian Kiesewetter.
December 15, 1789.

Dearest Herr Professor,

11:112

I should really feel ashamed that only now am I answering your kind letter, which gave me such extraordinary pleasure by providing unmistakable evidence that you think me worthy of your friendship. I had a great many things to do that kept me from writing.

My situation is as good as I could ever wish: my lectures on logic and on the *Critique of Pure Reason* are rather well attended; I have about 20 auditors attending the former, 25 for the latter, and even though not all of them pay, still, I calculate that the two courses together will bring in 100 thalers. My logic lectures are based on my own notes; for my lectures on the *Critiqiue* I use your book. As far as I can tell, people

11:113

are satisfied with my lectures, and this is all the more pleasing to me since I have a number of businessmen among my auditors. I also teach anthropology to the Princess Auguste's governess,[1] the Baroness von Bielefeld,[2] daily from 8 till 9 o'clock, and I repeat those lectures in four lessons a week that I give to the son of the book merchant Nicolai, the son-in-law of Councillor Klein.[3] I also teach mathematics an hour a day and, finally, I am reading Xenophon with Councillor Mayer.[4]

You see, dearest Herr Professor, that I cannot complain for lack of business and that I am earning my keep. But I fear that my weak physique is not going to endure this pace for long, and therefore I have been thinking of some ways of making it easier for me to support myself. Through the good offices of Baroness von Bielefeld, who is very important at court, I think I might make a closer connection to the court itself and perhaps become the tutor of Princess Auguste. That position is all the more important since there is a lifelong pension connected with it. Furthermore, Chancellor von Hoffmann,[5] Councillor von Irwing[6] of the Supreme Consistorial Court and the Baroness von Bielefeld von Bielefeld all promised to do their best to get me appointed as a chaplain in Berlin as soon as a position becomes vacant. You ask how I stand with Minister Wöllner.[7] I spoke to him and he assured me of his favor in the most pompous terms, but this assurance was given so readily that I fear he says the same thing to anyone who waits on him. People have warned me to be careful about my lectures, for there are eavesdroppers to record anything one might say against religion; I have been told to remind people casually that the Kantian philosophy is not opposed to Christianity. I acted on that suggestion

326

in my first lecture on the *Critique of Practical Reason* and emphasized throughout the lecture the agreement of the formal law with the teachings of Christianity. There was actually a young man present who transcribed every word I said, attracting everyone's attention by his industriously nervous behavior; and he never came again. Supreme Consistorial Court Councillor von Irwing has much influence with Wöllner and assures me that he is my friend. My influence with Wöllner via Chancellor von Hoffman is less, for even though they seem outwardly to be on good terms this is really not the case, because Hoffman is a confidant of Prince Heinrich[8] and Heinrich hates Wöllner.

I felt most uncomfortable when I read in the *Letters of a Minister* (Wöllner) to the King[9] (which everybody here says was written by Zedlitz) the part about you and your followers. I won't copy out the passage here since you have in all probability read the book. If by chance you have not yet read it and the book is unavailable in Königsberg just let me know and I will mail it to you right away. – They say that Wöllner's position is not as firmly established as it was, but we shall not gain much by a change if, as seems likely, he is replaced by Privy Councillor Lamprecht. – Zedlitz has quite unexpectedly come into a large inheritance, so that he can live entirely as a man of independent means.[10] I must admit that I was extremely upset when I heard that he had asked to be relieved of his position, for I am convinced that he was on my side. He wants to travel to England, but he had the misfortune of suffering a dangerous head wound during an attack of epilepsy.

Privy Councillor Oelrichs[11] introduced me to Minister Herzberg[12] who received me with great kindness, invited me to dinner, and praised you greatly.

As for the meetings of the high school faculty, there has been little activity so far. Just about the only topic of concern has been the determination of which teachers fall under the law that releases the children of school teachers from military duty. You may be assured that I shall do everything I can to bring about the results that you favor for the schools in Königsberg.

Prof. Herz[13] has asked me to convey to you his most devoted respects. I usually go to his home for tea and supper on Fridays and I must say that I enjoy myself greatly there. He is certainly one of your most enthusiastic admirers. I was introduced to Maimon[14] at Herz's house. His outer appearance is unprepossessing, all the more so since he speaks little and badly. I started to read his Transcendental Philosophy but I have not gotten very far into it; I can see right at the start that I don't agree with him. I think too that he often lacks precision.

The public here is divided about Herr Reinhold's Theory of the

11:114

11:115

Cognitive Faculty.[15] Some people praise it inordinately while others find a number of faults in it. I still cannot find the time to finish the book, but overall I do not agree with its author, and his demonstrations often seem to me to be flawed. For example, on p. 282 he offers a proof of the proposition *"Manifoldness^a is the Criterion of the Material ^b of Representation."* What he says is: In a representation that is to be distinguished from the subject, there must be the possibility of distinguishing something, and that which allows of being distinguished in the representation can only be the material, and everything material in a representation must be distinguishable, i.e., must be diverse. I find this demonstration most incomprehensible and I think it is open to several objections. Herr Reinhold, who is so dreadfully prolix on matters of far less importance than this one, is here short and obscure. The following proof, which I submit to your examination, seems to me easier and more comprehensible. Every material, if it is to become a representation, must receive form from my faculty of representation; this form is nothing else than combination,^c combination presupposes the manifoldness of what is capable of being combined; consequently, every representation must contain something manifold. – Herr Reinhold is carrying on rather strangely about this book; among other things, he wrote to Dr. Biester asking him to purchase it, read it, and defend it against the review that might appear in the *A [llgemeine] D [eutsche] Bibl[iothek]*. I would hardly believe this if Dr. Biester had not told it to me personally. I know also that he was pleased that you have not written anything to him about the book.

My lectures have given me a new opportunity to rethink the theory of space and time, and it occurred to me that the following line of argument might make it easier to grasp. I distinguish the representation of space from space itself; they are distinguished the way a representation is distinguished from what is represented. So the first question is, What is the representation of space? It must be either an intuition or a concept. It cannot be a concept, because synthetic propositions flow from it; so it must be an intuition. Now I continue with the following question: Is it a priori or a posteriori? It cannot be a posteriori, because it is necessary, and the propositions that derive from it carry apodictic certainty with them. It is therefore a pure intuition a priori. But now, what is space? It cannot be a thing in itself, or an objective characteristic of things in themselves, for then the representation of it would be empirical; so the representation of space must be grounded in the subjective constitution of our cognitive faculty. Since it is an intuition, it must be grounded in sensibility, and since it is only

11:116

---

^a *Mannigfaltigkeit* ^b *Stoff*
^c Verknüpfung

found with objects of outer sense, it must be given through outer sense. Since our cognitive faculty only supplies us with form, not with matter, it follows that space is the form of outer sense. – Please be so kind as to tell me what you think of this argument, dearest sir.

Manipulation[16] is attracting a great deal of attention here; from the enclosed essay you will see how far the matter has gone already. Being acquainted with Pastor Schleemüller gives me the chance to try some experiments myself and, as you will learn, I have already done so. Clearly there is fraud behind it, though it is difficult to tell who the author of this fraud is. I doubt that it is Prof. Selle; perhaps Lohmeier, the pensioner; or perhaps another gentleman entirely who plays a not insignificant role at our court and who is a member of the Straßburger Magnetic Society; at least he himself has distributed a guide to comfortable magnetizing. – I did my experiments without Selle's knowledge, so I must not let it be known in public, for otherwise Schleemüller might be compromised. – I would be grateful if you were to suggest some experiments to me. One question is especially important to me: are there criteria by which one can determine whether someone is asleep or merely pretending? If so, what are they? I think that there are no indubitable criteria of that sort.[17]

Forgive me, beloved and esteemed man, if my chatter has robbed you of a little half hour. It is an indescribable pleasure for me to converse, even if only in writing, with a man who possesses my whole heart and whom I love above all else. I am always deeply moved when I think of my happiness in your presence and I never cease to call up those memories. If only I could tell you just once what I feel and how much I cherish what you have given me.

My sincerest respects to your esteemed friend, Prof. Krause, and tell him how proud I would be if he were to honor me with his friendship.

Hoping that you remember me with your affection and good will, I am faithfully

your sincerest admirer,
J. G. C. Kiesewetter

Berlin, November 15, 1789

P.S. Here are the typographical errors in the *Critique of Practical Reason*.

November 17. Chancellor von Hoffmann, whom I mentioned just now, sends you his regards.

---

1   Princess Friederike Christiane Auguste (1780–1841) was the daughter of Friedrich Wilhelm II.

2 Baroness Elise von Bielefeld (1765–1825). She became the wife of the writer Franz Michael Leuchsenring in 1792 and went with him to Paris. Leuchsenring (1746–1827) was mocked as the "Apostle of sentimentality [*Empfindsamkeit*]" in Goethe's "Pater Brey" in *Dichtung und Wahrheit*, part III, book 13. He was a friend and correspondent of many important literary figures of the period, e.g., Herder, and he is mentioned and praised as a literary friend by Kant's friend J. C. Berens. (Cf. Berens' letter to Kant, Ak. [338].) Elise died in Paris, in 1825, after an unhappy marriage.

3 Ernst Ferdinand Klein, director of the University of Halle and of its law faculty. Member of the Berlin Academy (1744–1810). Klein was the author of several books on jurisprudence and the theory of punishment.

4 Johann Christoph Andreas Mayer, *Kammergerichtsrat* in Berlin.

5 Carl Christoph von Hoffmann, (1735–1801) chancellor of the University of Halle in 1786.

6 Karl Franz von Irwing (1728–1801), *Oberkonsistorialrat* (member of the High Consistory) in Berlin.

7 Johann Christoph Wöllner (1732–1800), favorite of Friedrich Wilhelm II and author of the religious censorship edicts that attempted to suppress liberal thinkers such as Kant.

   Wöllner, an orthodox theologian, was once characterized by Frederick the Great as "a deceitful, scheming priest and nothing more." (Cf. K. Vorländer, *Immanuel Kant's Leben*, [Leipzig: Felix Meiner, 1921 ed.] p. 157.

   Friedrich Wilhelm II put special trust in Wöllner, elevating him on July 3, 1788, to the position of minister of justice and head of the departments concerned with spiritual matters. He thus replaced Zedlitz, to whom Kant had dedicated the *Critique of Pure Reason*. Six days after receiving this appointment, the *Religionsedict* appeared, asserting that even Lutheran and Calvinistic teachers were aiming to destroy the basic truths of Holy Scripture and, under the pretense of enlightenment, were disseminating countless errors. The edict paid lip service to the Prussian tradition of toleration and freedom of conscience but insisted that people should keep their opinions to themselves and take care not to undermine other people's faith. On December 19, 1788, a new censorship edict followed, designed to limit "the impetuosity of today's so-called enlighteners" and the "freedom of the press, which has degenerated into insolence of the press." All writings published domestically or to be exported beyond the borders of Prussia were put under censorship. The king anticipated that the censorship would "put a check on those works that oppose the universal principles of religion, the state, and civil order." (Cf. Vorländer, op. cit., p. 158.)

8 Prince Heinrich was the brother of Frederick the Great.

9 Wöllner's "Letters of a Minister concerning Enlightenment" (*Briefe eines Staatsministers über Aufklärung*), published anonymously in Straßburg, 1789. In one letter, p. 41, there is a sentence that reads: "A second class of insolent agitators of the public teaches that God exists but that one cannot prove his existence mathematically; so one must believe that he exists. But this belief, sir, is quite a different thing from the ordinary, modest theological faith which I share with the unspoiled Christian church and with your majesty: it is a product of pure reason which, according to their view, precedes all faith rather than

following it." The danger of this doctrine is then made clear by an argument to the effect that the enlighteners also regard the existence of the king as indemonstrable so that the people may be led to disobey his edicts. *Letters*, pp. 41, ff., cited in Ak. 13:254.

10 Zedlitz resigned his position "for reasons of health" in Dec. 1789.

11 Johann Karl Konrad Oelrichs, *Legationsrat* in Berlin (1722–99).

12 Count Ewald Friedrich von Hertzberg (1725–95), *Staatsminister* from 1763.

13 Kant's friend and former student, the physician Marcus Herz. See Herz's letters to and from Kant, in this volume.

14 The philosopher Salomon ben Joshua, known as Salomon Maimon. See his letter to Kant, Apr. 7, 1789, Kant's letter to Herz, May 26, 1789, Maimon's subsequent letters to Kant, etc. On Maimon's philosophical significance, see Frederick C. Beiser, *The Fate of Reason* (Cambridge, Mass. and London, 1987), ch. 10.

15 Karl Leonhard Reinhold, *Versuch einer neuen Theorie des menschlichen Vorstellungsvermögens* (1789). On Reinhold, see the letter to Kant from C. G. Schütz, Feb. 18, 1785, Ak. [237], n. 2, along with the Kant-Reinhold correspondence in this volume.

16 Mesmerism. Mesmer used his alleged magnetic powers to produce cures of various ailments by manipulation and stroking with his hands. Schleemüller was a pastor at the Charité hospital, Lohmeyer a resident surgeon there. The Straßburger Magnetic Society was one of the German schools, a "Gesellschaft der Harmonie," that taught Mesmer's theory. The gentleman alluded to was, according to the conjecture in Ak. 13:255, Count Hans Moritz von Brühl, a member of this society.

17 Kant answers this question, perhaps jestingly, at the end of his responding letter to Kiesewetter, Feb. 9, 1790, Ak. [405a].

Letters 1790–1794

[405a–647]

1790

102 [405a][1]

To Johann Gottfried Carl Christian Kiesewetter.

February 9, 1790.

You have given me great pleasure with your letter, so full of information, dearest friend.[2] I take joy in your good prospects,[3] praise your industriousness, and worry about your preserving your health; but I hope that those worries will be removed by your soon receiving a well paying position or an appointment as chaplain which will not require you to expend your energies so much.

I did not overlook that spot in the "Letters of a Minister"[4] and I noticed at whom it was directed. But it didn't trouble me.

I noticed a certain animosity in Herr Reinhold's letter as well; he is vexed that I have not read his *Theory [of the Power of Representation]*.[5] I answered him and I hope he will be reconciled to my postponing a complete reading of his book because of my pressing projects. The proof that you give of his proposition concerning the material of representation is comprehensible and correct. If, when I refer to the "material" of a representation, I mean that whereby the object is given, then, if I leave out synthetic unity (combination), which can never be given but only thought, what remains must be the manifold of intuition (for intuition in space and time contains nothing simple).[6]

Your proof of the ideality of space as the form of outer sense is entirely correct; only the beginning is questionable. You distinguish between the representation of space (one ought rather to say the consciousness of space) and space itself. But that would bestow objective reality on space, a view that generates consequences wholly at odds with the *Critique*'s line of argument. The consciousness of space, however, is actually a consciousness of the synthesis by means of which we construct it, or, if you like, whereby we construct or draw the concept of something that has been synthesized in conformity with this form of outer sense.[7]

I have not had time yet to read Maimon's book.[8] I hope you will cultivate his acquaintance a bit. Self-educated minds commonly possess a certain originality which one can use to sharpen one's ways of conceiving things (which are usually due more to one's teachers than to one's own thinking) and often such people can give us a wholly new perspective for assessing things. Please give Professor Herz, with whose solid, friendly, and gracious mind I have long been acquainted, my devoted greetings.

I am very sorry to hear that the manipulation nonsense[9] has, through Herr Selle's supposed experiment, even overcome the disbelief of our good *Berlinische Monatsschrift* publisher [Biester]. (Selle's experiment, if it proved electricity, should have done so by demonstrating movement in little cork balls rather than by exciting the nerves of lascivious women by stimulating their imagination.) I fear that he will have to endure a great deal of mockery from his opponents. Dr. Elsner[10] says that common women often allow themselves to be put to sleep by having children grope through their tresses (delousing them, as it were). The test of whether someone's sleep is true or feigned is best done as follows: have someone nearby the subject, speaking softly yet audibly, say something that will embarrass, anger, or frighten her and watch her demeanor.

But I must close. Your intention to visit us in Königsberg during the coming dog-days will make many people very happy; most of all your loyal and devoted friend

I. Kant

P.S. Yesterday I sent almost the whole manuscript to Herr Delagarde. More next time.

---

1   This letter, mentioned in the Akademie edition of Kant's letters, was published by Peter Remnant and Christoph E. Schweitzer in *Journal of the History of Philosophy 3*, 1965, pp. 243–246, and then in the third edition (1986) of Kant's *Briefwechsel*, ed. by R. Malter and J. Kopper.

2   Kiesewetter to Kant, Dec. 15, 1789, Ak.[394]; the end of the letter says "15 November 1789" but since the lectures alluded to began Dec. 1, "November" must be a slip of the pen.

3   See the letter mentioned in n. 2.

4   Wöllner published, anonymously, a work called "Letters (addressed to the king) from a minister of state concerning enlightenment" (*Briefe eines Staatsministers über Aufklärung*, Strasbourg, 1789). It contained a reference to Kant's denial of the possibility of proving God's existence.

5 Reinhold, *Versuch einer neuen Theorie des menschlichen Vorstellungskraft.*
6 Cf. *Critique of Pure Reason*, A 523–7, B 551–5.
7 Cf. op.cit., B 137–8, A 713 B 741.
8 But cf. Kant to Herz, May 26, 1789, Ak. [362], in which Kant discusses Maimon's book in detail.
9 The reference is to Mesmer's quack medical treatments, involving manipulation, touching, a sort of hypnosis, supposedly brought about by Mesmer's "animal magnetism."
10 Christoph Friedrich Elsner (1749–1820), professor of medicine in Königsberg, the physician who cared for Kant in his last illness.

103 [411] (388)
To Ludwig Ernst Borowski.[1]

Between March 6 and 22, 1790.

You ask me what might be the source of the wave of mysticism[a] that is so rapidly gaining ground and how this disease might be cured. Both of these questions are as difficult for physicians of the soul as was the influenza epidemic that spread all around the world a few years ago (what the Viennese call "Russian catarrh") for physicians of the body. The influenza infected people one right after the other, but it soon cleared up by itself. I think the two sorts of doctors have much in common, incidentally, both being much better at describing illnesses than at locating their origin and prescribing the cure. Lucky indeed are the sick when the doctors' only prescription is to keep to a diet and take good, clean water, trusting Mother Nature to do the rest.

It seems to me that the universally prevailing *mania for reading*[b] [2] is not only the carrier that spreads this illness but the very miasmic poison that produces it. The more well-to-do and fashionable people, claiming their insights at least equal if not superior to the insights of those who have troubled to pursue the thorny path of thorough investigation, are content with reviews and summaries, superficially skimming the cream off of scientific treatises. These people would like to obscure the obvious difference between loquacious ignorance and thorough science, and this is easiest to do by snatching up incomprehensible things that are no more than airy possibilities and presenting them as facts that the serious natural scientist is supposed to explain. They

11:141

---

[a] *Schwärmerei*   [b] *Lesesucht*

11:142 ask him how he can account for tne fulfillment of this or that dream, premonition, astrological prophecy, or transmutation of lead into gold, and so on. For in matters of this kind, when once the alleged facts are on the table (and these people will never concede that the facts themselves may be in doubt) one man is as ignorant of the explanation as another. They find it hard to learn *everything* the natural scientist knows, so they take the easier road, attempting to dissolve the inequality between them and him by showing that there are matters about which neither of them knows *anything*, matters of which the unscientific man is therefore free to make definite pronouncements simply because the scientists cannot contradict them. This is where the mania begins, and from there it spreads to ordinary people as well.

I see only one remedy for this disease: thoroughness must be substituted for dilettantism in the curriculum, and the desire to read must not be eradicated but redirected so as to become purposeful. When this happens, the well-instructed man will enjoy reading only what will genuinely profit his understanding, and everything else will disgust him. In his *Observations of a Traveller*, a German physician, Herr Grimm,[3] finds fault with what he calls *"the French omniscience,"* but the voracious reading of the French is not nearly as tasteless as that of the German, who usually constructs a ponderous system that he becomes fanatically unwilling to abandon. The *Mesmer-show*[4] in France is only a fad and is bound to disappear sooner or later.

The customary trick that the mystic and dreamer uses to cover up his ignorance and give it the appearance of science is to ask, "Do you understand the real cause of magnetic force, or do you know the material stuff that produces such marvelous effects in electrical phenomena?" He thinks he is justified in expressing opinions on a subject that, on his view, the greatest natural scientist understands as little as he, and he ventures to hold forth even on the most likely effects of this force. But the scientist considers only those effects to be genuine that are susceptible of experimental testing, so that the object of investigation is brought wholly under his control. The mystic, on the other hand, snatches up effects that could have originated in the imagination of either the observer or the subject being observed, so that there is no possibility of experimental control.

11:143 There is nothing to be done about this humbug except to let the animal magnetist magnetize and disorganize, as long as he and his credulous fellows desire. But we can advise the police to watch out that these people keep away from moral issues and we can recommend that the single road of natural science, using experiment and observation to discover the properties of objects of outer sense, be pursued. Elaborate refutation here is beneath the dignity of reason and, furthermore, accomplishes nothing. Scornful silence is more appropriate toward

such madness. Movements of this kind, in the moral realm, have but a
short duration before they make way for new follies. I remain, etc.

---

1 Ludwig Ernst Borowski (1740–1832), one of Kant's first students and later,
with R. B. Jachmann and E. A. C. Wasianski, biographers. Borowski was an
army chaplain, then pastor at the Neu-Roßgärtischen Kirche in Königsberg.
He rose to a high rank in the Prussian church. Borowski's connection to Kant
was interrupted in 1762 when he left Königsberg but resumed in 1782 and
remained close for the following decade.
   The present letter is in response to Borowski's letter of Mar. 6, 1790, Ak.
[410], in which Borowski expresses concern about "the wave of mysticism that
has been sweeping the country" and asks Kant to write a short essay on the
topic to combat the influence of "these fanatic dreamers" on the public. Borowski published Kant's letter in his biography.
2 Historians of the *Sturm und Drang* period have noted the change in reading
habits and in readership during this period. Libraries and reading societies
made novels and romantic dramas available to the general literate public, while
among the educated upper bougeoisie there were societies devoted to reading
the latest publications aimed at the improvement of taste and morals. It is this
explosion of reading to which Kant must refer.
3 J. F. C. Grimm (1737–1821), of Weimar, *Bemerkungen eines Reisenden durch
Deutschland, Frankreich, England und Holland*, 3 Theile (Altenburg, 1775).
4 The reference is to the Austrian physician and mystic, Franz Anton Mesmer
(1734–1815), whose highly popular theory of "animal magnetism" – a supposed healing, magnetic power emanating from the body – had been investigated by a commission of scientists appointed by the French government in
1784. (Benjamin Franklin served on it.) Mesmer, who settled in Paris in 1778
after being accused of practicing magic in Austria, was viewed as a charlatan
not only by Kant but by many "enlightened" people, e.g., Wolfgang Amadeus
Mozart and his librettist Lorenzo Da Ponte. While "animal magnetism" as a
supposedly magical form of therapy was taken up throughout France, Mozart
satirized it in his opera *Così fan tutte*.

104 [413a]¹

To Johann Gottfried Carl Christian Kiesewetter.

March 25, 1790.

I am very disturbed to learn that your indisposition still continues,
dearest friend. The many tasks you have taken on at the same time

could well be part of the cause. But I am apprehensive about your undertaking so much mental work after dinner, studying I imagine late into the evening. This attacks one's mental and physical strength, if one is not blessed with an athletic constitution. I found this out in my own experience and gave up the practice when I was only 15 years old. For I find that it does not further the progress of knowledge or the mental concentration on one's tasks anyhow, though it may be possible, between periods of light reading in the evening, to assemble disconnected thoughts and to sketch ideas and write them down briefly, things that one wants to digest the following morning. All this can be easily accomplished if you get up early, as early as 4 in the morning in summer, assuming you go to bed at 9, being sure not to drink anything but cold water before retiring. A diet such as that, avoiding or greatly reducing the intake of warm drinks and warm soups, will do more for you in a few weeks than the medical arts.[2]

Herr Delagarde[3] will transmit to you the manuscript recently sent to him which contains the Introduction to the work now in press. I believe my summarizing of what you transcribed earlier has the advantage both of making it clearer and of not lengthening the time it takes to print it. The reason why you must see it right away before the typesetter gets hold of it is that you can cross out a note which, as I recall, is on Page 2 of Sheet VI of the Introduction (in the manuscript) and which is supposed to contain a Principle of Reflective Judgment, for it does not belong in the place where it occurs. It is written by me personally and one cannot fail to notice therefore that I wrote it hastily, for there are some words crossed out in it as well.[4] At the same time I beg you to take care of the page citation on Sheet X. Presumably Herr Delagarde will make it his business to expedite the printing in the best possible way.

If you have some free moments sometime please give me news of how things stand with the new catechism that is supposed to be introduced in all Lutheran congregations; they say that the order has now been rescinded.[5]

Every bit of news concerning your good health will bring genuine pleasure to

your devoted
I. Kant.

---

1 A version of this letter was published by Arnold Buchholz in *Kant-Studien* 55, Köln, 1964, pp. 242–243. Another version was discovered in the Moscow Historical Museum. The present translation is based on the Supplement to the third edition (1986) of Kant's *Briefwechsel*, ed. by R. Malter and J. Kopper.

2 Cf. *The Conflict of the Faculties* (*Streit der Fakultäten*, 1798), part 3, "Grundsatz der Diätetik." Kant's remarks about the ill effects of working after dinner are also given at the end of his letter to Herz, Ak. [166], in May 1781.

3 Kant means Lagarde, François Théodorede (1756–?), book merchant in Berlin and publisher of the *Critique of Judgment*.

4 Cf. *First Introduction to the Critique of Judgment*, Section VIII, Comment.

5 Kiesewetter's report in his letter of Mar. 3, 1790, Ak. [409], did not reach Kant until mid-April.

105 [414] (391)
To François de la Garde.[1]

March 25, 1790.

[*Kant instructs Lagarde to send hard-bound copies of the* Critique of Judgment *to nine persons: Count Windisch-Grätz*[2] *in Bohemia, F. H. Jacobi in Düsseldorf, Reinhold in Jena, Jacob in Halle, Blumenbach*[3] *in Göttingen, and to Wloemer, Biester, Kiesewetter, and Herz in Berlin. He asks that Kiesewetter be shown the manuscript of the Introduction, in which he will make a correction prior to its publication . . .*]

11:145

. . . Please greet Herr Abbot Denina[4] for me and tell him that I was extremely put off when in reading his intellectual history I came upon his pity-inspiring description of my domestic condition at the university prior to my succeeding to a full professor's salary. He has certainly been misinformed. For I have always had a full lecture hall from the very beginning of my academic career (in 1755) and never had to give private lessons (this must include the *privatissimum* seminar in one's own lecture room which was usually very well paid), consequently my income has always been ample, so that it sufficed not only for the rent on my two rooms and my very well laden table, without my having to ask for help from anyone, in particular not from my late English friend[5] who was my regular dinner guest without needing any special invitation, and besides this I was always able to afford my own servant. Those were just the most pleasant years of my life. And a proof of this is that I turned down four invitations to positions at other universities during that period. – When the opportunity arises for him to make corrections in his book, as he has indicated to you he means to strike the word "absurdités" in the article *"Eberhard"* (which I believe must be done, for it is inconsistent with a number of passages in the article

11:146

11:147

341

"Kant"), he could also, if he is willing, retract in general terms that error in the depiction of my life.[6]

. . . [Kant asks de la Garde to charge the shipping costs incurred by rapid delivery of the various copies of the *Critique of Judgment* against his honorarium.]

I remain your most devoted servant

I. Kant.

P.S. I have received the first three issues of the second volume of Eberhard's *Magazin*[7] and I see from the Hamburger correspondent that the fourth issue is also out; please send it to me by the next stagecoach, for it is very important to me. – I still have the *Examen politique d'un Ouvrage intitulé Histoire secrette* [*sic*] etc., as well as the *Briefe eines Staatsministers über die Auifklärung*.[8] What should I do with them? I shall deliver them to your brother.

---

1 François Théodore de la Garde (1756–?). There is no consistency in references to "de la Garde" or "Lagarde," the version of his name used in most German editions of Kant's letters, or, as Kant sometimes calls him, "Delagarde." He was a book merchant in Berlin and the publisher of Kant's *Critique of Judgment*.

2 See Kant to Jacobi, Ak.[375], n. 1.

3 Johann Friedrich Blumenbach (1752–1840) was a renowned anatomist and naturalist, professor of medicine in Göttingen. His *Über den Bildungstrieb* (On the formative impulse) is mentioned in the *Critique of Judgment*. See Kant's letter to him, Aug. 5, 1790, Ak.[438], below.

4 Carl Johann Maria Denina (1731–1813), member of the Berlin Academy of Sciences, author of *La Prusse littéraire sous Frédéric II* (two volumes, Berlin, 1790). The article on Kant states that Kant's parents were poor and that he was forced to sustain himself by fees from individual lessons. Kant's position as second librarian in Königsberg in 1755 hardly sufficed to pay the rent for his two rooms, according to Denina, and he dined regularly with his friend, an English merchant, to survive.

   Kant's rebuttal of this description paints a happier picture of his life as a young instructor than did his letter to Lindner, Ak.[13], above.

5 Joseph Green (c.1727–86) was Kant's close friend.

6 In the sentence "Dans la metaphysique il (Eberhard) ne donne pas dans les absurdités de Mr. Kant" Denina changed the word "absurdités" to "abstrusités," but made no change in describing Kant's life.

7 On Eberhard see Kant's letter to Reinhold, May 12, 1789, Ak.[359], n. 1. The *Philosophischen Magazin* founded by Eberhard was published 1788–9.

8 The precise title is Baron Frédéric de Trenk, *Examen politique et critique d'un ouvrage intitulé histoire secrette de la Cour de Berlin ou correspondance d'un Voyageur François depuis le 5 Juillet 1786 jusqu'au 19 Janvier 1787*, 2 volumes, 1789. The *Histoire secrette* referred to by Trenk was written by Mirabeau. Bahrdt's *Briefe*

eines Staatsministers über Aufklärung (Strasbourg, 1789) is mentioned also in Kiesewetter's letter of Dec. 15, 1789, Ak.[394].

106 [419] (396)
To Johann Gottfried Carl Christian Kiesewetter.
April 20, 1790.
[*Excerpt*]

... The criterion of a genuine moral principle is its unconditional practical necessity; thereby it differs entirely from all other sorts of practical principles. The possibility of freedom, if this be considered (as in the *Critique of Pure Reason*) prior to any discussion of the moral law, signifies only the transcendental concept of the causality of an earthly creature in general insofar as that causality is not determined by any ground in the sensible world; and all that is shown there is that there is nothing self-contradictory about this concept (it is not specifically the concept of the causality of a will). This transcendental idea [of freedom] acquires content by means of the moral law, and it is given *to the will* (the will being a property of a rational being – of human beings) because the moral law allows no ground of determination from nature (the aggregate of objects of sense). The concept of freedom, as causality, is apprehended in an affirmation, and this concept of a free causality is without circularity interchangeable with the concept of a moral ground of determination.[1]

11:154

11:155

---

1 This passage is one of the places where Kant tries to answer the charge that his arguments for freedom and the moral law are circular, each assuming the reality of the other. The circularity is only apparent, he explains, since "freedom" is used in two senses: first, to signify the negative, "transcendental" idea of independence from the determinism of nature (a concept whose non-contradictoriness Kant thinks he has shown in the antinomy of the first *Critique*), and second, to signify the positive concept of freedom as autonomy, a unique sort of causality possessed by rational beings. Cf. *Grundlegung zur Metaphysik der Sitten, Werke*, Ak. 4:450, where Kant offers a somewhat different solution: the activity of thinking, he maintains there, is itself a manifestation of freedom. The charge of circularity came from the critic Johann Friedrich Flatt (1759–1821), professor of philosophy in Tübingen.

107 [420] (397)
From Johann Gottfried Carl Christian Kiesewetter.
April 20, 1790.

11:156   Dearest, best Herr Professor,

[*Kiesewetter apologizes for not writing sooner and gives a somewhat lengthy account of his circumstances, his success as a private tutor and lecturer, and news of various mutual acquaintances. He tells of Professor Selle,*[1] *a physician in Berlin, who was about to publish an essay that, Selle hoped, would give the death blow to Kant's system.*]

11:157   ... As far as I have learned, his main argument is that even assuming that you had proved space and time to be forms of our sensibility, you could not have shown that they were *only* forms of sensibility, since it is still *possible* to imagine them to belong to things in themselves, a possibility that you are in no position to deny, in view of your claim that we can know nothing of things in themselves. Besides, can one answer the question, why we intuit in just these and no other forms?

11:158   In his opinion, space and time are subjectively necessary conditions of our intuitions, but there are also properties of things in themselves that correspond to them. – If it turns out that his whole attack contains nothing more significant than that, I shall not find it so frightening. How is Herr S. going to prove that space and time pertain to things in themselves? And if he admits that space and time are forms of sensibility, how can he claim that they are nevertheless dependent on things in themselves? For if they are given to us by the objects, they must be part of the matter of intuition, not its form. I shall gladly send you a copy as soon as the book appears.

Strange things are happening here nowadays. A week ago last Sunday the King got married to the Countess von Dehnhof,[2] in one of the rooms of the palace here. The probability is – virtually a certainty, to my mind – that Zöllner[3] performed the wedding. Minister Wöllner[4] and Herr von Geysau[5] attended the King; the mother and sister of the Countess and her stepbrother (or cousin, I forget which) attended the bride. The King arrived Saturday evening from Potsdam and the marriage took place Sunday evening at 6. The Countess was dressed in white (like the heroine of a novel), with hair unfurled. She resides in Potsdam now. It is presumed that the Elector of Saxony[6] will have to promote her to imperial princess. Formerly she was lady-in-waiting to the reigning queen. For almost a year the King has been carrying on negotiations with her, but her public behavior was such that one couldn't tell whether she gave him a hearing or not. About two weeks ago her mother came, or so the Countess has let it be circulated, to take her to Prussia, at her request. The Countess then publicly makes her farewells at court. The reigning queen makes her a present of a pair of brilliant earrings and tells her she will know best whether they should remind her of the Queen. Everybody thinks she has left, just as the marriage is taking place. The Queen has received the news rather calmly. What I have told you up to now is, apart from precise details, known to almost everyone, and it is causing a mighty sensation among the public. The crowd at Zöllner's sermons has diminished and even at an *introduction* that he recently held, where people used to come in droves, the church was empty. – The following facts are known only to a few persons. The King and Queen are divorced, a decree to which she agreed at the time of the "negotiations" with the late Ingenheim.[7] The King gave up all marital rights, and the Queen retained only the honorary title. Dr. Brown[8] declared her unbalanced, and this is very probably true, since insanity runs in the family. She often dances around on chairs and tables and sees spirits. What a misfortune it would be for our state if this defect had been transmitted to her children.

11:159

War preparations are still continuing here.[9] The most remarkable thing, though, is that the King and not the ministry wants war. The official plan is as follows: our army will be divided into four corps, the first, led by the King, with Möllendorf[10] commanding under him, will fight the Austrians; the second, led by the Duke of Braunschweig,[11] will oppose the Russians; Prince Friedrich[12] commands the reconnaissance corps against the Saxons; and besides these there is supposed to be a so-called flying corps. As far as Saxony is concerned, they say that at the time that the late Emperor was still alive a special envoy of the Emperor's who had come for a private audience with the Elector at the Saxon court was arrested. The audience was, however, granted, and the envoy inquired of the Elector how he would act if Prussia should go to war. The Elector replied that he would remain neutral. The envoy received this answer with pleasure and asked the Elector to make an official proclamation. But happily the Marquis Lucchesini[13] prevented this, though the Elector had given his answer orally. So now an army will compel the Elector to join our side . . .

[*Kiesewetter wishes Kant a happy 67th birthday tomorrow.*]

Your devoted servant,
J. G. C. Kiesewetter, Berlin

P.S. My last letter[14] told you the story of the catechism rejected by the Superior Church Council. Now Herr Silberschlag and Preacher

From Johann Gottfried Carl Christian Kiesewetter. April 20, 1790

Hecker[15] are reworking an old catechism, composed by the late Inspector Hecker,[16] containing a compilation of theological twaddle.

---

1 Christian Gottlieb Selle (originally Sell) (1748–1800), physician at the Berlin Charité, member of the Berlin Academy, an empiricist and one of the men to whom Kant sent complimentary copies of the *Critique*. The essay Kiesewetter heard Selle deliver, "De la Réalité et de l'Idéalité des objets de nos connaissances," was published by the Berlin Academy in 1792. Selle's central argument, as reported by Kiesewetter, anticipates the criticism of Kant made by Trendelenburg in his *Logischen Untersuchen* (1840), I, 128.

2 Sophie Juliane Friederike Wilhelmine, Countess von Dönhoff (1768–1834) married Friedrich Wilhelm II on Apr. 2, 1790. She is mentioned again in the letter from Kiesewetter of June 14, 1791, Ak.[474].

3 Johann Friedrich Zöllner, preacher and *Oberkonsistorialrat* (prior in charge of the principal church in the district) in Berlin (1753–1804). Zöllner argued warmly against the King's new catechism.

4 Johann Christoph Wöllner, favorite of Friedrich Wilhelm II (1732–1800). Wöllner, an orthodox theologian, was once characterized by Frederick the Great as "a deceitful, scheming priest and nothing more" (K. Vorländer, *Immanuel Kant's Leben* [Leipzig: Felix Meiner, 1921], p. 157).

Friedrich Wilhelm II put special trust in Wöllner, elevating him on July 3, 1788, to the position of minister of justice (replacing Minister Zedlitz, to whom Kant had dedicated the *Critique of Pure Reason*) and head of the departments concerned with spiritual matters. Six days later his *Religionsedikt* appeared, asserting that even Lutheran and Calvinist teachers were trying to destroy the basic truths of Holy Scripture and were disseminating countless errors under the pretense of enlightenment. The edict paid lip service to the Prussian tradition of toleration and freedom of conscience but insisted that everyone should keep his opinions to himself and take care not to undermine other people's faith. On December 19, 1788, a new censorship edict followed, designed to limit "the impetuosity of today's so-called enlighteners" and the "freedom of the press, which has degenerated into insolence of the press." All writings published domestically or to be exported beyond Prussia were put under censorship. The King anticipated that the censorship would "put a check on those works that oppose the universal principles of religion, the state, and civil order." (See Vorländer, op. cit., p. 158.)

At first, the edict had no effect. Liberal theologians preached more freely than ever, Kant's friend Berens wrote to him. One man wanted to print Luther's essay on freedom of thought, especially the sentence, "Knights, Bishops, and Nobles are fools if they meddle in matters of faith." Berens thought that similar passages written by the late Frederick the Great should be published as an appendix. He asked Kant (as had others before him) to express his views on the problem in Biester's journal, the *Berliner Monatsschrift*.

For a time, Wöllner pretended to be friendly to Kant, allowing Kiesewetter

to lecture on Kant's philosophy (though with his own spy sometimes in attendance). See Kiesewetter's letter of June 14, 1791, Ak.[474].
5 Levin von Geysau, a Prussian army officer.
6 Friedrich August III (1763–1817); after 1806, as king, Friedrich August I.
7 Julie von Voß, another mistress of Friedrich Wilhelm II, was "betrothed" to him – a so-called left-hand marriage (*Ehe an der linken Hand*, legally recognized concubinage) – and received the title Countess von Ingenheim in 1787. She died in 1789 at the age of 22.
8 Dr. Carl Brown, royal physician.
9 Against Austria.
10 W. J. H. von Möllendorf (1724–1816), general field marshal, governor of Berlin.
11 Carl Wm. Ferdinand (1735–1806), Prussian field marshal.
12 Duke of York (1763–1827).
13 Girolamo Lucchesini (1752–1825), Italian by birth, at that time sent to Warsaw by Friedrich Wilhelm II as an envoy extraordinary and minister plenipotentiary.
14 Mar. 3, 1790, Ak.[409].
15 Andreas Jakob Hecker (1746–1819), chaplain at the *Dreifaltigkeitskirche* and, from 1785, director of the united institutes of the royal *Realschule*.
16 Johann Julius Hecker (1707–68), founder of the *Realschule* in Berlin.

108 [426] (402)
From Ludwig Heinrich Jakob.
May 4, 1790.

Halle, the 4th of May, 1790

Esteemed Herr Professor,   11:168

First of all let me thank you most sincerely for the gift of your *Critique of Judgment*, sent to me via Herr Lagarde. I have not yet been able to study it thoroughly, since I don't even have all the pages; but the isolated glances I have given it have already opened up great and glorious insights for me.

Allow me at the same time to put a question to you concerning the concept, or rather the expression, "cognition",[a] a question over which Herr Reinhold and I have recently had some division. As far as I see,

[a] *Erkenntni*

347

you use the expression "cognition" in the *Critique of Pure Reason* in a double sense, sometimes meaning by it the genus[b] "objective representations," as opposed to sensation,[c] so that intuition and concept are species[d] of this genus, consequently themselves cognitions; but at other times the word "cognitions" means those representations that are formed by the synthesis of an intuition and a concept. Herr Reinhold uses the word always in the latter sense, and where the *Critique of Pure Reason* says that no cognition of supersensible objects is possible, the word "cognition" is also taken exclusively in this latter sense.

If I consider linguistic usage, it seems always to agree with the first meaning, so that the word "cognition" signifies any representation that one relates to an object. One ascribes cognitions to animals lacking reflection, notwithstanding the fact that one denies them understanding or the faculty of concepts. And on the other hand, an idea, even supposing that it is one for which admittedly no object could be given in experience and that it has no intuitional content, is called a cognition as soon as one has to admit that it is a representation that refers to something at all, something distinct from the representation. So, for example, the mere concept of an appearance leads to a something that is not appearance. I cannot materially determine this something, but it is still thought of as necessarily bound up with the representation of appearance. I therefore have a mere idea of this something, but even if I do not take this idea, say, for that which lies at the foundation of appearance, I can undoubtedly still interpret it in such a way that it refers to a real something in general, something that is in any case distinct both from the idea and from appearance, even though I cannot now determine whether this something is conceivable or inconceivable. The authority that compels me to assume such an object is my reason; but my reason requires me to posit the actuality[e] of a something that appears there, just as much as the senses require me to grant the actuality of appearances. In the one case, reason points me toward an object; in the other case, the senses present me with one. I can trust the authority of reason no less than I trust the senses. We thus really recognize through reason that there are things in themselves, and we do this through the Idea.[f] This Idea does not express anything about the things in themselves; it leaves them undetermined, but it does I think point to their reality.[g] However empty this Idea might be, as soon as it even points to a real object it can, I think, be called cognition. I am well aware that I cannot determine whether something is a *real being*, if I cannot deter-

11:169

[b] *Gattung*
[d] *Arten*
[f] *Idee*

[c] *Empfindung*
[e] *Wirklichkeit*
[g] *Dasein*

mine such a thing by means of a temporal relation to my faculty of perception; but the merely logical concept that I unite with it when I say "the thing in itself is there" and which says no more than that it contains the necessary ground of the reality of appearance, that concept is nevertheless a sign of a sort that would put me in a position (were I to have a faculty of intellectual intuition) to seek and find the thing in itself; it is a formal, provisional[b] concept but really never an objective representation, something like the way a deaf person can form anticipatory concepts of hearing for himself, concepts which, given the condition of deafness, can really only be formal, but which still would put him in a position (were he suddenly to acquire the power of hearing) to recognize that now he could hear. I don't see why one couldn't say that deaf people and blind people could have anticipatory cognitions (concepts) of hearing and seeing, even if they don't now have any intuitions.

My main aim with this suggestion is to see whether this sort of indulgence in the usage of expressions might not reconcile the disputing parties, since it is after all desirable for the *Critique*'s cause to get them to agree. Basically, people have already conceded a great deal to 11:170 the *Critique*. The main point of contention for its opponents seems to be that they are not supposed to have any cognition of God, immortality, etc. They generally admit that their cognition of these things could not be intuitive. If one now proves to them that the predicates "simple," "immaterial," etc., are intuitive predicates, they must give them up since they are not for us intuitive. If these people were to grant that we can only indicate relations of the unconditioned something to ourselves and to the sense world, then it seems to me that we can undoubtedly call the representation of these relations *cognitions* too; for it is granted that we do not merely think these relations (merely imagine them) – they are real, we take them to be objective, whether the ground that determines us to do this be the object or the subject. In my *Critical Essays concerning the First Volume of Hume*, I have made an attempt to present these concepts clearly. I am terribly eager to be instructed in this matter. I am not the only person who finds difficulties here. It would be an easy thing for you to offer resolutions of these linguistic ambiguities and to reconcile your usage of words to ordinary linguistic usage. I think that this certainly would further reconciliation a great deal.

By the way, I think you must be pleased to see Hume dressed as a German.[1] I think the basis of his reasoning can only be understood properly through your *Critique* and if I have accomplished anything, with the accompanying essays, towards making the correct judgment

---

[b] *vorläufiger*

easier, the greatest part of the credit for this is yours. So it is also with my prize essay which you will receive from a book dealer.² I wish nothing more than that you may judge your principles to have been well served and that you judge me not entirely incapable of contributing to the spread and advancement of the true philosophy. May Heaven yet grant you many years of power and strength, so that you can continue to impart your treasures to the world. Would that you would still decide to present us with an *Anthropologie*.

I am with the deepest respect and reverence

your

Jakob

---

1 The reference is to Jakob's translation of Hume, *David Hume über die menschliche Natur. Aus dem Englischen nebst kritischen Versuchen zur Beurteilung dieses Werks*, 3 volumes (Halle, 1790–2).

2 Jakob's *Beweis für die Unsterblichkeit der Seele aus dem Begriffe der Pflicht: Eine Preisschrift*, (Proof of the immortality of the soul from the concept of duty; Züllichau, 1790).

109 [427] (403)
From Salomon Maimon.
May 9, 1790.

11:171 Learned Sir,
Esteemed Herr Professor,

I trust you will forgive me for writing to you again. Not long ago I acquired and read the works of Bacon, and this led me to make a comparison between Bacon's and your own philosophical projects, which I published in the *Berlinisches Journal für Aufklärung*¹. Since I worry that I may have gone too far or not far enough, I beg you for your opinion. I shall be more pleased to have it than to have the opinion of any enthusiastic disciple or opponent. I know that one cannot be too careful in interpreting the thoughts of a somewhat ancient author, if one wants to avoid the charge of mangling the text on the one hand or of injecting new ideas into it on the other. I beg you, sir, not only to gratify my desire for your opinion but also to give me permission to publish your judgment in the aforementioned journal. With sincerest respect I have the honor of remaining

> your devoted servant
> Salomon Maimon

Berlin, May 9, 1790

---

1 Published by G. N. Fischer and A. Riem, vol. VII, issue #2, 1790, pp. 99–122. Maimon sees Bacon and Kant as reformers of philosophy who share the view that traditional formal logic is sterile. Maimon attempts to draw parallels between the three main divisions of the first *Critique* and Bacon's work. Bacon's warnings against hasty generalization and his view that contradictory errors may have a common cause are compared to Kant's doctrine, especially that of the resolution of the Antinomies. If these thinkers agree in certain respects, Maimon argues, their methods nevertheless differ. Maimon notes advantages and disadvantages in each. In Kant, there is a gap between the universal transcendental forms and the particular forms of things, and another gap between forms and matter in general. Maimon presents his own answer to this problem in his *Versuch über die Tranßcendentalphilosophie*. See Maimon's letter to Kant, Nov. 30, 1792, Ak. [548].

110 [430] (405)
From Salomon Maimon.
May 15, 1790.

Noble Sir,   11:174
Esteemed Herr Professor,

I thank you most sincerely and I am greatly obliged for the kind gift you have sent me, your *Critique of Judgment*. I treasure the gift also as evidence of your good opinion of me, which gives me cause to be proud. I have so far only been able to skim this important book, not having had time to give it the thorough reading and pondering that it deserves. However, the approbation you bestow on Privy Councillor Blumenbach induced me to read his excellent little essay[1] and called up an idea in me which, though not new, may seem quite paradoxical, viz., the idea of the world-soul and of how its reality might be determined. I venture to submit my thoughts on this for your examination.[2] I cannot be sure what exactly the ancients meant by this concept, whether they thought of it as God himself or as something distinct from God. Leaving that aside, here is how I think of it: The world-soul is a power inherent in matter in general (the material of all real objects), a power that affects matter in general in different ways according to the various ways that matter is modified. It is the ground of the particular sort of combination in each sort of matter (even in unorganized matter), the ground of the organization in every organized body, the ground of the life in an animal, of the understanding and reason in human beings, etc.; in short, the world-soul confers forms on all things according to the constitution of their matter, in such a way that it adapts matter, enabling it to change from a single form, to take on other forms, forms of a higher order. And since matter can undergo unlimited modification, so this entelechy too can supply an unlimited variety of forms. It is thus the ground of all possible agency.

I don't think that the newer philosophers have succeeded in repudiating this view entirely. Is the counter-argument supposed to be that we have no concept of this world-soul as an object? But we have just as little a concept of our own soul. Or is the problem that people fear Spinozism? If so, it seems to me that the definition I have given sufficiently forestalls this. For according to Spinozism, God and the world are one and the same substance. But it follows from the explanation I have given that the world-soul is a substance created by God. God is represented as pure intelligence, outside the world. This world-soul, by contrast, is indeed represented as an intelligence but as one that is essentially connected to a body (the world), consequently as limited and as subordinate to the laws of nature. If one speaks of substance as *thing in itself*, one can as little claim that there are several substances in the world as one can claim that there is only one. If we speak of phenomena, on the other hand, I think there are good grounds for deciding in favor of the latter alternative. For

a) the fact that the agency of so-called substances can be totally interrupted – e.g., thinking is interrupted by sleep – speaks against their being substantial. Locke maintained that the human soul does not think constantly; he gave this interruption as an example. Leibniz took refuge in his "obscure representations" and tried to prove the reality of the latter from the fact that representations that follow the interruption are connected with representations preceding it. But what are these obscure representations other than mere dispositions and residual traces of movements in the organs, movements that accompanied the ideas? The concept of a world-soul, by contrast, allows us to explain this connection in a comprehensible way. Each movement in the organs is accompanied by a corresponding representation, but there is a certain degree of intensity intrinsic to each. This intensity diminishes during sleep, so that this world-soul cannot then produce any representations. On awakening, however, the intensity is again increased, so that those movements in the body's organs are accompanied by their corresponding representations. And since the movements that follow sleep and those preceding it and those continuing while one is asleep cohere precisely according to natural laws, it follows that there must also be such a coherence among the representations corresponding to these movements.

b) It seems also that the nature of objective truth, which all human beings presuppose, necessarily requires the idea of a world-soul, one that explains the identity of the forms of thinking in all thinking subjects, and explains the agreement of the objects thought, in accordance with this form.   11:176

c) The doctrine of the purposiveness in nature (teleology) seems also to demand this idea. I believe, that is to say, that a purpose is not brought into being but that it is achieved by means of something already brought into being. I hold therefore that forms are purposes of nature which are realized, according to mechanistic laws, by objects that are brought into being in a definite manner. This proves therefore that there must exist a general ground of the connection of these forms among themselves, as particular purposes connected to a main purpose, and there must exist a general ground of the agreement of objects with these forms in general, objects, that is to say, which come into being according to natural laws. One can thus, from this point of view, liken the form-bestowing intelligence to a legislative intelligence, and liken the mechanistic laws of nature to the executive power of a well-constituted state.

These, in a few words, are roughly the arguments that I venture to submit to your grace's judgment. I await your verdict on them impatiently, and have the honor of remaining, sir,

your most obedient servant,
Salomon Maimon.

Berlin, the 15th of May, 1790.

---

1   On Blumenbach and the essay, see Kant's letter to Blumenbach, Aug. 5, 1790, Ak. [438], nn. 1–3.
2   Maimon's "Über die Weltseele" (On the world-soul) apppeared in the *Berliner Journal für Aufklärung*, 1789, i.e., prior to the writing of this letter.

111 [438]
To Johann Friedrich Blumenbach.[1]

August 5, 1790.

Königsberg, the 5th of August, 1790.

11:184

Esteemed Sir,

11:185

My erstwhile auditor Herr Jachmann, M.D., who has the honor of delivering this letter and who hopes to learn from you how profitably to spend his short stay in Göttingen, provides me with the chance to thank you most sincerely for your excellent essay *On the Formative Impulse*, which you sent me last year.[2] I have found much instruction in your writings, but the latest of them has a close relationship to the ideas that preoccupy me: the union of two principles that people have believed to be irreconcilable, namely the physical-mechanistic and the merely teleological way of explaining organized nature. Factual confirmation is exactly what this union of the two principles needs. I have tried to show my indebtedness for your instruction in a citation that you will find in the book that de Lagarde, the book merchant, will have sent you.

Please convey my respects to Privy Secretary Rehberg.[3] He requested, via Councillor Metzger, that I send him all my short essays. Please inform him that these have long since been out of my hands, for the direction that my thinking has taken is such that I am no longer concerned about them and, as far as the whole publication project is concerned, I am not eager to see some of them resurrected since they were written so hastily.

With best wishes for your welfare and good health, so that you may continue to instruct the world, I remain most respectfully

your most devoted servant,

I. Kant

---

1 On Blumenbach, see Kant to Lagarde, Mar. 25, 1790, Ak. [414], n.2, above.

2 *Über den Bildungstrieb* (On the formative impulse) was published in 1781 and 1789. Kant praises it and cites it in the *Critique of Judgment*, Ak. 5:424.

3 On Rehberg, See Schütz's letter of June 23, 1788, AK.[330], n. 1.

112 [439] (411b)
To Abraham Gotthelf Kästner.[1]

August 5 [?], 1790.

Illustrious sir,   11:186

Dr. Jachmann, M.D., a former auditor of mine who has the honor of transmitting this letter, hopes that my modest intercession will lead you, sir, to grant him a few moments of your busy time in order that he may be instructed by some of your suggestions during his short stay in Göttingen.

I did not want to pass up this opportunity to communicate my unbounded respect to the Nestor of all philosophical mathematicians of Germany.

At the same time permit me to explain that the efforts at criticism I have heretofore made are in no way meant (as they might appear to be) to attack the Leibniz-Wolffian philosophy (for I find the latter neglected in recent times). My aim is rather to pursue the same track according to a rigorous procedure and, by means of it, to reach the same goal, but only via a detour that, it appears to me, those great men seem to have regarded as superfluous: the union of theoretical and practical philosophy. This intention of mine will be clearer when, if I live long enough, I complete the reconstruction of metaphysics in a coherent system.

It is a genuine pleasure to see a man of intellect in his old age in good health and with a mind still freshly blossoming.

I would even accept him gladly as arbiter of the intellectual controversies to which I alluded if one were only permitted to expect the olive tree to release its oil in order to float above the trees.[2]

Nothing exceeds the respect with which I am, at all times, illustrious sir,

Your obedient servant,
Kann

---

1 Abraham Gotthelf Kästner (1719–1800), professor of physics and mathematics in Göttingen. His students included the mathematical physicist and aphorist G. C. Lichtenberg and the outstanding mathematician (often called "the prince of mathematics") J. F. C. Gauss. Kant admired Kästner also as a poet and sometimes quoted his verses. Herder was his friend in Leipzig, earlier in life. Kant wrote a commentary (unpublished in his lifetime, Ak. 20:410–23) on

essays that Kästner had published in Eberhard's *Magazin*. As Henry Allison points out, Kant respected Kästner (despite the connection with Eberhard) and saw that, unlike Eberhard, Kästner did not confuse the sensible with the intelligible, or space as an a priori intuition with an image. See Allison's *The Kant-Eberhard Controvesy*, pp. 12 f. and 84 f.

2 Kant makes a puzzling reference to an equally puzzling line from Wieland's *Empfindungen eines Christen* (Sentiments of a Christian), XXIV, "Der Ölbaum träufelte seine Fettigkeit auf ihr Haupt" (The olive tree lets fall its drops of oil upon her head).

113 [448] (418)
To August Wilhelm Rehberg.[1]

Before September 25, 1790.

11:207   The question is: Since the understanding has the power to create numbers at will, why is it incapable of thinking $\sqrt{2}$ in [rational] numbers? For if the understanding could *think* it, it ought to be able to *produce* it, too, since numbers are pure acts of its spontaneity, and the synthetic propositions of arithmetic and algebra cannot limit this spontaneity by the condition of intuition in space and time. It seems, therefore, that we must assume a transcendental faculty of imagination, one that, in representing the object independently even of space and time, connects synthetic representations solely in pursuance of understanding. From this faculty, a special system of algebra could be constructed, a knowledge of which (were it possible) would advance the method of solving equations to its highest generality.

This is how I understand the question put to me.

An Attempt to Answer This Question

(1) I can regard every number as the product of two factors, even if these factors are not immediately given to me or even if they could not be given in numbers. For, if the given number is 15, I can take one of the factors as 3, so that the other is 5, and $3 \times 5 = 15$. Or let the given factor be 2; then the second factor sought is 15/2. Or let the first factor be the fraction 1/7; the other factor is 105, and so on. It is thus possible, given any number as product and given one of its factors, to find the other factor.

(2) If neither of the factors is given but only a relationship between

them – for example, it is given that they are equal – so that we have a and the factor sought is x, where $1{:}x = x{:}\ a$ (that is, x is the mean proportional between 1 and a), then, since $a = x^2$, x must $= \sqrt{a}$. That is, the square root of a given quantity, for example, $\sqrt{2}$, is expressed by the mean proportional between 1 and the given number (in this case, 2). It is thus also possible to think a number such as that one.

Geometry shows us, by the example of the diagonal of a square, that the mean *proportional quantity* between the quantities 1 and 2 can be found and that $\sqrt{2}$ is consequently not an empty, objectless concept. So the question is only, why cannot a *number* be found for this quantity, a number whose concept would represent the quantity (its relation to unity) clearly and completely.

From the fact that every number could be represented as the square of some other number, *it does not follow* that the square root must be rational (that is, have a denumerable relation to unity). This can be seen by means of the principle of identity, if we consider the concepts basic to the question: the idea of two equal (but undetermined) factors of a given product. For there is no determinate relation to unity given in these concepts, only an interrelationship. It follows from paragraph 1 above, however, that this root, located in the series of numbers between two members of that series (let them be divided into decades, for instance), will always encounter still another intermediate number and thus another relation to unity. This must be so when one part of the root is found in this series. But the reason why the understanding, which has arbitrarily created the concept of $\sqrt{2}$, must content itself with an asymptotic approach to the number $\sqrt{2}$ and cannot also produce the complete numerical concept (the rational relationship of $\sqrt{2}$ to unity) – the reason for this has to do with time, the successive progression as form of all counting and of all numerical quantities; for time is the basic condition of all this producing of quantities.

It is true that the mere concept of the square root of a positive quantity, that is, $\sqrt{a}$, as represented in algebra, requires no synthesis in time. Similarly, one can see the impossibility of the square root of a negative quantity, $\sqrt{-a}$ (where the same relation would have to hold between the *positive* quantity, unity, and another quantity, x, as holds between x and a *negative* quantity,* if the condition of time did not enter into this insight. This can be seen from the mere concepts of quantities. But as soon as, instead of a, the number for which a stands is given, so that the square root is not simply to be *named* (as in algebra) but *calculated* (as in arithmetic), the condition of all producing of numbers, viz., time, becomes the inescapable foundation of the process. Indeed, we then require a pure intuition, in which we discover not only

11:209

---

* Since this is self-contradictory, the expression $\sqrt{-a}$ stands for an impossible quantity.

the given quantity but also the root, and we learn whether it can possibly be a whole number or can only be found as an irrational number by means of an infinite series of diminishing fractions.

The following consideration shows that what is needed for the concept of the square root of a *definite number*, for example, 15, is not the mere concept of a number, provided by the understanding, but rather a synthesis in time (as pure intuition): from the mere concept of a number, we cannot tell whether the root of that number will be rational or irrational. We have to *try it out*, either by comparing the products of all smaller whole numbers up to 100 with the given square, according to the multiplication table, or, in the case of larger numbers, by dividing them up, in accordance with demonstrated theorems, trying to find the components of the square or the parts of a twofold or *n*-fold root; and wherever the test of multiplying a whole number by itself does not yield the square, we increase the divisors of unity in order to obtain an infinite series of diminishing fractions, a series that expresses the root, though only in an irrational way (since the series can never be completed, though we can carry it out as far as we like).

Now if it were assumed to be impossible to explain or to prove a priori that *if the root of a given quantity cannot be expressed in whole numbers it also cannot be expressed determinately in fractions* (though it could be given as accurately as one wants), this would be a phenomenon concerning the relation of our power of imagination to our understanding, a phenomenon that we perceive by means of experiments with numbers but that we are totally unable to explain by means of the concepts of the understanding. But since we *can* explain it and demonstrate it, there is no need to assume this conclusion.

It seems to me that the puzzle about the mean proportional, which the penetrating author who questions the adequacy of our imaginative powers to execute the concepts of the understanding has discovered in arithmetic, is really based on the possibility of a *geometric construction* of such quantities, quantities that can never be completely expressed in numbers.

For the puzzlement one feels about $\sqrt{2}$ seems to me not to be produced by the proposition that, for every number, one can find a square root that, if not itself a number, is a rule for approximating the answer as closely as one wishes. What perplexes the understanding is rather the fact that this concept $\sqrt{2}$ can be constructed geometrically, so that it is not merely thinkable but also adequately visualizable, and the understanding is unable to see the basis of this. The understanding is not even in a position to assume the possibility of an object $\sqrt{2}$, since it cannot adequately present the concept of such a quantity in an intuition of number, and would even less anticipate that such a *quantum* could be given a priori.

11:110

The necessity of combining the two forms of sensibility, space and time, in determining the objects of our intuition – so that time, when the subject makes himself the object of his representation, must be imagined as a line, if it is to be quantified, just as, on the other hand, a line can be quantified only by being constructed in time – this insight concerning the necessary combining of inner sense with outer sense, even in the temporal determination of our existence, seems to me of aid in proving the objective reality of our representations of outer things (as against psychological idealism) though I am not able to pursue this idea farther at the moment.

---

1 The present letter is Kant's response to Rehberg's letter, Ak. [447], precise date uncertain, raising questions prompted by B 188 of the *Critique of Pure Reason*.

114 [451] (429)
From Abraham Gotthelf Kästner.

October 2, 1790.

Esteemed Sir,   11:213

Your letter sets a difficult task in practical philosophy for me, sir: to avoid the sin of pride.

I came to know and admire your insights and penetration even in my younger years. Your later philosophical achievements made me regret that my current condition did not permit me to make use of them as I would have wished.

I did not find in the Wolfian philosophy that I learned in my youth the certainty that Wolf[1] thought he had attained, not the certainty that I found in mathematics. Perhaps I undervalued Wolf in those days.

It gave me no pleasure to study more recent philosophical writings, e.g., those of the English who are lauded as great observers. In some that I read, I found nothing that I did not already know, or nothing that, if knowing it seemed important to me, I could not infer from things that I thought I knew. So I have more and more abandoned any serious pursuit of philosophy and I dare not make any judgments about it now.

I did observe at least this much: that after the decline of Wolfian philosophy there was a movement in the opposite direction, toward a kind of philosophy that aims to be totally unsystematic. The bad Wolfians advocated "system," by which they meant the memorizing of definitions and proofs they did not really understand and could not really test. Their detractors preferred "eclectic" philosophizing: using unexplained words, unattached to any definable concepts, throwing together opinions without asking whether they cohere with one another, declaiming instead of proving.

Lessing visited here for the last time on his return journey from the Pfalz. In our conversations concerning the current state of philosophy 11:214 he expressed the hope that things would soon change, for philosophy had become so shallow that even people who are not much inclined to reflection could not respect such shallowness for long.

It is to your great credit, sir, to have hastened the progress of knowledge away from this shallowness, leading philosophers to exert their minds and to try to think coherently once again. If your efforts are misunderstood, I think that this can be overcome through clear explanation and definition of words and figures of speech. Nowadays it is certainly common enough for an author to copy other people's uses of words without really understanding what they mean, a mistake at which one laughs when ordinary people for instance misuse a French expression, but now we can laugh at scholars doing the same thing. It becomes natural then for people to argue over words to which they do not attach the proper concept, and sometimes any concept at all. You once published an excellent explication, sir – I believe it was in the *Berliner Monatsschrift* – of what *orientation* means. It would be greatly to your credit if you were to perform a similar service on several fashionable terms in current philosophical jargon. The French have always given their witty writers freedom to use a well known word in some secondary sense that people are then supposed to guess (and perhaps they guess wrong) from the way the word is used. Then, when a German tries to use the word, naturally in a context different from the original one, asking for the meaning of the word becomes a question that has no clear answer. So we hear people who believe in "animal magnetism"[2] make pronouncements about "disorganizing" and "manipulating," etc., and now the statisticians quite commonly talk of "organization" and "manipulation" without being able to tell us what they mean by these words What I can make out is that France is pretty "disorganized" by the "manipulations" of the national assembly.

You often advise philosophers to pay attention to the procedure of mathematicians; since that procedure is what I know best, you will excuse my confining myself to it. Possibly the philosophers sometimes ask whether they might not do so as well? I don't think it is entirely possible, for in dealing with philosophical concepts, the understanding cannot so easily be assisted by sensible images.　　　　　　　11:215

I wish you long life and health to allow you to establish metaphysics coherently, and I hope that this project will benefit the sciences.

At a time when philosophy had deteriorated into mere talk and people were avoiding all intellectual exertion, a time when scholars became famous by writing books that one could finish, read and even consume as quickly as one smokes a pipe of tobacco, you, sir, succeeded in stimulating an interest in profound philosophical investigations and in getting writers to take such investigations seriously. This is certainly an achievement that distinguishes you, sir, and will make you unforgettable in the history of the sciences.

I remain with the greatest respect

your obedient servant
A. G. Kästner

Göttingen, October 2, 1790

1　"Wolf" = Christian Wolff.
2　The reference is to mesmerism. On Mesmer, the Austrian physician and mystic, see Kant's letter to Borowski, circa Mar. 6, 1789, Ak. [411], n. 4.

115 [452] (421)
From Johann Benjamin Jachmann.[1]
October 14, 1790.

[Abbreviated][2]

Dear Herr Professor, my eternally dear teacher and friend,　　　11:215

My brother's letters inform me in detail of the warm interest you take in my fate. I was fully convinced of this even without his telling me. The kindly confidence and favorable inclination with which you have honored me for several years now are so flattering and moving that I cannot help but feel justified in thinking you will forgive me for bothering you from time to time with a letter, and for feeling encouraged to send you news of my whereabouts and how I fare.

The fluctuations in my way of life, my frequent moves from one place to another and the huge distractions that these moves cause,

11:216 explain why I have not till now taken the liberty of writing to you again. Doubtless you have learned that, contrary to my previous decision to go to Göttingen by way of Holland and Hamburg, I have traveled via Paris; I hope that this will not displease you. The reasons that led me to this change of plan were that I calculated the difference in costs of the two routes to be inconsequential and that I would in any case arrive in Göttingen too late to be able to utilize the teachers and library here. But the main reason for my going to Paris was to be there during the principal epoch of its history, since I was so close by. Thus I was witness to the great celebration of the French union[3] and I attempted to use both eyes and ears to witness every important happening in Paris that occurred during my sojourn.

My first impression was that I was in the land of the blessed; for all the people, even the lowliest inhabitants, seemed to show by words and deeds that they felt as though they were living in a land that had totally thrown off the yoke and oppression of the mighty, a land where freedom and the rights of mankind were universally honored and cherished to the highest degree. I therefore did not hesitate to judge France in this regard now superior to the land of the proud British, who are contemptuous of all other nations and look upon them as slaves, even though one could point out a number of flaws in British freedom. For several days before and after the anniversary celebration one could see in Paris concrete examples of patriotism, solidarity of all ranks, etc., examples of which one would previously have hardly dared to dream. But this spirit seemed to reign only as long as the people were entertained with celebrations, dances, and banquets that buoyed them up with false promises. As soon as these were discontinued and the deputies from the provinces had drawn back, one heard complaints and discontent expressed from all sides, even from those who had declared themselves to be true friends of the revolution. A great many noble and middle-class families, even though patriotically minded, started to complain that the decrees and innovations of the National Assembly went too far, that it was much too early to abolish certain abuses by means of "absolute" laws, which the current constitution is supposed to do by making them null and void. Time itself would render those

11:217 abuses powerless and insignificant without arousing such resentment and displeasure among people – people who are weak enough as it is, so that they place value on certain inherited privileges, be they only nominal and illusory.

The tremendous and to my mind iniquitous reduction of pensions and salaries also arouses a highly audible grumbling and a lively discontent. And this discontent is inevitable, since there is hardly a family in all of France that does not lose out, directly or indirectly, that does not have a son or some relative whose income has been reduced by half.

And it takes more philosophy and patriotism to make such sacrifices for the common good than one can expect to find. On the other side, the rabble is unlimited in what it requests and demands. It is conscious of its power and influence now and misuses them, perhaps to its own ruin. Instead of guarding what it now possesses, that noble treasure, *freedom under law*, it strives for unbridled license. The rabble refuses to obey the laws any longer and insists on its arbitrary right to judge everything as it sees fit. One sees and hears examples of this in Paris every day. It is the rabble and one or two agitated heads that rule France at present. I have visited the National Assembly myself several times and seen the Assembly compelled to draw up certain decrees, because nobody was allowed to raise the slightest objection to them without being insulted by the rabble on the public rostrum and denounced as an "aristocrat." Many members of the National Assembly, in order to gain the affection and esteem of the common people, make proposals at the Assembly sessions which do not perhaps aim at the general welfare but which they know will get them general shouts of approval from the people, and these proposals are passed because nobody dares to oppose them. A good many members who are unhappy with this behavior have already quit the Assembly and will have nothing more to do with its business. Nobody dares to predict what the ultimate outcome of all this will be. Those who have the most optimistic view of the matter think that France will have to endure many 11:218 changes before its constitution is firmly established. Others who perhaps see everything in a pessimistic light fear that a national bankruptcy is unavoidable, with civil war the necessary consequence, especially since in certain provinces the peasants are supposed to have announced that they will not pay any of their taxes since they cannot see that they will have won anything from the present revolution if they do.

The fate of the country is the main topic of conversation in France so that one rarely gets to talk about anything else even with scholars; if they are under 60, they have another reason to be actively concerned, for all of them, like every other Frenchman, belong to the National Guard and are required to serve in the military. A musket, a grenadier's cap, and the national uniform thus customarily adorn the libraries of these gentlemen. I have made several pleasant acquaintances among them, especially among physicists and chemists. The renowned Charles[4] was the most interesting of the physicists, and Peletier[5] of the chemists. I worked with Peletier on the famous experiment,[6] converting two gases into water, an experiment really initiated by Herr von Jacquin,[7] who became my traveling companion to Strasbourg.

I left Paris in the company of Dr. Girtanner and Herr von Jacquin, and we were virtually eyewitnesses to the massacre at Nancy.[8] We were at least the first travelers who passed through the city after the gate was opened again and calm had been to some extent restored. We had already received some indefinite information about the story in Nancy from a messenger on horseback on his way to the National Assembly when we were still several miles outside the city. He painted a bloody picture for us, but said that he thought the violence was ended now. My traveling companions were frightened by this news and wanted to avoid Nancy but I persuaded them to continue on our route, for I suspected that the messenger had exaggerated a lot in his telling of the story. When we reached Toul, about two miles from Nancy, we thought we were in a war zone. At first we saw several cavalrymen looking extremely disturbed, but we didn't know what to make of this.

11:219   Soon the whole Mestre de Camp regiment appeared, as many as were left of them. The whole regiment had been hit and horribly knocked about, and now they had to flee Nancy. There were many wounded among them and often one man would be leading four or five horses, for the other horsemen had been killed. One can't imagine a more warlike scene. We did not know what to expect when we caught sight of them, for since they were defeated rebels we had everything to fear from them. But they let us pass quietly by, and we them. At this point my frightened traveling companions were determined to avoid unsettled Nancy and make their way via Metz. I, however, as a good Prussian, had no such fear and finally got them to agree to go one more stop, the last before Nancy, where we would get definite information about the situation in the city and could make our decision accordingly. My colleagues had already instructed the driver to head for the first station after Metz when I finally came upon a hussar who had fought under Boulli[9] [sic] in Nancy and who assured us that everything was quiet now and that we could travel there without danger. When we reached the gates of the city we were in fact rather sharply interrogated and our passports thoroughly scrutinized, but then we were quietly admitted into the city. Nancy looked totally like a conquered fortress. It was filled with an enormous number of soldiers, the victors. Most of the houses were shut up, many windows broken, and in some of the houses there were still musket-balls imbedded in the walls. Apart from soldiers there were very few men in the streets, but a great many women. Everything looked depressed and melancholy. We stayed a few hours in order to get information about the number of dead, etc., and the commanding officer estimated the number to be at least 700 but feared that it was higher. Soon after Nancy we encountered the Carabinier regiment out of Luneville, which had been through the same business as their comrades in Nancy, thrown into chains as prisoners and there delivered up. All along our way between Nancy and Strasbourg we were the bearers of news, for we were the first who

11:220   came through the cities after the engagement. When we entered these places we were immediately surrounded with hundreds of people who were eager to learn the fate of beautiful Nancy. In Strasbourg we stayed for several days; I visited the medical institution there and found teachers but nothing particularly interesting. I did not meet anyone who was especially involved with your writings. But in the bookstore at Koenig I found your latest works which I had not yet read and although I was not in a position to read them, I was still delighted to see something of yours again. In Paris I had already read with great interest the reviews in the *Jenaischen Lit. Zeitung* about several of your friends and opponents. My brother informed me that you were kind enough to make me a gift of your *Critique of Judgment*, for which I now offer my sincerest thanks.

Between Strasbourg and Mainz I stayed nowhere for more than a few hours or at most a night and half a day, as in Mannheim, e.g., so that I had no opportunity to look up any scholars about whom I could give you news. I stayed two and a half days in Mainz, mainly in Councillor Forster's[10] house. He is a most amiable and accommodating man. In his library I found again all your recent and even some of your earlier writings, but he regretted that his other literary work did not leave him enough time to study your writings as they deserve. He beseeched me to assure you of his boundless respect and asked me to commend him also to Prof. Kraus whom he still recalls with pleasure meeting in Paris. He regrets very much the tone he assumed in his controversy with you. Allow me to show you a few words from his letter to me: "Please express my veneration to the excellent Kant. My essay against him had an ill-tempered, polemical tone which I wanted to take back as soon as I saw it in print, for it is appropriate neither to the subject-matter nor to a man like Kant. To excuse myself I must say that everything I wrote in Vilna at that time had the same tone and I am enough of a materialist to think that the source of this was a physical indisposition which really existed then. – Don't forget to greet Prof. Kraus, etc."

Councillor Soemmering[11] also sends his regards.

I spoke to several medical practitioners in Frankfurt am Main but not profound philosophers. I visited Count von Kayserling[12] who is with the embassy here and he seemed pleased to see me again. He inquired warmly about you and your health and asked me to send you his best regards. After Frankfurt I went to Marburg where I stayed a whole day. Early in the morning I visited Prof. Bering[13], whose letter to you I still recall, the letter in which he declared himself to be a great admirer of yours and wished that he could come to Königsberg. He still has that wish and would surely satisfy it if Königsberg were not so far away, something of which a number of scholars have complained. He has now been named librarian, which chains him still further to

11:221

Marburg. He received me with great joy and warmth as a favorite of Kant's, and I had to tell him all sorts of things about you. He kept me there all morning and even through dinner. He told me also that he still lives rather "in ecclesia pressa" [secretly worshipful] with regard to your philosophy. He informed me that a certain Endemann[14] who is dead now was the author of that decree [in 1786] forbidding lectures on your philosophy. We also discussed your current controversy with Eberhard, and Prof. B. expressed his great regret that you have been forced into this; he thinks that if you had realized how little credit Eberhard has with the public you would not have felt it worth the trouble to refute him. I also want to tell you the following things about Professor B.'s person. He is a man near 40, with a very serious, reflective manner, resembling both facially and in his whole figure our Prof. Holtzhauer, but not as tall and not as lank, though he speaks just as sharply as Prof. H.

He promised to send me, in Leipzig, a little essay of his, published as a funeral oration for the prorector, which is supposed to contain various references to your writings; I should find it when I arrive there. After dinner he directed me to Professor Tiedemann,[15] but he was out of town so I have not been able to speak with him. Then he took me to another of your admirers, a convert, Court Councillor Jung,[16] who was very happy to see me for I could give him news of you; he asked to be remembered to you. Similarly Privy Councillor Selchow,[17] to whom Prof. B. took me, because S. is such a ridiculous person and he wanted me to get to know him thoroughly while I was in Marburg. Finally I went to see Baldinger who also would not let me go until evening.

Never have I seen humanity so deteriorated! I could write whole pages about him, but I shall wait and tell you orally. After Marburg I went to Cassel where I again stayed for a few days in order to see the sights, both natural and artistic, and in the environs as well as in the city. But I encountered no literary news there.

On September 21st I finally arrived in Göttingen. I visited my friend Prof. Arnemann right away and found there the letters from my friends in Königsberg for which I had yearned. They made it a veritable holiday for me. I was truly glad to find in all those letters the assurance that I was still well regarded in my father-city. But especially pleasing were the three letters through which you introduced me to the three most distinguished scholars in Göttingen, a new and treasured proof of your kindness and goodness to me. First I visited Privy Councillor Blumenbach the following morning, a kind and open man. He felt very flattered by your letter and offered to do anything he could for me during my stay. Saturday evening I dined with him. Sunday morning he led me to the museum, etc. He gave me the enclosed letter to you as well as the first issue of his *Beiträge zur Naturgeschichte*, which I shall keep until a convenient opportunity presents itself, for I think you have read it already. I think too that it is not important enough to mail. I presented my letters of introduction to Lichtenberg and Kaestner the same day. Privy Councillor Lichtenberg was giving lectures just then, and since it was half way through the lesson I didn't want to disturb him. So I just left the letter and my address. He drove to his garden 11:223 outside the city as soon as he had finished his lectures but sent his servant to me right away, saying that I should make use of him to show me around. He himself hoped that he could see me the following day. I visited him therefore in the morning, as soon as he got into town. I think, as you know, that he is a sickly, hunchbacked man who has several times been near death, though now he has recovered again. His happiness at your letter was great. He spoke with great warmth, with his lively and intelligent eyes sparkling, saying how long and how greatly he had admired you and known you even from your earliest writings. He said he would be delighted to do you or me any service. He also invited me to attend his lectures as often as I please. The next day he showed me his collection of instruments and I spent the whole afternoon with him and drank coffee with him. I went to all his lectures while I was in Göttingen. His topic was electricity. Once again he suggested I make use of his servant as much as I might like. I visited him every day and spoke with him, for he is such an extremely kind and gracious man. He will be sending you a letter soon. I heard from other professors as well that he was so very pleased to have received a letter from you. He referred to it as receiving a letter from the Prophet of the North.

I can't tell you how mistaken I was in how I pictured Privy Councillor Kaestner. The image I had of his person and demeanor from his epigrams and from other things I had read and heard about him was totally false. Instead of finding a man from whose cutting tongue one had to guard oneself, I found a tiny little man in a dressing gown and a round wig, sitting in front of a burning lamp in a very hot room, from whose face I could see that he was pleased to see me once I presented greetings from you and gave him your letter, but a man who was so obviously perplexed and fearful that he could not speak. More through signals than through words he indicated that I was to sit down; constantly wringing his hands and bowing his body he kept saying how 11:224 welcome I was since I brought news of you. He continued in the same way, asking about your age and health and about Prof. Krause, just as virtually all the professors, e.g., Heyne, Lichtenberg, Feder, inquired about Prof. Kant with great interest.

He asked how long I was staying in Göttingen and was sorry that my sojourn was so short, offered gladly to show me around, which I however refused since I had already found other friends who would do it. Finally, after a conversation broken off after 10 or 15 minutes, I took my leave from him and he asked me to visit him again and said he was sorry that I would not accept his offer of service. The day before my leaving Göttingen I visited him again and found him exactly as before. He regretted that you had to be involved in a controversy with Herr Eberhard and he asked me, if I write or see you again, to convey his great respect. He will write you himself very soon.

I also visited Privy Councillor Feder who received me very graciously as one of your pupils. He talked a great deal of his boundless respect for you and insisted that whenever he had contradicted you it was only out of love of truth; yes, he even convinced himself that your propositions and claims were not so very different from his own. He visited me a couple of times and I was at his house several times.

You have an enlightened disciple and defender of your philosophical principles in Göttingen in Prof. Buhle, with whom however I had no opportunity to converse. People don't think much of him, though.

I will say no more about the other people I met in Göttingen, for they were mainly medical professors. Because of the brevity of my stay there were a number of people I did not get to talk to whom I had wanted to see. Since it was vacation time, a number were absent. In the company of one of your most grateful pupils, Herr Friedländer from Königsberg, I left Göttingen and traveled to Hannover. Herr Friedländer sends his respects and assures you through me of his lively gratitude for your excellent teaching, which instructed his heart and his mind. We traveled together from Göttingen all the way to Halle and I found his company most interesting. The topic of our discussions was usually our beloved fatherland, in which we shared the same interest, in the man for whom both our hearts feel the most intense and unfeigned respect and esteem. Soon after my arrival in Hannover I visited Privy Secretary Rehberg, an ardent admirer and follower of yours. He is a young man of about 30 years but who at first did not greatly appeal to me. He seemed very reserved, somewhat cold, and very condescending, so I stayed only a few minutes with him. I saw a marble memorial bust of the renowned Leibnitz at his house.

The same day in the afternoon he visited me and was much more friendly and open and very talkative. He invited me to have dinner the next noon when I dined in the company of his estimable mother, his kind sister and the young Herr Brandes; I count that day among the pleasantest of my entire journey. Herr Rehberg is a very modest man in conversation, but one can see that he has a mind, originality and wide learning. I regard him as the finest mind among all your students that I have come to know up to now. He speaks of your *Critique of Practical Reason*, with greater warmth than I have ever heard a man

11:225

speak about a book. He intends to write on natural law and to show that there are just such antinomies of reason there as in speculative and moral philosophy. His modesty and his knowledge that you are so burdened by letters has kept him from writing to you; but now he has ventured to write a letter to Nicolovius containing certain questions that he hopes you will help him resolve when you have the chance.[18] I also visited the cavalier von Zimmermann in Hannover who received me most courteously. I was with him for over an hour on my first visit and he asked about your health and requested that I convey his respects. He returned the visit the next day and stayed over half an hour   11:226 with me. His treatment of me was most gracious for they say that he generally does not receive even counts and other high nobility. . . .

From Magdeburg I went to Halle where I have now spent several days, enjoying pleasant hours with your loyal admirer Prof. Jakob. Magister Beck, who sends his best regards, lives in the same house, and is our companion. I have already visited most of the professors here and even Herr Eberhard. I have been with him twice already, each time for over an hour. He has not made the slightest mention of you or of his controversy but only discusses political matters in France, which interest him greatly and about which I can give him some news. I cannot report much else to you about Halle, except that many professors send their respects, among them Herr Forster, Semler, etc., also Dr. and now beer-server Bahrdt.[19] . . .

---

1   Johann Benjamin Jachmann (1765–1832), like his younger brother, Reinhold Bernhard J., Kant's student and amanuensis. Kant secured a scholarship for him at the university. Eventually Jachmann practiced medicine in Königsberg.

2   Jachmann's letter may be found in its entirety in Kant's *Werke*, Ak. 11: 215–27. The abbreviated version of the letter in the *Philosophische Bibliotheque* edition (Hamburg: Felix Meiner, 1986) omits the part of the letter reporting Jachmann's visit to Paris and other cities in France a year after the start of the revolution. The present shortened version of the original letter includes this but omits some inconsequential passages later in this long letter.

3   July 14, 1790, the anniversary of the storming of the Bastille.

4   Jacques Alexandre César Charles (1746–1823), professor of physics and member of the Academy of Sciences in Paris.

5   Bertrand Pelletier (1761–97).

6   Jachmann may have been thinking of Lavoisier's research, in 1783.

7   Joseph Franz Edler von Jacquin (1766–1839).

8   An insurrection by soldiers in Nancy that was put down in a bloody fashion.

9   The forces that put down the revolt were under François Claude Amour Marquis de Bouillé (1739–1800).

10   Johann Georg Adam Forster (1754–94). On his argument with Kant, see

Kant's letter to Reinhold, Dec. 28 and 31, 1787, Ak. [313], and Kant's essay "On the Use of Teleological Principles . . ." Ak. 8: 157, ff. Forster's attack was directed against Kant's essay "Bestimmung des Begriffs einer Menschenrasse" (1785).

11 On Soemmering see Kant's letters to Soemmering of Aug. 10 and Sep. 17, 1795, Ak. [671] and [679].

12 Otto Alexander Heinrich Dietrich, Count von Keyserling (1765–1820).

13 Johann Bering (1748–1825), prof. of philosophy in Marburg, one of Kant's disciples. See Kant's letter to him, Apr. 7, 1786, Ak. [266], n. 1.

14 The theologian Samuel Endemann. See Bering's letter to Kant, Sept. 21, 1786, Ak. [279].

15 On Tiedemann see Kant's letter to Bering, Ak. [266], n. 2.

16 Jung-Stilling.

17 Johann Heinrich Christian von Selchow, chancellor of the university of Marburg.

18 See Rehberg's letter prior to Sept. 25, 1790, Ak. [447], and Kant's response, Ak. [448].

19 Karl Friedrich Bahrdt (1741–92), notorious theologian and free spirit, who lived in Halle from 1779, purchased and operated a beer garden.

161 [453] (422)
To Johann Friedrich Reichardt.[1]
October 15, 1790.

11:228 Dearest friend,

My modest efforts in your early philosophical instruction have their own reward if I may flatter myself that they contributed somewhat to the development of your talents and your present renown. I gratefully acknowledge your statement to this effect as a sign of friendship.

It is from that same perspective that I view your hoping to gain peace of mind from my writings,[2] albeit my work has had this effect on me, although, as I see from many examples, it is difficult to communicate this to others. Surely it is philosophy's thorny path that is to blame for this, but that path is unavoidable if one hopes to reach enduring principles.

It would please me if a connoiseur truly conversant with the products of the faculty of taste could give a more concrete and explicit account of the characteristics of that faculty, so difficult to fathom, that I have tried to outline. I have been content to show that without moral feeling there would be nothing beautiful or sublime for us, that our, as it were, lawful entitlement to approve of anything that bears these names is based on just this moral feeling, and that taste is that subjective [aspect] of morality in our nature which we consider under the name "moral feeling" as inscrutable. The ability to make judgments of taste, though not founded on objective concepts of reason, such as are required by evaluations according to moral laws, is still founded on an a priori principle of judgment (albeit an intuitive and not a discursive one) and is not in any way grounded on the contingencies of sensation.

The beautiful maps that you intended to present to me as a gift,[3] will be a memento of your friendship to me, and I remain, with total respect and friendship, 11:229

Your devoted servant,
I. Kant

Königsberg
October 15, 1790

---

1 On Reichardt see Kant's letter to Marcus Herz, May 1, 1781, Ak. [164], n. 2, and the biographical sketches in this volume. The present letter is in answer to Reichardt's letter of Aug. 28, 1790, Ak. [443].

2 In the letter just cited, Reichardt told Kant that he had been studying Kant's works seriously for the preceding three years, stimulated by the opposing works of his dear friends Jacobi and Selle.

3 Reichardt had promised to send Kant some excellent maps of the Kingdom of Naples that Reichardt had brought back from there.

1791

117 [461] (430)
To Christoph Friedrich Hellwag.[1]
January 3, 1791

11:244 Esteemed Sir,

Herr Nicolovius[2] who has the honor of delivering this letter to you, is a former auditor of mine and a very fine young man. He would like to make the acquaintance of some of the people in your circle of friends during his brief stay in Eutin. Getting to know such people is often impossible in large cities, yet so good for one's heart and mind. His modest demeanor ensures that his request will cause you no trouble.

The penetrating observations you made in your letter[3] will give me much food for thought. For the present, since I have not found the time to give sustained thought to your suggestions, I must beg you to be contented with my still unripe judgments.

11:245 First, concerning the analogy between colors and tones, you certainly bring into focus the issue of their relation to judgments of taste (which aim to be more than mere sensory judgments about what pleases or displeases). Your graduated scale of vowel sounds, the only sounds, you maintain, that can produce a distinct tone by themselves, seems to me to be unnecessary here. For no one can think music that he is not able, however clumsily, to sing – and this at the same time shows clearly the difference between colors and tones, since the former do not presuppose any such productive power of the imagination. But I am now too involved in other matters to be able to transfer my thoughts to the investigation required here. I must only remark that when I spoke, in the *Critique of Judgment*, of persons who with the best hearing in the world still cannot distinguish tones, I did not mean by this that they could not tell the difference between one tone and another but that they were absolutely incapable of distinguishing a tone from a mere sound. I had in mind my best friend, Herr Green, the English merchant who died four years ago; his parents noticed this deficiency in his childhood and therefore had him instructed in piano-playing with music. But he never succeeded in reaching the point where he could tell, when someone else played or sang an entirely different piece of music, that it was different. So tones were mere noises to him. And I read somewhere of a family in England whose members, even with the healthiest of eyes, saw all objects only as in an engraving, so that all of nature looked to them like nothing but light and shadow. It was noteworthy with my friend Green that this incapacity extended even to the distinction between poetry and prose, which he could never recognize except for the former's having a forced and unnatural arrangement of syllables. Therefore, while he enjoyed reading Pope's *Essay on Man*, he found it annoying that it was written in verses.

I shall think over your remarks on the consequences of the distinction between synthetic and analytic propositions,[4] with respect to conversion, *for logic*. In metaphysics, where we are not so much concerned with the place of concepts in a judgment (the question of what follows   11:246
from mere form) as with the question whether or not the concepts of certain judgments have any material content, your suggestions about convertibility are not relevant.

But as for the question, What is the ground of the law that matter, in all its changes, is dependent on *outer* causes and also the law that requires the equality of *action* and *reaction* in these changes occasioned by outer causes? – I could easily have given a priori[5] the universal transcendental ground of the possibility of such laws as well, in my *Metaphysical Foundations of Natural Science*. It might be summarized as follows.

All our concepts of matter contain nothing but the mere representation of outer relationships (for that is all that can be represented in space). But that which we posit as existing in space signifies no more than *a something* in general to which we must attribute no characteristics but those of an outer thing, insofar as we regard the thing as mere matter, consequently no *absolutely inner* properties such as the power of conception, feeling, or desire. It follows from this that, since every change presupposes a cause, and we cannot conceive of an absolutely inner cause (a life) in a merely material thing producing a change in outer relations, the cause of all such changes (from a state of rest to a state of motion and conversely, along with the determinations of such changes) must lie in external matter, and without such a cause no change can take place. It follows that no special *positive* principle of the conservation of motion in a moving body is required but only a *negative* one, viz., the absence of any cause of change.

As for the second law, it is based on the relationship of *active forces* in space in general, a relationship that must necessarily be one of reciprocal opposition and must always be equal (*actio est aequalis reactioni*), for space makes possible only reciprocal relationships such as these, precluding any unilateral relationships. Consequently it makes possible change in those spatial relationships, that is, motion and the action of bodies in producing motion in other bodies, requiring nothing but reciprocal and equal motions. I cannot conceive of a line drawn from body A to every point of body B without drawing equally as many lines in the opposite direction, so that I conceive the change of relationship in which body B is moved by the thrust of body A as a reciprocal and equal change. Here, too, there is no need for a special positive cause of reaction in the moved body, just as there was no such need in the case of the law of inertia, which I mentioned above. The general and sufficient ground of these laws lies in the character of space, viz., that spatial relationships are reciprocal and *equal* (which is not true of the relations between successive positions in time). I shall look over Lambert's opinion on this matter in his *Beyträgen*.[6]

I have sent your cordial greetings to Prof. Kraus, a worthy man who is a credit to our university. Our locality is so spread out that it inhibits visits with even the most amiable people, and that is why I am not yet able to report his responding greeting to you.

Please commend me to your excellent friends King's Counsel Trede,[7] Court Counselor Voß, and both the Herren Boie. I was very pleased to hear what you told me concerning the younger of these two gentlemen.[8] But his sort of preaching will not become universal until *integrity* of conscience also becomes universal among teachers (an integrity that is not content merely with good behavior, from whatever motive, but insists that purity of motive is all-important).

I wish you contentment in your domestic life, pleasure in your social life, and much success in your professional life for many years to come, and I remain with total respect

your most obedient servant,
I. Kant

Königsberg,
January 3, 1791.

---

1 Christoph Friedrich Hellwag (1754–1835), a physician in Eutin, friend of J. H. Voß and F. H. Jacobi.

2 Georg Heinrich Ludwig Nicolovius (1767–1839), younger brother of the book merchant Friedrich Nicolovius. His wife, Marie Anna Luise Schlosser, was the

daughter of Goethe's sister, Kornelie. There exists a draft of the present letter, different in many places; cf. Ak. 13: 293, ff.

3 Hellwag's long letter of Dec. 13, 1790 [460].

4 In his letter Hellwag suggested that convertible synthetic propositions would have analytic propositions as their converses, whereas the converse of an analytic proposition would in some instances be synthetic. For example, " 'All physical bodies are heavy' is synthetic; the synthesis of 'physical' and 'bodies' is the condition for the predicate 'heavy,' since it is not true that all physical things are heavy (a rainbow is physical but not heavy) or that all bodies, in a broad sense, are heavy (geometrical bodies are in a way bodies but are not heavy). Conversion yields two mutually independent analytic propositions: 'Everything heavy is a physical body' and 'Everything heavy is a body.' If we convert these [analytic] propositions, the subject of the converse synthetic propositions needs to be supplemented by the word 'certain': 'Certain physical things are heavy' and 'Certain bodies are heavy.' Another example: 'All bodies are extended' is analytic. Add to this 'All bodies are three-dimensional' – conversion yields the fully synthetic proposition 'All extended, three-dimensional things are bodies.' The connection of the two concepts in the subject of this proposition is the condition for the predicate, for not every extended thing is a body (a plane is extended) and not all three-dimensional things are bodies. . . ."

5 It is not clear in Kant's sentence whether "a priori" qualifies "could have given" or "such laws."

6 Lambert, *Beyträgen zum Gebrauche Mathematik und deren Anwendung* (Berlin, 1770). See Kant's *Werke*, Ak. 13: 292.

7 Trede, according to Hellwag's letter, testified that a certain chef, artistically preparing a dish, had declared, "It tastes good, but to me it's not pleasant." The anecdote was meant to support Kant's *Critique of Judgment* account of judgments of taste as disinterested.

8 Christian Rudolf Boie, deputy headmaster of a Latin school in Eutin, studied Kant's writings on ethics and preached a sermon that, according to Hellwag, exemplified Kant's suggestion on the teaching of virtue through examples of moral actions done in the absence of any foreign incentives. Cf. *Grundlegung*, Ak. 4: 411, n.

118 [466] (435)
To Johann Friedrich Gensichen.[1]
April 19, 1791.

Dear Magister Gensichen,   11:252

In order to give proper credit to everyone who has contributed to the history of astronomy, I wish you would add an appendix to your dissertation and explain how my own modest conjectures differ from those of subsequent theorists.

11:253

1. The conception of the Milky Way as a system of moving suns analogous to our planetary system was formulated by me six years before Lambert published a similar theory in his *Cosmological Letters.*[2]

2. The idea that nebulae[3] are comparable to remote milky ways was not an idea ventured by Lambert (as Erxleben[4] maintains in his *Foundations of Natural Philosophy* on p. 540, even in the new edition), for Lambert supposed them (at least one of them) to be dark bodies, illuminated by neighboring suns.

3. A long time ago I defended a view that has been supported by recent observations, namely, that the production and conservation of the ring of Saturn could be accounted for by the laws of centripetal force alone. This view now appears to be well confirmed. There is, it seems, a revolving mist whose center is that of Saturn, and this mist is composed of particles whose revolution is not constant but varies with their distance from the center. This also confirms the rate of Saturn's revolution on its axis, which I inferred from it, and its flatness.

4. The agreement of recent findings with my theory as to the production of the ring of Saturn from a vaporous matter moving according to the laws of centripetal force seems also to support the theory that the planets [great globes] were produced according to the same laws, except that their property of rotation must have been produced originally by the fall of this dispersed substance as a result of gravity. Herr Lichtenberg's approval of this theory gives it added force.[5] The theory is that prime matter, dispersed throughout the universe in vaporous form, contained the materials for an innumerable variety of substances. In its elastic state, it took the form of spheres simply as a result of the chemical affinity of particles that met according to the laws of gravitation, mutually destroying their elasticity and thus producing bodies. The heat within these bodies was sufficient to produce the illumination that is a property of the larger spheres, the suns, whereas it took the form of internal heat in the smaller spheres, the planets.

Appendix

Several inquiries, both public and private, concerning Kant's 1755 work, *Natural History and Theory of the Heavens,* have suggested that a new and unauthorized edition of the book may be coming out. With this in mind, the author has asked me to make an abstract of it, containing its essential points, taking into account the great progress of astronomy since its publication. I present that abstract here, reviewed by the author and with the author's approval.

Please do not be offended at my request, and do me the honor also of favoring me with your company at dinner tomorrow if you possibly can.

I. Kant

---

1 Gensichen (1759–1807) was one of Kant's dinner companions and a professor (*extraordinarius*) of mathematics. He was named executor of Kant's will and inherited Kant's library.

The original German version of this letter is not extant. A virtually incomprehensible English translation appeared in *Kant-Studien*, II (1897), 104 f., under the title "A New Letter of Kant, by Walter B. Waterman, Boston, Mass." The present translation is a reworking of this, with several obvious mistranslations corrected. It may nevertheless be false to the original here and there.

2 J. H. Lambert, *Kosmologische Briefe* (1761). Cf. Lambert's letter to Kant, November 13, 1765, Ak. [33].

3 An obvious mistranslation of the German *Nebelsterne* (foggy stars) appears here in the "English" version of this letter.

4 Johann Christian Polykarp Erxleben (1744–77), professor of physics in Göttingen, *Anfangsgründe der Naturlehre* (1772).

5 Georg Christoph Lichtenberg (1742–99). In 1791 Lichtenberg published an edition of Erxleben's book.

119 [474] (443)
From Johann Gottfried Carl Christian Kiesewetter.

June 14, 1791.

Dearest Herr Professor, 11:264

[*Kiesewetter apologizes for not writing. He sends Kant a copy of his new logic book, which he has dedicated to Kant.*][1]

... The fact that your [book on] Moral [Philosophy] has not ap- 11:265 peared at the current book fair has created quite a stir, since everyone was expecting it. People around here are saying (though it must be their imagination) that Woltersdorf, the new *Oberconsistorialrath*,[2] has managed to get the king to forbid you to write anymore. I myself was asked about this story at court. I talked with Wöllner[3] recently and his flattery made me blush. He tried to appear very favorably disposed toward me, but I don't trust him at all. People are now virtually convinced that he is being used by others who are forcing him to do things he otherwise would not do.

The king has already had several visions of Jesus; they say he is going to build Jesus a church in Potsdam for his very own. He is weak in body and soul now, and he sits for hours, weeping. Dehnhof[4] has fallen from grace and has gone to her sister-in-law, but the king has written to her again and in all probability she will come back soon. Rietz[5] is still an influential woman. The people who tyrannize over the king are Bischoffswerder,[6] Wöllner, and Rietz. A new edict on religion is expected, and the populace grumbles at the prospect of being forced to go to church and Holy Communion. For the first time they have the feeling that there are some things that no prince can command them to do. Caution is necessary, lest the spark ignite. The soldiers are also very discontented. They have received no new uniforms this past year, on account of Rietz, who took the money to go to Pyrmont. Besides that, the late king used to give them 3 gulden after every review, as a bonus, and now they get only 8 groschen.

Models for floating batteries are being built here, everything is being made battle-ready, and this time we are going to war even with our treasury. The Turkish ambassador,[7] one of the most insignificant men I have ever seen, is still here, boring himself and everybody else. There is much talk of a marriage of the Duke of York[8] and Princess Friederike, but the minor details of the story make it improbable. They say, namely, that the king wants to give two million toward effacing his debts and, in addition, to give her 100,000 thalers annually, even though the law allows only a total of 100,000 thalers for every princess's dowry.

11:266

But look at all that I have been chattering about to you – things that you either know already or have no desire to hear. Only the suspicion that these matters might interest you has induced me to write of them.

Literary news I have none, at least none that you have not got from the scholarly papers. Snell[9] has published an explication of your *Critique of Aesthetic Judgment*. It seems to me admirable. Spatzier[10] has published an abridgment of the *Critique of Teleological Judgment*, but it is not nearly as good. . . .

Your devoted friend and servant,

J. G. C. Kiesewetter

---

1 It may be of interest to readers that Kiesewetter's logic book must have made its way to Russia, for Tolstoy refers to it in his famous short story, "The Death of Ivan Ilych."

2 Theodor Carl Georg Woltersdorf (1727–1806) held this position from 1791.
3 Johann Christoph Wöllner. See Kiesewetter's letter of Apr. 20, 1790, Ak. [420], and notes.
4 Countess Dönhoff, mistress and then "wife" (the legality of the marriage is suspect) of Friedrich Wilhelm II. See Kiesewetter's letter, op. cit., n. 2.
5 Wilhelmine Enke (1752 or 1754–1820), another mistress of Friedrich Wilhelm II, who was betrothed to the court official Rietz; she was the daughter of a musician and later became Countess Lichtenau.
6 Johann Rudolf von Bischoffswerder (1741–1803), a favorite of the king's.
7 Ahmed Axmi Effendi.
8 Prince Friedrich, Duke of York (1763–1827) married Princess Friederike Charlotte Ulrike Katharine, daughter of Friedrich Wilhelm by his first wife.
9 Friedrich Wilhelm Snell (1761–1827), *Darstellung und Erläuterung der Kantischen Kritik der ästhetischen Urtheilskraft* (Mannheim, 1791 and 1792).
10 Karl Spatzier (1761–1805), *Versuch einer kurzen und faßlichen Darstellung der teleologischen Principien, ein Auszug aus Kants Kritik der teleologische Urtheilskraft* (Neuwied, 1791).

120 [478] (447)
From Maria von Herbert.[1]
[August?], 1791.

Great Kant,   11:273

As a believer calls to his God, I call upon you[2] for help, for solace, or for counsel to prepare me for death. The reasons you gave in your books were sufficient to convince me of a future existence – that is why I have recourse to you – only I found nothing, nothing at all for this life, nothing that could replace the good I have lost. For I loved an object who seemed to me to encompass everything within himself, so that I lived only for him. He was the opposite of everything else for me, and everything else seemed to me a bauble, and I really felt as if human beings were all nonsense,[3] all empty, well, I have offended this person, because of a protracted lie, which I have now disclosed to him though there was nothing unfavorable to my character in it – I had no viciousness in my life that needed hiding, the lie was enough, though, and his love has vanished. He is an honorable man, and so he doesn't refuse me friendship and loyalty. But that inner feeling that once unbidden led us to each other, it is no more. Oh my heart splits into a thousand pieces, if I hadn't read so much of your work I would certainly have taken my own life by now, but the conclusion I had to draw from your theory stops me – it is wrong for me to die because my life is tormented, and I am instead supposed to live because of my being, now put yourself in my place and either damn me or give me solace, I read the metaphysic of morals including the categorical imperative, doesn't help a bit, my reason abandons me just where I need it most, answer me, I implore you, or you yourself can't act according to your own imperative

11:274

My address is **Maria Herbert** in *Klagenfurt* Carinthia care of the white lead factory or perhaps you would rather send it via Reinhold because the mail is more reliable there.

---

1   Maria von Herbert (circa 1770–1803) lived in Klagenfurt, in the home of her brother, a factory owner and philosopher, Franz Paul von Herbert. J. B. Erhard's letter to Kant, Jan. 17, 1793, Ak. [557], discloses the background of Maria's letter, viz., her unhappy love affair.

In Aug. 1802 she left her brother's house and on May 23 of the following year, having put her affairs in order and, having arranged some sort of ceremony or celebration ("bei sich eine Festlichkeit veranstaltet"), she committed suicide in the Drau River. Her brother too took his own life, Mar. 13, 1811. According to Borowski, "Kant sent me the letter and remarked on an appended page that her letter had interested him far more than others because 'it spoke of truth and trust'" ("von Wahrheit und Zuverlässigkeit darin die Rede wäre"). Borowski (cf. Ak. [479]) returned Maria's letter to Kant and, moved by her words and by the fact that she read Kant's writings, urged him to respond and give her his counsel.

2   As though addressing God, Maria uses the *Du* rather than *Sie* form throughout.

3   "gwasch." Maria's phonetic spelling of what must be local dialect or Austrian pronunciation (*posten* becomes *bosten*, *handlen* is *handln*) has great charm. Her breathlessly uninterrupted run-on sentence contributes to the ring of genuineness in her cry for help.

121 [479] (448)

From Ludwig Ernst Borowski.

August (?) 1791.

I enclose most humbly the strange letter from Maria Herbert in Klagenfurt. Our last conversation was so engrossing that I absent-mindedly put the letter into my pocket where I found it today as I was undressing. If by answering her letter you could relieve even temporarily the distraction and suffering in which her spirit is trapped, or perhaps through your serious instruction remove it forever, you would truly have done something great and good. Anyone who is so eager to read your writings and who has such a powerful trust in you is worthy of your attention and care.

I am with the greatest esteem

yours,

122 [482] (451)
From Johann Gottlieb Fichte.[1]

August 18, 1791.

Esteemed man, 11:276

Let other titles be reserved for those to whom one cannot say "esteemed" and mean it with all one's heart.

I came to Königsberg to become more closely acquainted with a man who is respected by all Europe but who in all Europe is loved by few as much as I love him.

I introduced myself. Only later did I realize how presumptuous it 11:277 was to lay claim to an acquaintanceship with such a man when one cannot show the slightest entitlement to do this. I might have had introductions written for me. I want only those that I create for myself. Here is mine.

It is painful to me that I cannot transmit it to you in the happy frame of mind in which I wrote it. To a man whose specialty it is to look deeply into everything that is and everything that was, it cannot be a new experience to read a work that fails to satisfy him; and all of us others must be extremely modest in our anticipation of his pronouncement, for he is the human embodiment of pure reason itself. A man like that will perhaps forgive me – whose mind wandered around in many a confused labyrinth before becoming (and only very recently) a student of the *Critique*, and whose circumstances allowed so little time for such studies – will forgive me my work's imperfections if it be of less than acceptable quality, as perhaps my own conscience will forgive me. But can I be forgiven for giving you this book, knowing it to be defective in my own eyes? Can the forgiveness bestowed on my work be extended to me? I would have been frightened away by that great mind, but the noble heart that, united with it, was uniquely empowered to restore virtue and duty to mankind drew me to it. I myself have rendered judgment on the worth of my essay; whether I shall ever produce anything better is for you to judge. Please view it as the letter of introduction of a friend, or of a mere acquaintance, or of someone wholly unknown, or as nothing at all. Your greatness, excellent man, exceeds all conceivable human greatness to such a degree and is so God-like that one approaches it with confidence.

As soon as I can believe that my essay has been read by that greatness, I shall pay my respects to you personally in order to learn whether I may continue to call myself

your sincerely devoted admirer,

Johann Gottlieb Fichte

---

1 Fichte (1762–1814) arrived in Königsberg on July 1, 1791, on his return from Warsaw where he had held a position as private tutor for 18 days. The essay that he sent to Kant, *Versuch einer Kritik aller Offenbarung* (attempt at a critique of all revelation) published anonymously and mistaken for Kant's work (Königsberg, 1792), made him famous. See the subsequent correspondence between Fichte and Kant for further discussion.

123 [483] (452)
From Johann Gottlieb Fichte.
September 2, 1791.

11:278 Noble Sir,
Esteemed Herr Professor,

Please forgive me, sir, for again preferring to speak with you in writing rather than orally.

You have responded to my self-introduction with a kindness and warmth which I would not have dared to ask of you, a generosity of spirit that infinitely magnifies my gratitude and gives me the courage to reveal myself fully to you. Considering your character, I might have dared to do this earlier as well, but without more specific permission I felt reluctant to let myself do this – a reluctance that people who are not inclined to open themselves up to just anyone feel twice as strongly when they encounter a person of wholly good character.

Let me first assure you, sir, that my decision to come to Königsberg rather than go back to Saxony was only self-interested insofar as I wanted to satisfy my need to introduce myself to you and to reveal some part of myself to you. For you are the man to whom I owe all my convictions and principles and my character, even the striving to want to *have* character. I wanted to reveal some part of myself to you, as much as time allowed, and to use you, if it were possible, to the advantage of my future career. I did not count on exploiting your kindness for my current needs, partly because I imagined Königsberg to be such a rich place, even richer in opportunities than, e.g., Leipzig, and partly because, if I were really desperate for help, I have a friend who has a substantial position in Riga.[1] I thought that from here I could find a place in Livonia. I think I owe this explanation in part to myself, so as to remove the suspicion of an unworthy self-interestedness from my feelings, which flow purely from my heart, and in part I owe it to you, if it pleases you to receive spontaneous, open thanks from one whom you have instructed and improved.

For five years I was employed as a private tutor and because of the unpleasantness of that work – having to see imperfections in important matters and being frustrated in accomplishing anything good that I could have brought about – I decided, a year and a half ago, that I would give it up forever. The result is that I suffer anxieties when a well-intentioned person undertakes to give me a recommendation for another such position, for I must fear that things will not turn out exactly as he might wish. I allowed myself, without much reflection, to be hired again in Warsaw, acting on the unreasonable hope that the job would be better and perhaps unconsciously motivated by the prospect of more money and reputation; it was a decision whose thwarting I shall bless, if I can disentangle myself from the straits in which I now find myself. Instead of taking that job, I feel a need to make up for everything I have missed – missed as a result of the premature praise of kindly but not very wise teachers, because of an academic career that has been run through almost before the start of adolescence and, after that, because of my constant financial insecurity. I want to become educated in every subject for which I may have talent, before my youth is totally gone and I abandon all those ambitious demands that have frustrated me; I want to grow stronger every day and stop worrying about the rest. Nowhere can I be more certain of realizing this goal than in my fatherland. I have parents who have nothing to give me but with whom I can reside at very little expense. I can occupy myself there with writing – the true means of learning for me, since I am a person who must write down everything and who has too great a love of honor to publish anything of which he is not fully convinced. And living in Oberlausitz, my home province, I can most likely and most easily find

11:279

the spare time, perhaps taking a position such as a village vicarage, to devote myself fully to literary activity. That is want I want to do, until I have fully ripened. It seems best for me therefore to move back to my fatherland. But I lack the means to do it. I still have two ducats but they are not really mine, for I owe them for my rent and such things. There seems to be no solution for my rescue unless someone should turn up who will lend me the money to pay for my return journey, lend it against the collateral of my honor and with strictest confidence in the latter, until the time when I am certain to be able to repay it, viz., Easter of next year. I know no one to whom one could offer this pledge without fear of being laughed at in the face; no one but you, virtuous man.

11:280   It is a maxim for me never to ask anything of anyone without having investigated whether I myself would reasonably do the same for another if the circumstances were reversed; in the present instance I have found that, given the physical possibility, I would do it for anyone whom I could trust to have the principles that truly reside within me.

I take so seriously the actual giving of a pledge of honor that I feel some part of one's honor is lost through the necessity of having to secure something by means of such a pledge; and the deep sense of shame that I feel in this is the reason why I could never make a proposal of this sort orally, for I would not want anyone to witness it. My honor seems to me really problematic until the promise that is made has been fulfilled, since in the meantime it is always possible for the other party to think that I will not fulfill it. I know therefore that if you, sir, were to fulfill my wish, then even though I would always think of you with sincere esteem and gratitude, it would also be with a sense of shame, and I know that the fully joyful thought of an acquaintanceship that I have wanted all my life will become possible only when I shall have redeemed my word. These feelings stem from my temperament rather than from principles, I know, and they may be mistaken; but I don't wish to rid myself of them until my principles become so firmly established that these supplementary feelings are rendered wholly superfluous. But I can already trust my principles this far: I know that if I should be capable of breaking my word to you, I would despise myself forever and would have to avoid looking into my inner self, would have to abandon principles that remind me of you, and of my lack of honor, in order to rid myself of the most painful rebukes.

Were I to suppose that this way of thinking were present in someone, then *I* would certainly do for him what is here under discussion. But it is less clear to me *how* and *by what means* I could produce the conviction, if I were in your place, that this way of thinking is present in me.

If I may be permitted to compare something great with something very small, esteemed sir: I concluded from your writings, with total confidence, that your character is exemplary, and I would have wagered everything on this even without knowing the slightest thing about your everyday conduct of life. I have presented you with only a trifle, and at a time when it did not occur to me that I would ever make such use of our acquaintanceship, and my character, furthermore, is not yet firm enough to leave its imprint on everything I write. But you are an incomparable judge of human beings and you can see, perhaps, even in this trifle the love of truth and the honesty that may exist in my character. 11:281

Finally – and I am embarrassed to add this – if I should be capable of breaking my word, my honor in the eyes of the world is in your hands. I intend to become an author, using my own name; if I should return to Königsberg I will ask you for letters of introduction to various scholars. I think it would be a duty to inform these people, whose good opinion will then depend on you, of my dishonesty. And it would be a duty, I think, to warn the whole world of such an absolutely disreputable character, to prevent the harm that the pretended appearance of honesty can cause a man in an atmosphere of falsity, deceiving his sharp-sightedness and mocking virtue and honesty.

These are the considerations I thought about before I dared to write this letter to you. I am, more by temperament and by virtue of experience than because of principles, very indifferent to things that are not in my power. This is not the first time I have found myself in difficulties from which I see no escape; but it would be the first time that I have remained in them. What I usually feel in such circumstances is just curiosity as to how matters will develop. I simply grasp the means that my reflections identify as the best and calmly await the successful outcome. It is even easier for me to be calm now, since I have put my success in the hands of a wise and good man. But on the other hand I feel an unaccustomed heartbeat as I send off this letter. Whatever your decision may be, I shall lose something of value in your eyes. If your decision is favorable, I can recover what is lost someday; if it is negative then, I think, I shall never recover it.[2]

As I mean to close my letter, an anecdote about a noble Turk occurs to me. The Turk made a similar proposal to a Frenchman with whom he was not acquainted. The Turk addressed the Frenchman more directly and candidly than I am doing; he probably had not experienced with his people what I have experienced with mine, but then neither did he have the conviction that he was dealing with a noble man as I have. I am ashamed of the shame that prevents me, despite the feelings I have, from throwing this letter into the fire and going to see you and speak to you as the noble Turk did to the Frenchman. 11:282

I must not apologize to you, sir, for the tone that dominates this letter. It is after all a distinguishing characteristic of the wise that one can talk to them as one human being to another.

As soon as I can do so without disturbing you I shall wait upon you to learn your decision. With sincere respect and admiration I remain, sir

your most obedient
J. G. Fichte.

---

1 The friend was Fichte's countryman Karl Gottlob Sonntag, rector of the Lyceum in Riga beginning in 1789.

2 What Kant did was not lend Fichte the money but help Fichte to sell his manuscript; see the following letter, Kant to Borowski, Sept. 16, 1791, Ak. [485]. With the assistance of Court Chaplain Schultz Kant also secured a position as private tutor for Fichte, at the home of Count Heinrich Joachim Reinhold von Krockow in the town of Krockow bei Danzig (Gdansk).

124 [485] (454)
To Ludwig Ernst Borowski.
September 16, 1791.

11:284   Herr Fichte, the bearer of this letter, has developed such trust in you, as a result of the conversation which you were kind enough to have with him, that he now counts on your assistance with a problem about which he will inform you. It concerns his manuscript, *Essay Toward a Critique of Revelation [Versuch einer Critik der Offenbarung]* for which he must find a publisher who will give him an honorarium just as soon as he delivers the manuscript.

I have had time to read it only up to page 8, for other business keeps interrupting me; but as far as I have read I find it well worked out and quite appropriate to the current mood with respect to the investigation of religious matters. You will be in a better position than I to form an opinion of it if you take the trouble to read it through. Herr Fichte's hope is that, should you feel confident of the book's favorable reception, you try to persuade Herr Hartung[1] to buy it from him, so that Herr Fichte can buy himself the necessities he needs just now. He will tell you about his long-range hopes himself.

I beg you not to take offense at the burden I impose on you, though I know that it does not go against your generous character. I am most respectfully

your devoted servant
I. Kant.

The 16th of September, 1791.

---

1 Gottfried Leberecht Hartung (1747–97), book merchant in Königsberg.

125 [486] (455)

From Salomon Maimon.

September 20, 1791.

Dear Sir,   11:285
Esteemed Herr Professor,

I know how unjust is any man who robs you of the least bit of your time, so precious to the world. I know that nothing could be more important to you than to complete your work. Yet I cannot refrain from bothering you, with just this one letter.

I vowed some time ago that I would henceforth read nothing but your books. I am totally convinced by the skeptical part of your *Critique*. As for the dogmatic part, it can be accepted hypothetically and, even though I have constructed a psychological deduction of the categories and ideas (which I attribute not to the understanding and to reason but to the power of the imagination), I can nevertheless grant what you propound as at least problematical. Thus I have made my peace with the *Critique* very nicely.

Herr Reinhold, however (a man whose sagacity I value second only to your own), claims in his writings that he has given your system *formal completeness* and also that he has found *the only universally valid principle (si diis placet)*[1] on which the system can be founded. This claim attracted my total attention. After more careful investigation, however, I found my expectation deceived. I *value* every system that has *formal completeness*, but I can accept its *validity* only insofar as it has *objective reality* and according to its *degree of fruitfulness*.

Now as regards its systematic form, I find that Herr Reinhold's theory of the faculty of representation can hardly be improved. But I cannot subscribe in any way to this highly lauded universally valid principle (the proposition of consciousness) and still less can I bring myself to have any great expectations of its fruitfulness.

11:286   I question specifically whether in every conscious experience (even in an intuition or sensation, as Herr Reinhold maintains) the representation is distinguished from both the subject and the object and is at the same time related to both of these by the subject. An intuition, in my opinion, is not related to anything other than itself. It becomes a *representation* only by being united with other intuitions in a synthetic unity, and it is as an element of the synthesis that the intuition relates itself to that representation, that is, to its object. The determined synthesis to which the representation is related is the *represented object*; and any undetermined synthesis to which the representation could be related is the concept of an *object in general*. How, then, can Herr Reinhold claim that the proposition of consciousness is a universally valid principle? It can be valid, as I have shown, only in the consciousness of a representation, that is, an intuition related to a synthesis as part to whole. But, says Herr Reinhold, we are of course not always conscious of this relating of the intuition to the subject and object, though it always takes place. Just how does he know that? Whatever is not represented[2] in a representation does not belong to the representation. How can he then claim that this principle is the fact of consciousness that obtains universally? For anyone can easily deny this, on the basis of his own consciousness. It is a *delusion of the transcendent imagination* that every intuition is related to some substratum or other; because of the imagination's habit of relating every intuition, as representation, to a real object (a synthesis), the transcendent imagination finally relates it to no real object at all but to a mere *idea* that has been foisted in place of a real object.

The word "representation" has made much mischief in philosophy, since it has encouraged people to invent an objective substratum for each mental event. Leibniz made matters worse with his theory of *obscure representations*.[3] I admit the supreme importance of his theory for anthropology. But in a critique of the cognitive faculty, it is certainly worthless. "Obscure" representations are not states of mind (which can only be conscious) but rather of the body. Leibniz makes use of them only in order to fill in the gaps in the substantiality of the soul. But I do not believe that any independent thinker will seriously think he can manage it that way. "Obscure" representations are merely bridges with which to cross from soul to body and back again (though Leibniz had good reason to prohibit this passage).

I cannot be satisfied even with Herr Reinhold's definition of philosophy. He means by "philosophy" what you rightly placed under the special title of "transcendental philosophy" (the theory of the conditions of knowledge of a real object in general).

I wish you would comment on this, and on my dictionary[4] (which from all appearances will either be badly reviewed or not at all). Awaiting this, I remain, most respectfully,

Your wholly devoted servant,

Salomon Maimon

Berlin

---

1 if it pleases the gods

2 Or "Whatever we do not picture or think in a representation . . ." ("Was in der Vorstellung nicht vorgestellt wird . . .").

3 Maimon may be referring to Leibniz's theory of clear versus "confused perceptions."

4 Maimon, *Philosophisches Wörterbuch oder Beleuchtung der wichtigsten Gegenstände der Philosophie in alphabetischer Ordnung*, Part I (Berlin, 1791).

126 [487] (456)

To Karl Leonhard Reinhold.

September 21, 1791.

[Kant praises Reinhold, apologizes for not writing, and expresses regret that they 11:287 *can converse with each other only in letters.]*

. . . Since about two years ago my health has undergone a drastic 11:288 change. Without any actual illness (other than a cold that lasted three weeks) or any visible cause, I have lost my accustomed appetite, and although my physical strength and sensations have not diminished, my disposition for mental exertion and even for lecturing have suffered greatly. I can only devote two or three uninterrupted hours in the morning to intellectual work, for I am then overcome with drowsiness (regardless of how much sleep I have had the night before), and I am forced to work at intervals, which slows up my work. I have to look forward impatiently to a good mood without getting into one, being unable to exercise any control over my own mind. I think it is nothing but old age, which brings everyone to a standstill sooner or later, but it is all the more unwelcome to me just now when I foresee the completion of my plan. I am sure you will therefore understand, my kind friend, how this need to utilize every favorable moment, in such circumstances, leads one to a fatal postponement of many resolutions whose execution does not seem pressing, and every postponement tends to prolong itself.

I shall be happy to acknowledge and intend to acknowledge publicly one of these days that the further analysis of the foundations of knowledge, insofar as it consists in [your] investigations of the faculty of representation in general,[1] constitutes a great contribution to the critique of reason; [I plan to do this] as soon as I can get clear about those parts of your work that are still obscure to me. But I cannot conceal from you, at least not in a private communication, that I think it would be possible to develop the consequences of the principles [that I have] already laid down as basic, so as to show their correctness, perhaps using your excellent literary talents to make comments that would disclose just as much of your profounder investigations as would be needed to clarify the subject fully, without requiring the friends of the *Critique* to struggle through such an abstract work and thereby risk having many of them frightened off. – This is what I have been hoping for, but I am not now telling you what to do, nor, still less, am I issuing a public verdict that would put your meritorious efforts in an unfavorable light. – I shall have to postpone any public pronouncement a while longer, for, leaving aside my university business, I am presently working on a small but taxing job[2] and also on a revision of the *Critique of Judgment* for the second edition, which is being published next Easter, and what little strength I have is more than consumed by these projects.

Do remain well disposed toward me, in friendship and candid trust. I have never shown myself unworthy of it, nor ever shall. May I be included in the company of you and your true, merry, and clever friend, Erhard,[3] a company whose minds, I flatter myself, will forever be in accord.

With fondest devotion and respect, I am ...

11:289

---

1 The reference is to Reinhold's *Versuch einer neuen Theorie des menschlichen Vorstellungsvermögens* (1789), the beginnings of Reinhold's break with Kant over the need for a new "foundation" for the Critical Philosophy. See Kant's letter to Beck, Nov. 2, 1791, Ak. [496], for a more disingenuous statement of Kant's view of Reinhold's book, free of the polite circumlocutions in the present letter. There Kant refers to Reinhold's "obscure abstractions" and expresses concern about Reinhold's project.

2 Probably the first part of *Religion innerhalb der Grenzen der bloßen Vernunft (Religion within the Limits of Reason Alone)*.

3 J. B. Erhard (1766–1827). See Kant's letter to him, Dec. 21, 1792, Ak. [552].

127 [488] (457)
To Jacob Sigismund Beck.[1]

September 27, 1791.

From the enclosed letter to me from Hartknoch you will see, dearest friend, that I have recommended you to him. What he wanted was somebody competent who is willing and able to make an integrated summary of my critical writings, composing it in his own original way. Since you indicated in your last letter that you were inclined to undertake a study of this sort, I could think of no one more reliable and clever for his project.[2] Of course I have a personal interest in this suggestion. But I am also certain that, once you become involved, you will find this work an inexhaustible source of entertaining reflection during those periods when you need a rest from mathematics (which you must not, however, allow yourself to neglect), and conversely, when you are worn out by this project you will find mathematics a welcome relaxation. For, partly from my experience, partly (even more) from the example of the greatest mathematicians, I have become convinced that mere mathematics cannot fulfill the soul of a thinking man, that something more must be added (even if it is only poetry, as in Kästner's case)[3] to refresh the mind by exercising its other talents and also by providing it with a change of diet. Now what can serve better for this and for a lifetime than investigating something that concerns the whole vocation of man, especially if one has the hope of making some profit from time to time by a systematic effort of thought. Besides, the history of the world and of philosophy are tied up with this enterprise, and I am hopeful that, even if this investigation does not shed new light on mathematics, the latter may, inversely, by considering its methods and heuristic principles together with the entailed requirements and desiderata, come upon new discoveries for the critique and survey of pure reason. And the *Critique's* new way of presenting abstract concepts may itself yield something analogous to Leibniz's *ars universalis characteristica combinatoria*.[4] For the table of categories and the table of ideas (under which the cosmological ideas disclose

11:289

11:290

something similar to impossible roots [in mathematics])* are after all enumerated and as well defined in regard to all possible uses that reason can make of them as mathematics could ask, so that we can see to what extent they at least clarify if not extend our knowledge.

11:291   I gather from your letter, forwarded to me by Herr Hartknoch, that you do not totally reject his proposal. I think it would be advisable for you to get started right away, beginning with a rough outline of the system, or, if you have already thought of that, you might seek out and inform me from time to time of those parts of the system that give you trouble and tell me what your doubts or difficulties are. In this connection I would be pleased if someone, perhaps Prof. Jacob – please greet him sincerely for me – would help you examine all of the polemical writings against me, such as the essays and especially the reviews in Eberhard's *Magazine*, early articles in the *Tübinger gelehrte Zeitung*, and wherever else you find similar things, and find all the alleged contradictions in my use of words. For I found it so easy to rebut the misunderstandings in these criticisms that I would long ago have made a collection of them and refuted them, had I not forgotten to write them down and assemble them as they came to my notice. As for the Latin translation, we can think about that later on, after your German edition is published.

     As for the two treatises proposed to Hartknoch, namely the one concerning Reinhold's theory of the faculty of representation and the one comparing the Humean and the Kantian philosophy (with respect to the latter treatise, please look at the volume of Hume's *Essays* containing his moral principle, and see how it compares with mine; his aesthetic principle is also to be found there), if the second project did not take too much of your time, it would of course be preferable to work on the first topic just now. For Reinhold, an otherwise nice man, has become so passionately committed to his theory (which is really not yet intelligible to me) that if it should turn out that you were at odds with him about this or that part of his theory, or perhaps with his whole idea, it might make him feel let down by his friends. At the same time I really hope that nothing deters you from that examination or

11:292   from publishing it. Let me therefore suggest that I write to Reinhold and acquaint him with your character and your present work, so as to bring about a literary correspondence between the two of you, since you are so close to each other. Such an exchange would certainly please him and might bring about a friendly agreement with regard to what you wish to write about the aforementioned subject. When you honor

---

* If, in accordance with the principle "In the series of appearances, everything is conditioned," I seek the unconditioned and the highest ground of the totality of the series, it would be as if I were looking for $\sqrt{-2}$.

me with a reply to this letter, please include your opinion as to whether you would agree to my writing him.

If you give me a hint, I shall negotiate the honorarium for your work (philosophical and mathematical) with Hartknoch. You need not settle for less than 5 or 6 Reichsthaler per sheet.

I remain with the greatest respect and friendly attachment,

Your

I. Kant

Königsberg, 27 Sept., 1791.

P.S. I beg you again not to spare me in any way with regard to the postage.

---

1 Jacob Sigismund Beck (1761–1840) was born in Marienburg in western Prussia. He studied in Königsberg, obtained his teaching degree in Halle, and became professor of philosophy there in 1796 and in Rostock in 1799. His first letter to Kant in the Akademie edition, Ak.[371], from Berlin, is dated Aug. 1, 1789, and contains gossip about various Kantians and anti-Kantians in Berlin and Leipzig. Biester, librarian of the royal library, had helped Beck to gain access to Newton's works. Platner, professor of physiology in Leipzig, who is mentioned in a number of Kant's letters, is according to Beck "a pathetic person." If Kant replied, his letter is not extant. Kant did write to Beck in May 1791, Ak.[469], offering advice on Beck's career and praising his understanding of Kant's concepts. As their subsequent correspondence shows, Beck was not an uncritical disciple, though his sometimes obsequious tone might suggest this.

The English translation of some of Kant's correspondence with Beck by G. B. Kerferd and D. E. Walford, in *Kant, Selected Pre-Critical Writings and Correspondence with Beck* (Manchester University Press, 1968), has been helpful in preparing the translations presented here.

2 Beck's completed work was published in Riga in three volumes, 1793–6. It was entitled *Erläuternder Auszug aus den kritischen Schriften des Herrn Prof. Kant auf Anraten desselben.*

3 On Kästner see Kant's letter to him, Aug. 5, 1790, Ak.[439], n. 1. Kant addressed him as "the Nestor of all philosophical mathematicians in Germany."

4 See notes to Kant's letter to Schultz, Aug. 26, 1783, ak.[210].

128 [496] (464)
To Jacob Sigismund Beck.
November 2, 1791.

11:303   Dearest Herr Magister,

11:304   My reply to your pleasant letter of October 8 is somewhat late but not too late, I hope, to have caused you delay in your work. My responsibilities as dean and other business as well have taken up my time till now and even banished from my thoughts the intention of replying.

Your reluctance to associate yourself, just for the sake of profit, with that tiresome crowd of book publishers is entirely justified.[1] And very sensible too is your decision to make your contribution to the public capital of science even without the incentive of financial reward, just as your predecessors (on whose legacy you build) have done, if, as you say, you think you can present "something thoughtful and not useless" to the public.

I would have wished that you had chosen the first of the two treatises that you suggested to Herr Hartknoch to make your debut to the public. For Herr Reinhold's theory of the faculty of representation is so weighed down with obscure abstractions, making it impossible to explain what he means with examples, that even if the theory were correct in every part (which I am really unable to judge, since I have so far been unable to penetrate his thoughts), these difficulties would still make it impossible for it to have any extensive or permanent effect. And even though the sample of your work which you were kind enough to send me has convinced me very nicely of your gift for clarity, your judgment of Reinhold's work would not have been able to overcome the obscurity attending the matter itself.

Above all I don't want Herr Reinhold to get the impression from your work that I encouraged or commissioned you to write it. For it is really your own idea. Furthermore, I cannot, at least not yet, introduce you to him as I had intended, for he would then easily interpret my friendship for hypocrisy. Besides this I have no doubt whatsoever that the tone of your book will be such as to avoid hurting this good and otherwise alert man who is however, as it seems to me, somewhat splenetic.

Your intention to compose an abstract of my critical writings, dearest friend, is a very interesting prospect for me, since you indicate that you are convinced of the truth and utility of my work. Because of my age I felt disinclined to undertake such a project myself, and I prefer

above all that the person who does this be a mathematician. Please 11:305
disclose to me the difficulties that have occurred to you concerning
morality.[2] I shall be pleased to try to solve them for you, and I hope I
can, for I have crisscrossed the field of ethics often and at length and
in every direction.

I shall keep the sample of your abstract, since your letter did not
indicate that I was to send it back.

But I cannot understand what you say at the close of your letter,
i.e., that this time you have at my request omitted the postage. For the
letter arrived with postage on it. Please, on no account do this in the
future! The cost of our correspondence is trivial for me but not for
you, at least for the present and for some time to come. It would be a
loss for me if, because of the costs, our correspondence were to be
suspended from time to time.

It is one of Prof. Kraus's[3] firmly established principles that he would
like to convert into old bachelors all those scholars who tell each other
that, because so many children die so soon after being born, it is better
not to father any more children.[4] Of all people I am least in a position
to dissuade him from this conviction. As far as I am concerned you are
totally free to take either side on this issue. I don't want to share in the
sin of authorship and to bear the guilt that your conscience may inspire
in you or that other people may make you feel. I remain, with all
respect and friendship,

your most devoted servant,
I. Kant.

Königsberg, November 2, 1791.

---

1 Kant refers to Beck's letter of Oct. 6, 1791, Ak.[489], in which Beck reported
to Kant that the publisher Hartknoch, in Riga, had invited him to prepare an
abstract in Latin of Kant's complete writings. Beck declared himself insufficiently competent in Latin and expressed the opinion that "mere book publishers are all crooks." Though he may have been in need of the money, Beck
resisted the temptation to publish just for that reason. He did however express
a willingness to publish an examination of Reinhold's theory of the faculty of
representation, or a comparison of Hume and Kant, or an abstract of Kant's
Critique. Beck asked Kant to introduce him to Reinhold.

2 In the letter just alluded to, Beck states that while he is totally convinced by
the first *Critique* and takes the second *Critique* as his Bible, he has "certain
difficulties" with the latter work that concern "true morality" ("die eigentliche
Moral.")

3 Christian Jakob Kraus (1753–1807) professor of practical philosophy and political science in Königsberg, Kant's pupil, dinner companion, and friend.

4 I.e., scholars who claim that it would be better not to publish, because

publications are so soon forgotten, ought not to write books – or ought not to be scholars. Beck had explained his own reasons for wanting to become an author, viz., not for the sake of fame and fortune but to produce something of use to the world. He feared that Kraus would misunderstand his motives and be displeased with him.

129 [499] (467)

From Jacob Sigismund Beck.

November 11, 1791.

[*Beck tells of his examination of and misgivings about Reinhold's theory of the faculty of representation. Because of Reinhold's evident love of truth, Beck is inclined not to say anything strongly critical of him in public. Of much greater interest to Beck is his work on the abstract of Kant's critical writings.*]

11:311 . . . Allow me to ask whether in what follows I have understood you correctly. . . . The *Critique* calls "intuition" a representation that relates immediately to an object.[1] But in fact, a representation does not become objective until it is subsumed under the categories. Since intuition similarly acquires its objective character only by means of the application of categories to it, I am in favor of leaving out that definition of "intuition" that refers to it as a representation relating to objects. I find in intuition nothing more than a manifold accompanied by consciousness (or by the *unique* "*I think*"), and determined by consciousness, a manifold in which there is as such no relation to an object. I would also like to reject the definition of "*concept*" as a representation mediately related to an object.[2] Rather, I distinguish concepts from intuitions by the fact that they are thoroughly determinate whereas intuitions are not thoroughly determinate. For both intuitions and concepts acquire objectivity only after the activity of judgment subsumes them under the pure concepts of the understanding.

[*Kant's marginal comment:* The fashioning*a* of a concept, by means of intuition, into a cognition of the object is indeed the work of judgment; but the reference*b* of intuition to an object in general is not. For the latter is merely the logical use of representation insofar as a representation is thought to belong to cognition.[3] When, on the other hand, a single rep-

a Bestimmung, usually translated "determination."
b Beziehung

resentation is referred only to the subject, the use is aesthetic (feeling), in which case the representation cannot become a piece of knowledge.]

I understand the words "to connect"^{c} in the *Critique* to mean nothing more or less than to accompany the manifold with the identical "I think" whereby a *unitary* representation comes to exist. I believe that the *Critique* calls the original apperception the *unity* of apperception just because this apperception is what makes such a *unitary* representation possible. But am I right in regarding original apperception and the unity of apperception as the same thing or, rather, in finding the only difference between them to be that the *pure* "*I think*," though it can only be discovered in the synthesis of the manifold, is nevertheless thought as something independent of the manifold (since in itself it contains nothing manifold) whereas the unity of consciousness in its self-identity, on the other hand, is thought to be connected with the parts of the manifold? This unity seems to me to acquire the character of objective unity when the representation itself is subsumed under the category. Herr Reinhold speaks of a connection and a unity in the concept, a second connection and a second unity (a unity "to the second power," as he expresses it) in the judgment. Besides these, he has a third connection, in inferences. I don't understand a word of this, since I take "connection" to mean nothing more than accompanying the manifold with consciousness. Still, his discussion makes me doubt myself.

[*Beck then asks for Kant's advice.*]

^{c} *verbinden*

---

1 *Critique of Pure Reason*, A 19 = B 33.
2 *Critique of Pure Reason*, A 50 = B 74.
3 That is, relation to an object in general is part of the meaning of "representation" if we intend that word to stand for an item of knowledge.

1792

130 [500] (468)

To Jacob Sigismund Beck.

January 20, 1792[1]

11:313 Worthiest friend,

I have made you wait a long time for a response to your letter of December 9 of last year, but it is not my fault. For pressing labors hang about my neck and my age imposes on me a necessity I would not otherwise feel, to devote my thoughts to the project before me until I am finished with it. I must not let anything alien interrupt my thinking, for once I let go of the thread, I cannot find it again.

You have presented me with your thorough investigation of what is just the hardest thing in the whole *Critique*, namely, the analysis of an experience in general and the principles that make experience in general possible. – I have already made plans for a system of metaphysics to handle this difficulty and to begin with the categories, in their proper order (having first merely expounded, without investigating their possibility, the pure intuitions of space and time in which alone objects can be given to the categories); and I would demonstrate, at the conclusion of the exposition of each category (for example, Quantity and all predicables included under it, along with examples of their use), that no experience of objects of the senses is possible except insofar as 11:314 I presuppose a priori that every such object must be *thought* of as a magnitude, and similarly with all the other categories. Here I shall always remark that such objects can be represented by us only as *given* in space and time. Out of this there emerges a whole science of Ontology as *immanent* thinking, i.e., a science of things the objective reality of whose concepts can be securely established. Only afterwards, in the second section, will it be shown that in this same science all *conditions* of the possibility of objects are themselves *conditioned*, and yet reason is

398

unavoidably driven to seek the *unconditioned*, where our thinking becomes *transcendent*; i.e., involves concepts whose objective reality cannot be assured at all and by means of which, therefore, no *cognition* of
objects can take place. I wanted to show, in the Dialectic of Pure
Reason (setting up its antinomies), that those objects of possible experience are to be recognized as objects of the senses, appearances only,
not things in themselves. I wanted then to make the Deduction of the
categories comprehensible by showing its relation to the sensuous
forms of space and time, as the conditions of the uniting of these for a
possible experience; but I wanted to present the categories themselves
as concepts that make it possible to think of objects at all[2] (be the
intuition of whatever form it will), and then I wanted also to determine[3]
their extension beyond the boundaries of sense, an extension which
however yields no cognition. Well, enough of this.

You put the matter quite precisely when you say, "The union[a] of
representations is itself the object, and the activity of the mind whereby
this union of representations is represented[b] is what we mean by 'relating them to the object'." But one may still ask: How can a union of
representations, being *complex*, be represented? Not through the awareness that it is *given* to us; for a union requires *uniting* [c], *(synthesis), of the
manifold. It must thus, (since it is a union), be produced*, and produced
furthermore by an inner activity that is valid for a *given* manifold in
general and that precedes a priori the manner in which the manifold is
given. In other words, the union can only be *thought* in a concept by
means of the synthetic unity of consciousness – thought in a concept
(of object in general), a concept that is undetermined with respect to
the manner in which anything may be given in intuition, and this
concept, applied to[d] an object in general, is the category. The merely
subjective state of the thinking subject,[d] insofar as the manifold is given
to that subject in a particular manner (for composition and its synthetic
unity) is called "sensibility"; and this manner (of intuition, given a
priori), is called the sensible form of intuition. By means of this form
and with the help of the categories, objects are *cognized*[e] but only as
things in the realm of appearance and not as they may be in themselves.
Without any intuition they would not be cognized at all, though they
would still be thought; but if one not only abstracts from all intuition
but actually excludes it, then one cannot guarantee the objective reality

11:315

---

[a] *Inbegriff*
[b] Or "presented," "conceived" ("vorgestellt wird").
[c] Or "composition," Eckart Förster's suggested translation of *Zusammensetzung*. The verb
   Zusammensetzen that Kant uses here could also be rendered as "combining."
[d] Or "of the representing subject" "des Vorstellenden Subjects").
[e] *erkannt*

of the categories (that they in fact represent anything at all and are not empty concepts).

Perhaps you can avoid defining "sensibility" right at the outset in terms of "receptivity," that is, the kind of representations that occur in the subject insofar as the subject is affected by objects. Perhaps you can identify it rather as that which, in a cognition, constitutes merely the relation of the representation to the subject, so that its form^f, in this relation to the object of intuition, allows us to cognize no more than the appearance of this object. But that this subjective thing constitutes only the manner in which the subject is affected by representations, and consequently is nothing more than the receptivity of the subject, is already implied by its being merely a modification^g of the subject.

In short, since this whole analysis only aims to show that experience is only possible with certain a priori principles,[4] and this thesis cannot be made truly comprehensible until those principles are actually exhibited, I think it prudent to keep the work as brief as possible before these principles are presented. Perhaps the way I proceed in my lectures, in which I have to be brief, can be of some help to you.

I begin by defining "experience" in terms of *empirical cognition*. But cognition is the representation *through concepts* of a *given* object as such; it is empirical cognition if the object is given in the senses' representation (the latter includes both sensation and sensation bound up with consciousness, i.e., perception); it is a priori cognition if the object is given, but not given in a representation of the senses^h (which[5] thus nonetheless can always be sensible). Two sorts of representations are needed for cognition: 1) intuition, by means of which an object is given, 2) concept, by means of which it is thought. To make a single cognition out of these two *pieces of cognition* a further activity is required: the composition of the *manifold given in intuition* in conformity with the synthetic unity of consciousness, which is expressed by the concept. Since composition, either through the object or through its representation in intuition, cannot be *given* but must be *produced*, it must rest on the pure spontaneity of the understanding in concepts of objects in general (of the composition of the given manifold). But since concepts to which no corresponding objects *could* be given, being therefore entirely objectless, would not even be concepts (they would be thoughts through which I think nothing at all), just for that reason a manifold must be given a priori for those a priori concepts. And because it is given a priori, it must be given in an intuition without any thing as object, that is, given in just the form of intuition, which is just

11:316

---

^{f}"die Form derselben" is ambiguous: the form of sensibility or the form of the affecting objects.

^{g} *Bestimmung* ^{h} *Sinnenvorstellung* subjective (space and time); it is therefore in conformity with the merely sensible intuition, whose synthesis through the imagination, under the rule of the synthetic unity of consciousness, the concept expresses; for the rule of the schematism of concepts of the understanding is then applied to perceptions (in which objects are given to the senses by means of sensation).

I close herewith my hurriedly composed sketch and beg you not to let my delay in replying to your letter, a delay caused by random impediments, keep you from disclosing your thoughts to me at any time that you encounter difficulties. I am, with the greatest respect,

Your
I. Kant.

Königsberg, 20 January, 1792.

P.S. Please mail the enclosed letter right away.

---

1 This letter is an answer to Beck's letter (not extant) of Dec. 9, 1791.

2 Or, "I wanted to present the categories themselves as concepts that make it possible to think of objects in general" ("... Kategorien ... als Begriffen Objekte überhaupt zu denken").

3 Or, "I wanted to secure [ausmachen] the [non-cognitive] extension of the categories beyond the limits of the senses." Both the meaning and relation of "ausmachen" is ambiguous.

4 Or "is only a priori possible ..."; grammatically, "a priori" could modify either "principles" or "possible."

5 Grammatically, the word "which" (*die*) could refer either to "a priori cognition" or to "representation." As the remainder of this paragraph shows, Kant's point is that even a priori cognitions require something given, hence they are "sensible" in the way that pure intuitions are, though not "of the senses," i.e., empirical.

131 [503] (471)
To Johann Heinrich Kant.
January 26, 1792.

Dear brother,   11:320

Herr Reimer, the bearer of this letter, a relative [nephew] of your wife's, my dear sister-in-law,[1] visited me, and I could not refrain from putting aside my tremendous chores (which I seldom do) in order to send you greetings. Despite my apparent indifference, I have thought of you often and fraternally – not only for the time we are both still living but also for after my death,[2] which, since I am 68, cannot be far off. Our two surviving sisters,[3] both widowed, the older of whom has five grown and (some of them) married children, are provided for by me, either wholly or, in the case of the younger sister, by my contribution to St. Georgs-Hospital, where provision has been made for her. So the duty of gratitude for our blessings that is demanded of us, as our parents taught us, will not be neglected. I would be pleased to receive news of your own family and its situation.

11:321 Please greet my dear sister-in-law. I am, ever affectionately,

Your loyal brother,

I. Kant

---

1 Kant and his sister-in-law were unacquainted with each another, according to J. H. Kant's letter of Feb. 8, 1792, Ak. [505].
2 Kant had made his will on Aug. 29, 1791; but his brother did not survive him.
3 Marie Elizabeth Kröhnert (1727–96) and Katharina Barbara Theyer (1731–1807). Another sister, Anna Luise (b. 1730), had died in 1774.

132 [504] (472)
To Johann Gottlieb Fichte.

February 2, 1792.

You ask my advice, sir, on how your manuscript, rejected by the current strict censor, might be salvaged. My answer is, it can't be done! Although I have not read your book myself, I gather from your letter that its main thesis is "that faith in a given revelation cannot be rationally justified on the basis of a belief in miracles."[1]

It follows necessarily that a religion may contain no article of faith other than one that exists for pure reason as well. I think that this proposition is completely innocent and denies neither the subjective necessity of a revelation nor the fact of miracles (since one can assume that, if it is possible at all, the actual occurrence of such a thing could be rationally understood as well, without revelation, even though reason would not have *introduced* these articles of faith by itself. It is not necessary to base the belief in those articles on miracles, once they are established, even if a miracle was needed originally). But by today's assumed maxims, it seems that the censor would not allow you to say this. For according to those maxims, certain texts in the confession of faith are supposed to be taken so literally that the human understanding can barely grasp their sense, much less see their rational truth, with the result that they need perpetually to be supported by a miracle and could never become articles of faith prescribed by reason alone. That the revelation of such propositions was only intended, as an accom- 11:322 modation to our weakness, to provide a visible cloak for them, and that this revelation can have merely subjective truth, is not acknowledged by the censor. He demands that they be taken as objective truths.

There is one way still open to bring your book into accord with the (as yet not widely known) opinions of the censor: If you could manage to make him understand and find attractive the distinction between a *dogmatic* faith, elevated above all doubt, and a *purely moral assumption* that freely bases itself on moral grounds (the imperfection of reason in its inability to satisfy its own demands). For then the religious faith that the morally good conscience has grafted onto the faith in miracles says in effect: "Lord, I believe!" (that is, I gladly assume it, whether or not I or anyone else can adequately prove it); "Help Thou mine unbelief!" (that is, I have moral faith in relation to everything that I can extract from the historical miracle story for my inner improvement, and I wish, too, that I might possess faith in those historical events insofar as that would also contribute to my inner improvement). My unintentional *non-belief* is not an intentional *unbelief.* But you will have a hard time making this compromise *attractive* to a censor who, it would seem, has made the historical credo into an essential religious duty.

You may do whatever you think best with these hurriedly written but not unconsidered ideas of mine, as long as you do not explicitly or covertly indicate their author; I assume of course that you would first have persuaded yourself sincerely of their truth.

I wish you contentment in your present position,[2] and should you wish to move, I hope I shall have some means of helping you to improve your situation.

Respectfully and with friendship,

Your devoted servant,

I. Kant

---

1 In his letter of Jan. 23, 1792, Ak. [501], Fichte explained his position on faith and miracles. No miracle as such can be proved. There might be other good grounds for believing a revelation, however; namely, the miracles it reports

may inspire awe in the mind of someone who needs this inspiration. But a revelation can extend neither our dogmatic nor our moral knowledge, since it concerns transcendent objects of which we may believe the "that" but cannot know the "how." It might be "subjectively true" for someone who wants to believe it; but it is not knowledge. (*Werke*, Ak. 11: 317.)

Fichte's manuscript, *Versuch einer Kritik aller Offenbarung* (*Critique of All Revelation*), had been denied the imprimatur by J. L. Schulze, dean of the theological faculty in the University of Halle. Schulze's successor, G. C. Knapp, however, allowed the book to be published without any changes. Since the work appeared anonymously, and was published by the Königsberg publisher Hartung (at Kant's suggestion), many people believed it to be by Kant himself. This was the start of Fichte's career. As Kant indicates in the present letter, he had not actually read the book before recommending it to Hartung. See also Kant's letter to Borowski, Sept. 16, 1791, Ak. [485].

2 Although refusing to lend Fichte money, Kant had secured him a position as private tutor in the household of Count Reinhold of Krakow.

133 [505] (473)
From Johann Heinrich Kant.
February 8, 1792.

11:323 Dear brother,

I received your letter of January 26, this year, via Reimers, on February 3rd. It was a day of celebration for me, a day on which I saw once more my brother's extended hand and his expression of genuinely fraternal feelings for me, which made me feel truly joyous. My good wife who, though she has not met you, loves you sincerely and honors you, shared my feelings completely, and gave a lively account of your letter to our good children, who also love you sincerely and honor you.

Your generous assurance that you have thought of me in a brotherly way, in contemplation of your possible demise – may it be far removed! – moved us all to tears. Thank you, thank you sincerely, my brother, for this account of your benevolence; *may my loyal wife, and my truly good-hearted children share in the portion of your fortune that you have so kindly assigned to us*, if I, in accordance with the general rule, shall leave them behind when I die. Believe me when I wish you a good long life; this wish is genuine, it lives in my heart.

I share with joy in the fame that you as a philosopher of the first rank, as the creator of a new philosophical system, have earned. May God allow you to complete your work and live to see the spread of your influence outside Germany, beyond the Rhine and beyond the Pas de Calais. Of course, in one's 68th year one is fairly close to the end – but whenever I browse through a catalog of scholars who have lived to be over 80 I see that, other things being equal, old age seems to be the happy fate of thinkers and scholars; and that makes me hope that this lot will be my brother's as well; that you feel yourself weak and sickly does not disconfirm my hypothesis. Fontenelle felt that way ever since he was a child and yet he lived to be almost 90.[1]

I who am now in my 57th year, in splendid health and fully alive   11:324
and strong, would like to live perhaps another 15–20 years, so as not to leave my family totally empty-handed when I go. Last year I completed the repayment of the debts I incurred when I was rector in that expensive city of Mitau. Now I can save whatever is left over from my salary for my wife and children.

My situation was never prosperous enough to allow me to help my poor sisters and I thank you all the more for that reason, dear brother, for all that you have done for them. You were kind to ask about my family history. Here it is. In 1775 I married a good young woman without any fortune and with her I have produced five children: my good son Eduard lived only a year. Four children are still alive and give promise of long life and of becoming good human beings. My oldest daughter, *Amalia Charlotte*, was 16 on January 15th, a lively girl but one who craves wisdom and who *reads* a great deal. *Minna* will be 13 on August 24th. She combines in her quiet way the gifts of nature and an indefatigable industriousness.

Friedrich Wilhelm will be 11 on November 27th. He is honest and good-natured, an Israelite[2] in whom there is no guile. He will certainly never pursue a crooked course.

Henriette will be 9 on August 5th. Full of fire, with the best heart in the world.

I am educating these good children myself. For I tried to get some noble boarders who included two private tutors but I failed utterly in my attempts to keep them. Alas, nothing is less attractive in Courland than the education of the youth. The people who advertise themselves as private tutors are often rogues. They promise golden mountains and show themselves in the end to be frauds. That happened to me as well.

If I live and if God gives me the means, my son will be a physician. But he should study surgery and not be trained in a barber's shop like a mechanic. This profession will earn him bread even in his fatherland, for theology would be too insecure a job – there are too many theologians waiting for appointments here. Of those, more than a third languish in school dust.   11:325

Aunt and Uncle Richter must be in eternity by now. They were fatherly and motherly benefactors and nurturers to me, I bless their memory. *Sit illis terra levis* [May the earth rest gently upon them]. Please greet their surviving son, my cousin Leopold, for me, and just as sincerely my good sister and her children; my wife and children join in this greeting. Every bit of news of their welfare gives me pleasure. My wife is not a little proud that you greeted her in your letter as your dear sister-in-law. She embraces you, and thanks you again for sending her that fine book on housekeeping, *The Housewife*, some years ago.[3] The book is her encyclopedia. My children are anxious to be inscribed in their uncle's memory. Before you know it you will have a letter from them, one that will not rob you of as much time in the reading as this one does. It will be shorter. Forgive my prattle. My heart propelled my pen. And this heart says to you that I am your

loyal, loving brother,
J. H. Kant.

Altrahden, the 8th of Feb. 1792.

---

1 In fact Fontenelle (1657–1757) died in his 100th year.
2 John 1:47: "Jesus saw Nathanael coming to him and said of him, Behold an Israelite indeed, in whom is no guile."
3 Cf. Johann Heinrich's letter to Kant, Sept. 10, 1782, Ak. [180], n. 1.

134 [506] (474)
From Johann Gottlieb Fichte.

February 17, 1792.

Dear Sir,
Esteemed Herr Professor,

Your kind letter gave me genuine pleasure, both because of the kindness with which you so quickly fulfilled my request and because of its contents. I now feel entirely confident about the points that were discussed, a confidence that stems not only from my own conviction but from the authority given to my ideas by a man who is esteemed above all others.

11:326   If I have correctly understood your view, I have in my essay taken the intermediate path you suggested: distinguishing between a faith that is *asserted* and one that is *assumed* on the basis of morality. I have, that is to say, carefully sought to distinguish a faith in the divinity of a given revelation that, according to my principles, is the only possible sort of faith in accord with reason, from a faith that assumes these truths to be in themselves postulates of pure reason. It was a free assumption of the divine origin of a form of truth, an assumption one could neither prove to oneself nor to others, but which just as certainly could not be disproved. The assumption was grounded on the experience of the efficacy ^{a} of such a form of knowledge for moral redemption, thought as having a divine origin. This assumption is, like every faith, merely subjective, but unlike purely rational faith^b it is not universally valid, since it is grounded on a particular experience.

I believe I have made this distinction reasonably clear. What I sought to do finally was to bring out the practical consequences of these principles; for example, that they render illegitimate all our efforts to impose our subjective convictions on others, while at the same time these principles secure to all persons the imperturbable enjoyment of anything they may need to get out of religion for their own improvement. Both the antagonist and the dogmatic defender of positive religion are banished, condemned to silence.

I did not think that my principles would evoke the wrath of truth-loving theologians. But it has happened, and I am now determined to leave the essay alone as it is and let the publisher do whatever he wants with it. However, I hope that you, sir, to whom I owe all my convictions and especially the justification and fortification of the essential points discussed here, will kindly accept my assurance of respect and most complete devotion.

yours sincerely,

Krakow
February 17, 1792

J. G. Fichte

---

^{a} *Wirksamkeit* ^{b} *Vernunftglaube*

135 [507] (475)
To Christian Gottlieb Selle.[1]

February 24, 1792.

Esteemed Sir,   11:327

It is almost three months since I received your gift, the profoundly reflective essay *De la Réalité et dé l'idéalité*, etc., and I have failed to reciprocate this generosity in any way; the reason is certainly not any lack of respect for your consideration nor any lack of appreciation for the arguments directed against me. I wanted to publish a reply, and I would perhaps have done so by now, but all sorts of intersecting hindrances have continually interrupted me, and my age makes it very difficult to pick up the thread of reflections again and carry out my plans when there are frequent interruptions.

Recently however a New Order has been established which may frustrate my intended project completely. I refer to the restriction on the freedom to think aloud about matters which might even indirectly relate to theology. The pressures on an academic teacher are much greater than on other sorts of scholars in such a situation, and reasonable prudence dictates that one at least postpone all essays of this sort for the time being, at least until the threatening meteor either disintegrates or shows itself for what it is.

Despite my having this aversion to combat, you will find no shortage of opponents, e.g., from members of the dogmatic party, though their style is different from mine. For empiricism is just as intolerable to those people, though they certainly attack it in the most empty and inconsistent way (for they think empiricism is not to be accepted either in part or as a whole). Compared to their reasoning, your emphatic declaration in favor of this principle does you credit.

I beg you therefore, dearest sir: release me from this obligation or allow me to delay still longer my response to your criticisms, since for the present this work would be to all appearances a pure waste of time.

11:328

With the greatest respect for your talent and manifold merits I remain

your most devoted servant

I. Kant

Königsberg, February 24, 1792.[2]

---

1 Christian Gottlieb Selle (1748–1800) was professor and physician at the Charité in Berlin. He had studied in Göttingen, absorbed the empiricist spirit of the Lockeans there, and, like Locke, had taken up both medicine – he became personal physician to Frederick II – and philosophy. Selle wrote to Kant in late 1787.

2 In his letter to Kant, Dec. 29, 1787, Ak. [314], Selle presents himself as Kant's opponent but nevertheless his admirer as well. According to Kiesewetter, Ak. [420], Selle thought that his book, *De la Réalité et de l'Idéalité des objets de nos connaissances*, published by the Berlin Academy in 1792, had given the death-blow to Kant's system.

136 [508] (476)
From Johann Erich Biester.
March 6, 1792.

Esteemed Sir,

You are really too generous to ordinary political establishments if you ask what their maxims are or if you demand consistency in how they apply them. People often find themselves induced, perhaps even necessitated, to issue some decree or other, though they haven't thought through all the implications of their action. But humanity is better off when the regime perpetrates beneficial inconsistencies! Such things prove at least that people are not totally and deliberately out to do evil but are only ignorant about particular things.

To come closer to our question: there has to be some discoverable maxim underlying the final decision of the Villaume[1] case, an idea that is clearly expressed in it. The idea is this: the censor's approval of any book is a sanctioning of all the principles expressed in that book; but no principle can be sanctioned if its contradictory has previously been sanctioned or publicly favored. Therefore what is intolerable is only the printing here, before the censor's eyes; such a book could be printed abroad and then imported like any other book (apart from blasphemous or slanderous ones). Books from Leipzig are not subjected to any inspection and require no permission to be sold.

As far as my own situation is concerned, I make it a firm rule to stay within the limits of the law. It has never been against the law here to publish abroad. Yet I would regard it as wrong to take a paper that had been turned down by the royal censor here and have it published abroad, just to spite the censor (even though that is not forbidden). I would regard this as disreputable and a chaffing unworthy of me – or it would take some truly unusual circumstance to make me do this. But that is not my situation; I have never had dealings with the local censor. I have only had the *Berlinische Monatsschrift* printed in Berlin, by Spener until 1791 and by Mauke in Jena since 1792. Or I should say my publisher has arranged this. The reason why we do this? that is another question, a question that no one presumably has the right to ask about a legal activity.[2]

That is how things stand, dearest man; and it seems to me that you have no cause to be dissatisfied with this arrangement or to see it as illegal or unjust.

To satisfy every scruple of a man like you, I submitted your excellent

11:329

essay[3] to the local censor immediately after receiving your last letter. The essay cannot come out in March but will adorn the April issue. Since its content is ethical, it devolves on Privy Councillor and Councillor of the Consistory Hillmer. He sent it to me a few days later with his imprimatur, offering the following wise reason for giving his approval, viz., "after careful reading, I see that this book, like other Kantian works, is intended for and can be enjoyed only by thinkers, researchers and scholars capable of fine distinctions."

I would be ashamed of the slightest dishonesty with a man like you. Even if you thought that your essay had already been sent to Jena and I could leave you thinking this, I have – since the essay happened coincidentally still to be here – proceeded in accordance with your wishes. It was sent to Jena on the third. There you have the whole story of this affair. Men of great renown and scholarship have given me their essays since then, just as they did before. I hope you will do 11:330 so as well. In addition I await your precise decision as to whether in the future your essays for the *Berlinische Monatsschrift* should be submitted to the censor *here*.

It goes without saying that I shall fulfill your desires exactly, however you may decide.

May Providence sustain you in the future, for the sciences, for enlightenment, and for the noble betterment of moral thinking!

Biester

March 6, 1792.

Your letter to Herr Selle has just been sent off.

---

1 Peter Villaume (1746–1806), preacher at the court of Frederick II and later professor at the Joachimsthal *Gymnasium*, was forbidden to publish one of his books in Prussia but allowed to do so abroad. The censor's reasoning was "If the printing of such books is allowed in my country, such permission can be seen as an expression of approval of such writings, and this is far from my intention."

2 The reason must have been that after the cabinet order of Oct. 19, 1791, all periodicals had to be submitted to Gottlob Friedrich Hillmer for censorship.

3 "On the Radical Evil in Human Nature," which became Part I of Kant's *Religion within the Limits of Reason Alone*.

137 [510] (478)
To Maria von Herbert.

Spring 1792.[1]

[Draft]

Your deeply felt letter is the product of a heart that must have been created for the sake of virtue and honesty, since it is so receptive to instruction in those qualities, instruction that will not stoop to flattery. I am thus compelled to do as you asked, namely, to put myself in your place and to reflect on the prescription for a pure moral sedative (the only thorough kind) for you. The object of your love must be just as sincere and respectful of virtue and uprightness, the spirit of virtue, as you are, though I do not know whether your relationship to him is one of marriage or merely friendship. I take it as probable from what you say that it is the latter, but it makes no significant difference for the problem that disturbs you. For love, be it for one's spouse or for a friend, presupposes the same mutual esteem for the other's character, without which it is no more than a very perishable, sensual delusion.

11:331

A love like that, the only virtuous love (for the other sort is only a blind inclination), wants to communicate itself completely, and it expects of its respondent a similar sharing of heart, unweakened by any distrustful reticence. That is how it should be and that is what the ideal of friendship demands. But there is in human beings an element of self-interestedness, which puts a limit on such candor, in some people more than in others. Even the sages of old complained of this obstacle to the mutual outpouring of the heart, this secret distrust and reticence, which makes a person keep some part of his thoughts locked within himself, even when he is most intimate with his confidant: "My dear friends, there is no such thing as a friend!"[2] And yet the superior soul passionately desires friendship, regarding it as the sweetest thing a human life may contain. Only with candor can it prevail.

11:332

This reticence, however, this want of candor – a candor that, taking mankind en masse, we cannot expect of people, since everyone fears that to reveal himself completely would make him despised by others – is still very different from that lack of sincerity that consists in dishonesty in the actual expression of our thoughts. The former flaw is one of the limitations of our nature and does not actually *corrupt* our character. It is only a wrong that hinders the expression of all the possible good that is in us. The other flaw, however, is a corruption of our thinking and a positive evil. What the honest but reticent man says is true but not the whole truth. What the dishonest man says is, in

411

contrast, something he knows to be false. Such an assertion is called a *lie*, in the doctrine of virtue.[3a] It may be entirely *harmless*, but it is not on that account innocent. It is, rather, a serious violation of duty to oneself and one for which there can be no remission, since the transgression subverts the dignity of man in our own person and attacks the roots of our thinking. For deception casts doubt and suspicion on everything and even removes all confidence from virtue, if one judges virtue by its external character.

11:333   As you see, you have sought counsel from a physician who is no flatterer and who does not seek to ingratiate himself. Were you wanting a mediator between yourself and your beloved, you see that my way of defining good conduct is not at all partial to the fair sex, since I speak for your beloved and present him with arguments that, as a man who honors virtue, are on his side and that justify his having wavered in his affection for you.

As for your earlier expectation, I must advise you first to ask yourself whether in your bitter self-reproach over a lie that as a matter of fact was not intended to cloak any wicked act you are reproaching yourself for a mere imprudence or are making an inner accusation on account of the immorality that is intrinsic to the lie. If the former, you are only rebuking yourself for the candor of your disclosure of the lie, that is, you regret having done your duty on this occasion (for that is doubtless what it is when one has deceived someone, even harmlessly, and has after a time set him straight again). And why do you regret this disclosure? Because it has resulted in the loss, certainly a serious one, of your friend's confidence. This regret is thus not motivated by anything moral, since it is produced by an awareness not of the act itself but of its consequences. But if the rebuke that pains you is one that is really grounded in a purely moral judgment of your behavior, it would be a poor moral physician who would advise you to cast this rebuke out of your mind, just because what is done cannot be undone, and tell you merely to behave henceforth with wholehearted, conscientious sincerity. For conscience must focus on every transgression, like a judge who does not dispose of the documents, when a crime has been sentenced, but records them in the archives in order to sharpen the judgment of justice in new cases of a similar or even dissimilar offense that may appear before him. But to brood over one's remorse and then, when one has already caught on to a different set of attitudes, to make one's whole life useless by continuous self-reproach on account of something that happened once upon a time and cannot be anymore – that would

11:334   be a fantastic notion of deserved self-torture (assuming that one is sure of having reformed). It would be like many so-called religious remedies

---

a *Tugendlehre*

that are supposed to consist in seeking the favor of higher powers without one's even having to become a better human being. That sort of thing cannot be credited in any way to one's moral account.

When your change in attitude has been revealed to your beloved friend – and the sincerity of your words makes it impossible to mistake this – only time will be needed to quench little by little the traces of his indignation (a justified feeling and one that is even based on the concepts of virtue) and to transform his indifference into a more firmly grounded love. If this should fail to happen, the earlier warmth of his affection was more physical than moral and, in view of the transient nature of such a love, would have vanished in time all by itself. That sort of misfortune we encounter often in life, and when we do, we must meet it with composure, since the value of life, insofar as it consists of the enjoyment we can get out of people, is generally over-estimated, whereas life, insofar as it is cherished for the good that we can do, deserves the highest respect and the greatest solicitude in preserving it and cheerfully using it for good ends.[4]

Here then, my friend, you find the customary divisions of a sermon: doctrine, [b] discipline, [c] and solace [d], of which I beg you to pay attention somewhat more to the first two, since the last, and your lost content-ment with life, will surely be recovered by itself when once these others have had their effect.

[b] *Lehre* [c] *Strafe*

[d] *Trost*

---

1 Dating Kant's letter precisely is not possible, but his question to Erhard in a letter of Dec. 21, 1792, Ak. [552], asking whether Miss Herbert had been strenghtened by Kant's letter, provides a clue. Kant had shown Maria's letter to Borowski, remarking that it was far more interesting than many, because of its evident truth and honesty. Vorländer (*Immanuel Kant, Der Mann und das Werk*, II, 118) disagrees with the Akademie edition's dating and thinks Kant's reply was earlier. The importance Kant attached to this reply is shown by his making a precise copy of his letter.

2 One of Kant's favorite sayings, from Diogenes Laertius, V, I, 21. Cf. Kant's discussion of friendship in the *Metaphysics of Morals* (*Tugendlehre*), § 46.

3 Since Kant's *Doctrine of Virtue* was not published till 1797, it seems unlikely that he would here be using the word *Tugendlehre* as a book title.

4 Cf. *Critique of Judgment*, § 83, n. "If the value that life has for us is assessed merely in terms of *what we enjoy* ... that value falls below zero."

138 [515] (483)
From Jacob Sigismund Beck.
May 31, 1792.

Halle, May 31, 1792.

Dearest Herr Professor,

11:338
Today I had the pleasure of making the acquaintance of Herr Hart-knoch[1] personally. He stated that you would permit us to say, in the preface to my abstract of your critical writings, that my book was prepared with your knowledge. That is all well and good, but I am still not entirely at ease. This is my first venture before the public and I must be very judicious in presenting myself as a scholar in my own right if this venture is to do me any good. Would you allow me to send you my manuscript or, if that is too much to ask, would you ask Court Chaplain Schulz on my behalf to examine it? He knows me very well and might be inclined to do this out of friendship for me, at least if you yourself ask him.

I should like to know whether you agree with the following remarks. It seems to me that one ought not to define "intuition," in the Transcendental Aesthetic, as a representation immediately related to an object or as a representation that arises when the mind is affected by the object. For not until the Transcendental Logic can it be shown how we arrive at objective representations. The fact that there are pure intuitions also rules out such a definition. I really do not see where I err when I say: intuition is a thoroughly determinate representation in relation to a given manifold. In this way it also becomes clear to me that mathematics is a science dependent on the construction of concepts. For even in algebra we cannot prove theorems except by means of thoroughly determinate representations. I think we must also take care to distinguish the subjective and objective aspects of sensibility, in order that we may afterward see all the more clearly the unique function of the categories, which confer objectivity on our representations.

Second, I understand quite well that the objects of the sense world must be subjected to the principles of our transcendental faculty of judgment. To see this clearly, let someone try to subsume empirical intuitions under the schemata of the categories; he will see immediately that this is the only way they obtain objectivity; because the question
11:339
"How does it happen that *objects* must conform to those synthetic a priori propositions?" is terminated. For objects are objects only to the extent that their intuition is thought as subjected to the synthetic

connection^a of the schema. For example, I see the validity of the [First] Analogy that states that something permanent must underlie all appearances, because the intuition becomes objective just when I relate the schema of substantiality to that empirical intuition. Consequently the object itself must be subjected to this synthetic connection of substance and accident. But when I ascend to the principle of this whole matter, I find one place where I would gladly have more clarification. I say that the combination of representations in a concept differs from combination in a judgment in that the latter presupposes, in addition to the first synthesis, the further *activity*^{b} of objective relation, that is, the very activity through which one thinks an object. It is in fact quite different if I say "the black man" or "the man is black," and I think one is not incorrect if one says that the representations in a concept are united into a subjective unity of consciousness, whereas those in a judgment are united into an objective unity of consciousness. But I would give a great deal to be able to penetrate more deeply into this matter of the *activity of objective relation* and to form a clearer idea of it. In my last letter I mentioned this point as one that seems to me obscure. Your silence, dearest sir, made me fear that I had uttered some nonsense in connection with this. Yet the more I turn the matter over in my mind, the more I fail to find any error in asking you for instruction, and I beg you for it once more.

[*Kant's marginal remark:* The expression "the black man" means "the man insofar as the concept of him is given as determined in respect to the concept of blackness." But "the man is black" indicates my activity of determining.]

Third, the procedure of the *Critique of Practical Reason* seems extraordinarily illuminating and excellent. It takes its start from the objective practical principle that pure reason, independently of all the material of the will, must acknowledge as binding. This originally problematical concept obtains irrefutable objective reality by means of the fact^c of the moral law. But I confess that, although the transition from synthetic principles of the transcendental faculty of judgment to objects of the sense world (by means of the schemata) is quite clear to me, the transition from the moral law by means of its *typus* is not clear. I would feel myself freed from a burden if you would kindly show me the emptiness of this question: Can't one imagine the moral law commanding something that might contradict its *typus*? In other words, can't there be activities that would be inconsistent with a natural order but that nevertheless are prescribed by the moral law? It is a merely

11:340

---

^{a} *synthetischen Verknüpfung* ^{b} *Handlung*
^{c} *Faktum*

problematical thought, but it has this truth as its basis: the strict necessity of the categorical imperative is in no way dependent on the possibility of the existence of a natural order. Yet it would be a mistake to account for the agreement of the two as accidental.

Please do not be offended, dear teacher, on account of the perhaps obstreperous stance of my letter. I love and revere you inexpressibly and I remain with heart and soul

your
Beck.

---

1 Johann Friedrich Hartknoch (1768–1819), son of the book merchant Hartknoch who had died in 1789.

139 [518] (486)

From Johann Erich Biester.

June 18, 1792.

11:343 I could never truly understand why you, my esteemed friend, insist on submitting your work to the local censorship commission. But I was obedient to your wish and sent the manuscript[1] to Herr Hillmer.[2] He answered me then, to my not inconsiderable amazement, saying that "since it belongs entirely to Biblical theology, he and his colleague Herr Hermes[3] had examined it together and, since the latter *declined* to give his imprimatur, he, Hillmer, concurred with this decision." I wrote to Herr Hermes then and received the reply that "The Religion Edict is here his guiding principle and no further explanation can be given on this matter."

It must enrage everyone that a Hillmer and a Hermes think they are qualified to prescribe to the world whether or not it should read a Kant – This just happened. I am as yet completely in the dark as to what more can be done. But I feel I owe it to myself and to the sciences in our nation to do something against this.[4]

Be well, if you can endure such a corruption of our literature without being upset!

Biester

Berlin
June 18, 1792.

416

1   Kant's essay "Concerning the Conflict of the Good with the Evil Principle for Sovereignty over Man," later published as Book Two of *Religion within the Limits of Reason Alone.*

2   Gottlob Friedrich Hillmer (1756–1835), *Oberkonsistorialrat* and member of the Censorship Commission on Spiritual Affairs.

3   Hermann Daniel Hermes (1731–1807), pastor in Breslau and, from 1791, member of the Censorship Commission.

4   Biester complained to Hermes on June 15 but without success. On June 20 he petitioned the king directly, but again to no avail.

140 [519] (487)
To Prince Alexander von Beloselsky.[1]

Summer 1792.

[*Draft*]

The precious gift which Your Excellency deigned to present to me last summer was properly delivered and I have distributed two copies of it to men who are capable of appreciating its worth. I have not at all forgotten the thanks I owe you all this time, but unavoidable obstacles have made me postpone sending you my gratitude since I wanted also to say something about what I have learned from your gift. Even now I can mention only a few principal features of that.

For a number of years I have been trying to circumscribe the boundary of human speculative knowledge in general, limiting it to just the field of all objects of the senses. For speculative reason, when it ventures beyond this sphere, falls into those "imaginary spaces" – *espaces imaginaires*, as your tableau calls them – where speculative reason has neither ground nor shore, i.e., where absolutely no knowledge is possible for it.

What Your Excellency had in mind, however, was to settle this metaphysical boundary of human cognition, of human reason in its pure speculation – with which I have been occupied for a number of years – from a different, anthropological direction as well, an approach that instructs each individual what the boundaries of his appropriate sphere are and that does this by means of a display chart[a] founded on secure principles, a plan that is as novel and astute as it is attractive and illuminating.

11:344

---

[a] *Demarculum*

417

It is a splendid observation, never properly recognized and never so well worked out, that nature has defined an exclusive sphere for each individual's use of his understanding, a sphere in which he can expand himself, that there are four such spheres and that no one can overstep the bounds of his own without falling into the gaps, all of which are named very appropriately according to their neighboring spheres (leaving aside the sphere that man shares with the animals, namely that of instinct).

11:345 If I may be allowed . . . [2] under the universal genus of Understanding *(l'intelligence universelle)*, the Understanding in a more particular sense *(l'entendement)*, the power of judgment and reason, but then the union of these three faculties with the power of imagination, which constitutes genius . . .

First, the division of the faculty of representation into the mere apprehension of representations, *apprehensio bruta* without consciousness (that is only for the beast) and the sphere of apperception, i.e., of concepts; the latter constitutes the sphere of understanding in general. This is the sphere (1) of *intelligence*, of understanding, i.e., of representing things abstractly through general concepts; (2) the sphere of judging, of representing a particular concretely under the general that contains it, subsuming it according to general rules of the power of judgment; (3) the sphere of insight, *perspicere*, the derivation of the particular from the general, i.e., the sphere of reason. Above these the sphere of imitation, be it an "apprenticeship" of nature itself according to similar laws or be it originality, the imitation of the ideal "transcendence." The latter is either the sphere of the transcendent imagination or that of transcendent reason; i.e., the sphere of the ideal objects of the power of *imagination*, genius, spirit – "esprit" – which, if the forms of imagination contradict nature, are phantoms of the brain, of colossal fantasizing, or, in the sphere of transcendent reason, i.e., of the ideal of reason, they are nothing but empty concepts, if they involve the extension of speculation to things that are not at all objects of sense and that consequently cannot belong to nature. The sphere of enthusiasm [*Schwärmerei*] of those "who rave with reason" (*qui cum ratione insaniunt)*[3] returning the understanding to folly, namely, to the point where its idea is totally incomprehensible.

The instruction I draw from this excellent sketch is the following: Understanding ("*l'entendement*") in the general sense is what one usually refers to as the higher cognitive faculty, as opposed to "*sensualité.*" It is really the faculty of thinking, for "*sensualité*" is the faculty of looking or sensing without thoughts. The sphere of the latter (when there is an absence of understanding) you have very nicely named the sphere of "*betise,*" folly. Under that other sphere (i.e., understanding in the general sense) lies the understanding in the specific sense, the power of judgment, and reason. The first is the power of reason to understand (*"intelligence"*), the second is the power to judge (*"jugement"*), the third the power to comprehend (*"perspicacité"*). Through negligence a person can sometimes fall back from the sphere of understanding into the emptiness of folly or, through exaggeration, into empty sophistry, *"espace imaginaire."* Thus your division into five spheres actually leaves only three for the understanding {*"l'entendement"*). You correctly group together understanding, *l'intelligence*, and the power of judgment in a single sphere, even though they are wholly different powers; because the power of judgment is nothing more than the power of demonstrating one's understanding in concreto; it does not produce new cognitions but merely distinguishes how those that are on hand are to be employed. The name for this is *"bon sens"* which in actual fact depends mainly on the power of judgment. One might say: through understanding we are able to learn (i.e., to grasp rules), through the power of judgment we are able to make use of what we have learned (to apply rules in concreto), through reason we are able to discern how to think of principles for diverse rules. Therefore, if the two first powers under the heading *bon sens* (really the union of *"intelligence"* and *"jugement"*) constitute the first actual sphere of the understanding, then the sphere of reason, the ability to comprehend something, is rightly the second sphere. In that case, however, the sphere of inventing (*"de transcendence"*) is the third. The fourth belongs to the uniting of sensibility with the higher powers, i.e., the discovery, by means of the imagination, of what serves as a rule without being guided by rules, i.e., the sphere of genius, which really cannot be counted as part of the mere understanding.

The sphere of *perspicacité*, discernment, is that of systematic insight into the rational ordering of concepts in a system. The sphere of genius is that of the connection of the former with the originality of sensibility.

11:346

---

1   Alexander von Beloselsky (1757–1809), Russian diplomat and poet, was at this time envoy in Dresden. The work he sent to Kant was called *Dianologie ou tableau philosophique de l'entendement* (Dresden, 1790). Beloselsky divides the understanding (*"l'intelligence universelle"*) into subdivisions, using a series of concentric circles to indicate the various *"spheres."* The lowest circle represents a *"vague d'inertie,"* a "wave of inertia" where there is no structure or organization. Then come five sorts of mental activities, each with its particular subheadings:

I. *Sphere de betise* [folly] (instinct, memoir, sentiment, artifice);

II. *Sphere de simplicité ou de jugement* (intuition, *"sens commun"*, intelligence, *"bon sens"*);

III. *Sphere de raison (perspicuité, conséquence, prudence)*;

IV. *Sphere de perspicacité ou de transcendence (méditation, profondeur, intégralité, philosophie)*;

V. *Sphere d'esprit (sagacité, imagination, goût, génie)*.

Between the individual spheres lie the *"espaces d'erreur,"* and beyond the fifth sphere, *"espaces imaginaires."*

2   Kant's sentence is incomplete.

3   Terence, *Eunuchus* I, i. Cf. Kant's *Anthropologie*, § 43.

141 [520] (488)
To Jacob Sigismund Beck.
July 3, 1792.

11:346   It is certainly not indifference to the questions you posed, treasured friend, that has kept me from answering your latest letter. Rather, there were other tasks to which I had committed myself, and at my age I must not interrupt my reflections on one subject with issues of a 11:347 different sort, for if I do I shall not be able to recover the thread where I left off. –

The difference between the connection of representations in a concept and the connection of representations in a judgment – for example, "the black man" and "the man *is* black" (in other words, "the man *who* is black" and "the man *is* black"), lies, I think, in this: in the first, one thinks of a concept as *determinate;*[a] in the second, one thinks of the activity of my *determining*[b] of this concept. Therefore you are quite right to say that in the *synthesized* concept, the unity of consciousness should be *acknowledged*[c] as *subjectively* given, whereas in the *synthesizing* of concepts the unity of consciousness should be *acknowledged* as *objectively* made; that is, in the first, the man is merely *thought* as black (problematically represented), and in the second, he is *acknowledged* as black. Therefore the question arises, Can I say without contradicting myself: the black man (who is black at a certain time) is white (that is, he is white, has paled, at another time)? I answer no; for in this judgment I carry over the concept of black along with the concept of non-black, since the subject is thought as determinate with regard to

[a] *bestimmt*
[c] *erkannt*

[b] *die Handlung meines Bestimmens*

the first. Consequently, since the subject would be both black and non-black at once, the judgment would unavoidably contradict itself. On the other hand, I can say of the same man, "*He is black*" and also, "*Just this man is not black*" (namely, at some other time, when he has paled), since in both judgments only the activity *of determining*, which here depends on experiential and temporal conditions, is indicated. You will find more of this in the discussion of the principle of contradiction, in my *Critique of Pure Reason*.[1]

As for your definition of intuition as a thoroughly *determinate* representation in respect to a given manifold, I would have nothing further to add except this: the thorough determination here must be understood as objective, not merely as existing in the subject (since it is impossible for us to know all determinations of the object of an empirical intuition). For then the definition would only say that an intuition is the representation of a *given* particular. Now, since nothing composite[d] can *as composite*[e] be given to us – rather, the *composition*[f] [2] of the manifold is something we ourselves must always *produce*[g] – and since too the composition, if it is to conform to the object, cannot be arbitrary,[h] it follows that even if a composite cannot be given, nevertheless the form, i.e., the only form in accordance with which the given manifold can be composed, must be given a priori. This[3] form then is the merely subjective (sensible) aspect of intuition, which is indeed *a priori* but is not *thought* (for only *composition* as activity is a product of thinking); rather it must be *given* in us (space and time) and consequently it must be a *singular* representation and not a concept (a general representation, *repraesentatio communis*). It seems to me a good idea not to spend too much time on the most subtle analysis of elementary representations, for the discussion that follows makes them sufficiently clear through their use.

As for the question, Can there not be actions incompatible with the existence of a natural order but which are yet prescribed by the moral law? I answer, Certainly! If you mean, a *definite order of nature*, for example, that of the present world. A courtier, for instance, must recognize it as a duty always to be truthful, though he would not remain a courtier for long if he did. But there is in that *typus* only the form of a *natural order in general*, that is, the compatibility of actions as events in accord with *moral laws*, and as in accord too with *natural laws*, but only as regards *their generality*, for this in no way concerns the special laws of any particular nature.

But I must close. – I would be pleased to receive your manuscript. I

11:348

---

[d] *Zusammengesetztes*
[f] *Zusammensetzung*
[h] *wilkürlich*

[e] *als ein solches*
[g] *immer selbst machen müssen*

shall go over it with Court Chaplain Schultz as well. – Please thank Prof. Jacob for his letter,[4] and Magister Hoffbauer for sending me his Analytic.[5] Tell them both that I shall soon have the honor of answering their letters. I remain

Your

I. Kant

---

1 See "The Highest Principle of All Analytic Judgments" and "The Transcendental Ideal," *Critique of Pure Reason*, B 189 ff. and B 599 ff.

2 *Zusammensetzung*, as pointed out in earlier letters, e.g., Ak.[33] from Lambert and Ak.[500] to Beck, is sometimes translated "synthesis" or "combination," since Kant, at least in some passages in the *Critique of Pure Reason*, uses the word interchangeably with "synthesis" or the Latin "combinatio."

3 Kant's "this" (*Diese*) could grammatically refer back to *Zusammensetzung*, the composition, or to *Form*. That the latter is his meaning seems clear from the remainder of the sentence.

4 Ak.[502].

5 Johann Heinrich Hoffbauer (1766–1827), *Analytic der Urtheile und Schlüsse mit Anmerkungen meist erläuternden Inhalts* (Halle, 1792). A brief summary may be found in Ak. 13:323.

142 [522] (490)

To Johann Erich Biester.

July 30, 1792.

11:349 Your efforts, worthy friend, to obtain the censor's permission to publish my recent essay[1] in the *Berliner Monatsschrift* have to all appearances impeded its early return to me, which I requested. Now I repeat my request; for I wish to put the piece to another use, and soon. This is all the more necessary since the previous essay must create an unfavorable impression in your journal without the succeeding pieces. But the verdict of your three Inquisitors[2] seems to be irreversible. I therefore urgently beg that my manuscript be returned to me as soon as possible, by regular mail and at my expense, for I have not kept a copy of various marginal notes I made in the text and I would like not 11:350 to lose them.

From my earlier letter you can easily refresh your memory as to why I submitted my work to the Berlin censor: as long as the essays in your *Monatsschrift* (as has heretofore been the case) confine themselves within narrow limits and allow nothing to enter in that, in the private opinion of the censor, could seem offensive to matters of faith, it makes no difference whether they be printed within the royal territories or abroad. But since I had been somewhat worried about this in the case of my essay, if it were to appear in the *Monatsschrift* without the censors' approval, the natural consequence would be that these censors would raise objections, putting obstacles in the way of this detour around their censorship in the future, and they would cite my article (which without doubt they would not fail to slander all around) as justification for their petition to have this detour forbidden. And that would cause me considerable unpleasantness.

Leaving all this aside I shall not neglect to send you very soon, if you like, another essay in place of this one,[3] something entirely on moral philosophy, namely on Herr Garve's recently expressed opinion about my moral principle, in his *Essays*, Part I.[4] I am moreover with immutable esteem and friendship

Your
I. Kant

Königsberg, the 30th of July, 1792.

---

1 Cf. letter Ak. [518], n. 1.
2 Hermes, Hillmer, and Woltersdorf.
3 "On the Proverb: That May Be True in Theory but Is of No Practical Value" (1793).
4 Garve's *Versuche über verschiedene Gegenstände aus der Moral, der Literatur und dem gesellschaftlichen Leben* (1792–7).

143 [523] (491)

From Johann Gottlieb Fichte.

August 6, 1792.

Dear Sir,   11:350
Esteemed Herr Professor,

In a roundabout way (because the *Literatur-Zeitung* arrived very late) I received news of an indefinite sort to the effect that the *Literatur-Zeitung*'s Information Column had identified my essay as a work of *yours*, and that *you* had found it necessary to protest this announcement.[1] I cannot understand how anyone could say such a thing, and I am all the more confused since I know of this matter only vaguely. As flattering as such a misunderstanding must be to me, it frightens me a great deal to think that you or some part of the public could believe that through some indiscretion I myself might have been responsible for an injury to the esteem in which everyone must hold you, and that I might have been even remotely responsible for this occurrence.

I have assiduously tried to avoid anything that might make you regret your good offices – which I acknowledge – with regard to my first attempt at authorship. I have never said anything to anyone at all to contradict your statement that you have read only a small part of my essay and judged the remainder from that sample. Indeed I have said just that, and on many occasions. It eliminated from my Preface the almost imperceptible suggestion that I had been fortunate enough to be favorably judged by you at least in part. (I now wish, alas too late! that I had withdrawn the entire Preface.)

This is the assurance that I wanted to give you – not out of fear that you, without any cause, would view me as indiscreet, but out of the purely respectful desire to inform you about my role in this unpleasant affair. If you think an open declaration on my part is necessary, something that I cannot judge before I am fully informed about the affair and concerning which I beg your kind advice, I have no objection to making such a declaration.

Would you allow the Countess von Krakow, in whose house I spend so many happy days, a bit of curiosity? She asks me to convey her respect (and I think she herself deserves the respect of all the world). What she is curious about is this: she discovered a little while ago in the bishop's garden in Oliva a statue of Justice which had your name inscribed on it. She wanted to know whether you yourself had been there. Although I assured her that she could draw no conclusion from the inscription, since you certainly would never have written your name there, she could not get over the idea that she had been in a place where *you* too had once been, and insists that I ask you about this. I think though that this curiosity has another motive behind it. "If you were once in Oliva," she thinks, "then you might come there again when you have a vacation, and from there you might well come to Krakow." One of her cherished desires is to see you where she is and to give you a few days or even weeks of enjoyment; and I myself believe that she would certainly achieve this second part of her desire if she could have the first part.

I am with warm respect

your most obedient servant,
J. G. Fichte.

Krakow, August 6, 1792.

1 Kant published an "Open Declaration" stating that Fichte, not he, was the author of the *Critique of All Revelation (Versuch einer Kritik aller Offenbarung)*.

144 [526] (494)
To the Theological Faculty in Königsberg.[1]

Late August 1792.

[Draft]

I have the honor of sending to you, highly esteemed sirs, three   11:358
philosophical essays which, along with the essay in the *Berlin Monatsschrift*, make up a whole work. I submit these not to your censorship
but rather to solicit your judgment whether the Theological Faculty
can presume to be the appropriate censorship body for this work, so
that the Philosophical Faculty may exercise its right over this without
objection, in accordance with the title that this work bears. For since
pure philosophical theology is here discussed in relation to biblical
theology, the question being to what extent the former in its own
efforts at textual interpretation may trust itself to approach the latter
and to what extent, on the other hand, reason is inadequate or even
incompatible with the Church's interpretation, this is therefore an
uncontroversial right of that faculty within whose boundaries it re-
stricts itself, a right that does not in any way usurp the authority of
biblical theology. Just as little can one accuse the Faculty of Biblical
Theology of usurping the authority of another discipline when it utilizes as many philosophical ideas as it thinks to be useful to its own
activity or explication.

Even where philosophical theology seems to assume principles contrary to biblical theology, e.g., in regard to the doctrine of miracles, it
asserts and demonstrates that these principles are to be taken as only
subjectively and not objectively valid, i.e., these principles must be
assumed as maxims when we confine ourselves to the counsel of our
(human) reason in theological judgments, whereby miracles themselves
are not denied but are left undisturbed to the biblical theologian so far
as he wishes to make judgments purely in that capacity and rejects all
connection with philosophy.

Since in recent times the interest of biblical theologians as such has   11:359
become a state interest, while at the same time the interest of the

sciences is also an interest of the state insofar as these theologians, as university scholars (and not simply as divines) are not to be neglected, and since one of the faculties, e.g., the philosophical, is not to be restricted for the sake of the presumed advantage of the other faculty but, on the contrary, each is bound and authorized to extend itself, it is therefore manifest that, if it be determined that a written work belongs to biblical theology, the commission appointed to censor this field has the competence to censor, but if this has not yet been decreed and doubts have been raised about it, in that case the faculty of a *university* (which institution bears that name because one of its duties is to see that a given discipline does not extend itself to the disadvantage of another) to which the division of biblical theology belongs is the only institution having the competence to judge whether a work is usurping the territory of one of the disciplines entrusted to it or not and, in the latter case, if it finds no basis for the charge, the work's censorship must fall under that faculty to which the work itself claims to belong.

---

1   Another draft of this letter is reprinted in Ak. 13: 326, ff. The Theological Faculty in Königsberg declared that Kant's *Religion within the Bounds of Reason Alone* could be evaluated by a philosophical faculty. Kant then sent the manuscript to the philosophical faculty of the University of Jena, whose *Dekan* bestowed the imprimatur. Had Kant submitted it to his own university the decision would have been made by his friend Kraus who was then *Dekan* of the philosophical faculty. That was repugnant to Kant.

145 [527] (495)
From Jacob Sigismund Beck.
September 8, 1792.

Dearest Herr Professor,

You gave me permission to send you my manuscript and I now take advantage of that kind offer. Since I have composed it with great care and have spared no effort at reflection, I find I have the courage to submit it to you. As far as most of the difficulties that bothered me are concerned – I have already told you about some of them – I have managed gradually to overcome them for myself. I rediscover daily that even in the sciences honesty is the best policy, for every time I persuaded myself that I had understood something in the *Critique* which I really had not, this just delayed even longer my reaching my goal. These copy-books of my *Abstract of the Critique of Pure Reason* cover the material up to the Transcendental Dialectic. I had completed it once, but progress in my studies and the enlightenment I gained thereby made me want to discard my whole work and start over again. I must apologize for one bit of rudeness. I wrote out the manuscript as legibly as I could, but it was impossible to have it transcribed, since the people who do this work are soldiers and they are now stationed in France.

11:360

And so, dear, precious teacher, I certainly cannot expect that you will go over the whole of my scribbling yourself. But I must ask you the favor of looking over those pages that deal with the Deduction of the Categories and the Principles, for I am most concerned about these; please show me what I have misinterpreted or what I have not presented the way you wish. The printer demands that the manuscript reach him within eight weeks, so I must ask that you send it back by the end of November.

There is still a question I should like to put to you.[1] It is prompted by your *Critique's* extraordinarily illuminating remark that one can think of a space as entirely filled with matter and at the same time postulate an infinite gradation of the real[a] in space.[2] I have never been able to understand the kind of explanation Kästner,[3] Karsten[4] and others give, namely that we must think of matter as constituted by homogeneous molecules of equal gravity in order to explain the differences in weights of the same volume of different substances. The Critical Philosophy enlightened me on this point beyond measure. To explain that phenomenon to myself I came up with the following account: The earth attracts every body on its surface, as it is in turn attracted by every such body. But the body's attractive effect[b] on* the earth is infinitely small in comparison with the effect that the earth has on the body, and that is the reason why the heights of fall of bodies in vacuo[5] are exactly equal. If I suspend two bodies of equal volume from a balance, bodies in which we assume no empty spaces at all, then the effect that the earth has on both bodies will be neutralized; but the forces with which both bodies attract the earth remain

---

* on a part of the earth equal in mass to the body, but on the whole earth it [the attractive force] is equal [i.e., the same as the attractive effect of the earth on the body]; the velocity, however, that it [the attractive effect] imparts on the earth is different [than the velocity that the earth imparts on the body].

[a] *das Reale*　　　　　　　　　　[b] *Wirkung*

11:361   the same and it is now these forces alone that stand in a certain ratio. In vacuo, the ratio of the forces that make both bodies fall toward the earth = a + dx: a + dy = a:a, that is, a ratio of equality; but at the balance this becomes = dx : dy, a ratio different from one. But certainly if we were to raise both bodies, e.g., to the distance of the moon, their respective heights of fall would no longer be equal. Am I possibly right about this?

Magister Rath[6] asked me to convey the enclosed letter to you. He would like to translate the *Critique* into Latin and wants your permission. Since you are wholly unacquainted with this man, let me say a few words about him. He is not young but a man between 30 and 40. What motivates him to be an author is a pure love of science and this love, along with his intellectual honesty, has kept him from the sort of writing others pursue in order to make a quick name for themselves. I have heard his knowledge of ancient languages praised by people who are themselves experts. And I know of his success in studying the Critical Philosophy from my own close association, which has given me the rare opportunity to share my thoughts pleasurably with another human being.

This coming winter I shall be giving public lectures on practical philosophy, a prospect that delights me since I shall certainly end up wiser than when I begin.

I close herewith and commend myself to your Grace with respect and affection.

Your,

Beck.

[Kant's comments on Beck's letter]

The greatest difficulty is to explain how a definite volume of matter is possible when its parts are attracting each other in proportion to the inverse square of [i.e., inversely with the square of] their distances from each other, and when these parts are, at the same time, repelled from each other in proportion to the inverse [i.e., inversely with the] cube of these distances (hence in proportion to the volume itself), the repulsion affecting, however, only the contiguous parts (not the more distant ones). This is [difficult to explain] because the attractive power depends
11:362   on the density, but the density itself depends on the attractive power.[7] Furthermore, density[8] depends on the inverse[9] ratio of the repulsive forces, i.e., on the inverse ratio of the volumes. – Now the question is: if I consider a certain quantity of matter in isolation, a quantity of matter in which all of the parts attract each other, whatever their distance, according to the aforementioned law but whose parts repel

428

each other with a still greater force, is there a definite limit to the extension of that object, a point where attraction and repulsion are balanced; or, if, for a certain density, the repulsion is greater than the attraction, would not the repulsion remain greater with larger extension up to infinite distances? The decrease of the repulsion with the cube of the distance seems to support the former hypothesis. Now one can imagine many such aggregates separated from each other, each of which so to speak serves its own purposes, and which attract each other, thus increasing their density, but whose coming closer to each other, if it resulted from a certain original low-density state of the universe by a sudden release [letting the aggregates move freely], would bring about a perpetual concussion whereby the different aggregates of matter could form certain enduring lumps that were connected, i.e., which could have an attraction, an attraction not arising from the combined attraction of all their parts but only from the contiguous parts, so that this [attraction] would result not from pull but from pressure.

The forces with which those two bodies would attract the earth would always give the same velocity to the earth because, though the mass of the earth is greater, when they together pull [attract] the earth, they impress a greater pull on the earth, but to the same extent their own distance from the earth is reduced (because of the greater mass of the earth), which distance remains always the same as long as the common center of gravity remains only infinitesimally different from the center of the earth. – In order to explain the difference of densities one must assume that the same attractive force of a given quantity of matter operates against an infinitely variable repulsive force, but that the former [attraction] could not balance the latter [repulsion] (or the former could not bring about the reaction necessary to limit the extension of the isolated quantity of matter) if it [the attractive force] did not affect the whole universe. Since the attractive force, however, diminishes with the square of the distance, it [the attractive force] could not, because of the pressure exerted by the attracted matter [from all the rest of the universe], balance any given compression, were it not that the repulsion diminishes in proportion to the inverse of the cube of the distance. Since the cohering [of matter] cannot be explained by any pressuring forces, it can be accounted for only by the difference in quality of different matters, namely their different repulsive forces; for it is possible to conceive of repulsion without assuming that the repelling object is in a state of motion, consequently also without assuming difference in masses in objects of the same volume.[10] For this reason differences in quantity of different kinds of matter can be measured only by impact or pull and by means of a common measure, namely the pull of the earth. Hence it is not the number of the parts of

11:363

heterogeneous matters that allows us to measure the density in a given volume, but their weight.

The difficulty here is that one needs to keep in mind that which moves, but in experience, all one determines are the forces that act at or from a [given] place (forces that fill a space only to a certain degree), or [one determines] the distance from the center of one force to that of another force. But since points cannot occupy[11] a space (not individual points, thus not large numbers of them together either) so one cannot estimate the quantity of substance in a body by comparing the number of parts in one body with the number in others; and yet one has to conceive of them [the bodies] as homogeneous and as differing only in the number of their parts, for that is the only way we can make sense of the relation of different masses.

The quantity of matter in the same volume is to be measured neither by the resistance of the expansive force against compression, nor by a sling stone, i.e., by the resistance against the centrifugal force of the attraction of a thread. The former is ruled out because a small quantity of matter exerts just as much resistance by its expansive force as does a large quantity; the latter is ruled out because the volume determines nothing with regard to a body's dislocation. Rather, what provides the measure is the locomotive force in a scale (assuming equal volumes), or the locomotive force in the expansion or compression of an elastic or cohesive body, and hence the overcoming of a moment of the dead force (in the same volume) by the tendency of the body and of all its parts to move in the same direction.

11:364   The filling of a space is possible only by other spaces, not by points: neither by putting them side by side nor by a force that extends out into the space from every point, in which there would be no other similar point centers. Therefore, the impenetrability of matter does not properly imply that the substances are a collection of separate independently existing things, but only implies that separate things have certain spheres of activity, which are present in every point of a given space but not by filling that space. The points of attraction properly contain the substance. The attractive forces are equal in all points, but in each point the substance (as compared to other substances) is determined by the power of repulsion which can be different in that point; and the [quantity of] substance is greater, the smaller the repulsive forces of that same matter are, hence the density of the matter is [so much] greater. – Actually, only the body insofar as it fills space is the substance given immediately to the senses. But since this filling [of space] itself would not be actual (it would have to be by mere repulsion in empty space), and the attraction would make everything coalesce into a single point, it follows that the measure of the quantity of matter is the substance insofar as it has attractive force, because in it everything would be internal [*innerlich*] and within a single point, and what is external has to be measured, not again by something external but, eventually, by that which is internal, [and] which has the same external effect as that which is external.

If there were no repulsive force in a [given] space, there would also be no substance there that could pull, because it would not fill any space. One could, however, imagine a repulsive force filling a space [i.e., a substance] that would not be limited by the attractive force of its own parts but rather by external pressure; this could not, however, go on ad infinitum. Thus, the volume is determined by the repulsive force alone. – Thus, if we want to distinguish different densities we have first to conceive of the volumes as determined by repulsion. However, we are not thereby informed about the resistance that one kind of matter shows as against another that tries to move it from its place. We learn about this [resistance] therefore only from the attraction that the matter contained in a volume exerts on other bodies external to it (the earth) and which thereby brings about its own movement (through gravity). The greater the repulsion that is necessary to prevent a body from getting closer (to the earth), the more substance is contained in a given volume. One has to conceive of the attraction, however, as limited to a volume only by repulsion; hence the attraction by itself is always the same. We do not have to think of the volume as restricted by something external to it; we can think of it   11:365 as restricted by the attraction of its own parts – that the repulsion in a volume, whose inner parts do not pull each other, is brought about from outside [the volume] can be explained by the fact that the parts *do not repel each at a distance*, whereas they can attract each other directly at a distance: on the other hand it is impossible that the parts should attract each other only on contact, for this[12] already requires a repulsion, hence it presupposes a volume, and not merely a plane.

The degree of repulsion does not increase when the volume is increased continuously, but the degree of attraction does, and this is because in the former case the parts inside the volume cancel their respective motions and the expansive force acts only on the surface [of the volume] (the repulsion does not act at a distance), while the attractive forces [of the inner parts of the volume], on the other hand, will increase the external force by increasing the volume. Therefore the total force of a substance is to be estimated according to its attraction. The attractive force has to be regarded as uniform because by itself it would not constitute any matter at all; and because it is determined only by compression, which in turn is the same everywhere within a volume, it follows that the resulting density has to be equal. The repulsive force, on the other hand, can be originally different in a given volume. Since the density can vary infinitely in degree, and since this

431

cannot be due to any original difference in the attractive force, it follows that the density must depend on repulsion. Put differently: since the degree of repulsion depends on the differences in external compression, the degree of repulsion is not determined internally [to the volume] and can become variously greater or smaller.

One can give no reason why a given quantity of matter must originally have a certain density. – This question cannot be asked about an object whose volume is less than a certain amount. That the attractive force is not greater, or even as great or small as one wishes, does not depend on it itself, but on repulsion: the smaller the repulsion, the greater the density that results from the attractive force. The difference in density of a given quantity of matter, however, does not result from its own attraction, since that is too weak, but from the attraction of the whole universe.

---

1   The translator thanks Professor Alexander Rüger for assistance with the rest of this letter and with Ak.[537] and [545], letters whose translation requires knowledge not only of German and philosophy but of debates in physics in the eighteenth-century.

2   Cf. *Critique of Pure Reason*, B 214 ff., "Anticipations of Perception." Kant argues against scientists who claim "the real in appearances [i.e., matter] to be uniform, differing only in aggregation and extensive magnitude." (A 175=B 216.) All appearances are continuous magnitudes, he argues; no part of them is the smallest possible.

3   Abraham Gotthelf Kästner, *Anfangsgründe der angewandten Mathematik*, Part II, Section I, § 8 ff. (Göttingen, 1792).

4   Wenzeslaus Johann Gustav Karsten (1732–87), professor of physics and mathematics in Halle, *Lehrbuch der gesamten Mathematik*, part 3, § 5, ff. (Greifswald, 1790).

5   "in equal times," Beck must mean.

6   Rudolph Gottlob Rath, rector of a *Gymnasium* in Halle. In his letter to Rath Oct. 16, 1792, Ak.[536], Kant gives his blessings to the proposed Latin translation.

7   I.e., Density = mass/volume; mass is the source and measure of gravitational attraction. Thus, attraction depends on density (mass) and density (mass) is measured in terms of attractive power. (This is Alexander Rüger's suggested explanation.)

8   I.e., the densities of different substances.

9   According to Rüger Kant is in error here; density depends on the ratio of the repulsive forces. I.e., density 1: density 2 = volume 2: volume 1 = repulsive force 1: repulsive force 2.

10   Kant claims that objects of the same density (= same mass in the same volume) can have different repulsive forces.

11   Eckart Förster's suggestion for "einen Raum einnehmen können." Kant distinguishes between occupying and filling a space. A shadow, e.g., may occupy without filling a space. (The distinction is drawn in Kant's *Metaphysische Anfangsgründe*.)

12   "this contact" or "this attraction"; the grammar of Kant's sentence is here too vague to decide.

146 [536] (-)
To Rudolph Gottlob Rath.[1]
October 16, 1792.

Noble Sir,
Esteemed Magister,   11:374

It has long been my wish that someone might turn up whose knowledge of language and subject-matter were adequate to translate the *Critique* into Latin. A certain professor in Leipzig,[2] a man competent   11:375 in both ways, agreed to do this some years ago, but presumably (or so the late Herr Hartknoch thought) because of other pressing business that he had to undertake to augment his limited income, he abandoned the project. Professor Schütz in Jena, to whom this intention was conveyed at that time, thought that this Leipzig professor's writing might be too refulgent with authentic Latin elegance which could easily detract from the intelligibility of the book; Schütz himself was willing to oversee the translation at that time but for the reasons indicated this never came about.

From the sample that you were kind enough to include with your letter I can see that you avoid very well the difficulty I mentioned while at the same time you do not render the work unintelligible with Germanisms, the way Germans often do. Since you have made such a persevering study of this book I have just as complete a trust in your insight into its meaning.

Begin this labor confidently then, worthy man. Perhaps your acquaintance with these matters will make the job go more quickly than you expect, so that I shall still live to see its publication.

I add my wish for your good health and the flourishing of all your other projects and am with the most complete respect

your most devoted servant

Königsberg, the 16th of October, 1792.   I. Kant

1 Rath (1758–1814) was rector of the *Gymnasium* in Halle and a friend of J. S. Beck's.

2 Friedrich Gottlob Born (1743–1807), *außerordentlicher* professor of philosophy in Leipzig. See his letter to Kant, May 7, 1786, Ak.[269]. Born's *Immanuelis Kantii opera ad philosophiam criticam* only appeared in 1796.

147 [537] (504)
To Jacob Sigismund Beck.
October 16 (17), 1792.

Treasured friend,

I mailed back your manuscript the day before yesterday, October 15, wrapped in gray paper, sealed, and labeled To Magister Beck, but too hastily, as I now see. For my memory deceived me so that I thought

11:376 that the date by which you needed to have it back was the end of October rather than November, and in my eagerness not to miss the next postal departure I neglected to reread your letter to confirm this date. And since in browsing through the first pages of your *Deduction* of the Categories and Principles I had nothing important to say, I just left it in your good hands.

This mistake can still be remedied, if you think it necessary, by having the relevant pages quickly transcribed and sent to me by courier (at my expense, of course) so that my answer will still get back to you before the deadline. – In my judgment everything depends on this: since, in the empirical concept of *something composite*[a] the composition[b] itself cannot be given or represented by means of mere intuition and its apprehension, but can only be represented by means of the *self-active connection*[c] of the manifold given in intuition – that is, it can be represented only in a consciousness in general (which again is not empirical) – it follows that this connection and its functioning under a priori[1] rules, rules that constitute the pure thought of an object in general (the pure concept of the understanding) must be in the mind. The apprehension of the manifold must be subject to this pure concept of the understanding insofar as it constitutes *one* intuition and insofar

[a] *des Zusammengesetzten* [b] *Zusammensetzung*
[c] *selbsttätige Verbindung*

as it [the pure concept] constitutes the condition of all possible experiential knowledge of what is composite (or of what belongs to what is composite, i.e., something that requires a synthesis), experiential knowledge that is expressed by means of these principles. It is commonly supposed that the representation of a composite as such is *given*, included with the representation of the apprehended manifold, and that thus it does not entirely belong, as however it really must, to spontaneity, etc.

I was very pleased by your insight concerning the importance of the physics question about the varying density of matter that has to be conceivable if one disallows any appeal to empty interstices in explaining this. For very few people seem even to have understood the question properly. I think the solution to this problem lies in this: the attraction (the universal, Newtonian attraction) is originally equal in all matter; it is only the repulsive force that varies in different kinds of matter, and this is what determines differences in density. But this solution seems to lead to a kind of circularity.[2] I cannot see how to escape from this circularity and I must give it more thought.

11:377

Your own solution to the problem will not be satisfactory to you either if you just consider the following. – You say that the effect that a small body has on the whole earth is infinitely small compared to the attractive effect of the earth on that body. What you in fact should have said is: compared to the effect that this small body has on another body of *similar* (or *smaller*) size; for, to the same extent that the small body attracts the whole earth, the former will be set in motion (it will receive a certain velocity) by the earth's resistance [against attraction], a velocity that is just equal to the velocity that the small body would receive from the attraction of the earth alone, so that the small body's velocity is just twice the velocity that it [the body] would achieve in case it did not itself attract the earth. The earth, on the other hand, would have received a velocity through the resistance of the body that the earth attracts, [a velocity] twice as large as it would have received from that body alone if the earth itself did not have any attractive force. – But perhaps I have not fully understood your way of explaining this problem; I would be grateful for a more detailed explication.

By the way, I wonder whether you could shorten your extract, though without detracting from its completeness, in such a way that the book could serve as a basis for lectures. That would be highly advantageous to your publisher and to you too, especially since the *Critique of Practical Reason* is included. But I fear that the Transcendental Dialectic will take up a fair amount of space. However I leave all this to your discretion and I am with true friendship and esteem,

Your

most devoted servant

I. Kant

Königsberg   16 October, 1792

---

1 The placement of the word "a priori" makes it modify either "rules" or "in the mind."

2 Since Kant was worried about the circularity of making difference in density a function of difference in repulsive force of different kinds of matter, he must have thought that difference in repulsive force is a function of density. Attraction, in Newtonian physics, is the same for all substances, so that it cannot explain difference in densities. (The translator again expresses thanks to Professor Alexander Rüger for assistance here.)

148 [540] (507)

To Ludwig Ernst Borowski.

October 24, 1792.[1]

11:379   Your friendly idea of bestowing a public honor on me, dear sir, deserves my wholehearted gratitude, but at the same time it embarrasses me greatly. For, on the one hand, I am by nature inclined to avoid anything that looks like pomp (partly also because the eulogizer commonly brings out the faultfinder) and for this reason I would prefer to decline the honor intended for me; but on the other hand I can well imagine that it may not please you to have undertaken such an extended piece of work in vain.

11:380   If this project can still be set aside, you would thereby save me from a genuine unpleasantness, and if your effort were viewed as a *collection of materials for a posthumous biography* it would not be entirely in vain. But I would most urgently and earnestly object to the publication of these materials while I am still alive.[2]

With *that in mind* I have taken the liberty of striking out or altering certain words, as you gave me permission to do. The reason for these changes would require too much discussion here and I shall indicate it

436

to you orally when I have the chance. The parallel[3] that is drawn between Christian morality and my proposed philosophical morality, on the page before the last three (where I have made a crease in the paper), could be altered by a few words so that instead of those names [Christ and Kant], the first of which is hallowed while the other is by comparison that of a pathetic bungler trying to interpret the former as well as he can, one could use the expressions ["Christian morality" and "philosophical morality"] just quoted. For otherwise the comparison of the two [moralities] may be offensive to some people.[4]

I remain, with fullest respect and friendship,

your most devoted, loyal servant

I. Kant

Königsberg, the 24th of October, 1792.

---

1 On Oct. 12, 1792, Borowski sent Kant his manuscript, "Sketch for a future Biography" – *Skizze zu einer künftigen zuverlässigen Biographie des preussischen Weltweisen Immanuel Kant* was the full title, when the piece was eventually published along with biographical essays by Jachmann and Wasianski in 1804. The present letter, and Borowski's reply, were printed as part of the Preface.

2 Borowski did as Kant requested. He responded immediately in a letter of Oct. 24, 1792, Ak.[541], and assured Kant that no "urgent and earnest" request was necessary to secure his compliance. He would put aside the manuscript entirely and hope that if he should die before Kant a worthy biographer might be found.

3 The "parallel" drawn by Borowski, to which Kant refers, is: ". . . they [the young theologians] are convinced by his [i.e., Kant's] lectures that his morality in particular does not contradict Christian moral teachings, even if that precise harmony between the two, of which so many people persuade themselves, may not exist, i.e., that Christ and the Apostles say exactly the same thing that Kant says. It cannot be denied that in its results the Kantian doctrine of virtue agrees completely with the Christian; the motives for the latter are different, and so are its popularity and comprehensibility." L. E. Borowski (and R. B. Jachmann and A. Ch. Wasianski), *Immanuel Kant, sein Leben in Darstellungen von Zeitgenossen* (Darmstadt, 1978 edition), pp. 41, f.

4 Borowski quotes Kant's self-deprecating remark in a footnote, citing it as evidence of Kant's modesty.

149 [545] (512)
From Jacob Sigismund Beck.
November 10, 1792.

Worthiest Herr Professor,

11:384

I received your friendly letter of October 17 and then, a few days later, my returned manuscript. Allow me to send you once again those pages of it that deal with the Deduction of the Categories. I have had them transcribed and I include them here and I ask you most humbly to be so kind as to show me where I may have failed to hit your meaning. The printing is not scheduled until about the end of November, so a response from you in four weeks' time would not be too late.

Professor Garve was here a while ago, and Professor Eberhard told me something of his conversations with him about the Critical Philosophy. He says that even though Garve strongly defends the *Critique* he was still forced to admit that Critical Idealism and Berkeleyan Idealism are entirely the same. I cannot understand the way these worthy men think and I am in truth convinced of the opposite opinion. Even if we assume that the *Critique* should not even have mentioned the distinction between things in themselves and appearances, we would still have to recall that one must pay attention to the conditions under which something is an object. If we ignore these, we fall into error. Appearances are the objects of intuition, and they are what everybody means when they speak of objects that surround them. But it is the reality of just these objects that Berkeley denied and that the *Critique*, on the other hand, proved. If one once sees that space and time are the conditions of the intuition of objects and then considers what the conditions of the thinking of objects are, one sees easily that the dignity that representations acquire in referring to objects consists in the fact that thereby the synthesis of the manifold is thought as necessary. This determination of thought is, however, the same as the function in a judgment. In this way the contribution of the categories to our cognition has become clear to me, in that the investigation has made me see that they are the concepts through which the manifold of a sensuous intuition is presented as necessarily (valid for everyone) grasped together. Certain summarizers, as I see it, have expressed themselves incorrectly on this matter. They say, "To judge means to connect objective representations." It is quite another thing when the *Critique* tells us: To judge is to bring representations to an objective unity of consciousness, through which the activity of synthesis, represented as necessary, is expressed.

11:385

I would feel reassured if I could infer from my own conviction about these matters that my *Abstract* has captured your meaning. The presentation of the Deduction of the Categories went extremely well for me and I would be very grateful, dear teacher, if you would inspect it. In the meantime I shall keep reworking the whole MS so that what I publish will be as sensible a book as I can produce.

Allow me to raise my recent physics question one more time.[1] For a long time, before I really studied the *Critique*, I used to confuse in my mathematical readings the established (but for me always hard to grasp) concept of mass*a*. and the concept of the efficacious. Euler now gives us a definition of mass insofar as he calls it *vis inetiæ qua corpus in statu suo perseverare, qua omni mutationi reluctari conatur* [mass = the force of inertia with which a body seeks to remain in its state of motion and with which it resists every change], and by endowing [different] particles of matter with a different *vis inertiæ* he seems to explain the unequal weights of two bodies having the same volume without his having to have recourse to [the idea of] empty space. On the other hand, it does seem to be the case that all parts of matter are endowed with an equal quantity of inertia [*quantitas inertiæ*] since their fall-distances in equal times in a vacuum are the same. But then, if one is to explain the different weights of similar volumes [of matter] one is forced to have recourse to empty pores.*b* I have tried to resolve this problem for myself in the following manner: Let a = the attractive force of the earth in a particular region of its surface acting on a particular volume which we will consider to be filled with matter; the attractive forces of two bodies of a volume equal to the previous one and also filled throughout, acting on the earth, we call dx and dy, which I can view as differentials since I am considering them in relation to a.* Since I have in mind the mutual attraction of these bodies on the earth and of the earth on them, I can add up the forces and say that the earth attracts the one body with a force equal to a + dx, while it attracts the other body with a force equal to a + dy. From this it follows, however, that the fall-distances of the two bodies in a resistance-free space must be equal, since the ratio a + dx : a + dy is a ratio of equality. But on the scales, a against a would cancel out and there would remain the ratio dx : dy, which can well be a ratio of inequality even if a + dx : a + dy = 1:1. If I have made a gross error I beg you to forgive me.

Hartknoch has asked me via the printer Grunert to arrange to have

11:386

---

* The notion of these forces needs to be grounded on something. I ground it on the distances that are traversed in unit time.

a Masse   *b poris* my book announcement published in the *Literaturzeitung*. But it cannot be a matter of indifference either to him or to me whether this announcement mentions that you know about this book – for there are so many abstracts of the *Critique* published under so many titles that a mere announcement of one under my name may not be noticed at all. Would you perhaps allow me to mention your name in the announcement?[2] If so, I beg you to be so kind as to *specify the words* that would refer to you. I should like to entitle this book, *Explanatory Abstract from the Critical Writings of Professor Kant*,[3] and devote the second volume of this work to an abstract of the *Critique of Judgment* and an explanatory presentation of the *Metaphysical Foundations of Natural Science*. What do you think of this?

With the greatest respect and affection, I am

your

Beck

---

1 For assistance with the translation of the remainder of this letter, the translator again wishes to thank Prof. Alexander Rüger.

2 The announcement appeared in the *Intelligenzblatt* of the *A.L.Z.*, Feb. 16, 1793, without any special recommendation by Kant.

3 The full title of the published work is *Erläuternde Auszug aus den kritischen Schriften des Herrn Prof. Kant auf Anraten desselben*, the words "prepared in Consultation with the Same" (*auf Anraten desselben*) appended to satisfy Beck's request. The publisher was Hartknoch, in Riga, 1796. An English translation of Volume Three, containing Beck's "The Standpoint from which Critical Philosophy Is to Be Judged" has been published by George di Giovanni (*Between Kant and Hegel. Texts in the Development of Post-Kantian Idealism* (Albany, NY: State University of New York Press, 1985).

150 [548] (515)
From Salomon Maimon.
November 30, 1792.

11:389 Worthiest man,

Though I have received no answer from you to my previous two letters, may that not deter me from taking up my pen once more, since I seek only *instruction* from you. For, besides the fact that your failure to respond can be explained by your venerable age which all the world appreciates and by the overwhelming importance of your completing your immortal works, so as to further the critical project, I also suspect a kind of *displeasure* with my conduct, which I can only now understand.

My first letter concerned my comparison between Bacon's attempts and your own immortal attempts to bring about the *reformation of the sciences*. I not only believe but am entirely *convinced* that my comparison was *entirely devoid of partisanship*. In retrospect, however, this comparison itself might have been presented with greater *precision* and more *detail*. I remark there that while the two methods are in themselves *opposed*, both are nevertheless *indispensable* for the completion of scientific knowledge. The one method gets ever closer to the thoroughly defined, necessary and universally valid principle, by means of an *ever more complete induction*, without hoping ever to reach those principles completely in this way. 11:390

The other method seeks these principles in the original constitution of our cognitive power and installs them for future employment. Similarly, it does this without any hope of extending that employment to empirical objects as such.

Whatever Herr Reinhold may say, the Critical Philosophy is, in my opinion, both a *pure science* in itself and an *applied science* (however far its use may extend) which you have already brought to *completion*.

In my second letter, I expressed displeasure with Herr Reinhold's procedure. This penetrating philosopher keeps trying to show that your principles are not thoroughly defined and fully developed; his efforts to alleviate this supposed deficiency inevitably keep him *constantly revolving in a circle*.

His Principle of Consciousness already presupposes your deduction. Consequently it cannot be laid down as an *original fact* of our power of cognition, to serve as the foundation of this deduction. This is what I have shown (in the *Magazin zur Erfahrungsseelenkunde*, 9th volume, 3rd issue). And now, since I have read the second part of his *Letters*[1] I notice that his concept of *free will* leads to a totally inexplicable *indeterminism*.

You posit *free will* in the hypothetically assumed *causality of reason*. According to him, on the other hand, the *causality of reason* would in itself be a *necessity of nature*. He therefore explains free will as "a power of a person himself, with regard to the satisfying or frustrating of the selfish drive, to decide either *in accordance* or *in opposition* to the promotion of unselfishness." He does not bother about the question of the *determining ground* of the will in the slightest. But I don't want to detain you with this any longer.

My present wish is only to receive *instruction* from you on the

11:391   important point in your *Transcendental Aesthetic*, namely the deduction of the representations of time and space. I am fully convinced by everything you say there against the *dogmatic* approach to the problem. But there is still, to my mind, a possibility of *skepticism*, supported by psychological grounds. This too deviates somewhat from your view, though the *consequences* which can be drawn from it may not differ from your own.

You maintain that the representations of space and time are forms of sensibility, that is, necessary conditions of the manner in which objects of sense are represented in us.

I maintain on the contrary (on psychological grounds) that this is not universally true. Homogeneous objects of sense are represented by us neither in space nor in time. We can represent them in space and time only mediately, by means of a comparison with heterogeneous objects with which those homogeneous objects are bound up spatio-temporally. Time and space are thus forms of the diversity of [things represented by] sensibility, not forms of sensibility as such. The appearance of red or green is not represented in time or space any more than a concept of the understanding as such is thus represented. But we can represent a comparison of red with green and we can imagine the coexistence or succession of red and green only in space and time.

Time and space are therefore not representations of the properties and relations of things in themselves – as the critical philosophy has already demonstrated against the dogmatic philosophy. But neither are they conditions of the way in which objects-of-sense-in-themselves, prior to their comparison with each other, are represented in us. What are they then? They are conditions of the possibility of a comparison between objects of sense, that is, of the possibility of a judgment as to their relation to each other. Let me explain:

1. Different representations cannot coexist in the same subject at the same time (at exactly the same instant).

2. Every judgment concerning the relation of objects to each other presupposes the existence of a representation of each of them in the mind. The question therefore arises, *How is a judgment regarding the*

11:392   *relation of objects to each other possible?* – for example, the highly evident judgment that *red differs from green*? The individual representations of red and green would have to precede this judgment in the mind. But since they cannot be in the mind of one and the same subject at exactly the same moment, and the judgment nevertheless relates to both of them, uniting them in consciousness, the possibility of this judgment is inexplicable. Certain psychologists appeal to "traces" at this point, but to no avail. For the "traces" of different representations can no more occur simultaneously in the mind than can the representations themselves, if they are to retain their distinctness.

Only by means of the idea of a temporal succession, therefore, is this judgment possible.

Even if we ignore what objects are represented in it, a temporal succession is intrinsically a *unity in diversity.*[a] The earlier point of time is thus *as such a point distinguished* from the succeeding one. They are therefore not *analytically the same*, and yet neither one can be represented without the other. Thus they constitute a *synthetic unity.* The idea of a temporal succession is thus a necessary condition not of the possibility of *objects in themselves* (even of sensible objects) but rather of the possibility of a *judgment concerning their diversity.* Without [the idea of] temporal succession, such diversity could not be an object of our cognition.

On the other hand, *objective diversity* is a condition of the possibility of *temporal succession*, not only as object of our cognition, but also as object of intuition as such (since temporal succession is conceivable[b] only if this[2] becomes an object of our knowledge). The *form of diversity* (also *objective diversity itself*) and the idea of temporal succession are thus mutually related. If red were not, as an appearance as such, *different* from green, we could not represent them in a temporal succession. But had we no idea of such a temporal succession, we could never *recognize* them [as different] even if they *were* different objects of intuition.

This same relationship exists also between the form of *diversity*[c] and the representation of spatial separation.[d] The latter cannot be without the former. The former cannot be *recognized* by us without the latter.

The diversity of outer appearances is represented in time only if it is not represented in space, and vice versa. One and the same sensible substance (for example, this tree) is represented as *different from itself* (changed) in time, not in space. Distinct sensible substances are *as such* represented as distinct in space, not in time (in that the judgment of their distinctness connects them together in one and the same moment of time).

The form of time thus does not belong to all objects of outer intuition without distinction but only to those that are not represented in space; and vice versa, the form of space belongs only to those outer objects that are not represented in time (in a *temporal succession*, for the property of being simultaneous is not, I maintain, a *positive* time-determination but merely the *negation of the idea of temporal succession*).

These considerations border on my discussion of *transcendental illusion* (in the article, *Fiction*, in my *Philosophisches Wörterbuch*). I await

11:393

---

[a] *Einheit im Mannigfaltigen*   [b] *vorstellbar*
[c] *Verschiedenheit*   [d] *Aussereinanderseyns im Raum*

your assessment of them with the greatest eagerness, but I shall not detain you longer here.

Worthiest man! Since your reply to this letter is of the highest importance to me, since it will remove the skeptical obstacles in the way of my intellectual progress, pointing me in the right direction, and since I dedicate my whole life purely to the discovery of truth, my straying down the wrong path must at least be deserving of correction; I therefore beseech you, yes, I implore you *in the name of the holiness of your moral philosophy*ᵉ not to deny me this response. Awaiting this, I remain with highest esteem and sincere friendship

your most devoted
Salomon Maimon.

P.S. If your answer cannot be a thorough one, I would still appreciate your pointing me more or less in the right direction. Your letter can be addressed to me personally.³

ᵉ *der Heiligkeit Ihrer Moral*; possibly "by the holiness of your morality."

---

1   Reinhoed, "Briefe über die kantische Philosophie" (1786 ff).
2   The referent of "this" (*sie*) is not clear; it could refer to either objective diversity or temporal succession.
3   Kant did not answer either this letter or Maimon's earlier one, May 9, 1790. Ak.[427].

151 [549] (516)
To Jacob Sigismund Beck.

December 4, 1792.

11:394   I believe that the accompanying little remarks will not arrive too late, worthy man, since you gave me permission to put off my reply for four weeks and this letter exceeds that postponement by only a few days. – Please note that since I cannot assume that the lines and words in the transcript sent to me will correspond exactly to those in your copy, you will find the corresponding pages of your manuscript all right (since the transcriptions are uniform) by my citation of the opening words of a passage, which I indicate with quotation marks. For the delay would be excessive for you if I sent back the whole manuscript by regular mail, while the cost of courier delivery is a little excessive. Your last letter, containing the manuscript, cost me exactly two Reichsthaler postage, which the transcriber could easily have reduced by ¾ if he had not used such thick paper and had written more compactly.

On page 5 you say about the division: "If however it is synthetic, then necessarily it must be trichotomy." However, this is not unconditionally necessary, but only if the division is supposed to be 1) a priori, 2) according to concepts (and not, as in mathematics, by means of the construction of concepts). So, for example, the regular polyhedron can be divided a priori into five different bodies, by exhibiting the concept of the polyhedron in intuition. From the mere concept of the polyhedron however one would not be able even to see the possibility of such a body, still less recognize the possible diversity thereof.

P. 7. (Where the discussion concerns the reciprocal effect of sub- $\quad$ 11:395 stances on each other and the analogy between that sort of reciprocity and the reciprocal determination of concepts in disjunctive judgments), instead of the words "The former hang together since they" I would say "The former constitute a *whole* with the exclusion of several parts from it; in the *disjunctive judgment*," etc.

P. 8. Instead of the words at the end of the paragraph "The *I think* must accompany all the representations in the synthesis" "must *be capable of* accompanying."

P. 17. Instead of the words "An understanding whose pure *I think*": "an understanding whose pure *I am*," etc. (For otherwise it would be contradictory to say that its pure *thinking* would be an *intuiting*.)

You see that my reminders are only of small significance, dear friend; your presentation of the Deduction is furthermore correct. Explanations by means of examples would indeed have made understanding easier for many readers; but one had to take account of the limits of space.

Herren Eberhard's and Garve's opinion that Berkeleyan Idealism is identical to Critical Idealism (which I could better call "the principle of the *ideality* of space and time") does not deserve the slightest attention. For I speak of ideality in reference to the *form* of *representation* while they construe it as ideality with respect to the *matter*, i.e., ideality of the *object* and its existence itself. – Under the assumed name "Aenesidemus"[1] however, an even wider skepticism has been advanced, viz., that we really cannot know whether anything at all corresponds to our representation (as its object), which is about as much as to say: whether a representation really *is* a representation (i.e., represents *something*). For "representation" means a determination in us that we relate to something else (the former, as it were, substituting in us for the latter).

With regard to your attempt to explain the difference in densities (if one may be permitted to use this expression) of two bodies that completely fill their respective volumes, we must assume, I think, that the moment of acceleration of all bodies on earth is the same; therefore there is no difference between the accelerations analogous to the difference between dx and dy, as I pointed out in my last letter; hence, if this problem is to be solved, we must be able to conceive of the quantity of motion in one of the bodies as different from that in the other body (i.e., their masses are different); consequently we can, so to speak, conceive of the mass in the same volume[2] not as measured by the *number* of parts, but as determined by parts that are *specifically different in their degree*, so that different masses can be in motion with the same velocity but with different quantities of motion. If mass depended on the number [of parts], then all those parts would have to be thought of originally as homogeneous, and thus they would differ in their respective composition in the same volume only with regard to the empty spaces between the parts, (which is contrary to our hypothesis). – Toward the end of this winter I shall send you my attempted analyses of this topic, written while I was working on my *Metaphysical Foundations of Natural Science*, but which I discarded; you may use them before you start on your summary of that work.[3] – To help you with your projected abstract of the *Critique of Judgment* I shall soon send you a packet containing the manuscript of my earlier Introduction to that work, which I discarded only because it was disproportionately long for the text, but which still seems to me to contain a number of things that serve to render one's insight into the concept of a purposiveness in nature more complete. I shall send it by regular mail for your personal use.[4] – I also wanted to advise that, to help you with your work on this, you look at Snell's and even better Spazier's treatises or commentaries on my book.[5]

I entirely approve of your title: *Explanatory Extract from the Critical Writings of Kant. First Volume, which Contains the Critique of Speculative and Practical Reason.*

I wish you the greatest success in this as in all your undertakings and I remain with respect and devotion

Your

I. Kant.

Königsberg, the 4th of December, 1792.

---

1 Gottlob Ernst Schulze (1761–1833), known as "Aenesidemus-Schulze" because of his book *Aenesidemus*, which appeared anonymously in 1792, was professor of philosophy in Hemstädt. The full title of his work is *Aenesidemus; or On the Foundations of Professor Reinhold of Jena's Elementarphilosophie, together with a Defense of Skepticism against the Presumptions of the Critique of Pure Reason.* Schulze, who was later to a become Schopenhauer's teacher, was one of the

11:396

sharpest critics of Kant and Reinhold. Like Jacobi, he objected that it was inconsistent to make an unknowable thing in itself the cause of the "material" of experience, since causality is supposedly a mere form of the subject's thinking. Kant, Schulze claimed, betrayed the principles of his own Critical Philosophy by invoking an unknowable entity, "the mind," as the source or cause of a priori concepts. Schulze praises Kant's Paralogisms arguments but maintained further that Kant had refuted neither the skepticism of Hume nor the Idealism of Berkeley and that Kant's position was in fact "dogmatic." Excerpts from *Aenesidemus* may be found in a translation by George di Giovanni in di Giovanni and H. S. Harris's *Between Kant and Hegel* (Albany: State University of New York Press, 1985).

Fichte published a review of *Aenesidemus* in the *Allgemeine Literatur-Zeitung*, Feb. 11 and 12, 1794. Salomon Maimon too offered criticisms. These essays, or excerpts from them, have been translated by di Giovanni, op. cit.

2 i.e., density.

3 Kant's promise was not kept.

4 Kant sent this essay on Aug. 18, 1793. Beck published an abstract of it, under the title "Über Philosophie überhaupt, zur Einleitung in die Kritik der Urteilskraft" (On philosophy in general, toward an introduction to the *Critique of Judgment*). The full Introduction was not published until 1914, in Ernst Cassirer's edition of Kant's works.

5 Friedrich Wilhelm Daniel Snell (1761–1827), professor of mathematics (and later, history) in Giessen, published a commentary of Kant's third *Critique* in 1791. Kiesewetter, in a letter of June 14, 1791, Ak. [474], had praised the book to Kant.

Johann Gottlieb Karl Spazier (1761–1805), was a philosophy instructor and composer who also taught German and fine arts in Berlin, and, in 1792, founded the *Berlinische musikalische Zeitung*. He published on theological, musical, and philosophical topics, including a book on Kant's third *Critique*, *Versuch einer Kurzen und faßlichen Darstellung der teleologischen Prinzipien* (1791). Kiesewetter mentioned this abstract of Kant's work also, but in disparaging terms.

152 [552] (519)
To Johann Benjamin Erhard.[1]

December 21, 1792

Dearest friend,   11:398

[Kant apologizes for not answering Erhard's letter for over a year, citing the indisposition from which he often suffers, brought on by aging. He expresses regret that Erhard does not live closer to Königsberg.]

447

... Allow me to make a few remarks about Herr Klein's discussion of criminal justice.[2] Most of what he says is excellent and quite in accord with my own views. I assume that you have a numbered copy of the points in your letter. Concerning No. 5:[3] The scholastic theologians used to say of the actual punishment (*poena vindicativa*) that it is imposed not to *nullify the offense*[a] but *because there is an offense.*[b] Therefore they defined punishment as "physical evil inflicted *because of moral evil.*"[c] In a world governed according to moral principles (by God) punishments are categorically necessary (to the extent that transgressions occur there). But in a world governed by men, the necessity of punishments is only hypothetical, and that direct union of the concept of transgression and the concept of punishment being deserved serves rulers only as a *justification*, not as a prescription, for their decrees. So you are right in saying that moral penalty[d] (which perhaps

came to be called "avenging punishment"[e] because it preserves divine justice), is indeed a *symbol* of punishment being deserved, as far as the condition of authorization is concerned, even if its purpose is merely therapeutic[f] for the transgressor and the setting of an example for other people.

With reference to numbers 9 and 10:[4] Both propositions are true, though entirely misunderstood in ordinary moral treatises. They belong under the heading of *Duties to Oneself*, which I discuss in the Metaphysics of Morals on which I am at work, and in a manner quite different from what is customary.

With respect to No. 12:[5] Also well said. It is often claimed in [the theory of] natural law[g] that civil society is based on the desirability of the social contract.[h] But it can be demonstrated that the state of nature[i] is a state of injustice and, consequently, that it is a juridical duty to enter into the condition of civil society.[j]

Prof. Reuß of Würzburg who visited me this fall presented me with your Inaugural Dissertation as well as the happy news that you have entered into a marriage that will render your life joyful. I congratulate you sincerely on both of these.

I would like to hear from you, especially as to whether Fräulein **Herbert**[6] was encouraged by my letter. I am ever your respectful and devoted

I. Kant

---

[a] *ne peccetur*
[c] *malum physicum ob malum morale illatum*
[e] *vindicativa*
[g] *Naturrecht*
[i] *status naturalis*

[b] *quia peccatum est*
[d] *poena meremoralis*
[f] *medicinalis*
[h] *pactum sociale*
[j] *status civilem*

1 Johann Benjamin Erhard (1766–1827), physician, traveler, and friend of Kant, Reinhold, Schiller, and the von Herberts. Erhard was one of Kant's main disciples in southern Germany (Nürnberg).

2 Ernst Ferdinand Klein, a friend of Erhard's, whose views Erhard had summarized in a letter to Kant, Sept. 6, 1791, Ak.[497].

3 "Since the aim of punishment cannot be compensation for damages, or improvement, or example, neither can we say that it is the suffering of a physical evil as such on account of a moral transgression. Rather, punishment is the symbol of an action's deserving punishment [*Strafwürdigkeit*], by means of a mortification of the criminal that corresponds to the rights which the criminal has violated."

4 "9. The moral law prescribes to me not only how I should treat others but also how I should allow myself to be treated by others; it forbids not only that I misuse others but also that I allow them to misuse me, that is, that I destroy myself.

"10. Therefore I am just as much commanded not to suffer an injustice as not to commit injustice, but this is only possible for me (unaided) as far as the intention goes, not in its realization. Therefore I and all men have the task of finding a means of making my physical powers equal to my moral obligations. From this there derives the moral drive and the need for society."

5 "No. 12. Insofar as society's main purpose is to protect the right and to punish crime, it is called civil society. As such, it is not only useful but holy."

6 Maria von Herbert. See letters of Aug. 1791, Ak.[478], spring 1792, Ak. [510], Jan. 1793, Ak. [557], and Feb. 11, 1793, Ak. [599].

1793

153 [554] (521)

From Maria von Herbert.

[January] 1793.

Dear and revered Sir,

The reason I delayed so long in telling you of the pleasure your letter gave me is that I value your time too highly, so that I allow myself to pilfer some of it only when it will serve to relieve my heart and not merely satisfy an impulse, and this you have already done for me once, when my spirit was most turbulent and I appealed to you for help, you understood me so perfectly that because of your kindness and your precise comprehension of the human heart I am encouraged to describe to you without embarrassment the further progress of my soul. The lie on account of which I appealed to you was no cloaking of a vice but only a sin of omission, holding something back out of consideration for the friendship (still veiled by love) that existed then. The conflict I felt, foreseeing the terribly painful consequences and knowing the honesty one owes to a friend, was what made me disclose the lie to my friend after all, but so late. Finally I had the strength, and with the disclosure I got rid of the stone in my heart at the price of the tearing away of his love. I enjoyed as little peace before, when I begrudged myself the pleasure I possessed, as afterward, when my heart was torn apart by the suffering and anguish that plagued me and that I wouldn't wish on anyone, even someone who would want to prove his wickedness in a court of law. Meanwhile my friend hardened in his indifference, just as you predicted in your letter, but later he made up for it doubly and offered me his sincerest friendship, which pleases me for his sake, but leaves me still dissatisfied, because it is only pleasant and pointless, and with my clear vision I have the sense of constantly reproaching myself and I get an empty feeling that extends inside me

11:401

450

and all around me, so that I am almost superfluous to myself. Nothing attracts me, and even getting every possible wish I might have would not give me any pleasure, nor is there a single thing that seems worth the trouble of doing. I feel this way not out of malcontentment but from weighing the amount of sordidness that accompanies everything good. I wish I were able to increase the amount of purposeful activity and diminish the purposeless; the latter seems to be all that the world is concerned with. I feel as if the urge to really do something only arises in me in order to be smothered. Even when I am not frustrated by any external circumstances and have nothing to do all day, I'm tormented by a boredom that makes my life unbearable, though I should want to live a thousand years if I could believe that God might be pleased with me in such a useless existence. Don't think me arrogant for saying this, but the commandments of morality are too trifling for me; for I should gladly do twice as much as they command, since they get their authority only because of a temptation to sin and it costs me hardly any effort to resist that. It makes me think that if someone has become really clear about the commandments of duty he is not at all free to transgress them any more. For I would have to insult my sinful feeling itself if I had to act contrary to duty. It seems so instinctive to me that my being moral could not possibly have the slightest merit.

Just as little, I think, can one hold those people responsible who in all their lives do not reach a real self-awareness. Always surprised by their own sensuality, they can never account to themselves for their action or inaction; and if morality were not the most advantageous thing for nature, these people would probably challenge her to further duels.

11:402

I console myself often with the thought that since the practice of morality is so bound up with sensuality, it can only count for this world, and with that thought I could still hope not to have to live another life of empty vegetating and of so few and easy moral demands after this life. Experience wants to take me to task for this bad temper I have against life by showing me that almost everyone finds his life ending too soon and everyone is so glad to be alive. So as not to be a queer exception to the rule, I shall tell you a remote cause of my deviation, namely, my chronic poor health. I have not been well at all since the time I first wrote you. This sometimes causes a frenzy of mind that reason alone cannot cure. So I forgo being healthy. What I could otherwise still enjoy doesn't interest me. I can't study any of the natural sciences or the arts of the world, for I feel I have no talent for extending them. And for myself alone I have no need to know them. Whatever bears no relation to the categorical imperative and to my transcendental consciousness is indifferent to me, though I am all finished with thoughts on those topics, too. Taking all these things together, you can perhaps see why I want only one thing, namely, to shorten this so useless life of mine, a life in which I am convinced I shall become neither better nor worse. If you consider that I am still young and that each day interests me only to the extent that it brings me closer to death, you could see what a benefactor you would be to me and you would be greatly encouraged to examine this question in detail. I can ask it of you because my concept of morality is silent on this point, whereas it speaks very decisively on all other issues. But if you are unable to give me the negative good I seek, I appeal to your feeling of benevolence and ask you to give me something with which to end this unbearable emptiness of soul. If I become a useful part of nature and if my health will permit, I hope to take a trip to Königsberg in a few years, for which I beg permission in advance to visit you. You will have to tell me your life's story then, and whether it never seemed worth the trouble to you to take a wife or to give yourself to someone with all your heart or to reproduce your likeness. I have an engraved portrait of you by Bause[1] from Leibpzig [*sic*], in which I see a calm moral depth although I cannot discover there the penetration of which the *Critique of Pure Reason* above all else is proof and I am also dissatisfied not to be able to look you right in the face.

Will you guess what my sole sensuous wish is, and fulfill it, if it is not too inconvenient. Please do not become indignant if I implore you for an answer, which my jabbering will have discouraged. But I must ask you that, if you should trouble to reply and do me this greatest favor, you focus your answer on specific matters and not on general points that I have already encountered in your writings when my friend and I happily experienced them together – you would certainly be pleased with him, for his character is upright, his heart is good, and his mind deep and besides that fortunate enough to fit into this world. And he is self-sufficient and strong enough to abstain from everything, and that is why I am confident I can tear myself away from him. Do guard your health, for you still have much to give to the world. Would that I were God and could reward you for what you have done for us. I am with deepest respect and truly, reverently,

Maria Herbert

11:403

---

1 In 1791 Johann Friedrich Bause (1738–1814) made an etching of Kant, based on a 1789 drawing by Veit Hans Schnorr von Carolsfeld (1769–1841).

154 [557] (524)
From Johann Benjamin Erhard.

January 17, 1793.

Nuremberg, January 17, 1793.

My teacher and my friend,

Your letter[1] was a source of consolation to me. It caught me in a melancholy state from which I often suffer and which usually I soon conquer, though this time because of a heap of minor troubles it became very powerful. Your letter demolished much of the basis of my despondency by showing me that I still have a certain value in your eyes, and this enlivened my hope that other intelligent and sincere people might also come to see me as being worth something. The ebb and flow of my self-respect and of my faith in other people is a spiritual malaise that has afflicted me since my youth. I knew no better way to characterize it than to call it a moral fever, and my own disease then is a sort of intermittent fever. I find this analogy consoling, for I hope that just as a well-cured fever leaves no damaging trace in the body, so too my spiritual illness, if I should succeed in curing it, will leave no damage in the soul. These are the remedies I intend to use: 1) conform to custom, as long as my conscience doesn't forbid it; 2) work resolutely, and not simply when I feel inclined to work; so I shall try to develop a medical practice and get admitted to the local medical school; 3) force myself sometimes to endure insipid conversations. If these remedies turn out to be good, I shall need no further answer; if not, I beg you for advice as to better ones. Please allow me to pose an intimate question here, a question whose answer might give me comfort: has it cost you much pain to be nothing but a professor in Königsberg – which means, as I see it, devoting your talents entirely to the world and not to yourself? For me it takes a lot of effort to *forgo* seeking my good fortune in the world at large, i.e., to abstain from exploiting the weaknesses I observe in people.

Now back to your letter. I am happy that I shall soon receive the Metaphysics of Morals. I hope you will live to see the completion of your work and afterwards die in peace. For my part, even in my most cheerful hours I see death as something desirable, so that if I had accomplished all that, given my powers, I could in good conscience ask for, I would wish to be allowed to leave the scene. I find this feeling, this desire for death, to be quite different from the desire to commit suicide, which I have often felt. It strikes me that this subject, a *moral*

11:406

11:407

yearning for death, has hardly been touched on by contemporary writers. Only Swift, among the authors I know, in his Miscellaneous Thoughts, has expressed it: "No one who asks himself honestly whether he would repeat his role on earth would answer Yes." Originally I found this thought in your writings[2] and it seemed to me intuitively correct. I am grateful to you for your reminding me.

I can say little about Fräulein Herbert. I had candidly expressed my opinion of some of her actions to a few of her friends in Vienna, thereby spoiling our friendship so that she won't even speak to me. She takes me to be a man of no moral sensitivity for individual cases, who judges only according to prudential rules. I do not know whether she is better off now. She has capsized on the reef of romantic love, which I have managed to escape (perhaps more by luck than by desert). In order to actualize an idealistic love, she first gave herself to a person who misused her trust, and then, to achieve such a love with a second person, she confessed this to her new lover. That is the key to her letter. If my friend Herbert had more *délicatesse*, I think she could still be saved. Her present state of mind, in brief, is this: her moral feeling is totally severed from prudence and is therefore coupled with fantasy, a more subtle sensibility. I find something moving about this state of mind, and I pity people of that sort more than actual maniacs. Unfortunately this state of mind appears to be very common among people who escape fanaticism and superstition. They escape only by embracing hypersensitivity, private delusions, and fantasies (the steadfast determination to convert one's own chimeras, which one takes to be ideals, into real things), and they think that they are doing truth a service thereby.

I am very contented with my wife.

Be well. I shall consult you, the next time I write, about some of my research. I won't trouble you about topics about which your coming publications can enlighten me. I can call myself "yours" as sincerely as if you were actually my father, for you have affected me even more than a father.

your
Erhard.

P.S. Girtanner[3] always wants to know whether you have read his chemistry book and what you think of it.

---

1 Dec. 21, 1792, Ak. [552].

2 Cf. *Critique of Judgment*, §83, note: "For who indeed would want to start life over again under the same conditions . . . [if enjoyment were the point of life]."

Kant had expressed a similar thought in *Muthmaßlicher Anfang der Menschen-geschichte* (1786), Ak. 8:122.

3 Christoph Girtanner (1760–1800), a physician and friend of Jachmann's, was the author of *Anfangsgründe der antiphlogistischen Theorie* (Berlin, 1792). He was a follower of Lavoisier.

155 [559] (526)
To Elisabeth Motherby.[1]

February 11, 1793.   11:411

I have numbered the letters[2] which I have the honor of passing on to you, my dear mademoiselle, according to the dates I received them. The ecstatical young lady*ᵃ* did not remember to date them. The third letter, from another source,[3] is included only because part of it provides an explanation of the lady's curious mental derangements. A number of expressions, especially in the first letter, refer to writings of mine that she read and are difficult to understand without an explanation.

You have been so fortunate in the upbringing you have received that I do not need to commend these letters to you as an example of warning, to guard you against the aberrations of a sublimated fantasy.   11:412 Nevertheless they may serve to make your perception of that good fortune all the more lively.

With the greatest respect, I am
My honored lady's obedient servant,
I. Kant

ᵃ die kleine Schwärmerin

---

1 Daughter of Kant's friend Robert Motherby, an English merchant in Königsberg.
2 From Maria von Herbert.
3 J. B. Erhard to Kant, January 17, 1793, Ak.[557].

156 [564] (531)
To Carl Spener.[1]
March 22, 1793.

Highly esteemed Sir,

11:417

Your letter of March 9th,[2] delivered to me on the 17th, pleased me by allowing me to see in you a man whose heart is devoted to a nobler cause than mere business success. However, I cannot agree to the proposal to publish a new, separate edition of my essay in the *Berliner Monatsschrift*, "Idea for a Universal History from a Cosmological Point of View," least of all with addenda directed at current affairs. If the powerful of this world are in a drunken fit, be it the result of the breath of some god or emanations from a damped fire, then one must strongly advise a pygmy who values his skin to stay out of their fight, even if the encouragement to get mixed up in it should come in a most gentle and respectful entreaty. The main reason is that they would not listen to him at all, while those scandalmongers who do hear him would misinterpret what he says.

In another four weeks[3] I shall embark on my 70th year. What special influence can one still hope to have on people of spirit at that age? And on the common herd? It would be lost labor, even detrimental to their interests. The best advice for an old man in what remains of his last years is "These are not the defenders this hour needs"[4] and he should be advised to conserve his strength, which will leave him almost nothing to wish for except peace and quiet.

With this in mind I hope you will not interpret my refusal as insolence. I am ever with fullest respect

your wholly obedient servant,

I. Kant.

---

1 Johann Carl Philip Spener (1749–1837) was a book merchant in Berlin.

2 The letter, Ak.[563], reports that Spener is now indirectly Kant's publisher, for he is reprinting the issue of the *Berliner Monatsschrift* that included Kant's 1784 essay, *"Idea for a Universal History from a Cosmopolitan Point of View."* Spener effusively praises Kant's essay and asks for permission to reprint it separately, in the hope that some powerful prince would read it and be moved by Kant's political ideas.

3 Kant's birthday was Apr. 22, 1724.

4 "non defensoribus istis tempus eget"; Virgil, *Aeneid*, II, 521, f. Hecuba, seeing the aged Priam put on armor, says this.

157 [572] (539)
To Abraham Gotthelf Kästner.
May 1793.

Kindly accept my thanks, esteemed sir, for your instructive and   11:427
stimulating letter (and for the greetings transmitted to me by Dr.
Jachmann who visited you in Göttingen). This is the first opportunity
I could find of showing my gratitude, namely by sending you a copy of
my overdue essay.[1]

I have often recalled vividly your suggestion that the harsh, newly
contrived scholastic terminology that I could hardly avoid in the *Critique* ought to be replaced by ordinary language or at least be combined
with the latter. I felt this most keenly when I read the works of my
critics. The most important advantage this would gain would be to
render inexcusable the mischief caused by mindless followers who
throw words around to which they attach no – or at least not my –
meaning. I shall take the next available opportunity where a dry discourse is called for to undo this mischief and try to combine that
scholastic terminology with ordinary language.

What makes you so remarkable to me and to everyone is that your
writings, which one can recognize even without seeing your name on
them, still exude such intellectual penetration and youthfulness, displaying your characteristic sagacity in so many areas of science and of
taste. May heaven preserve you, even to the age of a Fontenelle,[2] and
as favored by the muses, without which a long life is no blessing to a
scholar. Unfortunately nature seems not to have decreed this for me
since, at the start of my 70th year, though I am not ill, I am starting to
feel the burdens of old age and the difficulty of mental labors.   11:428

With sincere esteem I remain always

your most obedient servant,
I. Kant.

---

1 *Religion within the Limits of Reason Alone.*
2 Bernard Le Bovier de Fontenelle (1657–1757), the French critic and poet.

158 [574] (541)
To Carl Friedrich Stäudlin.[1]

May 4, 1793.

11:429   ... The plan I prescribed for myself a long time ago calls for an examination of the field of pure philosophy with a view to solving three problems: (1) What can I know? (metaphysics). (2) What ought I to do? (moral philosophy). (3) What may I hope? (philosophy of religion). A fourth question ought to follow, finally: What is man? (anthropology, a subject on which I have lectured for over twenty years). With the enclosed work, *Religion within the Limits [of Reason Alone]*, I have tried to complete the third part of my plan. In this book I have proceeded conscientiously and with genuine respect for the Christian religion but also with a befitting candor, concealing nothing but rather presenting openly the way in which I believe that a possible union of Christianity with the purest practical reason is possible.

The biblical theologian can oppose reason only with another reason or with force, and if he intends to avoid the criticism that attends the latter move (which is much to be feared in the current crisis, when freedom of public expression is universally restricted), he must show our rational grounds to be weak, if he thinks ours are wrong, by offering other rational grounds. He must not attack us with anathemas launched from out of the clouds over officialdom. This is what I meant to say in my Preface on page xix. The complete education of a biblical theologian should unite into one system the products of his own powers and whatever contrary lessons he can learn from philosophy. (My book is that sort of combination.) By assessing his doctrines from the point of view of rational grounds, he shall be armed against any future attack.

Perhaps you will be alienated by my Preface, which is in a way rather violent. What occasioned it was this: the whole book was sup-
11:430   posed to appear in four issues of the *Berliner Monatsschrift*, with the approval of the censor there. The first part, "On the Radical Evil in Human Nature," went all right; the censor of philosophy, Privy Councillor Hillmer, took it as falling under his department's jurisdiction. The second part was not so fortunate, since Herr Hillmer thought that it ventured into the area of biblical theology (for some unknown reason he thought the first part did not), and he therefore thought it advisable to confer with the biblical censor, *Oberconsistorialrath* Hermes, who then of course took it as falling under his own jurisdiction (when did a mere priest ever decline any power?), and so he expropriated it and

458

refused to approve it. The Preface therefore tries to argue that if a censorship commission is in doubt over which sort of censor should judge a book, the author ought not to let the outcome depend on the commission's coming to an agreement but should rather submit the question to a domestic university. For while each individual faculty is bound to maintain its own authority, and resist the pretensions of the other faculties, there is an academic senate that can decide this sort of dispute over rights. To satisfy all the demands of justice, therefore, I presented this book in advance to the theological faculty, asking them to decide whether the book invaded the domain of biblical theology or whether it belonged rather to the jurisdiction of the philosophical faculty, which is how it turned out.

I am moved to disclose this incident to you, sir, so that you will be able to judge whether my actions are justified in case a public quarrel should arise over the case, and to show you, as I hope you will agree, the justification for what I have done. I am, with genuine respect,

Your most obedient servant,

I. Kant

---

1 Carl Friedrich Stäudlin (1761–1826), professor of theology in Göttingen, the liberal theologian to whom Kant dedicated his *The Conflict of the Faculties (Der Streit der Fakultäten*, 1798). A discussion of the publication of this work and of the problems surrounding it may be found in Mary Gregor's Introduction to her translation of the *Conflict of the Faculties* (New York: Abaris Books, Inc., 1979). Kant's correspondence with (and about) Biester, Gensichen, Hufeland (the physician), Nicolovius, Rehberg, and Tieftrunk is relevant to understanding both the content and the publication problems of the book's three essays.

159 [575] (542)
To Matern Reuß.[1]

[May 1793].

[Draft, in two fragments][2]

1. Once more accept my thanks, esteemed sir, for your visit and for 11:431 letting me make your acquaintance, an event which shall always remain one of the pleasantest memories of my life! I enclose with this acknowledgment a little essay, not really biblical-theological but philosophical-

theological in content. It is not meant to offend [the teachings and practices of][3] any church, since what it addresses is not the question "What faith is adequate for a human being in general?" but only "What faith is adequate for someone who aims to base his convictions purely on reason?" i.e., someone therefore who aims at a faith that rests purely on a priori grounds and whose validity can thus be maintained whatever one's particular beliefs may be. But as to this aim's fulfillment, as an object of experience that the ruling power of the universe meant to present to us, [my philosophical theology] does not close the door to an empirical belief in some revelation or other but on the contrary leaves the heart open to such a revelation as long as the latter is found to agree with the former . . . [4]

2. I do not say here that reason dares to affirm its sufficiency in matters of religion; I only maintain that if it is insufficient either in insight or in the power of execution, it must rely on the supernatural assistance of Heaven for everything that exceeds its power, though it is not allowed to know in what that assistance may consist.

---

1 Matern (or Maternus) Reuß (1751–98) was a physician who became a Benedictine friar in 1777 and, in 1782, professor of philosophy in Würzburg. An ardent disciple of Kant's, he journeyed with his friend Conrad Stang to Königsberg, a considerable trip in 1792. Reuß devoted his energies to the spread of Kant's philosophy among Catholics. See also his letter to Kant, Apr. 1, 1796, Ak.[699].

2 These fragments are to be found in Ak. 11:431. Another draft is printed in Ak. 23:496 f. Its content is much the same, with one or two additional or variant phrases.

3 This phrase occurs in the draft mentioned in n. 2.

4 The variant version of this sentence: "As to the means for realizing this Idea and producing such a disposition in the human race, a matter not of what we are required to do but of what God has done to make his moral governance of the universe appear to us, that is a matter of faith that rests solely on historical and empirical grounds and therefore it is left to be sought out by people who wish to join a church; nor is the pure philosophizing theologian closed off from revelation as long as what it prescribes does not conflict with what reason authoritatively demands as belonging to a pure moral disposition."

160 [576] (543)
To Friedrich Bouterwek.[1]
May 7, 1793.

You have given me unexpected pleasure, excellent sir, with the news   11:431
of your intention to give a course of lectures on the *Critique of Pure
Reason* in Göttingen and by the well-thought-out plan that you enclosed. In fact I always wished but dared not hope for a poetic mind   11:432
that would have the intellectual power to explain the pure concepts of
the understanding and make these principles more readily communicable; for to be able to unite scholastic precision in determining concepts with the popularizing of a flowering imagination is a talent too
rare to count on meeting up with very easily.

Since I saw from your outline that you have a thorough insight into
the essence and structure of the system, I was all the more convinced
that you have the capacity to carry out your plan. I therefore congratulate those who will participate in your course and I congratulate
myself for having found such a worthy collaborator. The glad and
spirited temper with which your poems have often delighted me did
not prepare me to expect that dry speculation might also be a stimulus
for you. But speculation invariably leads to a certain sublimity, the
sublimity of the Idea, which can[2] draw the imagination into play and
produce useful analogies, though of course the Idea cannot actually be
reached in this way. Your linguistic dexterity and mastery can help to
overcome the evil to which Councillor *Kaestner* calls attention: the
frequent misuse of new terminology by disciples who have no grasp of
its meaning. I wish you great progress with your undertaking and I
remain with full respect and devotion

your devoted servant,
I. Kant.

---

1   Bouterwek (1766–1828) was a philosopher, aesthetician, and poet in Göttingen. In a letter to Kant of Sept. 17, 1792, Ak. [529], Bouterwek informs Kant
of his plan to give a course of lectures on Kantian philosophy. He compliments
Kant effusively and declares himself to be the first to defend the *Critique of
Pure Reason* openly in Göttingen. Kant, in *Perpetual Peace*, Ak. 8:367, cites
Bouterwek's lines, "If you bend the reed too much, you break it; and he who
attempts too much attempts nothing."

2   "kann" is Ernst Cassirer's proposed addition to the text.

161 [578] (545)
To Johann Gottlieb Fichte
May 12, 1793.[1]

I congratulate you heartily on your good fortune in finding the spare time to devote to your work on important philosophical problems, worthy man, though you prefer to remain silent as to where and under what circumstances you hope to enjoy this leisure.

Your *Critique of All Revelation* does you honor but I have read it so far only in part and with interruptions. To judge it adequately I would have to go through the whole book in a continuous reading, for I have to keep in mind what I have read so that I can compare it to what follows. But till now I have found neither the time nor the disposition for this (for several weeks my health has not been favorable to intellectual labors). Perhaps by comparing your work with my new essay, *Religion within the Limits, etc.*, you can most easily see how our thoughts agree on this subject or how they differ.

I hope and wish for good fortune from your talent and industry in addressing the problem alluded to in the *Critique of Pure Reason*, p. 372, etc.[2] If my work on all my projects were not going so slowly – something for which my upcoming 70th year may be to blame – I would already have completed the chapter of my projected Metaphysics of Morals whose subject matter you have chosen as your topic; it would please me if you could make my work dispensable by stealing a march on me in this business.

However near or far the end of my life may be, I shall not be dissatisfied with my career if I can flatter myself with the thought that what my modest efforts have initiated will be brought ever nearer to completion by astute men zealously working to improve the world.

With my wish for your welfare and the wish to hear news from time to time of the happy progress of your efforts to advance the public good I am with total respect and friendship, etc.

I. Kant.

Königsberg, the 12th of May, 1793.

11:433

11:434

---

1 According to Ak. 13:346 this letter was first printed in an 1831 biography of Fichte, *Fichtes Leben und literarischer Briefwechsel.*
2 In his letter of Apr. 2, 1793, Ak.[565], Fichte spoke of his soul glowing with the great thoughts Kant expressed there, i.e., "A constitution allowing *the*

greatest human freedom in accordance with laws by which *the freedom of each is made to be consistent with that of all others* . . . is at least a necessary idea . . ." (B 373).

162 [580] (547)
From Johann Gottfried Carl Christian Kiesewetter.
June 15, 1793.

[*Kiesewetter thanks Kant for sending a copy of Kant's* Religion within the Limits of Reason Alone, *saying that it can bring endless benefits, if properly understood, at least by putting an end to the current witch-hunt and intolerance of dissent. Kiesewetter is eager to hear what the theologians and especially the inquisitors will say to it, since they have been unable to prevent its publication.*]   11:436

. . . I was delighted to hear from Herr Tilling[1] of Courland, who brought me regards from you, that you are feeling quite well. So now we can hope that your [Metaphysics of] Moral[s] will soon appear – no book is awaited more eagerly by so many people. The majority of thinking people have been persuaded of the correctness of the formal principle of morality, as could easily have been predicted; but the deduction of a system of duties and of various rights (for example, the right of property) is so fraught with difficulties, not successfully solved by any previous system, that everyone is truly anxious to see your system of morality appear, and all the more so just now since the French Revolution has stimulated a mass of such questions anew. I   11:437
believe that there are many interesting things to be said about the rationality of the basic principles on which the French Republic bases itself, if only it were prudent to write about such things. It is the topic of every conversation around here as well and the subject of every argument, though the disputes all tend to stray from the point at issue, either because people confuse the issue [of republicanism] with that of the merits of the current representatives of the institution, or because they try to establish or refute the validity of the ideas by appeal to experience, or they make impossible demands.

My situation has not changed much. I earn 600 reichsthaler per year as tutor to the royal children, for which however I have to teach 15 hours a week. My professorship so far provides no income, but I am required to give a course of public lectures on logic every year, the king has however promised me a salary as soon as they begin. Besides this I was earning 400 reichsthaler a year as *chargé d'affaires* to Princess Auguste,[2] but the position has been withdrawn and I have been promised only compensation. As long as the war[3] lasts there is little hope of my receiving more money, but I hear from a fairly reliable source that the king is inclined to make peace before the year is over

Professors Jakob and Fischer[4] have agreed to publish a philosophical journal with me, a *philosophische Bibliothek*[5] containing extracts from the best philosophical writings that come out at each book fair. It will not try to be critical but only put the readers in a position to understand better the drift of the authors' ideas and to grasp more easily whatever is novel in each. The aim is thus not so much to draw attention to the most important philosophical writings as to help people to read them.

My illness has kept me from completing the essay that was announced in the book fair catalogue. I now doubt that it will appear.[6]

---

1 Nicholas Tilling (1769–1823) studied theology in Mitau and Jena.
2 Princess August Friederike Christine, daughter of Friedrich Wilhelm II and Friederike Luise von Hessen-Darmstadt.
3 Prussia's First Coalition War, 1792–5, ended by the Peace of Basel.
4 Carl Friedrich Fischer (1766–1847), professor of history at the military academy in Berlin.
5 A single issue of the *Neue philosophische Bibliothek* was published by Kiesewetter and Fischer in Berlin (1794) containing three essays, two by Kiesewetter, one by Fisher.
6 Kiesewetter suffered from an inflammation in his arm that kept him from writing. The work to which he refers is his *Versuch einer Faßlichen Darstellung der wichtigsten Wahrheiten der neueren Philosophie für Uneingeweihte* (Attempt at an easy-to-understand presentation of the most important truths of recent philosophy, for the uninitiated), which was published in Berlin, 1795, and in a revised edition, 1798.

163 [584] (551)
To Jacob Sigismund Beck.

August 18, 1793.

I am sending you the essay I promised you, dearest sir. It was supposed to be a Preface to the *Critique of Judgment*, but I discarded it because it was too long. You may use it as you see fit, in your condensed abstract of that book. I am also enclosing the specimen of your abstract transmitted to me by Court Chaplain Schultz.

The essential theme of this Preface (which might be sufficient to make up half of your manuscript) concerns a unique and unusual presupposition of our reason: that Nature, in the diversity of her products, was inclined to make some accommodation to the limitations of our power of judgment, by the simplicity and noticeable unity of her laws and by presenting the infinite diversity of her species in conformity with a certain law of continuity that makes it possible for us to organize them under a few basic concepts, as though she acted by choice and for the sake of our comprehension – not because we recognize this purposiveness as such to be necessary but because we need it and hence are justified in assuming it a priori and in using the assumption as far as we can make shift with it.

You will be kind enough to forgive me, at my age and with all my complex labors, for not having had time to look at the specimen [of your manuscript] so as to give you any sound judgment about it. I can trust your own critical spirit to do this. Nonetheless I remain, with whatever assistance my powers can lend to your good wishes,

Your most devoted
I. Kant

164 [591] (557)
From Johann Gottlieb Fichte.
September 20, 1793.

11:451

With heartfelt joy, most esteemed patron, did I receive your letter, the proof that even from afar you find me worthy of your kind benevolence. My journey was directed toward Zürich, where during a previous visit a young and very deserving woman had deigned to bestow her special friendship on me. Even before my trip to Königsberg she wanted me to come back to Zürich and be united with her. What I had formerly regarded as impermissible, since at that time I had achieved nothing, I now thought possible; for it seemed that I had at least given promise of future accomplishments. Our marriage, previously postponed on account of unforeseen difficulties that the laws of Zürich impose on foreigners, will take place in a few weeks.[1] This marriage

465

would offer me the prospect of independent leisure to devote to my studies, were it not for the quite intolerable character of the people in Zürich – a character incompatible with my particular nature even if kind enough in itself. It is this that makes me want to change my residence.

I anticipate the same pleasure from the publication of your *Metaphysics of Morals*[2] that I have had in reading your *Religion within the Limits*, etc. My project concerning natural law, civil law, and political theory is progressing and I could easily use half a lifetime to carry it out. So I can look forward forever to making use of your work with this project. Would you permit me to ask your advice, if it should turn out that I run into difficulties in developing my ideas? Perhaps as they struggle to develop I shall put some of them before the public, anonymously of course, in various guises. I confess that I have already done something of this sort, though at present I do not want people to know of my authorship;[3] for I have zealously and with total candor denounced numerous injustices, even though I am not yet ready to offer any proposals for rectifying them without creating disorder. I have encountered *one* piece of enthusiastic praise[4] but so far no thorough examination of this book. If you would permit me this – should I say "this confiding" or "this confidence"? – I shall send you a copy for your evaluation just as soon as I receive the next installment from the printer. You are the only person, most esteemed sir, whose judgment and strict discretion I fully trust. When it comes to political issues, unfortunately, almost everyone in these confused times is partisan, even people who are capable thinkers; either they fearfully adhere to what is old or they hotly combat it just *because* it is old. If you were to give me your kind permission to send you this book – I would not dare to do so otherwise – I think that Court Chaplain Schulz could forward your letters to me.

No, great man, you who are so significant for the human race, your works will not perish! They will bear rich fruits; they will give humanity a new energy and bring about a total rebirth in its first principles, opinions, dispositions. There is nothing, believe me, that will be unaffected by the consequences of your work. And your discoveries open up glad prospects. I have sent some remarks about this to Court Chaplain Schulz, things that I wrote during my journey, and I have asked him to share them with you.

Great and good man, what must it be like, toward the end of one's earthly life, to be able to feel as you can feel! I confess that the thought of you will forever be my guiding spirit, driving me not to retire from the stage until, as far as my abilities allow, I have been of some service to humanity.

11:452

I commend myself to your continued benevolence and I remain   11:453
with greatest respect and esteem,

Faithfully yours,

Fichte.

Zürich, the 20th of September, 1793.

---

1 Fichte married Johanna Maria Rahn, a niece of the famous poet F. G. Klopstock, on Oct. 22, 1793.

2 Kant's *Metaphysik der Sitten* did not appear until 1797.

3 *Beiträge zur Berichtigung der Urteile des Publikums über die französische Revolution, I. Teil, zur Beurteilung ihrer Rechtmässigkeit*, published anonymously, 1793.

4 In the Intelligenzblatt (Notices) of the *A.L.Z.*, June 12, 1793.

165 [596] (562)
From Johann Erich Biester.[1]

October 5, 1793.   11:456

Finally I am able to send you the new issue of the *Berliner Monatsschrift*, most worthy friend. I do so with the deepest gratitude for your excellent September essay.[2] As you wished, it has been printed all in one piece, in a single issue. How abundantly full of significant lessons it is! The second section was especially pleasing to me, on account of its new, masterful way of presenting and developing the concepts. To speak quite openly, it pleased me all the more since it refuted the rumor (which I suspected from the start) that you had come out in favor of the ever increasingly repulsive French Revolution, in which the actual freedom of reason and morality and all wisdom in statecraft and legislation are being most shamefully trampled underfoot – a revolution that even shatters and annuls the universal principles of constitutional law and the concept of a civil constitution, as I now learn from your essay. Surely it is easier to decapitate people (especially if one lets others do it) than courageously to discuss the rational and legal grounds of opposition with a despot, be he sultan or despotic rabble. Till now, however, I see only that the French have mastered those easier operations, performed with bloody hands; I do not see that they have the power of critical reason.

11:457

In view of the purpose of your first section, I wish you would look at Schiller's essay, "Über Anmuth und Würde"[3] (in the second issue of *Thalia*, 1793, published separately as well), and notice what he says, quite speciously, about your moral system, viz., that the hard voice of duty sounds too strongly therein (duty being a law prescribed by reason itself but nevertheless in a way an alien law) and that there is too little attention to *inclination* . . . [4]

Biester

---

1   On Biester, see Kant's letter to Herz, Ak. [141], n. 3.

2   "Über den Gemeinspruch: Das mag in der Theorie richtig sein, taugt aber nicht für die Praxis" ("On the Common Saying: That May Be True in Theory but Not in Practice," 1793).

3   "On Grace and Dignity." In a footnote to *Religion within the Limits of Reason Alone* Kant calls Schiller's essay a "masterful treatise" and explains how he agrees and disagrees with Schiller. See Kant's *Werke*, Ak. 6: 23 f.

4   Kant defends himself against Schiller's interpretation in the second edition of *Religion within the Limits.*

166 [605] (571)

From Johann Gottfried Carl Christian Kiesewetter.

November 23, 1793.

Esteemed Herr Professor,

11:469

I took the liberty of sending you a little tub of Teltow carrots[1] about two weeks ago and I would have informed you sooner had I not wished to include the first issue of the *Philosophische Bibliothek*,[2] which Professor Fischer and I are publishing jointly. But since it is being printed outside Prussia and this will take a while longer, I decided to send it to you later on, so that the turnips will not arrive unannounced. I do hope they meet with your approval. I made sure that they really did come from Teltow.

You may wonder why the *Philosophische Bibliothek* is being published abroad. Herr Hermes[3] thought it dangerous to publish an extract from Heidenreich's *Natürliche Religion*.[4] On the first page of it Hermes made so many corrections that I was forced to decide in favor of foreign publication. His corrections are masterpieces; they would deserve to be printed as an official document of the Berlin Censorship Commission if I were not so lazy. He will not allow that God is an individual, and he says that one does not become worthy of blessedness through virtue but rather capable of blessedness, and other such stuff. I am waiting to see whether he will condemn the book. If so, I am determined to fight him. He has still been treating me with indulgence, but Professor Grillo,[5] a man of 60, wanted to publish a summary of your *Religion within the Limits of Reason* and Hermes treated him like a schoolboy, writing doggerel in the margins of his manuscript. If only Grillo were not so peace-loving.

You see, we have hard taskmasters. Hermes himself said to my publisher that he is only waiting for the war[6] to be over before issuing more cabinet orders, which he has in his desk. These gentlemen are now visiting schools and investigating the children. Among other things, people are talking about an examination that von Woltersdorf[7] gave in the school of the Gray Convent. It was really remarkable. It would be a waste of time to tell you the whole story, but here are the first two questions – WOLTERSDORF: How old are you, my son? CHILD: Nine years old. w: And where were you ten years ago, then? – ! The story is absolutely true and not something somebody made up.

The new law code[8] is now being introduced, but with four changes, one of which I forget. First, in the preface, the commendation of monarchy as the best form of government is omitted, for the reason that it is supposed to be self-evident. Second, the article on legally recognized concubinage [*Ehe an der linken Hand*] is taken out, and third, the article on the punishment of exorcists is removed.   11:470

Nobody knows how the war will go. I heard yesterday that we are demanding 45 million from Austria, in exchange for which we would prosecute the war by ourselves. It is certain that at the beginning of the war we made many loans to Austria, because they are not as efficient as we are. A special envoy from Austria is awaited. The princes are expected in a week and so is the king, who is now in Potsdam. Lucchesini,[9] Bischoffswerders'[10] brother-in-law, is going to Vienna as ambassador. Everyone longs for peace.

Your grateful pupil,
J. G. C. Kiesewetter

---

1   "Teltower Rüben." Kant was enormously fond of these carrots. Kiesewetter kept him regularly supplied for a number of years. Some of Kant's last letters discuss Teltow carrots, requesting more and discussing the proper way to cook them.

2 *Neue philosophische Bibliothek*, first (and last) issue, Berlin, 1794.
3 Hermann Daniel Hermes (1731–1807), member of the Censorship Commission on Spiritual Affairs in Berlin.
4 Karl Heinrich Heydenreich, *Betrachtung über die Philosophie der natürlichen Religion* (2 vols.; Leipzig, 1790–1), followed Kant's moral theology.
5 Friedrich Grillo (1739–1802).
6 The First Coalition War (French Revolutionary Wars), 1792–5.
7 Woltersdorf was another member of the Censorship Commission.
8 Allgemeine Landrecht, put into effect July 1, 1794.
9 Girolamo Lucchesini (1752–1825), an Italian in the Prussian diplomatic service.
10 Johann Rudolf von Bischoffswerder (1741–1803), a favorite of Friedrich Wilhelm II's.

167 [606] (572)
From Salomon Maimon.
December 2, 1793.

11:470   Full of the respect and reverence that I owe you, which are never out of my consciousness, aware too of my unseemly importunity, I still cannot bring myself to forgo sending you the enclosed copy of a little work of mine for your evaluation.[1]

Since you convinced me, worthy man, that all our cognitive claims must be preceded by a critique of the faculty of cognition, I could not help but be vexed by the following observation: since the appearance of the *Critique*, there have been several attempts to bring particular disciplines into accord with its requirements, yet no one has attempted 11:471 a reconstruction of logic. I am convinced that logic, as a science, is just as much in need of the *Critique*. *General* Logic must of course be distinguished from *Transcendental* Logic, but the former must be revised in light of the latter.

I think I have sufficiently shown the necessity and importance of such a treatment of logic in this little essay.

As I see it, logic can not only be *rectified* but also *expanded* and given a *systematic ordering*. The rectification of logic will occur when people see the error of *abstracting* logical forms from their use, an error that early logicians, even Aristotle, committed. Something foreign to logical forms still remains attached to them thereby. One must try to use *reflection* on the cognitive faculty to define and complete those forms. Logic can be expanded if we provide methods for resolving all possible composite forms into the simple ones. But to achieve the *systematic ordering* of logic one must not isolate the so-called operations of thinking and logical forms but show instead their reciprocal *dependence* on each other. This would yield a "family tree" of logic that one might justifiably call a *tree of cognition*.

I am now at work on a logic that carries out this idea;[2] I would therefore be grateful to have your opinion both of the project's worth and its feasibility. I would take your judgment as my guide. Awaiting your reply I remain, with all respect and sincere friendship,

your devoted servant

Berlin, December 2, 1793.   S. Maimon

---

1   *Die Kathegorien des Aristoteles. Mit Anmerkungen erläutert und als Propädeutik zu einer neuen Theorie des Denkens dargestellt* (Berlin, 1794).

2   *Versuch einer neuen Logik oder Theorie des Denkens. Nebst angehängten Briefen des Philaletes an Aenesidemus* (Berlin, 1794).

168 [609] (575)
To Johann Gottfried Carl Christian Kiesewetter.
December 13, 1793.

Esteemed Herr Professor,   11:476

Your friendly letter and the accompanying gift (which arrived intact) were doubly pleasing to me, and I wish for the opportunity to reciprocate both.

I have more confidence that your *Philos[ophische] Bibliothek* will be well received by the public than that it will please the appointed guardian of the public, a man who is eager to overstep the limits of his office as biblical theologian and extend his authority to purely philosophical works as well, works which ought to fall under the jurisdiction of the philosophical censor. The philosophical censor – and this is the most evil part of it – is unwilling to oppose the former's arrogation and instead has an understanding with him about this matter; this coalition has to be exposed sometime or other, not to mention the fact that it is one thing to censor a book and another to correct religious devotions, two distinct jobs that require entirely different warrants. Aside from

11:477

this, it is the tenor of the times to sound an alarm where there is nothing but peace and quiet, so one has to have patience, be precisely obedient to the law, and put off censure of the abuses of the literary police establishment until gentler times . . .

Your most devoted friend and servant

Königsberg,

the 13th of December, 1793   I. Kant.

169 [612] (578)

From Johanna Eleonora Schultz.[1]

11:481   December 22, 1793.

Please excuse my bothering you with this brief message "but it is a duty to give you the most accurate information about our success in finding a good and *honest* cook for your house."[2] The person I have found is the only one I dare recommend to you, for besides her culinary skills she has a *willing* and *honest soul*, qualities that make such a person treasurable. If I were still lucky enough to be choosing someone for my *father*, I would have selected this person and no other. I have a genuine and honest desire to see that besides your trusty Lampe you have a woman in your service who deserves this good fortune. I have informed her "of the *wages* you offered and she is quite satisfied, and I have given her a general idea of the *work* that needs to be done in your house, following the list of the good *Lehman*.[3] This too was agreeable to her and she understands that you have a woman who carries water and takes care of various things, as is the case in her present employment. However, she has set certain *conditions* which, from what I *know* of this *person*, I sincerely hope that you will fulfill. I believe that you will enjoy peace of mind thereby which, my dearest father," is so essential for you.

11:482

Please forgive me for speaking so intimately. The woman would naturally like to be in charge of *shopping* for everything that pertains to her *cooking*. Her second point, and she will not *move* into your house without your *consenting* to this, is that she wants to receive all the money she needs for this from you directly and not through Lampe. Madam *Barckley*, in whose house she has worked for four years, leaves everything to her, as did her previous employers. She has only one son, and he lives in Herr Schubert's house where he is well cared for, so that you have nothing to fear on that score. She used to be at my house often when her husband was alive, and I trusted her with everything. I have never known a better shopper nor a more honest person; she is careful to use things up. This is the recommendation she deserves. You will know how best to arrange things in your house so that the good *Lampe*[4] is not neglected.

... I am sure you will be spared much annoyance and that your life, so precious to us, will be lengthened as soon as you hire this person, but you must determine the most suitable time for her to start, when the present cook is away, because these people's chatter is unendurable.

your most devoted and obedient
J. E. Schultz, née Büttner.

December 22, 1793

---

1 Johanna Schultz (1751–95) was the daughter of Christian Büttner, an anatomist in Königsberg, and the wife of Kant's disciple, Court Chaplain Johann Schultz.

2 The original letter is evidently lost. Quotation marks here and later in the letter are found in the Akademie edition, without explanation. It may be that the transcription stems from more than one source, or that Frau Schultz meant literally what she says about writing to Kant as she would to her father.

3 Johann Heinrich Immanuel Lehmann, Kant's amanuensis.

4 Martin Lampe (1734–1806), Kant's servant for 40 years.

1794

170 [614] (580)
From Maria von Herbert.
Early 1794.

Klagenfurt, in the beginning of the year 1794

Honored and sincerely beloved man,

Please don't take offense and do grant me, with your customary good will, the pleasure of writing to you again. For when I write to you I feel the highest pleasure: the feeling of awe and of love for your person – you who ennoble humanity. And I need not prove to you that this is the feeling that makes us blessed, because you had the good fortune to locate for us this purest and most sacred of feelings and to rescue it forever from religious institutions. I must thank you most warmly for "Religion within the Bounds of Reason," thank you in the name of all who have managed to tear themselves loose from those ensnaring chains of darkness. Do not deprive us of your wise guidance so long as you think that there is still something we lack, for it is not our desire or our satisfaction that can judge what we need but only your perception of us. I felt myself wholly informed by the *Critique of Pure Reason*, and yet I found that your subsequent works were not in the least superfluous. Gladly would I have commanded the course of nature to stand still if that could assure me that you would have the time you need to complete what you have begun for us, and gladly would I attach the days of my future life to your own if I could thereby know that you were still alive when the end of the French Revolution comes about.

I had the pleasure of seeing Erhard. He told me that you had inquired about me, from which I inferred that you must have received

11:485

my letter of early 1793; for I have received no answer – I suppose because you understood better than I did that your writings had already paved the path that I must tread for myself. Since I assume that you are interested in the fate of anyone who owes as much to your guidance as I do, I want to tell you of my spiritual progress and my frame of mind. For a long time I tortured myself and couldn't make sense of many things; for I confused God's arrangement with the contingencies of fate, and I failed to be satisfied with just the feeling of being. There you can see immediately how things stood with me, for I wanted too much, I regarded the coincidental misfortunes of life as sent to me by God, and I bristled at the injustice, for my conscience was free of guilt. I thought: either God is unjust or my life is not at all arranged by him, and that thought made me lose my feeling for him. Finally I was in such turmoil that the antinomies which are the main source of my steady recovery could just as well have induced me to commit an irreversible act. For I could not come to terms with these thoughts, until from an entirely different quarter a moral feeling awoke in me – a feeling that remained steadfast in the face of the antinomies. From that moment on I felt that I had won and that my soul was in good health. Not that I lacked my share of wearisome adversities that tested my new outlook until finally, after strenuous effort, I achieved an imperturbable peace of mind. I came also to understand my desire for death, which had seemed to me before as a digging into myself, a perversion of nature, for my own extinction was exactly what I coveted. Even the joy of friendship, for which my heart always yearned, did not protect me from that urge. I saw friendship too as something I did not deserve and I wanted no other being to be burdened by it. For given that I am finite, no pleasure in the world could compensate for the fact that my life has no purpose. Now my desire is still with me but my view has changed. I think that death, from an egoistic point of view, must be the most pleasant thing for every true human being, and only if people take morality and friends into account can they with the greatest desire to die still wish for life and try to preserve it no matter what. There is much more I wanted to say to you, but my conscience bothers me for robbing you of time; my hope is still to visit you sometime, accompanied by my friend (from whom I shall now unfortunately be absent for more than a year and have been for a long time). Meanwhile I bless the thought of you with the warmest feeling of thanks, of love, and of respect. May heaven preserve you from all hardship so that you may have a long life on this earth! With all my heart.

11:486

your devoted
Maria Herbert

171 [620] (585)
To Karl Leonhard Reinhold.
March 28, 1794.

11:494

Eesteemed Sir,
Dearest friend,

[Kant extends his best wishes on Reinhold's decision to accept another professorship, in Kiel. He apologizes for not writing to offer his opinion of Reinhold's book on the principles of natural law, but says he was unable to do so.] . . . For the past three years or so, age has affected my thinking – not that I have suffered any dramatic change in the mechanics of health, or even a great decline (though a noticeable one) in my mental powers, as I strive to continue my reflections in accordance with my plan. It is rather that I feel an inexplicable difficulty when I try to project myself into other people's ideas, so that I seem unable really to grasp anyone else's system and to form a mature judgment of it. (Merely general praise or blame does no one any good.)

11:495

This is the reason why I can turn out essays of my own, but, for example, as regards the "improvement" of the critical philosophy by Maimon[1] (Jews always like to do that sort of thing, to gain an air of importance for themselves at someone else's expense), I have never really understood what he is after and must leave the reproof to others.

I infer that this problem is attributable to physical causes, since it dates from the time, three years ago, when I had a cold that lasted a week. A mucus made its appearance then, and after the cold was better, this material seems to have moved into the sinuses. It clears up momentarily when I am fortunate enough to sneeze but returns soon after, fogging my brain. Otherwise I am quite healthy, for a man of 70.

I hope that this explanation, which would be pointless to relate to a doctor, since they can do nothing about the consequences of aging, will serve to assure you of my friendship and devotion.

Now as to our friends – [Kant inquires about J. B. Erhard,[2] who was duped by a confidence man into cashing a large check and accepting a nonexistent position as surgeon with the American army].

---

1 Solomon Maimon. See letters of Apr. 7, 1789, Ak. [352], May 26, 1789, Ak. [362], and Sept. 290, 1791, Ak. [486].
2 See Kant's letter to Erhard, Dec. 21, 1792, Ak. [552], n. 1.

172 [621] (586)
To Johann Erich Biester.
April 10, 1794.

Here is something[1] for your M.S. [*Berliner Monatsschrift*], dearest friend, which may serve, like Swift's *Tale of a Tub*, to create a momentary diversion from the constant uproar over the same problem.

Herr Rehberg's essay[2] arrived only yesterday. In reading it, I found that, as regards the infinite disparity between rationalist and empiricist interpretations of concepts of justice the answering of his objections would take too *long;* with regard to his principle of justice grounded on power as the highest source of legislation, the answering would be too *dangerous;* and in view of his already having decided in favor of the powers that be (as on page 122),[3] the answering would be in *vain*. It can hardly be expected that a man of 70 would occupy himself with tasks that are burdensome, dangerous, and in vain.

Herr Rehberg wants to unite the actual *lawyer* [a] (who puts a sword onto the scales of justice to balance the side of rational grounds) with the *philosopher of law*[b] and the inevitable result is that the *application*[c] extolled as so necessary in order to render the theory adequate (so they pretend, though actually they want to substitute application for theory) will turn out to be *trickery*.[d] As a matter of fact, an essay of that sort forbids one at the outset to say anything against it.

That injunction presumably will soon be felt with its full force, since Herr Hermes[4] and Herr Hillmer[5] have taken their positions as overseers of secondary schools and have thereby acquired influence on the universities with respect to how and what is supposed to be taught there.

The essay I will send you soon is entitled "The End of All Things." It will be partly doleful and partly jolly to read.

Your devoted servant and friend,

I. Kant

11:496

11:497

---

1 Kant's "On the Influence of the Moon on Atmospheric Conditions" ("Etwas über den Einfluß des Mondes auf die Witterung") appeared in the May issue (1794) of the *Berliner Monatsschrift*.

[a] *Juristen* [b] *Rechtsphilosophen*
[c] *Praxis*
[d] *Praktiken*. Kant's word-play is lost in translation.

2 August Wilhelm Rehberg, "On the Relation of Theory to Practice" ("Über das Verhältnis der Theorie zur Praxis") in the *Berliner Monatsschrift* (1794). On Rehberg, see Schütz's letter to Kant, Ak. [330], n. 1. Rehberg claimed that Kant's proof of the highest principle of morality was valid but that it was impossible to derive any specific moral knowledge from it, since the formal law has no content and does not indicate any specific purpose at which human activity should aim. The principle needs to be supplemented with empirical knowledge. Kant's letter to him of around Sept. 25, 1790, Ak. [448], concerns the philosophy of mathematics rather than ethics.

3 Rehberg claimed that the principle that man must be treated as an end in himself is invalid. It holds only for man *qua* rational being, but in fact man is also a natural being, not governed by reason, and can therefore be treated as an object.

4 Hermann Daniel Hermes (1731–1807), a member of the Censorship Commission on Spiritual Affairs.

5 On Hillmer, see Kiesewetter's discussion of the censorship commission, Ak. [605].

---

173 [625] (590)
To Johann Erich Biester.

May 18, 1794.

11:500   I hasten, treasured friend, to send you the treatise[1] that I promised, before your authorship and mine are trampled down. In case that has
11:501   happened in the interim, please send it on to Professor and Deacon Ehrhard Schmidt[2] in Jena for his *Philosophisches Journal*. I thank you for your information. Convinced that I have acted at all times legally and scrupulously, I look forward calmly to the conclusion of these remarkable events. If new laws *command* what is not contrary to my principles, I will obey them at once; I shall do that even if they should merely *forbid* that one's principles be made public, as I have done heretofore (and which in no sense do I regret). Life is short, especially what is left of it after one has lived through 70 years; some corner of the earth can surely be found in which to bring it to an untroubled close. If you obtain any information that might interest me, not secret but perhaps not reliably or in a timely fashion available here, I would be very pleased to have you share it with me.

I remain

yours,

I. Kant.

P.S. I have indicated in one place in this treatise how *the typesetter* should remedy an error in the text made by my amanuensis;[3] please call his attention to it.

---

1 "Das Ende aller Dinge" appeared in the *Berliner Monatsschrift* in June 1794.
2 Karl Christian Erhard Schmid (1761–1812), professor of philosophy in Jena, author of an abstract of Kant's first *Critique* and of books on empricism, moral philosophy, and metaphysics. The *Philosophisches Journal für Moralität, Religion und Menschenwohl* was published by Schmid and Friedrich Wilhelm Daniel Snell in 1793/94.
3 Johann Heinrich Immanuel Lehmann (1769–1808), Kant's secretary.

174 [630] (595)
From Jacob Sigismund Beck.

June 17, 1794.

Esteemed teacher,

[*Beck asks Kant's opinion of the proposed third volume of his* Explanatory Abstract of the Critical Writings of Prof. Kant. *It is the work entitled* Einzig möglicher Standpunkt, aus welchem die critische Philosophie beurtheilt werden muss (*Only possible standpoint from which the critical philosophy is to be judged*).]

11:508

In your *Critique of Pure Reason* you lead your reader gradually to the highest point of the transcendental philosophy, viz., to the synthetic unity.[1] First, you draw his attention to the consciousness of a given, then make him attentive of concepts by means of which something is thought; you present the categories initially also as concepts, in the ordinary sense, and finally bring him to the insight that these categories are actually the activity of the understanding through which it *originally* creates for itself the concept of an object and produces the "*I think an object.*" I have become used to calling this production of the synthetic unity of consciousness "the *original attribution.*"[a] It is this activity, among others, that the geometer *postulates* when he starts his geometry from the proposition "Conceive of space"; and no discursive represen-

11:509

---

[a] *Ursprüngliche Beilegung*

tation whatsoever could take its place for this purpose. As I see the matter, the postulate "To conceive of an object by means of the original attribution" is also the highest principle of philosophy as a whole, the principle on which both general pure logic and the whole of transcendental philosophy rests. I am therefore strongly convinced that this synthetic unity is just the standpoint from which, if one has once mastered it, one can truly understand not only the meaning of "analytic" and "synthetic" judgment but what is actually meant by "a priori" and "a posteriori," what the *Critique* means when it attributes the possibility of geometric axioms to the purity of the intuition on which the axioms are based, what it really is that affects us – whether it is the thing in itself or whether this expression only means a transcendental Idea, or, instead, the object of empirical intuition itself, that

11:510   is, appearance – and whether the *Critique* argues circularly when it makes the possibility of experience into the principle of synthetic a priori judgments and yet conceals the principle of causality in the concept of this possibility. I say that one can only have a full understanding of all these things, and even of the discursive concept "possibility of experience" itself, when one has fully mastered this standpoint. So long as one still thinks of this "possibility of experience" purely discursively and does not follow up the original attributive activity[b] in just such an attribution[c] as this, one has insight into virtually nothing, having merely substituted one incomprehensible thing for another. Your *Critique*, however, leads your reader only gradually, as I say, to this standpoint, and thus, according to its method, it cannot clear up the matter right at the beginning, that is, in the Introduction. The difficulties that reveal themselves along the way ought to encourage the thoughtful reader to be persistent and patient. But since only a very few readers know how to master this highest standpoint, they attribute the difficulties to the style of the work and doubt that they can stick to it. Their difficulties would certainly be overcome, if they were once in a position to consider the challenge: produce the synthetic unity of consciousness. But a proof that even the friends of the *Critique* don't know what they are about is that they don't know where they ought to locate the object that produces sensation.

I have decided therefore to pursue this subject, truly the most important in the whole *Critique*, and am working on an essay in which the method of the *Critique* is reversed. I begin with the postulate of the original attribution, locate this activity in the categories, try to get the reader right into this activity itself, where the attribution discloses itself originally in the material of time representation. – Once I think I have the reader completely in the framework in which I want him, I shall

---

[b] *ursprünglich beilegende Handlung*   [c] *Beilegung*

then lead him to the assessment of the *Critique of Pure Reason*, its Introduction, Aesthetic, and Analytic. Then I shall let him evaluate the most important criticisms of it, especially those of the author of *Aenesidemus*.[2]

What do you think of this? Your age oppresses you, and I shall not ask you to answer me, though I must confess that your letters are most treasured gifts to me. But I do beg you to be kind enough to give your true opinion about this work to my publisher, for he shall base his decision on that. Of course I desire only that you tell him exactly what you think of the project, whether such a work of mine would be useful to the public.   11:511

Please excuse me if I seem too assertive. I must forward this letter via Hartknoch, and the mail is about to leave, so I have had to write somewhat glibly. May you remain well disposed toward

Your most respectful

Beck

---

1 See B 134 n.: "The synthetic unity of apperception is therefore that highest point, to which we must ascribe all employment of the understanding, even the whole of logic, and conformably therewith, transcendental philosophy."

2 See Kant's letter to Beck of Dec. 4, 1792, Ak.[549], n. 1, for further details about *Aenesidemus-Schulze*.

175 [634] (599)
To Jacob Sigismund Beck.
July 1, 1794.

Dearest friend,   11:514

Aside from remarking on the pleasure that your letters always give me, I have only the following little remarks to make concerning your proposed book on the "original attribution"[a1] (the relating of a representation, as a determination[b] of the subject, to an object distinct from it,[2] by which means it becomes a cognition and is not merely a feeling):

1. Could you also make clear what you mean by the word "Beile-   11:515

---

a Ursprüngliche Beilegung   *b Bestimmung* gung" in Latin? Furthermore, one cannot actually say that a representation *befits* another thing but only that, if it is to be a cognition, a *relation* to something else (something other than the subject in which the representation inheres) *befits* the representation, whereby it becomes *communicable* to other people; for otherwise it would belong merely to feeling (of pleasure or displeasure), which in itself cannot be communicated. But we can only understand and communicate to others what we ourselves can *produce*,[3] granted that the manner in which we *intuit* something, in order to bring this or that into a representation, can be assumed to be the same for everybody. Only the former is thus the representation of a *composite*. For –

2. The composition[c4] itself is not given; on the contrary, we must produce it ourselves: we must *compose* if we are to represent anything *as composed* (even space and time). We are able to communicate with one another because of this composition. The grasping (apprehensio) of the given manifold and its reception in the unity of consciousness (apperceptio) is the same sort of thing as the representation of a composite (that is, it is only possible through composition), if the synthesis of my representation in the grasping of it, and its analysis insofar as it is a concept, yield one and the same representation (reciprocally bring forth one another). This agreement is related to something that is valid for everyone, something distinct from the subject, that is, related to an object[d] since it lies exclusively neither in the representation nor in consciousness but nevertheless is valid (communicable) for everyone.

I notice, as I am writing this down, that I do not even entirely understand myself and I shall wish you luck if you can put this simple, thin thread of our cognitive faculty under a sufficiently bright light. Such overly refined hairsplitting is no longer for me; I cannot even get an adequate grasp of Professor Reinhold's thinking. I need not remind a mathematician like you, dear friend, to stay within the boundaries of clarity, both by using the most ordinary expressions and by furnishing easily grasped examples. – Herr Hartknoch will be very pleased with your projected book. Hold me dear as

11:516

Your sincere friend and servant,
I. Kant

[c] *Die Zusammensetzung*   [d] *auf ein Objekt bezogen wird*

---

1 As Kant indicates in the next paragraph, it is difficult to know how to translate Beck's word "Beilegung" (or "Beylegung," as Kant writes). Ordinary uses of the word in German seem pretty irrelevant to Beck's meaning.

2 I.e., an object distinct from that representation ("von ihr unterschiedenes Objekt").

3   This thought must have appealed to Kant in a number of different contexts. Cf. Ak. 16:344 and 345, Reflections 2394 and 2398. "Wir begreifen nur was wir selbst machen können" (We grasp only what we ourselves can produce). Kant makes a similar sounding claim in a letter, Ak.[692], to Johann Plücker, sometime *Bürgermeister* of Elberfeld: "Denn nur das, was wir selbst machen können, verstehen wir aus dem Grunde" (For only that which we ourselves can produce do we understand from its basis). The sense of the words is different, however: Kant's statement in the Plücker letter aims to contrast what we learn from others (of which, when it comes to spiritual matters, we can never be certain, he maintains) and what we achieve in the way of insight through our own efforts.

4   *Zusammensetzung* is sometimes used interchangeably with the Latin *combinatio* in the *Critique*, and sometimes with "synthesis" or "synthesizing" or "connection," since its root meaning of "putting together" is also that of *Verbinden* and *Verbindung*. In some places it is unclear whether it is the activity of putting together or the result of that activity that Kant means.

176 [636] (601)
From Friedrich August Nitsch.[1]
July 25, 1794.

London, the 25th of July, 1794.

Dear Sir,
Most honored Herr Professor,

    I am so happy to have found a favorable opportunity that enables me to write to my friends and benefactors in Königsberg without having to pay the expensive postage from London. And since I have this opportunity, I would never forgive myself were I to let it pass without writing to you. You were my teacher. You allowed me to attend your lectures *gratis*, enlightened my mind, improved and ennobled my principles and my heart and recommended me to people, not only in Königsberg but in Berlin. I have reflected on all these matters a great deal and I find that if there is anything worthwhile in me, if my insights in matters of duty are correct, if now I walk securely and lead others securely through what had previously been the meaningless wasteland of speculative reason, and if I have created anything of value in this world or shall do so in the future, I have only your instruction, example, and kindness toward me to thank for these things. How could I think all this and not write to you, not let some marks of gratitude

11:518 show themselves, gratitude to a man who will be and must be honored for millennia to come, and who has been my teacher, my friend, and my benefactor. God, I would be a villain if I were capable of such a thing, a thoughtless human being if I did not rejoice in it daily. I would be as unfeeling as the pen with which I write if tears of sincerest gratitude did not prove the love and respect that I owe for the friendship and great support of such a great man.

For over a year I have had to struggle against adversity in London. That is the reason why I have not written. I could not write because the postage was too costly for me and I had no other way to communicate.

As far as philosophy in England is concerned, it is, except for the mathematical and empirical part of it, thoroughly bad and could really not be worse. I have many friends and acquaintances in the Royal Society of Sciences here and I read the most popular philosophical writers in English. But I must say that what I have usually found is an amalgam of dogmatic skepticism, materialism, idealism and other opposing systems basted together. And this happy union is even regarded here as demonstrating the great advantage of healthy human understanding over speculative reason. The contradictions in practical principles and the distrust of reason seem here to be wide-ranging. Were the English not bound together by common entertainments and needs, I am fully convinced they would murder each other if they were allowed to behave in accordance with their principles. Those principles are full of mistakes and contradictions, because they all appeal to empirical determination of the will. I have the honor of being the first person in London to lecture on the Kantian philosophy, and I shall perhaps be the first to write an introduction to this remarkable system in English, following Reinhold. I say only that I am completely convinced that no one can undertake anything like this who does not feel totally at home in the job. It has to be done well or not at all. My lectures have had great and surprising acclaim. Until now, people were not even acquainted with the title of your immortal book, let alone its contents. If you allow me, I could send you further news about my important and honorable project in the future.

11:519 I have the honor of remaining, with deepest respect, veneration, and gratitude,

your wholly obedient and most devoted servant
Fr. Aug. Nitsch.

If there is anything you want in London, it would give me infinite pleasure to receive your orders. My mother will be happy to see that your letter gets to London. My address is: Mr. Nitsch No. 88 St. Martin's Lane, Charing Cross. London.

1 Nitsch, born in Gumbinnen, matriculated as a student of theology in Königs-
berg in Oct. 1785. As this letter indicates, he became the first person to lecture
on Kant's philosophy in England. He lectured for three years (1794–6) at
Number 18 Panton Square, Haymarket. Nitsch published his lectures as "A
General and Introductory View of Professor Kant's Principles concerning
Man, the World and the Deity, submitted to the consideration of the learned."
According to the editor of the Akademie edition of Kant's works, the lectures
are insignificant: "Das Buch hat keine Bedeutung" (Ak. 13: 370). Adolf Poschmann, in an article entitled "Die Ersten Kantianer in England" (in Ernst Bahr,
ed., *Studien zur Geschichte des Preussenlandes*, Marburg, 1963), thinks this judgment too harsh. A copy of Nitsch's book exists in the University of Würzburg
library, according to Poschmann.

177 [640] (605)
From Friedrich Wilhelm II.[1]
October 1, 1794.

Friedrich Wilhelm, by the Grace of God King of Prussia, etc., etc.,   11:525

Our gracious greetings, first of all. Worthy and most learned, dear
loyal subject! Our most high person has long observed with great
displeasure how you misuse your philosophy to distort and disparage
many of the cardinal and foundational teachings of the Holy Scriptures
and of Christianity; how you have done this specifically in your book,
"Religion within the Limits of Reason Alone," and similarly in other
shorter treatises. We expected better of you, since you yourself must
see how irresponsibly you have acted against your duty as a teacher of
youth and against our sovereign purposes, of which you are well aware.
We demand that you immediately give a conscientious vindication of
your actions, and we expect that in the future, to avoid our highest
disfavor, you will be guilty of no such fault, but rather, in keeping with
your duty, apply your authority and your talents to the progressive
realization of our sovereign purpose. Failing this, you must expect
unpleasant measures for your continuing obstinacy.

   With our gracious regards. By the most gracious *special* order of his
royal majesty.

                                        [signed] Woellner.
                                        Berlin, October 1, 1794

To Prof. Kant
in Königsberg

485

1 This draft of a royal proclamation or *Kabinettsorder* is signed by Woellner, Friedrich Wilhelm II's minister. Both the proclamation, differing from this draft only insignificantly, and Kant's reply, Ak.[642], were published by Kant in the Preface to *Streit der Fakultäten (The Conflict of the Faculties)*, 1798. The translation here is mainly that of Mary Gregor from her edition and translation of the *Streit* (New York: Abaris Books, Inc., 1979).

178 [642] (607)
To Friedrich Wilhelm II.[1]

After October 12, 1794

[*Draft*]

Your Royal Majesty's supreme order issued on October 1 and delivered to me October 12 enjoins me, as follows.[2] *First*, because of my misuse of philosophy in distorting and disparaging many of the basic teachings of the Holy Scripture and of Christianity, particularly in my book *Religion within the Limits of Reason Alone*[3] as well as in other smaller treatises and because I am guilty of overstepping my duty as an educator of the youth and guilty of opposing the very highest purposes of our sovereign, purposes that are supposedly well known to me, I am therefore duty-bound to bring forward a conscientious vindication of my conduct, and *Second*, I am not to repeat this sort of offense in the future. In regard to both of these obligations and with profound submissiveness I hope to show Your Royal Majesty sufficient proof of my previously demonstrated and further to be demonstrated obedience.

As for the *first* complaint against me, that I have misused my philosophy to disparage Christianity, my conscientious self-vindication is as follows:

1. As an *educator of the youth*, that is, in my academic lectures, I have never been guilty of this sort of thing. Aside from the testimony of my auditors, to which I appeal, this is sufficiently demonstrated by the fact that my pure and merely philosophical instruction has conformed to A. G. Baumgarten's textbooks, in which the subject of Christianity does not even occur, nor can it occur. It is impossible to accuse me of overstepping the limits of a philosophical investigation of religion in my teaching.

2. Nor have I, as an *author*, for example in my *Religion within the Limits* . . . opposed the highest purposes of the sovereign that were

11:527

11:528

486

known to me. For since those purposes concern the state religion, I would have had to write as a teacher of the general public, a task for which this book along with my other little essays is ill-suited. They were only written as scholarly discussions for specialists in theology and philosophy, in order to determine how religion may be inculcated most clearly and forcefully into the hearts of men. The theory is one of which the general public takes no notice and which requires the sanction of the government only if it is to be taught to schoolteachers and teachers of religion. But it is not against the wisdom and authority of the government to allow academic freedom. For the official religious doctrines were not thought up by the government itself but were supplied to it from these scholarly sources. The government would rather be justified in demanding of the faculty an examination and justification of religious doctrines, without prescribing what it is to be.

3. I am not guilty of disparaging Christianity in that book, since it contains no assessment of any actual revealed religion. It is intended merely as an examination of rational religion,[a] an assessment of its priority as the highest condition of all true religion, of its completeness and of its practical aim (namely, to show us what we are obligated to do) as well as of its incompleteness from the standpoint of the theoretical [reason] (an incompleteness that is the source of evil, just as the latter is the source of our transition to the good or the reason the certainty that we are evil is possible, and so on). Consequently the need for a revealed doctrine is not obscured, and rational religion is related to revealed religion in general, without specifying which one it is (where Christianity, for example, is regarded as the mere idea of a conceivable revelation). It was, I maintain, my duty to make clear the status of rational religion. It should have been incumbent on my accusers to point out a single case in which I profaned Christianity either by arguing against its acceptance as a revelation or by showing it to be unnecessary. For I do not regard it as a disparaging of a revealed doctrine to say that, in relation to its practical use (which constitutes the essential part of all religion), it must be interpreted in accordance with the principles of pure rational faith and must be urged on us openly. I take this rather as a recognition of its morally fruitful content, which would be deformed by the supposedly superior importance of merely theoretical propositions that are to be taken on faith.

11:529

4. My true respect for Christianity is demonstrated by my extolling the Bible as the best available guide for the grounding and support of a truly moral state religion, perennially suitable for public instruction in religion. Therefore I have not allowed myself any attacks or criticisms of the Bible based on merely theoretical beliefs (though the

[a] *Verrunftreligion*

faculties must be allowed to do this). I have insisted on the holy, practical content of the Bible, which, with all the changes in theoretical articles of faith that will take place in regard to merely revealed doctrines, because of their coincidental nature, will always remain as the inner and essential part of religion. The essential, practical essence of religion can always be recovered in its purity, as it was after Christianity had degenerated in the dark ages of clericalism.

5. Finally, I have always insisted that anyone who confesses a revealed faith must be conscientious, viz., he must assert no more than he really knows, and he must urge others to believe only in that of which he himself is fully certain. My conscience is clear: I have never let the Divine Judge out of my sight, in writing my works on religion, and I have tried voluntarily to withdraw not only every error that might destroy a soul but even every possibly offensive expression. I have done this especially because, in my 71st year, the thought necessarily arises that I may soon have to give an accounting of myself before a judge of the world who knows men's hearts. Therefore I have no misgivings in offering this vindication now to the highest authority in our land, with full conscientiousness, as my unchangeable, candid confession.

11:530

6. Regarding the second charge, that I am not to be guilty of such distortion and depreciation of Christianity (as has been claimed) in the future, I find that, as Your Majesty's loyal subject,[4] in order not to fall under suspicion, it will be the surest course for me to abstain entirely from all public lectures on religious topics, whether on natural or revealed religion, and not only from lectures but also from publications. I hereby promise this.

I am eternally Your Royal Majesty's most submissive and obedient subject.

---

1 This is Kant's response to the *Kabinettsorder* of Oct. 1, 1794. Both documents were subsequently published in the Preface to Kant's *Conflict of the Faculties* (*Der Streit der Facultäten*) (Königsberg, 1798), Ak. 7: 1–116. Three drafts of the present letter exist. Cf. *Werke*, Ak. 13:372–87.

2 The *Kabinettsorder* was signed by Woellner.

3 On Oct. 14, 1795, the King, or rather his ministers Woellner and Hillmer, issued an order to the academic senate in Königsberg forbidding all professors to lecture on Kant's book. (Schultz had announced a course of lectures.) (*Werke*, Ak. 13:371.)

4 Kant later interpreted this phrase as committing him to silence only insofar as he was a subject of Friedrich Wilhelm II. He therefore felt himself not in violation of his promise when he published on religious topics after the death of that monarch. He adds a footnote to the reprinting of the letter in *Streit der*

Fakultäten: "This expression, too, I chose carefully, so that I would not renounce my freedom to judge in this religious suit *forever*, but only during His
Majesty's lifetime." (Ak. 7:10,n.)

179 [643] (608)
To François Théodore de la Garde.[1]
November 24, 1794.

Your letter of November 8, which arrived here on the 22nd along
with a portion of the *Anacharsis* and one of Montaigne, together with
the gift of *Philosophie Sociale*, whose publication pleased me very much,   11:530
deserves my sincere thanks.[2] But I am not sure that you still owe me
anything toward the equivalent value of the complimentary copies,
especially if the sixth part of the Montaigne is to be included in a
future shipment; sending your company's catalog for this purpose
(which I did not however find in the packet) was therefore unnecessary.
Yet you do me an injustice in seeming to interpret my negligence in   11:531
letter writing as dissatisfaction on my part. I have no cause at all to be
dissatisfied.

The only reason I have not turned to you to publish some of my
recent articles is that in my withdrawn lifestyle I need to have an
adequate provision of new reading material every evening, as nourishment rather than just for the sake of pleasure, and for this purpose I
need the good will of one or another of the local book merchants –
which will not be the case unless I also give them something to publish.
I hoped that I could divide up this business so as to be able to deal
with you as well; I have not abandoned that hope, despite two obstacles. One of them is that, in my rather advanced years, my indisposition
makes the work of authorship proceed only slowly and with numerous
interruptions, so that I cannot specify a firm delivery date, at least not
at present. The other obstacle is that my subject is really metaphysics
in the widest sense and as such includes theology, morality (and thus
also religion) as well as natural law (including public law *[Staatsrecht]*
and international law *[Völkerrecht]*, though only to the extent that reason can address these subjects; but the hand of the censor lies heavily
on all of these topics and one cannot be sure that all one's work in any
of these fields will not be rendered futile by a stroke of the censor's
pen. I hope that once peace is established, which seems to be near, the
limits of what an author is allowed to write will be defined more

precisely, so that one can feel secure about what is permissible. Until then, worthy friend, you will have to have patience while with optimistic hopes I continue my labors.

I do have one favor to ask, namely, that you find out from Dr. Biester why I have received no issues of the *Berlin Monatsschrift* from him other than the first quarterly, i.e., that of January, February, March, not even the two issues that contain essays of mine, issues of which an author customarily receives a copy. I would rather have him write me a personal account of this matter, if he is willing, but if that is impossible I shall be content with an oral message. I beg you to send me an answer by the next post and at my expense, for I am impatient to hear his reply.

With total respect and friendship I remain ever

Your wholly devoted servant,

I. Kant

Königsberg,
the 24th of November 1794.

11:532

---

1 On Lagarde, see Kant's letter of Mar. 25, 1790, Ak. [414], n. 1, above.
2 In a letter of Sept. 20, 1793, Ak. [593], Kant had asked Lagarde to send either a book called *Travels of the younger Anacharsis through Greece (Reise des jüngern Anacharsis durch Griechenland*, Biester's translation of *Voyage du jeune Anacharsis en Grèce* by the Abbé Jean Jacques Barthelemy, Berlin, 1789–83, in 7 volumes) or Montaigne's *Thoughts and Opinions* (Johann Joachim Christoph Bode's translation of Montaigne, published in Berlin, 1793–5, under the title *Michel de Montaignes Gedanken und Meinungen über allerley Gegenstände*) as substitutes for complimentary copies of Kant's third *Critique*, which Lagarde had promised Kant. Lucius Junius Frey's *Philosophie sociale, dédiée au peuple français, par un citoyen de la section de la République française ci-devant du Roule* appeared in Paris, 1793.

180 [644] (609)
To Carl Friedrich Stäudlin.
December 4, 1794.

Highly esteemed Sir,
Dearest friend,

Reciprocating the valued affection you have shown me, I thank you for your kindness in sending me your now completed *History of Skepti-*

cism, a useful, carefully written and penetrating book.[1] I thank you as well for your long unanswered letter which pleased me very much; my neglect is not due to any lack of respect but to the indisposition if not yet illness that attends my age and forces me to put off many things for the sake of slow progress on more pressing business. I hope that my kind friends will forgive me for these omissions.

In regard to the proposal in your letter, I must tell you candidly how I feel.

I found this proposal – to include some of my writings in a theolog-   11:533
ical journal that you would publish,[2] allowing me, as you say, to count on the most unrestricted freedom of the press – not only praiseworthy but personally welcome. For even though I had no intention of utilizing this freedom in its fullest scope, still I thought that the esteem that [Göttingen], a university under the orthodox George III, has in the eyes of the equally orthodox Friedrich Wilhelm II, who is a friend of the former, could serve me as a shield to curb the disparaging attacks of the hyper orthodox (who are a danger) in our locality.[3]

With this idea in mind, I have therefore written an essay entitled "The Strife of the Faculties" and have had it ready for some time now, intending to send it to you. The work seems to me of interest because it does not only try to shed light on the right of the learned professions to submit all matters of state religion to the *Theological* Faculty, arguing also that the state authorities have an interest in granting this permission; but besides this the essay also argues for the *Philosophical* Faculty's right to sit as an opposition bench against the Theological Faculty. The authorization of an article of faith as a binding rule of duty or even of prudence of the established state religion must be in accord with the verdict of clerics instructed by both faculties and acting as officers of the church so far as they constitute an Ecclesiastical Council, while other religious associations are to be tolerated as *sects* as long as they do not offend against morality.

Even though this essay is really not theological but concerned with *public law*[4] (the legal principles concerning religious and ecclesiastical matters), I have had to give some examples which may be the only ones that make clear why a sectarian religion by its very nature is unfit to become an established religion and why certain articles of faith cannot be enforced by public authorities as part of a state religion but can only be the credo of a sect.

But I am afraid, not only on account of these examples but also on account of others that I introduce, that the censor (who is now very powerful in these parts) may take some of these things as aimed at him and denounce them. Therefore I have decided to refrain from publishing this work for now[5] in the hope that the approaching peace may   11:534
also bring with it an increased freedom for innocent judgments; when

that happens I shall submit the work to you for an assessment as to whether it should be viewed as belonging to theology or merely to public law.

I beg you most urgently to give my warmest thanks to your excellent Privy Councillor *Lichtenberg*;[6] his clear head, upright way of thinking and unsurpassable humor can accomplish more in the struggle against the evil of a miserable religious tyranny than others accomplish with their rational arguments. Thank him for his kind and undeserved gift, "Collection and Description of Hogarth's Copper Engravings", but I forbid him to assume the cost of the remainder of the collection.

When you have the chance, please pay my respects to Dr. Plank.[7] I cannot conceal my pleasure in finding that, since the freedom of thought we used to cherish has fled from here, it has found protection among such worthy men as you have in your university.

I remain always, with thoroughgoing respect and true affection,
Your most devoted servant,
Königsberg,
the 4th of December, 1794   I. Kant.

---

1 *Geschichte und Geist des Skeptizismus, vorzüglich in Rücksicht auf Moral und Religion* (History and spirit of skepticism, especially with respect to morality and religion; Leipzig, 1794). Stäudlin sent Kant the first volume June 14.

2 The journal was the *Göttingische Bibliothek der neuesten theologischen Literatur*, published by Johann Friedrich Schleussner and Stäudlin, Göttingen, 1794–1801, of which five volumes appeared.

3 Great Britain's King George II, father of George III, was a Hanoverian prince. It was under him that the University of Göttingen was founded; the university opened in 1737.

4 Kant parenthetically writes the Latin phrase here, "de iure principis circa religionem et ecclesiam."

5 *The Conflict of the Faculties* was published in 1798 and was dedicated to Stäudlin.

6 Georg Christoph Lichtenberg (1742–99), famous satirist and physicist, professor in Göttingen. For his relation to Kant, see, e.g., an article by Arno Neumann in Kant-Studien, IV, pp. 68, ff.

7 Gottlieb Jakob Planck (1751–1833), professor of theology in Göttingen.

181 [647] (612)
From Samuel Collenbusch.[1]
December 26, 1794.

My dear Herr Professor,

Herr Kant's rational faith is a faith *purified of all hope.*
Herr Kant's morality is a morality *purified of all love.*   11:536

Now the question arises: In what respects does the Devil's faith differ from that of Herr Kant? And in what respects is the Devil's morality different from that of Herr Kant?

S. Collenbusch, M.D.

Elberfeld,
the 26th of December, 1794.

---

1 Samuel Collenbusch (1724–1803) was a physician and an ardent Pietist who lived in the Rhineland. In addition to the present letter, he wrote several others to Kant (Ak.[649], [657], and [698]) proclaiming his Christian faith and up-braiding Kant for his ethics and philosophy of religion. Collenbusch found it incomprehensible that Kant did not adhere to Christian doctrines.

Letters 1795–1800

[656–867]

1795

182 [656] (621)
To Friedrich Schiller.[1]

March 30, 1795.

Esteemed Sir, 12:10

I am always delighted to know and engage in literary discussions
with such a talented and learned man as you, my dearest friend. I   12:11
received the plan for a periodical that you sent me last summer and
also the two first monthly issues. I found your *Letters on the Aesthetic
Education of Mankind* splendid, and I shall study them so as to be able
to give you my thoughts about them. The paper on sexual differences
in organic nature, in the second issue, is impossible for me to decipher,
even though the author seems to be an intelligent fellow.[2] There was
once a severely critical discussion in the *Allgemeine Literaturzeitung*
about the ideas expressed in the letters of Herr Hube of Thorn[3] concerning a similar relationship extending throughout nature. The ideas
were attacked as romantic twaddle. To be sure, we sometimes find
something like that running through our heads, without knowing what
to make of it. The organization of nature has always struck me as
amazing and as a sort of chasm of thought; I mean, the idea that
fertilization, in both realms of nature, always needs two sexes in order
for the species to be propagated. After all, we don't want to believe
that providence has chosen this arrangement, almost playfully, for the
sake of variety. On the contrary, we have reason to believe that propa-
gation is not possible in any other way. This opens a prospect on what
lies beyond the field of vision, out of which, however, we can unfortunately make nothing, as little as out of what Milton's angel told Adam
about the creation: "Male light of distant suns mixes itself with female,
for purposes unknown."[4] I feel that it may harm your magazine not to
have the authors sign their names, to make themselves thus responsible

497

for their considered opinions; the reading public is very eager to know who they are.

For your gift, then, I offer my most respectful thanks; with regard to my small contribution to this journal, your present to the public, I must however beg a somewhat lengthy postponement. Since discussions of political and religious topics are currently subject to certain restrictions and there are hardly any other matters, at least at this time, that interest the general reading public, one must keep one's eye on this change of the weather, so as to conform prudently to the times.

Please greet Professor Fichte and give him my thanks for sending me his various works. I would have done this myself but for the discomfort of aging that oppresses me, with all the manifold tasks I still have before me, which, however, excuses nothing but my postponement. Please give my regards also to Messrs. Schütz[5] and Hufeland.[6]

And so, dearest sir, I wish your talents and your worthy objectives the strength, health, and long life they deserve, and also the friendship, with which you wish to honor one who is ever

Your most devoted, loyal servant

I. Kant

12:12

---

1   Friedrich Schiller (1759–1805), the great poet and essayist, wrote to Kant from Jena, June 13, 1794, Ak. [628], asking Kant to contribute an essay to a new literary magazine, *Die Horen* (12 vols., 1795–7). Fichte wrote to Kant as well, supporting this request, "in the hope that the man who has made the last half of this century unforgettable for the progress of the human spirit for all future ages" might "spread his spirit over various other branches of human knowledge and to various persons." On June 17(?), 1794, Ak.[631] and again on Oct. 6, 1794, Ak. [641], Schiller assured Kant of his devotion to his moral system and expressed profuse gratitude to Kant for illuminating his spirit. On Mar. 1, 1795, Ak.[652], Schiller wrote again, repeating his request and sending two issues of *Die Horen*. He disclosed that he was the author of the *Letters on the Aesthetic Education of the Human Race*, a work he believed to be an application of Kant's philosophy and as such he hoped that Kant would like it.

2   The article was by Wilhelm von Humboldt (1767–1835): "Über den Geschlechts unterschied und dessen Einfluß auf die organische Natur." On Humboldt's understanding of Kant, see Kiesewetter's letter to Kant, Nov. 25, 1798, Ak. [827].

3   Johann Michael Hube (1737–1807), director and professor at the military academy in Warsaw, author of a book on natural science (*Naturlehre*).

4   The correct quotation is as follows:
    and other suns perhaps
    With their attendant moons thou wilt descry

Communicating male and female light,
Which two great sexes animate the world,
Stored in each orb perhaps with some that live.
Paradise Lost, Book VIII, ll. 148–52

5 Christian Gottfried Schütz. On Schütz, see Kant's letter of Sept. 13, 1785, Ak.[243].

6 Gottlieb Hufeland (1760–1817), professor of law in Jena. Hufeland was co-director of the *A.L.Z.* In addition to teaching at Jena, then Würzburg, Landshut, and Halle, he served for a short time as Bürgermeister of his home town, Danzig. Hufeland's *Versuch über den Grundsatz des Naturrechts* (Leipzig, 1785) was reviewed by Kant in the *A.L.Z.*, Apr. 18, 1786. (Hufeland was also a cousin of the physician Christoph Wilhelm Hufeland, inventor of "macrobiotics," the art of prolonging life.)

183 [668] (633)
To Carl Leonhard Reinhold.

July 1, 1795.

Your good letter, delivered by the very worthy Count von Purgstall,   12:27
gave me pleasure.[1] It made me see that your expression of a certain dissatisfaction with my silence about your progress in completing the Critical Philosophy by extending it to the very limits of its principles was not based on any true displeasure with me. I am pleased to see that your friendship persists as before.

Because of my age and certain physical infirmities inseparable from it, I am now compelled to leave to my friends any attempt to amplify this science. I must, though it is slow going, devote what little strength I have left to the additions that are still part of my plan.

Do maintain your friendship for me, dearest man, and rest assured that I shall always take the greatest interest in everything that concerns you.

Your loyal and devoted servant,
I. Kant.

---

1 Reinhold's letter is Ak.[655]. The count alluded to was Gottfried Wenzel von Purgstall (1733–1812) who traveled to Königsberg in order to meet Kant, having studied Kantian philosophy with Reinhold in Jena. He later praised

Kant's lectures and wrote a lively account of Kant's personality. "My first visit to Kant was on Apr. 18, 1795, at seven-thirty in the morning. I found him in a yellow dressing gown with a red silken Polish sash, wearing his sleeping cap – working. He received me politely of course, skimmed Reinhold's letter, talked a lot – almost chattered, mainly about little things, chatted with great wit and made some wholly original remarks about *Schwärmerei*, and especially about scholarly women and their illnesses . . . The conclusion of my observations about Kant is this: He is certainly honest, his soul is *pure*, he is childlike and does not at all take himself to be a great man . . ." Quoted in a footnote to Kant's letter in the *Philosophische Bibliothek* edition of Kant's *Briefwechsel*, ed. by Rudolf Malter (Hamburg, 1986), p. 879.

184 [671] (636)
To Samuel Thomas Soemmerring,[1]
August 10, 1795.

August 10, 1795.

12:30   You, dearest sir, the prime philosophical dissector of the visible in man, have honored me, dissector of the invisible in man, with the dedication of your excellent work, presumably to invite the union of our two enterprises towards a common goal.

With sincerest thanks for your trust I submit to you my draft concerning on the one hand the possibility and on the other hand the impossibility of uniting the two projects.[2] I leave it to your good judgment to publish what I say as you see fit.

Given your talent, your blossoming strength and your youth, science can hope for great contributions from you, to which I add my heartfelt hope for your health and comfort, while the ebbing tide of my own remaining years leaves little to expect other than to use the instruction of others as much as is possible.

Your
devoted admirer and most devoted servant
I. Kant.

Königsberg, the 10th of August, 1795.

---

1   Soemmerring (1755–1830) – the name is sometimes spelled with only one *r* – was a physician in Frankfurt, well known for his work on physiology and

anatomy. Three of Kant's drafts of the present letter, each slightly different, exist: see Ak. 13:398–412. The translation of Kant's essay on Soemmerring, "Concerning the Organ of the Soul" ("Über das Organ der Seele"), originally appended to the present letter, may be found in Günter Zöller's edition of Kant's *Anthropology, Philosophy of History and Education*, in the Cambridge Edition of the Works of Immanuel Kant.

2 Soemmerring's "On the Organ of the Soul" ("Über das Organ der Seele") was published with Kant's remarks included as an Appendix to the work. Soemmerring introduces them with the words: "The pride of our age, Kant, has been kind enough not only to endorse the central idea of this treatise but to develop it and refine it and thus to complete it. He has given me his kind permission to crown my work with his own words."

185 [679] (644)
To Samuel Thomas Soemmerring.
September 17, 1795.

Since Herr Nicholovius asked whether I wished to include anything 12:41 in his letter to you, dearest friend, the following occurred to me.

The main problem concerning a common organ of the senses is this: how to form a unified aggregate of sense representations in the mind, given their infinite diversity, or better, how to render that unity comprehensible by reference to the structure of the brain. This problem can be solved only if there is some means of associating even *heterogeneous* but temporally ordered impressions: e.g., associating the visual representation of a garden with the sonic representation of a piece of music played in that garden, the taste of a meal enjoyed there, etc. These representations would disarrange themselves if the nerve-bundles were to affect each other by reciprocally coming into contact. But the *water* that is in the brain cavities can serve to mediate the influence of one nerve on another and, by the latter's reaction, can serve to tie up in one consciousness the corresponding representation, without these impressions becoming confused – as little as the tones of 12:42 a polyphonous concert transmitted through the *air* are confused with each other.

But this idea must have occurred to you, so I will add nothing more except to say that I took the greatest pleasure in your expression of friendship and in the harmony of our ways of thinking, which I observed in your welcome letter.

I. Kant

186 [683] (648)
To Johann Gottfried Carl Christian Kiesewetter.
October 15, 1795.

12:45

You spoiled me so with last year's lovely Teltow carrots that my gums will no longer be contented with the local ones. Would you be kind enough again to send me a bushel of this domestic necessity? I could take care of the expenses for them and the freight if the shipment is addressed to the merchant Herr J. Conrad Jacobi, or I could repay you in any way that is convenient for you if you lay out the money. I would feel guilty if I made a habit of exploiting your politeness.

Your local friends and I were very pleased by your promise to visit us in perhaps a year and a half. A friend of yours, the wife of Court Chaplain Schultz, will not be here to meet you for she died on October 10 after a lengthy illness. Perhaps I too will expire before you come, since the seventies usually make short work of it, though I am for the present reasonably healthy.

Should you wish to be kind enough to honor me with a quick reply, I would love to be informed about the remarkable goings-on with the prize competition of the Academy of Sciences – for example, why the awards were not made, as is customary, on the king's birthday[1] rather than eight days later, and how it could come about that Schwab, Abicht, and Reinhold are assembled in a colorful arrangement,[2] and something harmonious brought forth out of so much dissonance, etc.

My reveries "On Perpetual Peace" will be sent to you through Nicolovius. With all the strife among intellectuals, it doesn't mean much if only they refrain from intrigues and make common cause with the politicians' trade, and like Horace's "atrum desinit in piscem"[3] conceal their ugly fishtails with their courtly manners.

With constant respect and friendship I remain
your most devoted servant,
I. Kant

Königsberg, October 15, 1795.

---

1 Kant was mistaken about this.

2 This is the competition devoted to the question "What actual progress [*Fortschritte*] has metaphysics made in Germany since the times of Leibniz and Wolff?" ("Welches sind die wirklichen Fortschritte, die Metaphysik seit Leibnitzens und Wolfs Zeiten in Deutschland gemacht hat?") The Academy

awarded first prize to Johann Christoph Schwab, and anti-Kantian, but also gave two equal awards to Johann Heinrich Abicht, Kant's disciple in Erlangen, and to Karl Leonhard Reinhold.

3 Horace, *Ars Poetica*, v. 3, f., speaks of a creature, presumably a mermaid, that appears as a lovely woman above and ends as an ugly fishtail.

187 [689] (654)
From Sophie Mereau.[1]
December 1795.

Even if my own feelings tell me that the step I am now prepared to take must be judged to be a daring one, I still find nothing in it that could be construed as an impropriety. I know moreover that with persons of higher quality one can boldly break the chains of that empty conventionality that adapts itself to differing circumstances and often sets up salutary barriers between ordinary people, and I know that more cultured persons focus on the matter at hand instead of remaining eternally caught up in empty formality, the way ordinary people do. It is with this presupposition that, without hesitation and without further concern about distance, gender, and intellectual dissimilarity, I feel I may present myself to you, *most estimable man*, in the simple role of a supplicant. 12:52

With the help of certain friends I intend to start a journal in the coming year; several local authors are planning to contribute to it. In an undertaking of this sort anyone who does not write just for profit must have more or less grandiose ideas. I must have very grandiose ideas, for I take it to be not impossible to win *you* to my cause. I would be content with some jottings out of your notebook that *you* perhaps think trivial, a few casual observations, to which your spirit lends light and your name lends luster. If you can do that, you will give support to my project. I dare not beg you more urgently, for I fear overstepping the delicate line that separates the unusual from the presumptuous. 12:53

If you should think it worth the trouble to become more closely acquainted with me, a woman who possesses sufficient courage to turn to you, then read the book which I enclose. Only this hope could move me to submit to the great Kant a literary work of whose deficiencies I am myself most intensely aware.

Would that I might receive your answer soon! I have turned to you trustingly – you must certainly be *kind*, however great and renowned you are.² What noble breath of humanity emanates from your *Perpetual Peace*! What power you have to kindle hope in the hearts of all well-disposed people! It depends entirely on you whether to my initial feeling of awe toward you, which I proudly nurture within my soul, I should add the sweeter feeling of gratitude.

Fare you well!

I am the wife of Professor Mereau in Jena.

---

1   Sophie Mereau (1770–1806), *née* Schubert, was married to a professor of law and librarian in Jena, Friedrich Ernst Karl Mereau, whom she later divorced. In 1803 she married the author and poetry editor (of *Knaben Wunderhorn* fame), Clemens Brentano. Her poetry was appreciated by Schiller and Goethe and was published in *Thalia*, the *Musenalmanach* and in *Die Horen*. She translated English, Italian, and Spanish novels, published reworkings of some French novels, and founded a women's magazine, *Kalathiskos* (little basket). She died in childbirth in Oct. 1806, at 33.

There is a beautiful portrait of her in Goethe's house in Frankfurt.

According to R. Reicke, writing in the *Altpreußische Monatsschrift*, XXII, p. 380 (quoted by Otto Schöndorffer in Kant's *Briefwechsel*, 3rd edition, edited by Rudolf Malter, p. 880), "Kant gave this letter as well as the accompanying book (probably her short stories, *Das Blütenalter der Empfindung*, Gotha, 1794) to the oldest daughter of his friend, Motherby, heartily delighted that she [i.e., Elisabeth Motherby] was no bluestocking." Kant's response to this talented woman, if Reicke's story is true, betrays an attitude of hostility or at least condescension toward intelligent women, a response similar to that shown in his reaction to Maria von Herbert's letters.

2   As the previous note shows, Sophie's confidence in Kant's kindness was not, in this instance, entirely justified.

1796

188 [699] (664)
From Matern Reuß[1]
April 1, 1796.

Dear Sir,   12:68

... Let me inform you at least in general terms of the state of the
critical philosophy in Catholic Germany. I continue to expound both   12:69
theoretical and practical philosophy according to your principles, without any opposition. Professor Andres[2] is teaching your aesthetics. Almost all the professors of theology and jurisprudence are modeling at
least their approaches if not the content of their teachings on your
principles, and even in religious instruction these principles are used to
teach catechism and sermons. Many foreigners come here just to hear
my lectures on the Kantian philosophy, and my prince[3] relieved me of
all my other duties so that I could devote myself to philosophy.

The prospects are not quite so bright in colleges in Bamberg, Heidelberg, and other Catholic schools, and the situation is even more
bleak in Bavaria, Swabia, and the Catholic part of Switzerland. I traveled through these three countries, and I hope I did some good. Since
their schools are largely run by monks who are strictly forbidden to
use a German textbook and certainly not a Protestant one, I wrote a
textbook of theoretical philosophy in Latin for the sake of these
schools. However, it has not been printed yet. In the Italian and French
parts of Switzerland, they also want a Latin exposition of Kant's philosophy. Professor Ith[4] in Bern asked me to give him one.

I cannot convey to you the enthusiasm for your ideas, even among
people who used to oppose them, and even the ladies here are taken
with you, since we read in a number of newspapers that you have been
called to France to act as lawgiver and patron of peace and that your
king has given you his consent. I myself am receiving many a friendly
glance from the ladies now, more than before.

I asked Court Chaplain Schultze to tell me whether the news is correct, since I know you have no time to write.

Your devoted servant,

Reuß, *Professor*

Herr Stang sends his best regards.[5]

------

1 Matern (or Maternus) Reuß (1751–98), a Benedictine, professor of philosophy in Würzburg, a disciple of Kant's. Reuß writes from Würzburg to tell Kant of the progress of Kant's philosophy in Catholic, that is, southern Germany.

2 Johann Bonaventura Andres (1743–1822), professor of philosophy in Würzburg.

3 Georg Carl, Freiherr von Fechenbach.

4 Johann Samuel Ith (1747–1813), professor of philosophy at the Akademie in Bern.

5 Conrad Stang. See the letter of Oct. 2, 1796, Ak.[715].

189 [715] (680)

From Conrad Stang.[1]

October 2, 1796.

12:97   [*Stang thanks Kant effusively for the honor of his acquaintance.*]

12:98   ... For a while I studied law, but I found it unbearably dry. I returned to philosophy, a more rewarding subject, which I had always loved. Granted, it is an unusual thing in a Catholic country, where people are used to leaving this auxiliary science to the clerics and no one really appreciates it as valuable in itself. But I also had to become a Mason (a synonym for Jacobin in this country as in other Catholic lands), and many people have busied themselves with warning me, pitying me, or even viewing me as dangerous. But I can laugh at them all, for I am wholly at peace, pursuing my philosophical studies of your works and finding truth in them and the feeling that you are with me as I read them. I enjoy practical philosophy most. And why not? For your tone here is so stirring, so moving, and this subject concerns the most important part of our lives.

Your system has been totally triumphant here, and no one dares to attack it. You know already how they used to intrigue against it, as Prof. Reuß wrote you earlier. Last year I made a trip to Vienna, returning by way of Salzburg and Munich. The many people I met enabled me to get an adequate picture of the condition of philosophy. The critical philosophy is regarded as an enemy in the Austrian monarchy, and woe to him who wants to teach it. The Emperor[2] is against it. When Herr von Birkenstock, the director of education in Vienna, told him about the critical system, the Emperor turned and said, "Once and for all, I don't want to hear any more of this dangerous system." In Vienna I heard about a Herr von Delling, who lost his professorship in Fünfkirchen, because he lectured on the principles of the critical philosophy. For three years they intrigued against him but he remained firm, but last summer the entire clergy of Hungary attacked him and he lost his position. The decree firing him charged him, among other things, with "furthering skepticism with his pernicious system" ["propter perniciosum Sistema ad Scepticism ducens"]. Other accusations were that he had tried to answer the charge (and they had actually asked him to defend himself) and had published a defense of the critical philosophy. Finally they said he had to be removed since, as his defense made clear, it was impossible to cure him of his allegiance to the critical principles. Nevertheless, the cause of the critical philosophy grows secretly as the Hungarian Protestants who study in Jena and Halle take the new principles home with them. Also in Vienna I met the rector of philosophy from Gratz, Herr von Albertini,[3] who had lost his position for defending the critical philosophy. People assure me that there are many in the Austrian monarchy who favor the new system. But nothing much can happen in Vienna, where there is a total lack of community among scholars, and the professors at the university do not know each other. Only by accident do they ever meet. The situation is better in Salzburg, where the worthy regent[4] of the seminary favors the critical philosophy. But many are still opposed, and not till Würzburg does one find a decent intellectual climate. The prince[5] has a hobbyhorse there; he wants to be known abroad as enlightened. That provides the aegis of the critical philosophy in Salzburg, which it will lose, however, when he dies. Munich is impossible for critical philosophy, since Stattler[6] lives and reigns there. Nevertheless there are individuals who study and try to make use of the critical philosophy in secret. Your books are contraband there as in Austria, but especially your work on religion. Alas, why must truth have to battle against so many enemies before its voice is half heard! But if the men are struggling so vigorously against the critical philosophy, its fortunes are somewhat better among the women. You can't guess how enthusiastically young ladies and women are taken with your system and how eager they all are to learn about it. There are many women's groups here in Würzburg,

12:99

12:100

where each one is eager to outdo the others in showing a knowledge of your system: it is the favorite topic of conversation. Yes, remarkable as it seems, they do not restrict themselves to practical philosophy but even venture into the theoretical part . . .

---

1 Conrad Stang, a Benedictine from Würzburg. Nothing further is known of him.
2 Joseph II.
3 Johann Baptist Albertini (1741–1820). He had actually been rector of philosophy in Innsbruck, not Gratz.
4 Matthäus Fingerlos (1748–1817).
5 Hieronymous Joseph Franz de Paula, Count of Colloredo (1731–1812).
6 Benedikt Stattler (1728–97), author of *Antikant* (2 vols.; Munich, 1788).

190 [731] (695)
To Johann Heinrich Kant.
December 17, 1796.

12:140 Dear Brother,

Our family here has recently suffered some changes. Last summer your older sister[1] died after a long illness, and therefore a pension which I had given for her support since 1768 fell vacant; I have doubled the amount and given it to her surviving children. In addition there is a pension for our one remaining sister, Barbara,[2] who is well cared for in St. George Hospital. Thus I have not allowed any of my siblings or any of their numerous children (some of whom already have children of their own) to be needy, and I will continue in this way until my own place in the world becomes vacant, at which time I hope to leave something more for my relatives and siblings, a not inconsiderable sum.[3]

Please give my friendly greetings to my niece, Amalia Charlotte, and take care of the enclosure. With brotherly dedication I am

your devoted
I. Kant

Königsberg, the 17th of December, 1796.

1   Maria Elisabeth Kröhnert (1727–96), married to a shoemaker named Christian Kröhnert, died in July 1795.

2   Katharina Barbara (1731–1807) was married to a wigmaker named Theuer. Kant's third sister, Anna Luise, b. 1730, had died in 1774. Her husband, Johann Christoph Schultz, was a toolmaker.

3   After Johann Kant's death in Feb. 1800, Kant supported his sister-in-law and her offspring with 200 Thaler a year. Kant also left half of his estate, approximately 20,000 Thaler, to them.

1797

191 [752] (715)
To Johann August Schlettwein.[1]

May 29, 1797.

[Open Declaration]

12:367   In a letter dated Greifswald, May 11, 1797, a letter recently made public, which is distinguished by its singular tone, Herr Johann August Schlettwein demands that I engage in an exchange of letters with him on the critical philosophy. He indicates that he already has various letters prepared on the subject and adds that he believes himself to be in a position to overthrow completely my whole philosophical system, both its theoretical and its practical parts, an event that should be pleasing to every friend of philosophy. But as for the proposed method whereby this refutation is to be carried out, namely, in an exchange of letters, either handwritten or printed, I must answer curtly: Absolutely not. For it is absurd to ask a man in his seventy-fourth year (when "packing one's bags" [*sarcinas colligere*] is really of the highest importance) to engage in a project that would take many years, just to make even tolerable progress with the criticisms and rejoinders. But the reason why I am making public this declaration (which I have already sent to him) is that his letter clearly had publicity as its object, and since his attack may be broadcast by word of mouth, those people who are interested in such a controversy would otherwise be left waiting empty-handed. Since Herr Schlettwein will not let this difficulty halt his projected overthrow of my system (probably with a massive assault, since he appears to rely on allies as well), and my declaration will make him regard me as his arch-enemy, he wisely has the foresight to ask "which one of the disputants[2] has really interpreted at least the main points of my system in the way I want them to be interpreted." My answer is, unquestionably the worthy court chaplain and professor of

510

mathematics here, Herr Schultz, whose book on the critical system, entitled *Prüfung*[3] etc. should be examined by Herr Schlettwein.

I would only add the qualification that the words of Court Chaplain Schultz are to be taken *literally according to the letter* and not according to some spirit ostensibly expressed in them (which would enable any-one to add any interpretation he pleases). Whatever ideas anyone else might have associated with the same expressions are of no interest to me or to the learned man to whom I commit myself. The sense that he attaches to those expressions is unmistakable in the context of the book as a whole. So now the feud may continue forever, with never a shortage of opponents for every disputant.

12:368

---

1 Johann August Schlettwein (1731–1802), prominent German physiocrat. This letter is a reply to an open letter to Kant, published by Schlettwein in the *Berlinische Blätter*, Sept. 1797 ([751] in Kant's *Werke*, Ak. 12:362–6). Schlettwein's letter is incredibly insulting, accusing Kant of contempt for his great predecessors and contemporaries, of pride, self-love, and self-seeking, the arrogant claim of infallibility and originality, and so on. He calls it a scandal that so-called critical philosophers dispute the sense and spirit of Kant's works and asks Kant to say which one of his disciples has understood him correctly. Schlettwein claims to have a refutation of Kant ready but does not in fact state any arguments. A hint of his own position is given in the assertion that "true philosophy teaches the incontrovertible doctrine of the reality of an infinite power, the forces of nature, and the marvelous and sublime properties and capacities of physical and spiritual man." He states that philosophy, in its practical part, should seek to bring people ever closer to God, "not by means of a loveless, despotic categorical imperative, contrary to the very nature of reason, but through the gentle, all-powerful tie of love that animates all things" (p. 366).

Kant's answer appeared in the *A.L.Z.* on June 14, 1797. Schlettwein responded with another open letter (Ak.[753], *Werke* Ak. 12:368–70). A lost letter of Kant's, of May 19, 1797, is alluded to in it.

2 Schlettwein had asked whether Reinhold, Fichte, Beck, or someone else was the correct interpreter.

3 *Prüfung der Kantischen Kritik der reinen Vernunft* (1789/92).

511

192 [754] (717)

From Jacob Sigismund Beck.

June 20, 1797

[abbreviated]

[*This letter is evidently a response to a letter from Kant, not extant but mentioned by Beck. Beck replies passionately to the charge made by Johann Schultz, Kant's favorite expositor, that Beck's* Grundriß der critischen Philosophie *(Halle, 1796) had totally misrepresented the Kantian philosophy. Beck is convinced that Kant will see his account of the critical philosophy to be correct.*]

12:164 ... I remark concerning the categories, *first*, that the logical employment of the understanding consists in using them as predicates of objects. For instance, we say that a thing *has* size, *has* factuality, that substantiality, causality, and so on, *belong to* it. I express this logical employment of the understanding also in a priori synthetic judgments: for example, "In all change of appearance, substance persists," "What happens has a cause," and so on. How then is the explanation of this synthesis of concepts to be approached? I notice the original procedure of the understanding in the category through which precisely that synthetic objective unity that I call the sense and meaning of my concept is produced. What is it, I ask, that requires the chemist, in his experiment of burning phosphorous in atmospheric air, to say that the weight by which the phosphorus has become heavier is just that by which the air has become lighter? I answer: His very own understanding, the *experiencing* in him, the original procedure of understanding to which I call someone's attention when I ask him to suspend all the objects in space and, after the passing of 50 years, posit a world again. He will assert that the two worlds are one and the same and that no empty time has passed, that is, that he can only conceive of time in connection with something persisting. Attention must be paid to this, in order to lay the ghost of Berkeleyan idealism. Just so, if I focus attention on the *experiencing* in me, whereby I arrive at the claim that something has happened, I notice that the causality that I connect with this is simply the determination of the synthesis of perceptions as a succession (the original positing of a something through which the event follows according to a rule). By means of this, the experience of an event is produced. In fact the explanation of all a priori synthetic judgments consists in this: the predicate that I connect with the subject, in such judgments, is the original activity of the understanding through which I arrive at the concept of an object. By recognizing this principle,

12:165 I think I have a clearer understanding than everyone else about the judgment, "My representation of the table before me conforms to the table; and this object affects me – it brings forth sensation in me," for others are conscious of this original activity of the understanding only in its application, not in abstraction; and thus I am certainly convinced that the division of the cognitive faculties – viz., into sensibility, as the subjective faculty (the capacity of being affected by objects) and understanding, the power of thinking objects (of relating the subjective element to an object) – can only be grasped with the requisite clarity after one has a proper perspective of the category, as an original activity of the understanding.

Jacobi of Düsseldorf says in his lecture "David Hume,"[1] "I must admit that this claim (namely, that objects produce sense impressions) made me hesitate more than a little in my studies of the Kantian philosophy, so that year after year I had to begin the *Critique of Pure Reason* once more from the beginning. For I was continuously confused, since without that assumption I could not enter the system, and with it I could not remain in it." If I were to give my judgment concerning this difficulty, which is certainly important to a great many people, and if I were to determine what your *Critique* actually means, when, on the first page of the Introduction, it speaks of objects that affect the senses[2] – whether it means by that things in themselves or appearances – I should answer that since the object of my representation is appearance, and since it is this representation in which determinations of the object are thought, determinations which I receive by means of the original activity of the understanding (for example, by means of the original fixation of my synthesis of perceptions as a successive one, whereby experience of an event becomes possible), the object that affects me must therefore be appearance and not thing in itself. But if someone should believe it possible to have an absolute employment of the categories, to regard them simply as predicates of things, disregarding the original activity of the understanding that lies in them (as you would say: to believe possible an application of them to objects without the condition of intuition), he would believe himself capable of cognizing things in themselves; and if I wanted to get a little bit angry with Herr Schultz, I would say that I have more right to accuse him of thinking he has an intellectual intuition than he has to make this accusation against me. In my view, human beings are capable only of the awareness of the relation of nature in general to a substratum of nature; we are conscious of this relation when we consider our moral disposition and are aware that our desires are determinable by means of the mere representation of an action's lawfulness. For in this awareness – it is exactly here that the synthetic practical principles arise, just as those synthetic a priori theoretical judgments arise out of the original activity of the understanding – we lift ourselves above

12:166

nature and place ourselves outside her mechanism. This is true even if, as human beings, we are also natural objects and our morality itself is something that had a beginning and thus presupposes natural causes. The mechanism of nature, which is continuous with a corresponding unity of purposes, adjusts us to this condition even more and encourages and strengthens the soul of a morally good person, even though he can only picture this substratum symbolically. The course of human events itself, of such natural events as, for example, the appearance of the Christian religion, concerning which, *qua* church doctrine, one can say that it carries in itself the principle of its own dissolution, natural events whose ostensible goal is to bring forth the pure moral faith in our species – all of these things lead the understanding to such a relation.

12:167 But I sound as if I wanted to tell you something new! . . . I have pointed out to the commentators of your *Critique* who make much of your words that in their mouths it seems to me entirely senseless to speak of a priori concepts; for they do not want to regard such concepts as innate, the way Leibniz did. I point this out solely to make conspicuous the important distinction between your claim, that the categories are a priori concepts, and the contention that they are innate, and in order to show that these categories are actually the activity of the understanding whereby I arrive at the concept of an object, arrive at the point at which I am in a position to say, "Here is an object distinct from me." No one can be more convinced of the correctness of his insights than I at this moment. What Herr Schultz blames me for never even occurred to me. It never occurred to me to try to construct an exegesis that would explain away sensibility. As I said, I could not close my eyes to the light I glimpsed when the idea came to me, to start from the standpoint of the categories and to connect what you are especially concerned with in your Transcendental Aesthetic (space and time) with the categories. Herr Reinhold had corrected you, when you

12:168 said: Space is an a priori intuition; his expert opinion was that you ought rather to have said, "The representation of space is an intuition." But I show him that space itself is a pure intuition, that is, the original synthesis of the understanding on which objective connecting (an object has this or that magnitude) rests. It never entered my mind to say that the understanding creates the object: a piece of naked nonsense! How can Herr Schultz be so unfriendly as to charge me with this. As I said, I wanted not a whit more than to lead people to this point: that we cannot objectively unify anything (or judge it – for example, assert "a thing has this or that size, this or that reality, substantiality, and so on") that the understanding has not previously united and that herein lies the objective relation. I want to lead everyone to this by the nose. How can one fail to see by this light! The object that affects me, that

stirs my senses, is called appearance and not thing in itself; of the latter
I can only construct the negative concept, a thing to which predicates
belong absolutely (entirely apart from this original activity of the understanding) – an Idea, and also the idea of an intuitive understanding,
which we get by negating the characteristic of our own understanding.
My intention was to bar the concept of the thing in itself from theoretical philosophy. Only in the moral consciousness am I led to that
unique mode of reality. . . . No one, of all the friends of the critical   12:169
philosophy, has stressed the distinction between sensibility and understanding more than I have. I do it under the expression: a concept has
sense and meaning only to the extent that the original activity of the
understanding in the categories lies at its basis – which in fact is the
same as your contention that the categories have application only to
what is directly experienced . . .³

---

1 Friedrich Heinrich Jacobi, "David Hume über den Glauben oder Idealismus
   und Realismus" in Jacobi's *Werke* II, p. 304 (1787). This is the oft-quoted
   criticism of Kant's supposed *Affektionslehre*, i.e., the attribution of causal agency
   to things in themselves in generating the "material" of sensation.

2 Beck alludes correctly to Kant's opening sentence: our cognitive faculty is
   "awakened" into action by objects that "stir" our senses: "durch Gegenstände,
   die unsere Sinne rühren . . ."

3 The remainder of Beck's letter tries to explain how the phrase "Prepared on
   the recommendation of Kant" ("auf Anraten K – ") came to appear on the
   title page of Beck's book. It was supposed to appear only on Beck's *Abstract* of
   Kant, not on his original interpretation of Kant's theory in the *Standpoint*, i.e.,
   vol. 3 of the *Abstract*, which was intended to be a separate work. Beck offers to
   set the matter straight by informing the public that only the abstract has Kant's
   approval. He fears, however, that the "enemies of the critical philosophy" will
   seize on his announcement, "smelling quarrel and dissension" among Kant's
   followers. Beck says that he has asked his friend Professor Tieftrunk to write
   to Kant on his behalf, in order to corroborate his contention that he is loyal to
   Kant's position. Beck adds an expression of disgust with Schlettwein, "this
   swaggerer who shoots off his mouth" ("dieser Rodomontadenmacher") and
   annoyance with Johann Schultz – Beck suggests that perhaps the latter's un-
   kindness to Beck was due to despondency over the death of Schultz's wife.
   Beck deplores the rivalry and jealousy among Kant's disciples, comparing it to
   that among some mathematicians.
      Beck's letter runs to ten full pages in the Akademie edition.

193 [755] (718)
From Johann Heinrich Tieftrunk.[1]

June 20, 1797

Esteemed Sir,

Professor Beck, who knows from our frequent philosophical conversations how interested I am in anything pertaining to philosophy and
how much I revere and admire you, venerable sir, was kind enough to
show me, in strictest confidence, your most recent letter concerning
the relation of his *Standpoint* to the *Critique of Pure Reason*. I value my
friend's confidence greatly, and I enjoyed learning from your letter the
opinion of worthy Court Chaplain Schulz, and thereby also your own
opinion, of Herr Beck's work concerning the *Critique*.

12:171

Since both the *method* and *content* of the *Critique* satisfied me completely, I have not been disconcerted by the attempts of other people
to refute your *Critique* or to provide it with a foundation or even to
abandon it in favor of new principles they try to discover and establish.
But my attention has been drawn to the peculiar perspective and standpoint that Herr Beck proposes for reaching the same goal as that of
the *Critique*. He and I have discussed this at great length but as yet I
have been unable to reach agreement with him.

12:172

I thought that you and Court Chaplain Schulz as well (please let me
take this opportunity to convey my respects to him) might be interested
to see how I, as a third party conversant with the critical philosophy,
assess the relationship of [Beck's] *Standpoint* to the *Critique of Pure
Reason*.

It seemed to me useful, with this in mind, to give you a little
specimen, as a test of my understanding of your *Critique*. I selected for
this purpose a topic that seems to me very important and, to my mind,
the most difficult in Transcendental Philosophy: the possibility of experience and, connected with that, the Deduction of the Categories.

First, I present the topic as I think the *Critique of Pure Reason*
intends; *then* I introduce Herr Beck's idea, of course only in outline
form but still sufficiently to give an idea of its direction. *Thirdly*, like a
suitor attracted to the *Critique* on account of its form and all its various
parts, I suggest *certain doubts about Herr Beck's approach*. My Beck knows
about my procedure in all this and it has his acquiescence.

You may however dispose of the enclosed pages entirely as you
wish: read them or throw them away. For I have written them only
with the thought that they might be useful to you or to Court Chaplain

Schulz, since they concern a matter with which you both seem currently to be occupied.

I have also read the announcement and explanation concerning Herr Schlettwein, and I was not very surprised by Herr Schlettwein's exaggerated bombast, for it seems to be his hobby-horse to pick a fight either with this person or that. He tried to start a similar quarrel with me about five years ago; but once I answered him, he never replied. I hope his letter of challenge to you will be the end of his storm against the *Critique of Pure Reason*.

I am sincerely overjoyed to observe the remarkable liveliness you still display in your advanced years. May Heaven preserve you for us for a long time to come; that is what I wish with all my heart.

Your respectful servant,
Joh. Heinr. Tieftrunk.

Halle, June 20, 1797.

12:173

---

1   Tieftrunk (1760–1837) was professor of philosophy in Halle from 1792. One of Kant's most steadfast disciples, he wrote on religion, *Einzig möglicher Zweck Jesu*, (1789) and *Versuch einer Kritik der Religion* (1790); philosophy of law, *Philosophische Untersuchungen über das Privat-und öffentliche Recht* (1797); and edited a collection of Kant's miscellaneous essays, *Kants vermischte Schriften* (1799).

194 [756] (719)
From Jacob Sigismund Beck.
June 24, 1797.

Esteemed Sir,

. . . You say that the purpose of your letter[1] is the swift and public removal of a disagreement over the fundamental principles of the critical philosophy. And Court Chaplain Schultz attributes to me the claim that "reality is the original synthesis of the homogeneous in sensation, which proceeds from the whole to its parts."[2] (The question must be *yours*, sir, when he asks, quite justifiably, in this connection, "What 'sensation' can mean, if there is no such thing as sensibility, I fail to

12:174 understand." Surely, excellent sir, if such a thing had ever occurred to me, this nonsense would have made me repulsive to myself.) And Schultz also quotes me as saying that "the understanding produces objects."[3] I infer from this that you and Herr Schultz have been discussing Herr Fichte's strange invention, since these expressions I quoted sound completely Fichtean to me. All I can do is to remind you of the following things and to offer a proposal that I have in mind.

I assure you, as I am an honest man, that my views are infinitely removed from this Fichtean nonsense. I only thought it essential to focus the attention of philosophers on the categories, as being an original activity of the understanding, to which your entire Deduction is directed, since the Deduction is an attempt to answer the question of how the categories are applicable to appearances. For I felt sure that disagreements would vanish when people came to see that the understanding cannot unify objectively anything that it has not already originally joined together.[4] When I say that the category of reality is the synthesis of sensation, proceeding from whole to parts (through remission), the only rational interpretation of my claim is this: the facticity[a] of a thing (the objective aspect[b] of the appearance that affects me and that produces this sensation in me) is necessarily an intensive magnitude, and therefore an absolute facticity such as Descartes supposes[5] – a thing that has no magnitude but is nevertheless a material substance, filling space just by its mere existence – would be meaningless. This original activity of the understanding, in the category of reality, converges with the activity in the category of existence, whereby I get beyond my own self and say, "Here is an object that affects me." But a proponent of the transcendental philosophy must distinguish these two aspects of the original activity. I thought it necessary to guide the reader's eye to each particular category. When someone asks me, "Suppose you suspend yourself in thought,[c] do you then also suspend everything existing outside you?" I will not be so stupid as to say yes to this silly idea. If I suspend myself, I am still considering myself under temporal conditions, and I can conceive of this passage of time only in relation to something enduring. To *turn my gaze away from* this original activity of the understanding is not the same as to *suspend* myself.

12:175 Indeed, I shall say, if I ignore the original synthesis of which I am conscious when I draw a line, I indeed lose all sense of the extensive magnitude that I attribute to an object, and just for that reason the object of my representations is called appearance and not thing in itself. Assuredly, excellent sir, if you would only honor me by examining my

[a] *Sachheit*
[b] *das Reale*
[c] *dich selbst in Gedanken aufhebst*

method, in which I descend from the standpoint of the categories, just as you proceed by ascending to them in your immortal book, you would see the feasibility of what I do. What is required is only that one get to feel at home with the whole system; then it is easy to show anyone who has interest and a bit of talent how to arrive at the true critical principles. I think my method is especially helpful for lectures. Court Chaplain Schultz, of whom I am ever fond and whose knowledge and sincerity I respect, has really been unfair to me, and I am depressed that this fine man could believe that I hold such absurd views as that the understanding creates the object. He would not have been able to think such things of me before, when he cherished me as his attentive pupil in mathematics.

But I know that Herr *Fichte*, who apparently wants disciples, has claimed that I agree with him, even though I strongly denied this in a review I published in Herr Jakob's *Annalen*⁶ and also in my *Standpoint*. When I visited him in Jena last Easter, he really did try to ensnare me. He actually started one conversation by saying, "I know it, you agree with me that the understanding creates the object." He said a number of foolish things, and since I saw through him immediately, he must have been highly perplexed by my friendly answers. I also wanted to say to you that *Fichte* told me that his new journal⁷ contains a revised version of his *Wissenschaftslehre* and will, among other things, treat philosophy as a *single* discipline, without assuming any distinction between theoretical and moral philosophy, since the understanding, through its absolute freedom, posits every object. (A stupid idea! Anyone who talks like that must never have mastered the critical principles); and he says he discusses my *Standpoint* at length there. I have not seen it yet, but I feel sure in advance that it will provide me with an occasion to explain myself, perhaps in Jakob's *Annalen*, so that I can point out, *first*, that I do not at all agree with him; *second*, that I believe I have given an accurate exposition of the *Critique* and therefore do not regard myself as deviating from it – for nothing concerns me more than to distinguish sensibility (the faculty of being affected by objects) from the understanding (the faculty of thinking objects, relating this subjective material of sensibility to objects); *third*, that nevertheless I do not at all intend to compromise the founder of the critical philosophy in the slightest way, since the *Standpoint* is entirely my own idea, which anyone is free to compare with your published works and make his own judgment. I don't want to antagonize Fichte personally, and I shall therefore be completely pleasant in discussing him. But in connection with the second point above, I want to express myself in detail and make clear what was badly stated in the *Standpoint*. Do you concur with me? I don't want to start anything until I have your approval. But

12:176

please don't be vexed with me. I am dedicated to philosophy and would be pained indeed by the thought that I have fallen from your favor.
Your
Beck

1　Kant's letter is not extant.

2　Beck in fact wrote that the category of reality is the original synthesis of the homogeneous, proceeding from the whole to its part. See Kant's *Werke*, 13: 452, and Beck's explanation in the next paragraph of the present letter.

3　Possibly an interpretation of Beck's claim that "the understanding originally posits a something [*Etwas*]."

4　Cf. *Critique of Pure Reason*; B 130.

5　Descartes, *Principles of Philosophy*, I, 53: "We can conceive extension without figure or action."

6　L. H. Jakob's *Annalen der Philosophie und des philosophischen Geistes von einer Gesellschaft gelehrter Männer* (Halle, 1795). Issues 16–18 contain a discussion of Fichte's *Über den Begriff der Wissenschaftslehre* and his "Grundlage der gesamten Wissenschaftslehre" (1794).

7　*Philosophisches Journal einer Gesellschaft Teutscher Gelehrten*, published by Fichte and F. J. Niethammer (Jena and Leipzig, 1797). Fichte praises Beck for "having independently liberated himself from the confusions of the age, in that he has come to see that the Kantian philosophy is a transcendental idealism and not dogmatism, since it maintains that the object is neither wholly nor partly given but rather produced . . ." See Kant's *Werke*, 13: 452 f., for a slightly fuller quotation.

---

195 [761] (724)
To Christian Gottfried Schütz.

12:181

July 10, 1797.

Though unsolicited by you, I am inspired by your letter to our mutual friend, the excellent Court Chaplain Schultz, to take this opportunity to tell you, dearest sir, how happy I am about your improved health, the rumor of which has been spreading recently. A man of such universal talents deserves a long and joyful life!

I am not offended by your criticism, in the aforementioned letter, of my recently advanced concept of "Rights to persons akin to rights to things."[1] For *Rechtslehre*, the Doctrine of Right based on pure reason, accepts the maxim "Entities are not to be multiplied beyond necessity"[2] even more than do the other branches of philosophy. Your suspicion might rather be aroused that I have deceived myself with verbal trickery, begging the question by surreptitiously assuming that what is practicable is also permitted. But no one can be blamed for mistaking a teacher's meaning if a new theory is alluded to without its grounds' being explained in detail. One can easily imagine that one sees errors then, when actually the complaint should only be that there is a lack of clarity.

I only want to touch on the criticisms in your letter and shall develop my comments more explicitly on another occasion.[3]

First: "You cannot really believe that a man makes an object out of a woman just by engaging in *marital* cohabitation with her, and vice versa. You seem to think marriage no more than a mutual subordination."[4] Surely, if the cohabitation is assumed to be marital, that is, lawful, even if only according to the Right of nature,[5] the authorization is already contained in the concept [of marriage]. But here the question is whether a marital cohabitation is possible, and how. So the discussion should center only on the matter of physical *cohabitation* (intercourse) and the conditions of its authorization. For the *mutuum adiutorium* is merely the necessary legal consequence of marriage, whose possibility and condition must first be investigated.

12:182

Second, you say: "Kant's theory seems to rest simply on a fallacious interpretation of the word, '*enjoyment*'. Granted, the *actual* enjoyment of another human being, such as in cannibalism, would reduce a human being to an object; but surely married people do not become interchangeable goods [*res fungibilis*] just by sleeping together." It would have been very weak of me to make my argument depend on the word "enjoyment." The word may be replaced by the notion of *using someone* directly (that is, sensuously – a word that has a different meaning here than elsewhere); I mean rendering her[6] an *immediately pleasurable* thing. An enjoyment of this sort involves at once the thought of her as merely *consumable (res fungibilis)*, and that in fact is what the reciprocal use of each other's sexual organs by two people provides. One or the other parties may be destroyed (consumed), through infection, exhaustion, or impregnation (a delivery can be fatal), and so the appetite of a cannibal differs only insignificantly from that of a sexual libertine.

So much for the relationship of man to woman. The relation of father (or mother) to child has not been subjected to possible objections.

Third, you ask, "Does it seem to you circular reasoning, a *petitio principii*, when Kant tries to show the right of master to servant or domestic to be a person-thing right [it should read: a property right (consequently, only formally a right over persons)][7] just because one is allowed to *seize* the runaway domestic servant again? But that is just the question at issue. How can it be shown that this is in fact allowed by natural law [*jure naturae*]?"

Certainly, this license is only the consequence and the mark of legal *possession*, when one person holds another as his own, even though the latter is a person. But one person's holding another as his own (that is, as part of his household) signifies a right to possession that may be exercised against any subsequent possessor (*jus in re contra quemlibet hujus rei possessorem*). The right to use someone for domestic purposes is analogous to a right to an object, for the servant is not free to terminate his connections with the household and he may therefore be brought back by force, which cannot be done to a day laborer who quits when his job is only half completed (assuming he takes nothing away with him that belongs to his employer). Such a man cannot be seized for he does not belong to the master the way a maid and a servant do, since the latter are integral parts of the household.

More on another occasion. I add only that every news of your health, success, and friendship for me would give me pleasure.

---

1 Or "rights *in rem* over other persons" ("auf dingliche Art persönlichen Rechts").

2 *entia praeter necessitatem non sunt multiplicanda*, the famous "principle of parsimony."

3 See Kant's "Anhang erläuternder Bemerkungen zu den metaphysschen Anfangsgründen der Rechtslehre" ("Supplement to the Metaphysical Principles of the Doctrine of Right"), in *Werke* 6: 357 ff.

4 *mutuum adiutorium*

5 "dem Rechte der Natur." There is an ongoing debate among Kant scholars as to the proper translation of *Recht, Rechte, Rechtslehre, Rechte der Natur*. The latter phrase in some contexts means "natural law" in the normative rather than physical sense. *Recht* can mean a right, justice, or normative law, shifting its meaning more or less as the French *droit* does.

6 It may be worth noting that Kant uses the feminine pronoun here.

7 Kant's parenthetical remark.

196 [762] (725)
To Johann Heinrich Tieftrunk
July 12, 1797

I am delighted that the discussion with Herr Beck concerning the proposal for a retraction[1] has led to a correspondence with you, worthy man.[2] And I am delighted as well by the use to which you have put my *Rechtslehre* in your most recent book on private and public Right. It would please me if, supposing that Herr Beck could convince himself of the correctness of your "Brief Presentation of an Essential Point in the Transcendental Aesthetic and Logic"[3] he were to alter his *Standpoint* and correct it accordingly. But if he cannot see his way to do this, it would be better to let the matter rest; for Herr Schlettwein or somebody else will interpret this silence as a confession of error and a justification of his attacks. If the attempt to correct is fruitless, why should others be publicly informed of the dissension?

Neither my own affection and respect for Herr Beck nor that of Court Chaplain Schultz should be diminished by this, though Herr Schultz noticed a certain alienating tone of bitterness in the letter from Herr Beck that I showed him; I hope that that tone will be modulated eventually into one of friendship. For what is the point of all our work and our controversies in philosophy if they lead us to forfeit kindheartedness?   12:184

I hope Herr Beck, to whom I beg you to give my friendly greetings, will soon explain his final resolution of the issue, either publicly or in a private letter. I would be pleased to receive news of this from you and any other important literary news as well. I am, with affection and respect,

your most devoted servant,
I. Kant.

Königsberg,
July 12, 1797.

---

1 *Liber retractationum*
2 Cf. Beck's letter to Kant, June 24, 1797, Ak.[756], especially the last paragraph, and Kant's letter to Tieftrunk, Oct. 13, 1797, Ak.[784]. Beck decided to announce that his *Standpoint* reflected his own views, not Kant's.
3 "Kurze Darstellung eines wesentlichen Punkts in der transc. Ästhetik u. Logik."

197 [764] (727)
From Christian Weiss.[1]

July 25, 1797.

Leipzig, July 25, 1797

12:185 My esteemed teacher,

You may be deluged with unsolicited letters, yet I dare to send you another one and count on your forgiveness. It is contrary to my whole personality to stay at a distance from people to whose writings, like yours, I owe so much instruction. I therefore seize the first opportunity that comes along to approach you. I offer you also an insignificant gift[2] which I dedicate to six of my best living teachers, without imagining that my gift will give you pleasure but just to tell you in a more concrete way that I am eternally in your debt.

It would be both imprudent and culpable to rob of his time a man of your age and with your preoccupations, or to bother him with complaints. As much as I would like to have it, I hesitate therefore to beg you for your written opinion of the little piece, really just an essay, that I am sending you. You would magnify my gratitude many times over if you were to find it possible to gratify my timid wish.

But there is another point on which I must ask you briefly to enlighten and correct me, dearest teacher. As you will immediately see, it is an affair of both the heart and the mind for me.

After long reflection and many unsuccessful attempts, it struck me a few months ago that Prof. Fichte in Jena has been the first to set forth 12:186 systematically the actual ground of the critical philosophy and to complete what your *Critique* had to leave unfinished, though his way of presenting his principles is unnecessarily obscure. Recently I heard from you, on the contrary, that you regard *only* Herr Schulz – whom I value exceedingly – as your true expositor.[3] But I know that you have also praised and acknowledged Professor Reinhold's theory of the faculty of representation as meritorious, a theory which he himself now declares to be in certain respects worthless. I find myself confused by all this.

You see, worthy man, that I do not ask you to spare me the pain of reflection. I have tried hard to find the answer and have so far come up with this:

"You arrived at your system by another route than Fichte took to his; therefore you used a different (and better) method than his to present it. The ground of your whole philosophy, however, if one asks for the highest and most complete ground of unity, can be no other than the *transcendental unity of the human mind*. It is the task of [Fichte's] *Wissenschaftslehre* to make this explicit. By its nature, the *Critique of Pure Reason* could only silently presuppose this and point to it. But *all truth* is grounded on that unity, which can be found (analytically) only by abstraction and can be proved (synthetically) only by means of an inner indestructible feeling that one calls pure inner intuition. Every *conviction*, and that means the conviction of the existence of something real in space, receives the character of necessity and immutability only through the transcendental transference of the *absolute* (not further *demonstrable* or *capable of mediation*) *reality* of the I to everything that sets itself over against that I as *real* and as something on which the I is to act. The *categories*, with their dichotomies and trichotomies, must actually be *deduced* from that unity (the absolute *Thesis*) and the *Antithesis* and *Synthesis* necessarily bound up with it, etc. In short, he who (as a philosopher) does not believe in himself, who is   12:187 not internally convinced of the real within him – for him there is no defensible ground of knowing or of believing that could be discovered anywhere else."

But now I beg you to tell me: have I, as I believe, captured the spirit of your teaching? Do truth and life come into us from the objects? Or does the mind rather bestow truth and life on things outside it (which are nothing at all without it)? Isn't Reinhold correct in what he says in the second volume of his Miscellaneous Writings?[4] And isn't this finally the same thing that the excellent Friedrich Heinrich Jacobi intends to convey? Does this spirit not radiate from his "Spinoza," his "David Hume," his "Allwill" and all his other works,[5] this high, exalted spirit which now begins to bless and uplift me as well?

Once more, worthy old man, forgive this twenty-three-year-old youth for following the urging of his heart and proceeding impatiently to the source, as he feels that he must.[6] Let me not have prayed in vain for a few words in reply, and allow me to call myself, with sincerest feelings of respect,

your grateful student and admirer   Christian Weiss.
Your letter can reach me in Leipzig up to Michaelmas. I live with my father, Dr. Weiss, deacon of the Nicolai Kirche.

---

1   Christian Weiss (1774–1833) was at the time of this letter a private teacher of philosophy in Leipzig.
2   *Fragmente über Seyn, Werden and Handeln* (Leipzig, 1797), "Dedicated to my Philosophy Teachers." The six teachers to whom Weiss refers probably included Kant, Reinhold, Fichte, Jacobi, and Schmid.

3 Kant's Declaration of May 29, 1797, asserts this.

4 Reinhold's *Auswahl vermischter Schriften*, in two parts (Jena, 1796/7).

5 The works alluded to are Jacobi's *Über die Lehre des Spinoza* (1785), *David Hume über den Glauben* (1787), and *Eduard Allwills Briefsammlung* (1792).

6 Kant wrote to Weiss in 1801. The letter is listed in a catalog published by J. L. Lippert (1853) as No. 1017. It is now evidently lost.

198 [783] (744)
To Jacob Axelson Lindblom.[1]

October 13, 1797.

12:205   Your Reverence,
Esteemed Sir,

12:206   Your efforts in the investigation of my genealogy, reverend sir, and your kindness in informing me of your results, deserve the highest thanks, even though there may be no utility in this work either for myself or for anyone else.

I have known for quite some time that my grandfather, who lived in the Prussian-Lithuanian city of Tilsit, came originally from Scotland, that he was one of the many people who emigrated from there, for some reason that I do not know, toward the end of the last century and the beginning of this one.[2] A large portion of them went to Sweden, and the rest were scattered through Prussia, especially around Memel. The families Simpson, Maclean, Douglas, Hamilton, and others still living there can attest to this. My grandfather was among that group and he died in Tilsit.* I have no living relatives on my father's side (other than the descendants of my brother and sisters). So much for my origin, which your genealogical chart traces back to honest peasants in the land of the Ostrogoths (for which I feel honored) down to my father (I think you must mean my grandfather). Your humanitarian desire to stir me to support my alleged relatives does not escape me, reverend sir.

For it happens that another letter came to me at the same time as yours, from Larum, dated July 10, 1797, with a similar account of my genealogy, but accompanied by a request from one who calls himself my "cousin," a request that I lend him eight or ten thousand thalers for a few years, which would enable him to achieve happiness.

---

* My father died in Königsberg, and in my presence.

But Your Reverence will acknowledge this and similar demands to be inadmissible when I tell you that my estate will be so diluted by legacies to my nearest relatives – I have one living sister;[4] my late sister left six children; I have a brother, Pastor Kant of Altrahden in Courland, who has four children, one of them a grown son who recently married – that there could hardly be anything left over for a remote relation whose relationship is itself problematic.

With greatest respect I am ever

      Your Reverence's

        Kant

---

1   Jakob Axelson Lindblom (1746–1819), Swedish bishop. This letter is in response to Lindblom's letter, in Latin (he identifies himself as "Jacobos Lindblom Episcopos Dioeces. Ostrogothicae in Svecia"), of Oct. 13, 1797, Ak.[772].

2   Kant's account of his genealogy is not uncontroversial. Notes to this letter in the Schöndörffer edition of the correspondence state that it was not Kant's grandfather but his great-grandfather, Richard Kant, who emigrated to Prussia from Scotland in 1630 and was certified as an innkeeper in Werden near Tilsit in 1648. Kant's grandfather, however, lived in Memel, not Tilsit, and died there.

3   In a draft of this letter, Kant adds a eulogy to his parents who, while leaving no fortune, nor any debts, managed to give him such an excellent moral education that he is filled with gratitude whenever he thinks of them.

4   Katherina Barbara Teyer is the sister to whom Kant refers.

199 [784] (745)
To Johann Heinrich Tieftrunk.

October 13, 1797.[1]

Treasured friend,   13:463

I am content with *Herr Beck's* decision to announce that his *Standpoint* is not my own position but his. Let me only remark on this point that when he proposes to start out with the categories he is busying himself with the mere form of thinking, that is, concepts without objects, concepts that as yet are without any meaning.[2] It is more natural to begin with the *given*, that is, with intuitions insofar as these are possible a priori, furnishing us with synthetic a priori propositions that disclose nothing but the appearances of objects. For then the claim that objects are intuited only in accordance with the form in which the subject is affected by them is seen to be certain and necessary.

I prefer that the Beck business be resolved not only in a friendly manner but with unanimity in our thinking, even though our approaches are different.

12:207 It gave me pleasure to hear of your discussions with Herr Beck (please convey my respects to him). I hope they may bring about a unanimity of purpose. I am also pleased to learn of your plans for an explanatory summary of my critical writings, and I appreciate your offering to let me collaborate on this work. May I take the opportunity to ask you to keep my hypercritical friends Fichte and Reinhold in mind and to treat them with the circumspection that their philosophical achievements fully merit.[3]

I am not surprised that my *Rechtslehre* has found many enemies, in view of its attack on a number of principles commonly held to be established. It is all the more pleasant therefore to learn that you approve of it. The Göttingen review (in issue No. 28) taken as a whole is not unfavorable to my system.[4] It induces me to publish a *Supplement*, so as to clear up a number of misunderstandings, and perhaps eventually to complete the system.

Please treat my friend Professor Pörschke[5] kindly, if you should have the opportunity. His manner of speaking is somewhat fierce, but he is really a gentle person. I suppose his fundamental law, *"Man, be a man!"* must mean, "Man, insofar as you are an animal, develop yourself into a moral being, and so on." But he knows nothing about your judgment or anything about my apology for him.

12:208 I agree to your proposal to publish a collection of my minor writings, but I would not want you to start the collection with anything before 1770, that is, my Dissertation "On the Form of the Sensible World and the Intelligible World, etc." [de mundi sensibilis et intelligibilis forma etc.]. I make no demands with regard to the publisher and I do not want any emolument that might be coming to me. My only request is that I may see all the pieces to be printed before they come out. . . .

It is possible that death will overtake me before these matters are settled. If so, our Professor Gensichen has two of my essays[6] in his bureau; one of them is complete, the other almost so, and they have lain there for more than two years. Professor Gensichen will then tell you how to make use of them. But keep this matter confidential, for possibly I shall still publish them myself while I live.

Your most devoted servant,
I. Kant.

1 The first two paragraphs translated here are taken from a draft of this letter, transcribed by a descendent of Tieftrunk's in 1853, which Kant did not send. The *Standpoint* reference is to J. S. Beck's *Only Standpoint from which the Critical Philosophy May Be Judged*. See the letters from Beck, Ak. [754] and Ak. [756].

2 Cf. *Critique of Pure Reason*, B 178 = A 139: "... Concepts are altogether impossible, and can have no meaning, if no object is given for them. ..." Kant altered this to "are for us without meaning."

3 This often quoted remark about Kant's "hypercritical friends," indicative of his disappointment with his erstwhile disciples, seems ironic in tone, but the corresponding lines in Kant's unsent draft do not. There he writes, "I hope your explanatory summary may lead my hypercritical friends back onto the path they once trod; but please do it in a friendly way." *Werke* Ak. 13: 463.

4 See Kant's *Werke*, Ak. 6: 356 ff. and 519. The review, which was published in the *Göttingische Anzeigen*, Feb. 18, 1797, was by Friedrich Bouterwek (1766–1828), a philosopher who also corresponded with Kant.

5 Karl Ludwig Pörschke (1751–1812), professor of poetry in Königsberg, wrote *Vorbereitungen zu einem populären Naturrecht* (1795). He asks, "How is natural right possible?" and answers, "Man ought to be, and has to be no more than, man; he is an animal and a rational being, and that he should remain." The principle "Man, be man!" is the rational foundation of all duties, according to Pörschke.

6 The "completed essay" was "Erneuerte Frage: ob das menschliche Geschlecht im beständigen Fortschreiten zum Besseren sei" ("An Old Question Raised Again: Is the Human Race Constantly Progressing," which became Pt. II of *Der Streit der Fakultäten* (*The Conflict of the Faculties*); the "almost complete" essay became Pt. I of that work, which was in fact published in 1798. Johann Friedrich Gensichen (1759–1807) was one of Kant's dinner companions and executor of his will. He was professor (extraordinarius) of mathematics. See the reconstruction of Kant's letter to him dated Apr. 19, 1791, Ak.[466].

200 [787] (748)
From Johann Heinrich Tieftrunk.
November 5, 1797
[*Fragment*]¹

12:212

... But it is possible to become aware of the fact that the original, pure apperception exists of itself and exists independently of all that is sensible, a unique function of the mind, indeed its highest function, from which all our knowledge begins, though it does not produce out of itself *everything* that belongs to our knowledge. The specific feature of the category of magnitude[2] (the feature that distinguishes it from space and time, the form of sensibility) is the activity of unifying*ᵃ* (*synthesis intellectualis*) that which is manifold but homogeneous. The fundamental condition of this activity of unification is synthesis into unity; thereby the synthesis of what *is* a unity *into* a unity becomes possible, that is, the synthesis of the many*ᵇ* and again of binding the many into a unity is totality.*ᶜ* So far there is no reference to space and time or any actual quantum. We have merely noted the rule or condition under which alone a quantum could be apperceived, viz., it must be possible to synthesize a homogeneous manifold into a unity, plurality,*ᵈ* or totality.

The greatest difficulty appears in connection with the category of quality, for it takes the most subtle thinking to distinguish the pure from the empirical here. Some people suppose that sensation and reality are the same thing and therefore believe that all [objects of] sensation, for example, even air and light, could be deduced a priori. Fichte does that. Other people hold these things to be wholly empirical, so that the category of reality is just the same thing as the production of the empirical. Herr Beck is an example. My view differs from both of these, and I think the *Critique of Pure Reason* must be interpreted otherwise as well. Here is my statement; I wish you would tell me whether it satisfies you and the problem and whether it is sufficiently clear.

Every sensation as such (as empirical consciousness) has two parts, one subjective, the other objective. The subjective part belongs to sense*ᵉ* and is the empirical aspect of the sensation (in the strongest sense of "empirical"); the objective part belongs to apperception and is the pure aspect of the sensation (in the stronger sense of "pure"). Now, then, what precisely is it that apperception as such contributes to every sensation? I answer that it is that whereby the sensation is a *quale* at all.* The function of self-consciousness referred to under the title "Quality" consists in positing.*ᶠ* The act of positing is the a priori condition of apperception and consequently the condition of the possibility of all empirical consciousness. Positing, as a function of mind, is spontaneity and, like all functions of self-consciousness, is a spontaneous *synthesis*[g3] and therefore a function of *unity*. The unity in positing

---

* At this point in Tieftrunk's letter, Kant wrote in, "sensation not mere intuition" ("Empfindung nicht blos Anschauung").

ᵃ Actus der Einheit
ᶜ Alles
ᵉ Sinne
ᵍ Zusammensetzen

ᵇ des Vielen
ᵈ Vielem
ᶠ setzen

is only possible because apperception may *determine* its positing. The determination of positing is[4] condition of the possibility of the unity of positing. The function of determination of positing consists, however, in the uniting[b] of positing and non-positing into a *single* concept (as act of spontaneity), that is, *the determination of a degree*[j] (gradation). The determined positing is thus the same as the determination of degree, and just as positing is the original function of apperception, so the determination of degree (gradation, limitation, uniting of positing and non-positing into a *single* concept) is the a priori condition of the unity of positing. The function of unity of this positing is called "determination of degree" (intension), and its product is a determined real[k] (intensive magnitude). The unity produced in this manner is not the unity of a collection,[l] by means of the synthesis of parts into a whole, but rather an absolute unity, achieved by the self-determining apperception in its act of positing. But this unity springs from the unification of positing (=1) and non-positing (=0) into a single concept. Since there are an infinite number of determinations of positing and non-positing into unity, between 0 and 1, so there are an infinite number 12:214 of degrees between 0 and 1, each of which must be, and must depend on being, a unity, and each of these is determined by apperception in accord with its positing, which conforms to an a priori necessary rule (of gradation). All existence[m] is therefore based on this original positing, and existence is actually nothing else than this being-posited.[n] Without the original, pure act of spontaneity (of apperception), nothing *is* or exists. The determination of degree in apperception is thus the principle of all experience, and so on. . . .

But whence comes the manifold of sensation, *the merely empirical* aspect of sensation? Apperception yields nothing but the *degree*, that is, 12:215 the unity in the synthesis of perception, which therefore rests on spontaneity and which is the *determination* of the material (of sensibility) according to a rule of apperception. Whence the material? Out of sensibility. But whence did sensibility obtain it? From the objects that 12:216 affect it? But what are these objects that affect sensibility? Are they things in themselves or – ?

One wrestles with endless questions here, and some of the answers are highly absurd. For me, there is no perplexity, since once the question becomes understood, the answer is obvious. However, it matters greatly how one understands the question, for ambiguities tend to creep in. Let me tell you briefly how I meet the difficulties.

---

[b] *Verknüpfung*
[j] *Gradesbestimmung*
[l] *Menge*
[n] *Geseztsein*

[i] *Nichtsetzens*
[k] *Reale*
[m] *Dasein*

The central thesis of the *Critique*, of which one must not lose sight, is this: a regression to discover the nature and conditions of our cognitive faculty is not a search for anything outside that faculty; it is not a playing with mere concepts but a presentation of how those elements of our cognitive faculty, as grasped in the act of cognizing,[o] can inform us about the essential problems of reason. It is a fact of consciousness[p] that there are two distinct sources of knowledge: receptivity and spontaneity. It is absurd to prove their reality, since they are fundamental.[q] One can only become aware of them and make them evident to oneself. Though they are two distinct, basic sources, nevertheless they belong to one and the same mind, and therefore they correspond to each other. Just as we assert that the representations of the understanding come into existence through spontaneity, so we assert that the representations of sensibility come to be through receptivity.

Sensibility *gives* representations, because it (or the mind whose faculty it is) is *affected*. When I say that the mind is affected, I subsume the existence[r] (that is, the fact that certain representations are posited) under the category of causality; I assert a relationship of the mind to itself, viz., receptivity, which relationship is distinct from others that the mind has to itself, for example, those in which the mind regards itself as spontaneous. If I ask further, What is it that affects the mind? I must answer, It affects itself since it is both receptivity and spontaneity.

The mind's spontaneity, however, imposes its conditions of synthesis (the categories) on the mind's receptivity, and the sense representations as such thereby acquire determination by the unity of apperception, that is, they acquire intellectual form, quantity, quality, relation, and so on. But whence does sensibility receive that which it gives out of itself? Whence the material and the empirical as such, if I abstract from that into which it has been transformed as a result of the influence of spontaneity and the forms of sensibility? Does sensibility produce this material out of its own stock, or is it perhaps produced by things in themselves, distinct and separate from sensibility? I answer: *Everything* given by sensibility (matter and form) is determined by its nature to be for us nothing but what it is for us. The properties of being *within* us or *external* to us are themselves only ways in which sensible representing takes place, just *as identity*[s] and *difference* are only manners of intellectual representing. If sensibility and the understanding were ignored, there would be no "internal" and "external," no "same" and "different." But since one cannot help but ask which of all the condi-

12:217

---

[o] *Erkennens*
[q] *ursprünglich*
[s] *das Einerlei*

[p] *Faktum des Bewußtseins*
[r] *das Sein*

tions of our sensibility (as to form and matter) is the ultimate condition, the ground of representations that is independent of apperception, the answer is this: that ultimate ground is, for our understanding, nothing more than a thought with negative meaning, that is, a thought without any corresponding object, though, as a mere thought, it is permissible and even necessary, since theoretical reason is not absolutely restricted, in its thinking, to that which is a possible experience for *us* and practical reason can offer grounds for admitting the reality (though only from a practical point of view) of such ideas. We cannot say of things in themselves (of which we have only a negative idea) that they affect us, since the concept of affection asserts a real relation between knowable entities, and therefore this concept can only be used when the related things are given and positively determined. Therefore it is also impossible to say that things in themselves transfer representations from themselves into the mind, since the problematic concept of "things in themselves" is itself only a point of reference for representations in the mind, a figment of thought. Our knowledge is thus exclusively of appearances; yet while we realize this, we posit in thought a something that is not appearance and thus leave open a space (by means of mere logical supposition) for practical knowledge. The chapter in the *Critique*, pages 294 f., makes the true view unmistakable[5] . . .

How is *intuition* distinguished from thinking? "The former is the representation that can be given prior to all thinking," says the *Critique*. . . . Thinking (as transcendental function) is the activity of bringing given representations under a consciousness in general, and it is prior to all intuition, a fact that accounts for the dignity of cognition.   12:218

One would like intuition and thinking to be one and the same thing, transcendentally speaking. Indirectly, it can be said that if intuition and thinking were one, there would be no such thing as transcendental logic and aesthetic; all concepts would be absolutely restricted to experience. But this is contradicted by apperception. I can at least form the negative concept of an experience that is not human experience, that is, form the concept of an *intuitive* understanding. But even this merely problematic concept would be impossible if the categories in and of themselves constituted experience. I could not transcend experience by means of experience; yet I do this in fact by means of the concept of unity of synthesis in general (in relation to the experiences that are possible and impossible for us to have). Moreover, if the understanding (in its categories) were of itself capable of experiencing, the transition to the practical realm would be impossible, for there it is by means of mere thought, without intuition, that laws, concepts, and objects are determined by the will.

One tends to confuse the sphere of application of the categories with the sphere of their functions as pure forms of apperception in

general. People suppose that because we become *aware* of the categories only by applying them in experience (where they are first put to
use, which is possible only in experience, in empirical consciousness)
that therefore they cannot be elevated beyond the sphere of their
application . . .

Your friend and servant,
J. H. Tieftrunk

1 Though no complete manuscript or copy of this letter is extant, it is an
   important example of Fichte's influence (Tieftrunk's critical remarks about
   Fichte notwithstanding) on Kant's disciples. The references to "positing"
   (*Setzen*) and "self-positing" (*Selbstsetzen*) echo Fichte's *Wissenschaftslehre*. The
   prospectus to Fichte's lectures on the idea of *Wissenschaftslehre* was published
   in 1794 and the lectures themselves, under the title *Grundlage der gesamten
   Wissenschaftslehre* (Foundations of the entire science of knowledge) in 1794/5.
   The idea of "self-affection" is prominent in Kant's *Opus postumum*. See Eckart
   Förster's introduction and notes to *Opus postumum* (Cambridge and New York:
   Cambridge University Press, 1993).
2 Tieftrunk may be thinking of the axioms of intuition, since magnitude is not
   one of Kant's categories. See *Critique of Pure Reason*, A 162 = B 202 ff.
3 Tieftrunk plays on the *setzen*, "positing" in *Zusammensetzen*, i.e., it is a "positing together." As has been pointed out in other letters, the word *Zusammensetzen* in Kant is also translatable as "combining" or "composing."
4 It is not clear from this sentence whether Tieftrunk means that positing is "a"
   condition or "the" condition of "the unity of positing."
5 "The Ground of the Distinction of All Objects in General into Phenomena
   and Noumena," bk. II, chap. III, B 294 ff. = A 235 ff.

201 [789] (750)
To Johann Gottlieb Fichte.
December 1797 [?].[1]

12:221 Treasured friend,

I could scarcely blame you if you were to take my nine months'
delay in responding to your letter as a sign of discourtesy and lack of
friendship. But you would forgive me if you knew how, for the past
year and half, my poor health and the frailties of age had forced me to

give up all my lecturing, and certainly not just out of concern for comfort. Now and then I can still communicate with the world via the *Berliner Monatsschrift;* and recently also through the *Berliner Blätter.* I regard such writing as a way of stimulating the little bit of vitality I still possess, though it is slow going and effortful for me and I find myself occupied almost exclusively with practical philosophy, gladly leaving the subtlety of theoretical speculation (especially when it concerns its new frontiers[2] to others to cultivate.

My choice of the journal *Berliner Blätter* for my recent essays will make sense to you and to my other philosophizing friends if you take my disabilities into account. For in that paper I can get my work published and evaluated most quickly, since, like a political newspaper, it comes out almost as promptly as the mail allows. I have no idea how much longer I shall be able to work at all.

Your writings of 1795 and 1796 arrived via Herr Hartung.[3]

I am especially delighted that my *Rechtslehre* has met with your approval.

If you are not too displeased about my delay in answering, please honor me again with your letters and tell me what is happening in the   12:222 literary world. I shall try to be more industrious about replying in the future, especially since I have observed the development of your excellent talent for lively and communicative writing in your recent pieces, and since you have made your way through the thorny paths of scholasticism and will not need to look back in that direction again.

With total respect and friendship I remain ever, etc.

I. Kant

---

1   This letter was published in the first edition of *Fichtes Leben* (1831), vol. II, pp. 174 ,f., misleadingly labeled as Kant's answer to Fichte's letter of Oct. 6, 1794. In the second edition of Fichte's biography the letter is identified as "late 1797." Fichte's letter to Kant, Jan. 1, 1798, may be an answer to it. Kant's reference to his publications in the journal *Berliner Blätter* help to date his letter. For a fuller discussion of the dating, see Kant's *Werke,* Ak. 13: 466, f. The most probable date, according to the latest scholarship by Werner Stark, is Oct. 13, 1797.

2   The phrase is *"äusserst zugespitzten Apices,"* literally, the tip of the apexes. Kant might be punning here on other sorts of "tips," e.g., the tip of a priest's cap or the tip of a king's crown, i.e., he leaves political and/or religious controversies to others. Possibly he means to say that he leaves acute sophistry *(Spitzfindig-keit),* to others.

3   *"Grundriss des Eigenthümlichen der Wissenschaftslehre"* (1795); *"Grundlage des Naturrechts nach Prinzipien der Wissenschaftslehre"* (1796). Both were published in Jena and Leipzig.

202 [790] (751)

To Johann Heinrich Tieftrunk.

December 11, 1797.

Treasured friend

Though I am distracted by a multitude of tasks that interrupt one another while I think constantly of my final goal, the completion of my project before it is too late, I am anxious to clarify the sentence in the *Critique of Pure Reason* that you mentioned in your kind letter of November 5, the sentence that occurs on page 177[1] and deals with the application of the categories to experiences or appearances. I believe I now know how to satisfy your worry and at the same time how to make this part of the system of the *Critique* more clear. My remarks here, however, must be taken as mere raw suggestions. We can make the discussion more elegant after we have exchanged ideas on it again.

The concept of the *composed* in general[2] is not itself a particular category. Rather, it is included in every category (as *synthetic* unity of apperception). For that which is composed cannot as such be *intuited*; rather, the concept or consciousness of composing[a] (a function that, as synthetic unity of apperception, is the foundation of all the categories) must be presupposed in order to think the manifold of intuition (that is, of what is given) as unified in one consciousness. In other words, in order to think the object as something that has been composed, I must presuppose the concept or the consciousness of *composing*; and this is accomplished by means of the schematism of the faculty of judgment, whereby composition is related to inner sense, in conformity with the representation of time, on the one hand, but also in conformity with the manifold of intuition (the given), on the other hand. All the categories are directed upon some material composed a priori; if this material is homogeneous, they express mathematical functions, and if it is not homogeneous, they express dynamic functions.[3] Extensive magnitude[4] is a function of the first sort, for example, a one in many. Another example of a mathematical function is the category of quality or intensive magnitude, a many in one. An example of extensive magnitude would be a collection of similar things (for example, the number of square inches in a plane); an example of intensive magnitude, the notion of degree[5] (for example, of illumination of a room). As for the dynamic functions, an example would be the synthesis of the manifold insofar as one thing's existence is subordinate to another's (the category

12:223

[a] *Zusammensetzens*

of causality) or one thing is coordinated with another to make a unity of experience (modality as the necessary determination of the existence of appearances in time).

Herr Beck (to whom I beg you to send my regards) could thus also quite correctly develop his "standpoint" on this basis, passing from the categories to appearances (as a priori intuitions). Synthesis of *composition* of the manifold requires a priori intuition, in order that the pure concepts of the understanding may have an object, and these intuitions are space and time.[6] – But in this changing of standpoint,[7] the concept of the composed, which is the foundation of all the categories, is in itself an empty concept; that is, we do not know whether any object corresponds to it – for example, whether there is anything that is an extensive *magnitude* while also having intensive magnitude, that is, reality; or in the dynamic division of concepts, whether anything corresponding to the concept of *causality* (a thing so situated as to be the ground of the existence of another thing) or anything corresponding to the category of *modality*, that is, any object of possible experience, that could be *given*. For these are mere forms of composition (of the synthetic unity of the manifold in general) and they belong to thinking rather than to intuition. – Now there are in fact synthetic a priori propositions, and it is a priori intuition (space and time) that make these propositions possible, and therefore they have an object, the object of a non-empirical representation, corresponding to them, (forms of intuition can be supplied for the forms of thought, thus giving sense and meaning to the latter). But how are such propositions possible? The answer is not that these forms of composition[8] present the object in intuition as that object is in itself. For I cannot use my concept of an object to reach out a priori beyond the concept of that object. So only in this way are synthetic a priori propositions possible: 12:224 The forms of intuition are merely subjective, not immediate or objective, that is, they do not represent the object as it is in itself but only express the manner in which the subject is affected by the object, in accordance with his particular constitution, and so the object is presented only as it *appears* to us, that is, indirectly. For if representations are limited by the condition of conformity to the manner in which the subject's faculty of representation operates on intuitions, it is easy to see how synthetic (transcending a given concept) a priori judgments are possible. And it is easy to see that such a priori ampliative judgments are absolutely impossible in any other way.

This is the foundation of that profound proposition: We can never know objects of sense (of outer sense and of inner sense) except as they appear to us, not as they are in themselves. Similarly, supersensible objects are not objects of theoretical knowledge for us. But since it is unavoidable that we regard the idea of such supersensible objects as at least problematic, an open question (since otherwise the sensible would lack a non-sensible counterpart, and this would indicate a logical defect in our classification), the idea belongs to pure practical cognition, which is detached from all empirical conditions. The sphere of non-sensible objects is thus not quite empty, though from the point of view of theoretical knowledge such objects must be viewed as transcendent.

As for the difficult passage on pages 177 ff. in the *Critique*, the explanation is this: The logical subsumption of a concept under a higher concept occurs in accordance with the rule of *identity* – the subsumed concept must be thought as *homogeneous* with the higher concept. In the case of *transcendental* subsumption, on the other hand, since we subsume an empirical concept under a pure concept of the understanding by means of a mediating concept (the latter being that of the synthesized material derived from the representations of inner sense), this subsumption of an empirical concept under a category would seem to be the subsumption of something *heterogeneous* in content; that would be contrary to logic, were it to occur without any mediation. It is, however, possible to subsume an empirical concept under a pure concept of the understanding if there is a mediating concept, and that is what the concept of something *composed* out of the representations of the subject's inner sense is, insofar as such representations, in conformity with temporal conditions, present something as a *composition*, i.e., as *composed* a priori according to a universal rule.

12:225 What they present is homogeneous with the concept of the composed in general (as every category is) and thus makes possible the subsumption of appearances under the pure concept of the understanding according to its synthetic unity (of composition). We call this subsumption a *schema*. The examples of schematism that follow [in the *Critique*] make this concept quite clear. (You will notice my haste and brevity here, which might be remedied in another essay.)

And so, estimable sir, I close now, so as not to miss the post. I enclose a few remarks on your projected collection of my minor writings. Please thank Professor Jacob for sending me his *Annalen* and do write again soon with another letter and excuse my delay in answering by attributing it to my poor health and the distractions that other demands make on me; but be assured of my eagerness to be of service to you in your work and of the respect with which I remain

Yours faithfully,

I. Kant

---

1 A 138 = B 177, "The Schematism of the Pure Concepts of Understanding." Tieftrunk's remark is not included in the fragment of his letter available to us,

but elsewhere he wrote: "In my letter of November 5, 1797, I called the worthy man's attention to a great problem in his doctrine of the schematism of pure reason (pp. 176, ff. in the second edition of the *Critique*). It concerns the question how pure concepts of the understanding can be applied to appearances. For this to be possible, says the *Critique*, there has to be some sort of homogeneity of the latter with the former; for only under that condition is a subsumption of an empirical concept under a pure concept of the understanding logically possible. But the *Critique* itself teaches us that pure concepts of the understanding have an entirely different *source* from that of sensible representations; the former are the work of the understanding while the latter are the product of our faculty of intuition. This difference in sources remains, be the intuitions pure or empirical, and nothing *homogeneous* can come either directly or indirectly from such different sources." The passage, from Reinhold's 1825 *Denklehre in reindeutschem Gewande*, is quoted in Malter's notes to the present letter, pp. 884, f. Kant's answer to Tieftrunk's question, Malter observes, leaves something to be desired in clarity.

2   In an earlier translation *(Kant's Philosophical Correspondence: 1755–1799, p. 145)* "des Zusammengesezten "was rendered "of the synthesized." The present translation generally follows Eckart Förster's suggestion, translating *Zusammensetzung* as "composition" and translating related terms, such as the verb *zusammensetzen* and the past participle *zusammengesetzt*, consistently with this decision – therefore "the composite" rather than "the synthesized," as a translation of Zusammengesetzten, though Kant translators such as Kemp Smith generally used "synthesis" for *Zusammensetzung*." Clearly one needs two words for a phrase such as "synthesis der Zusammensetzung" in the following paragraph of this letter, to avoid the absurdity of "synthesis of synthesis."

3   See *Critique of Pure Reason*, B 110.

4   See "Axioms of Intuition," *Critique of Pure Reason*, A 162 = B 202 ff.

5   See *Critique of Pure Reason*, A 166 = B 206 ff. and the section on anticipations of perception that follows.

6   In another draft, Kant writes "in space and time" here rather than "space and time."

7   It is not clear whether Kant means *Beck*'s "Standpoint" here.

8   or "forms of what has been composed" ("Formen des Zusammengesetzen").

203 [791] (752)
From Marcus Herz.
December 25, 1797.

Esteemed teacher,

The great and well-known Meckel[1] asks to be commended to the great, all-knowing Kant, via me, so little known, so little knowing. I would hesitate greatly to satisfy this superfluous desire, were it not an opportunity, long coveted, to call up in the mind of my unforgettable mentor and friend the name of Herz and to tell him once more how much the memory of those early years of my education under his guidance still spreads joy over my whole being and tell him how burning is my desire to see him again and to embrace him again while there is still time. Why am I not a great obstetrician, a cataract specialist, or healer of cancer, that I might be summoned to Königsberg by some Russian aristocrat? Alas, I have learned absolutely nothing! The little skill I possess can be found tenfold in any village in Kamchatka, and thus I must stay in Berlin, moldering, and abandon forever the thought of seeing you again before one or the other of us leaves this earth.

12:226

All the more consoling, therefore, is every little bit of news I get of you from travelers, every greeting passed on to me from letters to a friend. Revive me often, therefore, with this refreshment and preserve your health and your friendship for me.

Your devoted
Marcus Herz

---

1 Philipp Friedrich Meckel (or Maeckel) (1756–1803), professor of medicine in Halle.

1798

204 [794] (755)
From Johann Gottlieb Fichte.
January 1, 1798.

Esteemed friend and teacher,

I thank you sincerely for your kind letter[1] which did my heart good. My veneration for you is so great that you could not offend me in any way; certainly not by anything as easily explained as your delay in responding to me. But it would have depressed me, having achieved what I took to be your good opinion of me, to see it lost. I live in the midst of people who delight in gossip and story-mongering. I don't mean by that our Jena, where for the most part people have more serious things to do, but the whole area around here. For years I have heard anecdotes of all sorts. I can well imagine how one might finally get sick of philosophy. It is not the natural air for human beings to breathe – it is not the end but the means. A person who has achieved the end – full development of his mind and complete harmony with himself – will put aside the means. That is your situation, esteemed old man.

Since you yourself say that "you gladly leave to others the subtlety of theoretical speculation, especially when it concerns the outer apexes," I feel more at ease about the adverse judgments of my system which practically everybody in the multitudinous ranks of German philosophers claims to have heard from you. I hear by way of my auditors that Herr Bouterweck,[2] the modest reviewer of your *Rechtslehre* and of Reinhold's *Vermischten Schriften*, in the *Göttingischen Anzeigen*,[3] quite recently reported receiving such a judgment from you. So that is what my world is like.

It gives me the greatest pleasure to know that my style meets with your approval. I don't think I deserve it when that same Bouterweck (in the *Göttingschen Anzeigen*) branded it as barbaric. Style is very important to me and I am aware of exercising the greatest care on it so that my work will appear polished *in all cases where the subject-matter allows this*. But I am therefore far from inclined to throw out scholasticism. I pursue it gladly and find that it enhances and uplifts my strength. There is another important area which heretofore I have only skirted and not really examined carefully: that of the critique of taste.

With sincerest esteem,

your devoted
Fichte

Jena, January 1, 1798.

---

1 Kant's letter, Oct. or Dec. 1797, Ak. [789].
2 On Bouterweck, see Kant's letter to him, May 7, 1793, Ak. [576], n. 1.
3 *Göttinger Anzeigen*, Dec. 7, 1797.

205 [795] (756)
To Johann Schultz.
January 9, 1798.

12:231   I take the liberty of advising you, reverend sir, to avoid *committing* yourself to any correspondence with Schlettwein, whose letter[1] I include herewith. Your time is too valuable for that. Instead, I suggest the following: since he himself proposes an examination of the concept of space in the *Critique of Pure Reason*, just challenge him to refute the propositions of the Critical Philosophy as he has offered to do, but demand that he refute them in print, not merely in a letter, so that the public will not expect any rebuttal if it should turn out that his arguments do not deserve it. In that way his arguments will die a natural death rather than a violent one through counter-arguments.

For I have a well-grounded suspicion that Schlettwein is only out for profit with his worthless writing and expects that you, because of your interest in the honorarium, might be indulgent with him. But I think the notoriety of the issue promises to make for a significant loss. If, prior to his work, you had bound yourself in writing to answer him,
12:232   then, if no published response from you were to come out, he would

claim this to be a confession of impotence and say that his arguments were irrefutable.
I remain with fullest respect
Your faithful, devoted servant,
I. Kant

---

1 See Kant's open letter, May 29, 1797, Ak.[752]. Two long letters from Schlettwein may be found in Ak. 12:362 ff. and 368 ff.

206 [796]
To Christoph Wilhelm Hufeland.[1]
February 6, 1798.

Here, esteemed friend, you have the promised essay "On the Power of the Mind"[2] etc., which you have my permission to publish in your journal or, if you prefer, publish as a separate work, along with your Preface or annotation, but I want no one to think that I am trying to increase my income by means of this authorship.

If your enormous knowledge of medicine should include some remedy or relief for the indisposition I have described to you, it would please me if you would send me that information in a personal letter. But I must admit in all honesty that I am not very hopeful, and I think I have ample reason to take to heart Hippocrates' phrase, "The judgment is doubtful, the experiment dangerous." – It is a great sin to have grown old, but no one is spared the punishment for it: death.

May you encounter it only after a long and happy life!
Your admirer and faithful, devoted servant
I. Kant

---

1 On Hufeland, the renowned physician, see also Schütz's letter to Kant, Nov. 13, 1785, Ak.[253], n. 5.

2 "Von der Macht des Gemüts," which became section 3 of *The Conflict of the Faculties* (1798).
   In an earlier letter, Kant wrote to Hufeland, Apr. 19, 1797, Ak.[746], thanking him for his book on how to prolong one's life, *Die Kunst das menschli-*

che Leben zu verlängern (1797). Kant also writes in that letter: "It occurred to me to compose a diathetic and to address it to you – it should make comprehensible, from my own experience, '*The Power of the Mind to Master Its Morbid Feelings by Sheer Resolution.*' This matter deserves to be taken up in the study of medicine as a psychological remedy, an experimental treatment in its own right. By the end of the week I shall be embarking on my 74th year and I have been fortunate enough to ward off all real illness (for I do not count as illness such indispositions as the raging epidemic of head pressuring catarrh). The psychological experiment may well produce conviction and success." Kant explains that he is too busy to pursue the topic just then.

207 [805] (766)
To Johann Heinrich Tieftrunk.
April 5, 1798.

12:240   I read your letter with pleasure, dearest friend, and I am especially pleased at your determination to support the cause of the *Critique* in its purity, to explain it and to defend it resolutely, a decision that, as your success will show, you will never have occasion to regret. – I would be happy to write a preface to my minor essays, one that would express my approval not only of your bringing the book out but also of any commentary you might be adding; I could do this if it were possible for me to see the book before it is put together or published, which would please the Renger book dealers as well. – Now for another concern of mine.

Several years ago I planned to publish a work under the title "The Conflict of the Faculties, by I. Kant." However, it fell under the censorship of Hermes and Hillmer and had to be abandoned. Now the way lies open for it, but, alas, another unpleasantness has come in the way of an offspring of my genius, namely, my recent work entitled "An Old Question Raised Again: Is the Human Race Constantly Progressing?"[1] which I sent to the librarian Biester to be published in his *Berliner Blätter*, has somehow been submitted to *Stadtpräsident* Eisenberg[2] for censorship. This was done on October 23, 1797, that is, while the late king was still alive, and the book was denied the censor's imprimatur. It is incomprehensible to me that Herr Biester waited until 12:241   February 28, 1798, to report this incident to me. Everyone knows how conscientiously I have kept my writings within the limits of the law; but I am not willing to have the products of my careful efforts thrown away for no reason at all. Therefore I have decided, after inquiring of a lawyer, to send this work, together with the one censored by Eisenberg, to Halle, via my publisher Nicolovius, and to ask you to be so kind as to have it submitted to the censor there. I am sure it will not be condemned, and I shall try to write the Introduction to it in such a way that the two parts will compose one book. If you like, you may then publish the latter separately in your collection of my minor essays.

What do you think of Herr Fichte's *allgemeine Wissenschaftslehre?* He sent it to me long ago, but I put it aside, finding the book too long-winded and not wanting to interrupt my own work with it. All I know of it is what the review in the *Allgemeine Literaturzeitung* said.[3] At present I have no inclination to take it up, but the review (which shows the reviewer's great partiality for Fichte) makes it look to me like a sort of ghost that, when you think you've grasped it, you find that you haven't got hold of any object at all but have only caught yourself and in fact only grasped the hand that tried to grasp the ghost.[4] The "mere self-consciousness," and indeed, only as far as the mere form of thinking, void of content, is concerned, is consequently of such a nature that reflection upon it has nothing to reflect about, nothing to which it could be applied, and this is even supposed to transcend logic – what a marvelous impression this idea makes on the reader! The title itself (*Wissenschaftslehre*) arouses little expectation of anything valuable – Theory of Science – since every systematic inquiry is science, and "theory of science" suggests a science of science, which leads to an infinite regress. I would like to hear your opinion of it and also find out what effect it is having on other people in your territory.

Fare you well, dearest friend.

I. Kant.

The 5th of April, 1789, by stagecoach.

---

1 "Erneuerte Frage, ob das menschliche Geschlecht im beständigen Fortschreiten zum Bessern sei."
2 Friedrich Philip Eisenberg (1756–1804), chief of police and *Stadpräsident* in Berlin.
3 The editors of the Akademie edition conjecture that the reviewer was Kant's friend Johann Benjamen Erhard. Erhard, in a letter to Kant from Nuremberg, Jan. 16, 1797, Ak.[735], wrote to Kant, "Fichte's *Naturrecht* [Theory of natural law] has much merit in half of it, but the beginning is total raving [*Radotage*]. It really is a pity that Fichte loses himself in nonsense so much, just to make himself look deeply profound. Unfortunately I am supposed to review his writings and I have not yet decided exactly what tone of voice to adopt. Mr.

Beck too seems to have gone overboard in the third part of his Abstract; I couldn't abstain from reprimanding him, in the review, for his arrogance, as also I did not spare Schelling for his nonsense." (Ak. 12: 144.)

The review of Fichte took up five issues of the *A.L.Z.* from Jan. 4 to 8, 1798.

4 The subject of this sentence is the review of Fichte's work rather than Fichte or his theory. Yet it makes more sense to suppose that Kant intended to censure the latter rather than the review itself.

208 [807]
To Friedrich Nicolovius.[1]
May 9, 1798.

12:243   Noble Sir,

In response to your letter of May 2, 1798, I repeat that I really did give Professor Hufeland permission to publish, either in his journal or separately as he preferred, the philosophical-medical piece I sent him.[2] For at that time I had not yet thought of completing the book and presenting it as "The Conflict of the Faculties," organized systematically in three divisions, namely the *philosophy* faculty versus the faculty of theology, the faculty of law and the faculty of medicine, which is also how I portrayed it to you before you left. Please report this to 12:244 Prof. Hufeland[3] and ask him to forgive me, for the reason stated, for publishing as part of this book the piece that was actually meant for him.

I must also remark, concerning the second edition of the *Metaphysical Elements of Justice*, that two sorts of title pages have to be made for it; the one should just state "second edition"; the other, however, should read "Explanatory Notes to the Metaphysical Elements of Justice by I. Kant" so that people who already own the first book will only need to purchase the second.

You write that you are still missing the title for the whole book, *The Conflict of the Faculties*. I think I have already stated it:

The Conflict
of the Faculties
in
three divisions
by
Immanuel Kant.

Then there will be title pages for each of the three sections, e.g., "Part One, The Philosophy Faculty versus the Theology Faculty; Part Two, The Philosophy Faculty versus the Faculty of Law, etc.["]

Please tell the typesetter and the proofreader that, since I must have confused the letters c and k here and there, e.g., writing "practisch" as "praktisch," he should observe consistency in this matter and conform to the usage that he will find on the opening pages; also ask that the typographical errors be sent to me as soon as possible.

Toward the end of this book you will find a section entitled "Casuistical Questions." Please change the heading to *Historical Questions about the Bible.*

I remain your most devoted friend and servant

I. Kant

Königsberg, May 9, 1798.

---

1 Friedrich Nicolovius (1768–1836), a book publisher in Königsberg. The firm was in business from 1790 until 1818.
2 Kant's essay "On the Power of the Mind . . ." See his letter to the physician C. W. Hufeland above, Ak.[796], n. 1.
3 There is no general agreement on the English translation of Kant's title for Part One of the *Metaphysics of Morals,* the "metaphysische Anfangsgründe der Rechtslehre," often referred to simply as the *Rechtslehre.* Some translators refer to *Rechtslehre* as "Jurisprudence" and some call it "The Doctrine of Right"; the Cambridge Edition of Kant's *Practical Philosophy* uses the latter.

209 [808] (769)
From John Richardson.[1]

June 21, 1798.

Altenburg, June 21, 1798.

Along with this letter you will receive the first volume of your *Essays and Treatises* in which I have tried as best as I can to express your   12:245
meaning and to grasp the spirit of your writings. I don't know whether I have been fortunate enough to succeed in making clear to others matters that not only interest and instruct me mightily but that have

made me more enlightened and, I must say in all sincerity, into a better person.

Under the common title *"Essays"* I have hidden a good deal of metaphysics. That is how I hope to move my countrymen, who are still wallowing in empiricism, to study a philosophy that is better grounded and, in my opinion, the *only* well-grounded philosophy. The transition from empiricism to critical idealism seems to be very difficult (and I admit that I found it so myself, and am grateful for the help of my worthy and learned friend Prof. Beck). I shall therefore patiently endure the trifling criticisms of my countrymen for a few more years. Even in Germany where scholars have the advantage of reading your works in the original, your system remained unintelligible for at least 12 years and, what is even worse, occasioned absurd theories and monstrous confusions. A proof of this is *Fichte*. I was misled by the great reputation of this man to want to study philosophy under him. But in less than ten days I became so revolted by his philosophy that I could not bring myself to enter his lecture room.

A thousand thanks for your kind answer to the questions I presented to Prof. Jacob, and for your kind reference to me in your letter to Professor Beck.[2] But I must now ask a *great* favor of you, namely, a few words from your own hand in explanation, please, of the following passages:

In your *Observations on the Feeling of the Sublime and the Beautiful*, 12:246 p. 90, where you say of a beauty: *It is a pity that lilies do not spin.*[3]

In *The False Subtlety of the Four Syllogistic Figures*, toward the end of #5 where you draw a comparison to a colossus whose head is in the clouds of antiquity *and whose feet are of clay.*[4]

I would not have bothered you with these questions if I had only found someone else who could answer them for me. I shall not rob you of your valuable time any further but assure you that you have no greater admirer in the world and no one more sincerely grateful to you than I.

Joh. Richardson

P.S. My address is: c/o Baron von Mühlen in Altenburg.

---

1 John Richardson (dates uncertain), English translator of Kant and J. S. Beck. Richardson published *Principles of Kant's Critical Philosophy Commented on by Beck* (1797), a translation of J. S. Beck's *Grundriß der kritischen Philosophie*. Richardson's two-volume collection of 19 of Kant's essays, translated into English, was published under the title *Essays and Treatises on moral, political, and various philosophical subjects. By Emanuel Kant. From the German by the translator*

of the principles of critical philosophy (London; vol. I, 1798, vol. II, 1799). A discussion of Richardson, along with a translation of the present letter, may be found in Stephen Palmquist's edition of some of Richardson's translations, *Four Neglected Essays by Immanuel Kant* (Hong Kong: Philopsychy Press, 1994).

2 Neither letter is extant.

3 See Ak. 2: 247. "Es ist Schade, daß die Lilien nicht spinnen." Kant obviously plays on Matthew 6:28 here. In the section of the *Observations* cited by Richardson, Kant is discussing "moral beauty" ("das moralisch Schöne"), the "spirit" of the French, and how the attractive qualities of "the fair sex" in France nurture the noble qualities of French men and should be encouraged to do so. His remark suggests that a beauty would be even more cherishable if it were also productive, but Kant's "Schade" (a pity) may be ironic.

4 See Ak. 2: 57. Kant says that he would be flattering himself excessively were he to believe that a few hours' labor (i.e., his brief critique of the figures of the syllogism) could bring about the collapse of the colossus (symbolizing the traditional view of the importance of syllogistic logic) "who hides his head in the clouds of antiquity, and whose feet are feet of clay."

Unfortunately, Kant's answer to Richardson's letter is not extant. Only a small fragment of a draft in Kant's handwriting has been found.

210 [819] (780)
From Christian Garve.
Mid-September 1798.

Dearest friend, 12:254

As far as the book that I have dedicated and sent to you is concerned, I have already stated so fully in my Dedication how I feel about it and about you that I need add nothing more.[1]

I shall always respect you as one of our greatest thinkers, a master of the art of thinking, who trained me when I was still an apprentice and a beginner. And I am convinced as well, if one can know a man from his writings alone, that your judgment of me is not unfavorable and that you even feel a friendly inclination toward me.

This hidden, silent connection which has existed between us for so long should be made still firmer in our old age: that is the aim of my Dedication. Even if I cannot hope for any enduring pleasure from it anymore, it will still please me if I can live to see your judgment concerning this book, a book that contains the concentration of many 12:255 of my meditations, and if I also live to be reassured of your friendly feelings.

I would have wished also to have your judgment concerning the latest progress that several of your students, especially Fichte, think they have made in philosophy since the appearance of the *Critique*. But you must have good reasons for declining to express a decisive judgment either publicly or in private letters. I myself am only superficially instructed in these matters. I have conquered the difficulties of the *Critique* and I feel on the whole rewarded for my efforts. But I have neither the heart nor the strength to undertake the far greater challenges that reading [Fichte's] *Wissenschaftslehre* would make for me. The illness that afflicts me more and more each day makes such refined speculations impossible in any case. I would sketch my condition for you; it is in certain respects as remarkable and strange as it is wretched. But a precise depiction of it would take a long book, for which I haven't the strength; and without precise details, what purpose could such a sketch serve? About 13 years ago I had an external injury to my right nostril, not far from the corner of the eye. It seemed innocent – really not, according to all its symptoms, cancer, yet nevertheless wholly cancer-like, growing not only in its surface dimension but cubically, extending as deeply as it is wide, and resisting every sort of treatment; perhaps the proximity to the eye made it impossible to use the most effective remedies for such cases. This injury has now destroyed the whole right eye and a portion of the right cheek; it has bored an equally large cavity in the head and produced disturbances of a strange sort. It would seem impossible that a human being could survive in this condition; it seems even more impossible that he should be able to think in this condition, and even think with a certain penetration and with a kind of exaltation of spirit, and yet both are true. This improbable but fortunate circumstance has given me – one who is afflicted alternately by weakness and pain and who is removed from human society – the most excellent relief and consolation of my life. Never have I perceived the beauty of a verse, the validity of an argument, the charm of a narrative more clearly and felt it with more pleasure.

12:256

Yet with all this, how small is the compensation for the suffering that I have to endure from time to time! And how much longer must I still fight this fight!

In your letters to Hufeland you discussed the power of the mind over pain and even over diseases. I am totally in agreement with you about this and I know from personal experience that *thinking* is a remedy. But not everyone can use this remedy in the same way. Some people, of which you are one, relieve their distress by directing their attention away from it. I have relieved my pain most effectively, e.g., toothache, by concentrating my attention on it and thinking of nothing else but my pain. But such outer ills as those from which I now suffer are least subject to the power of the mind; they appear to be entirely mechanical and bodily. But they are subject to the power of Providence and the ruler of the universe. May he keep you healthy and strong, he who has let you enjoy advanced age. May he bring me to my life's goal with endurable pain, since an earlier release from it is impossible. I am most sincerely

your devoted friend,

C. Garve

---

1 Christian Garve, *Übersicht der vornemsten Prinzipien der Sittenlehre, von dem Zeitalter des Aristoteles an bis auf unsre Zeiten* (Breslau, 1798). The Dedication is reprinted as a letter to Kant, Ak.[818].

211 [820] (781)

To Christian Garve.

September 21, 1798.

I hasten, dearest friend, to report my receipt, on September 19th, of your book[1] so full of kindness and fortitude, and your letter[2] (whose date I seem to miss). The description of your physical suffering affected me deeply, and your strength of mind in ignoring that pain and continuing cheerfully to work for the good of mankind arouses the highest admiration in me. I wonder though whether my own fate, involving a similar striving, would not seem to you even more painful, if you were to put yourself in my place. For I am as it were mentally paralyzed even though physically I am reasonably well. I see before me the unpaid bill of my uncompleted philosophy, even while I am aware that philosophy, both as regards its means and its ends, is capable of completion. It is a pain like that of Tantalus[3] though not a hopeless pain. The project on which I am now working concerns the "Transition from the metaphysical foundations of natural science to physics." It must be completed, or else a gap will remain in the critical philosophy. Reason will not give up her demands for this; neither can the awareness of the possibility be extinguished; but the satisfaction of this demand is maddeningly postponed, if not by the total paralysis of my vital powers then by their ever increasing limitation.

12:257

551

My health, as others will have informed you, is less that of a scholar than that of a vegetable – capable of eating, moving about, and sleeping – and this so-called health, now that I am in my 75th year, is not sufficient for me to be able to follow your kind suggestion that I compare my present philosophical insights with those ideas of yours that we once disputed in a friendly fashion, unless my health should improve somewhat. I have not abandoned all hope of that since my present state of disorganization began, about a year and a half ago, with a head cold.

If there should be an improvement, it will be one of my pleasantest tasks to try such a harmonizing – I won't say of our intentions, for those I take to be unanimous, but of our approaches, in which perhaps we only misunderstood each other. I have made a start by carefully reading your book.

On skimming it, I came upon a note on page 339 to which I must protest. It was not the investigation of the existence of God, immortality, and so on, but rather the antinomy of pure reason – "The world has a beginning; it has no beginning, and so on, right up to the 4th [*sic*]: There is freedom in man, vs. there is no freedom, only the necessity of nature" – that is what first aroused me from my dogmatic slumber and drove me to the critique of reason itself, in order to resolve the scandal of ostensible contradiction of reason with itself.

12:258

With greatest affection and respect, I am

Your loyal, most devoted servant,

I. Kant

---

1 Garve, *Übersicht der vornehmsten Principien der Sittenlehre von dem Zeitalter des Aristoteles an bis auf unsre Zeiten* (Breslau, 1798). In this history of ethics, Garve discusses Kant's moral philosophy as well. After commending Kant's illumination of the field, the edification of his teachings, and the "sensitivity of his heart," Garve raises the following objections: 1) that Kant starts from unproven presuppositions and develops his ideas according to postulated goals, 2) that his rational law lacks motivational force, 3) that he ends by reuniting virtue and happiness after all, in contradiction to his own theory, and 4) that the moral law lacks content. Kant's *Opus postumum* contains a fragmentary answer to the first charge: "To Garve. My principles are not taken from a certain, previously extracted purpose, for example, what is best for everybody [*das Weltbeste*], but simply because that is the way it must be, without any conditions. It is in no way the assumption of a principle [*Grundsatz*]." See Ak. 13: 486 and Ak. 21:478, f.

2 Mid-Sept. 1798, Ak. [819].

3 In Greek mythology, Tantalus was a wealthy king who, for revealing the

secrets of Zeus, was punished by being made to stand in water that receded when he tried to drink and under branches laden with fruit too far away for him to reach.

212 [821] (782)
To Johann Gottfried Carl Christian Kiesewetter.
October 19, 1798.

Your informative letters certainly occasion many pleasant memories of our lasting friendship, dearest friend. Allow me now to stir up also my periodic recollection of Teltow carrots, a winter's supply of which you will, I hope, be kind enough to secure for me, though I would be happy to take care of any expenses you will incur.

The state of my health is that of an old man, free from illness, but nevertheless an invalid, a man above all who is superannuated for the performance of any official or public service, who nevertheless feels a little bit of strength still within him to complete the work at hand; with that work the task of the critical philosophy will be completed and a gap that now stands open will be filled.[1] I want to make the *"Transition from the Metaphysical Foundations of Natural Science to Physics"* into a special branch of natural philosophy [*philosophia naturalis*], one that must not be left out of the system.

You have steadfastly remained loyal to the critical philosophy, and you will not regret it. Although others who had also once dedicated themselves to it, motivated in part by a ridiculous fondness for innovation and originality, now seek to lay a trap out of sand and raise a cloud of dust all about them, like Hudibras,[2] it will all subside in a little while.

I have just received the news (though not yet sufficiently authenticated) that Reinhold has recently changed his mind again, abandoned Fichte's principles and been reconverted.[3] I shall remain a silent spectator to this game and leave the scoring to younger, more vigorous minds who are not taken in by ephemeral productions of this sort.

12:259

It would delight me to be regaled with news from your city, especially on literary matters. I am, with greatest friendship, respect, and devotion,

Your

I. Kant

1   On the "gap" and its filling, see Eckart Förster's Introduction to Kant's *Opus postumum* (Cambridge and New York: Cambridge University Press, 1993). The "Transition" (*Übergang*) project is mentioned also in Kant's letter to Garve, Ak. [820].

2   Samuel Butler, *Hudibras*, pt. I, canto I, vss. 157 ff.

3   In fact, the rumor was incorrect.

213 [827] (788)
From Johann Gottried Carl Christian Kiesewetter.

November 25, 1798.

[Abbreviated]

Sincerely beloved friend and teacher,

12:265   Don't be angry with me for answering your letter only now. I didn't want to write until I could report that the carrots were en route. There have been many other obstacles to my writing. You ought to receive the little barrel of carrots soon after this letter. The carrier who is bringing it is named Wegener and the little barrel is marked "H. P. K. in Königsberg in Prussia." Freight charges, tariff, and excise taxes have all been taken care of so that you can have your Lampe pick it up without any problem. You don't know how much it delights me to have a chance to serve you in some way. I just hope that the carrots meet with your approval. They are native Teltow carrots and those that I had cooked so I could try them out were very nice. Your cook must store them in a dry place, and when she cooks them she must wash them in warm water, not cold, and then right away boil them in hot meat stock or hot water. Don't worry about this advice: it comes not from me but from my mother, who is a fine old housewife.

Your *Conflict of the Faculties* and your *Anthropology* gave me infinite pleasure. The latter reminded me often of the happy days I enjoyed under your instruction, a time that will always be unforgettable to me. If I could only see you again and thank you in person. You are the creator of my good fortune; whatever I may know and whatever I may be I owe mainly to you, and the thought that I am not an unworthy pupil of yours gives me joy. O my dear friend, how infinite is the good you have brought about through your writings, and what a rich harvest the world can await from the seeds that you have scattered.

You have probably heard from Herr Nitsch what progress your

system is making in England.[1] I recently received some news on this topic from France that I want to share with you. Your essay *Perpetual Peace* attracted attention in Paris on account of the French translation of it from Königsberg, but people found the translation too rough so it didn't appeal to the disgusting Parisians until a Parisian scholar, whose name escapes me, wrote a summary of it in the French style and published it in a newspaper. An abstract of that came out in the *Moniteur*[2] whereupon everyone became enthusiastic and wanted to know more about your system. This desire was widespread especially among the members of the Institut National and after a while people asked the elder Herr von Humboldt[3] to give a lecture in the Institut on the results of your system. He agreed to do it, though he rather lacked the appropriate equipment for the job. He explained that the utility of the Critical Philosophy was negative, preventing reason from building supersensible castles in the air. The Parisian scholars answered that they had no wish to dispute that you had demonstrated the truth of this conclusion in a new and penetrating manner, but they insisted that this was no great victory since these things were already known, and they asked whether you had merely torn things down without building anything up. Just think: Herr von Humboldt really knew only the debris of the system that the *Critique* had demolished. *Si tacuisset, philosophus mansisset*[4] [He might have been taken for a philosopher, had he remained silent]. The envoy in Paris from the Hanseatic cities Hamburg, Bremen, Lübeck, and Frankfurt attended and, since he is not unacquainted with the critical writings, was greatly angered by this lecture. He disputed Humboldt's claim but was not in a position to give an account of your system himself. This envoy came to Berlin a few weeks ago and sought me out. He told me about this incident and utilized all his time in Berlin to become better acquainted with the spirit and conclusions of your system. He was enchanted with what he heard and wished for nothing more than to convert the Parisian scholars from their error. I promised that I would collaborate with him to this end . . .

12:266

I worry about tiring your patience, so I must end this letter. My best wishes for your health. May I hear from you soon? I pray you for this and pray that you have some affection for a man who loves and treasures you above all,

12:268

your grateful pupil

Berlin, November 25, 1798.   Kiesewetter.

---

1   Friedrich August Nitsch lectured on Kant's philosophy in London. See his letter to Kant, July 25, 1794, Ak.[636].

2 "Projet de paix perpétuelle, par Kant," *Gazette nationale ou le Moniteur universel*, Jan. 3, 1796.
3 Wilhelm, Freiherr (Baron) von Humboldt (1767–1835), a member of Schiller's circle in Jena, 1794–7. Renowned as a reformer of education, a political liberal, and a pioneer in linguistics, he founded the Friedrich-Wilhelm University in Berlin (called Humboldt-Universität since 1945).
4 From Boethius, *The Consolations of Philosophy*, II, 7, 71, f.

1800

214 [855] (815)
To Friedrich Nicolovius.
April 2, 1800.

Many thanks to Herr Nicolovius for the 16 Göttingen sausages,   12:300
which arrived yesterday and therefore must have been shipped immediately.[1] My household will be amply supplied for a whole year with
these wares.

I. Kant

---

1 In his previous letter to Nicolovius, Mar. 28, 1800, Ak.[854], Kant had asked
Nicolovius for "Göttinger Würste." Kant also specified to Nicolovius the coins
or notes with which his honorarium for the publication of the *Anthropologie*
should be paid.

215 [867] (827)
To Johann Gottfried Carl Christian Kiesewetter.
July 8, 1800.

Dearest old friend,   12:315

Your gift, the two-volume Refutation of Herder's *Metacritique*[1] (it
does equal honor to your heart and your head), revives my memory of
those pleasant days we used to enjoy together, days enlivened by what

is true and good and imperishable to both of us. Now, in my 77th year, plagued by physical weaknesses (which do not however point to an imminent farewell) that make my final project more difficult but not, I hope, null and void, these memories are no small tonic for me, in my condition – your gift is thus doubly pleasing.

Your concern lest the carrots you sent last autumn might have been damaged by the long and early frost that took place then has turned out to be unwarranted. For I consumed the last of them only the day before yesterday at Sunday dinner, as usual with two friends, and the carrots tasted fine.

12:316   Be happy, and continue your affection for your eternal friend. Let me hear something now and then of your situation and literary happenings.

With greatest devotion and friendship and respect I remain always your unwaveringly loyal friend and servant.

I. Kant

Königsberg, the 8th of July, 1800

---

1   Kiesewetter's *Prüfung der Herderschen metakritik zur Kritik der reinen Vernunft*, parts I and II (Berlin, 1799 and 1800, respectively). Kiesewetter sent Kant the first part on Nov. 15, 1799, saying that Herder's babble (*Geschwätz*) hardly deserved refuting, but for old Wieland's praise of Herder in his journal, the *Deutsche Merkur*. Cf. Kiesewetter's letter to Kant, Nov. 15, 1799, Ak.[848]. Herder's book was entitled *Verstand und Erfahrung. Eine metakritik zur Kritik der reinen Vernunft*, in two parts (Leipzig, 1799). Part II bore the subtitle *Vernunft und Sprache*.

Declaration concerning Fichte's *Wissenschaftslehre.*[1]

August 7, 1799.

Public Declarations, No. 6; *Werke*, Ak. 12: 370–1.

In response to the solemn challenge made to me by the reviewer of $\quad$ 12:370
Buhle's "Entwurf der Transcendental-Philosophie" in No. 8 of the
Erlangischen Litteraturzeitung, January 11, 1799, I hereby declare that I
regard *Fichte's Wissenschaftslehre*[2] as a totally indefensible system. For
pure theory of science[a] is nothing more or less than mere *logic*, and the
principles of logic cannot lead to any material knowledge, since logic,
that is to say, *pure logic*, abstracts from the content of knowledge; the
attempt to cull a real object out of logic is a vain effort and therefore
something that no one has ever achieved.[3] If the transcendental philosophy is correct, such a task requires a passing over into metaphysics.
But I am so opposed to metaphysics, as defined according to *Fichtean*
principles, that I have advised him, in a letter, to turn his fine literary
gifts to the problem of applying the *Critique of Pure Reason* rather than
squander them in cultivating fruitless sophistries. He, however, has
replied politely by explaining that "he would not make light of scholasticism after all." Thus the question whether *I* take the spirit of Fichtean
philosophy to be a genuinely critical philosophy is already answered by
Fichte himself, and it is unnecessary for me to express my opinion of
its value or lack of value. For the issue here does not concern an object
that is being appraised but concerns rather the appraising subject, and
so it is enough that I renounce any connection with that philosophy.

$\quad$ I must remark here that the assumption that I have intended to
publish only a *propaedeutic* to transcendental philosophy and not the $\quad$ 12:371
actual system of this philosophy is incomprehensible to me.[4] Such an
intention could never have occurred to me, since I took the complete-

---

[a] *Wissenschaftslehre*

ness of pure philosophy within the *Critique of Pure Reason* to be the best indication of the truth of that work. Since the reviewer finally maintains that the *Critique* is not to be taken *literally* in what it says about sensibility and that anyone who wants to understand the *Critique* must first master the requisite *standpoint*[5] (of Beck or of Fichte), because *Kant's* precise words, like Aristotle's, will destroy the spirit, I therefore declare again that the *Critique* is to be understood by considering exactly what it says and that it requires only the common standpoint that any mind sufficiently cultivated in such abstract investigations will bring to it.

There is an Italian proverb: May God protect us especially from our friends, for we shall manage to watch out for our enemies ourselves. There are indeed friends who mean well by us but who are doltish in choosing the means for promoting our ends. But there are also treacherous friends, deceitful, bent on our destruction while speaking the language of good will (*aliud lingua promptum, aliud pectore inclusum genere*),[6] and one cannot be too cautious about such so-called friends and the snares they have set. Nevertheless the critical philosophy must remain confident of its irresistible propensity to satisfy the theoretical as well as the moral, practical purposes of reason, confident that no change of opinions, no touching up or reconstruction into some other form, is in store for it; the system of the *Critique* rests on a fully secured foundation, established forever; it will prove to be indispensable too for the noblest ends of mankind in all future ages.

The 7th of August, 1799.

Immanuel Kant

---

1 Open letter, published in the *Intelligenzblatt* of the *Allgemeine Litteratur-Zeitung*, Aug. 28, 1799, was prompted by a review of Johann Gottlieb Buhle's *Entwurf der Transcendental-Philosophie* (Göttingen, 1798). The challenge stated: "*Kant* is the first *teacher* of Transcendental Philosophy and Reinhold the admirable *disseminator* of the critical doctrine: but the first true Transcendental Philosopher is undeniably *Fichte*. For Fichte has realized what the *Critique* proposed, carrying out systematically the transcendental idealism which *Kant* projected. How natural therefore is the public's desire that the originator of the *Critique* declare openly his opinion of the work of his worthy pupil!" The reviewer goes on to ask explicitly for Kant's view of Fichte's *Wissenschaftslehre*. Ak. 13:542–50 offers a detailed discussion of Kant's delay in answering the challenge and a lengthy account of the reactions of Kant's followers and apostates to this denunciation of Fichte and, in a passing allusion to "Standpoints," J. S. Beck. Fichte's public reaction (it too appeared in the *A.L.Z.*, a month after Kant's Declaration) was restrained – but privately, to Schelling, he expressed contempt for Kant's theory as "total absurdity," which Kant

understood as little as he understood Fichte's theory. Beck took a more tolerant attitude, excusing Kant in part, deploring the blabber (*Geschwätz*) of Reinhold, but criticizing Kant's tendency to flatter.

2   The title cited is imprecise, but Kant must mean Fichte's *Grundlage der gesamten Wissenschaftslehre*. Fichte, in a letter of Oct. 6, 1794, Ak.[641], asked Kant for his opinion of a "small part of my first attempt to carry out the project stated in my work, concerning the concept of *Wissenschaftslehre* etc. . . ." In a letter to Tieftrunk, Apr. 5, 1788, Ak. [805], Kant admits not having read Fichte's "allegmeine Wissenschaftslehre" and to know the work only from a review in the *A.L.Z.* On the basis of the review, Kant expresses great misgivings about Fichte and the idea of "self-consciousness" and he is put off even by the title, "Wissenschaftslehre." See above, p. 545. The editors of Ak. 13 dismiss as highly improbable the suggestion that Kant in fact read the book some time between the Tieftrunk letter and the writing of this open declaration. Fichte thought that Kant had read his *Zweite Einleitung in die Wissenschaftslehre* of 1797.

3   That Fichte never attempted to do what Kant accuses him of attempting is clear. In a letter to Schelling he explains that by the word "Wissenschaftslehre" he did not mean "logic" but "transcendental philosophy or metaphysics itself." See Ak. 13: 549.

4   Kant's claim here is contradicted by many passages in the first *Critique* as well as by his own "Transition" project of his final years.

5   The allusion is to J. S. Beck's *Only Possible Standpoint from Which the Critical Philosophy Must Be Judged*.

6   who think one thing and say another

561

Biographical Sketches

BASEDOW, *Johann Bernhard* (1723–90), renowned educational reformer of the Enlightenment and one of the so-called popular philosophers, was born in Hamburg, where he studied philosophy with the Wolffian, Herman Samuel Reimarus (father of Johann Albrecht Heinrich Reimarus and Elise [Margarete Elisabeth] Reimarus, Lessing's and Mendelssohn's friend). Basedow studied theology at Leipzig, under C. A. Crusius and, while working as a private tutor, became interested in problems of pedagogy. On Klopstock's recommendation, he was appointed professor of philosophy and rhetoric at Soro in Denmark, but his heterodox views brought on dismissal. Basedow moved to Altona in 1761 to teach at a *Gymnasium* but again he was dismissed and his writings banned. Leaving theology, he turned to the philosophy of education. His writings and textbooks brought renown and he was invited by Prince Leopold of Dessau to start an experimental school there. Basedow's school, the Philanthropinum, opened in 1774. Other schools, modeled on it, appeared in Switzerland and Germany.

In 1774 he published *Philalethie*, a work that echoes Crusius, Hume, and the French philosophes. (Georgio Tonelli, writing in the *Encyclopedia of Philosophy*, ed. P. Edwards, claims that it influenced Kant, Tetens, and others.) A theological treatise, *Examen in der alten natürlichsten Religion*, in which Basedow defends deism and rational, practical religion devoid of the dogmas of orthodox Christianity, appeared in 1776.

Basedow's educational theory was indebted to Locke and Rousseau. He maintained that education should be cosmopolitan, the same for all social classes, avoiding religious indoctrination in any specific sect. (The Philanthropinum admitted even Jewish pupils.) Instruction was given in the pupil's mother tongue and included physical education. Anticipating in at least one respect the doctrine of John Dewey, Basedow stressed the importance of some sort of connection between school studies and the outer world.

Basedow's other publications include *Praktische Philosophie für alle Stände* (1758), *Theoretisches System der gesunden Vernunft* (1765), *Methodischer Unterricht in der überzeugenden Erkenntnis der biblischen Religion* (1764), *Vorstellung an Menschenfreunde und vermögende Männer* (1768), *Methodenbuch für Väter und Mütter der Familien und Völker* (1776), and a treatise on education entitled *Elementarwerk* (1774). Goethe cites Basedow's visit to him in Frankfurt in Bk. 14 of *Dichtung und Wahrheit*. Impractical, quarrelsome, and inclined to drunkenness, Basedow was fired in 1776 and replaced by Wolke and Campe. The Philanthropinum closed in 1793.

BECK, *Jacob Sigismund* (1761–1840), was born in Marienburg in western Prussia. He studied mathematics and philosophy in Königsberg, then accepted a *Gymnasium* teaching position in Halle, in which city he became professor of philosophy in 1796. In 1799 he accepted a similar position in Rostock where he remained until his death.

As his correspondence with Kant shows, Beck was one of Kant's most ardent and astute disciples. Their letters are the most technical in this collection, treating fundamental issues in Kant's theory as well as topics in physics and mathematics. The critical questions Beck poses to Kant, concerning the positive role of the thing in itself in Kant's account of sensible intuitions, reflect the concerns of a number of Kant's students; but few were able to probe Kant as vigorously on a variety of scientific and metaphysical topics as did Beck. Beck insisted that Kant's doctrine of "objects" affecting our sensibility must be understood only in the empirical sense, not as an unknowable thing in itself acting on an unobservable I in itself, for the "I" (and its body) are themselves epistemological products of the human understanding. We cannot speak of intuitions being given by objects, as Kant does, antecedently to the subjection of sense intuitions to the categories. A unique a priori act of synthesis, which Beck calls the "Ursprüngliche Beilegung," must be presupposed. Though Kant was initially sympathetic, he became impatient with Beck's dogged self-explanation. Gradually the two men became estranged, an estrangement perhaps encouraged by the unflattering accounts of Beck's apostasy given to Kant by Johann Schultz. But Kant respected Beck and complimented him for the questions he raised – questions which Kant never clearly answers, at least in the letters – and praised him for investigating "the hardest thing" in the *Critique of Pure Reason*.

Beck's published works: 1. *Erläutender Auszug aus den critischen Schriften des Herrn Prof. Kant*, (Explanatory abstract from the critical writings of Herr Prof. Kant; Riga, 1793–6), three volumes, of which the third volume (1796) is *Einzig möglicher Standpunkt, aus welchem die kritische Philosophie beurteilt werden muß* (Only possible standpoint from which the Critical Philosophy must be judged). 2. *Grundriß der Kritischen Philosophie*, Halle, 1796. 3. *Kommentar über Kants Metaphysik der Sitten* (Halle, 1798). 4. *Lehrbuch der Logik*, and *Lehrbuch des Naturrechts* (Rostock, 1820).

BERENS [*sometimes spelled Behrens*], Johann Christoph (1729–92), merchant in Riga, friend of both Kant and Hamann, at least before the latter's conversion from deism to devout, "born again" Christianity.

BERING, *Johann* (1748–1825), a disciple of Kant's, became professor of logic and metaphysics in Marburg in 1785. It was Bering who informed Kant of the ban on teaching Kant's philosophy at the university in Marburg. See Kant's letter to him, April 7, 1786, AK. [266], n.1, for an account of the Marburg controversy. Bering's dissertation, *Dissertatio philosophica de regressu successivo* (1785), was directed largely against Dietrich Tiedemann's criticisms of Kant.

Biographical Sketches

BERNOULLI, *Johann* (1744–1807), mathematician and astronomer in Berlin, one member of the extraordinary Swiss family of scientists and mathematicians. This Bernoulli who corresponded with Kant is Johann III, oldest son of Johann II (1710–90), mathematician and jurist, brother of another brilliant Bernoulli, Daniel (1700–82). Johann III was educated by his father and his uncle; at age 13 he gave lectures, at 14 he was awarded an instructorship, and at 19 he completed a law degree, at which point Frederick the Great called him to Berlin to the Academy of Sciences. There Bernoulli did research in astronomy and translated Euler's *Vollständige Anleitung zu Algebra* into French.

Bernoulli met Kant at the home of Count Keyserling while journeying to St. Petersburg in June 1778. He published an account of his travels, *Reisen durch Brandenburg, Pommern, Preußen, Kurland, Rußland und Polen in den Jahren 1777 und 1778* (Travels through Brandenburg, Pomerania, Prussia, Courland, Russia and Poland in the Years 1777 and 1778; Leipzig, 1779). In Volume 3 he describes Kant: "This renowned philosopher is so lively and charming in conversation and so refined, that one would not easily guess the searching depth of his intellect; his eyes and facial expressions reveal his great wit, strikingly similar to D'Alembert's."

BIESTER, *Johann Erich* (1749–1816), sometimes grouped with the so-called popular philosophers, studied in Göttingen, taught at the *Pädagogium* and as privatdozent at the University of Bützow in Meklenburg-Schwerin. He became secretary of literary and pedagogical matters to Minister von Zedlitz in 1777 and first librarian of the Royal Library in Berlin. Biester was also a member of the Academy of Sciences. He founded and published the liberal journal *Berliner* [or *Berlinische] Monatsschrift*. Like Minister von Zedlitz, he was introduced to Kant's philosophy by Marcus Herz's lectures. It was Biester who urged Kant to take a stand on the pantheism controversy, prompting Kant's essay, "What Is Orientation in Thinking?" Biester was also fervently opposed to the "genius-craze" of the *Sturm und Drang* movement in the 1780s and asked Kant to speak out forcefully against the growing *Schwärmerei* which, by 1786, had become fashionable in philosophy.

BLUMENBACH, *Johann Friedrich* (1752–1840), famous anatomist, physiologist, anthropologist, and zoologist. His vitalist idea of a life force, *Bildungskraft*, and a "formative impulse" (*Bildungstrieb*) postulated to explain non-mechanistically how organized (i.e., living) bodies develop, was taken up by Kant, Fichte, Schelling, and Goethe. Born in Gotha, he studied in Jena, then Göttingen, where in 1776 he became professor of medicine, a position he held for over 60 years. He published widely, was elected to the Royal Academy of Sciences in 1784, made permanent secretary of its physical and mathematical division in 1812, knighted in 1816, and eventually elected to 78 learned societies. Among his many students was Alexander von Humboldt. In 1778 Blumenbach married and became the brother-in-law of C. G. Heyne, professor of rhetoric in Göttingen. Blumenbach's in-laws also included Georg and Ernst Brandes, important in the management of the university.

Blumenbach is regarded as the founder of physical anthropology, in the modern sense of the word. His interest in "the loves of animals" (1781) and "the natural history of serpents" (1788) led him to keep a kangaroo and various snakes in his home. Less amusingly, he performed experiments and vivisection on living animals in his public lectures. By dissecting the eyes of seals he discovered that the animal could shorten or lengthen the axis of its eyeball at will, enabling it to see just as clearly underwater as in air.

Blumenbach studied the anatomical characteristics of human beings as well and decided that variation in skulls (rather than color, e.g.) was the best basis for racial classification. Rather arbitrarily he identified five principal races of mankind as Caucasian (European), Mongolian, Ethiopian, American, and Malayan. Though he regarded the first as "primitive," "most beautiful," and "preeminent," and claimed that other races were "degenerate forms," he denied the inferiority of non-Caucasians, was outspoken against slavery, and rejected the view commonly held in his times that darker-skinned people were intellectually inferior "savages." Like Kant, whom he admired and claimed as a teacher, he saw all races as entitled to equal rights and privileges.

In addition to his philosophical works and his strictly scientific publications, Blumenbach corresponded with Goethe and Soemmerring. Kant also praises Blumenbach and cites his work in the *Critique of Judgment*, Ak. 5: 424.

Blumenbach's most influential anthropological writings were *De generis humani varietate nativa* (1775, 1781, and 1795, translated into English as "On the natural varieties of mankind," London, 1865; New York, 1969), *Handbuch der Naturgeschichte* (1779, 1780, 1830), *Handbuch der vergleichenden Anatomiehe* (several editions – Goethe read the third, 1824), *Geschichte und Beschreibung der Knochen des menschlichen Körpers* (1786, 2nd ed. 1807), and *Beiträge zur Naturgeschichte* (1790). The work Kant mentions and cites, *Über den Bildungstrieb* (On the formative impulse), appeared in 1781 and 1789.

BORN, *Friedrich Gottlob* (1743–1807), professor of philosophy in Leipzig, published a four-volume Latin translation of Kant's writings (Leipzig, 1796-8). See his letter to Kant, Ak.[269], n. 3, for the somewhat complicated story of Born's project and its completion. The saga of efforts to get a Latin translation of Kant's *Critique* published is complicated. Born did not complete his translation for ten years. It was finally published in 1796. Hartknoch, son of Kant's publisher in Riga, wrote to Kant that he thought Born was working on the translation and had received an advance of 150 thalers but that he was impossible to contact. Born wrote to Kant (Kant never answered him directly) on May 10, 1790, Ak.[429], addressing Kant as "Your Magnificence," expressing an interest in doing another book, a "pragmatic history of critical philosophy," and asking Kant to send him an autobiography. His translation work, he said, was interrupted by the need to work on a lexicon of church Latin. He explained to Kant that he needed the money and complained that Hartknoch's fee for Born's Kant translation, 3 thalers per page, was insufficient. Born asked whether Kant could get Hartknoch to agree to 5, in which case the first part of his book could be done by Michaelmas. Kant sympathized with Born's poverty, but, writing to Rudoph Gottlob Rath in Halle, (see Kant's letter of Oct. 16, 1792, Ak.[536]) he asked Rath to undertake the Latin translation, mentioning Schütz's offer to review it. Born's translations of Kant appeared in 4 volumes, Leipzig, 1796-8.

Biographical Sketches

BOROWSKI, *Ludwig Ernst* (1740–1832), one of Kant's first students and later, with R. B. Jachmann and E. A. C. Wasianski, one of his first biographers. As early as 1756 Borowski assisted in the dissertation defense required for Kant's promotion to university lecturer. Borowski was an army chaplain, then pastor at the Neu-Roßgärtische church in Königsberg. He rose to a high rank in the Prussian church. Borowski's connection to Kant was interrupted in 1762 when he left Königsberg but resumed in 1782 and remained close for the following decade. He published, anonymously, a work entitled *Cagliostro, einer der merkwürdigsten Abentheurer unsres Jahrhunderts. Seine Geschichte nebst Raisonnement über ihn und den schwärmerischen Unfug unsrer Zeit überhaupt* (Cagliostro, one of the most remarkable charlatans of our century. His history together with reflections on him and the fanatical nonsense of our time in general, 1790). Count Alessandro Cagliostro (really Giuseppe Balsamo, 1743–95) was a notorious magician and hypnotist who, like Mesmer, managed to "mesmerize" a good many prominent people with his occult experiments, persuading them to believe in his magical powers. A brief newspaper article on Cagliostro by Kant is reprinted by Borowski in an appendix to his Kant biography, under the heading *Raisonnement über einen schwärmerischen Abentheurer.*

Borowski is also the original source for our knowledge of Kant's letter concerning Swedenborg and the first letter he received from Maria von Herbert, both of which he published in appendices to his biography, the first entitled "Wie dachte Kant über Swedenborg im Jahre 1758?" (How did Kant think of Swedenborg in 1758?) although, as pointed out in notes to Ak. [29], the letter could not have been written in 1758. Kant's little essay, "Über Schwärmerei und die Mittel dagegen" (On *Schwärmerei* and the remedies for it), is appended to it.

BOUTERWEK, *Friedrich* (1766–1828), born near Hanover, studied law and became a philosopher, aesthetician and poet. He published a book of aphorisms defending Kant, *Aphorismen, den Freunden der Vernunft Kritik nach Kantischer Lehre vorgelegt* (Aphorisms, to friends of the *Critique of Reason* according to Kantian doctrine, 1793). In 1797 he was appointed professor of philosophy in Göttingen. A work entitled *Paullus Septimius* (Halle, 1795) shows Bouterwek's departure from Kant, under the influence of Jacobi and Reinhold. He writes there: "1. I exist, 2. So certain am I that there is something external to me . . . Our insight-philosophy and faith-philosophy are unified in the truth: *The world which is in itself real never was and never will be; it is only; it is eternal.*" (See. Ak. 13: 418 f., for these and other quotations.) Bouterwek's *Ideen zu einer allgemeinen Apodiktik* (1799) shows his further turn toward Jacobi.

In an effusively flattering letter to Kant, Sept. 17, 1792, Ak. [529], Bouterwek wrote with pride that he was the first instructor in Göttingen to dare to give a course of lectures on Kantian philosophy and to defend the *Critique of Pure Reason*. (Göttingen was a hotbed of empiricism, where the very idea of synthetic a priori knowledge raised eyebrows.) Later, Bouterwek reviewed Kant's *Rechtslehre* as well as Fichte's *Wissenschaftslehre* and Reinhold's *Vermischte Schriften*. The *Rechtslehre* review, which appeared in #28 of the *Göttinger Anzeigen*, Feb. 18, 1797, prompted Kant to write his Appendix (*Anhang*) to the

Rechtslehre, as he himself reports there, referring to Bouterwek as a "penetrating reviewer" (*Rechtslehre*, Ak. 6:356 ff.). In *Perpetual Peace* (Ak. 8: 367) Kant takes note of Bouterwek again, quoting his lines, "If you bend the reed too much, you break it; and he who attempts too much attempts nothing."

Bouterwek's objections to some of the ideas in Kant's *Rechtslehre* (specifically, to Kant's innovative concept of a right to a person analogous to a right to a thing) are answered in the Appendix and in Kant's letter to Schütz, July 10, 1797, Ak.[761], where Kant discusses Schütz's similar objections.

COLLENBUSCH, *Samuel* (1724–1803), a physician and an ardent Pietist who lived in the Rhineland. He wrote several letters to Kant in addition to the one included in this collection (they are Ak.[649], [657], and [698]) proclaiming his Christian faith and upbraiding Kant for his ethics and philosophy of religion. He found it incomprehensible that Kant did not adhere to Christian doctrines.

EBERHARD, *Johann August* (1738–1809), theologian and philosopher, a follower of Christian Wolff, was born in Halberstadt. He studied theology as well as philosophy and classical philology at the University of Halle, worked as a private tutor and preacher in Halberstadt, then Berlin. In Berlin he befriended Moses Mendelssohn and other Enlightenment thinkers such as Nicolai. Under Mendelssohn's liberalizing influence he published, in 1772, *Neue Apologie des Sokrates, oder Untersuchungen der Lehre von den Seligkeit der Heiden* (New apology for Socrates, or investigations of the doctrine of the salvation of the heathens; Berlin and Stettin, 1772; 2nd rev. ed., 1776; vol. 2, 1778; 3rd ed. of Vol. 1, 1788.) The book was an important contribution to the debate concerning the salvation of non-Christians. Eberhard portrayed Socrates as a model human being, a pagan whose acquisition of virtue required no supernatural revelation. Believers in the need for such a revelation (e.g., Leibniz) he accused of hypocrisy. Eberhard's theological liberalism, i.e., his heretical belief in the future eternal bliss even of pagans and Jews and his rejection of the dogma of eternal punishment in hell as both nonsensical and incompatible with God's wisdom and justice, led some to declare him unfit to be a preacher (his closeness to the Jew Mendelssohn was another disability), but his book was widely discussed and translated into several languages. Eberhard was attacked not only by orthodox theologians but also by the generally tolerant Lessing, who disagreed with his understanding of Leibniz (a charge that was to be echoed by Kant in his polemic against Eberhard).

Eberhard's *Allgemeine Theorie des Denkens und Empfindens* (General theory of thinking and of sensing) won the Berlin Academy's prize in 1776. It contained an attack on the doctrine of innate ideas that Eberhard attributed to Leibniz's *New Essays*. Partly as a result of this success Eberhard became Professor of Philosophy in Halle in 1778, where his students included Schleiermacher.

Students of Kant know Eberhard mainly as a fervent opponent of the critical philosophy and the object of Kant's scorn. He claimed that whatever was true in Kant's teachings had been anticipated and obviated by Leibniz and Wolff. Kant's letters to Reinhold of May 12 and 19, 1789, Ak. [359 and 360], answer Eberhard's charges. Kant's letters became part of his lengthy polemical essay on Eberhard, *Über eine Entdeckung nach der alle neue Kritik der reinen*

Vernunft durch eine ältere entbehrlich gemacht werden soll (On a discovery according to which any new *Critique of Pure Reason* has been made superfluous by an earlier one; 1790, Ak. 8:187–251 and 492–7). A full discussion of the issues raised in it may be found in Henry Allison, *The Kant-Eberhard Controversy* (Baltimore and London: The Johns Hopkins University Press, 1973).

Eberhard's *Vermischte Schriften* (Miscellaneous Writings) appeared in 1784. He also published several books based on his lecture courses: *Sittenlehre der Vernunft* (Ethics of reason, 1781); *Theorie der schönen Künsten und Wissenschaften* (Theory of fine arts and sciences, 1783); *Vernunftlehre der natürlichen Theologie* (Rational doctrine of natural theology, 1787); *Allgemeine Geschichte der Philosophie* (Universal history of philosophy, 1788); *Kurzer Abriß der Metaphysik mit Rücksicht auf den gegenwärtigen Zustand der Philosophie in Deutschland* (Short sketch of metaphysics with regard to the present condition of philosophy in Germany, 1794); various essays in 1788–9 in the *Philosophisches Magazin*, a journal he founded with J. G. Maaß and J. E. Schwab specifically devoted to attacking Kant's philosophy; and *Der Geist des Urchristenthums* (The spirit of original Christianity, 1808).

ELSNER, *Christoph Friedrich* (1749–1820), professor of medicine in Königsberg, attended Kant during his last illness. In the winter semester of 1795–6, he took over the duties of rector of the university, relieving Kant. An exchange of letters concerning this favor is in Kant's *Amtlicher Schriftverkehr*, Ak. 12: 437–8.

ERHARD, *Johann Benjamin* (1766–1827), physician and philosopher, was a friend of Kant as well as of Reinhold, Schiller, and the von Herbert family. Erhard was born in Nürnberg, studied in Würzburg, and was in close contact with Reinhold and Schiller in 1790–1. In 1799 he went to Berlin where he practiced medicine. His autobiography was published posthumously in 1830.

EUCHEL, *Isaac Abraham* (1758–1804), Jewish scholar, rabbi, biographer, and, according to Kant, one of Kant's brightest auditors. He published, from 1784 on, a journal called *Der Sammler* in which he sought to augment exclusively rabbinical learning and to spread German culture among the Jews. Kant's letter to the philosophical faculty recommends his temporary appointment as teacher of Hebrew, Letter #6 of Kant's official business correspondence (after Ak.[259]). This was in response to Euchel's appeal to Kant, at that time dean (*Dekan*) of the philosophical faculty. Despite Kant's personal recommendation, Euchel was turned down. The rejection was with Kant's concurrence, since the statutes of the university required that all members of the teaching faculty swear allegiance to the doctrines of the Augsburg Confession and Euchel was unwilling to convert to Christianity. No Jew was licensed to teach in Königsberg until 1848.

Euchel, who was a close friend of Joel Brill Loewe (Joel ben Rabbi Jehuda Leb Levi, 1762–1802), Mendelssohn's helper on the German translation of the Bible, grew up in Berlin and became an important scholar in both Hebrew and secular studies. He visited Mendelssohn in 1784 on his way from Königsberg to Copenhagen, his native city, and came to be part of Mendelssohn's inner circle. His magnum opus was *The Life of Mendelssohn*, written in Hebrew:

Toledot Rabbenu Ha-Hakkam Moshe Ben Menahem (Berlin, 1788; 2nd ed., Vienna, 1814). Translated excerpts from it, providing a vivid account of Mendelssohn's struggles and rise to fame as well as a depiction of eighteenth-century Jewish struggles for toleration and against such infamous attacks as the "blood libel," may be found in Alexander Altmann, *Moses Mendelssohn* (Philadelphia: Jewish Publication Society of America, 1973).

EULER, *Leonard* or *Leonhard* (1707–83), famous mathematician and physicist, well-known to students of logic for "Euler diagrams," was born in Basel, Switzerland, where he studied under Jean Bernoulli. Euler was elected to the St. Petersburg Royal Academy in 1727. He taught mathematics and physics at the university there until invited by Frederick the Great to Berlin. Elected to the Prussian Royal Academy of Sciences in 1741, he remained in Berlin until 1766, publishing numerous treatises, e.g., *Gedanken von den Element der Körper* (Thoughts concerning the elements of bodies, 1746), *Réflexions sur l'espace et le temps* (in *Mémoires de l'Académie des Sciences*, Vol. IV, 1748), *Dissertatio de principio minimae actionis* (Dissertation on the principle of least action, 1753), *Theoria motus corporum solidorum seu rigidorum ex primis nostrae cognitionis principiis stabilita* (Theory of the motion of solid or rigid bodies, based on the first principles of our knowledge, 1765). He returned to St. Petersburg in 1766, at the invitation of Catherine the Great, and continued to produce many significant physical and mathematical works, e.g., *Lettres à une princesse d'Allemagne sur quelques sujets de physique et de philosophie* (3 vols., St. Petersburg, 1768–72, [German translation, Leipzig, 1769]). Copies of Euler's *Mechanica* (St. Petersburg, 1736) and *Institutiones calculi differentialis* (Berlin, 1755) were found in Kant's library. Kant refers to "the celebrated" and "illustrious" Euler in several writings other than the letters, e.g., in *Attempt to introduce the concept of negative magnitudes into philosophy* [Ak. 2:168], in "Concerning the ultimate foundation of the differentiation of directions in space" [Ak. 2:378], in the Inaugural Dissertation [Ak. 2:414 and 419], in *Metaphysical Foundations of Natural Science* [Ak. 4:520], and in the discussion of colors in the *Critique of Judgment* [Ak. 5: 224].

Euler anticipated Kant in maintaining that space and time could not be derived from either experience or pure reasoning; they must be real, however, since motion and mechanics would be impossible without them. Euler also defended the idea that mathematical truth is sui generis.

FEDER, *Johann Georg Heinrich* (1740–1821), professor of philosophy in Göttingen from 1768, director of the Georgianum in Hannover from 1796, one of the founders of *Popularphilosophie* and one of the leading "enlighteners." Feder was a friend of Garve, Mendelssohn, Nicolai, Tetens, and was admired by Lessing and Lambert on account of his forceful opposition to the rationalistic metaphysics of Wolff. Kant students know him as co-author of a review, usually referred to as the "Garve-Feder review," of the *Critique of Pure Reason*, the review that prompted Kant's *Prolegomena*, in part to answer the charge that Kant's theory was a version of Berkeleyan idealism. Feder's major works: *Logik und Metaphysik* (1769 and 1790), *Institutiones logicae et metaphysicae* (1777), *Über Raum und Causalität, zur Prüfung der kantischen Philosophie* (1787), the latter a polemic specifically directed against the *Critique*. Equally or perhaps even more significant was Feder's role in introducing French and British writings into Germany, e.g., his *Der Neue Emil* (1768), based on Rousseau's work, and his reviews, the first in German, of Adam Smith's *Wealth of Nations* and Reid's *Essays on the Intellectual Powers of Man*. With Christian Meiners, another of the popular philosophers, Feder edited a journal mainly devoted to fighting Kantianism, the *Philosophische Bibliothek*. F. Beiser calls him "the Lockean Ringleader" in the empiricists' campaign against Kant's metaphysics, particularly Kant's theory of space and time in the Transcendental Aesthetic. Beiser's *The Fate of Reason*, ch. 6, "Attack of the Lockeans," contains a lively account of Feder's unsuccessful campaign. A somewhat different perspective on Feder may be found in E. Zeller's *Geschichte der deutschen Philosophie seit Leibniz* (2nd ed., Munich, 1875, pp. 252–66) where Feder's liberalism in theology and political theory is disclosed.

FICHTE, *Johann Gottlieb* (1762–1814) was born in Rammenau, the son of a peasant. Taken under the wing of a Baron Miltitz, he received a good education at Pforta, studied theology at the University of Jena, 1780, then in Wittenberg and, from 1781–4, Leipzig. In 1788 his patron died, leaving Fichte penniless and unemployed. About 1790, Fichte discovered Kant's works. "I have been living in a new world ever since reading the *Critique of Practical Reason*," he wrote to a friend, going on to praise Kant's *Critique of Judgment* and the essay against Eberhard, Kant's *On a Discovery. . . .*, works which Fichte judged more readable than the first *Critique*.

Fichte arrived in Königsberg on July 1, 1791, on his return from Warsaw, where he had held a position as private tutor for 18 days. He sent Kant his essay, "Versuch einer Kritik aller Offenbarung" (Attempt at a Critique of all Revelation) inscribed "To the Philosopher." Fichte hoped that Kant would lend him money. Kant, though he refused, assisted Fichte by arranging for the purchase and publication of the manuscript by his own publisher. Understandably, the piece – another *Kritik* – was mistaken for Kant's work, and Kant's public disclosure that it was Fichte's, not his, made Fichte famous. Kant's disclaimer, July 31, 1792, Ak.12:359, declares "theology candidate Fichte" to be the author and states that he, Kant, had no part in the essay, "either in writing or conversation. The honor of the work belongs entirely to the talented man himself."

Kant also helped Fichte secure a position as private tutor in the home of a Count Krockow, in a village near Danzig. In Danzig in 1793, Fichte published, anonymously, a defense of freedom of thought and expression and a treatise against German critics of the French Revolution, e.g., A. W. Rehberg. (See Kant's correspondence with and about the latter.) Fichte's interest in Reinhold and in the idea they shared of a "completion" and systematization of the Critical Philosophy stems from the Danzig period.

Fichte traveled through Königsberg, Berlin, and Weimar in the spring of 1793 to Zürich, where he became engaged to Johanna Rahn. He managed to obtain another position as private tutor. This year also saw the publication, in the *A.L.Z.*, of Fichte's review of *Aenesidemus* by G. E. Schulze, perhaps the first clear sign of Fichte's deviation from Kant. In 1794 he married Johanna. In that same year Goethe, who had been impressed by the *Critique of All Revelation*, helped Fichte obtain a professorship in Jena, where Fichte and his wife and father-in-law settled in the spring of 1794.

The five Jena years, turbulent but productive, saw the ascension of Fichte's reputation among liberal theologians, philosophers, and intellectuals generally. Schiller, Friedrich Schlegel, Schleiermacher, to name just a few, came under his spell. Yet even from his second semester, there were conflicts, controversial and tactless actions, portents of the conflicts that would lead to his dismissal in 1799. He chose to schedule his public lectures, on morality (or moral philosophy) for scholars (*Moral für Gelehrte*) on Sunday mornings, a decision that seemed to some irreverent even though the appointed hour was between church services. He denounced the student "orders" or fraternities for encouraging drunkenness, debauchery, and dueling. And he published not only abstruse works such as the *Wissenschaftslehre* (usually translated "science of knowledge" – *Über den Begriff der Wissenschaftslehre* and *Grundlage der gesamten Wissenschaftslehre* exist in different versions, beginning in 1794; *System der Sittenlehre nach den Principien der Wissenschaftslehre* appeared in 1798) but also easily comprehensible – and theologically radical – essays such as *Über den Grund unseres Glaubens an eine göttliche Weltregierung* (On the ground of our belief in a divine world order). The thesis of the latter essay, disturbing even to some of Fichte's liberal supporters, is that the concept of a personal God is logically absurd and belief in such a being is "idolatry" as Fichte calls it. Genuine belief in God means *only* the faith that moral beings can do their duty, abstaining from evil even when that appears to be impossible.

Fichte, short but commanding in stature, was an inspiring, often vehement teacher. His criticism of the student fraternities and concern for these students' moral welfare seems not to have pleased them. In 1795 they disrupted his lectures, insulted him and his wife, and stoned his house, nearly killing his father-in-law. He fled to a village, Osmannstädt, near Weimar. Returning to Jena in the fall – the students' rioting had been punished – Fichte was enormously popular and seemingly triumphant. In 1799, however, his denunciation of standard concepts of God led to the publication of an anonymous letter, "Letter to his student son regarding Fichtean and Forbergian atheism." The charge of atheism was discussed by administrators but Fichte, typically, refused to acknowledge the slightest criticism or rebuke, and, despite the attempted intervention of leading literary and philosophical figures, the liberal Weimar administration felt compelled to dismiss him.

The end of his brilliant Jena career did not mean that Fichte was finished. In 1800 he published *Die Bestimmung des Menschen* (The vocation of man) and *Der geschlossene Handelsstaat* (The closed commercial state), the latter advocating a form of state socialism. His philosophy of history appeared in 1806, *Grundzüge der gegenwärtigen Zeitalters* (Characteristics of the present age) along with *Die Anweisung zum seligen Leben, oder Religionslehre* (The way toward the blessed life, or doctrine of religion). Perhaps his most famous non-technical work, *Reden an die deutsche Nation* (Addresses to the German nation) appeared in the winter of 1807–8, after the siege of Jena and the Peace of Tilsit. This rallying of a "nation" that had no firm geographical or political unity was one of the important steps in the tragic development of *volkisch* thinking in Germany.

On leaving Jena, Fichte had come to Berlin where, until 1810, there was no university. He lectured in Berlin but left the city before the approaching army in October 1806 for Königsberg. He taught briefly at Erlangen and Königsberg before being appointed the first rector of the new University of Berlin. Fichte was immediately at odds with his colleagues over student discipline; the "misuse of academic freedom" needed suppression, he maintained.

Fichte wanted to join the troops as chaplain but was forced to remain in Berlin, under attack. His wife, nursing wounded soldiers, contracted typhus but recovered from the disease. Fichte came down with it as well; he died on January 27, 1814.

For further details of Fichte's life, career, and character, see Daniel Breazeale's Editor's Introduction, "Fichte in Jena," in Fichte, *Early Philosophical Writings*, translated and edited by Breazeale (Ithaca and London: Cornell University Press, 1988). Much of the foregoing biographical sketch is indebted to Breazeale's book and to Kuno Fischer's article, "Fichte," in *Allgemeine Deutsche Biographie* (Leipzig, 1877), vol. 6, pp. 761–72.

FORMEY, *Johann Heinrich Samuel* (1711–97), permanent secretary of the Berlin Royal Academy of Sciences. A follower of Wolff, as were many of the members of the Berlin Academy, he published a popular six-volume digest of Wolff's philosophy, specifically for ladies, *La Belle Wolfienne* (1741–53). Lewis Beck (*Early German Philosophy*, p. 315) calls Formey "this singular man," and quotes a description of him from Dessoir's *Geschichte der neueren deutschen Psychologie*, p. 192: "The man actually produced nearly 600 books besides an even to us frightful number of reviews that were much in demand, in part because he felt happy only in his work and in part *'pour donner un peu d'aisance à ses enfants.'* Besides that, Formey had the largest correspondence known in Germany since Leibniz's. And toward the end of his life he accomplished a stroke of genius: incapable of creative work but likewise incapable of doing nothing, he himself published his *Oeuvres posthumes.*"

Though little is now known of his personal or professional life, it seems that he was not on good terms with his colleague, Johann Sulzer. The Berlin Academy's competition in 1751, on Pope's metaphysical optimism – really a debate on Leibniz's "best of all possible worlds" theory – was won by an anti-Wolffian named A. F. Reinhard. The awarding of the prize to Reinhard led Sulzer to attack Formey's honor. He alleged that the award was dishonest since the mathematician Maupertuis, president of the academy, could not have read the submitted papers that were in German. (This was the same competition for which Mendelssohn and Lessing submitted their satiric *Pope ein Metaphysiker!*)

FRIEDLÄNDER, *David* (1750–1834) was born in Königsberg to one of the most prominent and highly educated Jewish families in town. A merchant, he moved to Berlin in 1771 where he befriended Mendelssohn and Herz. In Berlin he became a banker and *Stadtrat* (city councillor). Friedländer and his three brothers contributed to the art and book collections of Königsberg.

GARVE, *Christian* (1742–98). Born in Breslau, Garve became professor of moral philosophy in Leipzig in 1769, (succeeding C. F. Gellert, a popular author of verse fables, plays and novels, appreciated by such notables as Beethoven and Friedrich II). While a professor at Leipzig, Garve published a critique of Lessing's work in aesthetics, *Laocoon, An Essay on the Limits of Painting and Poetry.* Ill health plagued Garve much of his life; he resigned his position and returned to Breslaw to write. Garve's horrendous final illness is movingly depicted in his last letter to Kant, Ak. [819].

Garve is grouped with the Lockean (as opposed to the Wolffian) *Popularphilosophen,* and he was important in bringing British philosophers to the attention of German readers. He translated Adam Ferguson's *Institutes of Moral Philosophy (Grundsätze der Moralphilosophie,* 1772) as well as Edmund Burke's *Philosophical Inquiry into the Origin of our Ideas on the Sublime and Beautiful (Über den Ursprung unserer Begriffe vom Erhabenen und Schönen,* 1773). Schiller came to know Ferguson's ideas through Garve's German translation.

Garve's original works were *Über die Besorgnisse der Protestanten* (On the fears of Protestants, 1785), *Abhandlung über die Verbindung der Moral mit der Politik* (Treatise on the connection of morality with politics, 1788), *Versuche über verschiedene Gegenstände aus der Moral, der Litteratur und dem gesellschaftlichen Leben* (Essays on various topics of morality, literature and social life, 1792–1802), *Die Ethic des Aristoteles übersetzt und erläutert* (Aristotle's Ethics translated and explained, 1798 ff.), *Über Gesellschaft und Einsamkeit* (On society and solitude, 1797–1800). Kant students know him principally for his review, modified by Feder, of the *Critique of Pure Reason,* the review that prompted Kant's *Prolegomena.* It is sometimes referred to as "The Göttingen Review" and was published in the *Gothaische gelehrte Zeitungen,* Gotha, August 1782. Garve's original review appeared the following year in the *Allgemeine deutsche Bibliothek,* Appendix to vols. 37–52, 2nd Division, 1783, pp. 838–62. Both reviews, translated by James C. Morrison, may be found in Morrison's translation and edition of Johann Schultz, *Exposition of Kant's Critique of Pure Reason* (Ottawa: University of Ottawa Press, 1995).

GENSICHEN, *Johann Friedrich* (1759–1807) was one of Kant's dinner companions, the heir to Kant's library, and, in Kant's will of Feb. 27, 1798, the executor of his will. (Kant's later will, Dec. 14, 1801, names another friend, Wasianski, as executor.) He studied in Königsberg, received his license to teach in 1790, and became professor (*extraordinarius*) of mathematics in 1795. See the reconstruction of Kant's letter to him dated Apr. 19, 1791, Ak. [466]. Kant had Gensichen arrange for the publication of his essay "An Old Question Raised Again: Is the Human Race Constantly Progressing?" which became Part II of Kant's *Conflict of the Faculties,* and his essay "The Conflict of the Philosophy Faculty with the Theology Faculty," which became Part I of that work, published in 1798. Gensichen published an "authentic abstract" of Kant's 1755 *Allgemeine Naturgeschichte und Theorie des Himmels* in 1791.

GOETHE, *Johann Wolfgang* (1749–1832) needs no identification. What is striking is that there is not a single reference to him in any of Kant's own letters. But Kant must have known, or at least known of Goethe's *Sorrows of Young Werther* (1774). Hamann alludes to it in his note of Feb. 18, 1775 ("9:45 in the evening"), jokingly referring to Nicolai's take-off, "*Freuden des jungen Werthers;*

Leiden und Freuden Werthers des Mannes" (Joys of the young Werther, sorrows and joys of Werther as an adult) when he speaks of *"Leiden und Freuden über D. Göthe lieben Werther."* Of course Kant's familiarity with Nicolai's parody does not prove that he read Goethe's novel. Karl Vorländer writes of Kant: "As for Goethe, Kant is even more indifferent than he is to Schiller as a poet." Aside from *Werther*, Vorländer conjectures that Kant might have been acquainted with Goethe's famous *Prometheus* poem from Jacobi's work on Spinoza, and the verses "Edel sei der Mensch, hilfreich und gut."

That Goethe knew Kant's work is clear. A copy of Kant's *Critique of Pure Reason* with Goethe's marginal notes is reprinted in some editions of Goethe's collected works.

HAMANN, *Johann Georg* (1730–1788) was born in Königsberg, son of a barber-surgeon, a fact that may help to account for Hamann's lifelong hypochondriacal interest in medicine. Tutored at home by various students, he learned bits of French, Italian, Greek, and something of the fine arts. His father's policy was to keep children out of the public schools as long as possible. Eventually Hamann attended a "hedge-school" run by a deposed priest and then a regular school. "I could translate a Roman author into German without understanding either the language or the author's meaning," he later wrote. Hamann regretted his lack of instruction in history, geography, and writing. But his inability to organize and express his thoughts in standard ways may well have been a benefit rather than a handicap, in view of the wonderfully unique and fantastic prose style he developed.

Hamann attended the Knepphof *Gymnasium*, studied philosophy, mathematics, theology, and Hebrew on his own. At the university, he was listed as a student of theology but transferred to the faculty of law. "While I was wandering about in the vestibules of the sciences, I lost the calling which I had thought I had for divinity," he reported later, after his religious conversion. Like Kant, he found their teacher Martin Knutzen (1713–51) outstanding. (Knutzen sought to combine Pietism with Wolffian rationalism.)

Hamann's extracurricular activities included work on a weekly magazine for women, *Daphne*, published for about a year, patterned after English models such as *The Spectator*. Hamann learned to play the lute and continued to make music as a hobby for years. He developed friendships with men who were also friends of Kant: J. C. Berens and J. G. Lindner. In 1752 he dropped out of the university and became private tutor in the homes of various German noblemen, some in Riga, where eventually he was employed by the Berens family in their wholesale business. He translated French and English philosophical works and wrote, at Berens's urging, an essay on political economy (translated as "The Merchant" in *Prose Writers of Germany* [New York, 1856], pp. 121–7). It advocated trade and commerce rather than feudal privilege as productive of peace, liberty, civic virtue – Enlightenment ideals Hamann was later to repudiate as misguided secular materialism.

In June 1756, Hamann returned to Königsberg to attend his ill mother; she died in mid-July of that year. In October, he made his way to Berlin where he met such notables as Mendelssohn and Sulzer. From Berlin, he journeyed to Lübeck, then to Amsterdam, and finally to London, arriving

Apr. 18, 1757. Hamann had been sent there on business, at the expense of the Berens firm, and it was there in London, having lost his health and the Berens's money indulging in an "irregular" life, that he experienced a profound religious conversion. Hamann had tried to earn some money by lute-playing and became involved with an Englishman who was being supported by a wealthy friend "for immoral purposes." Some Hamann scholars believe that Hamann had a homosexual experience and conjecture that his feelings of guilt – in addition to his reading the Bible – may have occasioned or contributed to his conversion. (See James C. O'Flaherty, *Hamann's Socratic Memorabilia* [Baltimore: Johns Hopkins University Press, 1967], p. 51, n. 2 for various sources.)

Whatever its causes, the conversion experience was momentous for Hamann and perhaps for the cultural life of his times. Josef Nadler, twentieth-century editor of Hamann's works, writes: "With this experience of Hamann's in London there was born the new intellectual Germany of his century" (Nadler, *J. G. Hamann, Der Zeuge des Corpus mysticum*, Salzburg, 1949, p. 76). Hamann wrote of his experience soon after: "I could no longer conceal it from my God that I was the fratricide, the fratricide of his only begotten son. The spirit of God continued to reveal to me more and more the mystery of divine love and the blessing of faith in our gracious and only Savior in spite of my great weakness, in spite of the long resistance which I had until then offered to his testimony and his compassion." *(Thoughts Concerning My Life*, quoted in O'Flaherty, op. cit., p. 51.)

After his conversion, Hamann returned to Riga, July 1758, where the Berens family seems to have forgiven him. But Hamann's spiritual turn to evangelical Christianity did not please his friend J. C. Berens. In 1759 Hamann was again in Königsberg where he remained for the next four years. Berens, in St. Petersburg, was eager to rescue him from the "born again" faith that, to rationalist deists like Berens, meant superstitious nonsense. To restore Hamann to sanity, Berens enlisted the assistance of Kant, their mutual friend. In June, Kant and Berens visited Hamann. Hamann's letter to Kant of July 27, 1759, Ak. [11], was one result. Hamann's *Sokratische Denkwürdigkeiten* (Socratic memorabilia) "compiled for the Boredom of the Public by a Lover of Boredom" (Amsterdam, 1759), a work Hamann dedicated, with irony, "An die Zween" (To the two) – Kant and Berens – is another.

Unemployed, Hamann eventually took a position as chancery clerk and copyist. In early 1764, his father suffered a stroke and Hamann stopped work in order to care for him. He then took various tutorial jobs and, in 1765, became secretary to a lawyer in Mitau. There he was close to Herder, then employed at the cathedral school in Riga. The following twenty years Hamann lived in Königsberg, where Kant helped him obtain work as a translator and tax official.

Hamann's reputation grew, from publication of the *Sokratische Denkwürdigkeiten, Selbstgespräche eines Autors* (An author's soliloquies, 1773) and from his personal friendships with literary and philosophical figures, among them Kant, F. H.. Jacobi, Goethe, Moses Mendelssohn, a protégé of Lavater and apostle of *Sturm und Drang* named Christoph Kaufmann, J. H. Merk, critic and teacher of the young Goethe, J. F. Reichardt, Kant's auditor who became

Frederick the Great's *Kappelmeister* in Berlin, and F. von Moser, a Hessian statesman who first called Hamann "Magus im Norden" (the magus, or wizard, of the north). Hamann retired from his government job in 1787, with a small pension from the king. He had suffered a light stroke, Dec. 7, 1785. Hamann was invited to the Münster Circle in Westphalia and spent the last year of his life, 1788, there.

Never legally married, Hamann in 1763 became involved with a peasant girl, Anna Regina Schuhmacher, his housekeeper, with whom he then had four children in what turned out to be an enduring common-law marriage, happy though frowned upon as disreputable by Königsberg society. His earlier amorous relationships were not as felicitous. He had been in love with Katharina Berens, sister of J. C. Berens, when she was still a child, and he had believed that she was destined for him by the hand of God. The Berens family, though usually generously supportive of Hamann, had not approved.

Among his many literary achievements was a partial translation of Hume's *Dialogues concerning natural Religion* (1780); Kant praised it, but the translation was not published because someone else's was already in print. We can see Hamann's appropriation of Hume, for anti-rationalist purposes, in Hamann's 1759 letter to Kant.

It was Hamann who called Kant "The Prussian Hume" (in a letter to Herder, May 10, 1781) or more exactly, "Hume in Prussian dress" ("prussisch bekleidet"). Hamann's correspondence with Kant, other than the 1759 letter, concerns two main topics. One was their collaboration on a projected juvenile physics (or general science) textbook, the other, a dispute between Hamann and his friend Herder over the conjectural origin of human language. The former is of no great philosophical interest, though the idea of a science textbook by these brilliant but unlikely collaborators is amusing. Hamann thought that the order of topics in a science text should parallel the order of creation. His letters to Kant, urging that the writer must become like a child in order to write for a child, are delightful and revealing.

The second topic in their correspondence concerned the divine versus natural origin of human language, a lively issue for debate in Kant's day and not without parallel to current controversies over "the language of thought" and the possibility of pre-linguistic knowledge. Not only Herder but Dietrich Tiedemann wrote on this subject. Tiedemann, a philosopher in Kassel who later wrote on Kant, argued that language is not of divine origin. Hamann reviewed Tiedemann's book critically and hoped that Herder would do better, but Herder too advanced a naturalistic account of language. In the same year, 1772, in the *Königsbergsche Gelehrte und Politische Zeitungen*, Hamann reviewed Herder. He made fun of Herder's Berlin Prize essay, in which Herder had argued that animal/human language comes into being for the sake of the expression of emotion rather than thought. Thinking, according to Herder, comes with the power of "reflection" (*Bessonenheit*), which is not a separate faculty but "a disposition of nature" that organizes all human powers. We confront "the vast ocean of sensations" and single out, by reflection, one wave; we concentrate on it, and thereby we become self-conscious. That is where the invention of human language originates. Reflection too is the source of our capacity to represent the outer world. Hamann accuses Herder of Platonism because of Herder's belief in this "interior" process, but as we see in the letters it is really Herder's distance from Hamann's supernaturalism that troubles him.

Hamann's humor, irony, and rabid opposition to Enlightenment liberalism in religion was understandably admired by Kierkegaard, who quotes him on the frontispiece of *Fear and Trembling*. Hamann's "born again" Christian zeal was not without a streak of nastiness, as one can see in his letters to Kant and others. Though fond of quoting the Old Testament and friendly with at least some Jews (Mendelssohn), he did not abstain from the anti-Semitic jibes that were common in his and Kant's social circle. As Vorländer points out, Hamann was jealous of Marcus Herz's success in Berlin, where Herz gave popular lectures on Kant to groups of distinguished people. Hamann complained to Herder about "philosophische Schulfüchserei" (philosophical pedantry) in Berlin, mocking "Dr. Herz, Kant's circumcised auditor." (The passage is quoted by Karl Vorländer, *Immanuel Kant der Mann und das Werk*, Vol. I, p. 211.) Perhaps Jean Paul's remark, in *Vorschule der Aesthetik*, captures Hamann best: "The great Hamann is a deep sky full of telescopic stars with many a nebula which no eye will resolve."

HARTKNOCH, *Johann Friedrich*, the elder (1740–89), publisher of the *Critique of Pure Reason*, studied theology in Königsberg and became an assistant in Kanter's bookstore. He founded his own book business, first in Mitau, then in Riga. After his father's death, his son (same name, 1768–1819) asked Kant to use him as publisher for the *Critique of Judgment*. For reasons unknown to us, Kant declined the younger Hartknoch's request and turned instead to the publisher Lagarde, whereupon Hartknoch complained to Kant, citing Kant's promise from a letter of Sept. 5, 1789 (only a fragment is extant).

HELLWAG, *Christoph Friedrich* (1754–1835), doctor of medicine and philosophy, as he signs himself in a long letter to Kant, Ak. [460], (see Kant's reply, Jan. 3, 1791, Ak. [461]) came to Oldenburg near Bremen in 1782 as physician to the prince bishop of Lübeck and duke of Oldenburg. In 1784 he married and in 1788 moved to Eutin as privy councillor and physician. He was a friend of F. H. Jacobi and J. H. Voß (rector of the Eutin school, not the Berlin publisher Christian Friedrich Voß who launched Mendelssohn's career, nor the Prussian Minister Otto Karl Friedrich von Voß whose sister Julie von Voß, Countess Ingenheim, was a mistress of Friedrich Wilhelm II – there seem to be many Voß's mentioned in Kant's correspondence!) Hellwag continued to work in Eutin as a physician for over 50 years.

HENNINGS, *Justus Christian* (1731–1815) became a professor in Jena in 1765. In the winter semester of 1792–3 he approved the publication of Kant's *Religion within the Limits of Reason Alone*. Schütz mentions him in his letter of November 13, 1785, Ak. [253].

HERBERT, *Maria* von (1769–1803), and *Franz Paul* von (1759–1811), lived in Klagenfurt, a town in southern Austria, where their household was a rare oasis of Kant studies and religious liberalism in a country largely hostile to both. The Herberts came from a manufacturing family in Carinthia that was raised to the rank of nobility by Maria Theresa in 1767. Baron Franz Paul took over the family's white lead factory at the age of 20, improved it, married in 1785, then, in 1789, "driven by a philosophical itch" (as Vorländer puts it), traveled to Weimar to work with Wieland. In 1790 he went to Jena to study with Reinhold, abandoning his wife, child, and business for half a year in order to learn about Kant's philosophy. In the spring of 1791 he returned to Carinthia and "transplanted" the new philosophy into his circle. A young man named Forberg, later to be Fichte's most radical student, described the Herbert household, in a letter to Reinhold, May 14, 1791, as "a new Athens. Everyone fanatically discusses philosophy, and out of the highest of motives: to reform religion. Piety has been displaced by morality, to which all pay homage."

Maria, who was born Sept. 6, 1769, became part of this circle. She was called "Mizza" in family circles and is said to be very beautiful. Her passionate, despairing letter to Kant in the summer of 1791 is explained by Erhard a year later in his letter to Kant, Jan. 17, 1793, Ak.[557]. To actualize an ideal love ("eine idealische Liebe zu realisieren") she had thrown herself into the arms of a man who exploited her trust. She fell in love a second time and, fearing the loss of her new lover's esteem, did not disclose her first love to him for a long time. When she did, his ardor cooled and they became merely friends. Induced by her brother's and Forberg's worship of Kant, she wrote to Kant (Ak.[478]), who was so moved by her letter's truth and authenticity that he carefully copied and improved on the preliminary draft of his reply to her – unusual for Kant. Kant's letter (Ak.[510]), in the form of a sermon, offers Maria his views on friendship, candor, love, and marriage. It is a remarkable document in showing Kant in the role of father confessor and "moral physician," sensitive to the nuances of emotional states and moral psychology, the temptation to deceive and to self-deceive. Remarkable too are her response to it, Ak.[554], and her final letter to Kant, Ak.[614], discussing suicide, which in fact she later committed.

The intellectual curiosity, warmth, and clear-eyed vision that shows itself in Maria's letters to Kant cannot fail to move. Whether the numbness and deep pessimism leading to her suicide was somehow congenital – Franz Paul also took his own life – or had other sources, perhaps connected with the status of women in her society, where there was little that a talented, reflective woman could do with her life, we can only conjecture. (It is interesting that Erhard, Kant's main informant about the Herberts, also discusses suicide in his letter, Ak.[557]. Could Klagenfurt's gray skies have contributed to the prevailing melancholia?)

HERDER, *Johann Gottfried* (1744–1803), poet, folklorist, philosopher and leading theoretician of the *Sturm und Drang* movement's attack on Enlightenment rationalism, was born in Mohrungen and died in Weimar. He attended a Latin school, studied medicine, then theology and philosophy in Königsberg where he was Kant's pupil, 1762–4. Herder became a great friend of Hamann's and it may be that Herder's eventual antagonism to Kant was fostered by him. In 1764 Herder took a position at the cathedral school in Riga where he became preacher and teacher. There he developed an interest in the folk poetry and sufferings of Baltic peoples. (His collection of folk poetry, 1779, contains

Estonian songs lamenting the oppressed lives of serfs.) Herder left Riga in 1769, studied French and French literature in Nantes, visited Paris, then Brussels, Holland, Hamburg. In the course of his travels he met Diderot, Klopstock, Lessing, Reimarus, Basedow and, in Strasbourg, Goethe. From 1771 on he held ecclesiastical positions in Bückeburg and, with Goethe's assistance in 1776, Weimar, where he became superintendent of the Lutheran clergy. (The church in which he gave sermons was the same one, still standing, in which Johann Sebastian Bach had worked.) Herder was married and had four children. He was extremely prolific: his collected works run to thirty-three volumes.

With Wieland, Herder worked on the *Teutsche Merkur*, he collected folk poetry and wrote on literature, art history, and philosophy. In Weimar he was close to Schiller, cooperating with the latter on the journal *Horen*, 1794–5. The noted author Jean Paul stayed with Herder, 1798–1800, the year of Herder's *Kalligon*, a work directed at Kant's *Critique of Judgment*. His most significant philosophical work, the object of Kant's examination, was *Ideen zur Philosophie der Geschichte der Menschheit* (Ideas for a Philosophy of the History of Mankind, 1784–91). Herder's other philosophical writings included an attack on Spinozistic pantheism, *Gott. Einige Gespräche über Spinozas System, nebst Shaftesburys Natursystem* (1787 and 1800).

Kant's lack of sympathy for his erstwhile student's philosophical development may be seen in his reaction to Herder's *Älteste Urkunde des Menschengeschlechts* (1774), which Kant discusses in an exchange of letters with Hamann (see Ak.[86], [87], and [88]) and in Kant's published review of Herder's *Ideen*. Herder's *Gott. Einige Gespräche* (1787) also elicited a critical comment from Kant. See his letter to Jacobi, Ak. [389], where he calls Herder "dieser grosser Künstler von Blendwerken" (this great sleight of hand artist). Herder's 1799 *Eine Metakritik zur Kritik der reinen Vernunft* (Part 1 of his *Verstand und Erfahrung*) was criticized by Kant's disciple Kiesewetter, who called it "Herderish babbling, unworthy of refutation." Cf. Ak.[848].

Given the antagonism between Kant and Herder, the incompatibility of Kant's sober, meticulous rationalism and Herder's romantic anti-intellectualism, it is easy to forget the warm relationship that existed between them, early on, when Herder was his student and Kant delighted in Herder's putting Kantian ideas into verse. It was Herder, after all, who wrote most movingly of what it was like to be in Kant's classes:

"I have had the good fortune to know a philosopher. He was my teacher. In his prime he had the happy sprightliness of a youth; he continued to have it, I believe, even as a very old man. His broad forehead, built for thinking, was the seat of an imperturbable cheerfulness and joy. Speech, the richest in thought, flowed from his lips. Playfulness, wit, and humor were at his command. His lectures were the most entertaining talks. His mind, which examined Leibniz, Wolff, Baumgarten, Crusius, and Hume, and investigated the laws of nature of Newton, Kepler, and the physicists, comprehended equally the newest works of Rousseau . . . and the latest discoveries in science. He weighed them all, and always came back to the unbiased knowledge of nature and to the moral worth of man. The history of men and peoples, natural history and science, mathematics and observation, were the sources from which he enliv-

ened his lectures and conversation. He was indifferent to nothing worth knowing. No cabal, no sect, no prejudice, no desire for fame could ever tempt him
in the slightest away from broadening and illuminating the truth. He incited
and gently forced others to think for themselves; despotism was foreign to his
mind. This man, whom I name with the greatest gratitude and respect, was
Immanuel Kant." (Herder's eulogy is quoted by the late Lewis White Beck [d.
1997] in Beck's introduction to his translation of Kant's *Grundlegung* [*Foundations of the Metaphysics of Morals*, New York, 1959, p. xxii]. With one or two
amendments, the editor of the present volume would apply these words to
Lewis Beck as well.)

HERZ, *Marcus* (1747–1803), Kant's student and trusted friend, was born in
Berlin, the son of a synagogue scribe. As a boy he was educated in Talmudic
studies at the Ephraim School. At fifteen he came to Königsberg, apprenticed
to a merchant, but in 1776, supported by wealthy members of the Jewish
community, he enrolled in the university to study medicine and philosophy.
Herz came to know Kant and was asked by him to serve as respondent at
Kant's Inaugural Dissertation defense in 1770. Herz then returned to Berlin
and enrolled at the Collegium medico-chirurgicum. Two years later, supported
by David Friedländer, Herz matriculated at the University of Halle, an enlightened and tolerant university, where he completed his studies for a doctorate in
medicine in 1774. Except for a short visit to Königsberg in 1777, accompanied
by his friend Moses Mendelssohn, Herz spent the rest of his life in Berlin. His
previous association with Kant must have helped to gain him acceptance in the
intellectual life of the city. He served Kant by helping Kant's students and on
several occasions by providing Kant with medical advice. In 1779 he married
the beautiful young Henriette, *née* de Lemos, daughter of a Sephardic physician
who was head of the Hospital of the Jewish Community, a position which
Herz himself later assumed. The Herz home became the center of a salon that
was attended by some of the leading literary and philosophical figures, both
Jewish and non-Jewish, in Germany. Herz lectured at his home on philosophy
and physics. In 1780 he was stricken with a nearly fatal illness, given up by his
own physicians, but made a miraculous recovery. Herz's interest in possible
psychosomatic factors in illness were inspired by this sudden event. He published his research in psychology and physiology, became celebrated as a physician, and was given the title "Hofrat" (Kant addresses him as "Wohlgeborner
Herr Hofrat" in a letter, Ak.[254]), or counselor, in 1785. In 1787, Friedrich
Wilhelm II gave him the title professor and granted him an annual salary along
with the latter honor. In 1792, however, Herz's application for membership in
the Berlin Academy of Sciences was turned down, presumably because he was
a Jew. A controversy in 1801 over the justification of smallpox vaccination
injured his reputation. He died of a heart attack in January of 1803.

  Herz's career as philosopher and physician and his importance in the Jewish
Enlightenment of the late eighteenth century are surveyed in Martin L. Davies's interesting and sometimes provocative *Identity or History? Marcus Herz
and the End of the Enlightenment* (Detroit: Wayne State University Press, 1995).
Of special interest for students of Kant's development is Davies's departure
from Cassirer's well-known claim that Herz and Kant understood each other's

thinking. Davies argues that, despite their friendship and the warm nostalgia each expressed, Herz and Kant mutually misapprehended each other during the so-called silent decade of Kant's development and that Kant in fact paid no attention to Herz's writings.

Herz's publications:

Betrachtungen aus der spekulativen Weltweisheit (Königsberg, 1771). There is a recent edition of this book, ed. Elfriede Conrad, Heinrich P. Delfosse, and Birgit Nehren (Hamburg: Felix Meiner Verlag, 1990). The book is essentially a resumé of Kant's Inaugural Dissertation of 1770.

For a number of years beginning in 1778 Herz gave public lectures on philosophical and scientific topics.

De varia naturae energia in morbis acutis atque chronicis (Halle, 1774).

Versuch über den Geschmack und die Ursachen seiner Verschiedenheit (Leipzig and Mitau, 1776). Second, augmented edition (Berlin, 1790).

Briefe an Aerzte. Erste Sammlung (Mitau, 1777). Second edition (Berlin, 1784).

Manasseh Ben Israel Rettung der Juden. Aus dem Englischen übersetzt. Nebst einer Vorrede von Moses Mendelssohn. Published as an appendix to Christian Wilhelm von Dohm's *Ueber die bürgerliche Verbesserung der Juden* (Berlin and Stettin, 1782). Dohm (1751–1820), a Prussian military counsellor, was the first in Germany to portray Jews as a group in a favorable light.

Grundriß aller medizinischen Wissenschaften (Berlin, 1782).

Briefe an Aerzte. Zweyte Sammlung (Berlin, 1784).

Versuch über den Schwindel (Berlin, 1786)

Grundlage zu meinen Vorlesungen über die Experimentalphysik (Berlin, 1787).

Ueber die frühe Beerdigung der Juden (Berlin, 1787).

Herz also published numerous reviews, among them "Rezension über Platners *Anthropologie für Aerzte und Weltweise*" (Leipzig, 1772, and in the *Allgemeine deutsche Bibliothek*, 1773). He also translated an apocryphal prayer of Maimonides into German, to acquaint the Christian world with medieval Jewish spirituality.

HIPPEL, *Theodor Gottlieb von* (1741–96), novelist, essayist, political reformer, and public administrator, was one of Kant's close friends and dinner companions. He studied theology at Königsberg in 1756 but then accepted an offer to accompany a Russian officer to St. Petersburg. On returning to Königsberg Hippel gave up theology to study law at the university and embarked on a varied career as author (a one-act play, *Der Mann nach der Uhr*, 1757, drew praise from Lessing) and civil administrator. Though his reputation in philosophical circles is now mainly due to his close friendship with Kant (see, e.g., Kant's letter of July 9, 1784, Ak.[232], in which Kant asks him to get the prisoners in a nearby jail to stop singing hymns so noisily) he is also renowned as the first man of letters in Germany to advocate equal rights for women. English translations by Timothy F. Sellner of Hippel's work, *Über die Ehe* (On marriage) and his essay *Über die bügerliche Verbesserung der Weiber* (On Improving the civic status of women) are available. Hippel's "On Marriage" went through four editions during his life, the last two taking more progressive positions than the earlier ones.

He was honored as Erster Bürgermeister of Königsberg, chief of police, judge of the Hofhalsgericht, and was given the titles privy war-councillor (*Geheim Kriegsrat*) and president of the city (*Stadtpräsident*) in 1786. Like many public officials, he managed also to become wealthy. Hippel applied to the king and received a renewal of his family's patent of nobility in 1791. Some sources conjecture that he wanted this "von" in order to propose marriage to a very young noblewoman. A more plausible explanation is that he wished to join the royal cabinet in Berlin, perhaps as minister of justice, impossible for anyone not of the nobility. His bourgeois status also precluded the purchase of land outside the city limits, another of Hippel's hopes, eventually realized.

Hippel is best known in the history of German literature for his quasi-autobiographical novel *Lebensläufe nach aufsteigender Linie*, 4 vols. 1778–81. Because fragments of Kant's lectures on logic, moral philosophy, and especially *Anthropologie* appeared in the work, it was conjectured that Kant himself had written the novel. Some readers attributed Hippel's "On Marriage" to Kant as well. After Hippel's death, Kant therefore published an open declaration (Ak. 12:360 f.) stating that Hippel, not he, was the author of both books. Another novel by Hippel dealt with the excesses of freemasonry, as Hippel saw them, and defended "enlightenment" and good works. All of his publications appeared anonymously.

Hippel is also the author of an essay on the granting of civil rights to Jews, "Ueber die bürgerliche Verbesserung der Juden."

Hippel's relation to Kant has been thoroughly discussed by Hamilton H. H. Beck in his *The Elusive "I" in the Novel; Hippel, Sterne, Diderot, Kant* (New York, Bern: Peter Lang, 1987) and in "Kant and the Novel," *Kant-Studien*, 74/3 (1983). Beck discusses Hippel's essay on the status of Jews in "Neither Goshen nor Botany Bay: Hippel and the debate on improving the Civic Status of the Jews," in *Lessing Yearbook*, 1995. vol. xxvii, pp. 63–102.

HUFELAND, *Gottlieb* (1760–1817), professor of law in Jena. Hufeland was co-director of the *Allgemeine Literatur-Zeitung*. In addition to teaching at Jena, then Würzburg, Landshut, and Halle, he served for a short time as Bürgermeister of his hometown, Danzig. Kant's review of Hufeland's *Versuch über den Grundsatz des Naturrechts*, (Essay on the principle of natural right, 1785) was published in the *A.L.Z.* April 18, 1786. An English translation by Allen Wood may be found in the Cambridge edition of Kant's *Practical Philosophy*, 1996.

Hufeland was a cousin of the physician Christoph Wilhelm Hufeland, inventor of "macrobiotics," the art of prolonging life.

HUMBOLDT, *Alexander, Freiherr* (Baron) von (1769–1859), traveler and scientist – geographer, mineralogist, botanist – younger brother of Wilhelm von Humboldt. Both Humboldt brothers were acquainted with Goethe and Schiller in Jena. Alexander published in Schiller's *Die Horen*, the periodical to which Schiller asked Kant to contribute.

HUMBOLDT, *Wilhelm, Freiherr* (Baron) von (1767–1835), born in Potsdam, studied law in Berlin and Göttingen and later became part of Schiller's circle in Jena, 1794–7. He spent the years 1798–1801 in Paris. Famous for promoting reform of the Prussian school system, along the humanistic lines advocated by

Pestalozzi, he exerted an influence on American elementary education, and on J. S. Mill. Humboldt's political philosophy too was influential, a variety of liberalism coupled with respect for tradition. He believed in limited government and in the importance of recognizing diverse national characters. He wrote on the diversity of human languages and how this influences mankind's mental development.

Humboldt's ideas on education were influenced by Kant, Fichte, Schelling, and Schleiermacher. The ideal of a cultured personality (the German word is *Bildung*) realizing the human being's highest moral potential required a curriculum that featured humanistic studies, with Latin and Greek as essential features of secondary education. Professors and students were to exchange ideas in a communal setting. Humboldt stressed the autonomy of universities. He founded the Friedrich-Wilhelm University in Berlin (called Humboldt-Universität since 1945). He represented Prussia at the Congress of Vienna and served in other administrative and diplomatic capacities as well. He retired in 1819, in protest against the Carlsbad Decrees drawn up by Metternich to suppress liberal nationalism.

Kant alludes to an article of Humboldt's, *"Über den Geschlechts unterschied und dessen Einfluß auf die organische Natur"* (On sexual difference and its influence on organic nature) in a letter to Schiller, Ak.[656], though he does not mention Humboldt by name. On Humboldt's understanding of Kant, see Kiesewetter's negative judgment in his letter to Kant, Nov. 25, 1798, Ak.[827].

JACHMANN, *Johann Benjamin* (1765–1832), like his younger brother, Reinhold Bernhard Jachmann, was Kant's student and amanuensis. Kant secured a scholarship for him at the university. Eventually Jachmann practiced medicine in Königsberg.

JACHMANN, *Reinhold Bernhard* (1767–1843), like his brother Johann Benjamin, was Kant's student. He was also, along with Borowski and Wasianski, one of Kant's first biographers: *Immanuel Kant, geschildert in Briefen an einen Freund* (Immanuel Kant depicted in letters to a friend), the second part of *Immanuel Kant, Sein Leben in Darstellungen von Zeitgenossen (Immanuel Kant, his life in descriptions by contemporaries*, 1804). Jachmann came to the university in 1784 and soon became one of Kant's amanuenses. Trained as a pastor, he became royal director at the Conradischen Provinzial-Schul und Erziehungs-Institut near Danzig, rector of an academic school in Marienburg, then privy councillor and provincial school councillor in Königsberg. He was in almost daily contact with Kant until the spring of 1794.

Jachmann's contribution to the biographies just mentioned is composed in the form of 18 letters to a friend. Like the other two essays, it is rich in anecdotes, the authenticity of which is unfortunately not always supported by other people's recollections.

JACOBI, *Maria Charlotta*, née *Schwinck* (1739–95). Married to Kant's friend, a banker named Johann Conrad Jacobi (circa 1718–74) who was also a friend of Hamann's, 21 years her senior, June 6, 1752, when she was only 13. (Herr Jacobi is not the merchant Jacobi mentioned in Kant's letter to Kiesewetter, Oct. 15, 1795, and again mentioned as a friend in a note to Friedrich Stuart,

Apr. 9, 1803.) Divorced in 1768, she married mint director Johann Julius Gösche (1736–98) in the following year.

In addition to her tantalizing note to Kant, Ak.[25], included in this collection, there is another letter from her, Jan. 18, 1766, two years before her divorce, responding to a letter of Kant's (not extant) that evidently sought to reassure her that her husband was at peace and of good cheer – "may he never lack it," she writes. He had been called home to Königsberg – she writes from Berlin – by some unnamed problem. Frau Jacobi had eye trouble at the time and her physician would not let her accompany her husband. She calls Kant "mein werter Freund" and accuses him of doing her an injustice by denying her the hope of his company on a trip to Königsberg. She also expresses pleasure at her husband's having an entertaining time with Kant and the mint minister, i.e., her future husband. Frau Jacobi must have been quite educated or at least aware of cultural celebrities: she says people are looking forward to Voltaire's and Rousseau's rumored visits to Berlin. She also says that certain passages in his last letter were too flattering for her to be able to answer. Her friendship with Kant ended when she married Gösche.

JACOBI, *Friedrich Heinrich* (1743–1819), often referred to as the "philosopher of faith," was born in Düsseldorf, the son of a wealthy merchant. He studied philosophy in Geneva with teachers committed to naturalism and empiricism, a sharp contrast to his early Pietist upbringing. (One of his teachers, Charles Bonnet, inspired Lavater's challenge to Mendelssohn to "refute" Christianity.) In 1764 Jacobi collaborated with Christoph Martin Wieland in founding the *Teutscher Merkur*, a major literary journal of the Enlightenment. Jacobi is typical of the *Sturm und Drang* generation in Germany, with its enthusiasm for "genius" and the cult of feeling. Hamann, Herder, and Heine were his friends in the 1770s. He is best known to Kantians for his role in the Pantheism Controversy, his feud with Moses Mendelssohn, and for his criticism of Kant's "thing in itself" thesis in one common interpretation, viz., an unknowable transcendental object affects our sensibility and is the cause of our sense impressions. Jacobi's remark on this "affection" thesis is famous: "Without this assumption I could not get *into* Kant's system, and *with* it I could not remain." (The remark occurs in Jacobi's "Über den transzendentalen idealismus," appended to his *David Hume, Über den Glauben*.) Despite this criticism of Kant and Jacobi's highly un-Kantian defense of theism based on an appeal to direct, non-sensible intuition, he and Kant were for the most part on very friendly terms, as their correspondence shows.

Jacobi was also a novelist and an early defender of liberal economics in the sense of Adam Smith. His first novel, *Edward Allwills Papiere* (1775–6; it has recently been translated by George di Giovanni, 1994), showed his fondness for Goethe's *Sorrows of Young Werther*; like the latter work, it is a *Briefroman*, i.e., written in the form of letters. A second novel, *Woldemar* (1779, revised in 1794 and '96), dealt with another subject characteristic of Romanticism: a sensitive man attracted simultaneously to two women.

Jacobi's career began neither in philosophy nor in literature but in commerce. After his Geneva studies, he first went into the family business, then into civil administration in Frankfurt, Geneva, and eventually Düsseldorf and

Munich. His friendship with Goethe, in 1774, was later destroyed over Jacobi's opposition to Spinoza and his role in the Pantheism Controversy. Jacobi had visited Lessing in 1780 and kept notes on their conversations. In a letter to Mendelssohn, Jacobi reported that he had given Lessing a copy of Goethe's *Prometheus* ode in order to gain Lessing's support against the pantheism expressed in that poem. But Lessing had replied (according to Jacobi) that he himself was a Spinozist. Mendelssohn could not or did not want to acknowledge any scandalous Spinozism in his friend Lessing, and a strong exchange of letters followed, which Jacobi published as *Über die Lehre des Spinoza in Briefen an den Herrn Moses Mendelssohn* (1785).

Jacobi's attack on rational religion produced a storm of controversy. *Wider Mendelssohns Beschuldigungen* (Against Mendelssohn's accusations) followed in 1786, and the essay *David Hume über den Glauben, oder Idealismus und Realismus* (David Hume on faith or idealism and realism) in 1787. Jacobi rejected Spinoza because of the latter's denial of moral freedom and because Spinoza's celebration of "God" or infinite substance seemed to Jacobi really a radical form of atheism.

In 1794, Jacobi, though a political liberal, fled to Eutin in Schleswig-Holstein before the advancing French revolutionary army. He was called to Munich in 1804 to reorganize the Bavarian Academy of Sciences. From 1807–12, he served as its president but resigned because of a controversy with Schelling over Jacobi's insistence on faith as the foundation of all knowledge. In an argument suggestive of some "death of God" and "honest to God" theological debates in the late twentieth century, Jacobi accused Schelling of hypocrisy for defending pantheism while persisting in the use of traditional Christian terms to describe his idea of God. Jacobi died in Munich in 1819.

JAKOB, *Ludwig Heinrich* (1759–1827) studied at the Lutheran gymnasium in Halle, became an instructor at the university, and eventually professor of philosophy in Halle and, later, Russia. His examination of Mendelssohn's *Prüfung der mendelssohnschen Morgenstuden* (morning lessons) was published in 1786. In his *Grundriß der Allgemeinen Logik*, 1788, 2nd ed., 1791, Jakob attempted to provide a popular presentation of Kant's philosophy. (He hoped that Kant might use the book as a text for his lectures in place of Kant's customary texts by Meier and Baumgarten.)

The *Philosophischen Annalen*, or *Annalen der Philosophie und des philosophischen Geistes von einer Gesellschaft gelehrter Männer*, Halle, 1795–97, of which Jakob was the editor, was a principal publication of loyal Kantianism at a time when Kant's doctrines were under attack. In addition to Jakob himself, J. S. Beck was a significant contributor. (Beck was one of two reviewers in the *Annalen* of Reinhold's 1794 *Beyträge zur Berichtigung bisheriger Misverständnisse der Philosophen*.) Jakob's *Annalen* attacked Fichte's *Wissenschaftslehre* and criticized Schiller's writings on aesthetics, thus earning Jakob mockery from Schiller in *Xenien* where he is caricatured as a thief who stole 20 concepts from Kant.

JENISCH, *Daniel* (1762–1804), born in Heiligenbeil, he was a friend of Schultz and Hamann in Königsberg, and became pastor in the Nikolaikirche in Berlin. Schiller wrote to Goethe of him, Nov. 21, 1795, "That fool, that Jenisch in Berlin who has to stick his nose into everything." This judgment may be too harsh. Jenisch may have been a busybody but it is not clear that he was a fool. His letter to Kant, May 14, 1787, Ak.[297], consists mainly of flattery and gossip, reporting on the reception of Kant's work in various places. But Jenisch was only 25 at the time. The letter contains at least one interesting remark: "People are attacking your Grundlage [*sic*] zur Meta[physik] d[er] S[itten]. [i.e., the *Grundlegung*] more than your Kritik – they don't want to believe that nature has erected morality on such deep grounds. . . . The *Anfangsgr* [*ünde*] d[er] *Naturwissenschaft* ['Metaphysical Foundations of Natural Science,' 1786], that touchstone of your philosophical system, is not read very much and those who read it find it much more difficult than the *Kritik* itself, except for the chapter on the Deduction." Jenisch informed Kant that H. A. Pistorius, translator of Hartley's, *Observations on Man, his frame, his duty and his expectations* (1749) was the author of a review of the *Grundlegung*. (Pistorius and Rehberg were the Kant critics who argued that Kant's account of the Highest Good involved an inconsistency when Kant spoke of "happiness" being apportioned to virtue, since happiness pertains to the body rather than to whatever survives the body's death.)

Jenisch published a translation of Aeschylus' *Agamemnon* (1786). He assembled some of Mendelssohn's essays and published them as *Moses Mendelssohns Kleine philosophische Schriften* (1789). Jenisch's work on the significance of Kant's discoveries in metaphysics, ethics, and aesthetics, *Über Grund und Werth der Entdeckungen des Herrn Professor Kant in der Metaphysik, Moral und Aesthetik* (in which he praises Kant over Wolff and Leibniz for giving a full account of the necessary conditions of thought), was published by the Berlin Academy, 1796.

On the other hand, Schiller may have been right about him. Jenisch liked to make up stories. In *Moses Mendelssohns Kleinen Philosophische Schriften* he attributes to Kant a witty remark that Kant (writing to Jacobi, Ak.[393]) claims he never spoke or even thought or could have thought. The remark was "the greatest philosopher of the Germans said, with as much truth as wit, 'It's Mendelssohn's fault that Jacobi thought of himself as a philosopher'." Jacobi asked Kant for an explanation, which prompted the denial Kant sent but Jacobi never used. A letter of Kiesewetter to Kant, Nov. 15, 1799, Ak.[848], refers to another of Jenisch's fictions. In a work entitled *Diogenes Laterne* (1799) Jenisch satirizes important contemporaries and important causes, e.g., the French Revolution, the Enlightenment, Rousseau, Schiller. He tells a supposedly witty story about Kant that in fact never happened. "In the company of the Königsberg philosopher, someone asked him [i.e., Kant] why he had not published his opposition or at least his opinion of Reinhold? The esteemed old man replied, 'Reinhold has done me too much good for me to want to say anything evil of him; Reinhold had done me too much evil for me to want to say anything good of him.' Of Fichte he said: "*Fichte* is an unfortunately ominous name for a philosopher. For there is a German expression, 'to lead someone behind the pine trees [*Fichten*]' meaning to cheat somebody, and in Latin 'Beweise von Fichten' (argumenta ficulnea) means proofs that are weak, soft (argumenta infirma)." A Kantian remark about Herr Beck in Halle, the author of the theory of the "Standpoint," is the following: "The good fellow stumbled over his own feet from his new standpoint." And then another remark: "The reason for this is that the Herren Pupils sit themselves down [a pun on 'sich selbst setzen' – posit themselves] and stand ['stellen' – possibly another pun, they come forward, i.e., assert themselves]." These stories are reported in the notes to Ak.[848], Ak.13:501 f.

Jenisch suffered from depression and committed suicide by drowning himself in the Spree river at age 42. By coincidence, one of his letters to Kant mentions a theologian named Jerusalem (a man who at 81 thought himself too old to follow Kant's arguments but loved Kant's essay "On Orientation"); this man's son, Karl Wilhelm Jerusalem, shot himself in 1772 and became the model for Goethe's famously suicidal *Werther*.

JENSCH, *Christian Friedrich*, died in 1802 (his birthdate is not given in either the Akademie or Schöndörffer editions of Kant's correspondence); *Kriminalrat* (criminal investigator) in Königsberg, a dinner companion of Kant's. He entered the university in 1763, registered as "Jenisch aus Norkitten bei Insterburg." Jensch was co-author, with Hippel, of a work on the emancipation of women, *Über die Bürgerliche Verbesserung der Weiber* (1792) at least according to Abegg, *Reisetagebuch*, p. 199. In addition to being Kriminalrat, he was, according to Kant's June 29, 1794, letter to Biester, Ak.[633], city councillor and Oberbillietier der Stadt Königsberg. Kant refers to him warmly as "mein vieljähriger, wohldenkender, aufgeweckter und im literärischen Fache wohlbewanderter, zuverlässiger Freund" (my trustworthy, clear-headed, enlightened and splendidly literate friend of many years[!]).

JUNG, *Johann Heinrich*, or JUNG-STILLING, or, as he called himself in his autobiography, STILLING (1740–1817) came from a humble, Pietist family (his father was a tailor) in Siegerland. He worked as a schoolmaster and, at 29, turned to the study of medicine. In 1772 he practiced in Elberfeld and became skillful at cataract operations. He took up economics in 1778 and became professor of economics (or political science) in Kaiserslautern, then Heidelberg, Marburg and again Heidelberg. He died in Karlsruhe where he lived from 1806 to 1817, with a pension from the Margrave of Baden. Renowned as an author, mystic, and cataract surgeon, he was a friend also of Goethe, who portrayed him in *Dichtung und Wahrheit* (Bk. 16) and from whom he received 140 Reichsthaller for a manuscript, assistance which Jung-Stilling attributed, as everything in his life, to God. Some scholars associate Jung-Stilling with Jacobi's defense of feeling and faith as inner revelations. The name "Stilling" was evidently chosen by Jung-Stilling from its close connection with "Stillen im Lande," a Pietist society. Often impoverished, the death of his second wife caused him more financial woes, producing a depression further aggravated by his "conversion" to determinism from studying Leibniz and Wolff. Kant rescued him from this despair, he maintained, by showing the incompetence of natural reason to speak on spiritual matters. Kant's letter reassured him also that the Gospels were a source of truth! Jung-Stilling's troubled life is depicted in his six-volume autobiography. His friendship with Goethe had led to his rejection by Pietist friends. Money problems plagued him. His academic positions – which he viewed as direct gifts of God – rescued him again. He traveled widely, performing cataract operations, endeavoring to support his five children and the fifteen people in his household. At 51, he married for the third time.

In addition to mystical writings such as "Scenes from the Realm of Spirits" he was the author of a four-volume novel, *Das Heimweh* (Homesickness, translated into virtually all European languages) and of several other novels and much poetry, not to mention writings on veterinary science, ophthamology, and political economy (he was influenced by Adam Smith). According to the *Allgemeine deutsche Biographie*, his religious writings were still read in Christian homes in the late nineteenth century.

KÄSTNER, *Abraham Gotthelf* (1719–1800), mathematician and astronomer, became professor of mathematics at Göttingen in 1756 and director of the observatory there. His students included the mathematical physicist and aphorist G. C. Lichtenberg and the outstanding mathematician (often called "The Prince of Mathematics") J. F. C. Gauss.

Kästner was remarkably literate. He knew 12 languages and authored numerous books on mathematics and physics, both technical and popular (Kant's library contained a number of his works); he was also impressive as a teacher, though it appears that Lichtenberg thought him vain and disliked him on that account (see Ak.[439], n. 1).

Kant admired Kästner also as a poet and sometimes quoted his verses. Herder was his friend in Leipzig earlier in life. Kant wrote a commentary (unpublished in his lifetime; see Ak. 20:410–23) on essays that Kästner had published in Eberhard's *Magazin*. As Henry Allison points out (in his *The Kant-Eberhard Controversy*, pp. 12 f. and 84 f.), Kant respected Kästner, despite the latter's connection with Eberhard, Kant's philosophical adversary.

KANT and KANT'S FAMILY. See the Introduction to this volume, pp. 5–7.

KANTER, *Johann Jakob* (1738–86), book merchant, lottery director, publisher of many of Kant's works and, for a time, Kant's landlord. His weekly periodical, *Königsberger Gelehrte und Politische Zeitungen*, brought him into contact with prominent scholars and political figures in Königsberg.

KIESEWETTER, *Johann Gottfried Carl Christian* (1766–1819), studied in Halle, where he was converted to Kant by Kant's disciple, Jakob. On recommendation of the philosophy faculty, Kiesewetter, with a 300 Thaler travel grant, was sent by the government to Königsberg to attend Kant's lectures and meet him personally. Returning to Berlin, Kiesewetter was appointed to teach Friedrich Wilhelm II's children mathematics and philosophy. In 1790 he received his doctorate from Halle and in 1793 he was named professor of philosophy in Berlin. Kiesewetter was required to teach at a medical school that, in 1798 became a division of the military academy. In 1807, Kiesewetter taught at the newly founded war college, and in the following year he was sent to study the military training schools in France, Switzerland, Italy and throughout Germany. He volunteered for service in the Prussian War of Liberation (1813–15) but was taken ill in Weimar. He returned to Berlin and died there two years later.

Kiesewetter published several works aimed at popularizing Kant's philosophy, and he lectured at the court to ladies and others on a variety of subjects including Kant's philosophy. One of his books was a logic text; it is mentioned in Tolstoy's "Death of Ivan Ilytch," when Ivan speaks of reading "in Kiezewetter's *Logic* that All men are moral, Caius is a man, therefore Caius is mortal

Biographical Sketches

... etc." but not that Ivan Ilytch is mortal. The book to which Tolstoy refers was probably *Logik zum Gebrauch für Schulen* (1797), which evidently remained in use long after Kiesewetter's death. Other writings include *Über den ersten Grundsatz der Moralphilosophie* (1788), *Grundriß einer reinen allgemeinen Logik* (1791), *Versuch einer faßlichen Darstellung der wichtigsten Wahrheiten der neueren Philosophie* (1795), *Gedrängter Auszug aus Kants Kritik der reinen Vernunft* (1795), *Die ersten Anfansgründe der reinen Mathematik,* (1799), and *Prüfung der Herderschen Metakritik,* (1799/1800).

Kiesewetter's letters are a great source of gossip concerning the counter-Enlightenment machinations and personal peccadilloes of Friedrich Wilhelm II and his court. He is also informative about Kant's erstwhile students and their apostasy, and about the proper preparation of Kant's favorite vegetable, carrots from Teltow, which he arranged to ship to Kant even in Kant's last years.

KNOBLOCH, *Fräulein Charlotte Amalie von* (1740–1804), daughter of major General Carl Gottfried von Knobloch and Sophie Louise Constanze, *née* von Droste. Fräulein Knobloch married a Prussian officer named Friedrich Wilhelm, baron von Klingspor. It was she to whom Kant wrote his famous account of Swedenborg's incredible powers of telepathy, clairvoyance, and communication with spirits. See his letter to her, Aug. 10, 1763, Ak.[29].

KRAUS, *Christian Jacob* (1753–1807), one of Kant's most talented pupils, dinner companions and friends, matriculated as a theology student in 1771. In 1777–8 Kraus was *Hofmeister* (private tutor) at the home of Count Keyserling. Eventually he became professor of practical philosophy and political science [*Staatswissenschaft*] in Königsberg.

LAGARDE, *François Théodore de la Garde* (1756– ?). (There is no consistency in references to "de la Garde" or "Lagarde," the version of his name used in most German editions of Kant's letters, or, as Kant sometimes calls him, "Delagarde".) He was a book merchant in Berlin and the publisher of Kant's *Critique of Judgment.* Lagarde was acquainted with Kant's friends in Berlin, e.g., Biester, Herz, Kiesewetter, and Wloemer, as well as various philosophers in Göttingen, Halle, and Jena.

LAMBERT, *Johann Heinrich* (1728–77), renowned Swiss-German mathematician, physicist and philosopher, was born in Mulhause, Alsace. Self-educated – he taught himself not only mathematics and philosophy but also Oriental languages – Lambert became a tutor to a Swiss family, a position that enabled him to travel with his pupils throughout Europe. Through numerous publications and correspondence he was able to establish a formidable reputation as a scientist. In 1759 he was invited by the Elector of Bavaria to help establish the Bavarian Academy of Sciences. In 1764, the year of publication of his *Neues Organon (New Organon)*, Lambert visited Berlin and was appointed by Frederick the Great to the Prussian Academy of Sciences. In the following year he was appointed government surveyor of public works. He held that position until his death in 1777.

In addition to the *New Organon*, the full title of which is *Neues Organon, oder Gedanken über die Erforschung und Beziehung des Wahren und dessen Unter-*

590

scheidung von Irrthum und Schein (New organon, or thoughts on the inquiry into and the relation of the true and its distinction from error and illusion; Leipzig, 1764), his most important publications include *Kosmologische Briefe über die Einrichtung des Weltbaues* (Cosmological letters on the structure of the universe; Augsburg, 1761), a work which Kant had in his library, and *Insigniores orbitae cometarum proprietates* (The chief characteristics of the orbits of the comets; Augsburg, 1761). Kant also owned Lambert's *Die freye Perspective, oder Anweisung, jeden perspectivischen Aufriss von freyen Stücken und ohne Grundriss zu verfertigen* (Free perspective, or, instructions on how, freely and without a plan, to prepare any perspectival outline; Zurich, 1759).

In mathematics, Lambert is known for developing hyperbolic trigonometry and for proving that when x is a rational number,e^x and tan x are irrational. He is cited also, along with Girolamo Saccheri (1667–1773), in the history of non-Euclidean geometries, for his study of quadrilaterals having at least three right angles (these are now named after him), an approach to the problem of proving the parallel postulate. Lambert deduced a number of non-Euclidean propositions from what Saccheri called "the inimical acute angle hypothesis." Lambert is also mentioned in the history of logic for his attempt to make a calculus of logic and for his experiments, like those of Leibniz, with sets of ruled and dotted lines to illustrate the relationships of syllogistic terms, an attempt to correct a defect in Euler's circle diagrams.

Lambert's collected writings, *Philosophische Schriften*, in 9 volumes, including the volume of correspondence mentioned in one of the Kant letters, were published in Berlin in 1782 and have been republished (Hildesheim, 1968).

LAVATER, *Johann Caspar* (1741–1801), Swiss theologian, born and died in Zürich, where he entered the church and campaigned successfully against corruption in the government of Canton Zürich. His travels in Germany brought him into contact with renowned writers such as Klopstock and Mendelssohn. Lavater was a poet, mystic, and physiognomist. He became most famous for the latter "science," the interpretation of people's characters, souls, etc., from their facial characteristics. (Lavater and his theory were satirized by, among others, G. C. Lichtenberg in his 1778 *Über Physiognomik, wider die Physiognomen* [On physiognomy, against the physiognomists] and in a parody that became well known, *Fragment von Schwänzen* [A fragment on tails, 1783].) Lavater published devotional poetry, e.g., *Gereimte Psalmen* (1768) and *Zwey Hundert Christliche Lieder* (1771). He edited a weekly journal, *Der Erinnerer*. In 1779 he took the position of deacon at an orphanage in Zürich.

Lavater's *Aussichten in die Ewigkeit* (Vistas of Eternity, 1768), spoke of a millennial kingdom to begin with Christ's Second Coming and the conversion of the Jews. Having befriended Moses Mendelssohn, Lavater challenged him in 1769 to either refute Christianity (as, according to Lavater, it had been demonstrated by a compatriot, the scientist Charles Bonnet) or convert to Christianity. Mendelssohn, thought Lavater, was one of those "intelligent Jews who are familiar with their prophets [and who] are waiting with so much confidence for an appearance of the Messiah totally different from the one that we want to obtrude upon them as the only one." (Quoted by Alexander Altmann, *Moses Mendelssohn*, p. 206. Altmann's book contains a detailed and fascinating account of the Lavater affair in Mendelssohn's life and in the life of Berlin's intellectual society.)

Lavater published a Pietistic "secret diary". *Geheim Tagebuch von einem Beobachter seiner selbst* (1771). The work for which he became best known, *Physiognomische Fragmente zur Beförderung der Menschenkenntnis und Menschen-liebe*, was published, in 4 volumes and with illustrative engravings, in 1775–8. In 1778 he was appointed pastor of St. Peter's church in Zürich. His friendship with Goethe, begun in 1774 when the two men took a Rhine journey together, ended in 1786 when Goethe gave him up. Goethe and Schiller ridiculed him in their *Xenien* and Goethe in *Faust*, Part One, where Lavater becomes the crane in the *Walpurgisnachtstraum* scene.

Lavater tried to use his physiognomy in anthropological studies: *Pontius Pilatus oder der Mensch in allen Gestalten* (1782–5). He died in 1800, shot by a French soldier during the occupation of Zürich.

Lavater exerted a considerable influence on the poet William Blake. A reprint of Blake's annotated copy of Lavater's *Aphorisms on Man* (originally published by J. Johnson, London, 1788) has been made available by Scholars' Facsimiles & Reprints (Delmar, NY, 1980). The translation of Lavater's text is by Henry Fuseli, born in Canton Zürich in 1741 as was Lavater. This small book of maxims provoked Blake to profound reflections on men, manners, and morals. See Blake's comments in David V. Erdman's edition of *The Complete Poetry and Prose of William Blake* (Berkeley, CA: University of California Press, 1982).

LEHMANN, *Johann Heinrich Immanuel* (1769–1808) Kant's amanuensis, late in life. He sent Kant sausages, dried fruit, and gossip about Lichtenberg, Stäudlin, and Kästner. There is an amusing, perhaps disconcerting anecdote reported by Kant's colleague F. T. Rink concerning Kant's reaction when the shipment of dried fruit was consumed by the ship's captain, in order to save his life and that of his crew from starvation: "No punishment would be severe enough for such an outrage!" Kant exclaimed. (Rink's story is quoted in Ak. 13:492.) But some of the dried fruit must have survived the perilous voyage, for Kant thanks Lehman, via his father Johann Gottfried Lehmann, in a letter or note, autumn 1800, Ak. [878].

LICHTENBERG, *George Christoph* (1742–99), famous satirist and scientist, professor of physics in Göttingen, was born in Oberramstadt near Darmstadt. Crippled by an accident in childhood, he became a man of wide intellectual interests: mathematics, physics, art criticism, and politics. He studied mathematics – Kästner was his teacher – and science at Göttingen. Visits to England led to an interest in Hogarth's engravings – he published an interpretation of several – and in English life generally. He discovered the so-called Lichtenberg electrical figures in 1777, published the *Göttingischer Taschenkalender* and *Göttingischen Magazins der Wissenschaften und Literatur*, containing many satirical, scientific, and literary essays. He applauded the French Revolution, though not its excesses – his ideal was a limited monarchy – and he sought to combat police state absolutism, religious intolerance, mysticism, obscurantism and superstition, using witty aphorisms as his weapons.

Lichtenberg's private life was unconventional. His mistress, Maria Dorothea Stechard, who lived with him from 1777 until her death in 1782, was only 13 when Lichtenberg took her into his house. After her death he brought home another companion, Margarete Kellner, whom he married in 1789.

Kant's informants who visited Lichtenberg in Göttingen spoke disparagingly of his conversational abilities, surprising for a writer with such cleverness as Lichtenberg's aphorisms manifest. The latter were collected in his *Vermischte Schriften*, published posthumously (1800–5). In aesthetics, he favored realistic representations of nature and human life, rather than the *Sturm und Drang* works of Goethe and the adherents of "genius." Like Goethe, however, he opposed Lavater's faith in physiognomy and "the crassest superstition," as Goethe called it.

Concerning his relation to Kant, readers of German may wish to see, in addition to the letters, an article by Arno Neumann, in *Kant-Studien*, IV, pp. 68, ff.

LINDBLOM, *Jakob Axelson* (1746–1819), Swedish bishop, wrote to Kant, Oct. 13, 1797, Ak. [772], concerning Kant's supposed genealogy, evidently aiming to get Kant to send money to his relatives. See Kant's response to him, Oct. 13, 1797, Ak. [783], offering Kant's own account, possibly not quite accurate, of his ancestry.

LINDNER, *Johann Gotthelf* (1729–76), friend of Kant and Hamann, studied in Königsberg and became a teacher at the Friedrichs-kollegium in 1748, lecturer in philosophy (*magister legens philosophiae*) in 1750, rector of the cathedral school in Riga, 1755, and professor of poetry in Königsberg, 1765.

MAIMON, *Salomon ben Joshua* (1753–1800). As indicated in Herz's letter, Ak. [351], n. 1, Herz and Kant spelled Maimon's name "Maymon." In his autobiography, Maimon referred to himself as "Solomon" and he was sometimes addressed as "Herr Solomon."

Maimon's life is told in his remarkable *Autobiography*, first published in 1792–3 and translated eventually into a number of languages. There is a highly readable though somewhat abridged version of an English translation by J. Clark Murray (London, 1888), edited by Moses Hadas (New York: Schocken Books, 1947). The *Autobiography* presents a fascinating picture not only of Maimon but of Jewish culture in Eastern Europe and the ignorance, superstition – and persecution – from which Maimon sought to escape. Maimon vividly captures the conflict between "enlightened" Jews and the ascetic Hasidism and rabbinical orthodoxy of his day.

He was born near Nieswiez, Lithuania (at that time Poland) in great poverty. He received a rabbinical education and was recognized even before adolescence as an extraordinary Talmudic scholar. His languages were Hebrew and the dialect, a mixture of Polish, Latvian, Lithuanian and Russian, that was spoken in his region. (Maimon's ignorance of correct Polish and German became a great obstacle when he sought acceptance outside his *stetl*.) Although the only books available to him were Talmudic and Old Testament studies, he was a precocious learner, evidently blessed with a photographic memory. At a young age, he read Maimonides and Ibn Ezra. His autobiography tells the complex story – poignant yet comic – of his arranged marriage at the age of eleven and of his attempts to run away from it. He became a father at fourteen. At 25 he made his way to Berlin as a penniless beggar. Rejected by Jewish elders at the gates of Berlin on account of his tattered dress and disreputable appearance, rejected also by a rabbi whose zealous orthodoxy Maimon offended, he managed to reach Posen (Posnan) and to be hired as a private tutor in a Jewish family appreciative of his learning. He taught himself written German and Latin but his spoken language other than Hebrew – a medley of Yiddish, Polish, and Lithuanian, as he describes it – was unintelligible to the people he met. Three years in Hamburg studying languages while tutoring various subjects, supported by a Jewish sponsor, prepared him for his second trip to Berlin. This time he succeeded in meeting Moses Mendelssohn and, largely through him, in gaining entrance to Jewish intellectual circles. He absorbed philosophy, e.g., Wolff's *Metaphysics*, a copy of which he rescued from a butter shop where its pages were being used for wrapping paper, and then, in German translation, Locke, on whom he immediately offered to lecture. He could not assent to Wolff's derivation of God's existence from the Principle of Sufficient Reason and disclosed his misgivings to Mendelssohn, who was impressed. New friends were made and soon alienated. Mendelssohn gave him a favorable recommendation but did not resist his leaving Berlin.

Maimon journeyed again to Hamburg, then to Amsterdam and The Hague, where his skepticism offended a patron who believed in the Kabbalah and where Maimon found himself pursued by a woman who had fallen in love with him. He returned to Hamburg and briefly entertained the thought of converting to Christianity, but only for economic reasons (not an unusual practice, as we see even in the life of a son of Mendelssohn). Now Maimon was pursued by his abandoned wife, and managed to offended the chief rabbi by parading his liberal or heretical views and tactlessly calling a *Shofar* a ram's horn. He did however receive a certificate from the director of the Gymnasium and thereupon embarked for Berlin a third time.

On this visit Maimon wrote a mathematics textbook in Hebrew, hoping that this example of rationality might be a start in bringing enlightenment to pious but uneducated Jews. The book, based on a Latin work by Wolff, was never published. He made the acquaintance of Christian scholars, including Garve, with whom he discussed philosophy, and he received a monthly allowance from a Jewish banker named Meier. Maimon obtained another house-tutor position and considered, briefly, a career in medicine. He met teachers in the Jesuits' College at Breslau, taught Euler's *Algebra* and the rudiments of German and Latin to a few pupils, was again pursued by his wife, to whom he now granted a divorce, then returned a fourth time to Berlin.

Having mastered Spinoza, Hume, and Leibniz by, as he puts it, thinking himself into their systems, Maimon now resolved to study Kant's *Critique of Pure Reason*. He composed what he called "explanatory observations" on the *Critique* and presented them to Marcus Herz. Herz admitted to Maimon that he himself was not in a position to judge either the *Critique* or any work dealing with it but he sent Maimon's manuscript, *Versuch über die Transzendentalphilosophie mit einem Anhang über die symbolische Erkenntnis und Anmerkungen*

(Essay concerning transcendental philosophy, with an appendix concerning symbolic cognition and annotations); Berlin, 1790), to Kant. (See Herz's letter, April 7, 1789, Ak. [351].) On Herz's advice Maimon asked for Kant's opinion of the book. Kant answered Maimon's criticisms in detail in a letter to Herz, May 26, 1789, Ak. [362], saying that Maimon's work was full of "the most subtle investigations" and written by an astute critic who had understood him better than any other. Maimon wrote to Kant again in July 1789, Ak. [370], expressing his gratitude for Kant's rejoinder, but he was not satisfied with Kant's answers to his criticisms. He wrote several times in 1790, May 9, Ak. [427], and May 15, Ak. [430], and again in 1791, 1792, and 1793 (see his letters Ak. [486], [548], and [606] in this volume) but, despite – or perhaps because of – Maimon's obsequies, apologies and protestations, Kant did not answer him. With this letter of December 2, 1793, Ak. [606], Maimon included a copy of his essay on Aristotle's Categories (Berlin, 1794) and outlined his provocative ideas concerning a reform of traditional logic. Clearly Kant thought highly of Maimon, praising him for his "penetrating observations" and great insight. (There is however a discrepancy in Kant's statements about his reading of Maimon's book. To Kiesewetter, February 9, 1790 – a letter not in the *Akademie* edition (it is numbered Ak. [405a]) Kant said he had not had time to read Maimon's book yet. But in the letter to Herz, May 26, 1789, nine months earlier, Kant wrote detailed comments on Maimon's theory, saying he had read the first two parts. Kant must have forgotten this letter – and his observations on Maimon's theory – when he wrote to Kiesewetter.) But when Maimon ignored Kant's suggestion that he rethink his criticisms of Kant's position before publishing them, Kant's respect gave way to annoyance, even provoking Kant to make one of his rare anti-Semitic remarks. (See Kant's letter to Reinhold, Ak. [620].) Perhaps the remark, "Isn't it just like a Jew to try to make a reputation for himself at someone else's expense," should be overlooked, on the grounds that Kant was always hypersensitive to criticism and, at that point in his life, concerned about the apostasy of his followers. The year 1794 was a bad one for him not only on that account but also because of his troubles with the official proscription of his work on religion. The persecution from which Kant suffered seemed serious enough to Kant's friends to warrant an offer of asylum from one of them (the educator J. H. Campe).

Maimon's criticism of Kant in 1789 already pointed the way to Fichte and the various post-Kantian idealisms that were soon to take center stage. He denied Kant's basic distinction between passive sensibility and the active, spontaneous understanding. He maintained that the human mind is part of an infinite world-soul that produces not only the form but also the content of experience. The human understanding is intuitive, not merely discursive. Maimon accepted the negative, anti-dogmatic part of Kant's theory (the "limitation" thesis) as correct but rejected as inconceivable the positive theory of a "thing in itself" (which Maimon mistakenly interpreted to mean that Kant claimed existence for a thinkable entity without any determinate characteristics). We cannot form a clear concept of either an object-in-itself or of a subject-in-itself, Maimon maintained. The "thing in itself" thus loses any character of "thinghood," in Maimon's view, and becomes merely an irrational limit of rational cognition, the idea of an endless task whose completion is constantly retreating as knowledge advances. The "self-contradictory" assumption of the existence of things independent of all consciousness arose in the attempt to explain the origin of the "content" of appearances; but there is in fact no content or material of experience independent of form. The distinction between the matter and form of knowledge is only a contrast between a complete and an incomplete consciousness of what is present to us, the incomplete consciousness being what we refer to as the given, that irrational residue that we distinguish from the a priori forms of consciousness. The contrast is only one of degree; form and matter are the terminal members of an infinite series of gradations of consciousness. The given is therefore only an idea of the limit of this series.

Maimon's other major works include *Versuch einer neuen Logik oder Theorie des Denkens* (Essay toward a new logic or theory of thinking; Berlin, 1794 and 1798), which he mentions in his letter to Kant, Ak. [606], *Kritische Untersuchungen über den menschlichen Geist oder das höhere Erkenntniss-und Willensvermögen* (Critical investigations concerning the human mind or the higher faculty of cognition and will; Leipzig, 1797), a philosophical dictionary, *Philosophisches Wörterbuch* (1791), a discussion of Bacon, *Bacons von Verulam Neues Organon* (1793), and a book on Aristotle's Categories, *Die Kategorien des Aristoteles* (1794). (Excerpts from the first of these are translated in George di Giovanni's *Between Kant and Hegel*.)

Maimon's *Autobiography* ends with his account of the exchange of letters with Kant and a summary of some of his writings: his essays in the *Journal für Aufklärung*, an article "Truth" and one comparing Bacon and Kant as reformers of philosophy, contributions to a Hebrew periodical called *Hameassef* (The Collector) attempting to overcome religious prejudices by "rational exegesis" of passages in Scripture (though he believed that the Jewish "aristocracy under the appearance of theocracy" would not be changed by such means). A number of his essays, including one on the commentary of Maimonides on the Mishnah, appeared in the *Berlinische Monatsschrift*.

Maimon's patrons in Berlin forsook him. His intellectual arrogance, heterodox beliefs, and Bohemian manners made him intolerable to both pious and "enlightened" Jews, and certainly to those striving for respectability in German society. He was taken in by a young Count Adolf von Kalckreuth in Silesia where he continued to philosophize – and drink – until his death.

MEINERS, *Christoph* (1747–1810), professor of philosophy in Göttingen. Meiners was one of Kant's Lockean empiricist opponents. Kant's follower Johann Bering in Marburg reported that Meiners accused Kant's *Critique* of containing "nothing but skepticism." Of course Meiners was not alone in thinking Kant's position a threat to religion and morality, but the accusation, coming from a philosopher, was even more irksome to Kant's followers than when it came from political personages such as the ministers appointed by Friedrich Wilhelm II.

Meiners published essays on aesthetics, psychology (*Grundriß der Seelenlehre*, 1786), and an outline of the history of philosophy (1786). (Without access to his writings, it is difficult to determine their merit. Plessing, Kant's student, thought that Meiners's history of philosophy seriously distorted the Greeks;

but Plessing himself entertained some questionable theories about them, e.g., he hated Aristotle, regarded him as a plagiarist, and thought that Plato's metaphysics had existed a thousand years before Plato.) An unidentified writer informed Kant in a letter in 1774 of Meiners's essay "Einige Betrachtungen über den guten Geschmack" (Some reflections on good taste) in his *Gemein-nützige Abhandlungen*, (1774). For Meiners's views about "barbaric" non-European nations, see the notes to Kant's letter to Plessing, Feb. 3, 1784, Ak.[218].

MENDELSSOHN, *Moses* (1729–86) (known in the Jewish community of his day as Moses ben Mendel Dessau). Born in Dessau, the son of a Torah copyist and teacher, Mendelssohn received a Jewish education, studying the Bible and commentaries in the Talmud and by Maimonides. He arrived in Berlin in 1743 following his teacher, Rabbi David Herschel Fränkel, who enabled him to stay despite the boy's "unprotected" status. (Frederick the Great, who was far from enlightened when it came to Jews, had in 1750 set up a complex economic and social stratification of Prussian Jews, with four different classes of "protected" Jews [*Schutzjuden*], and a fifth and sixth class whose presence in Berlin was merely tolerated; Mendelssohn initially belonged to none of these classes.) Impoverished and sickly (he suffered from curvature of the spine and "Nervenschwäche," some sort of nervous debility) he was placed in the home of a Jewish silk manufacturer, Isaak Bernhard, as a tutor. Mendelssohn was an autodidact: he taught himself German, English, French, and Latin. He read Locke and Shaftesbury, Wolff, then Leibniz and Spinoza. (A few years later, in 1761, he translated Shaftesbury into German.) In 1754, his employer promoted him to be his bookkeeper and secretary, a position that left more time for study, and led eventually to Mendelssohn's success as a business manager. That same year he met and befriended the great Gotthold Ephraim Lessing who later used Mendelssohn as the model for his play *Nathan the Wise*. Through Lessing he became a friend also of Friedrich Nicolai, founder of the *Allgemeine deutsche Bibliothek* and, with Mendelssohn, co-founder of the periodical *Bibliothek der schönen Wissenschaften* (Library of the fine arts, 1757).

Mendelssohn soon became known as a writer and spokesman for Enlightenment concerns. Like Kant and Lessing, he was a great champion of religious tolerance and freedom of conscience. (Kant praises him on this score in his letter of August 16, 1783, Ak. [206].) Mendelssohn's first love as an author was poetry – he wrote Hebrew poems at the age of ten – and some of his first published work was in aesthetics: *Briefe über die Empfindungen* (Letters on the sensations, 1755). In Nicolai's *Bibliothek* Mendelssohn published, along with various reviews, an essay on the source and connections of the fine arts and sciences, *Betrachtungen über die Quelle und die Verbindungen der schönen Künste und Wissenschaften*. The essay was later retitled *Über die Hauptgrundsätze der schönen Künste und Wissenschaften* (On the primary principles of the fine arts and sciences). A poetic essay of 1758, *Über das Erhabene und Naïve in der schönen Künste* (On the sublime and the naïve in the fine arts), full of citations of poetry and the classics, impressed Schiller.

A few years earlier, with Lessing's collaboration, Mendelssohn wrote *Pope ein Metaphysiker!* (1755), a satire inspired by the Berlin Academy's proposal in

1753 that Pope's "system" be examined. The academy's charge encapsulated Pope's metaphysical position in the proposition "Alles ist gut," i.e., in the Leibnizian thesis, that this is the best of all possible worlds. Mendelssohn and Lessing argued that poetry was not the proper medium for philosophical arguments. At Lessing's urging, Mendelssohn published, anonymously, a German translation of Rousseau's *Discours* on the origin of inequality and on the question whether natural law sanctioned inequality. Though he had high regard for Rousseau, Mendelssohn did not share what he took to be Rousseau's radical and revolutionary ideas, e.g., that all civilized nations are degenerate, inferior to orangutans; that private property should be abolished, society dissolved, and everyone return to the forests, etc.

In 1762 Mendelssohn married Fromet Gugenheim, the daughter of a Hamburg merchant. Of their eight children, two died in infancy. Three sons and three daughters survived, of whom one son, Abraham, was to become the father of the composers Felix and Fanny Mendelssohn. These grandchildren of Moses, along with their sister Rebecca, were raised as Protestants by their parents, Abraham and Lea, who also subsequently converted to Christianity. Lea and her brother took the name "Bartholdy" from the name of the previous tenant of their Berlin house, becoming Mendelssohn-Bartholdy to distinguish themselves from the Jewish branch of the family.

With the assistance of the Marquis d'Argens, Mendelssohn and his wife received the protection privileges of *Schutzjuden* from Friedrich II in 1763. However, when the Berlin Academy voted to make Mendelssohn a member (Sulzer had proposed the election of "le juif Moses") Friedrich vetoed Mendelssohn's elevation by simply ignoring the academy's petition. The academy held a second vote, reaffirming its support of Mendelssohn, but various members feared offending the king, so the matter was not pressed. (Sulzer told Mendelssohn that he was "puzzled.") Friedrich also turned down Mendelssohn's request that his *Schutzjude* status be continued after his death. Only in 1787, under Friedrich's successor, Friedrich Wilhelm II (a monarch not otherwise famed for religious toleration or liberalism – witness his censorship of Kant – but less hostile to Jews), did Mendelssohn's widow again receive protected status.

Mendelssohn's 1763 *Abhandlung über die Evidenz in den metaphysischen Wissenschaften* (Treatise on evidence in the metaphysical sciences) was written for another competition sponsored by the Berlin Academy, the same competition for which Kant submitted his "Inquiry concerning the distinctness of the principles of natural theology and morality." The Academy's question was "Is metaphysical truth capable of the same evidence as mathematics?" Kant's essay received approval and acknowledgment ("Accessit") while Mendelssohn's won First Prize. (But Mendelssohn modestly wrote to Thomas Abbt, a friend and fellow competitor, that his prize essay would have been burned or left in his desk if he had known Lambert's *Neues Organon* at that time.)

Phädon, a paraphrase and extension of Plato's arguments on the immortality of the soul in the *Phaedo*, appeared in 1767. The first dialogue is a free, sometimes literal translation of Plato; the second and third dialogues supply additional arguments, from Plotinus, Descartes, Leibniz, Wolff, Baumgarten, Reimarus, et al. The book was confiscated by the censor in Austria on account of its excessively theistic stand, but elsewhere it went through many editions, winning Mendelssohn fame and affection from liberal theologians and philosophers such as Garve and Eberhard but hostility from more conservative Christians such as Spalding and Lavater. Lavater, in 1769, demanded "in the name of the God of Truth" that Mendelssohn either refute the arguments for Christianity formulated by Charles Bonnet (whose work Lavater had sent to Mendelssohn two years earlier) or become a Christian. Bonnet (1720–93) was a notable Swiss scientist – he is mentioned in Kant's 1768 essay on the differentiation of directions in space. He was the discoverer of parthenogenesis in aphids and did other significant research in botany, anticipating the theory of evolution. Like Lavater, he was a devout Christian. Unlike Lavater, he deplored the challenge to Mendelssohn.

Lavater's open letter, appended to a German translation of Bonnet's *Palingénésie*, provoked furious discussion among enlightened theologians and friends of Mendelssohn. A reply from Mendelssohn refused to accept the challenge: he *could* not accept Christianity but he *would* not refute Bonnet's arguments. Mendelssohn offered a plea for tolerance, stated his conviction of the truth of Judaism as the religion of reason, though he admitted that his religion, like other religions, contained some "harmful man-made additions" and superstitious abuses that obscure its rational core.

A number of prominent intellectuals (e.g., Herder) came to Mendelssohn's defense, and Lavater's own reputation was sullied. But agitation over the Lavater affair affected Mendelssohn badly. He suffered a nervous breakdown, and only gradually could he return to work. *Philosophische Gespräche* (Philosophical dialogues) defending Leibniz against Voltaire's *Candide* satire and other objections, had been his first philosophical work (it was not published but Herz alluded to it in a 1770 letter to Kant, Ak. [58]). Now he returned to it and a revised form appeared in *Philosophische Schriften* (Philosophical writings) in 1771.

By 1776 Mendelssohn was able travel to Dresden and, in the summer of 1777, to Königsberg, to visit such notables as Kant and Hamann. In 1778 he again turned to writing, now concentrating on Jewish subjects. His interest in broadening the horizons of his own people led him to translate the Torah and the Psalms into German. He wrote on Jewish rituals and laws concerning marriage, inheritance, etc. His translation of the Torah, composed between 1780 and 1783, was originally intended for his children, but in 1783 he allowed it to be published, with the Hebrew original alongside the German and with a Hebrew commentary on the text. His translation of the Psalms, begun ten years earlier, also appeared in 1783. Banned by some rabbis as sacrilegious, these translations (said by some Christian scholars to be more accurate than Luther's) became powerfully influential among Jews of all ranks in Germany.

Another religious issue made its appearance: Mendelssohn was asked by the Jews of Alsace to support their emancipation. Mendelssohn and his friend Christian Wilhelm von Dohm agreed to help and Dohm published *Über die bürgerliche verbesserung der Juden* (On the civil improvement of the Jews, 1781) defending emancipation. However, Dohm also argued that the state should defend the synagogue's power to excommunicate its members. Mendelssohn, through association with Dohm, was faced with hostile reactions from liberal members of the public. He denounced excommunication in a preface he published to a work by Manasseh ben Israel, *Vindiciae Judaeorum* (Vindication of the Jews, 1782). In the following year, he published *Jerusalem oder über religiöse Macht und Judentum* (Jerusalem, or concerning religious power and the Jewish people), a powerful defense of religious toleration, freedom of conscience, and the separation of religion and the state. *Jerusalem* was written in answer to an anonymous writer who accused Mendelssohn of subverting the Mosaic law. Mendelssohn argued that the state may use force to control actions but not thoughts. This is the work praised by Kant in his letter Ak. [206] as "the announcement of a great, overdue reform" (though Kant later took issue with one of its points, Mendelssohn's contention that the human race will never make moral progress. Cf. "On the common saying: That may be correct in theory, but it is of no use in practice," 1793). Herder, Garve, and Mirabeau also spoke favorably of Mendelssohn's view, but Hamann expressed his opposition to it in *Golgatha und Scheblimini*.

The controversy that caused the greatest pain in Mendelssohn's life was occasioned by the *Pantheismusstreit* – the so-called Pantheism Controversy that came to involve so many prominent intellectuals and artists in Germany and into which Kant himself was finally drawn, though initially he dismissed it as trivial. The background of this notorious feud is rather complicated. By their mutual friend Elise Reimarus, Mendelssohn was told that Lessing, in 1780, a few months before his death, had said in conversation with Jacobi that he, Lessing, was a Spinozist, one of the *All-Einer* or "All-is-one-ists," as the followers of Spinoza were called. This report was tantamount to an accusation of atheism against Lessing and, by association, his close friend Mendelssohn. In "To the Friends of Lessing," whose publication Mendelssohn did not live to see, Mendelssohn attempted to rescue Lessing from this charge of atheism. (See his letter to Kant of Oct. 16, 1785, Ak.[248]. For Kant's opinion of the controversy as "nothing serious – an affectation of inspired fanatics," see his letter to Herz, Apr. 7, 1786, Ak.[267].) Kant's essay, "Was Heißt; Sich im Denken Orientieren?" (What does it mean to orient oneself in thinking?) contains his answer to the disputants, both of whom had attempted to gain his support.

The controversy took its toll; knowing the precarious state of his health, Mendelssohn hastened the publication of his *Morgenstunden, oder Vorlesungen über das Dasein Gottes* (Morning lessons, or lectures on the existence of God, 1785). In that work he continued his defense of rationalism, examining Leibnizian proofs of the existence of God and, in part 2, offering a theodicy. *Morning Lessons* is the work that Kant calls "a masterpiece of reason's self-deception," in his letter to Schütz, Ak.[256]. Since it defends proofs such as the ontological argument, proofs which Kant thought himself to have demolished, e.g., the inference from "most perfect being" to "existence," it is easy to understand Kant's disdain.

Kant's supposed intention to publish a refutation of Mendelssohn was announced in the periodical *Gothaer Gelerte Zeitungen*, Jan. 25, 1786. But Kant left his task to his disciples Schütz and Jakob; the latter's *Prüfung der Mendelssohnischen Morgenstunden* appeared in Oct. 1786, with Kant's note after the Preface: "Einige Bemerkungen zu Ludwig Heinrich Jakobs Prüfung . . ." (See

Biographical Sketches

Ak. 8: 151–5.) Schütz's review of *Morgenstunden* appeared earlier, in the Jan. 1786 issue of the *A.L.Z.*, with Kant's letter to Schütz, Ak.[256], appended to it. Mendelssohn died on Jan. 4, 1786. His death was blamed by some on the controversy with Jacobi. (See Herz's letter to Kant, Ak.[260], n. 5, for the details of this additional controversy.)

To see Mendelssohn's philosophical importance and his relation to Kant in greater detail, Lewis White Beck's *Early German Philosophy* and Frederick C. Beiser's *The Fate of Reason* are invaluable. For an understanding of his connection with liberal theologians and other Enlightenment philosophers, Kant's friends and opponents who show up in Kant's correspondence (e.g., Daniel Jenisch, Friedrich Nicolai, J. H. Eberhard, Feder, Engel), and Mendelssohn's tremendous role in the history of Jews in Germany, their emancipation and Germanization, the massive and splendidly readable biography of Mendelssohn by Alexander Altmann (University of Alabama Press, 1963) is indispensable.

MEREAU, *Sophie* (1770–1806), *née* Schubert or Schubart, born in Altenburg, the daughter of an "Obersteuerbuchhalter" – presumably a senior tax accountant. In 1793 she was married to a librarian and professor of law in Jena, Friedrich Ernst Karl Mereau, whom she divorced in 1801. In 1803 she married the famous author and folk-poetry editor (of *Des Knaben Wunderhorn* fame), Clemens Brentano, with whom she lived in Marburg and Jena, and then, in 1804, Heidelberg.

Her poetry and her novels were praised by Schiller and Goethe. Some were published in *Thalia*, the *Göttinger Musenalmanach* on which she collaborated with Schiller, and in Schiller's periodical *Die Horen*. She translated English, Italian, and Spanish novels, published reworkings of some French novels, and founded a women's magazine, *Kalathiskos* (Little basket). She died in childbirth in October 1806, at 33, after a turbulent marriage. There is a beautiful portrait of her in Goethe's house in Frankfurt.

NICOLAI, *Christoph Friedrich* (1733–1811), writer, book publisher, and merchant in Berlin, one of the *Popularphilosophen* and author of a famous satire on Goethe's *The Sorrows of Young Werther: Freuden des jungen Werthers; Leiden und Freuden Werthers des Mannes; voran und zuletzt ein Gespräch* (Joys of the Young Werther; Sorrows and Joys of Werther the Man; a Conversation from Beginning to End; Berlin, 1775). He also satirized Herder's cult of folksong in *Eyn feyner kleyner Almanach vol schönerr echterr liblicherr Volckslieder, lustigerr Reyen undt kleglicher Mordgeschichte* (A lovely little almanac full of beautiful, authentic, lovely folksongs, jolly journeys and plaintive murder stories; 1777–8 – the ridiculously anachronistic spelling is essential to the satire).

A good friend of Lessing and Mendelssohn, Nicolai edited the *Bibliothek der schönen Wissenschaften und der freien Künste*, which had writers such as Mendelssohn among its contributors. From 1765 he founded and edited the *Allgemeine deutsche Bibliothek*, the most important organ of the *Popularphilosophen*, a journal in support of the older, rationalistic Enlightenment, opposed to Kantianism. With Mendelssohn, he co-founded the periodical *Bibliothek der schönen Wissen-schaften* (Library of fine arts, 1757–60). With both Lessing and Mendelssohn, Nicolai published *Briefe, die neueste Litteratur betreffend* (Letters concerning the newest literature, 1761–6). Like his fellow *Popularphilosophen*, he fought against

601

authority in religion and what he regarded as "extravagance" in literature and philosophy, the Romanticism of Goethe, Schiller, Herder, and Fichte. Nicolai also opposed the reunification of Catholic and Protestant churches. (Reinhold, himself a former monk, agreed with Nicolai on this issue.)

Nicolai's distaste for Kant's philosophy and style was shown also in his novel *Geschichte eines dicken Mannes* (The story of a fat man, 1794), and in *Leben und Meinungen Sempronius Gundiberts, eines deutschen Philosophen* (The life and opinions of Sempronius Gundibert, a German philosopher, 1798). A takeoff on Kant, this work, along with Nicolai's publishing of a volume by Justus Möser (who defended the hereditary privileges of the nobility) prompted Kant to write an essay, "Über die Buchmacherei: Zwei Briefe an Herrn Friedrich Nicolai" (Ak. 8:431–8). (Kant's essay has been translated by Allen Wood as "On Turning Out Books, Two Letters to Mr. Friedrich Nicolai," in the Cambridge edition of Kant's *Practical Philosophy*, 1996.)

Nicolai was himself mocked in Goethe and Schiller's *Xenien* for his opposition to new ideas and for his ineffective parodies. He is ridiculed most cleverly as the "Proktophantasmist" in Goethe's *Faust*, Part One, ll. 4144–75, in the Walpurgisnacht episode. Nicolai had expressed opposition to the use of supernatural devices in literature, but it was said that he himself thought he was visited by a ghost in Tegel, a suburb of Berlin. Tegel is referred to in line 4161. The "cure" for being haunted was supposedly an application of leeches to the rear end; thus Goethe's lines about the prokto – the Greek word for "anus" – phantasmiac: "And when the leeches feast on his behind / He's cured of spirits and spiritual urges."

NICOLOVIUS, *Friedrich* (1768–1836) was a publisher and, later, banker. After three years at the university, he became an apprentice in the bookstore of Friedrich Hartknoch the elder in Riga, publisher of the *Critique of Pure Reason*. From 1790 to 1818 he ran a book and publishing business in Königsberg. He was the publisher of all of Kant's works after the *Critique of Judgment*.

NITSCH, *Friedrich August*, born in Gumbinnen (date uncertain), he matriculated as a student of theology in Königsberg in Oct. 1785. Nitsch met Kant, became a teacher of Latin and mathematics in the Collegium Fridericianum, went to Berlin in 1792 and then to London. As his letter from London, Ak.[636], indicates, he became the first person to lecture on Kant's philosophy in England. He lectured for three years, 1794–6, at Number 18 Panton Square, Haymarket. Nitsch published his lectures as "A General and Introductory View of Professor Kant's Principles concerning Man, the World and the Deity, submitted to the consideration of the learned" (1796). According to the editor of the Akademie edition of Kant's works, the lectures are insignificant: "Das Buch hat keine Bedeutung" (Ak. 13: 370). Adolf Poschmann, in an article entitled "The First Kantians in England" ("Die Ersten Kantianer in England," in Ernst Bahr, ed., *Studien zur Geschichte des Preussenlandes* [Marburg, 1963]) thinks this judgment too harsh. A copy of Nitsch's book exists in the University of Würzburg library, according to Poschmann.

PLESSING, *Friedrich Victor Leberecht* (1749–1808), born in Belleben (Wernigerode) where his father was a preacher and, later, church administrator. After studying in various universities, Plessing came to Königsberg in 1779 and matriculated there, concentrating on ancient history and philosophy. In Apr. 1783, Kant petitioned the faculty to accelerate his promotion to instructor status, though Plessing had not entirely satisfied the degree requirements and was 10 Thalers short of the 50 Thalers normally charged for degrees conferred in absentia. (Kant stated his willingness to forgo his own portion of the fee and to pay for the publication of Plessing's thesis himself. Kant's official letter is not among the Akademie edition correspondence but may be found in notes, Ak. 13: 116, f.). Kant described him, in a letter to the university rector, as "well mannered, industrious and clever" ("wohlgesitteten, fleißigen und geschickten Mann").

Two years earlier, in 1777, Plessing had encountered Goethe, who described him, after their meeting in the Harz mountains, in rather different terms: "He never took any notice of the outer world but, through manifold reading, he has educated himself; yet all his energy and interest are directly inwardly and, since he has found no creative talent in the depths of his life, he has virtually condemned himself to destruction."

It was Goethe who immortalized Plessing: reclusive, neurotic, troubled, he provided the inspiration for Goethe's *Harzreise im Winter* and thus, indirectly, for Johannes Brahms's *Alto Rhapsody*, which utilizes some of Goethe's text, descriptive of the despairing Plessing whom Goethe sought to restore to human society.

Kant aided Plessing not only academically but personally, when Plessing was required to make child support payments. (See letters Ak.[226] and Ak.[228].) In 1788, Plessing became professor of philosophy in Duisberg, where Goethe visited him again in 1792 and where Plessing remained until his death.

Plessing's letters are extremely long-winded and effusive, but he must have felt very close to Kant. He expresses convincingly his distress when he cannot repay the money he owes Kant, and he shares with Kant his intimate tales of woe, family illnesses, his father's gout, palsy, and mental illness, etc. His gratitude for Kant's assistance and instruction is expressed with rhetorical flourishes – "O my benefactor! My generous friend! Never think me capable of ingratitude! The very thought disturbs my peace of mind. Be not angry with me – How can I express the noble concept which you have implanted in my soul?" (Ak.[214], 10:258.) Notwithstanding Plessing's passionate prose, he was, like Kant, alert to the dangers of *Schwärmerei*, which, he warned Kant in 1783, was on the ascendancy.

PÖRSCHKE, *Karl Ludwig* (1751–1812), professor of poetry in Königsberg and author of *Vorbereitungen zu einem populären Naturrecht* (Preliminaries to a popular presentation of natural law, 1795). Kant's letter to Tieftrunk, Oct. 13, 1797, Ak.[784], discusses "my friend Herr Professor Poerschke" and his theory and asks that he be treated gently.

REHBERG, *August Wilhelm* (1757–1836), a writer and statesman in Hannover, for some time an ally of Kant's in his struggle with the followers of Wolff's philosophy. Rehberg published a review of the *Critique of Practical Reason* in the *Allgemeine Literatur-Zeitung*, (1788) questioning the possibility of deriving applications of the moral law to human actions, given the formal, contentless nature of Kant's law, and rejecting Kant's account of the feeling of "respect" as unsatisfactory in explaining how pure practical reason could generate action. Rehberg also challenges the imperative that man be treated only as an end in itself; he claims that that proposition is valid only for rational beings, but since human beings are also "natural" beings, they may be treated as things.

As with other followers and students of Kant, there appears to be a shift of loyalty in the course of their careers. Jachmann, writing to Kant of a visit to Rehberg in 1790, Ak.[452], describes him as "one of your most excellent devotees and disciples" and gives a glowing account of Rehberg's mind and modesty. In 1789, Rehberg and Reinhold both sought to aid Kant in his philosophical battle with Wolffians such as Eberhard. In 1790 Kant exchanged interesting letters with Rehberg on mathematics (see Ak.[448]). But a few years later, writing to Biester, Apr. 10, 1794, Ak.[621], Kant is strongly critical – indeed, almost contemptuous – of Rehberg's position in ethics and jurisprudence.

Rehberg's writings included *Über das Verhältnis der Metaphysik zu der Religion* (On the relation of metaphysics to religion, 1787), a review, mentioned above, of Kant's second *Critique*, published in the *A.L.Z.* (1788), reviews of the first two issues of Eberhard's *Magazin* and of Reinhold's *Versuch einer neuen Theorie des Vorstellungsvermögens*, both in *A.L.Z.*, 1789, an essay on the French Revolution (1793), and the essay that prompted Kant's hostile remarks, *Über das Verhältnis der Theorie zur Praxis* (On the relation of theory to practice) in the *Berliner Monatsschrift* (1794). See Ak.[621].

REICHARDT, *Johann Friedrich* (1751 or 2–1814), composer, author, *Kapellmeister* (music director). Born in Königsberg, Reichardt entered the university at the age of 15, attended Kant's lectures and kept in touch with him even after becoming Frederick the Great's *Kappelmeister* in Berlin in 1775. He was one of the people who helped Kant distribute the first copies of the *Critique*. He wrote to Kant on various occasions and he attempted to distill from Kant's *Critique of Judgment* some lessons concerning the aesthetics of music, *Von der Methodenlehre des Geschmacks im musikalischen Kunstmagazin* (On the methodology of Taste in musical art, 1791). Reichardt was prolific: his other works include *Lyzeum der schönen Künste* (1797), several journals, over 40 operas and other musical stage works, as well as 7 symphonies, 14 piano concertos, and numerous pieces of chamber music. Kant wrote to him, Oct. 15, 1790, Ak.[453], in response to Reichardt's letter of Aug. 28, 1790, Ak.[443]: Kant's letter is significant for one lovely remark: "I have been content to show that without moral feeling there would be nothing beautiful or sublime for us: that moral feeling is the foundation of what one might call the lawful entitlement to assent to the application of these terms to anything, and that the subjective [aspect of] morality that is in our being, the inscrutable thing we call 'moral feeling' [*or* which, under the name 'moral feeling' is inscrutable], is the thing that demands (though not on the basis of objective concepts of reason) that we judge according to moral laws . . ." Kant expressed the wish that someone like Reichardt, someone who was really knowledgeable about the arts, could present "the principles of our faculty of taste" more explicitly and precisely than he himself had been able to do.

Reichardt ended up in a village near Halle, as inspector of the salt works. He had lost his royal *Kappelmeister* position in 1794 because of his sympathies for the French Revolution. (By then, his employer was Friedrich Wilhelm II, the anti-Enlightenment nephew of Frederick the Great.) Reichardt's political liberalism also cost him his friendship with Goethe, whose poems he had earlier set to music (over 60 of them. Goethe and Schiller disliked him – Schiller said it was impossible to get rid of the man – and the two poets made fun of him in *Xenien*).

Reichardt was no philosopher but he revered Kant and wrote appreciatively of his memory of Kant's lectures, e.g., on physical geography and *Anthropologie*, and on Kant's conversational style of lecturing, his wide reading and un-quenchable thirst for more knowledge, e.g. of foreign lands – Reichardt made him a gift of some beautiful maps of the kingdom of Naples which he had brought from there, as a token of gratitude to Kant. Reichardt's life ended in poverty – as it began: Kant allowed him to attend his lectures *gratis*.

REINHOLD, *Karl Leonhard Reinhold* (1757–1823), devoted disciple and popular-izer of Kant, was Viennese by birth. Educated by Jesuits, he joined their order as novice in 1772 but became a Barnabite monk when the Jesuit order was dissolved one year later. He studied philosophy and theology at two Barnabite colleges in Vienna, was ordained a priest in 1780, and for a time taught philosophy, mathematics, and physics in the Barnabite St. Michael College. Through one of his teachers he had become acquainted with English Enlight-enment authors, in particular John Locke, the start of his apostasy. Along with his Viennese friends, Reinhold joined the Freemasons and the secret order of the Illuminati, institutions supportive of Joseph II's anti-clerical reforms and of the Enlightenment's ideal of freedom of thought. For some reason, possibly romantic, possibly religious, Reinhold fled to Germany in 1783, gave up his religious vows, and converted to Protestantism. In Weimar, where Herder was his pastor, Reinhold was received by the famous writer Christoph Martin Wieland, publisher of *Der Teutsche Merkur*. In 1784, he married Wieland's daughter Sophie. Reinhold became editor of the supplements (*Anzeiger*) to the *Merkur*, in which he published an enthusiastic review of Herder's *Ideen* and a critique of Kant's review of that work. Soon after, however, Reinhold under-went one of his several philosophical conversions and became a devoted disci-ple of Kant's. Through the publication of "Briefe über die Kantische Philoso-phie," published first in *Der Teutsche Merkur*, 1786–7, he contributed greatly to the spread of Kantianism. Reinhold's transformation into an ardent Kantian is explained in his letter of October 12, 1787, Ak.[305]. The *Letters on the Kantian Philosophy*, warmly endorsed by Kant, earned Reinhold his appoint-ment to the University of Jena's chair in philosophy, 1787. *Versuch einer neuen Theorie des menschlichen Vorstellungsvermögens* (Essay on a new theory of the human faculty of representation), the work that Kant and several loyal Kantians found indecipherable, appeared in 1789.

Eventually (in 1793 and the years following up to 1799, when Reinhold again changed his views) Reinhold became convinced that Fichte, not Kant, was the philosopher to worship. In 1794 Reinhold gave up his position in the University of Jena for a full professorship in Kiel. His move was evidently prompted by political considerations: Kiel was under Danish rule and offered a less turbulent scene than Germany, where Reinhold was at odds with various responses to the French Revolution. Scholars differ as to what Reinhold's own position on the French Revolution was. Like Kant, he opposed the idea of a right of revolution and gave a central place to the concept of property in political theory. Unlike Kant, he defended the retention of the nobility's special privileges, because to abolish them would be, he argued, to violate their right of ownership. Some scholars see Reinhold as denying basic human rights to some classes of society; others see this as a misinterpretation of Reinhold's opposition to the Reign of Terror after 1792.

In Kiel Reinhold composed his *Elementarphilosophie*, the "fundamental philosophy" which aimed to lay out the presuppositions of any scientific cognition. During the final period of his career, the philosophy of language and the reform of metaphysics were his dominant interests, though he continued to write on religion and moral philosophy as well.

A work of 1805, *Umleitung zur Kenntnis und Beurteilung der Philosophie in ihren sammtlichen Lehrgebäuden*, is said to show again Reinhold's move away from Kant. In 1820, Reinhold wrote on the renewed controversies regarding revelation and human reason.

There is little of Reinhold's work available in English, and even the German texts are difficult to find in the United States apart from Harvard's Widener Library. Reinhold's *Gedanken über Aufklärung* (Thoughts on Enlightenment) is included in James Schmidt, ed., *What Is Enlightenment?* (Berkeley, Los Angeles, and London: University of California Press, 1996) in a translation by Kevin Paul German. That essay dates from August 1784 and was published originally in the *Teutsche Merkur*. Sabine Roehr, *A Primer of German Enlightenment* (Columbia, MO: University of Missouri Press, 1995) contains a translation of Reinhold's *Verhandlungen über die Grundbegriffe und Grundsätze der Moralität aus dem Gesichtspunkte des gemeinen und gesunden Verstandes* (Fundamental concepts and principles of ethics from the point of view of the common and healthy understanding). George di Giovanni and H. S. Harris, eds., *Between Kant and Hegel* (Albany: State University of New York Press, 1985) include excerpts from Reinhold's *Über das Fundament des philosophischen Wissens* (The foundation of philosophical knowledge, 1794). Of secondary sources, Frederick Beiser's *The Fate of Reason*, ch. 8, is very useful; the book contains a detailed bibliography of Reinhold's writings. Daniel Breazeale, "Between Kant and Fichte: Karl Leonhard Reinhold's 'Elementary Philosophy'" in *Review of Metaphysics* 35 (June 1982) probes the relation between Reinhold and Fichte.

REUß, *Maternus* (1751–98), a Benedictine, professor of philosophy in Würzburg, a disciple of Kant's. See Ak.[699].

RICHARDSON, *John* (dates uncertain, though evidence indicates that he must have been born before 1775 and to have died after 1836), English translator of Kant and J. S. Beck. Little is known of his life. He was, according to Kant's disciple Jakob, a Scotsman who studied Kant in Halle, with Beck and Jakob.

While residing in Jakob's house, he undertook a translation of Kant's *Rechtslehre*. His travels took him also to South Carolina during the American Revolution, which he mentions in a note to his translation of Kant's *Observations on the Feelings of the Beautiful and the Sublime*. Richardson published *Principles of Kant's Critical Philosophy commented on by Beck* (1797), a translation of J. S. Beck's *Grundriß der kritischen Philosophie*. Richardson's two-volume collection of nineteen of Kant's essays, translated into English, was published under the title *Essays and Treatises on moral, political, and various philosophical subjects. By Emanuel Kant. From the German by the translator of the principles of critical philosophy* (London. Vol. I, 1798; Vol. II, 1799). A discussion of Richardson may be found in Stephen Palmquist's edition of some of Richardson's translations, *Four Neglected Essays by Immanuel Kant* (Hong Kong: Philopsychy Press, 1994).

RINK (OR RINCK), *Friedrich Theodor* (1770–1811), studied in Königsberg, 1786–9, during which time he attended some of Kant's lectures but became a pupil of the Orientalist, Johann Gottfried Hasse (1759–1806). He left Königsberg but returned in the spring of 1792 and lectured as a *Privatdozent*. For a time he took a position as private tutor in Kurland but toward the end of 1794 he returned to Königsberg where he became *außerordentlicher* professor of Oriental languages in 1794, full professor in 1797. He served as a pastor in Danzig after 1801. Rink was or said he was Kant's dinner companion, 1792–3 and 1795–1801, and Kant entrusted him with the editing of some of his lectures for publication, e.g., the "Physical Geography," 1802. In 1805 he published *Ansichten aus Immanuel Kants Leben* (Views from Kant's life). While there are no interesting letters extant between Rink and Kant, a short note from Kant indicates that Rink was asked to see to the publication of Kant's declaration against Fichte in the *Intelligenz-blatt* of the Jena *A.L.Z.* (Kant to Rink, Aug. 8, 1799, Ak.[841]).

SCHILLER, *Friedrich* (1759–1805), the great poet, dramatist, and essayist, was born in Marbach, Württemberg, the son of an army lieutenant turned horticulturist, employed by the duke of Württemberg, Karl Eugen. The Duke's despotic ways – he decreed that Schiller was to study law and medicine at a military academy and made him take a position as regimental physician – provided Schiller with the theme of several of his plays: the abuse of aristocratic power masked as paternalism. When Karl Eugen forbade Schiller's playwriting, Schiller fled Stuttgart for Mannheim where he received assistance from Baron von Dalberg. An unhappy attachment to a married woman, Charlotte von Kalb, occasioned his move to Leipzig where he was befriended and supported by Christian Gottfried Körner. *Die Räuber, Fiesco, Kabale und Liebe*, and *Don Carlos* secured Schiller's reputation as the outstanding poet in German-speaking lands. In addition to works for the theater Schiller published *Rheinische Thalia*, from 1785 onward, of which Issue #2 included his famous "Ode to Joy": *An Die Freude*; issue #3 contained part of the drama *Don Carlos*. Partly on the strength of his history of the Netherlands' revolt against Spain – a part of the plot of *Don Carlos* involves this struggle – Schiller became professor of history in Jena, a position he retained from 1789 to 1799. Schiller's historical writings include also a history of the Thirty Years' War. He was married in 1790 to Charlotte von Lengefeld, with whom he had two sons and two daughters.

Overwork brought illness, but it was during his recuperation, 1793–1801, that Schiller's serious study of Kant occurred. Schiller wrote on aesthetic activity, its relation to society and to morality: *Über Anmut und Würde* (On moral grace and dignity), *Über das Erhabene* (On the sublime), *Über naive und sentimentalische Dichtung* (On the naive and sentimental in literature), and *Briefe über die aesthetische Erziehung des Menschen* (Letters on the aesthetic education of human beings), the last two published in *Die Horen*.

In 1788 Schiller had met Goethe and subsequently collaborated with him on a number of projects. Their friendship ripened his art and his wisdom. One of their joint efforts was *Xenien* (1796), a set of satirical epigrams. The book is mentioned in a number of Kant letters, e.g. in correspondence from Kant's amanuensis, Lehmann, Jan. 1, 1799, Ak.[832]. Kant's disciple Ludwig Heinrich Jakob, in Halle, having published some negative opinions about Schiller's aesthetic theories in Jakob's *Philosophische Annalen*, was mocked by Schiller in *Xenien* as a plagiarizer of Kant. Cf. Jakob's letter, Ak.[264], n. 1.

Notwithstanding his now famous objection to Kant's ethics – the joke that "I must try to hate my friends so that my doing them good, which now I gladly do, will acquire moral worth" – Schiller appreciated Kant enormously. Unfortunately the reverse cannot be said, and their correspondence is disappointingly meager. Schiller wrote to Kant from Jena, June 13, 1794, Ak.[628], asking Kant to contribute an essay to a new literary magazine, *Die Horen* (Goddesses of the seasons) (12 vols., 1795–7). Fichte, who was friendly with Schiller, wrote to Kant as well, supporting Schiller's request, "in the hope that the man who has made the last half of this century unforgettable for the progress of the human spirit for all future ages" might "spread his spirit over various other divisions of human knowledge and to various persons" (June 17(?), 1794, Ak.[631], and again Oct. 6, 1794, Ak.[641]). Schiller assured Kant of his devotion to Kant's moral system and expressed profuse gratitude to Kant for illuminating his mind. On Mar. 1, 1795, Ak.[652], Schiller wrote again, repeating his request and sending two issues of *Die Horen*. He confessed that he was the author of the *Letters on the Aesthetic Education of the Human Race* (1795: *Über die aesthetische Erziehung des Menschen*), a work he believed to be an application of Kant's philosophy and hoped that Kant would like. Schiller claimed that art was a civilizing influence on sensuous barbaric human beings, who become rational, free, enlightened, able to overcome desires, etc., through aesthetic education. It is interesting to notice that Schiller and Fichte were colleagues at Jena during these years. Vorländer points out that Kant's one letter to Schiller shows his lack of appreciation of Schiller's stature as one of Germany's most renowned poets. Kant took a year to answer Schiller's letter and then referred to Schiller politely as a "learned and talented man," ending with the friendly wish that his "talents and good intentions shall be accompanied by appropriate strength, health, and long life." Kant's lack of awareness and understanding of Schiller's poetic personality is shown more strikingly in these phrases than through any other evidence. (As for Goethe, Vorländer remarks that Kant is even more indifferent.)

Schiller's last work, the great drama *Wilhelm Tell*, echoes his first, *Die*

Räuber, with its resounding cry, "Tod dem Tyrannen" – "Death to tyrants!" He remains even in the twentieth century the most widely quoted poet in the German language. Lines such as "Freude, schöner Götterfunken" or the opening of his *Lied von der Glocke* or, from Wallenstein, "In deiner Brust sind deines Schicksals Sterne" – "Your fortune's stars lie within your breast" – are familiar to every student of German culture.

SCHLETTWEIN, *Johann August* (1731–1802), prominent German physiocrat. In an open letter to Kant, published by Schlettwein in the *Berlinische Blätter*, Sept. 1797 (Ak.[751]; 12: 362–6) Schlettwein demanded that Kant inform the public which of Kant's disciples has understood him correctly. The letter is incredibly insulting, accusing Kant of contempt for his great predecessors and contemporaries, of pride, self-love, and self-seeking, the arrogant claim of infallibility and originality, etc. He calls it a scandal that so-called critical philosophers dispute the sense and spirit of Kant's works and asks Kant to adjudicate the disputes among his interpreters. Schlettwein claims to have a refutation of Kant prepared but he does not in fact state any arguments. A hint of his own position is seen in the assertion that "true philosophy teaches the incontrovertible doctrine of the reality of an infinite power, the forces of nature, and the marvelous and sublime properties and capacities of physical and spiritual man." He states that philosophy, in its practical part, should seek to bring people ever closer to God, "not by means of a loveless, despotic categorical imperative, contrary to the very nature of reason, but through the gentle, all-powerful tie of love that animates all things" (12:366).

Since Schlettwein asked whether Reinhold, Fichte, Beck, or someone else was Kant's correct interpreter, Kant felt called upon to reply. His answer, "Schultz!" appeared in the *A L.Z*, on June 14, 1797.

SCHMID, *Carl Christian Erhard* (1761–1812), *Magister* (instructor) in Jena, later professor of philosophy. In 1786 he published an introduction and lexicon to the *Critique: Kritik der reinen Vernuft im Grundrisse zu Vorlesungen nebst einem Wörterbuch zum leichteren Gebrauch der Kantischen Philosophie*. He became involved in a bitter feud with Fichte in 1793.

SCHULTZ, *Johann* (1739–1805), court chaplain and professor of mathematics in Königsberg; Kant's most trusted expositor. He served as pastor in Löwenhagen near Königsberg, was appointed court chaplain in 1775 and professor of mathematics in 1786. In 1784 he published *Erläuterungen über des Herrn Prof. Kant Kritik der reinen Vernunft* (Exposition of Kant's *Critique of Pure Reason*) and in 1789/92 *Prüfung der Kantischen Kritik der reinen Vernunft* (in two volumes). He discussed Kant's Inaugural Dissertation in the *Königsberger Gelehrten und Politischen Zeitungen* in the issues of Nov. 22 and 25, 1771.

Schultz's *Exposition* has been translated by James C. Morrison (Ottawa: University of Ottawa Press, 1995).

SCHULZE, *Gottlob Ernst*, (1761–1833), known as "Aenesidemus-Schulze," became professor of philosophy in Helmstedt, 1788, where he was one of Artur Schopenhauer's teachers; when the university in Helmstedt was dissolved in 1810, Schulze moved to Göttingen. His book, *Änesidemus oder über die Fundamente der von dem Herrn Prof. Reinhold in Jena gelieferten Elementarphilosophie*

(1792) (the full title is Aenesidemus or concerning the foundations of the philosophy of the elements issued by Prof. Reinhold in Jena, together with a defense of skepticism against the pretensions of the *Critique of Reason*) was published anonymously. An excerpt from it is available in an English translation by George di Giovanni in his *Between Kant and Hegel* (Albany, NY: State University of New York Press, 1985). Schulze is known for his attack, following Jacobi's lead, on the idea of the thing in itself. Fichte, who reviewed *Aenesidemus*, was influenced by him. Schulze also published a review of Fichte's *Critique of All Revelation* (1793).

SCHÜTZ, *Christian Gottfried* (1747–1832), philologist and professor of rhetoric and poetry in Jena from 1779. In 1785 he co-founded, with Bertuch, the *Allgemeine Literaturzeitung*-(A.L.Z.) devoted to the defense of Kantian philosophy. Schütz became one of Kant's strongest unwavering disciples. His son, F. K. J. Schütz, published a biography of him, in two volumes: C. G. Schütz, *Darstellung seines Lebens, nebst einer Auswahl aus seinem literarischen Briefwechsel* (Halle, 1834/5), but it is not to be found in American libraries.

SELLE, *Christian Gottlieb* (1748–1800), physician and professor at the Charité hospital in Berlin, anonymous author of *Philosophische Gespräche* (Philosophical dialogues, 1780) and several other works including one on animal magnetism. He was a member of the Berlin Academy and one of the first people to whom Kant sent copies of the first *Critique*. Although he regarded himself as Kant's philosophical opponent, he respected him greatly. On Dec. 29, 1787, Ak.[314], he wrote to Kant and sent his essay aiming to prove that there are no a priori cognitions at all. As the editors of the Akademie edition notice (13:209 f.), Selle confounds the distinction, so important to Kant, between "quid facti?" and "quid juris?" questions. Selle's Göttingen training had made him a confirmed Lockean. On his critique of Kant and Kant's response, see Kiesewetter's letter, Ak.[420], and Kant's letter to Selle, Feb. 24, 1792, Ak.[507]. As the latter hints, in matters of politics, e.g., resentment of Friedrich Wilhelm II's "new order" and its restrictions on freedom of thought and the press in matters of theology, Selle and Kant were in close agreement.

SOEMMERING, *Samuel Thomas* (1755–1830), a physician in Frankfurt, known for his research on physiology and anatomy. Soemmering's *Über das Organ der Seele* (On the organ of the soul, 1796) is the subject of Kant's essay appended to his letter, Ak.[671]. Three drafts of Kant's essay, each somewhat different, may be found in Ak. 13: 398–412.

STANG, *Conrad*, a Benedictine Kantian from Würzburg. Nothing further is known of him.

STÄUDLIN, *Carl Friedrich* (1761–1826), professor of theology in Göttingen, author of *Geschichte und Geist des Skeptizismus, vorzüglich in Rücksicht auf Moral und Religion* (History and spirit of skepticism, especially with respect to morality and religion; Leipzig, 1794).

SUCKOW, *Simon Gabriel* (1721–86), professor of mathematics and physics in Erlangen, in charge of conveying to Kant the invitation to accept a position there.

SULZER, *Johann Georg* (1720–79), aesthetician, educated in Switzerland, he became a member of the Berlin Academy of Sciences and a friend to Moses Mendelssohn whose membership in the academy he attempted unsuccessfully to bring about. Sulzer was one of the men to whom Kant sent his 1770 Inaugural Dissertation for review. (His letter to Kant of Dec. 8, 1770, Ak.[62], comments on Kant's theory of space and time.) His essay, "Récherches sur l'origine des sentiments agréables et desagréables" (Investigation of the origin of pleasant and unpleasant sensations, also known by its German title, "Untersuchung über den Ursprung der angenehmen und unangenehmen Empfindungen") was published in the proceedings of the Berlin Academy, 1751–2. In this early work Sulzer argued that pleasure is an active state of the soul, connected with the intellectual faculty. All pleasures, even those of the senses, derive not from the object but from the intellect. Sulzer's later theory, as in his *Allgemeine Theorie der schönen Künste* (General theory of the fine arts, 1771–4) departs from this "intellectualist" aesthetic and maintains that aesthetic experience involves a different faculty than cognition. We need not understand the purpose of an object in order to delight in it. Beauty is experienced as an emotional response rather than a cognition, but it is not only that, for it is aroused by the representations of a faculty of representation (*Vorstellungsvermögen*) which is not the faculty of mere feeling (*Empfindungsvermögen*). As Lewis Beck points out (*Early German Philosophy*, pp. 296 ff.). Sulzer's aesthetic theory was an important step in the "emancipation" of the artistic faculty from the cognitive, an emancipation carried further by Mendelssohn and accomplished by Kant. Alexander Altmann's *Moses Mendelssohn* offers more details on Sulzer's philosophical and personal interaction with Mendelssohn and his response to the latter's criticisms.

Kant wrote no letters to Sulzer but often sent greetings – and copies of his books. That he thought highly of Sulzer is shown also in his note in the *Groundwork of the Metaphysics of Morals*, Ak. 4:410, addressing a question which "the late excellent Sulzer" had asked him. It may also be Sulzer's translation of Hume's *Enquiry* (1756) to which Kant was indebted for his knowledge of some of Hume's arguments concerning the principle of causality.

An interesting fact not mentioned in philosophical accounts of Sulzer: Anton Graff, a famous Romantic painter, became Sulzer's son-in-law.

SWEDENBORG, *Emanuel* (1688–1772), originally "Svedberg" until 1719 when, in recognition of his engineering services to the state, he was ennobled. Born in Uppsala, where his father was a bishop and professor, he studied the natural sciences at Uppsala University. From 1710–14 he traveled, visiting Germany, Holland, France, and England. On returning to Sweden, he was appointed assessor in the Royal College of Mines in 1716, a position he held until 1747 when, following a religious crisis and revelation, he resigned in order to devote himself to spiritual matters.

Swedenborg is famed not only for his theology and clairvoyant powers – he predicted the precise moment of his own death – but also for a variety of scientific activities, e.g., the discovery of the function of endocrine glands. His scientific writings include studies of the brain in human beings and animals and a treatise on the world-system, *Principia* (1734). He published the first work on algebra in Swedish, helped to found the science of crystallography, devoted himself for 30 years to metallurgy, and is said to have made suggestions toward the invention of the submarine and the airplane.

His mystical religious experiences began around 1736 and culminated in 1745 with a vision of God and a world of spirits "opened" to him. Visions, communications with angels and other spirits, including the Second Coming of Christ followed. He believed that the correct interpretation of Scripture had been given to him directly by God. In the years 1749–56 he published his exegesis of Genesis and Exodus, *Arcana Coelestia* (Celestial mysteries, in 8 volumes). Numerous religious writings followed, many of them translated into other languages. The New Jerusalem Church, following his religious and spiritualist teachings, was founded by some of his disciples in London around 1784 and still has branches today, one of them in Cambridge, Massachusetts, next to Harvard University.

As mentioned in the notes to Kant's letter to Fräulein Knobloch, Ak.[29], there is now a fairly extensive literature, mainly in German, on the relation between Swedenborg and Kant. Kant's *Dreams of a Spirit-seer* (1766) alludes to some of the same stories about Swedenborg's supernatural powers that are reported in the Knobloch letter and mocks them, but the letter states that he had been a skeptic about Swedenborg's supernatural powers until he learned of the incidents reported in this letter and became convinced of their credibility. It is difficult to reconcile the critical tone of *Dreams of a Spirit-seer* and Kant's lifelong hostility to *Schwärmerei* with his taking seriously Swedenborg's allegedly occult powers.

Regarding Swedenborg, see also the translation and discussion of Kant's *Dreams of a Spirit-Seer* in Volume One of *The Cambridge Edition of the Works of Immanuel Kant, Theoretical Philosophy*, 1755–1770, translated and edited by David Walford and Ralf Meerbote (Cambridge University Press, 1992).

TETENS, *Johann Nicolaus* (1736–1807) was born in Schleswig (there is some doubt concerning the precise town) and studied at the University of Kiel, where he became professor of philosophy until 1789, when he took a position in Copenhagen with the finance ministry of the Danish government. His teacher in Kiel had been Johann Christian Eschenbach, the first German translator of Berkeley. Lewis Beck (*Early German Philosophy*,p. 412) reports that Tetens was called "the German Locke." His three-faculty theory of human psychology (knowing, feeling, and willing) was accepted by Kant who in turn influenced Tetens, though not sufficiently to lead him away from a rationalistic, pre-Humean view of causation.

In his letter to Herz, Ak.[134], Kant alludes critically to Tetens' discussion of freedom in the latter's *Philosophische Versuche über die menschliche Natur und ihre Entwicklung* (Philosophical essays on human nature and its development, 2 volumes, 1776). Kant was also interested in Tetens' article on how to protect oneself best against thunderstorms. He mentions the lightning rod and Tetens in his letter to C. D. Reusch, a physics professor in Königsberg, May or June 1774.

Tetens' principal work, other than the *Philosophische Versuch*, was *Über die allgemeine speculativische Philosophie* (On general theoretical philosophy, 1775).

Biographical Sketches

TIEDEMANN, *Dietrich* (1748–1803), professor at the Collegium Carolinum in Kassel, one of Kant's critics, published an essay on the nature of metaphysics, attacking the *Critique of Pure Reason* and the *Prolegomena*. "Über die Natur der Metaphysik; zur Prüfung von Herrn Prof. Kants Grundsätzen," in *Hessische Beiträge zur Gelehrsamkeit und Kunst*, vol. I, (Frankfurt, 1785). Notwithstanding Kant's low opinion of Tiedemann (he complained that Kant was hard to understand, rejected Kant's intuitional view of space and time, held that mathematical propositions are analytic, interpreted "a priori" psychologically, and charged Kant with idealism), Tiedemann is of historical interest. In the speculative debate in the eighteenth century over the origin of language, Tiedemann held, against Herder, that human beings have pre-linguistic knowledge. (Hamann's exchange of letters with Kant, discussing Herder's theory of language, concerns this controversy. They show Hamann to have a third position, viz., that human language is of divine origin.)

TIEFTRUNK, *Johann Heinrich* (1760–1837) was professor of philosophy in Halle from 1792. One of Kant's most steadfast disciples, he wrote on religion, *Einzig möglicher Zweck Jesu* (1789), *Versuch einer Kritik der Religion* (1790), the philosophy of law, *Philosophische Untersuchungen über das Privat- und öffentliche Recht* (1797), and he edited a collection of Kant's miscellaneous essays, *Kants vermischte Schriften* (1799).

ULRICH, *Johann August Heinrich* (1744–1807) was professor of philosophy in Jena. Although Kant did not correspond with him, there is one extant letter, Ak.[239], from Ulrich to Kant. Ulrich was initially a follower of Kant, though with reservations: his letter thanks Kant for the gift of a book (probably the *Grundlegung*) and sends Kant his own, saying that it shows how carefully he has studied Kant. Ulrich's textbook is entitled *Institutiones logicae et metaphysicae* (Jena, 1785; Ak. 13:144–6 has an extended summary of it, showing that he was indeed strongly influence by Kant). It was reviewed by Johann Schultz in the *A.L.Z.*, Dec. 13, 1785. (See Kant's note in the Preface to *Metaphysische Anfangsgründe der Naturwissenschaft*, Ak. 4:474–6, and the editor's comment, 4:638 f.). As Kant's popularity in Jena increased, Ulrich became strongly antagonistic to Kant, and to Reinhold as well, thereby (according to Reinhold) ruining his own reputation. See Reinhold's letters, Ak.[305] and [318].

Ulrich's defense of what Kant calls "comparative" or "empirical" freedom, *Eleutheriologie* (1788) – the title derives from one of Jupiter's names, "liberator") – was reviewed by Kant's friend C. J. Kraus, who claimed that his review was based on an essay by Kant himself. The review is therefore included in Kant's works, Ak. 8:453–60, and it can be found in the Cambridge volume of Kant's *Practical Philosophy*.

WASIANSKI, *Ehregott Andreas Christoph* (1755–1831), the third (with Borowski and R. B. Jachmann) of Kant's first biographers, was born in Königsberg, attended the university in 1772 and studied medicine, natural science, then theology. He became pastor and deacon of the Tragheim Church in Königsberg. Kant engaged him as one of his amanuenses in 1784. From that time on he had general charge of Kant's house and possessions. One of Wasianski's achievements was the construction of a grand piano (*ein Bogenflügel*), which Kant and Hippel came to hear in 1795.

In Kant's declining years, Wasianski was his daily companion and physical caretaker. In Dec. 1801, Kant named him the executor of his will and literary remains and left him 2,000 Thaler. An additional legacy of one-twentieth of Kant's estate was added by him in May 1803. Wasianski's account of Kant's last years, "I. Kant in seinen letzten Lebensjahren," was published in the year of Kant's death, 1804.

WIELAND, *Christoph Martin* (1733–1813), poet, philosophical novelist, essayist, translator of Shakespeare, Horace, Cicero, Lucian, and publisher of the journal *Neuen Deutschen* (or *Teutchen) Merkur*. Kant published one essay, "Über den Gebrauch teleologische Prinzipien in der Philosophie" (On the employment of teleological principles in philosophy, 1788) in the *Merkur*. Wieland, sometimes called "the German Voltaire," was born near Biberach in Würtemberg to a Pietist family. He studied in Erfurt and Tübingen. Though Wieland's interests were broadly literary, he had studied law in Erfurt where he was later appointed professor of philosophy. Wieland's *Merkur* was announced in Königsberg in spring 1773. Though Kant did not respond to all of Wieland's letters (the first date from Dec. 25, 1772, and Feb. 1, 1773, Ak.[73] and [74]), Kant often asked Reinhold to transmit cordial, respectful regards to "your excellent father-in-law" (Wieland). Later in life, Wieland's defense of Herder (he liked Herder's *Metakritik*) made Kant less friendly.

WINDISCH-GRAETZ, *Joseph Nicolaus*, Reichsgraf von (1749–1802), political philosopher and philanthropist. See also Kant's letter to Jacobi, Ak.[375], n. 1.

WIZENMANN, *Thomas* (1759–87), instructor of philosophy and friend of Jacobi's. He studied philosophy and theology in Tübingen, under Gottfried Ploucquet. Wizenmann wrote to Hamann that the works of Oetinger had deepened his understanding of the "philosophy of the Bible" and that Herder had made him understand biblical history. He read Mendelssohn, Locke, Leibniz, Wolff, and Boehme while a preacher in Essingen. Mendelssohn's *Phaedon* seemed to him full of sophisms and he planned to refute it. Apparently he remained respectful of Mendelssohn (as a private tutor in Barmen he wrote an ode on Mendelssohn's death) though he was strongly critical of Mendelssohn's appeal to "sound common sense."

Wizenmann was the author of *Die Resultate der Jacobischen und Mendelssohnschen Philosophie* (1786), which caused a stir and contributed to the pantheism controversy. Jacobi praised him enthusiastically, saying that his "Critical investigation of the results of Jacobi's and Mendelssohn's philosophies" "presents with admirable clarity my own opinion in its total and fundamental aspect, and it reveals an independent thinker of the first rank, a man in the noblest sense of the word." Kant praises Wizenmann too – "What Is Orientation in Thinking?" refers to him as "the penetrating author of the *Resultate*" and a footnote in the *Critique of Practical Reason* (Ak. 5:143) refers to him as "a fine and bright mind whose early death is to be regretted" – but Wizenmann's belief in the Bible as superior in historical truth to all metaphysical arguments could hardly have appealed to Kant. (See Biester's letter, Ak. [275], n. 3, and

Beiser, *The Fate of Reason*, ch. 4.) Like Jacobi and Hamann, Wizenmann defended a kind of irrationalism, freedom from the constraints of reason.

WLÖMER, *Johann Heinrich* (1728–97). Born in Pilkallen, he became privy financial councillor (*Finanzrat*) in Berlin. Wlömer was a school friend of Kant's, and possibly the only person outside Kant's family to call him "Du." (But Kant's biographer Wasianski claimed this unique distinction for Johann Gerhard Trummer, another school friend of Kant's and the physician who attended Kant in his final days.) He addresses Kant as "Dearest Brother" in his two extant letters (Ak.[403] and [464]; neither of these are otherwise of much interest). Wlömer was a member of the Berlin society of liberal theologians, Berlin Academy members, and enlighteners that, according to Mendelssohn, included Mendelssohn, Biester, Engel, Klein, Nicolai, Gedike, Dohm, von Irwing, von Beneke, and other notables.

There is an amusing anecdote about Wlömer in a letter of Zelter's to Goethe, Dec. 4–6, 1825 (Borowski and Jachmann refer to it in their biographies of Kant). Wlömer was once sent to Königsberg to revise the banking procedures. There, after 40 years' separation, he found his former *Stubenbursche*, old Kant. Kant asked him, "Do you, a businessman, ever wish to read my books?" "Oh yes, and I'd do it more, but I haven't enough fingers," he replied. Kant: "How's that?" Wlömer: "Well, dear friend, your prose style is so full of brackets and stipulations on which I have to keep my eye, what I do is put a finger on one word, then the second, third, fourth, and before I can turn the page my fingers are all used up."

Kant's brother mentions him, Ak.[403], as "your former academic friend" and says that Wlömer's sister was present at the baptism of Kant's niece.

WÖLLNER, *Johann Christoph* (1732–1800) became minister of spiritual affairs and of education under Friedrich Wilhelm II. He took the office of *Staatsminister* on July 3, 1788, replacing the liberal Baron von Zedlitz. On July 9, Wöllner issued the notorious edict on religion, threatening any state employee who deviated from orthodox teachings with civil penalties and discharge. He was active in the Berlin lodge *Zum Roten Löwen*, which, under his leadership, became the main seat of the Rosicrucian Order in Germany. Though officially an orthodox Lutheran theologian, he accepted the secret teachings of the Rosicrucians concerning magic, alchemy, and communion with spirits, as did his colleague Bischoffswerder who initiated the crown prince, Friedrich Wilhelm, into the order in 1782.

Wöllner's deceitful character and his role in Kant's censorship problems are discussed or referred to in a number of letters. See, e.g., the notes to Kiesewetter's letter to Kant of Apr. 20, 1790, Ak.[420]. As pointed out in the notes to Kant's earlier letter to Kiesewetter, Ak.[405a], Wöllner published, anonymously, a work called *Briefe eines Staatsministers über Aufklärung* (Letters from a minister of state concerning enlightenment, 1789). It contained a reference to Kant's denial of the possibility of proving God's existence.

With the death of Friedrich Wilhelm II in November, 1797, Wöllner's fortunes changed. The commission in charge of religions examinations was closed and Wöllner, reprimanded by the new king, was fired in March 1798. His edict though not officially repealed was allowed to fade away.

ZEDLITZ, *Freiherr (Baron) Karl Abraham von* (1731–93), minister of justice in the cabinet of Friedrich II, 1770, then minister of church and educational affairs, 1771, the man to whom Kant dedicated the *Critique of Pure Reason*. Zedlitz's intellectual curiosity and enlightened spirit are shown in his letter to Kant, Aug. 1, 1778, Ak.[137]: "This winter I shall take a course in rational anthropology with your former pupil, Herr Herz . . . Mendelssohn has vouched for Herz' talent . . . and on this man's voucher, I might undertake anything, especially since I know that you respect Herz and are conducting a kind of correspondence with him." In 1778 he invited Kant to accept a professorship in Halle, with a salary of 600 Reichsthaler.

Friedrich II died in 1786 and Zedlitz submitted his resignation as minister of education to the new king, Dec. 1, 1789, "for reasons of health," and on Dec. 3 his dismissal became official. Zedlitz's departure was a great loss to religious liberals. Johann Christoph Wöllner, the man who wrote the notorious *Religionsedikt* and, a few years later, the cabinet order against Kant's philosophy of religion, had already replaced him as *Staatsminister*, July 3, 1788, and had issued his edict on July 9, 1788. It demanded that Protestant preachers adhere strictly to orthodox doctrines and it established censorship of theological publications. The attack on Kant, accusing him of misusing his philosophy to depreciate fundamental dogmas of Holy Scripture and Christianity, was issued on Oct. 1, 1794. (See Ak.[640].) By then Zedlitz had died.

Glossary

Abfolge	succession
abhängig	dependent
ableiten	derive
Absicht	purpose, intention, aim
absondern	separate, abstract, set aside
Abstoßungskraft	repulsion (physics)
abstrahieren	abstract
Achtung	respect
Affekt	emotion, feeling
Akt	act (cf. Handlung)
allgemein	universal, general
allgemeingültig	universally valid
Allmacht	omnipotence
anerkennen	recognize; acknowledge
Anfangsgründe	foundations
anhängend	dependent
Anlage	predisposition, constitution
Anmut	grace, gracefulness; elegance
Annehmung	assumption, adoption
Anschauen	intuit, inspect directly, visualize
anschaulich	intuitive, evident
Anschauung	intuition, sometimes "a thoroughly determinate representation"
Anstoß	collision (physics)
Anthropologie	anthropology, social psychology
Antrieb	impulse
Anziehung	attraction
Anziehungskraft	attraction, attractive force (in physics)
Apperzeption	apperception
Art	kind, way, species
Auflösung	solution; resolution; dissolution

617

Aufrichtigkeit	sincerity, candor, veracity
Ausdehnung	extension
Auslegung	exegesis, interpretation
ausmachen	constitute; make out; settle
äußere	external
bedeuten	signify, mean
Bedeutung	meaning, significance
bedingt	conditioned
Bedingung	condition
Befugnis	authorization; warrant
Begebenheit	occurrence
Begehrungsvermögen	faculty of desire
Begierde	desire
Begriff	concept, a general representation (*repraesentatio communis*)
begründen	to found, establish, prove, confirm, justify, give a reason for
Begründung	foundation, establishment, proof, argument, motivation, reason
beharrlich	constant, persistent, abiding
beilegen	ascribe
Beilegung	attribution
bekennen	acknowledge
Bemerkung	observation, remark
Beobachtung	observation
Beschaffenheit	property, state, condition, characteristic
Besitz	possession
besonder	particular; special
beständig	constant
bestätigen	confirm
bestehen	exist; consist
bestimmen	determine
bestimmt	determinate, definite
Bestimmung	modification, determination, vocation
Betrachtung	consideration
beurteilen	judge; assess
Bewegung	motion
Bewegungsgrösse	momentum
Bewegungsgrund	motive
Beweis	proof, evidence
Bewußtsein	consciousness
Beziehung	relation, reference
Bild	picture, image
Bildung	education, culture

billigen	approve
Blendwerk	illusion, deception
bloß	mere, merely; pure
Böse	evil
bürgerlich	civil
Darstellung	presentation, exhibition
Dasein	existence
Dauer	duration
Denken	thinking
Denkungsart	way of thinking
Deutlichkeit	distinctness; clarity
Deutung	interpretation
Ding	thing
dunkel	obscure
durch	through; by
durchgängig	thoroughgoing
Eigenschaft	attribute, property
eigentliche	actual
Einbildung	imagination
Einbildungskraft	power of imagination
Eindruck	impression
einerlei	same
einfach	simple
Einfluß	influence
einförmig	simple
Einheit	unity
Einschränkung	limitation
einsehen	have insight into; understand
Einsicht	insight
Einstimmung	agreement
Einteilung	division
Empfänglichkeit	receptivity
Empfindung	sensation, feeling
empirisch	empirical
endlich	finite
Endzweck	final end, purpose
enthalten	contain, include, embody, express
entschließung	decision
entstehen	arise
Ereignis	occurrence, event
Erfahrung	experience
erkennen	recognize, cognize
Erkenntnis	cognition, knowledge
Erklärung	explanation, declaration

Erläuterung	clarification, elucidation
Erörterung	exposition
Erscheinung	appearance, phenomenon, manifestation
erzeugen	produce, generate
Existenz	existence
Fähigkeit	capacity
Faktum	fact
Folge	sequence; consequence
folgen	follow
Folgerung	consequence, conclusion, inference
Fortschritt	progress, advance
Fortsetzung	continuation
Freiheit	freedom, liberty
Ganze	whole; entirety
gänzlich	entirely
Gattung	species, genus, race
Gebrauch	use, employment
Gedanke	thought, intention, plan, idea
Gedankending	conceptual or imaginary entity, thought-entity (*ens rationis*)
Gedankenverkettung	association of ideas
gedenkbar	conceivable
Gefühl	feeling
gegeben	given
Gegenstand	object
Gegenwirkung	reaction
Geist	spirit, mind
Geistlicher	clergyman
gemein	common
Gemeinschaft	community
Gemüt	mind
Genie	genius
Genieseuche	genius-epidemic
geschehen	happen
Geschmack	taste
Geschwindigkeit	velocity, speed
Gesetz	law
Gesetzgebung	legislation, law giving
Gestalt	shape, configuration
Gewohnheit	habit; custom
Glaube	belief; faith
gleichartig	homogeneous, similar
gleichförmig	homogeneous, uniform
Glückseligkeit	blessedness; happiness

Grad	degree
Grenze	bound, boundary
Grund und Folge	ground and consequent
gründlich	thorough
Grundsatz	principle
gültig	valid
Handlung	activity, act, action
Hirn	brain
Hirngespinst	fantasy, phantom of the brain, chimera
Inbegriff	union, sum total
Inhalt	content
innerlich	internal
kennen	know; be acquainted with
Kenntnis	knowledge; acquaintance
konstruieren	construct
Körper	body
Kraft	strength; force (physics); power
Lage	position
lediglich	solely
Lehre	doctrine, teaching, theory
Lehrsatz	theorem
Leitfaden	key; clue
mannigfaltig	manifold (adj.), diverse
Mannigfaltige	manifold (n.), manifold of elements; diversity
Mannigfaltigkeit	manifold (n.), diversity, variety, multiplicity
Materie	material, stuff
Meinung	opinion
Menge	multiplicity; amount
Mensch	human being
Mittel	means; remedy
möglich	possible
nach	according to; in accordance with; after
nachfolgen	succeed, follow
Naturanlage	natural predisposition
Naturgeschichte	natural history
Naturgesetz	natural law (physics)
Naturrecht	natural law (ethics), natural right
Neigung	inclination
Not	privation
notwendig	necessary, necessarily
nützlich	useful
Obersatz	major premise
oberst	supreme
Objekt	object, thing, fact

Offenbarung	revelation
Ort	place, location; village, region
Pflicht	duty
Probe	experiment, test
Probestück	specimen, sample
probieren	try, attempt; test
Probierstein	touchstone
Quale (Latin)	sort, kind
Quelle	source
Rasse	race
Raum	space
Reale	real
Recht	right, the law, justice
Reihe	series
rein	pure
Religionswahn	fanaticism
Rückgang	regress
Sache	thing; fact
Satz	proposition; sentence; principle
Schätzung	appraisal
Schein	illusion
schlechthin	absolutely
schließen	infer, conclude
Schluß	conclusion, inference
Schranke	limitation
Schwärmerei	enthusiasm, mysticism, daydreaming, fanaticism, fantasy
schwer	heavy
Schwere	gravity
Schwerkraft	gravitational attraction or force
selbständig	independent; self-sufficient
Selbstbewußtsein	self-consciousness
selbsttätig	self-active
setzen	posit; place; put
Sinn	sense, meaning
Sinnenvorstellung	sense representation
sinnlich	sensible
Sinnlichkeit	sensibility
Sitten	morality, manners, practices
Sittengesetz	moral law
Steigerung	increase
Stoff	material, matter
Straffe	punishment, discipline
Stunden	hours; lessons
Teil	part

teilbar	divisible
Teilung	division
Triebfeder	incentive
Trost	solace, consolation
Übergang	transition
übergeben	pass (into)
Überlegung	reflection, consideration
übersinnlich	supersensible
Überzeugung	conviction
Umfang	domain
Undurchdringlichkeit	impenetrability
unendlich	infinite
unerforschlich	inscrutable
unerweislich	indemonstrable
ungereimt	absurd
Unlust	displeasure
unmittelbar	immediate, immediately, direct
unschädlich	innocent
Unschuld	innocence
Untersatz	minor premise
Unterscheidung	distinction
Unterschied	difference
Urbild	archetype
Ursache	cause
ursprünglich	original
Ursprüngliche Beylegung	original (act of) attribution, authorization (J. S. Beck)
urteilen	to judge
Urteilskraft	power or faculty of judgment
Urwesen	primordial being
Veränderung	alteration
Verbindung	connection
Vereinigung	union, association
Verhältnis	relation
Verknüpfung	connection
Vermögen	faculty, power
Verpflichtung	obligation
Verschiedenheit	difference, diversity
Verstand	understanding
Verstandesbegriff	concept of the understanding; category
verstehen	understand
vollständig	complete
Voraussetzung	presupposition
vorgestellt	presented, conceived

vorhergehen	precede
vorstellbar	conceivable
Vorstellung	representation, presentation, thought
Wahn	delusion, madness
Wahrheit	truth
Wahrnehmung	perception
Wärmestoff	caloric (heat-substance)
Warscheinlichkeit	probability
Wechsel	change, exchange
wechselseitig	reciprocal
Wechselwirkung	interaction
Welt	world
Weltall	world-whole
Weltganze	world-whole
Weltkörper	heavenly body
Weltweisheit	philosophy
Wesen	being; essence
Widerlegung	refutation, rebuttal, disproof
Widerspruch	contradiction
Widerstreit	conflict; opposition
Wiederholung	repetition
wirkende Kraft	active force
Wirklichkeit	actuality, reality
Wirkung	effect
Wissen	knowledge
Wissenschaft	science
Wunder	marvel, miracle
Wurzel	root
Zahl	number
Zeit	time
Zeitfolge	temporal sequence
Zensur	censorship
Zergliederung	analysis; dissection
Zerteilung	disintegration
zufällig	contingent
Zurechnung	imputation
zureichend	sufficient
zureichenden Grund	sufficient reason
Zurückstoßung	repulsion (physics)
Zurückstoßungskraft	repulsive force
zusammengesetzt	composed, synthesized, composite
zusammengesetzter Begriff	complex concept
Zusammenhang	connection; interconnection
zusammensetzen	to combine, synthesize, compose

Zusammensetzung.	composition, combination, synthesis
Zusammenstellung	juxtaposition
Zustand	state; condition
Zwang	coercion; compulsion
Zweck	purpose; end
zweckmäßig	purposive; suitable

ENGLISH-GERMAN

absolutely	*schlechthin*
abstract	*abstrahieren*
absurd	*ungereimt*
according to; in accordance with; after	*nach*
acknowledge	*bekennen*
act, activity, action	*Akt, Handlung*
active force	*wirkende Kraft*
actual	*eigentliche*
actuality, reality	*Wirklichkeit*
affirm, maintain, assert, claim	*behaupten*
agreement	*Einstimmung*
analysis; dissection	*Zergliederung*
analytic	*analytisch*
anthropology, social psychology	*Anthropologie*
appearance, phenomenon, manifestation	*Erscheinung*
apperception	*Apperzeption*
application	*Anwendung*
appraisal	*Schätzung*
approve	*billigen*
archetype	*Urbild*
arise	*entstehen*
ascribe	*beilegen*
association of ideas	*Gedankenverkettung*
assume	*annehmen*
assumption, adoption	*Annehmung*
attack; assault	*Angriff*
attraction	*Anziehung*
attraction, attractive force (physics)	*Anziehungskraft*
attribute, property	*Eigenschaft*
attribution	*Beilegung*
authorization; warrant	*Befugins*
being; essence	*Wesen*
belief, faith	*Glaube*
blessedness; happiness	*Glückseligkeit*
body	*Körper*

boundary	*Grenze*
brain	*Hirn*
caloric (heat-substance)	*Wärmestoff*
capacity	*Fähigkeit*
category, concept of the understanding	*Verstandesbegriff*
cause	*Ursache*
censorship	*Zensur*
change (alteration	*Veränderung*
change (exchange)	*Wechsel*
civil	*bürgerlich*
claim, demand	*Anspruch*
clarification, elucidation	*Erläuterung*
clergyman, ecclesiastic	*Geistlicher*
coercion; compulsion	*Zwang*
cognition, knowledge	*Erkenntnis*
collision (physics)	*Anstoß*
combine, synthesize, compose	*zusammensetzen*
common	*gemein*
community	*Gemeinschaft*
complete	*vollständig*
complex concept	*zusammengesetzter Begriff*
composed, synthesized, composite	*zusammengesetzt*
composition, combination, synthesis	*Zusammensetzung*
conceivable	*vorstellbar, gedenkbar*
concept, a general representation	*Begriff*
conceptual or imaginary entity, thought-entity	*Gedankending*
conclusion, inference	*Schluß*
condition	*Bedingung*
conditioned	*bedingt*
confirm	*bestätigen*
conflict; opposition	*Streit, Widerstreit*
connection, interconnection	*Verbindung, Verknüpfung, Zusammenhang*
consciousness	*Bewußtsein*
consequence	*Folgerung*
consideration	*Betrachtung*
constant, persistent, abiding	*beharrlich, beständig*
constitute; make out; settle	*ausmachen*
construct	*konstruieren*
contain, include	*ethalten*
content	*Inhalt*
contingent	*zufällig*
continuation	*Fortsetzung*
contradiction	*Widerspruch*

conviction	*Überzeugung*
decision	*Entschließung*
degree	*Grad*
delusion, madness	*Wahn*
dependent	*abhängig, anhängend*
derive	*ableiten*
desire	*Begierde*
desire, faculty of	*Begehrungsvermögen*
determinate, definite	*bestimmt*
determine	*bestimmen*
determining	*bestimmens*
difference, diversity	*Unterschied, Verschiedenheit*
disintegration	*Zerteilung*
displeasure	*Unlust*
distinction	*Unterscheidung*
distinctness; clarity	*Deutlichkeit*
divisible	*teilbar*
division	*Einteilung, Teilung*
doctrine, teaching	*Lehre*
domain	*Umfang*
duration	*Dauer*
duty	*Pflicht*
education, culture	*Bildung*
effect	*Wirkung*
emotion, feeling	*Affekt*
empirical	*empirisch*
enthusiasm, mysticism, daydreaming	*Schwärmerei*
establish, prove, confirm, justify	*begründen*
ethical, moral	*sittlich, moral*
evil	*Böse*
exegesis, interpretation	*Auslegung*
exist; consist	*bestehen*
existence	*Dasein, Existenz*
experience	*Erfahrung*
experiment, test	*Probe*
explanation, declaration	*Erklärung*
exposition	*Erörterung*
extension	*Ausdehnung*
external	*äußere*
fact	*Faktum, Sache*
faculty, power	*Vermögen*
fanaticism	*Religonswahn*
fantasy, phantom of the brain, chimera	*Hirngespinst*
fastidious, pretentious	*Anspruchsvoll*

feeling	*Gefühl*
final end, purpose	*Endzweck*
finite	*endlich*
follow	*folgen*
force, power	*Kraft*
foundation, establishment, proof, reason	*Begründung, Anfangsgrund*
freedom	*Freiheit*
genius	*Genie*
genius-epidemic	*Genieseuche*
genus	*Gattung*
given	*gegeben*
grace, gracefulness; elegance	*Anmut*
gravitational force	*Schwerkraft*
gravity	*Schwere*
ground and consequent	*Grund und Folge*
habit; custom	*Gewohnheit*
happen	*geschehen*
heavenly body	*Weltkörper*
heavy	*schwer*
homogeneous	*gleichartig, gleichförmig*
hours; lessons	*Stunden*
human being	*Mensch*
illusion, deception	*Schein; Blendwerk*
imagination	*Einbildung*
immediate, immediately, direct	*unmittelbar*
impenetrability	*Undurchdringlichkeit*
impression	*Eindruck*
impulse	*Antrieb*
imputation	*Zurechnung*
incentive	*Triebfeder*
inclination	*Neigung*
increase	*Steigerung*
indemonstrable	*unerweislich*
independent; self-sufficient	*selbständig*
infer, conclude	*schließen*
infinite	*unendlich*
influence	*Einfluß*
innocence	*Unschuld*
innocent	*unschädlich, unschuldig*
inscrutable	*unerforschlich*
insight	*Einsicht*
interaction	*Wechselwirkung*
internal	*innerlich*
interpretation	*Erklärung, Auslegung, Deutung*

intuit, inspect directly, visualize, view	*anschauen*
intuition, view	*Anschauung*
intuitive, evident	*anschaulich*
judge; assess	*urteilen, beurteilen*
juxtaposition	*Zusammenstellung*
key; clue	*Leitfaden*
kind, way, species	*Art*
know (be acquainted with)	*kennen*
know (know that; propositional knowing)	*wissen*
knowledge	*Erkenntnis, Wissen, Kenntnis*
law	*Gesetz*
legislation, law-giving	*Gesetzgebung*
limitation	*Einschränkung, Schranke*
major premise	*Obersatz*
manifold (adj.), diverse	*mannigfaltig*
manifold (n.), diversity	*Mannigfaltigkeit, Mannigfaltige*
marvel, miracle	*Wunder*
material, matter, stuff	*Stoff, Materie*
meaning, significance	*Bedeutung, Sinn*
means; remedy	*Mittel*
mere, merely; nothing but	*bloß*
mind	*Gemüt, Geist*
minor premise	*Untersatz*
modification, determination, vocation	*Bestimmung*
momentum	*Bewegungsgrösse*
moral law	*Sittengesetz*
morality, morals	*Sitten, Sittlichkeit, Moral, Moralität*
motion	*Bewegung*
motive	*Bewegungsgrund*
multiplicity; amount	*Menge*
natural history	*Naturgeschichte*
natural law (ethics), natural right	*Naturrecht*
natural law (physics)	*Naturgesetz*
natural predisposition	*Naturanlage*
necessary, necessarily	*notwendig*
number	*Zahl*
object, thing, fact	*Objekt, Gegenstand*
obscure	*dunkel*
observation	*Beobachtung*
observation, remark	*Bemerkung*
occurrence, event	*Begebenheit, Ereignis*
omnipotence	*Allmacht*
opinion	*Meinung*

original	*ursprünglich Beylegung*
original (act of) attribution (J. S. Beck)	*Ursprüngliche Beylegung*
part	*Teil*
particular; special	*besonder*
pass (into)	*übergeben*
perception	*Wahrnehmung*
philosophy	*Weltweisheit, Philosophie*
picture, image	*Bild*
place, village, region, location	*Ort*
posit; place; put	*setzen*
position	*Lage*
possession	*Besitz*
possible	*möglich*
power of imagination	*Einbildungskraft*
power or faculty of judgment	*Urteilskraft*
precede	*vorhergehen*
predisposition, constitution	*Anlage*
presentation, exhibition	*Darstellung*
presented, conceived	*vorgestellt*
presupposition	*Voraussetzung*
primordial being	*Urwesen*
principle	*Grundsatz, Satz*
privation	*Not*
probability	*Warscheinlichkeit*
produce, generate	*erzeugen*
progress, advance	*Fortschritt*
proof, evidence	*Beweis*
property, state, condition, characteristic	*Beschaffenheit*
proposition; sentence; principle	*Satz*
punishment, discipline	*Straffe*
pure	*rein, bloß*
purpose, intention, aim	*Absicht*
purpose; end	*Zweck*
purposive; suitable	*zweckmäßig*
reaction	*Gegenwirkung*
real	*Reale*
receptivity	*Empfänglichkeit*
reciprocal	*wechselseitig*
recognize, cognize; acknowledge	*erkennen, anerkennen*
reflection, consideration	*Überlegung*
refutation, rebuttal, disproof	*Widerlegung*
regress	*Rückgang*
relation	*Verhältnis*
relation to, reference	*Beziehung*

repetition	*Wiederholung*
representation, presentation, thought	*Vorstellung*
repulsion (physics)	*Abstoßungskraft*
repulsive force	*Zurückstoßungskraft*
respect	*Achtung*
revelation	*Offenbarung*
right, the law, justice	*Recht*
root	*Wurzel*
science	*Wissenschaft*
self-active	*selbsttätig*
self-consciousness	*Selbstbewußtsein*
sensation, feeling	*Empfindung*
sense representation	*Sinnenvorstellung*
sense, meaning	*Sinn*
sensibility	*Sinnlichkeit*
sensible	*sinnlich*
separate, abstract, set aside	*absondern*
sequence; consequence	*Folge*
series	*Reihe*
shape	*Gestalt*
signify, mean	*bedeuten*
simple	*einfach, einförmig*
simultaneity	*Zugleichsein*
sincerity, candor, veracity	*Aufrichtigkeit*
solace, consolation	*Trost*
solely	*lediglich*
solution; resolution; dissolution	*Auflösung*
sort, kind	*Quale (Latin)*
source	*Quelle*
space	*Raum*
species, genus, race	*Gattung*
specimen, sample	*Probestück*
spirit, mind	*Geist*
state; condition	*Zustand*
strength, force (physics)	*Kraft*
succeed, follow	*nachfolgen*
succession	*Abfolge*
sufficient	*zureichend*
sufficient reason	*zureichenden Grund*
supersensible	*übersinnlich*
superstition	*Aberglaube*
supreme	*oberst*
taste	*Geschmack*
temporal sequence	*Zeitfolge*

631

theorem	*Lehrsatz*
thing; fact	*Ding, Sache*
thinking	*Denken*
thorough	*gründlich*
thoroughgoing	*durchgängig*
thought, intention, plan, idea	*Gedanke*
through; by	*durch*
time	*Zeit*
touchstone	*Probierstein*
transition	*Übergang*
truth	*Wahrheit*
try, test, attempt	*probieren*
understand	*verstehen, begreifen, einsehen*
understanding	*Verstand*
union, association	*Vereinigung*
union, sum total	*Inbegriff*
unity	*Einheit*
universal, general	*allgemein*
universally valid	*allgemeingültig*
use, employment	*Gebrauch*
useful	*nützlich*
valid	*gültig*
velocity, speed	*Geschwindigkeit*
whole; entirety	*Ganze*
world	*Welt*
world-whole	*Weltganze, Weltall*

Index of Persons